NE GOLFGUIDE

THE DIRECTORY FOR PUBLIC PLAY™

OUR 15TH YEAR
OF BRINGING YOU THE BEST INFORMATION
ON NEW ENGLAND'S PUBLIC COURSES

366 River Road   Carlisle, MA 01741
phone: (800) 833-6387
fax: (978) 287-0125
golfguide@earthlink.net
www.newenglandgolfguide.com

Publishers:	Leona Curhan
	Irwin Garfinkle
Editor:	John DiCocco
Contributing Author:	Paul Harber
Designer:	Diane Novetsky/Nova Design
Consultant:	Rick Walsh
Contributors:	Alan Pollard, Frank Procopio
Publisher's Asst:	Meghan Savage

©2003 *New England GolfGuide*

ISBN 0-9744438-0-8

Printed in Canada

A Word from the Publishers

15th Anniversary Edition

During these 15 years, the *New England GolfGuide*© has grown from 450 public golf courses in the 1990 edition to 663. The basic data sheet for each course has expanded so that the overall size of the book is larger and thicker. Included now are web addresses, tee time phone numbers, fees for twilight and all day play. There is more info about schools, clinics, junior and senior discounts, and women friendly courses. Every year we include a number of tables for open year round, ratings, the unofficial handicap calculator, and much more.

The maps have been updated with 16 new golf courses. In addition to the scorecard and detailed information about each course, there are 258 discount coupons for greens fees, plus discounts for driving ranges, merchandise and services. In these 15 years, the *New England GolfGuide*© and public golfing in New England have come a long way!

The 2004 edition focuses on "Courses." Our cover story is on the Quarry Hills Golf Course and the recycled Big Dig. Paul Harber, Boston Globe golf editor, focuses on how to determine what's the best course for you, not for the experts, but for you. Our editor John DiCocco, in one article, outlines the 5 rules every golfer should memorize, in another article suggests tips on managing your game on the course, and finally, presents "A Course to Remember: Golf Architecture 101."

First time readers will note that the book is divided into 10 geographic areas. The golf course locations are on the chapter maps and are then alphabetically arranged in the chapter. An index at the back of the coupon section lists courses alphabetically by state.

And finally, congratulations to Michael Williams, the winner of the drawing for 2 nights and golf at Mount Snow in Vermont. Thanks to the many readers who commented on and rated the courses they played. We want and need to hear from you.

Leona Curhan & Irwin Garfinkle
The Publishers

Contents:
Features, Indexes, Directories and Coupons

Contents: The Golf Courses

GB
CC/
MA

NE/
CTRL
MA

W
MA

SE
MA
/RI

NH

S
ME

N
ME

VT

NE
CT

SW
CT

Granite Links at Quarry Hills.
The Big Dig Meets a Big Idea.

You want stunning views with your golf? You don't have to leave Boston anymore. Go play Granite Links at Quarry Hills.

Granite Links is a sparkling upscale golf course, housing development, and public athletic complex rising from the landfills and abandoned quarries of Quincy and Milton. The course opened just 9 holes in 2003, but they are spectacular. The conditions rival that of courses several years older. The views as you get to the higher elevations on the course are striking: the Blue Hills in one direction, the Boston skyline and harbor in another. Another 9 should be open in the Spring of 2004, and the third and final 9 is planned for 2005. John Sanford of Jupiter, FL is the architect.

Thirty years ago Chick Geilich looked at the Quincy and Milton landfills and dreamed of doing something useful with all that open acreage. But the landfills had to be capped and the adjacent Quincy quarries presented logistical problems of their own.

Geilich sat with his idea for years. Then the Big Dig came along, and the resulting need to get rid of millions of tons of fill. Geilich called on developers Bill and Peter O'Connell, no stranger to big projects. (They developed the Boston World Trade Center, for one.) Together with Geilich they formed Quarry Hills Associates and went to work. Most courses take about three years to develop start to finish. It has taken the Quarry Hills group twelve years to get through the permitting process, designs, lawsuits, negotiations with abutters and environmentalists, and the construction is still ongoing. The original estimate to haul away the Big Dig fill was $300 million. It took the O'Connells 18 months of negotiations to convince the Big Dig contractors to let them take the dirt for only $100 million. (No one ever accused the Digmeisters of being cost-sensitive!)

Over the years, 900,000 truckloads brought more than 13 million tons of Big Dig fill. Because the slopes on the site are so severe, some of the holes required terracing fills of up to 90 feet deep.

The clubhouse, which will be perched on the highest point of the site, won't be completed until late 2004. So for 2003 and 2004, the course will operate out of a trailer and is accessed by a road through Milton. When the clubhouse is ready, the entrance will be off the Southeast Expressway.

Another view of Granite Links at Quarry Hill.

Because of its still rustic situation, the *New England GolfGuide*© is only granting two stars, but when it adds the clubhouse and opens another nine, it will certainly move higher.

The current nine is comprised of holes that eventually will be divided among the Granite and Milton nines. The shot values are wonderful, with many of the holes forcing you to make risk-reward decisions. The fairways are wide, but you'd best stay on them, because the rough is deep and extremely penal. In some places, smart players will take unplayables before trying to hack it out. There are carries over gorgeous marshes, and testing tee shots to slanted fairways guarded by ledge outcroppings or heather on one side and traps or steep dropoffs on the other. The traps, by the way, are dazzlingly white, made from pulverized limestone, and play beautifully, wet or dry. The undulating greens make for some adventurous putting. Look for a slope in the 128-132 range when a full 18 is open.

Granite Links is semi-private, with memberships still available. The daily player's green fees are rather high for a nine-holer ($75 on weekends, $60 Monday through Thursday, both including a cart), but Milton and Quincy residents get discounts. Even so, our advice is to play it before the rest of Greater Boston discovers it. And be forewarned: the views are so entrancing, you may forget to watch your ball.

A Course to Remember: Golf Architecture 101

by John DiCocco

"Angles angles angles," Brian Silva is saying, his arms karate-slashing the air. "Angles make the hole intriguing. They make you make choices. They dare the golfer—they make him decide to go for it or lay up. Angles—you need to love 'em and use 'em a lot."

Brian Silva can design. Brian Silva can teach. Brian Silva can make you laugh and learn at the same time. I had the great good fortune to sit in on the annual Harvard Design School two-day class on golf architecture, co-taught by Silva and Andy Staples. Silva is a partner in Cornish, Silva, Mungeum Inc., (CSM) and Staples is a partner in Robert Muir Graves & Damian Pascuzzo Ltd. Together these two firms have had and continue to have an enormous influence on modern course design.

The class is a two-day golf junkie's dream. From 9 am Monday, it's 40 straight hours (believe me: you're dreaming contours and wedge distances all night) of golf-talk, golf-think, golf-plotting. It's a grass-blade thin peek into a career we all covet, and believe we could do—if we just had a chance.

Silva and Staples are definite anglers. Both like to set the greens on an angle to the fairway, making you think backwards to the tee: "What tee shot will get me to the best spot to approach this green?" They like to angle a stream or a pond across a fairway. "How much can I challenge the water and still keep my ball dry?" They like to set a fairway at an angle on the hillside across a gulley. "How far is the closest safe landing area over there? How far is my optimal landing area?"

"Put together a good golfer and good angles and you'll have a hole where you can fail positively." Silva says, "If you read the land, you can use *your* game."

The class was originated by their elder partners, Geoffrey Cornish and Robert Muir Graves, and they developed a book, Golf Course Design, to help teach it.

Silva's best known new work is RedTail in Devens, MA. RedTail was named a 2003 *Golf Magazine* Top 10 New Course in the US. Staples is known for his renovation of La Quinta, and locally he designed the new private in Kingston, MA, named Indian Pond.

Low handicap players only make up about 15% of the actual golfing public, though by definition, they are the core and the opinion leaders. Architects design with the A player in mind, all the while knowing it's the B-C-D players who will make up the majority of customers and pay the most greens fees over time. So with a very few exceptions, designers seek to make a course "challenging but fair."

The two men show slide after slide of examples of good and bad holes, and classics that have stood the test of time. In their

Andy Staples, right, comments on student drawings.

work, they make multiple variations of each hole and then multiple variations of each green. They fuss over the placement and size and shape of each trap, and when those are done, they go back and widen the fairway here, and squeeze it a bit there. They fiddle with things a lot. Moans Silva, "Please don't make me walk around a course I designed 15 years ago. I'd want to change 80% of it."

The real meat of the class, and the part we were itching for, is the hands-on design. In preparation for the course, we students were required to read the Cornish & Graves book to have a working vocabulary when we arrived. In fact, several of those in attendance were superintendents, apprentice designers, or amateur designers looking to get a leg up on a career change. Some had wonderful drawing skills, others like me used colored pencils like bricks. But it was the enthusiasm that counted.

They had us take a large elevation plan of a fairly rectangular site, about five hundred acres with several elevation changes—a nice juicy plot. Our overnight assignment was to conceive of a routing plan, one that obeyed the several rules they laid out for us: include a driving range that faced north, a first hole that didn't face the east into the morning sun, an 18th hole that didn't face west into the setting sun, a clubhouse close to the main street (to keep road-building costs to a minimum), vary the length of holes to create a good sense of pace, create a finishing hole that can decide a match, and others. (But you could break any of the rules if you had a good reason.)

The routing plan laid down the bones in preparation for day two's assignments. Routing was an arduous task of measuring and converting yards into inches and back, trying to site good landing areas, trying to make a hole demanding enough for an A player, but fun enough for the 20-handicapper. (I had great empathy for the latter.) Should we use the hill or run around it? Flow a couple of holes down and back through a natural canyon, or splay one over the top of the big mound for a demanding blind-shot par five? Choices, choices.

It soon became abundantly clear how many hundreds of choices could be made on one piece of land.

Each student had an opportunity to show his routing plan and listen to the class's critique. As a group, most were pretty exciting to see. While many of us started holes in the same direction, by the third or fourth, people laid holes into spots others avoided. One fellow forgot a hole, and only had 17 in his plan. We all had enough flaws of our own not to laugh.

We covered the three major types of holes or overall course strategies: penal design, strategic design, and heroic design. Staples and Silva talked about eye appeal, balance, rhythm, harmony, proportion, and emphasis. What to do with tees, fairways, bunkers, and greens. And where and where not to plant or leave trees. And on and on. We couldn't get enough of it.

That's another thing that's so cool about this game of ours. There's so much to learn about playing golf. But if you're a course design fanatic, there's a whole other realm to jump into. Sure, baseball players have their fantasy week camps. But give me a couple of days like this, anytime.

To sign up in 2004, visit www.gsd.harvard.edu

What is the Best Course for *You?*

by Paul Harber

Are hot dogs better than hamburgers? Does Bud Lite have it over Coors Light? Top-Flite or Titleist? Which has the best golf ball? It's all a matter of personal choice and the same can be said about golf course rankings.

What makes one course better than another?

The first ratings lists conceived probably had to do with exclusivity and desire. Everybody tells you that The Country Club in Brookline ranks among the best in the United States. Why? Two basic reasons are its exclusivity and historical significance. You can't just walk in and play. Augusta National is as beautiful and well manicured an 18-hole layout as you will find. But why does it deserve to be called one of the top courses in America?

From golfers' 19th hole listings, ratings went to the golfing periodicals. It was easy to do, made a nice tease on a magazine cover and certainly created a buzz in the golfing community. Of course, when the magazines first decided to put together a list of best courses, they polled some of the top players and golf executives in America.

Later, the magazine editors refined the process and graded golf courses on six or seven factors, such as playability, aesthetics, design, historical significance and shot-making value.

By this time, golf course owners realized there was money to be made by having their course on the lists. What did these savvy owners do? They hired public relations companies to promote their courses and politic with the powers that be.

Eventually, magazines relented. What began as the Top 100 courses was diluted to Top 100 courses in the World and Top 100 courses in America. That was further diluted to many more lists such as Top 100 courses you can play and Top 100 courses built after World War II, etc. to Top 100 Resort Courses to Top 100 Municipal Courses.

It makes it difficult to determine what really is a good golf course.

The golf architects of the world live by the words of their patron saint, Donald Ross, who said that God creates golf courses and the architects simply reveal them, meaning that it is the nature of the landscape, the ocean vistas and mountain views, the dramatic change in the topography that makes one course better than another. Why else would golfing pilgrims make our way to California to play Pebble Beach, paying a king's ransom for the privilege?

Ross was correct in believing that the parcel of land was a primary factor in building a great course. However, there are only a few golf course locations on prime real estate. Basically, it is because of economics. If there is a parcel of land with magnificent vistas and dramatic topography, a developer can make millions of dollars more by transforming it into house lots instead of a golf course. Historically, thousands of courses around the nation—and hundreds in New England—no longer exist today because developers purchased the golf facilities, closed them, and built housing developments.

Ross should have added an addendum to his theory about what makes great courses. Besides topography, the most important fact in developing great golf courses is money. It is simple. If two tracts of land are equal, the golf course developer who puts more money into his project during the construction of the golf course, will end up with a better course.

Fifty years ago, typically, courses were built on old farm sites. Sons and daughters of New England farmers, who had no desire to continue their agricultural heritage, would seek out Geoffrey

Cornish, a professor at the Turf School at the University of Massachusetts. Today, the Pete Dyes and Jack Nicklauses of the world demand an upfront $1 million fee to design a course. Cornish was more benevolent and less mercenary. He would ask the prospective client, "How much can you spend on a golf course?" They would offer an amount, and he would go to work with the money he was given. Just by looking at his courses, you can see the variety of price tags.

The courses that had more money to spend, most likely, would have more land to spread the course out on. They would have more earth moved to make the settings around the greens more playable, with more greenside and fairway bunkers and more sets of tees. However, do not malign those pedestrian courses with small greens and no sand bunkers.

I remember my first time on a golf course. My aunt and uncle, Peg and Maurice Bresnahan, probably the worst golfers ever to play the game, would drag me, a youngster, along with them when they would play Harwichport on Cape Cod. They loved the simple little course. Sure, they were slow. In fact, instead of letting one group play through, they would allow a pack of foursomes to go through as we'd sit down to the side of one of the tees and have a picnic lunch of sandwiches and soda that my aunt had packed in her bag. They wouldn't have had fun playing a Pine Valley or a Pebble Beach; Harwichport was their special place.

That was the best course for them. What is the best course for you? It depends on you. There is a golf course for everyone. You just have to find the right fit.

Best courses for women? Most courses built in the last 15 years are more accommodating to women that ever before in the history of the game. Some actually have two sets of tees for women. Many of the good women golfers are bored by the forward tees that are so close to the green and offer little or no challenge. For want of a challenge, some women go back to the next set of tees, but there are no handicap ratings for women. If they have a handicap, they cannot post a score. Good courses for women have two sets of well-designed tees and offer course ratings from both sets.

Another easy way to tell if a golf course is concerned about women's play is simply to look at the scorecard. If the handicap holes from the men's tees are different than they are from the women's tees, some thought went in to assigning the stroke holes.

The beautiful 18th hole of the 4-star rated Red Tail Golf Club in Devens, MA.

Obviously, what is a difficult hole from the men's tee does not necessarily offer the same difficulty from the women's tee. Other women-friendly factors range from the construction of the teeing ground to the placement of restrooms on the course.

Best courses for seniors? Avoid courses where you have to keep your carts on the paths. It seems that your balls are always on the opposite side of the fairway and usually require an arduous 50-foot climb uphill or downhill.

Avoid courses that demand too many forced carries.

When I think of retirement golf, which is not that many years to go, I used to believe I wanted to belong to a golf club that offered heroic challenges where you had to hit the ball a ton and have several exciting holes over water. That philosophy has changed along with my loss of distance off the tee. I want to play golf where I can have fun, not lose a ton of golf balls and threaten par with an occasional chance at a birdie. When I pick a retirement course, it will be a course where I can reach at least half the par-4 holes in regulation. The standards for seniors, juniors and beginners are similar.

Short courses and par-3s are wonderful places to start. (*See page 15*). My first experiences at golf courses were south of Boston at Ridder Farms in Whitman and Cedar Hill in Stoughton. They were perfect places to begin. The front nine at Ridder is wide open. I will never forget standing on the first tee that first Sunday afternoon. The straightaway par-4 seemed so long, the green seemed a mile away. Today, it seems like the easiest hole in the world. It measures only about 300 yards and the green is huge and inviting. It was the first place to begin my golfing career and it would be a wonderful place to finish it, too.

Short Courses - Par 3

Course	Yards	Course	Yards
Connecticut		**Maine**	
Guilford Lakes Golf Course	1165	Loons Cove Golf Course	1214
Highland Greens GC	1398	Merriland Farm Par 3 Golf	838
Hillside Links LLC	932	Pine Ridge Golf Course	2570
Mile View Par 3	722	**New Hampshire**	
Short Beach Par 3 Golf Course	1270	Alpine Ridge	950
South Pine Creek Par 3 GC	1240	Applewood Golf Links	1367
Twin Lakes GC	835	Fore-U-Golf Center	1031
Villa Hills Golf Course	1158	Hickory Pond Inn and Golf Course	1006
Massachusetts		Kona Mansion Inn	1170
Cyprian Keyes Golf Club, Par 3	1230	Twin Lake Villa Golf Course	1356
Executive Par 3 at Swansea CC	1196	**Rhode Island**	
Fore Kicks GC & Sports Complex	1003	Button Hole	780
Murphy's Garrison Par 3 GC	1005	Windmill Hill Golf Course	1191
Rolling Green GC	1500		
Shadow Brook Golf Course	752		
Stoneham Oaks	1125	**Vermont**	
Stony Brook Golf Course	1287	Arrowhead Golf Course	1330
Woodbriar CC	1410	Barcomb Hill At Apple Tree Bay Rst	1108
		Stonehedge GC	1107

Course	Yards	Course	Yards
Executive Courses		**Executive Style Courses**	
Connecticut		**Connecticut**	
Birch Plain Golf Course	2666	Gainfield Farms GC	1384
Cedar Ridge GC	3025	Miner Hills Family Golf, LLC	1769
Massachusetts		Portland West Golf Club	3620
Blue Rock Golf Club	2563	Quarryview Golf Course	1576
Heritage Hill CC	2575	The Orchards Golf Course	1625
Holly Ridge Golf Club	2715	Willow Brook Golf Course	2613
Lost Brook Golf Club	3002	**Massachusetts**	
MGA Links at Mamantapett	2421	Challenger 9 at Waverly Oaks	2022
Middleton Golf Course	3000	Fire Fly Country Club	3083
Pine Knoll Par 3	1567	Lakeview Golf Club	1836
Rockland CC	3014	Paul Harney GC	3315
Twin Brooks GC At Sheraton	2621	Southers Marsh Golf Club	3694
Village Links	1986	Willowdale Golf Course	1935
Maine		Woodbriar CC	1410
White Birches GC	1922	**New Hampshire**	
Vermont		Balsams-Coashaukee Golf Course	3834
Sitzmark Golf Course	2300	Ponemah Green	4320
Rhode Island		**Vermont**	
Lindhbrook GC	2869	The Links at Lang Farm	
		Wilcox Cove GC	1732

The five rules you should memorize.

The following are among the most frequent occurrences on a golf course. Yet many players continually make things up as they go. Remember these, and you won't be scrambling for a Rules book, or confusing your fellow players.

1. Lateral hazards—red stakes. From a lateral hazard, you get two club-lengths relief from the point of entry into the hazard, not nearer the hole. Mark an area with a tee that's two club lengths from the line, real or determined, that defines the hazard. Drop a ball between the tee and the hazard line and add one stroke for the drop. You may also hit a ball from where you originally hit it, or on a line equidistant from your entry point on the other side of the hazard.

2. Water hazards—yellow stakes. From a water hazard, you can go back only, not sideways, as far as you want from the point a ball first crosses the hazard, on a line between the hole (not the tee) and the entry point. So if, from the tee, you hit over a pond, and the ball then hits a hillside and rolls back into the pond, you must take it back and drop it from the tee side of the pond, not the "rolling in" side. *(See illustration A)* Add one stroke.

3. Cart paths. If your ball is on a cart path, or your ball is in such a place that your stance is on the cart path, you are entitled to get one club-length free relief, on the nearest side of relief, not nearer the hole. If you elect to take relief in any situation, you must take full relief. In other words, if you see a nice grassy patch next

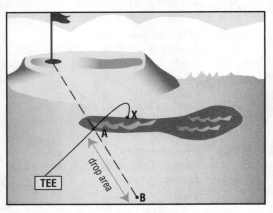

Illustration A

What if your tee shot safely crosses the water hazard, but then hits a sidehill, and rolls back into the pond, at Point X? What do you do? You must determine the point where the ball FIRST crossed the hazard (point A). Then on an imaginary line between A and the hole (not the tee), you may drop anywhere along that line between A & B. There is no limit to how far back B can be.

to the cart path, but dropping a ball there would mean that your foot is still on the path, then you cannot drop there. Also, if you decide to take a drop off the cart path, you must drop on the same side the ball is closest to, even if that means worse conditions than the other side. (Also, if the only drop you can take puts you behind a tree, that's too bad.) Sometimes the better choice is to hit off the path. In any case, make a decision BEFORE lifting your ball, because once you lift, you must take relief—or take a penalty stroke.

4. Advice? Don't ask; don't tell. One of the most common errors is asking or giving information that could be construed as opinion or advice. This is okay among friends in a casual round, but in a tournament, it will cost you two strokes per infraction. Ask or tell *facts* only. Yes: "This sprinkler head is marked 127 yards." No: "You're about 130 yards away." You also may not ask or tell what club you or another player has hit (except to your partner).

Other examples of what you cannot say:
"Your backswing is too fast."
"Your putt will break about three balls to the left."
"You're about 170 yards from the hole."
"That's a two-club wind in our face."
"Am I lined up to the hole?"

What you *can* say:
"There is a pond on the other side of this hill, on the left."
"Blue flags mean the pin is in the back third of the green."
"The flag is on a direct line over that rock."(Except on a putting green, you can indicate the line of play to another player.)
And in a team match, you can share info with your partner or partners about any of the above.

5. Provisionally speaking. A provisional ball is a ball you should hit when you think the ball you hit previously went out of bounds or may be lost for any reason. You must declare it is a provisional ball before you hit it; otherwise, it becomes the ball in play. You may continue to play the provisional until you reach the area where the original ball is likely to be. If you find the original, the provisional is null and void and costs you no strokes. But if you abandon the original, the provisional becomes the ball in play. If you later find your original ball, it doesn't matter. Add one penalty stroke for using a provisional ball.

Want lower scores?
Manage your game better.

Almost every golfer, including the pros, will make a bad decision or two on the course. Most of us make more than few. By playing a little smarter, we might improve our score by 5-7 strokes—without even changing our swing. We sought the advice of New England professionals to provide a few helpful hints.

Recognize trouble and take your medicine.

Head pro Ron Beck of Fox Hopyard in East Haddam, CT, says "Never follow a bad shot with a stupid shot. When you hit a bad shot, take your medicine, get the next shot back in play, and play one shot at a time." He says too many people will hit one into the woods and then attempt a low-percentage recovery by threading the needle between five trees, under a branch, and over a trap—usually resulting in hitting one of the trees, catching the overhanging branch, and if you make it that far, landing in the trap. Suddenly, you're looking at triple bogey. "A much better play," Beck says, "is to hit sideways, safely out into the fairway. You'll lose one stroke, but not two or three."

Factor in the wind more.

Even a small breeze behind you or in your face can have a full club's effect. On high trajectory shots, look around. Even if you can't feel a breeze on the ground, watch the tops of trees where your ball is going to be traveling. Consider this: the pros, when they play Pebble Beach, may hit anything from a wedge to a 4 iron to the 17th green. These are people who know much more about wind than you do—and they're making decisions that could win or lose them thousands of dollars. Here's what to do. Ralph Lenihan, head pro at Laurel Lane, in West Kingston, RI, says, "Most golfers swing too hard into a headwind. I teach people to take an easier swing, maybe three-quarters, widen their stance for stability, and be sure to follow through. For a breeze, add one club. For a strong wind, add two clubs, choke down two inches on the grip, and try to punch the ball under the wind." When the wind is to your back, Lenihan advises teeing it higher off the tee to let nature help you. Off the fairway, go down one club, and again take a three-quarters swing. "You don't want the ball to get too high in the air because the wind will take the spin off of it, making it much harder to stop on the green."

Where is the flag?

"Pin placement is one of the most overlooked aspects of course management ·for mid-to-high-handicappers," says John Tuffin, head pro at The Pinehills in Plymouth, MA. "If you want to be closer to the hole more often, remember all yardage markers measure shots to the center of the green. On long greens, the pin up front, middle, or back might call for three different clubs. Many golfers never think of this, thus mis-clubbing the shot. If the pin is in a safe area, go for it." But Tuffin points out that higher handicappers often suffer the opposite brain cramp. They shoot for the flag tucked behind a trap when they should be aiming at the safe part of the green. "Even the pros take the risky part of the green out of play sometimes. Most players should do so more often."

Buried lie? "Floating" in the rough?

All rough is not equal, according to Harry Parker, head pro at Ocean Edge in Brewster, MA. "In thick rough, if the grass is lying toward the pin, your biggest worry is getting the club away clean on your takeaway. On your downswing, you should generally make good contact with the ball." When your ball is down in thick grass that is lying in the direction away from the hole, Parker says you have to make several adjustments. "The most important thing is to try to get the clubface on the ball with as little grass as possible getting in the way. So you need to stand closer, take a steeper swing, and usually, swing harder." If you're more than 160 yards out, this is not the shot where you go for the pin—you just want to get it back in play. Use a lob wedge or pitching wedge, not a mid or long iron.

Forget lag putts.

Bob Rotella, sports psychologist, advises his players to always aim for the cup. When you hit a lag putt, the common thought is to get within a three-foot circle. The result often means you're left with a three-foot putt, the most dreaded shot in golf. Rotella advises players to pick as small a target as possible on each and every shot, 40-foot putts included. The same goes for chip shots. Don't just try to get it close—try to sink it. He says that even if you don't sink many, chances are you'll start having much shorter putts.

Handicap Calculator

A handicap is a golfer's personal rating. It is a number which "levels" the playing field, allowing a golfer of any ability to compete with any other golfer. Your handicap lets you subtract strokes from your score. The higher your handicap, the more strokes you may subtract. "Scratch" golfers subtract zero. You can get an official handicap at most public golf clubs by joining their inner club, or by joining a traveling tournament club.

The USGA has a patented handicap formula, which is based upon a number of your scores. The more scores you enter into the system, the more accurate it is likely to be. An official USGA handicap is issued by an authorized club.

To determine your own unofficial handicap, you must first determine your handicap index, by making the following calculations:

1. Subtract the course rating (found on the scorecard) from your score.
2. Multiply that difference by 113.
3. Divide the answer in Step 2 by the course Slope Rating (also found on the card). This answer is called the "differential" for that round.
4. Calculate the differentials for your last 20 rounds by repeating steps 1 to 3 for each of these 20 rounds. (If you have less than 20 rounds, talk to the administrator of the handicap system at your club.)
5. Add the lowest 10 differentials, of your last 20 rounds.
6. Divide the total of step 5 by ten to get the average.
7. Multiply the average by 0.96 and round to the nearest 10th.
8. This is your handicap index, but it NOT your handicap to use everywhere.
9. Using your handicap index, your handicap for the course you are playing depends of the degree of difficulty (the slope) of the course. Your handicap may be more or less than your index.

The terms course handicap, handicap index, slope, and USGA are registered trademarks of the United State Golf Association.

Most Difficult Courses
by Slope from the Back Tees

Course	Slope	Course	Slope

Connecticut

Great River Golf Club	143
Pistol Creek Golf Club	136
Laurel View CC	135
Lyman Orchards GC (Player)	134
Whitney Farms	134
Richter Park GC	134
Fox Hopyard Country Club	131

Massachusetts

Crumpin-Fox Club	141
The Ranch Golf Club	140
Ballymeade CC	139
Red Tail Golf Club	138
Norton Country Club	137
Farm Neck Golf Club	135
Pinehills Golf Club, Jones Course	135
Crosswinds Golf Club	133
Dennis Pines GC	133
Ledges Golf Club	133
Maplegate Country Club	133
New Seabury CC, Ocean Course	133
Westminster CC	133
Blackstone National Golf Club	132
Bradford Country Club	132
Cyprian Keyes Golf Club	132
Quashnet Valley CC	132
Captains GC, The Port Course at	131
Pinehills Golf Club, Nicklaus Course	131
Shaker Hills Golf Club	131
Westover Golf Course	131
Whaling City GC	131
Butternut Farm GC	130
Country Club of Wilbraham	130
Far Corner Golf Course	130
New England CC	130
Ocean Edge GC	130
Sheraton Hotel & Colonial Golf Club	130
Stow Acres CC (north)	130
Waverly Oaks Golf Club	130

Maine

Sugarloaf Golf Club	151
Belgrade Lakes GC	142
Sable Oaks Golf Club	138
Point Sebago Golf Club	135
Dunegrass Golf Club	134
Bethel Inn & Country Club	133
Boothbay Region CC	133
The Ledges Golf Club	133
Fox Ridge Golf Club	132
Natanis Golf Course	132
Samoset Resort GC	130

New Hampshire

Shattuck GC, The	145
Atkinson Resort and Country Club	140
Laconia Country Club	139
Stonebridge Country Club	138
Bretwood Golf Course (North)	136
Canterbury Woods CC	136
Ragged Mountain Golf Club	136
Windham Country Club	135
Apple Hill Golf Club	134
CC of New Hampshire	134
Breakfast Hill Golf Club	133
Bretwood Golf Course (South)	133
Newport Country Club	133
Owl's Nest Golf Club	133
Passaconaway CC	132
Eastman Golf Links	131
Lochmere Golf & CC	131
Balsams Panorama GC, The	130
Hanover Country Club	130

Rhode Island

Fenner Hill Golf Club	131
Foxwoods Golf CC	131

Vermont

Green Mountain National GC	138
Mount Snow Golf Club	133
Vermont National CC	133
Okemo Valley Golf Club	130
Country Club of Vermont	130

TPC Brings The Pros Back.

It was Labor Day Weekend 2003, and the eastern New England area was abuzz because the PGA made its return to the area, to the TPC at Boston (actually in Norton, very close to the Rhode Island border). The big names were there: Jim Furyk, Greg Norman, Justin Rose, Vijay Singh, Tiger Woods, and of course New England's own Brad Faxon. The tournament winner was Adam Scott who took the lead on Saturday afternoon and held on through the Monday finish. Rocco Mediate was second.

But the real winners were the Greater Boston/ Providence/ Worcester fans who have gone without their heroes ever since Pleasant Valley lost its long-running, multi-named event. Make no mistake, the Greater Hartford Open is a first class tournament, one of the Tour's best run and best attended stops and well worth the drive from anywhere else in New England. But this felt different, because it was closer to the biggest metropolitan area north of Manhattan, the big banks were there, the big limos were there, and the big crowds had that familiar "go Tigah" accent.

For a relatively flat piece of land, Arnold Palmer designed an intriguing, varied course, with some intimidating fairway obstacles, daring carries, and sinister greens. The pros played the par-71 layout at more than 7400 yards (when will the madness stop?) and by the 16th they were plenty bushed. Anyone following them was pretty beat, too. It seemed about driver, three wood, three wood to get from some of the holes to the next. Even the players got rides. But if you brought comfortable shoes, you could walk along every hole and the TPC did an excellent job of providing good or great views of every fairway and green. Superintendent Tom Brodeur did an exceptional job of getting this brand new course ready for the ever-critical pros. The bentgrass greens ran true and fast. The bentgrass fairways looked lush. Give it two more years and it will be sensational.

There were plenty of food stations, contests, vendor displays, port-a-lets, greenside bleachers, and helpful volunteers to point the way. If you get an opportunity to visit in 2004, don't miss it. If you want to actually play the course without joining (it is, after all, a private), become a volunteer. One of the perks is a free round, the day after the event.

When you're there, you might also want to stop right at the entrance and visit the headquarters of the Massachusetts Golf

Association and the William F. Connell Golf House and Museum, displaying many of the significant moments of Bay State golf.

The Deutsche Bank Classic has only a two-year commitment to the Norton site, but it seems pretty obvious this event at this venue will draw big crowds year after year. If you come out with your family in 2004, we can keep it around a long, long time. Hope to see you there.

The Green Room of the William F. Connell Golf House and Museum in Norton, MA.

The Women's U.S. Open Comes to Western Mass.

July 1-4, the Women's US Open comes to The Orchards, in South Hadley MA, just a short hop from Amherst. Defending champion Hilary Lunke and her fellow competitors will find a Donald Ross classic that has undergone a considerable amount of tweaking in the past two years. The relentless rains of 2003 delayed till September much of what the superintendent hoped would be done by July. It didn't seem to hurt the thick US Open-style rough, however. Tucked away behind a quiet neighborhood, The Orchards lies on just 160 acres of rolling countryside.

The greens are small and offer typical Ross characteristics: the breaks are subtle, and you don't ever want to be long. There are several of the master's patented false front bunkers as well: they appear to be greenside, but could be 30 yards short or more. From the higher elevations of the course, the pros will have dramatic views of Mt. Tom and others in the region.

The players will have some interesting shotmaking decisions on almost every hole, but the spectators will be better off finding one good vantage point and spending the day there, or following a group of lesser known players, because unless the course takes down 400-500 trees, movement between holes will likely create several bottlenecks. Hopefully the people from Palmer Management Group, who manage the course, will have the layout in prime shape when the best women in the world once again visit New England.

Help us Rate the Courses

We need your input. Tell us what You think!
You Are The Expert On Courses You Play.

We can't visit every course every year, and course conditions change from year to year. We received over 160 reader-suggested ratings and comments on courses they liked and didn't like. Thank you! Your comments are published in the course listings as "Players' comments". For this year we hope that more of you will rate and comment on 2 star and un-rated courses.

We want to hear from golfers at all levels. Tell us your handicap, how often you play, and your ratings and comments. Make your ratings on a NEGG scale of 2 to 4 stars.

✪✪✪✪ Four Stars means the course competes with any course, public or private in the nation.

✪✪✪ Three Stars are awarded for excellent courses our consultants and readers have enjoyed and highly recommend.

✪✪ Two Stars are earned by offering great golfing experiences in nearly every category.

The Ratings Take Into Account Three Main Factors:

1. Course layout. Is it interesting and varied? Will you remember several holes a few days later? Is it challenging but also fair?

2. Course condition. Is there grass on the tees or is it worn off? Is the rough cleaned out? Are the fairways green? Are the greens conducive to putting true? Are the greens in good shape?

3. Staff and ownership service attitude. Are carts required? (If so, this is a negative point.) Are the prices fair for greens fees and pro shop merchandise? Is the signage on the course helpful? Is there enough drinking water on the course? Are the clubhouse personnel friendly and helpful? (Poor service attitude can hurt a rating.)

Contact us by:
U.S. Mail: 366 River Road Carlisle, MA 01741
Email: golfguide@earthlink.net
Fax: 978-287-0125
Web: www.newenglandgolfguide.com

18 hole Courses

✪✪✪✪-Four Star

Massachusetts
Crumpin-Fox Club
Farm Neck Golf Club
New Seabury CC, Ocean Course
Pinehills Golf Club
Red Tail Golf Club
Shaker Hills Golf Club
Taconic Golf Club
The Ranch Golf Club
Waverly Oaks Golf Club

Maine
Belgrade Lakes GC

Connecticut
Richter Park GC

✪✪✪-Three Star

Massachusetts
Atlantic Country Club
Blackstone National Golf Club
Captains GC
Cranberry Valley GC
Cranwell Resort, Spa and Golf Club
Cyprian Keyes Golf Club
Hickory Ridge CC
Kettle Brook Golf Club
Poquoy Brook GC
Southers Marsh GC
Wahconah CC

Maine
Northeast Harbor GC
Point Sebago Golf Club
Sable Oaks Golf Club
Samoset Resort GC
Sugarloaf Golf Club
The Ledges Golf Club

New Hampshire
Atkinson Resort and Country Club
Balsams Panorama GC, The
Canterbury Woods
Eastman Golf Links
Laconia CC
Owl's Nest Golf Club
Passaconaway CC
Portsmouth CC
Stonebridge Country Club

Rhode Island
Richmond Country Club

Vermont
Country Club of Vermont
Green Mountain National G. C.
Killington Golf Resort
Stratton Mt.
Vermont National CC

Connecticut
Fox Hopyard Country Club
Great River Golf Club
Pistol Creek Golf Club

✪✪-Two Star

Massachusetts
Acushnet River Valley Golf Course
Ballymeade CC
Beverly Golf & Tennis
Blissful Meadows GC
Braintree Muni. GC
Butternut Farm GC
Cape Cod CC
Chemawa Golf Course
Chicopee Municipal GC
Country Club of Greenfield
Dennis Pines GC
Far Corner Golf Course
Foxborough Country Club
Gardner Municipal GC
Glen Ellen
Granite Links at Quarry Hills
Hampden Country Club
Hickory Hill GC
Juniper Hill GC
Ledges Golf Club
Maplegate Country Club
New England CC
New Seabury CC, Dunes Course
Oak Ridge Golf Club
Ocean Edge GC
Olde Barnstable Fairgrounds GC
Olde Scotland Links
Quashnet Valley CC
River Bend CC
Sandy Burr CC
Swansea Country Club
Tekoa Country Club
The Meadow at Peabody
The Meadows Golf Club
Townsend Ridge Country Club
Trull Brook Golf Course
Veteran's Golf Club

Wachusett CC
Wayland Country Club
Woods of Westminster CC

Maine
Bar Harbor Golf Course
Bethel Inn & Country Club
Brunswick Golf Club
Cape Arundel Golf Club
Cape Neddick County Club
Dunegrass Golf Club
Mingo Springs GC
Naples Golf and Country Club
Natanis Golf Course
Nonesuch River Golf Club
Palmyra Golf Course
Spring Meadows GC
The Links at Outlook
Va-Jo-Wa Golf Club
Waterville Country Club

New Hampshire
Amherst Country Club
Androscoggin Valley CC
Beaver Meadow GC
Breakfast Hill Golf Club
Bretwood Golf Course
Campbell's Scottish Highlands
CC of New Hampshire
Green Meadow GC
Hanover Country Club
North Conway CC
Overlook GC
Pease Golf Course
Shattuck GC, The
Souhegan Woods GC
Tory Pines Resort
Windham Country Club

Rhode Island
Beaver River Golf Club
Cranston Country Club
Exeter Country Club
Fenner Hill Golf Club
Foxwoods Golf CC
Laurel Lane GC
North Kingstown Muni.
Triggs Memorial GC
Winnapaug Golf Course

Vermont
Crown Point CC
Equinox Country Club
Haystack Golf Club

Mount Snow Golf Club
Mt. Anthony CC
Okemo Valley Golf Club
Rutland Country Club
Stowe Country Club
Woodstock Inn & Resort

Connecticut
Blackledge CC - Anderson's Glen
Crestbrook Park GC
Fairview Farm Golf Course
Hunter Golf Club
Lyman Orchards GC (Jones)
Manchester CC
Pequabuck Golf Course
Pine Valley Golf Course
Portland Golf Club
Putnam Country Club
Quarry Ridge GC
Rockledge CC
Sterling Farms GC
Tallwood Country Club
Tashua Knolls CC
Timberlin Golf Club
Topstone Golf Course
Tunxis Plantation CC
Willimantic CC

9 hole Courses

✪✪✪-Three Star
Massachusetts
Challenger 9 at Waverly Oaks
Greenock Country Club

Maine
Wilson Lake CC

✪✪-Two Star
Massachusetts
The Links at Bayberry
Hopedale CC
Rockport Golf Course
Scituate Country Club
Swanson Meadows
Touisset Country Club
Webster Dudley Golf Club

Southers Marsh GC in Plymouth, MA.

Maine
Dexter Municipal GC
Grindstone Neck GC
Limestone CC
Piscataquis CC

New Hampshire
Hales Location Country Club
Hooper Golf Club
Pinehurst CC

Connecticut
Hotchkiss School GC
Woodstock Golf Course

✪✪✪-Executive Three Star
Paul Harvey GC - MA
Portland West GC - CT

✪✪-Executive Two Star
Executive Par 3 at Swansea - MA
Squirrel Run CC - MA

The Links at Lang Farm - VT
Williston Golf C - VT
Pattonbrook CC - CT
Westwoods GC - CT
Willow Brook GC - CT

✪✪✪-Par 3, Three Star
Massachusetts
Blue Rock GC
Cyprian Keyes GC, Par 3
Holly Ridge GC
Middleton GC
Twin Brooks GC at Sheraton

✪✪-Par 3, Two Star
Shadow Brook GC - MA
Village Links- MA
Merriland Farm Par 3 Golf - ME
Applewood Golf Links - NH
Button Hole - RI
Guilford Lakes GC - CT

Golf Geocenters

Courses geographically clustered. Take your pick!

Plymouth, Massachusetts

Atlantic Country Club
Challenger 9 at Waverly Oaks
Crosswinds Golf Club
Pinehills Golf Club, Jones
Pinehills Golf Club, Nicklaus
Southers Marsh Golf Club
Squirrel Run Country Club
Village Links
Waverly Oaks Golf Club

Springfield & Southwick Massachusetts

Edgewood Golf Club
Southwick Country Club
The Ranch Golf Club
Franconia Muni Golf Club
Veteran's Golf Club

Rehoboth, Massachusetts

Hidden Hollow Country Club
Hillside Country Club
Middlebrook Country Club
Pine Valley Golf Course
Rehoboth Country Club
Sun Valley Country Club

Portland & Westbrook, Maine

River Meadow GC
Riverside Municipal Golf Course
Sable Oaks Golf Club
South Portland Municipal
Sunset Ridge
Twin Falls Golf Course

Amherst, NH

Amherst Country Club
Buckmeadow Golf Club
Ponemah Green
Souhegan Woods Golf Club

Hope Valley & Richmond, Rhode Island

Beaver River Golf Club
Fenner Hill Golf Club
Foxwoods Country Club
Lindhbrook Golf Club
Meadow Brook Golf Course
Richmond Country Club
Wood River Golf

Hartford Area Connecticut

Buena Vista Golf Club
East Hartford Golf Club
Gillette Ridge
Goodwin Golf Course
Keney Golf Club
Rockledge Country Club
Wintonbury Hills Golf Course

Open Year Round

Weather permitting, or function facility and clubhouse remain open.

Connecticut
Airways Golf Course
Alling Memorial GC
Cedar Knob GC
E. Gaynor Brennan GC
Fairchild Wheeler GC
Goodwin Golf Course
Hunter Golf Club
Keney Golf Club
Laurel View CC
Leisure Resort At Banner Lodge
Meadowbrook CC
Pistol Creek Golf Club
Rolling Meadows Country Club
Shennecosset GC
Short Beach Par 3 Golf Course
Tallwood Country Club

Massachusetts
Ballymeade CC
Bass River Golf Course
Bay Pointe CC
Blissful Meadows GC
Brookline GC at Putterham
Brookside Club, The
Cape Cod CC
Captains GC
Chelmsford Country Club
Clearview Golf Course
Cotuit-Highground GC
Crosswinds
Cyprian Keyes Golf Club
Cyprian Keyes Golf Club, Par 3
D.W. Fields Golf Course
Dennis Highlands/Dennis Pines GC
Easton Country Club
Falmouth Country Club
Far Corner Golf Course
Fire Fly Country Club
Fore Kicks Golf Course & Sports Complex
Franklin Park, (William J. Devine GC)
Glen Ellen CC
Heather Hill CC
Heritage Country Club
Heritage Hill CC
Highland Links
Holly Ridge Golf Club
Hyannis Golf Club
Lakeview Golf Club
Lakeville Country Club
Little Harbor CC
Maplegate Country Club
Marion Golf Course

MGA Links at Mamantapett
Middleton Golf Course
Mill Valley Links
Mink Meadows GC
Newton Commonwealth GC
Northampton CC
Norwood Country Club
Ocean Edge GC
Poquoy Brook GC
Quashnet Valley CC
Rehoboth Country Club
Sagamore Spring GC
Sandwich Hollows Golf Club
Squirrel Run CC
St. Anne Country Club
Stone-E-Lea Golf Course
Strawberry Valley GC
Swansea Country Club
Tekoa Country Club
Tewksbury CC
Touisset Country Club
Twin Brooks GC At Sheraton
Wampanoag Golf Club
Woodbriar CC
Woods of Westminster CC

Maine
Bath Country Club
Biddeford & Saco CC
Maple Lane Inn and Golf Club
Samoset Resort GC

New Hampshire
Applewood Golf Links
Owl's Nest Golf Club
Windham Country Club
Woodbound Inn GC

Rhode Island
Country View Golf Club
Cranston Country Club
Laurel Lane GC
Montaup Country Club
Pinehurst CC
Rose Hill Golf Course
Triggs Memorial GC
Weekapaug Golf Club
Winnapaug Golf Course
Wood River Golf

Vermont
Lake Morey CC

New Course Indicator

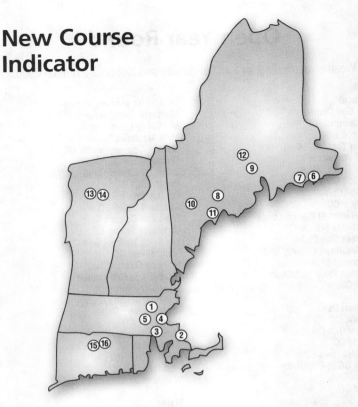

Course	Location	holes/par	Chapter/Page
1. Butter Brook GC	Westford, MA	18 / par 36	2 / p. 85
2. Crosswinds	Plymouth, MA	18 / par 72	1 / p. 44
3. Forekicks	Norfolk, MA	9 / par 27	4 / p. 156
4. Granite Links	Quincy, MA	18 / par 72	1 / p. 49
5. Shining Rock	Northbridge, MA	18 / par 72	2 / p. 111
6. Barren View	Jonesboro, ME	9 / par 34	7 / p. 261
7. Bonnie Blink	Sorrento, ME	9 / par 36	7 / p. 263
8. Highland Greens	Topsham, ME	9 / par 35	6 / p. 239
9. Rocky Knoll	Orrington, ME	9 / par 36	7 / p. 284
10. Sunday River	Bethel, ME	18 / par 72	6 / p. 252
11. Toddy Brook	Yarmouth, ME	9 / par 36	6 / p. 254
12. White Tail	Charleston, ME	9 / par 34	7 / p. 289
13. Links at Long Farm	Essex, VT	18 / par 60	8 / p. 317
14. Woodbury	Woodbury, VT	9 / par 27	8 / p. 320
15. Gillette Ridge	Bloomfield, CT	18 / par 72	9 / p. 330
16. Wintonbury Hills	Bloomfield, CT	18 / par 70	9 / p. 348

Courses that closed: Pine Acres, MA, Pocassett CC, RI, Woodland Terrace GC ME, Marble Island CC, VT., Canton Public GC, CT

New Course Listings

Less than 450 courses were listed in the first edition of the *New England GolfGuide*© in 1990. The 15th edition in 2004 lists 663 courses, an increase of 213. That averages over 14 new listings per year. In some years when there was a golf course building boom, as many as 29 new listings were recorded. This year there are 16. The USGF reported that there are 30 courses under

Crosswinds is the 9th public course in Plymouth, MA.

construction or awaiting permits. Permits were refused for three proposed courses in Western Massachusetts and two in Connecticut because of ecological problems. Construction of the back 9 of Butter Brook in Westford, Massachusetts was halted because of an endangered salamander. Last year the "E" word was Economics. This year its either Environmental or Estate as in real estate development.

There are 5 new courses in Massachusetts. The Big Dig provided millions of tons of fill that enabled the construction of a truly beautiful 27 hole championship golf course, **Granite Links at Quarry Hills**. (Story, pages 6-7). **Shining Rock Golf Community** in Northbridge is an 18 hole, 7010 yard course that includes a large real estate development. **Butter Brook** in Westford, hopes to have 18 holes when its EPA problems are resolved. **Crosswinds**, an

The fifth hole at Butter Brook Golf Course in Westford, MA.

18 hole municipal course with professional management, is the 9th public course in Plymouth. **Fore Kicks** in Norfolk is an excellent example of the trend of multi-sports complexes. The links style par 3 also has lights for night play.

There are six new 9 hole golf courses in Maine: **Barren View** in Jonesboro; **Bonnie Blink** in Sorrento; **Highland**

Sunday River's 18th hole in Bethel, Maine.

Green in Topsham; **Rocky Knoll** in Orrington; and **Toddy Brook** in North Yarmouth. **Sunday River** in Bethel, Maine is an 18 hole resort course designed by Rees Jones.

There are two new 18 hole courses in Connecticut, coincidentally both in Bloomfield: **Gillette Ridge,** an Arnold Palmer design, and **Wintonbury Hills,** a Peter Dye design.

In Vermont, the **Links at Lang Farm** in Essex is an 18 hole, championship par 60 course. **Woodbury GC** in Woodbury is a 9 hole, 1200 yard course, family owned and family run.

CHAPTER 1

Boston & South Shore

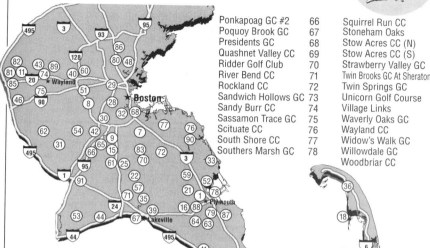

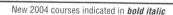

New 2004 courses indicated in **bold italic**

Atlantic Country Club

✪✪✪

Plymouth, MA (508) 759-6644
www.atlanticcountryclub.com

Club Pro: Don Daley, PGA
Pro Shop: Full inventory
Payment: Cash , MC, Visa
Tee Times: 2 days in advance
Fee 9 Holes: Weekday: $25.00 M-Th
Fee 18 Holes: Weekday: $45.00 M-Th
Twilight Rates: Yes, after 3 pm
Cart Rental: $15pp/18 $7pp/9
Lessons: $30.00/ half hour **Schools:** No
Clinics: Junior **Day Camps:** No
Other: Soft drinks/ Snack Bar / Banquet Facilities

Tees	Holes	Yards	Par	USGA	Slope
BACK	18	6262	72	70.8	127
MIDDLE	18	5840	72	69.0	119
FRONT	18	4918	72	68.3	116

Weekend: $30.00 F/S/S/H
Weekend: $55.00 F/S/S/H
All Day Play: No
Discounts: None
Junior Golf: No **Membership:** Waiting List
Driving Range: Yes

COUPON

Players' Comments: "Great track at a reasonable price. Many great holes with challenging tee box selection. Compares right up there with the best in Massachusetts." "Great putting greens."

	1	2	3	4	5	6	7	8	9
PAR	4	3	4	5	4	5	3	4	4
YARDS	302	144	410	475	343	467	134	387	345
HDCP	11	17	3	7	13	9	15	1	5
	10	11	12	13	14	15	16	17	18
PAR	4	3	4	4	5	4	5	3	4
YARDS	336	156	310	281	460	330	491	105	364
HDCP	8	12	4	18	6	14	10	16	2

Directions: Take Route 3 to Exit 2. Right onto Long Pond Road. Left onto Carter's Bridge Road. Right onto Upland Road to Little Sandy Pond Road. Course is 1 mile on left.

Ballymeade CC

✪✪ 2

N. Falmouth, MA (508) 540-4005
www.ballymeade.com

Club Pro: Jody Shaw, GM
Pro Shop: Full inventory
Payment: Cash and credit cards
Tee Times: 1 week adv.
Fee 9 Holes: Weekday: $40, cart incl.
Fee 18 Holes: Weekday: $58, cart incl.
Twilight Rates: Yes, after 3 pm
Cart Rental: see 'fees '
Lessons: $35.00/half hour **Schools:** No
Clinics: Women **Day Camps:** No
Other: Restaurant / Clubhouse / Bar-lounge / Lockers / Snack Bar / Showers

Tees	Holes	Yards	Par	USGA	Slope
BACK	18	6928	72	74.3	139
MIDDLE	18	6358	72	71.7	134
FRONT	18	5001	72	69.9	119

Weekend: $45, cart incl.
Weekend: $76, cart incl., f/s/s
All Day Play:
Discounts: None
Junior Golf: Yes **Membership:** Yes
Driving Range: $6.00/lg. bucket

Players Comments: "Superb in every way. Challenging. Scenic." Hole 11: Highest point on Cape; can see the Bay, New Bedford, over Marion to Fairhaven, all the boats in between. Seasonal rates. Open all year.

	1	2	3	4	5	6	7	8	9
PAR	4	3	5	4	3	4	4	5	4
YARDS	355	183	464	333	164	419	367	464	390
HDCP	17	11	9	7	13	1	5	15	3
	10	11	12	13	14	15	16	17	18
PAR	5	3	4	4	3	4	4	4	5
YARDS	500	164	403	415	380	331	156	367	503
HDCP	8	6	2	10	14	16	18	12	4

Directions: Over Bourne Bridge to Route 28 South. Take the North Falmouth Route 151 exit, 9 miles from the bridge. Turn right off the exit ramp. Course is less than 1 mile on right.

Bass River Golf Course

So. Yarmouth, MA (508) 398-9079
www.golfyarmouthcapecod.com

Club Pro: Fred Ghioto
Pro Shop: Full inventory
Payment: Visa, MC, Disc
Tee Times: 7 days adv. (508) 398-4112
Fee 9 Holes: Weekday: No
Fee 18 Holes: Weekday: $50.00
Twilight Rates: Yes, after 2 pm
Cart Rental: $30.00/18 $18.00/9
Lessons: Yes **Schools:** No
Clinics: No **Day Camps:** No
Other: Clubhouse / Snack bar / Bar-lounge

Tees	Holes	Yards	Par	USGA	Slope
BACK	18	6129	72	69.3	122
MIDDLE	18	5734	72	67.7	117
FRONT	18	5343	72	69.9	115

Weekend: No
Weekend: $50.00
All Day Play: N/R
Discounts: None
Junior Golf: No **Membership:** No
Driving Range: No

New irrigation system in fall 2003. Proximity to river creates constant breezes. Donald Ross designed.

	1	2	3	4	5	6	7	8	9
PAR	4	4	4	3	5	3	3	4	4
YARDS	329	348	282	105	464	139	190	282	391
HDCP	8	9	17	18	5	13	7	14	2

	10	11	12	13	14	15	16	17	18
PAR	4	4	5	5	3	4	5	4	4
YARDS	247	386	450	500	140	333	474	319	339
HDCP	16	1	4	3	15	6	11	12	10

Directions: Take Exit 8 off of Route 6 East. Take left onto Regional Ave. Turn right at second stop sign to entrance.

Bay Pointe CC

Onset, MA (508) 759-8802, 1-800-24T-TIME
www.baypointecc.com

Club Pro: Rusty Gunnarson
Pro Shop: Full inventory
Payment: Most major
Tee Times: 1 week in advance.
Fee 9 Holes: Weekday: $20.00
Fee 18 Holes: Weekday: $35.00
Twilight Rates: After 3 pm
Cart Rental: $15pp/18 $7.50pp/9
Lessons: $50.00/half hour **Schools:** No
Clinics: No **Day Camps:** No
Other: Clubhouse / Lockers / Showers / Snack bar / Restaurant / Bar-lounge /Pool / Tennis

Tees	Holes	Yards	Par	USGA	Slope
BACK					
MIDDLE	18	6201	70	71.6	125
FRONT	18	5380	72	71.3	125

Weekend: $25.00 after 3 pm
Weekend: $40.00
All Day Play: Yes
Discounts: Senior & Junior
Junior Golf: No **Membership:** Yes
Driving Range: No

COUPON

Typical Cape course, superbly manicured, excellent greens and fairways. Great rates for juniors and seniors. Weekday special $35 for 18, with 3 day advance tee time, includes cart. Open year round.

	1	2	3	4	5	6	7	8	9
PAR	5	4	4	3	4	4	3	3	5
YARDS	481	465	384	189	452	283	101	227	517
HDCP	5	1	7	15	3	13	17	11	9

	10	11	12	13	14	15	16	17	18
PAR	3	4	3	4	3	5	4	5	4
YARDS	195	391	203	360	208	526	337	492	390
HDCP	10	2	12	14	16	6	18	8	4

Directions: I-495 turns into Route 25. Take Exit 1 from Route 25. At 7th light go right, course 2/3 mile on right. From Route 3 South take Route 6 at Sagamore Rotary toward Wareham. Cross Buttermilk Bay into Wareham and go left a first light. Course 2/3 mile on right.

Bayberry Hills GC/ Bayberry Links

▶ 5

S. Yarmouth, MA (508) 394-5597
www.capecodgolf.com/bayberryhills

Club Pro: Don Geay, Golf Dir.
Pro Shop: Full inventory
Payment: Visa, MC, Disc
Tee Times: 7 days adv. (508) 398-4112
Fee 9 Holes: Weekday: $32.50 cart incl.
Fee 18 Holes: Weekday: $52.50 cart incl.
Twilight Rates: Yes, after 2 pm
Cart Rental: included
Lessons: $35.00/half hour **Schools:** No
Clinics: N/R **Day Camps:** No
Other: Clubhouse / Bar-lounge / Restaurant

Tees	Holes	Yards	Par	USGA	Slope
BACK	18	6523	72	71.7	125
MIDDLE	18	6067	72	69.6	119
FRONT	18	5323	72	69.4	111

Weekend: $32.50 cart incl.
Weekend: $52.50 cart incl.
All Day Play: N/R
Discounts: None
Junior Golf: No **Membership:** No
Driving Range: $10/lg. $7/md. $4/sm.

27 holes includes Links Course (9 holes, par 36, 2926 yards). Depending on volume / tee time availability, two of the three tracks may be assigned. Playable for all skill levels. Off season rates.

	1	2	3	4	5	6	7	8	9
PAR	4	5	3	4	4	4	5	3	4
YARDS	375	485	140	336	335	350	505	146	350
HDCP	3	9	17	7	15	13	1	11	5
	10	11	12	13	14	15	16	17	18
PAR	4	4	3	4	4	5	4	3	5
YARDS	372	384	130	320	352	503	349	160	475
HDCP	4	2	18	16	8	10	6	14	12

Directions: Take Exit 8 off Route 6 East. Turn south onto Station Avenue. Take right at second traffic light, Old Townhouse Road to 4-way stop. Cross into Bayberry Hills.

Blue Rock Golf Club

✪✪✪ ▶ 6

S. Yarmouth, MA (508) 398-9295
www.bluerockgolfcourse.com

Club Pro: Pat Fannon, PGA
Pro Shop: Full inventory
Payment: Visa, MC, Cash, Check
Tee Times: 7 days adv.
Fee 9 Holes: Weekday: $45.00
Fee 18 Holes: Weekday: $45.00
Twilight Rates: After 2 pm
Cart Rental: $5.00 Pull cart
Lessons: $40/half hour **Schools:** Yes
Clinics: Yes **Day Camps:** Yes
Other: Clubhouse / Snack bar / Restaurant / Bar-lounge / Hotel / Tennis / Pool / Golf School / Golf Clinic

Tees	Holes	Yards	Par	USGA	Slope
BACK	18	2890	54	56.4	83
MIDDLE	18	2563	54	56.4	83
FRONT	18	2170	54	55.8	80

Weekend: Breakfast Club-$23
Weekend: $45.00
All Day Play: No
Discounts: None
Junior Golf: Yes **Membership:** Yes
Driving Range: Members only

Rated "Top 3 par 3 in US" *Golf Digest*. "Top short course in US.", *Sports Illustrated*

	1	2	3	4	5	6	7	8	9
PAR	3	3	3	3	3	3	3	3	3
YARDS	103	127	118	125	247	145	170	165	165
HDCP	17	15	13	11	1	9	5	7	3
	10	11	12	13	14	15	16	17	18
PAR	3	3	3	3	3	3	3	3	3
YARDS	150	117	190	147	185	185	144	129	173
HDCP	10	18	2	12	6	8	14	16	4

Directions: Take Mid Cape Highway East to Exit 8. Turn right off the ramp. First left White's Path, right to intersection, turn left Great Western Road. Course is 1/4 mile on right.

Braintree Muni. GC

Braintree, MA (781) 843-6513
www.braintreegolf.comm

Club Pro: Bob Beach
Pro Shop: Full/discount
Payment: Cash, Visa, MC
Tee Times: 3 days adv.

Tees	Holes	Yards	Par	USGA	Slope
BACK	18	6569	72	71.3	128
MIDDLE	18	6237	72	70.4	126
FRONT	18	5454	72	71.0	114

Fee 9 Holes: Weekday: None
Fee 18 Holes: Weekday: $30.00
Twilight Rates: Yes, after 4 pm $17.00
Cart Rental: $26.00/18 $14.00/9
Lessons: $40.00/40 minutes **Schools:** Yes
Clinics: Special Olympics **Day Camps:** Yes
Other: Restaurant / Clubhouse / Snack Bar

Weekend: None
Weekend: $37.00
All Day Play: No
Discounts: Senior & Junior
Junior Golf: Very active **Membership:** Res. only
Driving Range: No

Player's Comments: "Walkable. Challenging. Well maintained." New forward tees completed. PGA Professional offers lessons for challenged golfers.

	1	2	3	4	5	6	7	8	9
PAR	4	4	3	4	3	5	4	5	4
YARDS	325	335	171	310	192	494	383	500	364
HDCP	16	14	12	18	10	4	2	6	8

	10	11	12	13	14	15	16	17	18
PAR	5	4	3	5	4	4	3	4	4
YARDS	481	408	172	465	411	391	174	347	314
HDCP	5	1	15	13	3	7	17	11	9

Directions: Route 93 to Exit 6. Take Route 37 South for 2 miles. Make right on Jefferson St. Club on right.

Brookline GC at Putterham

Brookline, MA (617) 730-2078

Club Pro: B. Bain, PGA, J. Neville, Dir.
Pro Shop: Full inventory
Payment: Visa, MC, Amex, Cash
Tee Times: 3 days adv.

Tees	Holes	Yards	Par	USGA	Slope
BACK	18	6307	71	70.2	123
MIDDLE	18	6003	71	68.3	118
FRONT	18	5414	72	70.6	118

Fee 9 Holes: Weekday: $20 M-Th til 7:30am
Fee 18 Holes: Weekday: $35.00 M-Th
Twilight Rates: Yes, after 4 pm
Cart Rental: $30.00/18 $20.00/9
Lessons: $35.00/half hour **Schools:** Jr.Yes
Clinics: Yes **Day Camps:** No
Other: Restaurant / Clubhouse / Bar-Lounge

Weekend: No
Weekend: $38.00 F/S/S/H
All Day Play: Yes
Discounts: Senior & Junior M-Th
Junior Golf: Yes **Membership:** No
Driving Range: No

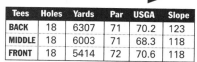

Sig. Hole: #12. Tight fairways, elevated greens, low terrain, small hills, and lots of brooks. Many trees. Dress code: collared shirts. Weekday 9 hole special until 7:30 am. Open year round.

	1	2	3	4	5	6	7	8	9
PAR	5	4	3	4	3	5	4	4	4
YARDS	460	335	148	317	177	506	340	390	365
HDCP	12	10	18	16	14	8	4	2	6

	10	11	12	13	14	15	16	17	18
PAR	4	4	3	4	4	5	4	3	4
YARDS	330	290	119	380	400	520	330	160	391
HDCP	11	13	17	5	1	7	9	15	3

Directions: From I-95 N & S to Rte 9 E, 4 miles to Chestnut Hill Mall on left. Exit onto Hammond Street. Go to rotary; 4th right to Newton St. 100 yrds on left. From Boston: Rte 9 to Hammond St. Turn left. 1 mi. to rotary — 4th right to Newton St. 100 yrds on left.

Brookmeadow CC

Canton, MA (781) 828-4444
www.brookmeadowgolf.com

Club Pro: Steve Lamdi
Pro Shop: Full inventory @ discount
Payment: Cash , Visa, MC
Tee Times: 5 days adv.

Tees	Holes	Yards	Par	USGA	Slope
BACK	18	6659	72	71.7	123
MIDDLE	18	6309	72	70.1	118
FRONT	18	5606	72	71.2	114

Fee 9 Holes: Weekday: $20 M-Th after 2pm **Weekend:** $20 before 6:30am
Fee 18 Holes: Weekday: $40.00 **Weekend:** $45.00
Twilight Rates: Yes, after 5:30 pm **All Day Play:** No
Cart Rental: $15.00/18 **Discounts:** Sr & Jr. $5 off M-Th before 10:30.
Lessons: $40.00/half hour **Schools:** No **Junior Golf:** Yes **Membership:** Yes
Clinics: Yes **Day Camps:** No **Driving Range:** $5.00/med. bucket
Other: Clubhouse / Lockers / Showers / Snack bar / Bar-lounge / Function Room

Sig. Hole: #2, 420 yd. par 4. Demanding dogleg right with an elevated green surrounded by 4 bunkers. "A joy to par." J.M.

	1	2	3	4	5	6	7	8	9
PAR	4	4	4	3	4	3	4	5	5
YARDS	376	387	308	168	346	151	385	475	522
HDCP	7	1	13	15	9	17	5	11	3
	10	11	12	13	14	15	16	17	18
PAR	4	3	5	4	4	3	5	4	4
YARDS	348	179	458	349	358	190	528	344	404
HDCP	6	18	8	14	12	10	2	16	4

Directions: Exit 11A (Neponset St.-Canton) off Route 95. Go 1 mile and take a right before Viaduct (stone bridge) onto Walpole St. Club is 1 mile on right.

Brookside Club, The

Bourne, MA (508) 743-4653
www.thebrooksideclub.com

Club Pro: Dwight Bartlett Jr.
Pro Shop: Full inventory
Payment: Visa,MC,Amex,Dis. and checks
Tee Times: 7 days adv.

Tees	Holes	Yards	Par	USGA	Slope
BACK	18	6300	70	71.1	126
MIDDLE	18	5814	70	68.1	124
FRONT	18	5130	70	69.6	118

Fee 9 Holes: Weekday: N/A **Weekend:** N/A
Fee 18 Holes: Weekday: $50 M-Th, cart incl. **Weekend:** $60 F/S/S/H Cart inc.
Twilight Rates: Yes, after 3 pm **All Day Play:** Replay, $15
Cart Rental: $15pp/18 **Discounts:** Sr., Jr., Ladies-Thurs.
Lessons: $40/30 min **Schools:** No **Junior Golf:** Yes **Membership:** No
Clinics: Yes **Day Camps:** No **Driving Range:** $5.00
Other: New Clubhouse in Spring / Bar

Course noted for scenic ocean views and unique terrain. Carts are required on the weekends.

	1	2	3	4	5	6	7	8	9
PAR	4	3	4	4	5	3	4	4	4
YARDS	379	156	359	365	503	96	361	421	332
HDCP	9	15	13	5	3	17	7	1	11
	10	11	12	13	14	15	16	17	18
PAR	5	4	4	3	4	4	4	3	4
YARDS	576	336	330	155	354	306	313	130	342
HDCP	2	10	6	16	4	12	14	18	8

Directions: Routes 495/25 over Bourne Bridge to Route 28 South. Golf Course is 1.4 miles on right.

Butternut Farm GC ⚙⚙ 11 ▶

115 Wheeler Rd., Stow, MA (978) 897-3400
www.butternutfarm.com

Club Pro: Trevor Page.
Pro Shop: Full inventory
Payment: Most major
Tee Times: 5 days
Fee 9 Holes: Weekday: $25.00
Fee 18 Holes: Weekday: $33.00
Twilight Rates: Yes, after 4 pm
Cart Rental: $26.00
Lessons: No **Schools:** No
Clinics: No **Day Camps:** No
Other: Clubhouse / Bar-Lounge / Snack Bar

Tees	Holes	Yards	Par	USGA	Slope
BACK	18	6302	70	71.2	130
MIDDLE	18	5755	70	69.3	126
FRONT	18	4778	70	67.6	117

Weekend: N/A
Weekend: $45.00
All Day Play: No
Discounts: Senior & Junior
Junior Golf: No **Membership:** Inner Club
Driving Range: No

Renovated clubhouse 2004 opening. Carolina type fairways real tight, bent grass on fairways and tees, tall trees. "Great shape. Challenging, fair, moderate prices." F.P. Open April - November.

	1	2	3	4	5	6	7	8	9
PAR	4	3	4	3	4	4	5	4	5
YARDS	314	155	375	150	403	383	434	268	452
HDCP	16	18	2	14	6	4	12	8	10

	10	11	12	13	14	15	16	17	18
PAR	5	3	4	3	4	4	3	4	4
YARDS	600	128	351	190	364	325	173	340	350
HDCP	1	17	5	13	3	9	15	7	11

Directions: Take 495 to Exit 27. Take Route 117 East for approx. 4 mi. Take right onto Wheeler Rd. (or) Route 2 West to Route 62 West. Follow through Stow center to 1st set of lights. Take left. 2nd right is Wheeler Rd.

Cape Cod CC ⚙⚙ 12 ▶

N. Falmouth, MA (508) 563-9842

Club Pro: C. Holmes, Golf Dir., J. Munroe, PGA
Pro Shop: Full inventory
Payment: Cash , MC, Visa
Tee Times: Fri.for following Fri -Sun
Fee 9 Holes: Weekday: $26 after 3 pm
Fee 18 Holes: Weekday: $41.00 M-Th
Twilight Rates: Yes, after 3 pm
Cart Rental: $14.00pp/18
Lessons: $35.00/half hour **Schools:** No
Clinics: No **Day Camps:** No
Other: Clubhouse / Snack bar / Bar-lounge

Tees	Holes	Yards	Par	USGA	Slope
BACK	18	6404	71	71.7	129
MIDDLE	18	6018	71	69.6	125
FRONT	18	5348	72	71.0	120

Weekend: $32.00 after 3 pm
Weekend: $55.00 F/S/S
All Day Play: Yes
Discounts: Tue/Ladies, Wed./Sr.
Junior Golf: No **Membership:** No
Driving Range: No

Sig. Hole: #14, The Volcano, is the most talked about hole. Course plays longer than the scorecard statistics. The impeccable fairways are lined with pine trees.

	1	2	3	4	5	6	7	8	9
PAR	4	3	5	4	4	5	4	4	3
YARDS	307	175	460	419	360	509	300	407	156
HDCP	11	13	17	1	7	5	15	3	9

	10	11	12	13	14	15	16	17	18
PAR	4	5	3	5	4	3	3	4	4
YARDS	405	515	220	461	351	180	183	300	310
HDCP	4	6	8	12	2	14	10	18	16

Directions: Take Route 28 South of Bourne Bridge, take right onto Route 151. Course is approximately 3 miles on right.

Captains GC, The Port Course at ✪✪✪ ▶ 13

Brewster, MA (508) 896-1716
www.captainsgolfcourse.com

Club Pro: Mark O'Brien
Pro Shop: Full inventory
Payment: Visa, MC
Tee Times: 5 days adv.
Fee 9 Holes: Weekday: N/A
Fee 18 Holes: Weekday: $60.00
Twilight Rates: Yes, after 4 pm
Cart Rental: $30.00/18
Lessons: Yes **Schools:** Yes
Clinics: Yes **Day Camps:** Yes
Other:

Tees	Holes	Yards	Par	USGA	Slope
BACK	18	6724	72	72.1	131
MIDDLE	18	6164	72	69.1	124
FRONT	18	5345	72	70.5	119

Weekend: N/A
Weekend: $60.00
All Day Play: No
Discounts: Senior
Junior Golf: Yes **Membership:** For Residents
Driving Range: $7/lg $4/sm volume discount

COUPON

Cornish and Silva successfully intregated old course with new course. Championship layout. " Holes 12 through 16 (all new) are a spectacular sequence." A.P.

	1	2	3	4	5	6	7	8	9
PAR	4	4	3	4	3	5	4	5	4
YARDS	321	374	160	361	141	508	427	529	337
HDCP	11	5	15	7	17	3	9	1	13
	10	11	12	13	14	15	16	17	18
PAR	4	3	5	5	4	3	4	3	5
YARDS	357	177	515	408	353	153	336	197	510
HDCP	10	18	2	12	6	16	8	14	4

Directions: Route 6 to Exit 11. Right off exit ramp and travel 1.5 miles to Freeman's Way on right. Turn onto Freeman's and course is 1.5 miles on right.

Captains GC, Starboard Course at ✪✪✪ ▶ 14

Brewster, MA (508) 896-1716
www.captainsgolfcourse.com

Club Pro: Mark O'Brien, Director of Ops.
Pro Shop: Full inventory
Payment: Visa, MC
Tee Times: 5 days adv.
Fee 9 Holes: Weekday: N/A
Fee 18 Holes: Weekday: $60.00
Twilight Rates: Yes, after 4 pm
Cart Rental: $30.00/18
Lessons: Yes **Schools:** Yes
Clinics: Yes **Day Camps:** No
Other:

Tees	Holes	Yards	Par	USGA	Slope
BACK	18	6776	72	71.5	122
MIDDLE	18	6198	72	68.8	120
FRONT	18	5359	72	70.6	118

Weekend: N/A
Weekend: $60.00
All Day Play: No
Discounts: None
Junior Golf: Yes **Membership:** For Residents
Driving Range: $7/lg $4/sm volume discount

COUPON

Player's Comments: "Excellent layout. Best conditioned course I've played."

	1	2	3	4	5	6	7	8	9
PAR	4	3	5	4	3	4	5	4	4
YARDS	352	131	491	401	178	287	507	370	322
HDCP	11	17	3	5	13	5	1	7	9
	10	11	12	13	14	15	16	17	18
PAR	4	3	4	5	4	4	4	3	5
YARDS	344	182	326	481	378	361	427	156	504
HDCP	2	16	14	8	6	12	10	18	4

Directions: Route 6 to Exit 11. Right off exit ramp and travel 1.5 miles to Freeman's Way on right. Turn onto Freeman's and course is 1.5 miles on right.

Cedar Hill Golf Club

1137 Park St., Route 27. Stoughton, MA (781) 344-8913
www.stoughton.com

Club Pro: No
Pro Shop: Limited inventory
Payment: Cash only
Tee Times: No
Fee 9 Holes: Weekday: $17.00
Fee 18 Holes: Weekday: $17.00
Twilight Rates: Yes, after 4 pm
Cart Rental: $22.00/18 $12.00/9
Lessons: No **Schools:** No
Clinics: No **Day Camps:** No
Other: Snack bar / Bar-lounge / Clubhouse

Weekend: $18.00
Weekend: $22.00
All Day Play: No
Discounts: Senior & Junior
Junior Golf: No **Membership:** Yes
Driving Range: No

Tees	Holes	Yards	Par	USGA	Slope
BACK	9	4416	33	61.2	105
MIDDLE	9	2155	33	61.2	105
FRONT					

Sig. Hole: #1, 258 yard par 4. Owned by town of Stoughton, "nice place to come to."

	1	2	3	4	5	6	7	8	9
PAR	4	4	4	4	3	4	3	3	4
YARDS	258	302	286	268	120	324	140	176	281
HDCP	3	5	6	9	8	1	7	2	4
	10	11	12	13	14	15	16	17	18
PAR									
YARDS									
HDCP									

Directions: Route 24, Exit 18B, turn onto Route 27. Course is on left.

Challenger 9 at Waverly Oaks ✪✪✪

Plymouth, MA (508) 224-6016
www.waverlyoaksgolfclub.com

Club Pro: Tracy Djerf, LPGA
Pro Shop: Full inventory
Payment: Visa, MC, Amex
Tee Times: Walk-up 7days a week
Fee 9 Holes: Weekday: $25 cart inc. M-Th
Fee 18 Holes: Weekday: $40 cart inc. M-Th
Twilight Rates: No
Cart Rental: Included
Lessons: Yes **Schools:** Yes
Clinics: Yes **Day Camps:** Yes
Other: Men, Women, Junior leagues / Corporate & Small Group Shotgun Outings

Weekend: $30.00 cart inc. F/S/S/H
Weekend: $45 cart inc. F/S/S/H
All Day Play: Replay, $15 with cart.
Discounts: Junior
Junior Golf: Tuesday **Membership:** No
Driving Range: $5.00/lg. $3.00/sm.

Tees	Holes	Yards	Par	USGA	Slope
BACK	9	2264	33		
MIDDLE	9	2022	33		
FRONT	9	1691	33		

Three sets of tees. Executive course layout is great for golfers of all abilities. "Several par 4's reachable from tee. Nicely done." R.W. "Pure fun! #1 a great opening hole." A.P. 1st come/ 1st serve, 7days a week.

	1	2	3	4	5	6	7	8	9
PAR	4	4	4	3	4	4	4	3	3
YARDS	292	294	200	106	331	263	283	153	100
HDCP	2	3	9	7	1	5	4	6	8
	10	11	12	13	14	15	16	17	18
PAR									
YARDS									
HDCP									

Directions:

4✪ =Excellent 3✪ =Very Good 2✪ =Good   **Greater Boston/South Shore/Cape Cod 41**

Chatham Seaside Links

Chatham, MA (508) 945-4774

Club Pro: John Giardino, Head Pro, PGA
Pro Shop: Limited inventory
Payment: Cash , MC, Visa
Tee Times: No
Fee 9 Holes: Weekday: $17.00
Fee 18 Holes: Weekday: $28.00
Twilight Rates: No
Cart Rental: $22.00/18 $13.65/9
Lessons: Schools: No
Clinics: Call **Day Camps:** No
Other: Snacks

Tees	Holes	Yards	Par	USGA	Slope
BACK					
MIDDLE	9	4930	68	65.6	107
FRONT	9	4800	68	65.6	109

Weekend: $17.00
Weekend: $28.00
All Day Play: Yes
Discounts: Senior & Junior
Junior Golf: No **Membership:** Yes
Driving Range: No

Links style golf course with ocean views. Course irrigated. Open April 1 - October 31.

	1	2	3	4	5	6	7	8	9
PAR	4	4	3	3	4	4	4	4	4
YARDS	295	285	150	140	350	305	325	295	320
HDCP	3	11	17	7	1	13	5	15	9
	10	11	12	13	14	15	16	17	18
PAR	4	4	3	3	4	4	4	4	4
YARDS	295	285	150	140	350	305	325	295	320
HDCP	3	11	17	7	1	13	5	15	9

Directions: Route 6 to Exit 11 (Route 137.) Go left to Route 28 and left again to Main Street Chatham. Take Seaview off Main Street to course.

Chequessett Yacht & CC

Wellfleet, MA (508) 349-3704
www.cycc.net

Club Pro: Barbara Boone
Pro Shop: Full inventory
Payment: Visa, MC
Tee Times: Unlimited w/CC
Fee 9 Holes: Weekday: $30.00
Fee 18 Holes: Weekday: $44.00
Twilight Rates: Yes, after 5 pm
Cart Rental: $28.00/18 $16.00/9
Lessons: $45/45 min. **Schools:** No
Clinics: Junior **Day Camps:** No
Other: Snack Bar (seasonal)

Tees	Holes	Yards	Par	USGA	Slope
BACK					
MIDDLE	9	5288	70	66.1	107
FRONT	9	4773	70	67.9	110

Weekend: $30.00
Weekend: $44.00
All Day Play: No
Discounts: Junior
Junior Golf: Yes **Membership:** Wait List
Driving Range: No

Sig. Hole: #3, 368 yd. par 4. Elevated tee guarded by small creek and waste area. 2nd shot to small undulating green. Gorgeous view of bay.

	1	2	3	4	5	6	7	8	9
PAR	4	3	4	5	3	4	4	4	4
YARDS	234	127	368	435	109	314	373	380	281
HDCP	17	15	3	9	11	7	1	5	13
	10	11	12	13	14	15	16	17	18
PAR	4	3	4	5	3	4	4	4	4
YARDS	234	151	343	449	164	297	373	390	266
HDCP	18	14	4	12	8	10	2	6	16

Directions: Turn left at red light on Route 6 toward center, take first left toward Town Harbor - follow road approx. 2 miles.

Cotuit-Highground GC

Cotuit, MA (508) 428-9863

Club Pro: Steve Heher, PGA
Pro Shop: Limited inventory
Payment: Cash only
Tee Times: No
Fee 9 Holes: Weekday: N/A
Fee 18 Holes: Weekday: $15.00
Twilight Rates: Yes, after 4 pm
Cart Rental: Some available
Lessons: Yes **Schools:** N/R
Clinics: Yes **Day Camps:** No
Other: Bar-Lounge / Snack Bar

Tees	Holes	Yards	Par	USGA	Slope
BACK					
MIDDLE	9	1360	28		
FRONT	9	1215	28		

Weekend: N/A
Weekend: $15.00
All Day Play: Yes
Discounts: Senior & Junior after 4pm
Junior Golf: Yes **Membership:** Yes
Driving Range: No

Player's Comment: " Good value. Great bar, very interesting people." Family fun. Links-style course, very tight greens. Accuracy is very important. Open year round.

	1	2	3	4	5	6	7	8	9
PAR	3	3	4	3	3	3	3	3	3
YARDS	115	180	290	130	140	110	100	180	115
HDCP									
	10	11	12	13	14	15	16	17	18
PAR									
YARDS									
HDCP									

Directions: Take Route 6 to Exit 2 (Route 130 South), left onto Route 28, right onto Main Street in Cotuit Center. Take right onto School Street then second left onto Crocker Neck Road.

Cranberry Valley GC

✪✪✪

Oak St., Harwich, MA (508) 430-5234
www.cranberrygolfcourse.com

Club Pro: Dennis Hoye
Pro Shop: Full inventory
Payment: Cash, Visa, MC
Tee Times: 2 days adv.: 430-7560/mem
Fee 9 Holes: Weekday: No
Fee 18 Holes: Weekday: $60.00
Twilight Rates: Yes, after 2:30pm
Cart Rental: $14.00pp/18
Lessons: $45.00/30 min **Schools:** Jr.
Clinics: Junior **Day Camps:** No
Other: Restaurant/Bar

Tees	Holes	Yards	Par	USGA	Slope
BACK	18	6745	72	71.9	129
MIDDLE	18	6296	72	70.4	125
FRONT	18	5518	72	71.5	115

Weekend: No
Weekend: $65.00
All Day Play: No
Discounts: None
Junior Golf: Yes **Membership:** Yes, residents
Driving Range: $4.00-$6.00

#18,493 yard par 5. Excellent finishing hole with bunkers and doglegs guarding the green. Large teeing areas and 53 sand bunkers. Open Mar. - Dec. Seasonal rates."Very fine play, great condition." BB(player)

	1	2	3	4	5	6	7	8	9
PAR	4	5	4	3	4	4	3	5	4
YARDS	357	473	382	188	424	323	164	502	378
HDCP	9	11	3	15	1	13	17	7	5
	10	11	12	13	14	15	16	17	18
PAR	4	4	4	3	5	4	4	3	5
YARDS	350	345	361	165	439	303	438	211	493
HDCP	6	14	8	18	12	16	2	10	4

Directions: Take Exit 10 off Route 6. Take a right off the ramp and take first left at the flashing yellow light (Queen Anne Road). Take third right (Oak Street). 1/2 mile on left.

Crosswinds Golf Club

21

Long Pond Rd., Plymouth, MA (508) 830-1199
www.golfcrosswinds.com

Tees	Holes	Yards	Par	USGA	Slope
BACK	18	6523	72	72.1	133
MIDDLE	18	6036	72	70.2	129
FRONT	18	5371	72	71.7	126

Club Pro: Mike Pry, PGA
Pro Shop:
Payment: Visa, MC, Amex
Tee Times:
Fee 9 Holes: Weekday: $30 M-Th
Fee 18 Holes: Weekday: $45 M-Th
Twilight Rates: No
Cart Rental: $10pp
Lessons: $35/30 **Schools:** Yes
Clinics: Yes **Day Camps:**
Other: Snack cart / Bar

Weekend: $40 F/S/S/H
Weekend: $60 F/S/S/H
All Day Play: Replay
Discounts:
Junior Golf: Yes **Membership:** No
Driving Range: $6/3

New Entry 2004. "Real gem, every bit as good (or better) than its renowned neighbors."A.P. All holes featrue dramatic elevation changes. Clubhouse, 3rd nine under construction.

	1	2	3	4	5	6	7	8	9
PAR	5	4	4	4	5	3	4	3	4
YARDS	490	355	317	326	491	141	340	162	360
HDCP	11	13	7	5	1	17	9	15	3
	10	11	12	13	14	15	16	17	18
PAR	4	3	4	5	5	4	4	3	4
YARDS	370	138	376	475	471	398	296	164	366
HDCP	14	18	2	10	12	6	8	16	4

Directions: Route 3 South to Exit 5. Right off Exit onto Long Pond Road. Follow Long Pond Road 4 miles. Crosswinds Golf Club entrance on left.

D.W. Fields Golf Course

22

Brockton, MA (508) 580-7855

Tees	Holes	Yards	Par	USGA	Slope
BACK	18	5972	70	68.4	120
MIDDLE	18	5630	70	66.9	116
FRONT	18	5370	70	70.1	111

Club Pro: Brian Mattos, PGA
Pro Shop: Full inventory
Payment: Visa, MC
Tee Times: 7 days, 1 day adv.
Fee 9 Holes: Weekday: No
Fee 18 Holes: Weekday: $22.00 (M-Th)
Twilight Rates: Yes, after 4 pm
Cart Rental: $14.00/pp
Lessons: Yes **Schools:** No
Clinics: Yes **Day Camps:** Yes
Other: Snack bar

Weekend: No
Weekend: $26.00
All Day Play: No
Discounts: Junior, $16
Junior Golf: Yes **Membership:** $300
Driving Range: No

Sig. Hole: #13 is a 415 yard par 4. Hits uphill to tree-lined fairway. Sloping green is well bunkered. Considered an easy walker. Open year round. Rates could change.

	1	2	3	4	5	6	7	8	9
PAR	4	5	5	4	3	4	4	3	4
YARDS	305	485	485	300	165	340	335	135	355
HDCP	18	4	6	2	10	12	14	16	8
	10	11	12	13	14	15	16	17	18
PAR	4	4	4	4	3	4	4	3	4
YARDS	315	340	360	405	125	300	345	175	360
HDCP	15	9	3	1	17	13	5	11	7

Directions: Take Route 24 to Exit 18B, 3 sets of lights and take a right onto Oak St. Course is 1.5 miles on the left.

Dennis Highlands

Dennis, MA (508) 385-8347
www.dennisgolf.com

Club Pro: Jay Haberl, PGA
Pro Shop: Full inventory
Payment: MC, Visa, Cash
Tee Times: 4 days adv.
Fee 9 Holes: Weekday: $30.00
Fee 18 Holes: Weekday: $55.00
Twilight Rates: Yes, after 3 pm
Cart Rental: $28.00/18 $19.00/9
Lessons: $30.00/half hour **Schools:** Yes
Clinics: Junior **Day Camps:** Yes
Other: Clubhouse / Restaurant / Bar-lounge

Tees	Holes	Yards	Par	USGA	Slope
BACK	18	6500	71	70.9	120
MIDDLE	18	6071	71	68.5	117
FRONT	18	5187	71	67.8	112

Weekend: $30.00
Weekend: $55.00
All Day Play: N/R
Discounts: None
Junior Golf: Yes **Membership:** Residents
Driving Range: $7.00/lg., $4.00/sm.

COUPON

Bunkers have all been rebuilt. Putting is key to good round. Open year round.

	1	2	3	4	5	6	7	8	9
PAR	4	5	3	4	4	4	3	5	3
YARDS	309	494	151	331	347	409	160	472	141
HDCP	16	4	15	14	9	1	12	7	18

	10	11	12	13	14	15	16	17	18
PAR	4	3	4	4	4	5	3	4	5
YARDS	371	151	365	392	383	529	170	377	519
HDCP	9	17	10	7	11	3	13	5	2

Directions: Take Route 6 to Exit 9. Take left off ramp, follow 1/2 mile. Take left onto Bob Crowell Rd., at end take right onto Old Bass River Road, course is 2 miles up on left.

Dennis Pines GC

Rt. 134, S. Dennis, MA (508) 385-8347
www.dennisgolf.com

Club Pro: Jay Haberl, PGA
Pro Shop: Full inventory
Payment: MC, Visa, Cash
Tee Times: 4 days adv.
Fee 9 Holes: Weekday: $30.00
Fee 18 Holes: Weekday: $55.00
Twilight Rates: Yes, after 3 pm
Cart Rental: $28.00/18 $19.00/9
Lessons: $30.00/half hour **Schools:** Yes
Clinics: Junior **Day Camps:** Yes
Other: Snack bar / Restaurant / Bar-lounge

Tees	Holes	Yards	Par	USGA	Slope
BACK	18	7029	72	74.2	133
MIDDLE	18	6525	72	72.1	131
FRONT	18	5845	72	73.6	126

Weekend: $30.00
Weekend: $55.00
All Day Play: N/R
Discounts: None
Junior Golf: Yes **Membership:** Yes
Driving Range: $7.00/lg., $4.00/sm.

COUPON

Tees have all been rebuilt. One of Cape's busiest courses.

	1	2	3	4	5	6	7	8	9
PAR	4	4	5	3	5	4	3	4	4
YARDS	373	369	471	188	476	423	187	442	389
HDCP	9	7	11	17	13	5	15	1	3

	10	11	12	13	14	15	16	17	18
PAR	4	4	5	3	4	5	4	3	4
YARDS	351	357	518	172	405	472	344	183	405
HDCP	8	10	2	16	4	14	12	18	6

Directions: Take Route 6 to Exit 9, take left off ramp, follow Route 134 for 2 miles, course is on right.

Easton Country Club

S. Easton, MA (508) 238-2500
www.eastoncountryclub.com

Club Pro: Chandler Phinney, PGA
Pro Shop: Full inventory
Payment: MC, Visa, Disc., Cash
Tee Times: 2 days adv.
Fee 9 Holes: Weekday: No
Fee 18 Holes: Weekday: $35.00 (M-Th)
Twilight Rates: Yes, after 2 pm
Cart Rental: $11pp/18
Lessons: $35/30 min **Schools:** No
Clinics: No **Day Camps:** No
Other: Clubhouse / Lockers / Showers / Snack bar / Bar-lounge / Function room

Tees	Holes	Yards	Par	USGA	Slope
BACK	18	6328	71	68.9	119
MIDDLE	18	6050	71	67.5	114
FRONT	18	5271	71	70.2	112

Weekend: No
Weekend: $40.00
All Day Play: Yes
Discounts: None
Junior Golf: No **Membership:** Junior
Driving Range: $4.00 / bucket

A par 4 over water, a par 3 over a creek, and two long par 4's have taken the wheels off of many a good round. Twilight rates.

	1	2	3	4	5	6	7	8	9
PAR	4	5	4	3	4	3	4	4	5
YARDS	390	486	269	136	382	159	411	304	488
HDCP	2	10	12	16	6	8	4	18	14
	10	11	12	13	14	15	16	17	18
PAR	4	4	4	5	3	4	3	4	4
YARDS	331	353	330	519	140	361	162	410	419
HDCP	13	11	17	9	15	3	7	1	5

Directions: Take Route 24 South to Exit 17B. Take Route 123 West to Route 138 South to Purchase Street on right (approx. 2 miles). Take a right onto Purchase Street, course is 7/10 mile on left.

Falmouth Country Club

Falmouth, MA (508) 548-3211
www.falmouthcountryclub.com

Club Pro: No
Pro Shop: Full inventory
Payment: All major cards
Tee Times: 7 days adv.
Fee 9 Holes: Weekday: $25.00
Fee 18 Holes: Weekday: $35.00 M-F
Twilight Rates: Yes, after 2 pm
Cart Rental: $30.00/18, $15.00/9
Lessons: No **Schools:** No
Clinics: No **Day Camps:** No
Other: Clubhouse / Snack bar / Bar-lounge

Tees	Holes	Yards	Par	USGA	Slope
BACK	18	6665	72	70.0	118
MIDDLE	18	6234	70	68.8	114
FRONT	18	5551	72	74	125

Weekend: $25.00
Weekend: $50.00 S/S/H
All Day Play: No
Discounts: None
Junior Golf: No **Membership:** No
Driving Range: $15/lg., $10/med., $6/sm.

Now **27** holes. Separate 9 hole, 3267 yard, par 37 course. Teaching pro available at driving range.

	1	2	3	4	5	6	7	8	9
PAR	4	3	4	4	4	3	4	5	4
YARDS	380	155	365	351	353	151	282	488	393
HDCP	8	18	12	10	6	14	16	4	2
	10	11	12	13	14	15	16	17	18
PAR	5	4	3	4	3	5	4	3	4
YARDS	483	362	135	401	535	495	370	165	370
HDCP	8	18	12	10	6	14	16	4	2

Directions: Take Route 28 South into Falmouth. Take right onto Route 151 East, follow 3.5 miles to Sandwich Road on right. Look for signs, left onto Carriage Shop Road.

Farm Neck Golf Club   ✪✪✪✪   27 ▶

Oak Bluffs, MA (508) 693-3057

Club Pro: Mike Zoll, PGA
Pro Shop: Full inventory
Payment: Visa, MC, Amex, Cash
Tee Times: 2 days adv.

Tees	Holes	Yards	Par	USGA	Slope
BACK	18	6815	72	72.8	135
MIDDLE	18	6301	72	70.5	133
FRONT	18	4987	72	64.3	118

Fee 9 Holes: Weekday: $85 In Season   **Weekend:** $85 In Season
Fee 18 Holes: Weekday: $135 In Season   **Weekend:** $135 In Season
Twilight Rates: Yes, after 4 pm   **All Day Play:** No
Cart Rental: $28.00/18 $13.20/9   **Discounts:** None
Lessons: $40.00/half hour **Schools:** No   **Junior Golf:** Yes **Membership:** Waiting List
Clinics: Yes **Day Camps:** No   **Driving Range:** $9/lg $7/med $5/sm
Other: Restaurant / Bar-Lounge / Snack bar / Lockers / Showers

Scenic, splendid, and challenging with ocean breezes and views, meadows and interior woodlands.
Player's Comments: "No wonder Bill Clinton keeps coming back." Off season: $45/18 holes, $30/9 holes.

	1	2	3	4	5	6	7	8	9
PAR	4	5	4	3	4	3	4	5	3
YARDS	378	490	340	157	325	189	371	486	175
HDCP	2	8	18	16	12	10	6	4	14
	10	11	12	13	14	15	16	17	18
PAR	4	5	4	4	4	3	4	4	5
YARDS	376	519	379	343	331	163	388	368	523
HDCP	5	11	1	15	17	13	9	3	7

Directions: On Country Road in Oak Bluffs, Martha's Vineyard.

Franklin Park, (William J. Devine GC)   28 ▶

Dorchester, MA (617) 265-4084
www.sterlinggolf.com

Club Pro: George Lyons
Pro Shop: Full inventory
Payment: Visa, MC, Amex, Disc
Tee Times: F/S/S 2 days adv

Tees	Holes	Yards	Par	USGA	Slope
BACK	18	6009	70	69.8	120
MIDDLE	18	5622	70	68.6	113
FRONT	18	5040	72	69.3	109

Fee 9 Holes: Weekday: $16.00   **Weekend:** $16.00 after 3:30
Fee 18 Holes: Weekday: $26.00   **Weekend:** $34.00
Twilight Rates: No   **All Day Play:** No
Cart Rental: $26.00/18 $15.00/9   **Discounts:** Senior & Junior
Lessons: $35/30 minutes **Schools:** No   **Junior Golf:** Yes **Membership:** Yes, waiting list
Clinics: Yes **Day Camps:** Yes   **Driving Range:** No
Other: Clubhouse / Snack Bar / Lockers / Function facility

Sig. Hole: #12 was played by Bobby Jones. Improvements include new tees and bunkers. Second oldest public course in United States, a Donald Ross design. Managed by Sterling Golf.

	1	2	3	4	5	6	7	8	9
PAR	4	4	4	3	4	4	4	3	4
YARDS	378	302	404	163	344	334	370	149	331
HDCP	7	13	3	15	11	5	1	17	9
	10	11	12	13	14	15	16	17	18
PAR	4	5	4	3	4	3	4	4	5
YARDS	299	502	382	118	338	152	327	267	462
HDCP	8	2	4	18	10	16	12	14	6

Directions: Follow signs to Franklin Park Zoo. Take 93 North/South. Take Columbia Rd. Exit.
Follow Columbia Rd. to Franklin Park.

Fresh Pond Golf Club

Cambridge, MA (617) 349-6282
www.freshpondgolf.com

Club Pro: R. Carey, Golf Dir., B. Golden, PGA
Pro Shop: Full inventory
Payment: Cash, Check
Tee Times: No
Fee 9 Holes: Weekday: $18.00
Fee 18 Holes: Weekday: $28.00
Twilight Rates: No
Cart Rental: $13 pp/18 $8 pp/9
Lessons: 45/half hour **Schools:** No
Clinics: Junior **Day Camps:** Yes
Other: Snack bar

Tees	Holes	Yards	Par	USGA	Slope
BACK	9	5988	70	70.2	120
MIDDLE	9	5656	70	67.5	112
FRONT	9	5266	70	70.2	122

Weekend: $23.00
Weekend: $35.00
All Day Play: No
Discounts: Senior & Junior
Junior Golf: Yes **Membership:** Yes
Driving Range: No

Improved tees and bunkers. Great course for intermediates and beginners. Season tickets available. Off-season rates. Open Apr. - Dec.

	1	2	3	4	5	6	7	8	9
PAR	4	4	3	4	5	3	4	3	5
YARDS	417	312	169	401	476	221	370	147	465
HDCP	1	13	17	5	3	11	9	15	7
	10	11	12	13	14	15	16	17	18
PAR	4	4	3	4	5	3	4	3	5
YARDS	417	312	169	401	476	221	370	146	465
HDCP	2	14	18	6	4	12	10	16	8

Directions: Take Route 2 to Huron Avenue to course.

George Wright GC

Hyde Park, MA (617) 364-2300

Club Pro: Scott Allen
Pro Shop: Full inventory
Payment: Visa, MC
Tee Times: S/S 2 days adv
Fee 9 Holes: Weekday: $16.00
Fee 18 Holes: Weekday: $27.00
Twilight Rates: No
Cart Rental: $28.00/18 $15.00/9
Lessons: $40/ 1/2 hour **Schools:** No
Clinics: Jr. July **Day Camps:** No
Other: Snack bar / Bar-lounge

Tees	Holes	Yards	Par	USGA	Slope
BACK	18	6367	70	69.5	126
MIDDLE	18	6166	70	68.6	123
FRONT	18	5054	70	70.3	115

Weekend: $18.00
Weekend: $33.00
All Day Play: No
Discounts: Junior rate $8.00/18 (M-F)
Junior Golf: Yes **Membership:** Yes
Driving Range: No

Improvements include new sprinkler system. Challenging front 9. Varied back 9. Reduced resident rates.

	1	2	3	4	5	6	7	8	9
PAR	4	4	5	3	4	4	4	3	4
YARDS	367	313	480	150	400	380	387	162	440
HDCP	11	13	5	17	3	7	9	15	1
	10	11	12	13	14	15	16	17	18
PAR	4	4	4	4	3	5	4	3	4
YARDS	449	347	399	369	182	493	318	158	372
HDCP	2	10	6	8	16	4	14	18	12

Directions: Take Route 1 to Washington Street (left) in Hyde Park. Take a right onto Beach Street. Follow signs to course.

Glen Ellen CC ✪✪ ········ 31 ▶

Rt.115, Millis, MA (508) 376-2775
www.glenellencc.com

Club Pro: Micheal Albrecht, Pro
Pro Shop: Full inventory
Payment: Visa, MC, Amex
Tee Times: 7 days adv.
Fee 9 Holes: Weekday: $19.00 M-F
Fee 18 Holes: Weekday: $29.00 M-F
Twilight Rates: Yes, after 3:30 pm (F/S/S)
Cart Rental: $30.00/18 for 2 people
Lessons: $25/$30/$35/half hour **Schools:** No
Clinics: Yes **Day Camps:** No
Other: Snack bar/ Showers/ Bar-Lounge

Tees	Holes	Yards	Par	USGA	Slope
BACK	18	6633	72	72.0	125
MIDDLE	18	6210	72	70.1	123
FRONT	18	5148	72	69.4	122

Weekend: $24.00 after 3:30pm
Weekend: $39.00
All Day Play: No
Discounts: Sr. (50+) Jr.(16 under)
Junior Golf: Yes **Membership:** Yes
Driving Range: $4.00/ bucket

COUPON

Course has undergone a 2 million dollar renovation. Architect Ron Pritchard and Assoc. specialize in classical golf course architecture. 23 bunkers and 16 new tees have been added.

	1	2	3	4	5	6	7	8	9
PAR	4	3	4	4	4	5	4	3	5
YARDS	428	155	375	315	346	506	335	119	445
HDCP	1	15	5	13	7	3	11	7	9

	10	11	12	13	14	15	16	17	18
PAR	5	4	3	4	4	4	4	5	3
YARDS	500	407	178	382	353	332	363	428	145
HDCP	2	4	14	10	16	12	8	6	18

Directions: Take I-495 to Route 109 East (Exit 19). Left at 3rd light (4 miles) onto Holliston. Right after 2 miles onto Goulding Street. Course is 1 mile on left.

Granite Links GC at Quarry Hills ✪✪ ····· 32 ▶   NEW 2004

Quarry Lane, Milton, MA, (617) 296-7600
www.granitelinksgolfclub.com

Club Pro: Chris Sleeper
Pro Shop: Yes
Payment: Visa, MC, Amex, Disc
Tee Times: 7 days adv.
Fee 9 Holes: Weekday: $50 w/cart
Fee 18 Holes: Weekday: $60 w/cart
Twilight Rates: Yes, after 3 pm
Cart Rental: Included
Lessons: Yes **Schools:** Yes
Clinics: Yes **Day Camps:** Yes
Other: Restaurant / Clubhouse / Lockers / Showers / Bar-Lounge

Tees	Holes	Yards	Par	USGA	Slope
BACK	18	6858	72		
MIDDLE	18	6497	72		
FRONT	18	4798	72		

Weekend: $60 w/cart
Weekend: $85 w/cart
All Day Play: No
Discounts: Senior & Junior
Junior Golf: Yes **Membership:** Yes
Driving Range: Yes

New Entry 2004. 27 hole championship links style golf course with dramatic views of Boston skyline, Harbor and Blue Hills. Challenging fairways and exceptional greens. "The completed project to be spectacular!" AP

	1	2	3	4	5	6	7	8	9
PAR	5	4	4	3	4	4	3	5	4
YARDS	570	409	436	205	385	359	185	487	367
HDCP									

	10	11	12	13	14	15	16	17	18
PAR	4	3	4	5	4	3	4	4	5
YARDS	480	179	452	516	383	223	364	349	509
HDCP									

Directions: I-93 to Exit 8 (Furnace Brook Parway). Follow signs to Quarry Hills main entrance.

Green Harbor Golf Club

Marshfield, MA (781) 834-7303

Tees	Holes	Yards	Par	USGA	Slope
BACK	18	6251	71	69.1	115
MIDDLE	18	6211	71	67.3	111
FRONT	18	5355	71	69.3	109

Club Pro: Gerry Mackedon, PGA
Pro Shop: Full inventory
Payment: Cash or VISA.
Tee Times: 3 days adv.
Fee 9 Holes: Weekday: $20.00 M-Th
Fee 18 Holes: Weekday: $32.00 M-Th
Twilight Rates: Yes, after 5:30 pm
Cart Rental: Pull carts $4.00
Lessons: Yes **Schools:** No
Clinics: No **Day Camps:** No
Other: Clubhouse / Snack bar / Lounge

Weekend: $22.00 F-S
Weekend: $38 F-S
All Day Play: No
Discounts: None
Junior Golf: Yes **Membership:** No
Driving Range: No

Flat, open course. Water on five holes. Features velvet bent grass. Open March 15 - December 15.

	1	2	3	4	5	6	7	8	9
PAR	4	4	4	4	3	4	5	3	4
YARDS	404	357	401	307	175	333	544	176	333
HDCP	3	9	5	13	17	11	1	15	9
	10	**11**	**12**	**13**	**14**	**15**	**16**	**17**	**18**
PAR	4	5	3	4	5	4	4	3	4
YARDS	381	523	199	292	484	375	402	173	352
HDCP	4	2	14	16	10	6	8	18	12

Directions: Take Route 3 to Exit 12 (Route 139). 139 East 4.5 miles. Right on Webster Street, 1 mile on left.

Harwich Port Golf Club

Harwich Port, MA (508) 432-0250

Tees	Holes	Yards	Par	USGA	Slope
BACK					
MIDDLE	9	2538	34		
FRONT					

Club Pro: No
Pro Shop: Limited inventory
Payment: Cash only
Tee Times: No
Fee 9 Holes: Weekday: $19.00
Fee 18 Holes: Weekday: $29.00
Twilight Rates: No
Cart Rental: Pull carts, $3.00
Lessons: No **Schools:** No
Clinics: No **Day Camps:** No
Other: Snack bar

Weekend: $19.00
Weekend: $29.00
All Day Play: No
Discounts: None
Junior Golf: No **Membership:** Yes
Driving Range: Members only

The course is considered an easy walker. Recommended for beginners and senior citizens. Members only after 5:30.

	1	2	3	4	5	6	7	8	9
PAR	4	3	4	4	4	4	3	4	4
YARDS	358	170	340	330	325	255	155	295	310
HDCP	1	9	7	11	3	15	17	5	13
	10	**11**	**12**	**13**	**14**	**15**	**16**	**17**	**18**
PAR									
YARDS									
HDCP									

Directions: Take Route 6 to Exit 9 or 10. Take Route 28 to South Street. Course 200 yards.

Heritage Hill CC

Lakeville, MA (508) 947-7743
www.heritagehillcc.com

Club Pro: B.Raynor & J. Baptista
Pro Shop: Full inventory
Payment: Visa, MC, Amex, Disc
Tee Times: Yes
Fee 9 Holes: Weekday: $15.00
Fee 18 Holes: Weekday: $25.00
Twilight Rates: Yes, after 3 pm
Cart Rental: $10pp/9, Pull $3.00
Lessons: No **Schools:** No
Clinics: No **Day Camps:** No
Other: Leagues

Tees	Holes	Yards	Par	USGA	Slope
BACK	18	3012	54	54.7	84
MIDDLE	18	2575	54	54.7	84
FRONT	18	2155	54	54.7	84

Weekend: $20.00
Weekend: $29.00
All Day Play: No
Discounts: Senior & Junior
Junior Golf: No **Membership:** Yes
Driving Range: No

COUPON

Sig. Hole: #16, 145 yard par 3. Tee shot against wind to 2 tiered green. Beginner friendly certified by NGCOA. Open all year round.

	1	2	3	4	5	6	7	8	9
PAR	3	3	3	3	3	3	3	3	3
YARDS	155	190	160	140	145	155	115	170	145
HDCP	5	1	11	15	13	7	17	3	9

	10	11	12	13	14	15	16	17	18
PAR	3	3	3	3	3	3	3	3	3
YARDS	140	130	125	110	145	120	145	160	125
HDCP	8	4	15	18	12	14	2	6	10

Directions: Exit 5 from Route 495. Go south on Route 18. 3 1/2 miles to second traffic light. Continue through light, take next right (Highland Rd.). Take first right onto Heritage Hill Drive.

Highland Links

N. Truro, MA (508) 487-9201

Club Pro: Jim Knowles, PGA
Pro Shop: Full inventory
Payment: Cash only
Tee Times: Yes
Fee 9 Holes: Weekday: $24.00
Fee 18 Holes: Weekday: $40.00
Twilight Rates: No
Cart Rental: $24.00/18 $12.00/9
Lessons: $30.00/half hour **Schools:** No
Clinics: Jr. Sun. **Day Camps:** No
Other: Club house / Snack bar

Tees	Holes	Yards	Par	USGA	Slope
BACK					
MIDDLE	9	5299	70	65.0	103
FRONT	9	4587	72	66.6	109

Weekend: $24.00
Weekend: $40.00
All Day Play: Yes
Discounts: None
Junior Golf: Yes **Membership:** Yes, $500
Driving Range: No

Sig. Hole: #2, 460 yard par 5. Hitting into valley with fairway enclosed by hills. Green is guarded by 3 bunkers. Keep tee shot to right and go to green on 2nd shot. Non-seasonal rates also.

	1	2	3	4	5	6	7	8	9
PAR	4	5	3	4	4	5	3	4	3
YARDS	250	460	160	346	380	464	171	353	136
HDCP	11	7	15	5	1	3	13	9	17

	10	11	12	13	14	15	16	17	18
PAR	4	4	3	5	4	5	3	4	3
YARDS	242	377	118	415	361	453	159	349	105
HDCP	12	6	16	4	2	10	14	8	18

Directions: Take Route 6 to Truro. Course is just past the Truro elementary school. (Look for signs on Route 6.)

Holly Ridge Golf Club ✪✪✪ ▶ 37

S. Sandwich, MA (508) 428-5577
www.hollyridgegolf.com

Club Pro: J. Enright, Head Pro/J. Frost, Inst. D
Pro Shop: Full inventory
Payment: Visa, MC, Amex
Tee Times: 7 days

Tees	Holes	Yards	Par	USGA	Slope
BACK	18	2952	54	N/A	N/A
MIDDLE	18	2715	54	N/A	N/A
FRONT	18	2194	54	N/A	N/A

Fee 9 Holes: Weekday: $18.00
Fee 18 Holes: Weekday: $29.00
Twilight Rates: Yes, after 3:30 pm
Cart Rental: $20.00/18 12.00/9
Lessons: $50/30 **Schools:** Yes
Clinics: Yes **Day Camps:** Yes
Other: Restaurant / Bar-lounge / Outings

Weekend: $18.00
Weekend: $29.00
All Day Play: No
Discounts: Senior & Junior
Junior Golf: Yes **Membership:** No
Driving Range: $9/ lg,$6.50/ med, $3.75/ sm.

COUPON

Player's Comments: "Top 100 Practice Facility," *Golf Range Magazine.* "Awesome course. Very pro female." Jane Frost, LPGA, Director of Golf Instruction. Open year round

	1	2	3	4	5	6	7	8	9
PAR	3	3	3	3	3	3	3	3	3
YARDS	163	183	142	158	120	184	187	130	202
HDCP	9	5	13	11	17	7	3	15	1
	10	**11**	**12**	**13**	**14**	**15**	**16**	**17**	**18**
PAR	3	3	3	3	3	3	3	3	3
YARDS	124	167	183	128	189	188	211	138	155
HDCP	16	10	6	18	8	4	2	14	12

Directions: Take Route 3 South over Sagamore Bridge, follow Route 6 to Exit 2. Go South on Route 130 for 1.6 miles, take left onto Cotuit Road for 1.4 miles , and left onto Farmersville Road for 1.6 miles. Follow signs for HRGC.

Hyannis Golf Club ▶ 38

Hyannis, MA (508) 362-2606
www.golfcapecod.com

Club Pro: Mike Borden, Dir. of Golf
Pro Shop: Full discount shop
Payment: Visa, MC, Amex, Disc.
Tee Times: 12 months!

Tees	Holes	Yards	Par	USGA	Slope
BACK	18	6711	71	69.4	121
MIDDLE	18	6002	71	68.2	115
FRONT	18	5149	72	69.7	125

Fee 9 Holes: Weekday: $30.00 (M-Th)
Fee 18 Holes: Weekday: $50.00
Twilight Rates: 2 pm wkdys, 4 pm wknds
Cart Rental: $16pp
Lessons: $70.00-$100/hr **Schools:** Jr. & Sr.Yes
Clinics: Yes **Day Camps:** Yes
Other: 3 practice greens / Restaurant / Bar -lounge / Snack bar / Lockers / Outings

Weekend: $35.00 after 2
Weekend: $60.00
All Day Play: Yes
Discounts: Sr. Days, Tues & Thurs
Junior Golf: Yes **Membership:** Yes
Driving Range: $6.00/bucket

COUPON

Sig. Hole: #2, 420 yd. par 4. Awarded 4 stars from *Golf Digest!* Outings are our specialty. Twilight rates offered daily.

	1	2	3	4	5	6	7	8	9
PAR	4	4	4	4	5	4	3	3	4
YARDS	342	388	326	392	528	332	144	195	406
HDCP	13	1	9	7	5	15	17	11	3
	10	**11**	**12**	**13**	**14**	**15**	**16**	**17**	**18**
PAR	5	3	4	4	5	3	4	4	4
YARDS	455	125	367	315	515	138	308	338	388
HDCP	8	16	4	12	2	18	14	10	6

Directions: Take Route 6 (Mid-Cape Highway) to Exit 6 (Route 132). Go south on Route 132 for 1/4 mile and golf course is on left.

Lakeville Country Club

Lakeville, MA (508) 947-6630
www.lakevillecountryclub.com

Tees	Holes	Yards	Par	USGA	Slope
BACK	18	6335	72	70.6	125
MIDDLE	18	5890	72	68.6	123
FRONT	18	4863	72	67.4	111

Club Pro: No
Pro Shop: Full inventory
Payment: Visa, MC
Tee Times: 1 week adv.
Fee 9 Holes: Weekday: $23.00 M-Th   **Weekend:** $26.00 F/S/S
Fee 18 Holes: Weekday: $35.00 M-Th   **Weekend:** $40.00 F/S/S
Twilight Rates: Yes, after 2 pm   **All Day Play:** No
Cart Rental: $15pp/18, $10/9   **Discounts:** Senior
Lessons: No **Schools:** No   **Junior Golf:** No **Membership:** No
Clinics: No **Day Camps:** No   **Driving Range:** No
Other: Restaurant / Clubhouse / Snack bar / Bar-lounge

Early bird special before 8:30 am. Enthusiastic, friendly staff.

	1	2	3	4	5	6	7	8	9
PAR	4	3	4	4	5	5	3	5	3
YARDS	334	216	351	432	533	538	216	521	166
HDCP	9	13	11	1	7	3	15	5	17

	10	11	12	13	14	15	16	17	18
PAR	4	4	5	4	5	4	3	3	4
YARDS	339	380	500	324	463	335	139	178	370
HDCP	4	12	8	14	6	10	18	16	2

Directions: Take I-495 to Exit 5. Go south on Route 18 . Take left at first light to Route 79, then first right on to Clear Pond. Entrance is 1/2 mile on right.

Leo J. Martin GC

40

Weston, MA (781) 894-4903

Tees	Holes	Yards	Par	USGA	Slope
BACK	18	6320	72	69.6	120
MIDDLE	18	6140	72	68.8	115
FRONT	18	6140	75	69.7	115

Club Pro: Mike Wortis, PGA
Pro Shop: Full inventory
Payment: Visa, MC
Tee Times: S/S 2 days adv
Fee 9 Holes: Weekday: $17.00   **Weekend:** $25.00
Fee 18 Holes: Weekday: $22.00   **Weekend:** $25.00
Twilight Rates: No   **All Day Play:** No
Cart Rental: $26.25/18 $14.00/9   **Discounts:** Sr & Jr Weekdays
Lessons: $45.00/half hour **Schools:** Jr.Yes   **Junior Golf:** Yes **Membership:** No
Clinics: Yes **Day Camps:** Yes   **Driving Range:** $11/lg., $6/sm.
Other: Snack bar

Course has summer academy. Considered an easy walker. Excellent for beginners and seniors. One rate on weekends for 9 or 18 holes.

	1	2	3	4	5	6	7	8	9
PAR	4	5	3	5	3	4	4	4	4
YARDS	315	500	155	525	140	360	325	355	265
HDCP	9	7	13	1	15	3	11	5	17

	10	11	12	13	14	15	16	17	18
PAR	3	4	3	4	4	4	5	4	5
YARDS	140	290	240	400	420	360	530	260	560
HDCP	16	14	10	8	4	12	6	18	2

Directions: Take Mass Pike to Weston Exit (Route 30), take first left onto Park Road to course on left.

4✪ =Excellent **3✪** =Very Good **2✪** =Good **Greater Boston/South Shore/Cape Cod 53**

Little Harbor CC

41

Wareham, MA (508) 295-2617

Club Pro: Shawn Lapworth
Pro Shop: Full inventory
Payment: Visa, MC, Cash
Tee Times: 3 days adv.

Tees	Holes	Yards	Par	USGA	Slope
BACK					
MIDDLE	18	3038	56	54.4	79
FRONT	18	2692	56	51.9	72

Fee 9 Holes: Weekday: $16.00   **Weekend:** $17.00
Fee 18 Holes: Weekday: $23.00   **Weekend:** $25.00
Twilight Rates: Yes, after 3 pm   **All Day Play:** No
Cart Rental: $20.00/18 $10.00/9   **Discounts:** Senior & Junior
Lessons: $45.00/45 minutes **Schools:** No   **Junior Golf:** Yes **Membership:** No
Clinics: Junior **Day Camps:** No   **Driving Range:** No
Other: Clubhouse / Snack bar

COUPON

Sig. Hole: #18 is scenic with water left and right. Aim for Old Glory. Holes range from 110 yards to 315 yards. Course and greens are in great condition. Open year round.

	1	2	3	4	5	6	7	8	9
PAR	3	3	3	3	3	4	4	3	3
YARDS	100	135	142	138	225	291	275	162	189
HDCP	17	15	13	7	1	5	9	11	3
	10	**11**	**12**	**13**	**14**	**15**	**16**	**17**	**18**
PAR	3	3	3	3	3	3	3	3	3
YARDS	205	125	140	132	183	100	156	132	208
HDCP	4	10	14	12	6	18	8	16	2

Directions: Take Route 6 to Depot Street. Follow Great Neck Road 2.5 miles. Go right on Stockton shortcut.

Lost Brook Golf Club

42

Norwood, MA (781) 769-2550
www.lostbrookgolfclub.com

Club Pro: No
Pro Shop: Limited inventory
Payment: Cash only
Tee Times: Weekends

Tees	Holes	Yards	Par	USGA	Slope
BACK					
MIDDLE	18	3002	54		
FRONT	18	2468	58		

Fee 9 Holes: Weekday: $15, $13 Senior   **Weekend:** $17.00
Fee 18 Holes: Weekday: $23, $18 Senior   **Weekend:** $25.00, $22.00 Senior
Twilight Rates: Yes, after 4 pm   **All Day Play:** No
Cart Rental: Yes (Pull carts) $2.00   **Discounts:** Senior & Junior
Lessons: No **Schools:** No   **Junior Golf:** No **Membership:** No
Clinics: No **Day Camps:** No   **Driving Range:** No
Other: Clubhouse / Snack Bar

Expertly maintained Par 3 golf course. Tree lined fairways surround the elevated greens.

	1	2	3	4	5	6	7	8	9
PAR	3	3	3	3	3	3	3	3	3
YARDS	90	208	212	210	141	158	170	190	102
HDCP	15	5	3	1	13	11	9	7	17
	10	**11**	**12**	**13**	**14**	**15**	**16**	**17**	**18**
PAR	3	3	3	3	3	3	3	3	3
YARDS	162	171	168	167	126	148	202	190	187
HDCP	8	14	12	10	18	16	2	4	6

Directions: Take Route 128 to Exit 13. Follow Univertsity Ave. approx. 1.5 miles to course located at Meditech, greens on the left.

Maynard Country Club

Maynard, MA (978) 897-9885
www.maynardcc.com

Club Pro: John Gordon, PGA
Pro Shop: Full inventory
Payment: Visa, MC
Tee Times: Wknds after 2:30
Fee 9 Holes: Weekday: $25.00
Fee 18 Holes: Weekday: $40.00
Twilight Rates: No
Cart Rental: $27/18 $17/9 $5/pull cart
Lessons: Yes **Schools:** No
Clinics: Yes **Day Camps:** No
Other: Clubhouse / Lockers / Showers / Snack bar / Bar-lounge

Tees	Holes	Yards	Par	USGA	Slope
BACK					
MIDDLE	9	5379	69	66.1	121
FRONT	9	5024	69	69.5	121

Weekend: $25.00
Weekend: $40.00
All Day Play: Yes
Discounts: None
Junior Golf: Yes **Membership:** Yes
Driving Range: No

Hole #2 now par 5. The course has narrow fairways with two significant water hazards. Some holes are very close together.

	1	2	3	4	5	6	7	8	9
PAR	4	5	3	4	4	3	4	4	4
YARDS	375	358	143	311	353	204	342	328	290
HDCP	6	10	17	15	2	7	4	12	14

	10	11	12	13	14	15	16	17	18
PAR	4	4	3	4	4	3	4	4	4
YARDS	375	358	143	345	353	141	342	328	290
HDCP	5	9	16	8	1	18	3	11	13

Directions: Take Route 2 East or West to Route 27 South. 3 miles on left.

MGA Links at Mamantapett

Rt. 123, Norton, MA (508) 222-0555
www.mgalinks.org

Club Pro: Mike Haberl, PGA
Pro Shop: No
Payment: Cash only
Tee Times: No
Fee 9 Holes: Weekday: $15.00
Fee 18 Holes: Weekday: $20.00
Twilight Rates: No
Cart Rental: $5/18, $3/9 pull carts only
Lessons: No **Schools:** No
Clinics: Junior **Day Camps:** No
Other: Lounge

Tees	Holes	Yards	Par	USGA	Slope
BACK					
MIDDLE	18	2421	54		
FRONT	18	2321	56		

Weekend: $15.00
Weekend: $20.00
All Day Play: No
Discounts: Junior
Junior Golf: Yes **Membership:** Yes
Driving Range: No

Good course for women, seniors, short game and irons practice. First Tee and MGA ForeKids Program Tues.-Fri. 9 holes available for adult public play daily. Open year round. Formerly Wading River GC.

	1	2	3	4	5	6	7	8	9
PAR	3	3	3	3	3	3	3	3	3
YARDS	117	135	82	140	93	91	115	136	108
HDCP	12	4	18	14	6	15	8	3	10

	10	11	12	13	14	15	16	17	18
PAR	3	3	3	3	3	3	3	3	3
YARDS	131	138	125	203	141	113	147	233	173
HDCP	17	5	13	11	9	16	7	1	2

Directions: Take I-495 to Exit 10 (Route 123 W). Go approximately 4 miles. Course is on left.

Miacomet Golf Club

Nantucket, MA (508) 325-0333
www.miacometgolf.com

Club Pro: Michael Merril, PGA
Pro Shop: Full inventory
Payment: Visa, MC, Amex, Disc
Tee Times: 4 days adv.
Fee 9 Holes: Weekday: $41.00
Fee 18 Holes: Weekday: $75.00
Twilight Rates: No
Cart Rental: $42.00/18 21.00/9
Lessons: $50.00/half hour **Schools:** Yes
Clinics: Yes **Day Camps:** No
Other: Restaurant / Clubhouse / Snack bar / Bar-lounge

Tees	Holes	Yards	Par	USGA	Slope
BACK					
MIDDLE	9	6674	74	72.7	116
FRONT	9	6004	76	71.6	115

Weekend: $41.00
Weekend: $75.00
All Day Play: No
Discounts: Senior
Junior Golf: Yes **Membership:** No
Driving Range: $5.00/lg. bucket

18 holes in 2004. Resident, non-resident fee schedules. Fees subject to change.

	1	2	3	4	5	6	7	8	9
PAR	4	4	4	4	3	4	5	4	5
YARDS	370	337	391	370	175	413	471	386	472
HDCP	3	15	9	5	17	1	3	7	11

	10	11	12	13	14	15	16	17	18
PAR	4	4	4	3	3	4	5	4	5
YARDS	370	337	391	370	175	413	471	386	472
HDCP	4	16	10	6	18	2	14	8	12

Directions: Nantucket is an island 25 miles off the coast of Cape Cod. Airport and ferry boat dock are in Hyannis.

Millwood Farm Golf Course

Framingham, MA (508) 877-1221

Club Pro: No
Pro Shop: Limited inventory
Payment: Visa, MC
Tee Times: 5 days advance
Fee 9 Holes: Weekday: $22.00 (14)
Fee 18 Holes: Weekday:
Twilight Rates: Yes, after 5 pm
Cart Rental: $17.00
Lessons: No **Schools:** No
Clinics: No **Day Camps:** No
Other: Snack bar

Tees	Holes	Yards	Par	USGA	Slope
BACK					
MIDDLE	14	3798	53	31.4	102
FRONT					

Weekend: $25.00 (14)
Weekend:
All Day Play: No
Discounts: Senior (M-Th, $17)
Junior Golf: No **Membership:** No
Driving Range: No

Sig. Hole: #5, 363 yard par 4 with dogleg right. Pond in front of tee and green. A friendly family owned course, with 14 holes. Added traps on 7th hole. Open April to November.

	1	2	3	4	5	6	7	8	9
PAR	4	3	4	4	4	3	4	4	5
YARDS	338	112	306	230	363	156	281	312	438
HDCP	3	14	10	11	1	8	6	9	5

	10	11	12	13	14	15	16	17	18
PAR	4	3	4	3	4				
YARDS	362	160	295	138	307				
HDCP	2	12	4	13	7				

Directions: Route 9 West from Route 128 to Route 30 exit (Edgell Road). At light, make right onto Edgell Road for 1 mile. Turn left onto Belknap Road, then third right onto Millwood Street.

Mink Meadows GC

Vineyard Haven, MA (508) 693-0600
www.minkmeadows.com

Club Pro: Allan Menne
Pro Shop: Full inventory
Payment: Visa, MC, checks, cash
Tee Times: 2 days adv.

Tees	Holes	Yards	Par	USGA	Slope
BACK					
MIDDLE	9	6206	71	69.9	126
FRONT	9	5458	71	71.7	123

Fee 9 Holes: Weekday: $46, $35 off season **Weekend:** $46.00
Fee 18 Holes: Weekday: $66, $48. off season **Weekend:** $66.00
Twilight Rates: No   **All Day Play:** Yes
Cart Rental: $28.00/18 $22.00/9   **Discounts:** Jr- discount only
Lessons: $40/30 min. **Schools:** Yes   **Junior Golf:** Yes **Membership:** Yes
Clinics: Jrs. Thurs. **Day Camps:** No   **Driving Range:** $6/lg. $3/sm.
Other: Snack Bar

COUPON

Easy to walk, beautiful challenging course. Weekday specials include golf cart, lunch and sleeve of balls.

	1	2	3	4	5	6	7	8	9
PAR	4	4	4	4	3	4	3	5	4
YARDS	349	328	355	424	186	394	166	500	376
HDCP	13	11	7	1	15	3	17	9	5
	10	**11**	**12**	**13**	**14**	**15**	**16**	**17**	**18**
PAR	4	4	4	5	3	4	3	5	4
YARDS	342	319	341	479	170	429	194	499	366
HDCP	14	12	6	4	16	2	18	10	8

Directions: From ferry, proceed to Main St. in Vineyard Haven. Take 2nd left and proceed to 2nd right (Franklin St.). Go 1.25 miles down Franklin St. to club entrance on left.

Mt. Hood Golf Course

Melrose, MA (781) 665-6656
www.mthoodgolf.com

Club Pro: Mike Farrell, PGA
Pro Shop: Full inventory
Payment: Visa, MC, Amex, Disc
Tee Times: Weekends, 2 days adv.

Tees	Holes	Yards	Par	USGA	Slope
BACK					
MIDDLE	18	5553	69	65.7	107
FRONT	18	5318	74	NA	NA

Fee 9 Holes: Weekday: $20.00   **Weekend:** $23.00
Fee 18 Holes: Weekday: $33.00   **Weekend:** $38.00
Twilight Rates: No   **All Day Play:** No
Cart Rental: $26.00/18 $14.00/9   **Discounts:** Senior & Junior
Lessons: $30.00/half hour **Schools:**   **Junior Golf:** No **Membership:** For residents
Clinics: No **Day Camps:** Yes   **Driving Range:** No
Other: Clubhouse / Lockers / Showers / Snack bar / Restaurant / Bar-lounge

Hole #12 redone, overlooks Boston Skyline. Now under Friel Management. New patios, new trees, much of irrigation system has been replaced.

	1	2	3	4	5	6	7	8	9
PAR	5	4	3	5	4	4	3	4	3
YARDS	477	340	202	532	303	338	215	362	183
HDCP	15	11	17	1	13	9	3	7	5
	10	**11**	**12**	**13**	**14**	**15**	**16**	**17**	**18**
PAR	3	4	4	4	5	3	4	4	3
YARDS	140	282	386	332	450	210	321	304	166
HDCP	18	12	4	10	2	6	8	14	16

Directions: Route 1 North. Take left onto Essex Street then left onto Waverly Avenue. Take left onto Slayton Road.

4❂ =Excellent **3❂** =Very Good **2❂** =Good   **Greater Boston/South Shore/Cape Cod 57**

New Seabury CC, Dunes Course ✪✪ ▶ 49

Mashpee, MA (508) 539-8322
www.newseabury.com

Club Pro: Brendan J. Reilly, PGA
Pro Shop: Yes
Payment: Visa, MC, Amex
Tee Times: 1 day adv.

Tees	Holes	Yards	Par	USGA	Slope
BACK	18	6340	70	71	125
MIDDLE	18	6000	70	69.3	121
FRONT	18	4748	68	67.8	114

Fee 9 Holes: Weekday: $70 incl. cart M-Th **Weekend:** $80.00 incl. cart
Fee 18 Holes: Weekday: $70 incl cart M-Th **Weekend:** $80.00 incl. cart
Twilight Rates: Yes, after 3 pm **All Day Play:** Replay 434
Cart Rental: Cart included **Discounts:** None
Lessons: Yes **Schools:** No **Junior Golf:** Yes **Membership:** Yes
Clinics: Day Camps: No **Driving Range:** Yes
Other: Restaurant / Clubhouse / Hotel / Bar-lounge / Snack Bar / Lockers / Showers / Resort

The course is relatively narrow with tree-lined fairways and no water holes. Rates vary seasonally. Call for play availability. Teaching Professional, Bob McGraw.

	1	2	3	4	5	6	7	8	9
PAR	4	3	4	4	4	4	4	3	5
YARDS	397	191	266	311	198	282	309	167	387
HDCP	1	15	13	5	9	11	7	17	3
	10	11	12	13	14	15	16	17	18
PAR	3	5	4	4	4	5	3	3	4
YARDS	408	166	380	216	323	430	162	160	352
HDCP	4	18	6	12	10	2	16	14	8

Directions: Route 3 to Route 6 East over Sagamore Bridge. Take Exit 2, follow signs to New Seabury.

New Seabury CC, Ocean Course ✪✪✪✪ ▶ 50

Mashpee, MA (508) 539-8322
www.newseabury.com

Club Pro: Brendan J. Reilly, PGA
Pro Shop: Yes
Payment: Visa, MC, Amex
Tee Times: 1 day adv.

Tees	Holes	Yards	Par	USGA	Slope
BACK	18	7140	72	75.8	133
MIDDLE	18	6789	72	73.9	131
FRONT	18	5731	72	74	129

Fee 9 Holes: Weekday: TBD **Weekend:** TBD
Fee 18 Holes: Weekday: TBD **Weekend:** TBD
Twilight Rates: Yes, after 3 pm **All Day Play:** Replay $35.00
Cart Rental: Cart included **Discounts:** None
Lessons: Yes **Schools:** No **Junior Golf:** Yes **Membership:** Yes
Clinics: Day Camps: No **Driving Range:** Yes
Other: Restaurant / Clubhouse / Hotel / Bar-lounge / Snack Bar / Lockers / Showers / Resort

Championship caliber with spectacular ocean views. For open play dates and seasonal rates, it is best to call. Resort guests and members only June 16th to September 15th.

	1	2	3	4	5	6	7	8	9
PAR	5	4	4	3	5	4	4	3	4
YARDS	487	390	393	172	480	365	386	195	410
HDCP	9	7	1	15	5	11	13	17	3
	10	11	12	13	14	15	16	17	18
PAR	5	3	4	4	3	5	4	4	4
YARDS	480	163	358	383	167	526	377	397	379
HDCP	8	18	14	4	16	2	6	10	12

Directions: Route 3 to Route 6 East over Sagamore Bridge. Take Exit 2, follow signs to New Seabury.

Newton Commonwealth GC

Newton, MA (617) 630-1971
www.sterlinggolf.com

Club Pro: Bob Travers,PGA
Pro Shop: Full inventory discounted
Payment: Cash and most credit cards
Tee Times: 4 days adv.
Fee 9 Holes: Weekday: N/A
Fee 18 Holes: Weekday: $28.00 M-Th
Twilight Rates: Yes, after 5 pm
Cart Rental: $26.00/18 $15.00/9
Lessons: $45/40 min **Schools:** No
Clinics: Yes **Day Camps:** No
Other: Snack bar / Twilight golf after league play $18 everyday

Weekend: N/A
Weekend: $35.00
All Day Play: Yes
Discounts: Senior & Junior
Junior Golf: Yes **Membership:** Yes
Driving Range: No

COUPON

Tees	Holes	Yards	Par	USGA	Slope
BACK	18	5336	70	67.0	125
MIDDLE	18	5009	70	66.0	122
FRONT	18	4349	70	69.4	118

Resident fees applicable. Well stocked pro shop. Friendly staff. Open year round. Operated by Sterling Golf Management, Inc.

	1	2	3	4	5	6	7	8	9
PAR	4	5	3	3	5	4	3	5	3
YARDS	252	476	179	110	435	255	162	473	197
HDCP	15	1	5	17	3	9	11	7	13
	10	**11**	**12**	**13**	**14**	**15**	**16**	**17**	**18**
PAR	4	5	3	4	4	4	4	3	4
YARDS	231	422	130	367	355	259	295	148	263
HDCP	10	6	18	4	2	14	8	12	16

Directions: From Route 128, take Exit 12 , Route 30 East. Follow 4.8 mi. to Grant Ave. Go left and follow the Golfer Logo signs.

North Hill CC

Duxbury, MA (781) 934-3249

Club Pro: Bill Allen, PGA
Pro Shop: Yes
Payment: Visa, MC
Tee Times: 5 days adv.
Fee 9 Holes: Weekday: $16.00
Fee 18 Holes: Weekday: $27.00
Twilight Rates: No
Cart Rental: $28.00/18 $15.00/9
Lessons: Private and Group **Schools:** No
Clinics: No **Day Camps:** No
Other: Snack bar / Bar-lounge / Clubhouse

Weekend: $18.00
Weekend: $30.00
All Day Play: No
Discounts:
Junior Golf: Yes **Membership:** Yes
Driving Range: Limited

Tees	Holes	Yards	Par	USGA	Slope
BACK	9	7002	71	71.6	121
MIDDLE	9	6610	72	70.5	115
FRONT	9	4984	74	N/A	N/A

Improvements include new irrigation system and sand traps. Sig. Hole: #3, 426 yard par 4. Elevated green with out-of-bounds to right. Sloping green protected by bunkers.

	1	2	3	4	5	6	7	8	9
PAR	5	4	4	3	4	5	4	3	4
YARDS	540	465	445	165	440	495	410	235	440
HDCP	3	5	1	17	15	9	13	11	7
	10	**11**	**12**	**13**	**14**	**15**	**16**	**17**	**18**
PAR	5	4	4	3	4	5	4	3	4
YARDS	540	465	445	165	440	495	410	235	440
HDCP	4	6	2	16	14	10	12	18	8

Directions: Route 3 to Exit 11, get on to Route 14 East, course is approximately 2 miles on right (Merry Avenue).

Norton Country Club

53

Norton, MA (508) 285-2400

Tees	Holes	Yards	Par	USGA	Slope
BACK	18	6545	71	72.2	137
MIDDLE	18	6201	71	69.9	132
FRONT	18	5040	71	71.0	124

Club Pro: Tony DiGiorgio
Pro Shop: Full inventory
Payment: Visa, MC
Tee Times: 3 days advance
Fee 9 Holes: Weekday: $23.00 M-Th
Fee 18 Holes: Weekday: $35, $48 w/cart
Twilight Rates: Yes, after 4 pm
Cart Rental: $13pp/18 $8pp/9
Lessons: $35/30 min **Schools:** No
Clinics: Yes **Day Camps:** No
Other: Clubhouse / Lockers / Showers / Snack bar / Bar-lounge

Weekend: N/A
Weekend: $58 F/S/S w/cart
All Day Play: No
Discounts: Lunch specials M-Th
Junior Golf: Yes **Membership:** Yes
Driving Range: No

COUPON

Course, completely redone by Cornish & Silva, is for serious golfers. **Players' Comments:** ""Beautiful course, great condition." "Not too long but tough. Management a must especially for first 6 holes." .

	1	2	3	4	5	6	7	8	9
PAR	4	4	3	5	5	4	3	4	4
YARDS	346	426	143	500	492	419	105	383	313
HDCP	15	1	17	5	9	3	13	7	11
	10	**11**	**12**	**13**	**14**	**15**	**16**	**17**	**18**
PAR	4	4	3	4	5	4	3	4	4
YARDS	328	344	138	298	489	414	120	358	389
HDCP	14	10	6	12	4	2	18	16	8

Directions: Take Route 123 (Exit 10) off I-495. Take 123 W toward Norton Center to Oak Street . Club is 1 mile on the left.

Norwood Country Club

54

Norwood, MA (781) 769-5880
www.norwoodgolf.com

Tees	Holes	Yards	Par	USGA	Slope
BACK	18	6292	71	67.1	112
MIDDLE	18	6092	71	65.9	108
FRONT	18	5950	71	68.7	108

Club Pro: Jeff Bailey, PGA
Pro Shop: Full inventory
Payment: Cash only
Tee Times: 1 week adv.
Fee 9 Holes: Weekday: $16.00 after 2 pm
Fee 18 Holes: Weekday: $25.00
Twilight Rates: 2 pm wkdys
Cart Rental: $28.00/18 $16.00/9
Lessons: $40.00/half hour **Schools:** No
Clinics: Adult/Jr **Day Camps:** No
Other: Clubhouse / Lockers / Showers / Bar-lounge

Weekend: N/A
Weekend: $30.00
All Day Play: No
Discounts: Senior
Junior Golf: No **Membership:** Inner Club
Driving Range: $9/lg., $7/med., $5/sm.

COUPON

It is basically a straightaway tract. Excellent course for seniors and beginners.

	1	2	3	4	5	6	7	8	9
PAR	4	4	4	4	5	4	3	3	5
YARDS	360	280	320	395	435	320	156	130	450
HDCP	5	13	9	1	7	11	15	17	3
	10	**11**	**12**	**13**	**14**	**15**	**16**	**17**	**18**
PAR	4	4	5	3	4	3	4	4	4
YARDS	300	305	480	150	347	130	390	330	367
HDCP	12	10	4	16	8	18	2	14	6

Directions: Route 128 to Route 1 South to Norwood. Note: course is on the northbound side of Route 1. To change direction, go to Norwood exit and then go around rotary and head north.

Ocean Edge GC ✪✪ ▶ 55

Brewster, MA (508) 896-5911
www.oceanedge.com

Club Pro: Harry Parker, PGA
Pro Shop: Full inventory
Payment: Visa, MC, Amex
Tee Times: 7 days in advance.
Fee 9 Holes: Weekday: $40.00
Fee 18 Holes: Weekday: $64.00
Twilight Rates: Yes, after 4 pm
Cart Rental: $15.00pp/18 $7.50pp/9
Lessons: $40.00/half hour **Schools:** Yes
Clinics: Yes **Day Camps:** Yes
Other: Hotel / Clubhouse / Lockers / Showers / Snack bar / Restaurant / Bar-lounge

Tees	Holes	Yards	Par	USGA	Slope
BACK	18	6602	72	72.6	130
MIDDLE	18	6079	72	70.2	124
FRONT	18	5109	72	69.6	118

Weekend: $40.00
Weekend: $64.00
All Day Play: Replay-Cart fee
Discounts: Under 16
Junior Golf: No **Membership:** Yes
Driving Range: $4.00 bucket

COUPON

Public welcome, call for starting time 7 days in advance. **Player's Comments:** "Great scenery and views."

	1	2	3	4	5	6	7	8	9
PAR	4	4	4	4	4	4	3	5	4
YARDS	291	400	320	381	339	306	155	546	350
HDCP	11	3	17	5	9	13	15	1	7

	10	11	12	13	14	15	16	17	18
PAR	4	4	3	5	4	4	4	3	5
YARDS	301	345	131	521	342	293	398	174	480
HDCP	16	12	18	6	8	14	4	10	2

Directions: Route 6 East (Cape Cod), Exit 11, turn right on Route 137. Follow 2 miles, Ocean Edge is on right side.

Olde Barnstable Fairgrounds GC ✪✪ ▶ 56

Marstons Mills, MA (508) 420-1141
www.obfgolf.com

Club Pro: Gary Philbrick, PGA
Pro Shop: Full inventory
Payment: Cash , MC, Visa
Tee Times: Yes
Fee 9 Holes: Weekday: N/A
Fee 18 Holes: Weekday: $50.00 Mon-Thurs
Twilight Rates: Yes, after 4 pm
Cart Rental: $15.00 per person
Lessons: $35.00/half hour **Schools:** Jr.
Clinics: N/R **Day Camps:** No
Other: Restaurant / Clubhouse / Bar-Lounge

Tees	Holes	Yards	Par	USGA	Slope
BACK	18	6479	71	70.7	123
MIDDLE	18	6113	71	69.1	120
FRONT	18	5122	71	69.2	118

Weekend: N/A
Weekend: $60.00 F/S/S
All Day Play: No
Discounts: Jr.(18 & under) after 12 pm $20
Junior Golf: Yes **Membership:** For residents
Driving Range: $7.00/lg., $5.00/sm. bucket

"Very enjoyable" - *Golf Digest.* **Player's Comments:** "From 1st tee to 18th green, a great test of golf. Great Cape Cod conditions." Rates may change.

	1	2	3	4	5	6	7	8	9
PAR	5	3	5	3	4	4	4	4	4
YARDS	485	140	503	158	365	351	430	317	385
HDCP	9	17	5	13	3	15	1	11	7

	10	11	12	13	14	15	16	17	18
PAR	5	4	3	4	4	3	4	3	5
YARDS	510	335	157	340	380	172	395	155	535
HDCP	6	14	18	12	10	8	4	16	2

Directions: Sagamore Bridge Route 6, Exit 5, take right off ramp. Bear right on Route 149. Course is 1/2 mile on left.

Olde Scotland Links

●● ▶

Bridgewater, MA (508) 279-3344
www.oldescotlandlinks.com

Tees	Holes	Yards	Par	USGA	Slope
BACK	18	6790	72	72.6	126
MIDDLE	18	6306	72	70.3	124
FRONT	18	5396	72	70.9	117

Club Pro: Holly Taylor, PGA
Pro Shop: Yes
Payment: Visa, MC, Amex, Discover
Tee Times: 7 days adv.
Fee 9 Holes: Weekday: $21.00   **Weekend:** $25.00
Fee 18 Holes: Weekday: $38.00   **Weekend:** $43.00
Twilight Rates: No   **All Day Play:** No
Cart Rental: $28.00/18 $15.00/9   **Discounts:** Senior & Junior M-Th
Lessons: $35/30 min. **Schools:** Yes   **Junior Golf:** Yes **Membership:** No
Clinics: Yes **Day Camps:** No   **Driving Range:** $5.00/bucket
Other: Snack Bar

COUPON

Players' Comments: "Well maintained. Nice layout." "Beautiful design, affordable and not crowded."
Noted for spectacular greens. Playability for all golfers. Open March 15-Dec. 24.

	1	2	3	4	5	6	7	8	9
PAR	4	4	3	4	4	5	4	3	5
YARDS	400	372	154	302	372	519	359	189	456
HDCP	4	2	12	18	16	6	10	8	14
	10	**11**	**12**	**13**	**14**	**15**	**16**	**17**	**18**
PAR	4	4	5	3	4	4	3	4	5
YARDS	435	359	520	205	357	362	130	321	494
HDCP	1	11	7	5	13	3	17	15	9

Directions: Follow Route 24 to Exit 15. Follow Route 104 east for about 1/2 mile to first set of lights. Take right onto Old Pleasant St. and follow for 2 miles. Course is on the right.

Paul Harney GC

●●● ▶

East Falmouth, MA (508) 563-3454

Tees	Holes	Yards	Par	USGA	Slope
BACK	18	3570	59	58.9	91
MIDDLE	18	3315	59	56.7	89
FRONT	18	3200	61	61.0	89

Club Pro: Mike Harney, PGA
Pro Shop: Limited inventory
Payment: Cash, Check
Tee Times: No
Fee 9 Holes: Weekday: $35.00   **Weekend:** $35.00
Fee 18 Holes: Weekday: $35.00   **Weekend:** $35.00
Twilight Rates: No   **All Day Play:** No
Cart Rental: $24.00/18, $12.00/9   **Discounts:** None
Lessons: $35/30 min. **Schools:** Yes   **Junior Golf:** Yes **Membership:** No
Clinics: Women **Day Camps:** No   **Driving Range:** Yes
Other: Bar-Lounge / Snack bar

A true test for all golfers. Executive-style course.

	1	2	3	4	5	6	7	8	9
PAR	4	3	3	3	3	3	4	3	3
YARDS	345	155	160	220	155	180	260	160	170
HDCP	15	17	5	1	13	2	11	9	6
	10	**11**	**12**	**13**	**14**	**15**	**16**	**17**	**18**
PAR	3	3	3	3	4	4	3	3	4
YARDS	175	225	150	100	250	270	160	170	255
HDCP	3	4	12	18	16	10	8	7	14

Directions: From Bourne Bridge take Route 28 East. Then take Route 151 towards Mashpee. Go 3-4 miles and see course on left. Take Fordham Road to clubhouse.

Pembroke Country Club

Pembroke, MA (781) 826-5191
www.pembrokecc.com

Club Pro: Russ Champoux, PGA
Pro Shop: Full inventory
Payment: Visa, MC, Cash, Check
Tee Times: Wed Am for S/S

Tees	Holes	Yards	Par	USGA	Slope
BACK					
MIDDLE	18	6532	71	71.1	124
FRONT	18	5887	75	73.4	120

Fee 9 Holes: Weekday: No
Fee 18 Holes: Weekday: $35 walk, $45 ride
Twilight Rates: Yes, after 5 pm
Cart Rental: Included
Lessons: $45.00/half hour **Schools:** Jr.Yes
Clinics: Yes **Day Camps:** No
Weekend: No
Weekend: $53 walk, $63 ride
All Day Play: Yes
Discounts: None
Junior Golf: No **Membership:** Yes
Driving Range: $5.00/bucket
Other: Clubhouse / Snack bar / Restaurant / Bar-lounge / Junior memberships

Greatly improved irrigation system. '

	1	2	3	4	5	6	7	8	9
PAR	5	4	3	4	4	4	3	4	4
YARDS	531	341	221	434	421	349	143	436	344
HDCP	11	13	7	3	1	15	17	5	9
	10	**11**	**12**	**13**	**14**	**15**	**16**	**17**	**18**
PAR	4	3	4	5	4	4	4	3	5
YARDS	415	168	431	564	341	370	345	188	490
HDCP	4	14	2	6	10	8	12	16	18

Directions: Take Route 3 to Exit 13, right onto Route 53 South, take right at 5th light onto Broadway, take left at island onto Elm Street, course is 2 miles on right.

Pine Meadows GC

Lexington, MA (781) 862-5516
www.pinemeadowsgolfclub.com

Club Pro: No
Pro Shop: Yes
Payment: Cash only
Tee Times: 7 days adv.

Tees	Holes	Yards	Par	USGA	Slope
BACK					
MIDDLE	9	2759	35	64.5	110
FRONT	9	2405	35	69.2	117

Fee 9 Holes: Weekday: $18, $15/residents
Fee 18 Holes: Weekday: No
Twilight Rates: No
Cart Rental: $13.00pp/9
Lessons: No **Schools:** No
Clinics: Yes **Day Camps:** No
Other: Snack bar
Weekend: $20,$17/residents
Weekend: No
All Day Play: No
Discounts: Srs. & Jrs. (M-Th)
Junior Golf: No **Membership:** No
Driving Range: No

The course open fairways and is excellent for beginners and intermediate players.

	1	2	3	4	5	6	7	8	9
PAR	5	5	4	3	4	3	4	4	3
YARDS	484	481	241	225	336	201	324	301	166
HDCP	2	1	8	5	3	6	7	4	9
	10	**11**	**12**	**13**	**14**	**15**	**16**	**17**	**18**
PAR									
YARDS									
HDCP									

Directions: Take Route 128 to Exit 31A, through 2 lights, right onto Hill Street, right onto Cedar Street.

Pine Oaks GC

S. Easton, MA (508) 238-2320

Club Pro: Leigh Bader, PGA
Pro Shop: Full inventory
Payment: Visa, MC, Dis, Cash, Check
Tee Times: No
Fee 9 Holes: Weekday: $20.00   **Weekend:** $21.50
Fee 18 Holes: Weekday: $27.50   **Weekend:** $31.50
Twilight Rates: After 4:30 pm, Wknds   **All Day Play:** Yes
Cart Rental: $22.00/18, $13.00/9   **Discounts:** Senior M-F
Lessons: $40.00/35min **Schools:** No   **Junior Golf:** Yes **Membership:** Yes
Clinics: Yes **Day Camps:** Yes   **Driving Range:** No
Other: Clubhouse / Lockers / Snack bar / Bar-lounge / Discount Golf Shop

Tees	Holes	Yards	Par	USGA	Slope
BACK	9	5945	68	67.0	115
MIDDLE	9	5824	68	67	111
FRONT	9	5000	68	67.0	111

New short game practice area. Plenty of water for a nine hole course. Pro shop is one of the best in the country.

	1	2	3	4	5	6	7	8	9
PAR	4	5	4	3	4	3	3	4	4
YARDS	326	558	407	175	378	245	149	302	372
HDCP	11	1	4	15	8	9	17	12	6
	10	11	12	13	14	15	16	17	18
PAR	4	5	4	3	4	3	3	4	4
YARDS	326	558	407	175	378	245	149	302	372
HDCP	10	3	2	18	7	14	16	13	5

Directions: Take Route 24 to Exit 16-B. Take Route 106 West approximately 3 miles. 200 yards on right hand side.

Pinecrest Golf Club

Holliston, MA (508) 429-9871
www.pinecrestgolfclub.org

Club Pro: Andy Ingham
Pro Shop: Limited inventory
Payment: Cash or Credit
Tee Times: Fri, Sat, Sun
Fee 9 Holes: Weekday: $15.00, $13 Senior   **Weekend:** $18.00
Fee 18 Holes: Weekday: $24.00, $18 Senior   **Weekend:** $29.00, $23 after 12
Twilight Rates: After 5 wkdy, 4 wknd   **All Day Play:** No
Cart Rental: $26.00/18 $14.00/9   **Discounts:** Senior & Junior Wkdays
Lessons: Yes **Schools:** No   **Junior Golf:** Yes **Membership:** Residents only
Clinics: Yes **Day Camps:** No   **Driving Range:** Yes, grass
Other: Clubhouse / Snack bar / Bar-lounge / Restaraunt

Tees	Holes	Yards	Par	USGA	Slope
BACK	N/A				
MIDDLE	18	5003	66	63	103
FRONT	18	4300	66	63.2	103

The course is relatively level and easy to walk. Very tight greens that are a true test of one's iron shot accuracy. The par 3s are fairly long. Most golfers are able to play 18 holes in under 4 hours.

	1	2	3	4	5	6	7	8	9
PAR	4	3	5	4	4	4	3	3	3
YARDS	279	205	472	245	405	290	227	200	222
HDCP	15	17	3	9	1	11	5	13	7
	10	11	12	13	14	15	16	17	18
PAR	4	3	4	3	4	3	4	4	4
YARDS	398	165	275	153	340	190	317	325	295
HDCP	2	18	14	16	4	12	8	6	10

Directions: Take Route 495 to Route 85 Exit 20 toward Holliston. Follow 3 miles to first flashing yellow light. Take right onto Chestnut Street, look for signs.

Pinehills Golf Club, Jones ✪✪✪✪

Plymouth, MA (508) 209-3000
www.pinehillsgolf.com

Club Pro: John Tuffin, PGA
Pro Shop: Full inventory
Payment: Visa, MC, Amex, Checks
Tee Times: 7 days adv.

Tees	Holes	Yards	Par	USGA	Slope
BACK	18	7175	72	73.8	135
MIDDLE	18	6762	72	72.4	131
FRONT	18	6201	72	69.6	125

Fee 9 Holes: Weekday:
Fee 18 Holes: Weekday: $85 inc. cart/ balls
Twilight Rates: Yes, after 3:30 pm
Cart Rental: Included
Lessons: Yes **Schools:** Yes
Clinics: Yes **Day Camps:** Yes
Other: Clubhouse / Grille / Bar / Banquet Facilities / Lockers / Showers / Restaurant

Weekend:
Weekend: $95.00 inc. cart/range balls
All Day Play: No
Discounts: None
Junior Golf: Yes **Membership:** No
Driving Range: Natural Grass

Player's Comments: "Could be a pro course. Excellent layout. Challenging but fair for men or women." "Friendliest staff, best service ever encountered." A.P.

	1	2	3	4	5	6	7	8	9
PAR	4	4	5	3	4	4	3	4	5
YARDS	348	404	501	177	403	431	165	397	552
HDCP	13	3	11	15	5	1	17	7	9

	10	11	12	13	14	15	16	17	18
PAR	4	5	4	4	3	5	4	3	4
YARDS	360	548	420	370	219	495	401	169	402
HDCP	14	2	4	12	16	10	6	18	8

Directions: Route 3 South, Exit 3. Turn left and follow signs.

Pinehills Golf Club, Nicklaus ✪✪✪✪

Plymouth, MA (508) 209-3000
www.pinehillsgolf.com

Club Pro: John Tuffin, PGA
Pro Shop: Full inventory
Payment: Visa, MC, Amex, Checks
Tee Times: 7 dys adv. (866) 855-4653

Tees	Holes	Yards	Par	USGA	Slope
BACK	18	6640	72	71.7	131
MIDDLE	18	6129	72	69.3	125
FRONT	18	5185	72	69.4	123

Fee 9 Holes: Weekday:
Fee 18 Holes: Weekday: $85 inc cart/ balls
Twilight Rates: Yes, after 3:30
Cart Rental: Included
Lessons: Yes **Schools:** Yes
Clinics: Yes **Day Camps:** Yes
Other: Clubhouse / Grille / Bar / Banquet Facilites / Lockers / Showers / Restaurant / Caddy Program

Weekend:
Weekend: $95.00 inc. cart/range balls
All Day Play: No
Discounts: None
Junior Golf: Yes **Membership:** No
Driving Range: Natural Grass/Mats

Players Comments: "Beautiful track. Easier than Jones." "' As close to first choice as you can get." "Best Nicklaus course I've played. Placement of approach shots are vital to score." R.W.

	1	2	3	4	5	6	7	8	9
PAR	4	5	3	4	4	5	3	4	4
YARDS	357	500	199	365	357	491	145	343	326
HDCP	13	5	7	3	9	1	17	11	15

	10	11	12	13	14	15	16	17	18
PAR	4	5	4	3	4	3	5	4	4
YARDS	365	486	403	165	280	144	486	344	373
HDCP	8	10	4	18	16	14	6	12	2

Directions: Route 3 South, Exit 3. Turn left and follow signs.

Ponkapoag GC #1

Canton, MA (781) 401-3191

Club Pro: Michael Fleming, PGA
Pro Shop: Full inventory
Payment: Visa, MC, Cash
Tee Times: S/S/H 2 days

Tees	Holes	Yards	Par	USGA	Slope
BACK	18	6728	72	72.0	126
MIDDLE	18	6256	72	69.8	120
FRONT	18	5523	74	70.8	115

Fee 9 Holes: Weekday: $17.00 **Weekend:** $17.00
Fee 18 Holes: Weekday: $22.00 **Weekend:** $25.00
Twilight Rates: No **All Day Play:** No
Cart Rental: $26.00/18 $15.00/9 **Discounts:** Sr & Jr Weekdays
Lessons: $40/30 min **Schools:** Jr.Yes **Junior Golf:** Yes **Membership:** Limited, Juniors
Clinics: Junior **Day Camps:** Yes **Driving Range:** $6.00/lg. bucket
Other: Restaurant / Clubhouse / Beer & wine / Showers

Sig. Hole: #13, 490 yard par 5. Elevated tee with sharp dogleg left. Plays to small, slightly elevated green. Beautiful setting. A Donald Ross designed course. Open April - December.

	1	2	3	4	5	6	7	8	9
PAR	4	3	5	4	4	4	4	3	5
YARDS	393	169	532	332	395	437	402	192	520
HDCP	11	17	1	13	9	5	7	15	3
	10	**11**	**12**	**13**	**14**	**15**	**16**	**17**	**18**
PAR	4	5	3	5	4	4	3	4	4
YARDS	406	480	182	489	375	402	221	386	413
HDCP	8	2	18	8	14	10	16	12	6

Directions: Course is 1 mile south of Route 128 on Route 138.

Ponkapoag GC #2

Canton, MA (781) 401-3191

Club Pro: Michael Fleming, PGA
Pro Shop: Full inventory
Payment: Visa, MC, Cash
Tee Times: Weekends

Tees	Holes	Yards	Par	USGA	Slope
BACK	18	6332	71	70.3	116
MIDDLE	18	5769	71	67.5	112
FRONT	18	5114	72	68.5	113

Fee 9 Holes: Weekday: $17.00 **Weekend:** $17.00
Fee 18 Holes: Weekday: $22.00 **Weekend:** $25.00
Twilight Rates: No **All Day Play:** No
Cart Rental: $26.00/18 $15.00/9 **Discounts:** Senior & Junior
Lessons: $40/30 min **Schools:** Jr.Yes **Junior Golf:** Yes **Membership:** Limited, Juniors
Clinics: Junior **Day Camps:** Yes **Driving Range:** $6.00/lg.
Other: Restaurant / Clubhouse / Beer & Wine / Showers

Sig. Hole: #16, 382 yard par 4. Narrow fairway guarded by 3 bunkers and doglegs to right. Green fronted by sand and surrounded by pines. Great Par 71 course designed by Donald Ross.

	1	2	3	4	5	6	7	8	9
PAR	4	4	3	5	4	4	4	3	4
YARDS	385	434	202	473	266	412	341	188	416
HDCP	9	3	15	1	13	7	11	17	5
	10	**11**	**12**	**13**	**14**	**15**	**16**	**17**	**18**
PAR	5	3	4	5	4	3	4	4	4
YARDS	498	166	351	482	401	192	402	323	408
HDCP	2	18	12	4	10	16	6	14	8

Directions: Course is 1 mile south of Route 128 on Route 138.

Poquoy Brook GC

✪✪✪ 67 ▶

Lakeville, MA (508) 947-5261
www.poquoybrook.com

Club Pro: Jim Bottary, PGA
Pro Shop: Full inventory
Payment: Cash, All major credit cards
Tee Times: M-F, 7 days. adv., S/S, 2 days.
Fee 9 Holes: Weekday: $22.00
Fee 18 Holes: Weekday: $37.00
Twilight Rates: $18 after 5 pm
Cart Rental: $14pp/ 18, 9pp/ 9
Lessons: $40.00/half hour **Schools:** Yes
Clinics: Yes **Day Camps:** No

Tees	Holes	Yards	Par	USGA	Slope
BACK	18	6762	72	72.4	128
MIDDLE	18	6286	72	69.9	125
FRONT	18	5415	73	71.0	114

Weekend: $25.00
Weekend: $43.00
All Day Play: No
Discounts: Junior
Junior Golf: Yes **Membership:** No
Driving Range: $5.00/lg. $3.0/sm.

COUPON

Other: Clubhouse / Lockers / Showers / Snack bar / Restaurant / Bar-lounge

Players' Comments: "Good conditions, good staff, nice clubhouse." "Interesting layout with great holes."
Open year round. Check on pm starting times and rates w/wo cart.

	1	2	3	4	5	6	7	8	9
PAR	4	4	3	4	5	4	4	3	5
YARDS	351	385	176	307	518	326	381	180	485
HDCP	9	1	17	15	5	7	3	13	11

	10	11	12	13	14	15	16	17	18
PAR	4	4	3	4	5	3	4	4	5
YARDS	372	336	185	366	436	173	426	428	455
HDCP	6	12	14	8	18	16	4	2	10

Directions: I-495 South - take Exit 5, Route 18 South. Bear right off exit. Take first right (Taunton Street) and then first left onto Leonard Street. Course on right.

Presidents Golf Course

68 ▶

Quincy, MA (617) 328-3444
www.presidentsgc.com

Club Pro: Don Small, PGA
Pro Shop: Full inventory
Payment: Cash only
Tee Times: 2 days adv. for Fri/Sat/Sun
Fee 9 Holes: Weekday:
Fee 18 Holes: Weekday: $28.00 M-Th
Twilight Rates: Yes, after 4 pm
Cart Rental: $13.00pp/18
Lessons: $35.00/half hour **Schools:** No
Clinics: Yes **Day Camps:** Yes

Tees	Holes	Yards	Par	USGA	Slope
BACK	18	5645	70	66.8	114
MIDDLE	18	5055	70	66.4	108
FRONT	18	4425	70	65.0	107

Weekend:
Weekend: $35.00 F/S/S/H
All Day Play: Yes
Discounts: Senior & Junior
Junior Golf: Yes **Membership:** Yes
Driving Range: No

Other: Clubhouse / Lockers / Showers / Snack bar / Restaurant /Putting green

New bunkering on 4 holes. **Players' Comments:** "Home of Norfolk County Classic. 5950 yard layout, is a true test of your short game. Greens are sloping and fast. You have to have the short stick working well."

	1	2	3	4	5	6	7	8	9
PAR	4	3	4	3	5	4	3	4	4
YARDS	300	90	270	150	440	355	120	350	285
HDCP	7	15	9	13	5	1	17	3	11

	10	11	12	13	14	15	16	17	18
PAR	3	4	5	3	4	5	5	4	3
YARDS	150	260	465	165	365	460	425	300	105
HDCP	16	12	6	14	4	2	8	10	18

Directions: From I-93 South, take Exit 11A. Take left at first light (Approx. 1 mile). Take left at next light . From I-93 North, take Exit 9. Go straight approx. 1 mile. Right 1 mile at lights. Left at next light.

Quashnet Valley CC

Mashpee, MA (508) 477-4412
www.quashnetvalley.com

Tees	Holes	Yards	Par	USGA	Slope
BACK	18	6601	72	71.7	132
MIDDLE	18	6093	72	69.1	126
FRONT	18	5094	72	70.3	119

Club Pro: Bob Chase, PGA
Pro Shop: Full inventory
Payment: Visa, MC
Tee Times: 1 wk, Prepay 6 mos.
Fee 9 Holes: Weekday: $18.00 M-Th.
Fee 18 Holes: Weekday: $35 M-Th $45 F
Twilight Rates: After 2 pm
Cart Rental: $15pp/18 $7.50pp/9
Lessons: $35.00/half hour **Schools:** Yes
Clinics: No **Day Camps:** No
Other: Clubhouse / Showers / Snack bar / Bar-lounge / Banquet facilities

Weekend: $23 F; $30 S/S/Hldy
Weekend: $60.00 Sat/Sun/Hldy
All Day Play: No
Discounts: None
Junior Golf: Yes **Membership:** Limited.
Driving Range: No

COUPON

The experience begins and ends with challenging par 5s. Players' Comments: "Excellent layout. Great shape. Must play when on Cape." "Friendly staff."

	1	2	3	4	5	6	7	8	9
PAR	5	3	4	4	3	4	5	3	4
YARDS	505	135	328	310	153	420	488	173	349
HDCP	1	17	13	9	15	3	5	11	7
	10	11	12	13	14	15	16	17	18
PAR	4	4	4	5	4	4	4	3	5
YARDS	302	390	322	530	354	360	339	155	480
HDCP	14	6	16	4	10	8	12	18	2

Directions: Take Route 6 East to Exit 2. Take right onto Route 130 South, follow 7.2 miles then take a right onto Great Neck Road. Follow 1.6 miles, take right onto Old Barnstable Road. Course is on left at the end.

Ridder Golf Club

Whitman, MA (781) 447-9003

Tees	Holes	Yards	Par	USGA	Slope
BACK	18	5909	70	68.1	113
MIDDLE	18	5857	70	66.3	110
FRONT	18	4981	70	67.1	107

Club Pro: Jeff Butler, PGA
Pro Shop: Full inventory
Payment: Cash, Checks
Tee Times: 2 days adv.
Fee 9 Holes: Weekday: $22.00
Fee 18 Holes: Weekday: $35.00 M-Th
Twilight Rates: No
Cart Rental: $12.50pp/18 $6.25pp/9
Lessons: $45.00/half hour **Schools:** Jr.
Clinics: Yes **Day Camps:** Yes
Other: Restaurant / Snack bar / Bar-lounge

Weekend: $25.00
Weekend: $45.00 F/S/S/H
All Day Play: No
Discounts: Junior
Junior Golf: Yes **Membership:** Yes, Annual Fee
Driving Range: Yes

Sig. Hole: #14. Junior summer program. Marked improvements, more challenging. Open March - Dec.

	1	2	3	4	5	6	7	8	9
PAR	4	4	3	4	4	4	4	3	4
YARDS	334	368	154	289	384	299	257	197	387
HDCP	16	7	14	15	5	17	18	8	4
	10	11	12	13	14	15	16	17	18
PAR	4	5	4	3	4	3	4	5	4
YARDS	312	468	370	166	427	225	385	476	359
HDCP	12	10	6	13	1	3	2	11	9

Directions: Take Route 3 to Route 18 South to Route 14 Whitman / East Bridgewater Line.

River Bend CC

W. Bridgewater, MA (508) 580-3673

Club Pro: Lyman J. Doane II, PGA
Pro Shop: Full inventory
Payment: Most major. No check
Tee Times: 7 days adv.
Fee 9 Holes: Weekday: $20.00 M-Th
Fee 18 Holes: Weekday: $37.00 M-Th
Twilight Rates: Yes, after 4 pm
Cart Rental: $14.00pp/18
Lessons: No **Schools:**
Clinics: No **Day Camps:** No
Other: Bar-lounge / Snack Bar

Weekend: $24.00 after 2pm
Weekend: $48.00
All Day Play: No
Discounts: Sr. & Jr. M-Th
Junior Golf: No **Membership:** Yes, Inner Club
Driving Range: No

Tees	Holes	Yards	Par	USGA	Slope
BACK	18	6312	71	69.9	125
MIDDLE	18	5773	71	67.6	124
FRONT	18	4915	71	67.7	120

Sig. Hole: #17, 162 yd. par 3. "...manicured magnificently, very fair greens." R.W. **Player's Comments:** "Great conditions for such a young course. The greens hold and putt wonderfully."

	1	2	3	4	5	6	7	8	9
PAR	4	5	4	3	4	4	4	3	4
YARDS	330	436	286	113	333	345	337	166	361
HDCP	9	11	15	17	3	7	1	13	5
	10	**11**	**12**	**13**	**14**	**15**	**16**	**17**	**18**
PAR	4	4	4	4	3	4	5	3	5
YARDS	358	326	363	317	171	340	501	162	516
HDCP	8	14	6	12	18	10	2	16	4

Directions: Route 128 to Route 24 South. Take Exit 16A on to Route 106 East for 2.5 miles. Course is on the right.

Rockland CC

Rockland, MA (781) 878-5836
www.rocklandgolfcourse.com

Club Pro: Brad Meekins, PGA
Pro Shop: Full inventory
Payment: Visa, MC, Disc
Tee Times: 3 days adv.
Fee 9 Holes: Weekday: $15.00
Fee 18 Holes: Weekday: $25.00
Twilight Rates: Yes, after 6 pm
Cart Rental: $13.65/18
Lessons: $40.00/half hour **Schools:** Jr.Yes
Clinics: Ladies/Juniors **Day Camps:** Yes
Other: Clubhouse / Snack bar / Restaurant / Bar-lounge

Weekend: $15.00
Weekend: $26.00
All Day Play: Yes
Discounts: Sr & Jr. Weekdays
Junior Golf: Yes **Membership:** Yes
Driving Range: No

Tees	Holes	Yards	Par	USGA	Slope
BACK	18	3300	54	56.0	78
MIDDLE	18	3014	54	58.0	87
FRONT	18	2100	60	N/A	N/A

Longest par 3 course in the nation. Tees and greens are in fine shape, but rough areas can balloon your scores. "Nice course, very forgiving. Easy to play, easy to walk." F.P.

	1	2	3	4	5	6	7	8	9
PAR	3	3	3	3	3	3	3	3	3
YARDS	212	136	202	137	146	152	171	95	207
HDCP	2	14	4	16	8	12	10	18	6
	10	**11**	**12**	**13**	**14**	**15**	**16**	**17**	**18**
PAR	3	3	3	3	3	3	3	3	3
YARDS	227	202	137	145	162	228	152	132	171
HDCP	3	9	15	1	13	5	7	17	11

Directions: Take Route 3 to Exit 16B. Left onto Route 139 for 3 to 4 miles. Course is on right.

Sandwich Hollows Golf Club

E. Sandwich, MA (508) 888-3384
www.sandwichhollows.com

Club Pro: Mick Herron, PGA
Pro Shop: Full inventory
Payment: MC, Visa, Check
Tee Times: 3 week adv.
Fee 9 Holes: Weekday: $17.00
Fee 18 Holes: Weekday: $35.00
Twilight Rates: After 2, after 4
Cart Rental: $15.00pp
Lessons: Yes **Schools:** Adult Introductory
Clinics: Yes **Day Camps:** Yes
Other: Clubhouse / Restaurant / Lounge / Function Facilities

Tees	Holes	Yards	Par	USGA	Slope
BACK	18	6220	71	70.4	124
MIDDLE	18	5891	71	68.6	120
FRONT	18	4894	71	68.1	115

Weekend: $22.00 after 2 pm
Weekend: $59 w/cart
All Day Play: Yes
Discounts: None
Junior Golf: Yes **Membership:** Full/seasonal
Driving Range: $5 bucket, all grass tees

The course is hilly and tight. Accurate shots are essential. Open year round. All day special on Wednsday includes greens fee and cart.

	1	2	3	4	5	6	7	8	9
PAR	5	4	3	4	4	5	3	4	4
YARDS	485	325	120	305	347	570	177	340	401
HDCP	9	11	17	15	3	7	5	13	1
	10	**11**	**12**	**13**	**14**	**15**	**16**	**17**	**18**
PAR	4	4	3	4	5	3	4	4	4
YARDS	300	380	175	285	520	160	340	355	330
HDCP	18	6	12	14	8	10	16	2	4

Directions: Located between Exits 3 and 4 on Route 6 (Mid-Cape Hwy) on service road.

Sandy Burr CC

✪✪

Wayland, MA (508) 358-7211
www.sandyburr.com

Club Pro: Charles Estes
Pro Shop: Full inventory
Payment: Most major
Tee Times: 7 days/week
Fee 9 Holes: Weekday: $29.00
Fee 18 Holes: Weekday: $42.00
Twilight Rates: Yes, after 5 pm
Cart Rental: $16pp/$13pp Sr.
Lessons: $40/30 min **Schools:** No
Clinics: No **Day Camps:** No
Other: Clubhouse / Snack bar / Bar-lounge / Showers

Tees	Holes	Yards	Par	USGA	Slope
BACK	18	6412	72	70.8	125
MIDDLE	18	6229	72	69.9	122
FRONT	18	4561	72	66.2	110

Weekend: $29.00 after 5pm
Weekend: $49.00
All Day Play: No
Discounts: Senior & Junior
Junior Golf: No **Membership:** No
Driving Range: No

Players' Comments: "A great Donald Ross course with a good mix of holes." "Good staff. Good Shape. Challenging." Early bird and midday 9 hole rate. Off season twilight rates.

	1	2	3	4	5	6	7	8	9
PAR	5	5	3	4	3	4	4	4	4
YARDS	471	491	147	429	220	409	335	353	281
HDCP	15	5	17	3	13	1	7	9	11
	10	**11**	**12**	**13**	**14**	**15**	**16**	**17**	**18**
PAR	3	5	4	3	4	4	4	5	4
YARDS	193	450	384	185	369	352	409	521	406
HDCP	10	18	8	14	16	12	4	6	2

Directions: Take Route 128 to Route 20 West Exit, at Wayland Center take left onto Route 27 S. Course is 1/4 mile on right.

Sassamon Trace Golf Course

Natick, MA (508) 655-1330
www.sterlinggolf.com

Club Pro: Pete Meagher, PGA
Pro Shop: Full inventory
Payment: Visa, MC, Amex, Cash
Tee Times: 4 days adv.
Fee 9 Holes: Weekday: $20.00
Fee 18 Holes: Weekday: $32.00
Twilight Rates: No
Cart Rental: $28.00/18 $14.00/9
Lessons: $50/45 min **Schools:** No
Clinics: By appt. **Day Camps:** No
Other: Restaurant / Clubhouse

Tees	Holes	Yards	Par	USGA	Slope
BACK	9	2383	32	31.7	111
MIDDLE	9	2167	32	30.9	107
FRONT	9	1744	32	29.8	96

Weekend: $22.00
Weekend: $35.00
All Day Play: No
Discounts: Senior & Junior (M-Th)
Junior Golf: Yes **Membership:** No
Driving Range: No

COUPON

Built on unique topography. Expansive greens place a premium on putting. Operated by Sterling Golf Management. " Mixes links and traditional." DW (player) "Fast running fairways." R.W.

	1	2	3	4	5	6	7	8	9
PAR	3	4	3	5	3	4	3	3	4
YARDS	158	326	180	529	162	341	177	143	367
HDCP	8	5	3	1	7	6	4	9	2
	10	11	12	13	14	15	16	17	18
PAR									
YARDS									
HDCP									

Directions: From I-95 (Route 128), take Exit 20 (Route 9 West) and follow for 6.5 miles to Route 27 South. Course is 3 miles south of Route 9 on right.

Scituate Country Club

✪✪

Scituate, MA (781) 545-9768
www.scituatecc.com

Club Pro: John M. Kan, PGA, R. Hayes
Pro Shop: Full inventory
Payment: Cash only
Tee Times: 2 days adv.
Fee 9 Holes: Weekday: $22 after 11am Mon
Fee 18 Holes: Weekday: $32 after 11am Mon
Twilight Rates: No
Cart Rental: $13pp/18, $8pp/9
Lessons: $50.00/half hour **Schools:** No
Clinics: No **Day Camps:** No
Other: Restaurant / Clubhouse / Bar-Lounge / Showers / Lockers / Snack Bar

Tees	Holes	Yards	Par	USGA	Slope
BACK					
MIDDLE	9	6051	70	69.7	121
FRONT	9	5407	72	71.6	119

Weekend: No public play
Weekend: No public play
All Day Play: No
Discounts: None
Junior Golf: No **Membership:** Yes
Driving Range: No

Open to the public on Mondays only after 11 am. Beautifully maintained seaside golf links with rolling terrain. Open April - November.

	1	2	3	4	5	6	7	8	9
PAR	4	3	5	4	4	4	4	3	4
YARDS	407	156	504	373	308	359	357	124	386
HDCP	2	6	12	8	16	4	10	18	14
	10	11	12	13	14	15	16	17	18
PAR	4	3	5	4	4	4	4	3	4
YARDS	422	165	525	385	320	370	365	130	395
HDCP	1	5	11	7	15	3	9	17	13

Directions: Take Route 3 to Exit 13. Go left off exit. Go to first set of lights, take right onto Route 123. Go to end, go straight across Route 3A. Go onto Driftway Road. Course is 1 mile on right.

South Shore CC

Hingham, MA (781) 749-8479

Tees	Holes	Yards	Par	USGA	Slope
BACK	18	6444	72	71.0	128
MIDDLE	18	6197	72	69.9	124
FRONT	18	5064	72	69.3	116

Club Pro: Bill Allen, PGA
Pro Shop: Full inventory
Payment: Visa, MC, Cash, Check
Tee Times: 4 days adv.
Fee 9 Holes: Weekday: $24 M-Th $29/F   **Weekend:** N/A
Fee 18 Holes: Weekday: $35 M-Th $40/F   **Weekend:** $44, $40 after 11am
Twilight Rates: Yes, after 5 pm   **All Day Play:** Yes
Cart Rental: $25.00/18 $15.00/9   **Discounts:** Sr & Jr Weekdays
Lessons: $65.00/ 45 minutes **Schools:** Jr.Yes   **Junior Golf:** Yes **Membership:** No, Waiting list
Clinics: Yes **Day Camps:** Yes   **Driving Range:** Yes
Other: Snack bar / Restaurant / Bar-lounge / Clubhouse / Lockers / Showers

Superb 18 hole championship golf course. 15th hole redone.

	1	2	3	4	5	6	7	8	9
PAR	4	3	5	4	4	4	4	3	5
YARDS	277	156	521	319	371	410	360	197	502
HDCP	13	17	1	15	3	5	7	11	9
	10	11	12	13	14	15	16	17	18
PAR	4	3	4	4	4	5	4	3	5
YARDS	295	179	372	401	327	530	380	148	452
HDCP	14	16	6	4	12	2	8	18	10

Directions: Take Route 3 to Exit 14 onto Route 228 North; Continue 4 miles through flashing red light to flashing yellow light. Turn left, 1/2 mile to club on left hand side.

Southers Marsh Golf Club ✪✪✪

Plymouth, MA (508) 830-3535
www.southersmarsh.com

Tees	Holes	Yards	Par	USGA	Slope
BACK	18	4111	61		
MIDDLE	18	3694	61		
FRONT	18	2907	61		

Club Pro: Hugh Connett
Pro Shop: Limited inventory
Payment: Visa, MC, Amex, Disc, No checks
Tee Times: 7 days adv.
Fee 9 Holes: Weekday: **Weekend:**
Fee 18 Holes: Weekday: $30.00 (M-Th)   **Weekend:** $35.00 (F/S/S)
Twilight Rates: Yes, after 3 pm   **All Day Play:** No
Cart Rental: $10.00/18   **Discounts:** Sr. & Jr. (M-Th)
Lessons: $30.00/half hour **Schools:** Yes   **Junior Golf: Membership:** No
Clinics: Yes **Day Camps:** No   **Driving Range:** Yes
Other: Restaurant / Clubhouse / Bar-lounge

COUPON

Player's comments: "Executive course with real golf holes. There are no easy hole...birdies wil be earned." "User friendly, a must try." Voted Plymouth's Best Golf Course 2003. Noted for cranberry bogs.

	1	2	3	4	5	6	7	8	9
PAR	4	3	3	4	3	4	3	4	3
YARDS	300	139	175	353	138	285	129	263	158
HDCP	5	17	3	9	13	7	15	1	11
	10	11	12	13	14	15	16	17	18
PAR	3	3	3	4	3	4	3	3	4
YARDS	123	121	97	304	121	314	157	165	352
HDCP	12	14	10	6	18	16	4	2	8

Directions: From Route 3, take Exit 6 onto Route 44 West. At second light, turn left onto Pilgrim Hill Rd. Turn right at light onto Federal Furnace Rd. After 4 miles, SMGC on left. Also minutes from Exit 2 off Route 495.

Squirrel Run CC

Plymouth, MA (508) 746-5001
www.squirrelrungolf.com

Club Pro: David Moore
Pro Shop: Full inventory
Payment: Visa, MC, Cash
Tee Times: 7 days adv.

Tees	Holes	Yards	Par	USGA	Slope
BACK	18	2859	57	55.4	85
MIDDLE	18	2338	57	53.7	82
FRONT	18	1990	57	56.0	83

Fee 9 Holes: Weekday: No   **Weekend:** No
Fee 18 Holes: Weekday: $25.00   **Weekend:** $28.00
Twilight Rates: Yes, after 4 pm   **All Day Play:** N/R
Cart Rental: $20.00/18   **Discounts:** Senior & Junior
Lessons: Yes **Schools:** No   **Junior Golf:** Yes **Membership:** No
Clinics: Yes **Day Camps:** N/R   **Driving Range:** No
Other: Restaurant / Clubhouse / Bar-Lounge / Snack Bar

COUPON

Tees and greens are immaculate. "A challenge to anyone's short game." (Paul Harber — Boston Globe). Sister course, Village Links.

	1	2	3	4	5	6	7	8	9
PAR	4	3	3	3	4	3	3	3	4
YARDS	286	105	125	90	263	98	131	123	206
HDCP	1	13	3	17	7	9	11	5	15

	10	11	12	13	14	15	16	17	18
PAR	3	3	3	3	3	3	3	3	3
YARDS	99	78	102	102	140	100	116	74	100
HDCP	14	18	12	8	2	10	6	16	4

Directions: From Route 3 take Exit 6 to Route 44 West. Go Approx. 2 miles to course on left. Look for Squirrel Run sign.

Stoneham Oaks

Stoneham, MA (781) 438-7888

Club Pro: Kent Pratt, PGA
Pro Shop: Limited inventory
Payment: Cash only
Tee Times: No

Tees	Holes	Yards	Par	USGA	Slope
BACK					
MIDDLE	9	1125	27	N/A	N/A
FRONT					

Fee 9 Holes: Weekday: $8.00 after 12pm   **Weekend:** $14.00
Fee 18 Holes: Weekday: $8.00 after 12pm   **Weekend:** $14.00
Twilight Rates: No   **All Day Play:** Yes
Cart Rental: $2.00/pull cart   **Discounts:** Senior & Junior
Lessons: $40/ 30min **Schools:** No   **Junior Golf:** No **Membership:** No
Clinics: No **Day Camps:** No   **Driving Range:** No
Other:

A par 3 course. Very hilly, many trees. Very Scenic. Various reduced weekday rates between 7:00 am and 2:00 pm.

	1	2	3	4	5	6	7	8	9
PAR	3	3	3	3	3	3	3	3	3
YARDS	89	147	179	128	95	113	153	139	82
HDCP	17	7	1	11	9	15	5	3	13

	10	11	12	13	14	15	16	17	18
PAR									
YARDS									
HDCP									

Directions: From I-93, take exit 36, Stoneham, Montvale Ave., 1 block. Course is at rear of the Stoneham Ice Rink.

Stow Acres CC (north) ✪✪ ▶ 81

Randall Rd., Stow, MA (978) 568-1100
www.stowacres.com

Club Pro: Dave Carlson
Pro Shop: Full inventory
Payment: Visa, MC, Amex
Tee Times: 5 days adv.
Fee 9 Holes: Weekday: N/A*
Fee 18 Holes: Weekday: $42.00 M-Th
Twilight Rates: Yes, after 4 pm
Cart Rental: $15pp
Lessons: $80.00/hr. **Schools:** Yes
Clinics: Yes **Day Camps:** Yes
Other: Clubhouse / Snack bar / Bar-lounge

Tees	Holes	Yards	Par	USGA	Slope
BACK	18	6939	72	72.8	130
MIDDLE	18	6310	72	70.5	127
FRONT	18	6011	72	72.5	130

Weekend: N/A
Weekend: $54.00 F/S/S/H
All Day Play: No
Discounts: Senior & Junior wkdys
Junior Golf: Yes **Membership:** Gold Card Mem
Driving Range: $9/lg. $7/med $5/sm.

PGA Tour Qualifier site. Championship layout. Top 50 public — *Golf Digest*. Black tees added. Open mid Mar. - mid Dec. **Player's Comments:** "Course continues to improve. Good practice area." *Play bef. work special.

	1	2	3	4	5	6	7	8	9
PAR	5	4	4	4	5	3	4	3	4
YARDS	503	374	354	387	472	180	318	165	426
HDCP	5	11	13	3	7	9	15	17	1
	10	**11**	**12**	**13**	**14**	**15**	**16**	**17**	**18**
PAR	4	4	5	3	4	4	3	4	5
YARDS	359	392	424	169	340	369	166	376	536
HDCP	4	6	18	16	14	8	12	10	2

Directions: Take Route I-95/128 to Route 20/117 Exit. Go west on Route 117 approx. 15 miles; left in Stow Center onto 62 West, follow signs from Route 62.

Stow Acres CC (south) ▶ 82

Randall Rd., Stow, MA (978) 568-1100
www.stowacres.com

Club Pro: Dave Carlson
Pro Shop: Full inventory
Payment: Visa, MC, Amex
Tee Times: 5 days adv.
Fee 9 Holes: Weekday: N/A *
Fee 18 Holes: Weekday: $42.00 M-Th
Twilight Rates: Yes, after 4 pm
Cart Rental: $15pp
Lessons: $80/ hour **Schools:** Yes
Clinics: Yes **Day Camps:** Yes
Other: Clubhouse / Snack bar / Bar-lounge

Tees	Holes	Yards	Par	USGA	Slope
BACK	18	6520	72	71.8	120
MIDDLE	18	6105	72	70.5	118
FRONT	18	5642	72	72.5	120

Weekend: N/A
Weekend: $54.00 F/S/S/H
All Day Play: No
Discounts: Senior & Junior wkdys
Junior Golf: Yes **Membership:** Yes, waiting list
Driving Range: $9/lg. $7/med $5/sm.

Rated in top 100 golf shops. Variety of instructional packages: schools, clinics and lessons for juniors. *Play before work special

	1	2	3	4	5	6	7	8	9
PAR	4	4	3	4	5	5	3	4	4
YARDS	375	416	123	301	476	487	212	346	368
HDCP	13	1	17	9	5	7	3	15	11
	10	**11**	**12**	**13**	**14**	**15**	**16**	**17**	**18**
PAR	5	3	4	4	5	3	4	3	5
YARDS	543	127	366	292	441	151	407	167	507
HDCP	4	18	10	14	16	12	2	8	6

Directions: Take Route I-95/128 to Route 20/117 Exit. Go west on Route 117 approx. 15 miles; left in Stow Center onto 62 West, follow signs from Route 62.

Strawberry Valley GC

Abington, MA (781) 878-8584

Club Pro: Tony Morosco, PGA
Pro Shop: Full inventory
Payment: MC, Visa, Cash
Tee Times: Daily 6am-8am
Fee 9 Holes: Weekday: $15.00
Fee 18 Holes: Weekday: $25.00
Twilight Rates: Scrambles
Cart Rental: $21.00/18 $12.00/9
Lessons: $45.00/ 1/2 hour **Schools:** No
Clinics: Yes **Day Camps:** No
Other: Snack bar

Tees	Holes	Yards	Par	USGA	Slope
BACK					
MIDDLE	9	4638	69	66.9	99
FRONT					

Weekend: $17.00
Weekend: $26.00
All Day Play: No
Discounts: None
Junior Golf: Yes **Membership:** Limited
Driving Range: No

Player friendly. Features senior, junior and beginner play. New management. Open year round.

	1	2	3	4	5	6	7	8	9
PAR	4	4	4	4	4	3	3	4	4
YARDS	228	357	385	233	215	119	132	302	309
HDCP	17	3	1	9	11	15	13	7	5
	10	11	12	13	14	15	16	17	18
PAR	4	4	5	4	4	3	3	4	4
YARDS	223	336	475	233	243	103	148	288	309
HDCP	18	4	2	12	10	16	14	8	6

Directions: Take Route 3 to Route 18 South. Course is approximately 7 miles on right.

Twin Brooks GC At Sheraton ✪✪✪

Hyannis, MA (508) 775-7775
www.twinbrooksgolf.com

Club Pro: No
Pro Shop: Full inventory
Payment: Visa, MC, Amex, Diner's, Cash
Tee Times: 2 days adv.
Fee 9 Holes: Weekday: $19.00
Fee 18 Holes: Weekday: $38.00
Twilight Rates: After 4 pm
Cart Rental: $22.00/18
Lessons: Available **Schools:** No
Clinics: No **Day Camps:** No
Other: Restaurant / Hotel / Bar-lounge / Showers

Tees	Holes	Yards	Par	USGA	Slope
BACK					
MIDDLE	18	2621	54		
FRONT					

Weekend: N/A
Weekend: $38.00
All Day Play: No
Discounts: Sr. $22, Jr. $20
Junior Golf: No **Membership:** Yes
Driving Range: No

COUPON

Course was rated the toughest Par 3 on Cape Cod by *Golf Digest*. Very challenging layout. Open year round.Five water holes. Pizza Scramble Fri. nights. Rates subject to change.

	1	2	3	4	5	6	7	8	9
PAR	3	3	3	3	3	3	3	3	3
YARDS	135	90	165	144	110	102	175	140	135
HDCP	6	18	4	12	14	16	2	10	8
	10	11	12	13	14	15	16	17	18
PAR	3	3	3	3	3	3	3	3	3
YARDS	190	140	150	115	170	215	150	160	135
HDCP	3	13	7	15	5	1	9	11	17

Directions: Take Route 6 to Exit 6 (Hyannis), follow Route 132 to Hyannis, follow signs to West End Hyannis. At rotary, you will see the Sheraton.

Twin Springs Golf Club

Bolton, MA (978) 779-5020
www.twinspringsgolf.com

Club Pro: Robert Keene
Pro Shop: Full inventory
Payment: MC, Visa, Amex
Tee Times: 1 week in advance
Fee 9 Holes: Weekday: $14.00
Fee 18 Holes: Weekday: $22.00
Twilight Rates: No
Cart Rental: $12/18pp, $7/9pp.
Lessons: $60.00/ hour **Schools:** Yes
Clinics: Yes **Day Camps:** Yes
Other: Snack bar

Tees	Holes	Yards	Par	USGA	Slope
BACK					
MIDDLE	9	2592	34	64.8	113
FRONT	9	2432	35	67.2	106

Weekend: $16.00
Weekend: $26.00
All Day Play: Yes
Discounts: Senior & Junior
Junior Golf: Yes **Membership:** Senior
Driving Range: Yes

COUPON

Sig. Hole: #4 is a devilish par 3 with a great view of Wachusett Mountain, fronted by a creek.

	1	2	3	4	5	6	7	8	9
PAR	4	4	4	3	3	4	4	4	4
YARDS	327	294	300	140	161	318	368	320	384
HDCP	7	9	13	15	11	3	1	17	5
	10	11	12	13	14	15	16	17	18
PAR									
YARDS									
HDCP									

Directions: Take I-495 to Exit 27 to Route 117 West into center of Bolton. Go straight for .7 of a mile. Turn left up hill at Wilder Rd. Course is 2 miles on right.

Unicorn Golf Course

Stoneham, MA (781) 438-9732

Club Pro: Carl Marchio
Pro Shop: Yes
Payment: Cash only
Tee Times: No
Fee 9 Holes: Weekday: $16.00
Fee 18 Holes: Weekday: No
Twilight Rates: No
Cart Rental: $13.00/9
Lessons: No **Schools:** No
Clinics: No **Day Camps:** No
Other: Snack bar

Tees	Holes	Yards	Par	USGA	Slope
BACK	9	6468	70	70.8	126
MIDDLE	9	6370	70	69.6	121
FRONT	9	5804	74	73.0	124

Weekend: $17.00
Weekend: No
All Day Play: No
Discounts: Senior & Junior Wkdays
Junior Golf: No **Membership:** No
Driving Range: No

Sig. Hole: #5 - rolling fairways, tree lined. The course is relatively level. Reduced fees for residents.

	1	2	3	4	5	6	7	8	9
PAR	4	4	4	3	4	5	4	3	4
YARDS	389	326	335	168	395	499	448	178	447
HDCP	5	13	11	17	1	9	3	15	7
	10	11	12	13	14	15	16	17	18
PAR	4	4	4	3	4	5	4	3	4
YARDS	389	326	335	168	395	499	448	178	447
HDCP	6	14	12	18	2	10	4	16	8

Directions: Take I-93 to to Montevale Avenue. Follow to end. Left onto Route 28, left at next set of lights (Williams Street.). Course is 1/4 mile on left.

Village Links ✪✪✪

Plymouth,MA (508) 830-4653
www.villagelinksgolf.com

Club Pro: David L. Moore, PGA
Pro Shop: Full inventory
Payment: Visa, MC
Tee Times: 7 days adv.
Fee 9 Holes: Weekday: N/A
Fee 18 Holes: Weekday: $25.00
Twilight Rates: Yes
Cart Rental: Yes
Lessons: $40.00/30min. **Schools:** Yes
Clinics: Yes **Day Camps:** Yes
Other: Restaurant / Clubhouse / Bar-lounge

Tees	Holes	Yards	Par	USGA	Slope
BACK	18	2407	54		
MIDDLE	18	1986	54	52.8	78
FRONT					

Weekend: N/A
Weekend: $28.00
All Day Play: No
Discounts: Senior & Junior
Junior Golf: Yes **Membership:**
Driving Range:

18 hole par 3, executive style. Associated with Pinehurst Village. Sister course to Squirrel Run. "Excellent holes include #4, 5, 8, 11, 15, 17." A.P.

	1	2	3	4	5	6	7	8	9
PAR	3	3	3	3	3	3	3	3	3
YARDS	134	141	159	57	114	124	113	60	76
HDCP									
	10	11	12	13	14	15	16	17	18
PAR	3	3	3	3	3	3	3	3	3
YARDS	133	112	130	84	79	96	136	74	164
HDCP									

Directions: From Rte. 3: Exit 6 West (Rte. 44). Turn left at the 3rd set of lights onto Seven Hills Rd. Turn right at the 1st set of lights onto South Meadow Rd. Village Links is 2.5 miles on the right.

Waverly Oaks Golf Club ✪✪✪✪

Plymouth, MA (508) 224-6016
www.waverlyoaksgolfclub.com

Club Pro: Tracy Djerf, LPGA
Pro Shop: Full inventory
Payment: Visa, MC, Amex
Tee Times: 7 days adv.
Fee 9 Holes: Weekday: $40 inc. cart after 4
Fee 18 Holes: Weekday: $75.00 cart incl.
Twilight Rates: No
Cart Rental: Included
Lessons: $35.00/half hour **Schools:** No
Clinics: Adult/Jr **Day Camps:** No
Other: Full Restaurant / Clubhouse / Bar-Lounge / Showers / Corporate Outings/ Sm group outings

Tees	Holes	Yards	Par	USGA	Slope
BACK	18	7114	72	73.5	130
MIDDLE	18	6682	72	71.3	126
FRONT	18	5587	72	71.4	127

Weekend: $40 inc. cart after 4pm
Weekend: $85.00 cart included
All Day Play: Replay Discount
Discounts: None
Junior Golf: Yes **Membership:** Season pass
Driving Range: $5/lg. $3/sm.

Top 100 you can play. One of NE best, ZAGAT Rating. **Players' Comment:**" Best course all round I've played." "Not a blemish." "$$$ worth it." Improvements at 17th hole. "A gem." R.W.

	1	2	3	4	5	6	7	8	9
PAR	4	4	3	5	5	4	4	3	4
YARDS	325	394	191	502	515	432	410	184	353
HDCP	13	5	7	15	17	3	1	9	11
	10	11	12	13	14	15	16	17	18
PAR	4	4	4	5	3	4	5	3	4
YARDS	386	372	311	512	163	449	606	221	356
HDCP	16	14	18	8	10	4	2	6	12

Directions: From the north, Route 3 South to Exit 3. Right off ramp. Right at first stop sign. Entrance two miles on right.

Wayland Country Club ✪✪ ▶ 89

Wayland, MA (508) 358-4775
www.waylandgolf.com

Club Pro: Joe Potty, PGA
Pro Shop: Top 100 in U.S.
Payment: Cash only
Tee Times: Call Mon. for wknd.dys in adv.

Tees	Holes	Yards	Par	USGA	Slope
BACK	18	5836	70	67.9	113
MIDDLE	18	5974	70	67.3	112
FRONT	18	4875	71	70.0	120

Fee 9 Holes: Weekday: $20 1pm-3pm, M-Th **Weekend:** No
Fee 18 Holes: Weekday: $36.00 (M-Th) **Weekend:** $45.00
Twilight Rates: Yes, after 6 pm **All Day Play:** Yes
Cart Rental: $26.00/18 $13.00/9 **Discounts:** Senior & Junior (M-Th)
Lessons: $60-$70/hour **Schools:** No **Junior Golf:** Yes **Membership:** No
Clinics: Yes **Day Camps:** Yes **Driving Range:** No
Other: Restaurant / Clubhouse / Snack bar / Bar-lounge

Course is fairly flat and wide open. Extensive pro shop open year round. National ranking in best 100 golf shop operations.

	1	2	3	4	5	6	7	8	9
PAR	5	4	4	3	4	3	4	3	4
YARDS	443	412	384	139	353	188	260	153	405
HDCP	11	1	5	15	13	9	17	7	3
	10	11	12	13	14	15	16	17	18
PAR	4	4	5	4	3	4	4	3	5
YARDS	320	326	500	346	174	378	400	198	457
HDCP	16	12	8	10	18	4	2	6	14

Directions: Take Route 128/95; take Route 20 West; right onto Route 27 North; approximately 1 mile right.

Widow's Walk Golf Course ▶ 90

Scituate, MA (781) 544-7777
www.widowswalkgolf.com

Club Pro: Bob Sanderson, PGA
Pro Shop: Yes
Payment: Visa, MC, Amex, Cash
Tee Times: 4 days adv.

Tees	Holes	Yards	Par	USGA	Slope
BACK	18	6403	72	71.2	129
MIDDLE	18	6062	72	69.6	127
FRONT	18	4562	72	66.2	113

Fee 9 Holes: Weekday: $19.00 M-Th **Weekend:** $22.00 F/S/S
Fee 18 Holes: Weekday: $32.00 M-Th **Weekend:** $42.00 F/S/S
Twilight Rates: No **All Day Play:** Replay rates
Cart Rental: $26.00/ 18 $14.00/ 9 **Discounts:** Senior & Junior M-Th
Lessons: $40.00/ 30 minutes **Schools:** No **Junior Golf:** Yes **Membership:** Residents M-Th
Clinics: Yes **Day Camps:** No **Driving Range:** $3.50/bucket
Other: Restaurant / Bar

Player's Comment: "Excellent shape, well developed. Use smart judgement. Nice view. great elevated tee boxes." (F.P.) Environmentally correct and also an affordable course. *Golf Digest.* Lodging partner.

	1	2	3	4	5	6	7	8	9
PAR	5	3	4	4	4	5	3	4	5
YARDS	504	126	350	351	302	486	167	313	481
HDCP	7	17	5	11	13	1	15	9	3
	10	11	12	13	14	15	16	17	18
PAR	4	3	4	4	3	5	4	3	5
YARDS	425	140	313	412	183	486	312	191	520
HDCP	4	18	8	2	14	6	12	16	10

Directions: Route 3 to Exit 13, Route 53 North to Route 123 East. Go straight through Route 3A intersection. Take first right after .1 mile and proceed to stop sign. Go straight. Course is 7/10 mile on left.

Willowdale Golf Course

Mansfield, MA (508) 339-3197

Club Pro: No
Pro Shop: Limited inventory
Payment: Cash only
Tee Times: No
Fee 9 Holes: Weekday: $12.00
Fee 18 Holes: Weekday: $15.00
Twilight Rates: No
Cart Rental: $2.00/pull cart
Lessons: No **Schools:** No
Clinics: No **Day Camps:** No
Other: Snack bar / Bar-lounge / Clubhouse

Tees	Holes	Yards	Par	USGA	Slope
BACK					
MIDDLE	9	1935	30		
FRONT					

Weekend: $14.00
Weekend: $17.00
All Day Play: No
Discounts: Senior M-F $1 off
Junior Golf: Yes **Membership:** No
Driving Range: No

Executive-style course, considered an easy walker. Open April 1 - December 1.

	1	2	3	4	5	6	7	8	9
PAR	4	3	3	4	4	3	3	3	3
YARDS	265	180	190	320	285	180	100	210	205
HDCP	2	5	8	3	1	7	9	4	6
	10	11	12	13	14	15	16	17	18
PAR									
YARDS									
HDCP									

Directions: Take I-95 to Mansfield Exit. Route 140 to Mansfield Center, School Street Exit. First right on Willow Street.

Woodbriar CC

Falmouth, MA (508) 495-5500

Club Pro: No
Pro Shop: No
Payment: Visa, MC, Personal checks
Tee Times: No
Fee 9 Holes: Weekday: $20.00
Fee 18 Holes: Weekday: $20.00
Twilight Rates: Yes, after 4 pm
Cart Rental: $4.00/pull cart
Lessons: Yes **Schools:** No
Clinics: Yes **Day Camps:** No
Other: Snack bar

Tees	Holes	Yards	Par	USGA	Slope
BACK					
MIDDLE	9	1410	27		
FRONT					

Weekend: $20.00
Weekend: $20.00
All Day Play: $7 after 18 holes
Discounts: Special
Junior Golf: Yes **Membership:** Yes
Driving Range: Practice net

COUPON

Sig. Hole: #5, 217 yard par 3. Hitting to green surrounded by bunkers with prevailing wind occasionally against you. Executive-style 9 hole course, good for beginners. Open year round.

	1	2	3	4	5	6	7	8	9
PAR	3	3	3	3	3	3	3	3	3
YARDS	142	129	115	139	270	162	168	127	158
HDCP	5	9	6	7	1	3	4	8	2
	10	11	12	13	14	15	16	17	18
PAR									
YARDS									
HDCP									

Directions: Take Route 28 to Brick Kiln Road Exit, take left at end of off-ramp, take right at first red light onto Gifford Street, course is 2.5 miles on left.

CHAPTER 2

Central Massachusetts & Boston's North Shore

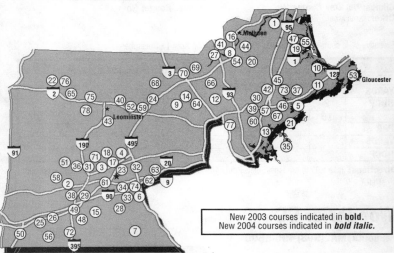

New 2003 courses indicated in **bold**.
New 2004 courses indicated in ***bold italic***.

Amesbury Golf & CC

Monroe St., Amesbury, MA (978) 388-5153

Club Pro: Butch Mellon
Pro Shop: Full inventory
Payment: Cash, personal checks
Tee Times: 5 days adv.
Fee 9 Holes: Weekday: $16.00
Fee 18 Holes: Weekday: $28.00
Twilight Rates: No
Cart Rental: $28.00/18 $14.00/9
Lessons: $30.00/half hour **Schools:** No
Clinics: No **Day Camps:** No
Other: Clubhouse / Lockers / Showers / Snack bar / Bar-lounge

Tees	Holes	Yards	Par	USGA	Slope
BACK					
MIDDLE	9	6095	70	70.5	125
FRONT	9	5381	70	71.9	126

Weekend: $18.00
Weekend: $30.00
All Day Play: No
Discounts: None
Junior Golf: Yes **Membership:** Yes
Driving Range: No

Newly constructed #9 green. Great 1st tee panorama. Featured in *Yankee Magazine*.

	1	2	3	4	5	6	7	8	9
PAR	4	3	4	4	5	4	4	3	4
YARDS	381	170	349	309	524	299	365	162	380
HDCP	7	17	11	13	3	9	1	15	5
	10	**11**	**12**	**13**	**14**	**15**	**16**	**17**	**18**
PAR	4	3	4	4	5	4	4	3	4
YARDS	387	230	354	324	530	335	414	181	395
HDCP	8	16	12	14	4	10	2	18	6

Directions: Take I-95 North to Route 110 West; then take right at lights near Burger King; take right onto Monroe Street. Course is 1/3 mile on left.

Bay Path Golf Course

East Brookfield, MA (508) 867-8161

Club Pro: No
Pro Shop: Full inventory
Payment: Cash or check
Tee Times: No
Fee 9 Holes: Weekday: $13.00
Fee 18 Holes: Weekday: $19.00
Twilight Rates: No
Cart Rental: $25.00/18, $13.00/9
Lessons: No **Schools:** N/R
Clinics: N/R **Day Camps:** No
Other: Clubhouse / Snack bar / Bar-lounge

Tees	Holes	Yards	Par	USGA	Slope
BACK					
MIDDLE	9	2640	36	69.5	113
FRONT					

Weekend: $15.00
Weekend: $23.00
All Day Play: No
Discounts: None
Junior Golf: No **Membership:** Yes, limited
Driving Range: No

Player's Comments: "Great deal for the money. Nice friendly staff and lounge.". Very flat and easy to walk for Central Mass. Open April - until it snows.

	1	2	3	4	5	6	7	8	9
PAR	4	4	5	4	3	5	4	3	4
YARDS	297	273	456	305	131	426	270	151	331
HDCP	8	7	2	1	4	5	9	6	3
	10	**11**	**12**	**13**	**14**	**15**	**16**	**17**	**18**
PAR									
YARDS									
HDCP									

Directions: Mass. Pike to Route 20 East (Sturbridge exit). Then take Route 20 East to Route 49 North to Route 9 West to Route 67 North (North Brookfield Road). Course is approximately 1/4 mile on left.

4✪ =Excellent 3✪ = Very Good 2✪ = Good   **Boston's North Shore & Central MA 81**

Bedrock Golf Club

3

Rutland, MA (508) 886-0202

Club Pro: Joe Carr, PGA
Pro Shop: Limited inventory
Payment: Visa, MC, Cash
Tee Times: Weekends
Fee 9 Holes: Weekday: $15.00
Fee 18 Holes: Weekday: $25.00
Twilight Rates: After 3 pm, 1 pm wknds
Cart Rental: $16.00pp/18 $8.00pp/9
Lessons: No **Schools:** No
Clinics: No **Day Camps:** No
Other: Clubhouse / Bar-Lounge / Snack Bar

Tees	Holes	Yards	Par	USGA	Slope
BACK					
MIDDLE	9	6013	72	69.8	127
FRONT					

Weekend: $25.00
Weekend: $40.00
All Day Play: Yes
Discounts: Junior, Wkdays
Junior Golf: No **Membership:** Yes
Driving Range: No

Gently rolling, narrow landing areas. Small, undulating greens, challenging. Collared shirts required. Open April - November.

	1	2	3	4	5	6	7	8	9
PAR	4	5	4	3	4	5	3	4	4
YARDS	340	460	380	184	355	487	166	348	411
HDCP	15	17	1	11	3	7	9	13	5
	10	11	12	13	14	15	16	17	18
PAR	4	5	4	3	4	5	3	4	4
YARDS	327	410	356	165	335	433	139	323	394
HDCP	14	18	2	8	6	10	12	16	4

Directions: Mass Pike to Auburn Exit (10). Then take Route 20 W to Route 56 N to Route 122. In Paxton. Course is 4 miles on left.

Berlin Country Club

4

25 Carr Rd., Berlin, MA (978) 838-2733

Club Pro: No
Pro Shop: Full inventory
Payment: Cash only
Tee Times: No
Fee 9 Holes: Weekday: $14.00
Fee 18 Holes: Weekday: $20.00
Twilight Rates: N/R
Cart Rental: $20.00/18 $12.00/9
Lessons: No **Schools:** No
Clinics: No **Day Camps:** No
Other: Clubhouse / Snack bar / Bar-lounge / Banquet Facility

Tees	Holes	Yards	Par	USGA	Slope
BACK	9	2433	33	62.9	108
MIDDLE	9	2233	33	62.9	108
FRONT	9	2183	33	62.9	108

Weekend: $14.00
Weekend: $20.00
All Day Play: N/R
Discounts: Senior & Junior
Junior Golf: No **Membership:** Yes
Driving Range: No (Close-by)

Mildly sloping fairways with challenging greens. Golf shirts and golf shoes required. Golf school and driving range near-by. Rates subject to change. Monday- Thursday 6am- 1pm special, call.

	1	2	3	4	5	6	7	8	9
PAR	4	4	4	3	4	4	3	4	3
YARDS	312	326	332	127	264	349	108	282	133
HDCP	13	5	3	15	11	1	17	9	7
	10	11	12	13	14	15	16	17	18
PAR									
YARDS									
HDCP									

Directions: From I-495 take Route 62 to Berlin Center and follow signs. From I-290 take Solomon Pond Mall Rd. to Berlin Center and follow signs.

Beverly Golf & Tennis ✪✪ 5 ▶

Beverly, MA (978) 922-9072
www.johnsongolfmanagement.com

Club Pro: Don Lyons
Pro Shop: Full inventory
Payment: All major
Tee Times: 7 days adv.

Tees	Holes	Yards	Par	USGA	Slope
BACK	18	6237	70	70.1	123
MIDDLE	18	5966	70	69.2	121
FRONT	18	5429	73	70.3	113

Fee 9 Holes: Weekday: $21.00
Fee 18 Holes: Weekday: $37.00
Twilight Rates: Call
Cart Rental: $28.00/18 $15.00/9
Lessons: $65/hour **Schools:** Yes
Clinics: Yes **Day Camps:** No
Weekend: $23.00 after 5pm
Weekend: $44.00
All Day Play: Yes
Discounts: Senior & Junior
Junior Golf: Yes **Membership:** Yes. $500/Res
Driving Range: No
Other: Clubhouse / Lockers / Showers / Snack bar / Restaurant / Bar-lounge

Player's Comment: "Course in good condition. Several long par 4's. Good challenge." Members weekends until 1:30. Resident discount.

	1	2	3	4	5	6	7	8	9
PAR	4	4	3	4	4	3	4	5	4
YARDS	431	413	147	390	271	159	372	571	300
HDCP	3	5	13	9	17	11	7	1	15

	10	11	12	13	14	15	16	17	18
PAR	4	3	3	5	4	3	4	5	4
YARDS	266	235	193	462	347	143	382	500	384
HDCP	16	6	12	4	14	18	8	2	10

Directions: Take Route 128 to Exit 20B, Right off Ramp, Go through fork keeping Henry's Market on your right. Next fork go left, 1/2 mile on right.

Blackstone National Golf Club ✪✪✪ 6 ▶

Sutton, MA (508) 865-2111
www.bngc.net

Club Pro: James Bombard, PGA
Pro Shop: Full inventory
Payment: Visa, MC, Amex, Disc.
Tee Times: 5 days adv.

Tees	Holes	Yards	Par	USGA	Slope
BACK	18	6909	72	73.5	132
MIDDLE	18	6396	72	71.2	127
FRONT	18	5203	72	70.0	122

Fee 9 Holes: Weekday: $30.00
Fee 18 Holes: Weekday: $54.00
Twilight Rates: After 1 pm, 1:30 wknds
Cart Rental: $19.95pp/18 $10.50pp/9
Lessons: Yes **Schools:** No
Clinics: Yes **Day Camps:** No
Weekend: $35.00
Weekend: $69.00
All Day Play: Yes
Discounts: Junior
Junior Golf: Yes **Membership:** Yes
Driving Range: $8.50/bucket
Other: Full Restaurant / Clubhouse / Lockers / Showers / Bar-Lounge / Henry Griffitt's Golf Club Fitting

Players' Comments: "Fun to play. Great condition. Greens hard. Long course to handle. Wonderfully built and kept." "Nice scenery."

	1	2	3	4	5	6	7	8	9
PAR	4	5	3	4	4	4	3	5	4
YARDS	331	575	154	393	346	425	196	480	363
HDCP	15	1	13	3	17	5	7	9	11

	10	11	12	13	14	15	16	17	18
PAR	4	3	4	3	4	4	5	4	5
YARDS	396	160	358	190	387	481	568	372	480
HDCP	6	18	14	10	12	2	4	16	8

Directions: Mass Pike to Exit 10A to Route 146 South. Go 6 miles and take Central Turnpike towards Oxford 3 miles to 4-way stop. Take left. GC on top of hill.

Blissful Meadows GC

7

Uxbridge, MA (508) 278-6113
www.blissfulmeadows.com

Club Pro: J.Griffin, D.Johnson, Head Pros
Pro Shop: Full inventory
Payment: Visa, MC, Amex
Tee Times: 2 days adv.

Tees	Holes	Yards	Par	USGA	Slope
BACK	18	6601	72	71.3	128
MIDDLE	18	6190	72	68.7	124
FRONT	18	5065	72	69.1	122

Fee 9 Holes: Weekday: $18.00 M-Thurs **Weekend:** $26.00, $22.00 Fri
Fee 18 Holes: Weekday: $29.00 M-Thurs **Weekend:** $43.00, $38.00 Fri
Twilight Rates: Yes, after 4 pm **All Day Play:** No
Cart Rental: $14.00 pp **Discounts:** Senior & Junior
Lessons: $30.00/half hour **Schools:** No **Junior Golf:** Yes **Membership:** Yes
Clinics: Yes **Day Camps:** Yes **Driving Range:** $6.00/lg. $4.00/sm.
Other: Meadowview Tavern / Clubhouse / Bar-lounge / Available for outings

Rolling hills, fifty tree varieties, and scenic country setting. Bent grass greens and tees.
Players' Comments: "Nice course. Feels like just you and your foursome playing." "Ladies League"

	1	2	3	4	5	6	7	8	9
PAR	4	3	5	4	3	4	4	5	4
YARDS	325	148	528	343	132	368	312	572	334
HDCP	7	15	3	13	17	5	11	1	9
	10	**11**	**12**	**13**	**14**	**15**	**16**	**17**	**18**
PAR	5	4	4	3	4	3	5	4	4
YARDS	499	343	375	143	306	176	515	373	398
HDCP	8	10	2	16	14	18	12	6	4

Directions: Take Route 146 to Route 16 West. Take first left on to West Street. Follow signs 3 miles. Take right at dead end.

Bradford Country Club

8

Bradford, MA (978) 372-8587
www.bradfordcc.com

Club Pro: Mark Mangion, PGA
Pro Shop: Full inventory
Payment: Visa, MC, Amex, Disc
Tee Times: 5 days adv.

Tees	Holes	Yards	Par	USGA	Slope
BACK	18	6311	70	72.4	132
MIDDLE	18	5697	70	69.6	127
FRONT	18	4614	70	67.6	123

Fee 9 Holes: Weekday: $17.00 **Weekend:** $21.00
Fee 18 Holes: Weekday: $32.00 **Weekend:** $40.00
Twilight Rates: Wknds after 3 pm **All Day Play:** No
Cart Rental: $15pp/18, $9pp/9 **Discounts:** Senior & Junior
Lessons: $35/30 min $50/60 min **Schools:** No **Junior Golf:** Yes **Membership:** Yes
Clinics: No **Day Camps:** No **Driving Range:** No
Other: Clubhouse / Bar-lounge / Restaurant / Lockers / Outings / Leagues

Player's Comment: "Difficult back 9." Open March - November.

	1	2	3	4	5	6	7	8	9
PAR	4	4	3	4	4	3	4	5	4
YARDS	368	346	156	375	382	146	353	491	479
HDCP	13	7	15	9	5	17	11	3	1
	10	**11**	**12**	**13**	**14**	**15**	**16**	**17**	**18**
PAR	4	3	5	4	4	4	4	3	4
YARDS	427	195	510	413	418	401	410	171	428
HDCP	10	16	2	4	8	14	12	18	6

Directions: Route 495 to Exit 48. North on Route 125 to Salem St. Turn right. Right onto Boxford Road (1st street after Bradford House Restaurant). Take first right on Chadwick Road to Clubhouse.

Butter Brook Golf Club

9 ▶

157 Carlisle Rd., Westford, MA (978) 692-6560
www.butterbrookgc.com

Club Pro: TBA
Pro Shop: Limited inventory
Payment: Visa, MC, Amex, Disc
Tee Times: 7 days adv.
Fee 9 Holes: Weekday: TBA
Fee 18 Holes: Weekday: TBA
Twilight Rates:
Cart Rental:
Lessons: No **Schools:** No
Clinics: No **Day Camps:** No
Other: Clubhouse / Bar-lounge

Tees	Holes	Yards	Par	USGA	Slope
BACK	9	3600	36		
MIDDLE	9	3375	36		
FRONT	9	2710	36		

Weekend: TBA
Weekend: TBA
All Day Play:
Discounts: None
Junior Golf: No **Membership:** Yes
Driving Range: No

New Entry 2004. Created on over 180 acres of serene rolling hills, tall pine trees, beautiful ponds and a babbling brook.

	1	2	3	4	5	6	7	8	9
PAR	5	4	3	4	3	4	5	3	5
YARDS	565	341	129	408	151	435	552	183	611
HDCP	3	8	9	6	7	2	4	5	1

	10	11	12	13	14	15	16	17	18
PAR									
YARDS									
HDCP									

Directions: Route 95(128N) to Exit 31B (Bedford/ Carlisle) Routes 4/225. Follow through Bedford Center. Stay on Routes 4 & 225. At Gammy's Gas Station, take left and stay on Route 225. Go 2.7 miles. Cross Route 27. Course is 500 ft on left.

Candlewood Golf Club

10 ▶

Rt. 133, Ipswich, MA (978) 356-5377

Club Pro: Bob Robinson
Pro Shop: Yes
Payment: Cash only
Tee Times: No
Fee 9 Holes: Weekday: $13.00
Fee 18 Holes: Weekday: $19.00
Twilight Rates: Yes, after 5 pm
Cart Rental: $15.00/18 10.00/9
Lessons: $25.00/hour **Schools:** No
Clinics: No **Day Camps:** No
Other: Snack Bar

Tees	Holes	Yards	Par	USGA	Slope
BACK					
MIDDLE	9	2108	32		
FRONT					

Weekend: $14.00
Weekend: $20.00
All Day Play: No
Discounts: Senior M-F
Junior Golf: No **Membership:** Yes
Driving Range: No

Course is easy to walk and good for senior citizens and beginners.

	1	2	3	4	5	6	7	8	9
PAR	4	4	3	3	3	4	4	4	3
YARDS	350	350	120	140	135	253	290	280	190
HDCP									

	10	11	12	13	14	15	16	17	18
PAR									
YARDS									
HDCP									

Directions: Take Route 128 to Route 1A North. Take Route 133 South towards Essex.

4✪ =Excellent **3✪** = Very Good **2✪** = Good

Cape Ann Golf Club

Rt. 133, Essex, MA (978) 768-7544
www.capeanngolf.com

Club Pro: No
Pro Shop: Limited inventory
Payment: Cash or credit card
Tee Times: No
Fee 9 Holes: Weekday: $17.00
Fee 18 Holes: Weekday: $32.00
Twilight Rates: Yes, after 5 pm
Cart Rental: $28.00/18 $15.00/9, $3/pull
Lessons: No **Schools:** No
Clinics: No **Day Camps:** No
Other: Bar-lounge / Snack Bar

Weekend: $19.00
Weekend: $35.00
All Day Play: Yes
Discounts: Senior & Junior
Junior Golf: No **Membership:** No
Driving Range: No

Tees	Holes	Yards	Par	USGA	Slope
BACK					
MIDDLE	9	5866	69	67.2	110
FRONT	9	4608	69	65.2	102

Many improvements include irrigation system, new putting green, pro shop stocked, new tee on hole #1 and #7 championship hole is now 258 yard, par 3.

	1	2	3	4	5	6	7	8	9
PAR	4	4	3	4	4	4	3	4	4
YARDS	359	351	170	437	330	280	258	379	341
HDCP	7	5	15	1	9	11	13	3	17
	10	11	12	13	14	15	16	17	18
PAR	4	4	3	5	4	4	3	4	4
YARDS	367	389	181	463	348	289	234	410	349
HDCP	8	6	18	12	14	10	4	2	16

Directions: Take Route 128 North to Exit 15 (School Street), follow signs toward Essex.

CC of Billerica

Billerica, MA (978) 667-9121 ext. 22
www.countryclubofbillerica.com

Club Pro: Steve Miller
Pro Shop: Full inventory
Payment: Cash or credit card
Tee Times: Yes. Call 10am TH for S/S/H
Fee 9 Holes: Weekday: $17.00
Fee 18 Holes: Weekday: $27.00
Twilight Rates: Yes, after 6 pm
Cart Rental: $26.00/18 $16.00/9
Lessons: $45.00/half hour **Schools:** Yes
Clinics: Junior **Day Camps:** No
Other: Restaurant / Bar-lounge / Clubhouse

Weekend: $19.00
Weekend: $29.00
All Day Play: No
Discounts: None
Junior Golf: Yes **Membership:** Yes
Driving Range: $7 lg./ $5/sm.

Tees	Holes	Yards	Par	USGA	Slope
BACK	18	5640	69	66.7	121
MIDDLE	18	5360	69	66.0	117
FRONT	18	4545	69	66.9	116

Challenging and affordable for all!

	1	2	3	4	5	6	7	8	9
PAR	5	3	4	5	3	4	3	3	4
YARDS	465	160	371	470	85	376	147	138	392
HDCP	4	14	8	6	18	10	12	16	2
	10	11	12	13	14	15	16	17	18
PAR	4	4	4	3	4	4	3	5	4
YARDS	296	360	234	153	292	294	190	552	382
HDCP	13	3	9	17	11	15	5	1	7

Directions: Take Route 128 to Route 3A North. Take Route 3A North into Billerica Center. Take right before Friendly's restaurant and at the end of the road, take a right and then the third left onto Baldwin Street. Course is on right.

Cedar Glen Golf Club

Saugus, MA (781) 233-3609

Club Pro: No
Pro Shop: Limited inventory
Payment: Cash only
Tee Times: No
Fee 9 Holes: Weekday: $16.00
Fee 18 Holes: Weekday: $26.00
Twilight Rates: No
Cart Rental: $22.00/18 $12.00/9
Lessons: No **Schools:** N/R
Clinics: No **Day Camps:** No
Other: Clubhouse / Snack bar

Tees	Holes	Yards	Par	USGA	Slope
BACK					
MIDDLE	9	5890	35	67.0	107
FRONT	9	1500	35	67	107

Weekend: $17.00
Weekend: $27.00
All Day Play: Yes
Discounts: Senior & Junior wkdys
Junior Golf: No **Membership:** No
Driving Range: No

Sig. Hole: #3 is a 225 yard, par 3 with an elevated tee to a green with a series of bunkers. New watering system.

	1	2	3	4	5	6	7	8	9
PAR	4	5	3	4	4	3	4	4	4
YARDS	350	475	220	335	380	135	310	340	400
HDCP	3	2	4	7	1	9	8	6	5
	10	11	12	13	14	15	16	17	18
PAR									
YARDS									
HDCP									

Directions: Take I-95 to Walnut Street. Follow Walnut Street east to Water Street. Take right, course is on left.

Chelmsford Country Club

66 Park Rd., Chelmsford, MA (978) 256-1818
www.sterlinggolf.com

Club Pro: Stephen Clancy
Pro Shop: Limited inventory
Payment: Visa, MC, Amex, Dis, Cash,
Tee Times: 4 days adv.
Fee 9 Holes: Weekday: $16.00
Fee 18 Holes: Weekday: $21.00
Twilight Rates: Yes, after 4 pm
Cart Rental: $24.00/18 $15.00/9
Lessons: Yes **Schools:** No
Clinics: No **Day Camps:** No
Other: Snack bar / Bar-lounge / Function Hall

Tees	Holes	Yards	Par	USGA	Slope
BACK					
MIDDLE	9	4894	66	64.2	108
FRONT	9	4404	68	66.1	109

Weekend: $18.00
Weekend: $25.00
All Day Play: No
Discounts: Senior & Junior
Junior Golf: Yes **Membership:** Yes
Driving Range: Yes

COUPON

A fun golf course for all playing levels. Two new tees built in 2003. Overall enhanced conditions. Managed by Sterling Golf Management, Inc.

	1	2	3	4	5	6	7	8	9
PAR	4	3	3	5	4	3	4	4	3
YARDS	237	196	140	453	352	120	318	415	196
HDCP	14	4	16	8	10	18	12	2	6
	10	11	12	13	14	15	16	17	18
PAR	4	3	3	5	4	3	4	4	3
YARDS	241	200	144	457	358	124	323	420	200
HDCP	13	3	15	7	9	17	11	1	5

Directions: Take Route 3 or Route 495 to Route110 to Chelmsford Center. Then take Route 27 S. Take left onto Park Road. Course is 200 yards on left.

Clearview Golf Course

15

Millbury, MA (508) 754-5654

Club Pro: Bill Chisholm
Pro Shop: Full inventory
Payment: Visa, MC, cash
Tee Times: 1 week adv.
Fee 9 Holes: Weekday: $13.00
Fee 18 Holes: Weekday: $20.00
Twilight Rates: N/R
Cart Rental: $13pp/18 $7pp/9
Lessons: Yes **Schools:** No
Clinics: No **Day Camps:** No
Other: Snack bar / Bar-lounge

Tees	Holes	Yards	Par	USGA	Slope
BACK					
MIDDLE	9	5569	71	66.3	107
FRONT	9	5236	71	67.7	112

Weekend: $16.00
Weekend: $23.00
All Day Play: No
Discounts: Seniors $1.00, Wkdys
Junior Golf: No **Membership:** Yes
Driving Range: No

COUPON

Best greens in Central Mass. Pre- 9 AM discounts available:$5 for 9 holes.

	1	2	3	4	5	6	7	8	9
PAR	3	5	5	3	5	3	4	4	3
YARDS	147	472	484	192	477	135	348	290	179
HDCP	18	8	2	10	6	16	4	12	14
	10	11	12	13	14	15	16	17	18
PAR	3	5	5	3	5	4	4	4	3
YARDS	160	485	491	207	489	304	365	305	193
HDCP	17	7	1	9	5	15	3	11	13

Directions: I-90 (Mass Pike) to Exit 10A (Route 146). Look for Route 20 East. At first traffic light, go right onto Park Hill Ave. Course is 1/2 mile on left.

Crystal Springs CC

16

N. Broadway, Haverhill, MA (978) 374-9621

Club Pro: Ed Tompkins, PGA
Pro Shop: Full inventory
Payment: Cash only
Tee Times: Wknds 7 days
Fee 9 Holes: Weekday: $13.00
Fee 18 Holes: Weekday: $23.00
Twilight Rates: No
Cart Rental: $23.00/18 $13.00/9
Lessons: $35.00/half hour **Schools:** No
Clinics: Yes **Day Camps:** No
Other: Snack bar / Restaurant / Bar-lounge

Tees	Holes	Yards	Par	USGA	Slope
BACK	18	6706	72	72.0	112
MIDDLE	18	6436	72	70.8	114
FRONT	18	5596	72	71.1	116

Weekend: $13.00
Weekend: $27.00
All Day Play: No
Discounts: None
Junior Golf: No **Membership:** Yes
Driving Range: yES

Sig. Hole: #4 is a 401 yard, par 4 with a view of Crystal Lake and winds to the left. Requires two mid-iron shots to green. Golfers who hit for distance will enjoy Crystal Springs.

	1	2	3	4	5	6	7	8	9
PAR	4	3	4	4	5	3	4	5	4
YARDS	367	213	351	395	472	207	387	475	415
HDCP	5	15	7	1	11	17	9	13	3
	10	11	12	13	14	15	16	17	18
PAR	4	5	4	3	4	4	3	4	5
YARDS	389	491	394	210	332	316	135	415	472
HDCP	6	8	4	16	10	12	18	2	14

Directions: Route 495 North to Exit 50 (Route 97). At end of ramp, go across Route 97 to monument. and turn left at the blinking red light. Course 2.5 miles on left.

Cyprian Keyes Golf Club ✪✪✪

Boylston, MA (508) 869-9900
www.cypriankeyes.com

Club Pro: Terry O'Hara, PGA
Pro Shop: Full inventory
Payment: Visa, MC, Amex, Disc
Tee Times: 3 days adv.
Fee 9 Holes: Weekday: N/A
Fee 18 Holes: Weekday: $49.00 M-Th
Twilight Rates: Yes, after 4 pm
Cart Rental: $16pp/18
Lessons: Yes **Schools:** Yes
Clinics: Yes **Day Camps:** Yes
Other: Restaurant/ Function facilities

Tees	Holes	Yards	Par	USGA	Slope
BACK	18	6871	72	72.7	132
MIDDLE	18	6134	72	69.7	127
FRONT	18	5029	72	69.2	119

Weekend: N/A
Weekend: $59.00F/S/S/H
All Day Play: No
Discounts: Junior
Junior Golf: Yes **Membership:** No
Driving Range: $6.00 /bucket

Sig. Hole: Too many to choose from. The short but risky 13th, the picturesque 15th, the challenging 11th, or even the downhill 6th with its great views.

	1	2	3	4	5	6	7	8	9
PAR	4	4	5	5	4	3	4	4	3
YARDS	332	367	510	476	376	180	357	369	155
HDCP	13	11	5	7	3	15	1	9	17

	10	11	12	13	14	15	16	17	18
PAR	5	3	4	4	4	4	3	4	5
YARDS	486	175	350	318	406	348	162	297	470
HDCP	10	8	14	4	2	6	18	16	12

Directions: Route 290 to Exit 23B (Route 140 North). Go 1 mile and take third right onto East Temple Street.

Cyprian Keyes Golf Club, Par 3 ✪✪✪

Boylston, MA (508) 869-9900
www.cypriankeyes.com

Club Pro: Terry O'Hara, PGA
Pro Shop: Full inventory
Payment: Visa, MC, Amex, Disc
Tee Times: 3 days
Fee 9 Holes: Weekday: $14.00 M-Th
Fee 18 Holes: Weekday:
Twilight Rates: No
Cart Rental: Pull, $3.00
Lessons: Yes **Schools:** Yes
Clinics: Yes **Day Camps:** Yes
Other: Clubhouse/ Restaurant/ Function facilities

Tees	Holes	Yards	Par	USGA	Slope
BACK					
MIDDLE	9	1230	27		
FRONT					

Weekend: $17.00 F/S/S/H
Weekend:
All Day Play:
Discounts: $10 (under 18) Mon-Sun
Junior Golf: Yes **Membership:** Junior
Driving Range: $6.00 bucket

Sig. Hole: #9 is a picturesque 165 yard hole framed by trees with water to the left. It provides the golfer with many options.

	1	2	3	4	5	6	7	8	9
PAR	3	3	3	3	3	3	3	3	3
YARDS	155	85	165	105	135	120	155	145	165
HDCP									

	10	11	12	13	14	15	16	17	18
PAR									
YARDS									
HDCP									

Directions: Route 290 to Exit 23B (Route 140 North). Go 1 mile and take third right onto East Temple Street.

Evergreen Valley GC

▶ 19

Newburyport, MA (978) 463-8600
www.evergreenvalleygolf.com

Club Pro: On call
Pro Shop: Limited inventory
Payment: Cash only
Tee Times: No
Fee 9 Holes: Weekday: $14.00
Fee 18 Holes: Weekday: $25.00
Twilight Rates: No
Cart Rental: $22.00/18 $12.00/9
Lessons: Yes **Schools:** No
Clinics: Yes **Day Camps:** No
Other: Snack Bar and deck

Tees	Holes	Yards	Par	USGA	Slope
BACK					
MIDDLE	9	5681	70	67.4	110
FRONT					

Weekend: $16.00
Weekend: $27.00
All Day Play: No
Discounts: Senior, $11.00
Junior Golf: No **Membership:** Yes
Driving Range: No

COUPON

New management. Overall course improvements on greens, hazards and landscaping. Open April - November.

	1	2	3	4	5	6	7	8	9
PAR	4	4	4	5	3	4	4	3	4
YARDS	370	300	420	460	155	390	305	165	215
HDCP	4	6	1	5	7	3	8	2	9
	10	**11**	**12**	**13**	**14**	**15**	**16**	**17**	**18**
PAR	4	4	4	5	3	4	4	3	4
YARDS	385	310	430	475	171	410	315	185	220
HDCP	5	7	2	6	8	4	9	3	10

Directions: I-95, Exit 57. Go east. Take left at Friendly's, then left at stop sign,. 300 ft. on left is entrance to club.

Far Corner Golf Course

✪✪ ▶ 20

W. Boxford, MA (978) 352-8300
www.farcorner.com

Club Pro: J. O'Connor, PGA B.Flynn, Golf Dir.
Pro Shop: Full inventory
Payment: Cash, MC, Visa
Tee Times: 5 days in adv
Fee 9 Holes: Weekday: $17.50
Fee 18 Holes: Weekday: $35.00
Twilight Rates: After 4 wknds
Cart Rental: $13.00pp/18 $6.50pp/9
Lessons: $40/30 min. **Schools:** Yes
Clinics: Yes **Day Camps:** Yes
Other: Snack bar / Restaurant / Bar-lounge / Clubhouse / Showers

Tees	Holes	Yards	Par	USGA	Slope
BACK	18	6719	72	72.9	130
MIDDLE	18	6189	72	70.9	126
FRONT	18	5655	73	71.4	115

Weekend: $20.00
Weekend: $40.00
All Day Play: No
Discounts: Senior & Junior
Junior Golf: Yes **Membership:** No
Driving Range: $5.00/med. All grass.

Now 27 holes - 3rd nine: Yardage: 3092 , Championship Par: 36 , Rating: 35.1 , Slope: 131. Open year round.

	1	2	3	4	5	6	7	8	9
PAR	5	4	4	3	4	4	3	4	5
YARDS	510	350	310	190	460	330	170	390	450
HDCP	7	3	17	15	1	9	13	5	11
	10	**11**	**12**	**13**	**14**	**15**	**16**	**17**	**18**
PAR	4	5	4	5	4	3	4	3	4
YARDS	270	470	360	530	380	170	320	135	390
HDCP	14	10	12	2	4	14	18	16	6

Directions: From I-95 North, take Exit 53B to Route 97 Georgetown. Follow to Route 133 West to West Boxford Village. Go right onto Main Street. Course is 2 miles on left.

Gannon Muni. GC

Lynn, MA (781) 592-8238
www.gannongolfclub.com

Club Pro: Mike Foster, PGA
Pro Shop: Full inventory
Payment: Cash only
Tee Times: No
Fee 9 Holes: Weekday: $18.00
Fee 18 Holes: Weekday: $32.00
Twilight Rates: Yes, after 3:30 pm
Cart Rental: $26.00/18 $13.00/9
Lessons: No **Schools:** No
Clinics: Yes **Day Camps:** No
Other: Snack bar / Grille

Tees	Holes	Yards	Par	USGA	Slope
BACK	18	6106	70	69.9	118
MIDDLE	18	6036	70	67.9	113
FRONT	18	5215	71	68.8	115

Weekend: $20.00 after 3:30 pm
Weekend: N/A
All Day Play: No
Discounts: None
Junior Golf: Yes **Membership:** Residents only
Driving Range: No

Player's Comment: "Beautiful well maintained course. Very busy." Municipal course. Resident rates. Strong junior golf program. 14th hole and 12th hole tee box redone.

	1	2	3	4	5	6	7	8	9
PAR	4	4	4	4	4	3	4	4	3
YARDS	346	309	357	404	333	187	318	414	216
HDCP	5	15	7	1	9	17	11	3	13

	10	11	12	13	14	15	16	17	18
PAR	4	4	4	4	3	5	3	4	5
YARDS	309	335	401	383	158	486	228	319	588
HDCP	12	16	4	6	18	8	10	14	2

Directions: Route1North. Take Route 129 East (towards Lynn). Stay on Route 129 E (Lynnfield St.) for 2 mi. Course is on the right.

Gardner Municipal GC

⊙⊙

Gardner, MA (978) 632-9703

Club Pro: Mike Egan, PGA
Pro Shop: Full inventory
Payment: Cash only
Tee Times: Weekends, Holidays
Fee 9 Holes: Weekday: N/A
Fee 18 Holes: Weekday: $30.00
Twilight Rates: Yes, after 4 pm
Cart Rental: $23.00/18 $13.00/9
Lessons: $35.00/half hour **Schools:** N/A
Clinics: Yes **Day Camps:** No
Other: Clubhouse / Snack bar / Restaurant / Bar-lounge

Tees	Holes	Yards	Par	USGA	Slope
BACK	18	6106	71	68.9	124
MIDDLE	18	5857	71	67.6	120
FRONT	18	5557	75	71.7	122

Weekend: N/A
Weekend: $35.00
All Day Play: Yes
Discounts: Junior
Junior Golf: Yes **Membership:** Yes
Driving Range: Yes

Fast greens. New tees #8 and #17. Irrigation system fully operational. Hosted NEPGA Pro AM and MA PubLinx Qualifier. Open April 15 – snow.

	1	2	3	4	5	6	7	8	9
PAR	4	4	3	4	5	3	5	3	4
YARDS	320	297	215	316	525	137	530	142	406
HDCP	11	13	7	9	5	17	1	15	3

	10	11	12	13	14	15	16	17	18
PAR	4	5	4	4	3	5	3	4	4
YARDS	300	450	323	370	136	478	207	352	353
HDCP	14	12	16	2	18	4	10	6	8

Directions: Route 2 West to Exit 24B-Route 140 North, follow signs to Mt. Wachusett Comm. College. Course is across College.

4⊙ =Excellent 3⊙ =Very Good 2⊙ =Good **Boston's North Shore & Central MA 91**

Green Hill Municipal GC

23 ▶

Worcester, MA (508) 799-1359
www.usegolf.com

Tees	Holes	Yards	Par	USGA	Slope
BACK	18	6487	72	70.4	122
MIDDLE	18	6110	72	68.6	116
FRONT	18	5547	71	69.9	116

Club Pro: Matthew Moison
Pro Shop: Full inventory
Payment: Visa, MC, Cash
Tee Times: 2 days (508) 799-1545
Fee 9 Holes: Weekday: $15.00   **Weekend:** $17.00
Fee 18 Holes: Weekday: $23.00   **Weekend:** $28.00
Twilight Rates: No   **All Day Play:** No
Cart Rental: $13pp/18 $8pp/9   **Discounts:** None
Lessons: $40.00/hour **Schools:** Yes   **Junior Golf:** Yes **Membership:** Yes, $160.00
Clinics: Yes **Day Camps:** No   **Driving Range:** No
Other: Clubhouse / Lockers / Showers / Snack bar

	1	2	3	4	5	6	7	8	9
PAR	4	4	5	4	4	3	4	3	5
YARDS	375	334	455	357	342	192	340	157	475
HDCP	1	17	4	3	13	7	11	15	5
	10	11	12	13	14	15	16	17	18
PAR	4	3	4	5	4	3	5	4	4
YARDS	358	196	328	482	380	131	458	371	379
HDCP	4	12	16	2	14	18	8	6	10

Directions: Take I-290 to Exit 20. Take left onto Lincoln Street, take right onto Marsh Avenue.

Groton Country Club

24 ▶

Groton, MA (978) 448-2564
www.grotoncountryclub.com

Tees	Holes	Yards	Par	USGA	Slope
BACK	9	6006	70	66.5	116
MIDDLE	9	5418	70	66.5	116
FRONT	9	4818	72		

Club Pro: B. Durrin, R. VanGuilder
Pro Shop: Full inventory
Payment: MC, Visa, Discover
Tee Times: 7 days adv.
Fee 9 Holes: Weekday: $14.00   **Weekend:** $16.00
Fee 18 Holes: Weekday: $20.00   **Weekend:** $26.00
Twilight Rates: No   **All Day Play:** No
Cart Rental: $24/18, $13/9   **Discounts:** Senior & Junior
Lessons: $140/ 5 lessons **Schools:** Yes   **Junior Golf:** Yes **Membership:** Yes
Clinics: Yes **Day Camps:** No   **Driving Range:** $5.00/lg $3.00/sm
Other: Full Restaurant / Clubhouse / Bar-Lounge / Snack Bar / Showers

COUPON

Resident discounted rates. Cart rentals available for single rider: $13/18 single and $7/9 single. Collared shirts are required. Open April - November.

	1	2	3	4	5	6	7	8	9
PAR	4	4	4	3	3	4	4	5	4
YARDS	330	260	325	140	210	326	335	450	300
HDCP	7	17	1	15	3	11	5	9	13
	10	11	12	13	14	15	16	17	18
PAR	4	4	4	3	3	4	4	5	4
YARDS	330	260	325	140	210	326	335	450	300
HDCP	8	18	2	16	4	12	6	10	14

Directions: The course is located six miles from I-495 on Route 119 in Groton.

Hemlock Ridge GC

Fiskdale, MA (508) 347-9935

Club Pro: No
Pro Shop: No
Payment: Cash only
Tee Times: No
Fee 9 Holes: Weekday: $13.00
Fee 18 Holes: Weekday: $21.00
Twilight Rates: No
Cart Rental: $20.00/18 $10.00/9
Lessons: No **Schools:** No
Clinics: No **Day Camps:** No
Other: Clubhouse / Snack bar / Showers

Tees	Holes	Yards	Par	USGA	Slope
BACK					
MIDDLE	9	6272	72	70.6	117
FRONT	9	5206	72	69.0	109

Weekend: $15.00
Weekend: $24.00
All Day Play: Yes
Discounts: Senior. $1.00 off
Junior Golf: Yes **Membership:** Yes
Driving Range: No

NE/ CTRL MA

Hilly scenery. Conditions good for both fairways and greens. No dress code. Open April 1 - November 1.

	1	2	3	4	5	6	7	8	9
PAR	4	4	3	4	4	5	4	3	5
YARDS	308	382	154	449	370	471	317	170	515
HDCP	15	3	17	1	7	9	11	13	5
	10	11	12	13	14	15	16	17	18
PAR	4	4	3	4	4	5	4	3	5
YARDS	308	382	154	449	370	471	317	170	515
HDCP	16	4	18	2	8	10	12	14	6

Directions: Take Route 20 West through Sturbridge to Holland Road, turn left. Course is 1 mile up Holland Road.

Heritage Country Club

Charlton, MA (508) 248-5111
www.heritagecountryclub.com

Club Pro: John Aldrich, PGA
Pro Shop: Full inventory
Payment: Cash, Credit Card
Tee Times: 7 days adv.
Fee 9 Holes: Weekday: $19.00 after 4 pm
Fee 18 Holes: Weekday: $29.00
Twilight Rates: Yes, after 4 pm
Cart Rental: $24.00/18 $14.00/9
Lessons: $30.00/half hour **Schools:** No
Clinics: Ladies/Jr/Sr **Day Camps:** No
Other: Clubhouse / Lockers / Showers / Snack bar / Bar-lounge

Tees	Holes	Yards	Par	USGA	Slope
BACK	18	6500	71	69.3	118
MIDDLE	18	6450	71	69.7	113
FRONT	18	5415	72	70.6	114

Weekend: $23.00 after 3 pm
Weekend: $35.00
All Day Play: No
Discounts: Senior & Junior
Junior Golf: Yes **Membership:** Yes
Driving Range: $5.00/ bucket

COUPON

30 new bunkers, 10 new tees. Redesigned in 2001. Course is easy to walk. Home of the Professional Central MA. Open. Open April 1-Nov 1.

	1	2	3	4	5	6	7	8	9
PAR	4	4	3	4	4	5	3	4	4
YARDS	355	385	195	350	360	385	190	330	460
HDCP	8	4	18	10	12	6	16	4	2
	10	11	12	13	14	15	16	17	18
PAR	4	4	5	3	4	4	3	5	4
YARDS	400	375	590	160	305	365	193	570	360
HDCP	10	11	1	17	13	7	15	3	9

Directions: Located on Route 20 in Charlton. 3 miles east of Old Sturbridge Village.

Hickory Hill GC

Methuen, MA (978) 686-0822

Club Pro: Michael Spencer
Pro Shop: Limited inventory
Payment: Visa, MC, Cash
Tee Times: Monday after 9 am
Fee 9 Holes: Weekday: $22.00 M-Th
Fee 18 Holes: Weekday: $40.00 M-Th
Twilight Rates: Yes, after 3 pm
Cart Rental: $26.00/18 $16.00/9
Lessons: $40/ 45 min, $150/5 **Schools:** No
Clinics: Junior **Day Camps:** No
Other: Clubhouse / Showers / Bar-lounge

Tees	Holes	Yards	Par	USGA	Slope
BACK	18	6276	71	69.2	122
MIDDLE	18	6017	71	67.9	119
FRONT	18	5397	71	73.2	127

Weekend: $26.00 F/S/S/H
Weekend: $45, $35 after 3 pm
All Day Play: No
Discounts: None
Junior Golf: No **Membership:** No
Driving Range: $6.00/sm.

Sig. Hole: #6 is a 513 yard, par 5. Has dogleg left, water to right and out-of-bounds to left of well bunkered green. Straight tee shots essential.

	1	2	3	4	5	6	7	8	9
PAR	4	3	5	4	4	5	4	3	4
YARDS	349	173	511	382	379	513	367	155	348
HDCP	13	15	3	5	7	1	11	17	9
	10	11	12	13	14	15	16	17	18
PAR	5	4	4	3	4	4	4	3	4
YARDS	489	390	340	141	326	357	304	114	379
HDCP	2	6	8	16	12	10	14	18	4

Directions: Take Route 93 to Exit 46. Take Route 113 West, follow 1.5 miles, course is on left.

NEW 2003

Highfields Golf & CC

Grafton,MA (508) 839-1945
www.highfieldsgolfcc.com

Club Pro: Roger Adams
Pro Shop: Yes
Payment: Cash, Visa, MC
Tee Times: Yes
Fee 9 Holes: Weekday: $20.00
Fee 18 Holes: Weekday: $50.00 inc. cart
Twilight Rates:
Cart Rental: included
Lessons: Yes **Schools:**
Clinics: Yes **Day Camps:** Yes
Other: Clubhouse to open early '04

Tees	Holes	Yards	Par	USGA	Slope
BACK	9	3272	36		
MIDDLE	9	2829	72		
FRONT	9	2475	36		

Weekend: $25.00
Weekend: $55.00 inc. cart
All Day Play: No
Discounts: Senior & Junior
Junior Golf: Yes **Membership:** Many levels
Driving Range: Yes

COUPON

2003 Entry. Cornish, Silva and Mungeam design compliments a beautiful residential project. Breathtaking views all around. Playable for all levels and abilities. Well manicured.

	1	2	3	4	5	6	7	8	9
PAR	5	3	4	4	3	4	4	4	5
YARDS	516	138	399	365	218	389	383	339	570
HDCP									
	10	11	12	13	14	15	16	17	18
PAR	4	3	4	4	4	5	4	3	5
YARDS	411	145	325	385	321	501	441	121	507
HDCP									

Directions: Mass Pike to Exit 11 (Route 122) Route 122 South 4.5 miles. Entrance on left Magill Dr.

Hillcrest Country Club

Leicester, MA (508) 892-0963

Club Pro: No
Pro Shop: Full inventory
Payment: Cash only
Tee Times: Suggested
Fee 9 Holes: Weekday: $12.00
Fee 18 Holes: Weekday: $18.00
Twilight Rates: No
Cart Rental: $20/18 $12/9 wknds
Lessons: No **Schools:** No
Clinics: No **Day Camps:** No
Other: Clubhouse / Snack bar / Restaurant / Bar-lounge

Tees	Holes	Yards	Par	USGA	Slope
BACK	9	6136	70	67.1	103
MIDDLE	9	5977	70	67.1	103
FRONT	9	4775	72	67.2	113

Weekend: $14.00
Weekend: $22.00
All Day Play: N/R
Discounts: None
Junior Golf: No **Membership:** No
Driving Range: No

Easy but interesting golf course layout with a laid back bar surrounded by a friendly staff and personnel.

	1	2	3	4	5	6	7	8	9
PAR	5	4	4	4	3	5	3	3	4
YARDS	500	402	345	340	355	475	110	136	475
HDCP	18	4	8	6	12	14	10	16	2
	10	11	12	13	14	15	16	17	18
PAR	5	4	4	4	3	5	3	3	4
YARDS	500	402	345	340	155	475	170	136	475
HDCP	17	3	7	5	11	13	9	15	1

Directions: Take Mass Pike to Auburn Exit (Exit 10). Take right onto Route 12, follow 3 miles, take right onto Route 20, follow 3 miles take right onto Route 56, 4 miles.

Hillview Golf Course

No. Reading, MA (978) 664-4435

Club Pro: Chris Carter, PGA
Pro Shop: Full inventory
Payment: Cash only
Tee Times: Weekends
Fee 9 Holes: Weekday: $17.00
Fee 18 Holes: Weekday: $32.00
Twilight Rates: No
Cart Rental: $24.00/18 $12.00/9
Lessons: $50.00/half hour **Schools:** No
Clinics: N/R **Day Camps:** N/R
Other: Snack bar / Restaurant / Bar-lounge / Clubhouse

Tees	Holes	Yards	Par	USGA	Slope
BACK	18	5802	69	67.4	120
MIDDLE	18	5251	69	65.2	118
FRONT	18	4500	69	66	110

Weekend: $20.00
Weekend: $35.00
All Day Play: No
Discounts: Sr. & Jr. AM only (M-W)
Junior Golf: N/R **Membership:** No
Driving Range: $5.00/lg., $2.50/sm.

A popular course in a good location. Interesting layout.

	1	2	3	4	5	6	7	8	9
PAR	5	3	4	4	4	4	4	5	3
YARDS	484	170	410	325	357	323	394	539	191
HDCP	11	7	5	15	17	13	3	1	9
	10	11	12	13	14	15	16	17	18
PAR	4	4	4	4	3	4	3	4	3
YARDS	372	310	346	355	180	324	236	239	173
HDCP	8	10	2	14	12	6	4	18	16

Directions: Take Exit 40 off I-93, and follow Route 62 East 1-1/2 miles. Turn left on North Street. Course is 1/2 mile up on left.

Holden Hills CC

Holden, MA (508) 829-3129
www.holdenhillsgolf.com

Club Pro: Gary Hall
Pro Shop: Full inventory
Payment: MC, Visa
Tee Times: Weekends, 1 week adv.

Tees	Holes	Yards	Par	USGA	Slope
BACK	18	6022	71	71.9	126
MIDDLE	18	5826	71	71.9	125
FRONT	18	5241	74	74.9	116

Fee 9 Holes: Weekday: $16, $29 ride
Fee 18 Holes: Weekday: $22, $35 ride
Twilight Rates: Yes, after 3 pm
Cart Rental: $13pp/18 $7pp/9
Lessons: Schools: No
Clinics: No **Day Camps:** Yes
Other: Clubhouse / Snack bar / Restaurant / Bar-lounge

Weekend: $22, $35 ride
Weekend: $32, $35 ride
All Day Play: No
Discounts: Senior, M-Th
Junior Golf: Yes **Membership:** Yes
Driving Range: No

Picturesque course set among hills, ponds and streams. While not long, the holes demand good placement and are challenging. Early bird before 8 am.

	1	2	3	4	5	6	7	8	9
PAR	4	5	3	4	4	3	4	5	4
YARDS	354	592	163	309	312	147	340	478	348
HDCP	9	1	15	13	5	17	7	3	11
	10	**11**	**12**	**13**	**14**	**15**	**16**	**17**	**18**
PAR	3	4	4	5	4	4	4	4	3
YARDS	164	269	278	433	359	341	414	327	216
HDCP	14	16	18	6	12	4	2	10	8

Directions: Route 290 to Route 190 North. Take second exit (Holden). Go straight through lights, then bear right. Bear left at next light, up hill. Right on Main Street to Route 122A North. Course is 5 miles on right.

Indian Meadows Golf Club

Westboro, MA (508) 836-5460
www.indianmeadowsgolfclub.com

Club Pro: Art Billingham
Pro Shop: Full inventory
Payment: Cash and check
Tee Times: 4 days adv.

Tees	Holes	Yards	Par	USGA	Slope
BACK	9	6530	72	71.7	124
MIDDLE	9	6038	72	69.4	119
FRONT	9	4936	72	69.0	

Fee 9 Holes: Weekday: $17.00
Fee 18 Holes: Weekday: $27.00
Twilight Rates: No
Cart Rental: $13.00/18 $6.50/9
Lessons: Yes **Schools:** Yes
Clinics: Yes **Day Camps:** Yes
Other: Restaurant / Clubhouse / Bar-lounge / Snack Bar

Weekend: $19.00
Weekend: $31.00
All Day Play: No
Discounts: Senior & Junior
Junior Golf: Yes **Membership:** Yes
Driving Range: No

Private conditions noted by club professional. Water on every hole. Shirts with collars required. Open April - December. Semi-private.

	1	2	3	4	5	6	7	8	9
PAR	5	4	4	4	3	5	4	3	4
YARDS	451	340	420	316	136	455	415	173	313
HDCP	5	15	1	13	17	7	3	11	9
	10	**11**	**12**	**13**	**14**	**15**	**16**	**17**	**18**
PAR	5	4	4	4	3	5	4	3	4
YARDS	451	340	420	316	136	455	415	173	313
HDCP	6	16	2	14	18	8	4	12	10

Directions: The course in on Route 9 (Turnpike Road) in Westboro, 3 miles west of 495.

Juniper Hill GC (Lakeside) ✪✪ ▶33

Northboro, MA (508) 393-2444
www.juniperhillgc.com

Club Pro: Ken Chzran, PGA
Pro Shop: Full inventory
Payment: Visa, MC, Cash, Check
Tee Times: 7 days adv.

Tees	Holes	Yards	Par	USGA	Slope
BACK					
MIDDLE	18	6282	71	69.9	127
FRONT	18	4707	71	65.3	102

Fee 9 Holes: Weekday: $19.00   **Weekend:** $22.00
Fee 18 Holes: Weekday: $33.00   **Weekend:** $38.00
Twilight Rates: No   **All Day Play:** No
Cart Rental: $28.00/18 $18.00/9   **Discounts:** Before 1 pm, Sr. (M-Th) & Jr.
Lessons: Yes **Schools:** Jr. & Sr.   **Junior Golf:** Yes **Membership:** No
Clinics: Yes **Day Camps:** Yes   **Driving Range:** Practice green
Other: Clubhouse / Lockers / Showers / Snack bar / Bar-lounge / Teaching facility

Eighteen holes of championship caliber with a lot of character. Collared shirts required. Noted for Golf Professional and friendly staff.

	1	2	3	4	5	6	7	8	9
PAR	3	5	4	4	3	4	5	3	4
YARDS	187	524	313	392	169	314	522	146	307
HDCP	10	6	12	2	14	8	4	16	18

	10	11	12	13	14	15	16	17	18
PAR	4	4	4	4	3	5	4	5	3
YARDS	377	365	336	420	206	482	441	602	179
HDCP	9	15	17	7	1	11	5	3	13

Directions: Take Mass Pike to 495 North. Exit to Route 9 West and continue onto Route 135 West. Follow for 1.4 miles. Right onto Brigham Street. Follow for 1 mile to course.

Juniper Hill GC (Riverside) ✪✪ ▶34

Northboro, MA (508) 393-2444
www.juniperhillgc.com

Club Pro: Ken Chzran, PGA
Pro Shop: Full inventory
Payment: Visa, MC, Cash, Check
Tee Times: 7 days adv.

Tees	Holes	Yards	Par	USGA	Slope
BACK					
MIDDLE	18	6266	71	70.4	123
FRONT	18	5263	71	70.2	117

Fee 9 Holes: Weekday: $19.00   **Weekend:** $22.00
Fee 18 Holes: Weekday: $33.00   **Weekend:** $38.00
Twilight Rates: No   **All Day Play:** No
Cart Rental: $28.00/18 $18.00/9   **Discounts:** Before 1 pm, Sr.
Lessons: Yes **Schools:** Jr. & Sr.   **Junior Golf:** Yes **Membership:** No
Clinics: Yes **Day Camps:** Yes   **Driving Range:** Practice green
Other: Clubhouse / Lockers / Showers / Snack bar / Bar-lounge / Teaching facility

Player's Comment: "36 holes well maintained for public play." Some open fairways let you let loose with the driver.

	1	2	3	4	5	6	7	8	9
PAR	4	4	5	4	3	4	3	4	4
YARDS	370	336	495	387	193	330	156	405	350
HDCP	4	6	2	8	12	16	18	10	14

	10	11	12	13	14	15	16	17	18
PAR	5	4	4	4	4	3	4	3	5
YARDS	490	391	367	381	371	157	391	220	476
HDCP	1	5	7	13	15	17	9	3	11

Directions: Take Mass Pike to 495 North. Exit to Route 9 West and continue onto Route 135 West. Follow for 1.4 miles. Right onto Brigham Street. Follow for 1 mile to course.

4✪ =Excellent **3✪** =Very Good **2✪** = Good

Kelley Greens By The Sea

Nahant, MA (781) 581-0840 ext. 101
www.kelleygreens.com

Club Pro: Richard Spinelli, PGA
Pro Shop: Yes
Payment: Cash & Credit cards
Tee Times: 3 day adv.

Tees	Holes	Yards	Par	USGA	Slope
BACK	9	3880	60	60.0	103
MIDDLE	9	3784	60	57	87
FRONT	9	3342	60	60.0	103

Fee 9 Holes: Weekday: $16.00 M-F   **Weekend:** $18.00
Fee 18 Holes: Weekday: $26.00   **Weekend:** $28.00
Twilight Rates: No   **All Day Play:** Replay
Cart Rental: $25.00/18 $15.00/9   **Discounts:** None
Lessons: $35 /30 min **Schools:** No   **Junior Golf:** Yes **Membership:** Yes
Clinics: Yes **Day Camps:** No   **Driving Range:** No
Other: Snack bar / Restaurant / lounge

COUPON

The course is fairly flat and considered an easy walker. An average golfer can usually cover nine holes in under 2 hours. Resident's discount.

	1	2	3	4	5	6	7	8	9
PAR	3	3	3	3	3	4	4	4	3
YARDS	137	179	186	142	213	325	260	249	174
HDCP	17	3	5	13	1	7	11	15	9
	10	11	12	13	14	15	16	17	18
PAR	3	3	3	3	3	4	4	4	3
YARDS	137	179	186	142	213	325	260	249	174
HDCP	18	4	6	14	2	8	12	16	10

Directions: Take Route 1A North to Lynn Center. Go toward Nahant over causeway (Nahant Road). Follow signs to course.

Kettle Brook Golf Club ✪✪✪

Paxton, MA 508-799-4653
www.kettlebrookgolfclub.com

Club Pro: No
Pro Shop: Limited inventory
Payment: Visa, MC, Amex, Cash, Checks
Tee Times: 7 days adv.

Tees	Holes	Yards	Par	USGA	Slope
BACK	18	6912	72	73.1	125
MIDDLE	18	6203	72	70.3	121
FRONT	18	5105	72	70.2	118

Fee 9 Holes: Weekday: $19.00 Twilight   **Weekend:** $22.00 Twilight
Fee 18 Holes: Weekday: $32.00 M-Th   **Weekend:** $54 w/cart after 10am F/S/S/H
Twilight Rates: Yes, after 3:30 pm   **All Day Play:** No
Cart Rental: $14 pp   **Discounts:** Senior & Junior
Lessons: No **Schools:** No   **Junior Golf:** No **Membership:** wknd club
Clinics: No **Day Camps:** No   **Driving Range:** No
Other: Clubhouse / Bar / Snack Bar / Function room for outings

Players' Comments: "Very good course that will be exceptional with maturity. Poor man's private golf course. Challenging but fun. Playable and friendly. Awesome test of golf. Needs a practice tee."

	1	2	3	4	5	6	7	8	9
PAR	4	5	4	4	4	3	5	3	4
YARDS	366	522	359	327	339	170	485	132	452
HDCP	7	3	9	15	13	11	5	17	1
	10	11	12	13	14	15	16	17	18
PAR	4	5	3	4	5	4	4	3	4
YARDS	346	485	164	251	481	338	379	196	411
HDCP	6	14	10	18	12	16	8	4	2

Directions: From Worcester center off Route 290, exit Route 9. Follow signs to Worcester airport. Take left off of Route 122 into airport rotary. First right to Bailey St. Go 3 miles on right. See website.

Lakeview Golf Club

Wenham, MA (978) 468-6676
www.lakeviewgc.com

Club Pro: Michael Flynn
Pro Shop: Yes
Payment: Cash,MC/Visa
Tee Times: Yes
Fee 9 Holes: Weekday: $15.00
Fee 18 Holes: Weekday: $17.00
Twilight Rates: No
Cart Rental: $17.00
Lessons: Private and Group **Schools:** No
Clinics: No **Day Camps:** No
Other: Snack Bar

Tees	Holes	Yards	Par	USGA	Slope
BACK	9	2001	31		
MIDDLE	9	1836	31	59.3	91
FRONT	9	1550	31		

Weekend: $22.00
Weekend: $24.00
All Day Play: No
Discounts: Senior
Junior Golf: Yes **Membership:** No
Driving Range: No

Executive-style golf course. Monday and Tuesday senior rates, $10.00 for 9 holes.

	1	2	3	4	5	6	7	8	9
PAR	4	3	3	4	3	4	3	3	4
YARDS	325	215	165	320	125	255	150	160	325
HDCP	1	9	11	3	17	7	15	13	5
	10	11	12	13	14	15	16	17	18
PAR									
YARDS									
HDCP									

Directions: Take Route 128 North to Exit 20 North (Route 1A). The course is 2 miles on the right.

Leicester Country Club

Leicester, MA (508) 892-1390 Ext. 12
www. leicestercc.com

Club Pro: Richard Carroll, PGA
Pro Shop: Limited inventory
Payment: Visa, MC
Tee Times: 5 days adv.
Fee 9 Holes: Weekday: $16.00
Fee 18 Holes: Weekday: $22.00
Twilight Rates: No
Cart Rental: $12pp/18 $6pp/9
Lessons: Yes **Schools:** No
Clinics: No **Day Camps:** No
Other: Snack bar / Bar-lounge / Banquet Facility /

Tees	Holes	Yards	Par	USGA	Slope
BACK					
MIDDLE	18	6026	70	69.8	126
FRONT	18	4559	70	67.4	121

Weekend: $19 after 3 pm
Weekend: $28.00
All Day Play: Yes
Discounts: Senior & Junior
Junior Golf: Yes **Membership:** No
Driving Range: No

New holes #14 & #15. Expanded new tees, irrigation system installed 2002! Noted for excellent conditions of greens.

	1	2	3	4	5	6	7	8	9
PAR	4	5	3	4	4	4	3	4	3
YARDS	437	489	201	345	371	328	179	309	173
HDCP	6	4	12	10	2	18	16	8	14
	10	11	12	13	14	15	16	17	18
PAR	4	4	3	4	5	4	5	3	4
YARDS	314	317	165	411	545	403	515	183	341
HDCP	17	15	11	1	3	7	5	13	9

Directions: Take Mass Pike to Route 9 West to Main Street in Leicester Center. Course is 1 mile West.

Lynnfield Center GC

39

Lynnfield, MA (781) 334-9877

Tees	Holes	Yards	Par	USGA	Slope
BACK	9	5120	68	63	
MIDDLE	9	4970	68	63	
FRONT	9	4480	68	63	

Club Pro: Bob Baker
Pro Shop: Limited inventory
Payment: Cash only
Tee Times: No
Fee 9 Holes: Weekday: $15.00
Fee 18 Holes: Weekday: $26.00
Twilight Rates: Yes
Cart Rental: $20.00/18 $12.00/9
Lessons: No **Schools:** No
Clinics: No **Day Camps:** No
Other: Clubhouse/Bar-lounge/Snack Bar

Weekend: $17.00
Weekend: $27.00
All Day Play: No
Discounts: Senior
Junior Golf: No **Membership:** Senior
Driving Range: No

Player's Comment: "Wide open fields and an island par 3." A good place to practice. Dress code.

	1	2	3	4	5	6	7	8	9
PAR	4	4	3	4	5	3	4	4	3
YARDS	350	355	225	260	476	139	270	340	145
HDCP	5	2	1	8	4	7	3	6	9
	10	11	12	13	14	15	16	17	18
PAR	4	4	3	4	5	3	4	4	3
YARDS	350	355	225	260	476	139	270	340	145
HDCP	5	2	1	8	4	7	3	6	9

Directions: Take Route 128 to Exit 41, follow to Main Street in Lynnfield Center.

Maplewood Golf Course

40

Lunenburg, MA (978) 582-6694

Tees	Holes	Yards	Par	USGA	Slope
BACK	N/A				
MIDDLE	9	5370	70	63.9	106
FRONT	9	5040	70	66.5	105

Club Pro: Joe Benevento, Head Pro, PGA
Pro Shop: Full inventory
Payment: Visa, MC
Tee Times: Weekends only
Fee 9 Holes: Weekday: $13.00
Fee 18 Holes: Weekday: $19.00
Twilight Rates: No
Cart Rental: $7.00pp/9
Lessons: No **Schools:** No
Clinics: N/R **Day Camps:** No
Other: Clubhouse / Snack bar

Weekend: $15.00
Weekend: $24.00
All Day Play: No
Discounts: Senior
Junior Golf: No **Membership:** No
Driving Range: No

Affordable and enjoyable golf. Proper golf attire required. Open April - November.

	1	2	3	4	5	6	7	8	9
PAR	4	4	4	4	3	4	5	4	3
YARDS	350	320	310	340	175	350	480	230	130
HDCP	1	7	11	9	15	3	5	13	17
	10	11	12	13	14	15	16	17	18
PAR	4	4	4	4	3	4	5	4	3
YARDS	350	320	320	340	175	350	480	230	130
HDCP	2	8	12	10	16	4	6	14	18

Directions: Route 2 to Route 13 North. Go past Whalom Park to stop sign. Take right, 1/8 mile to top of hill. Take left back on Route 13 North, go 2 miles to Northfield Road. Take left, go 1/2 mile. Clubhouse on right.

Merrimack Valley GC

Methuen, MA (978) 685-9717

Club Pro: Stephen Kattar
Pro Shop: Limited inventory
Payment: Cash only
Tee Times: F/S/S/H
Fee 9 Holes: Weekday: $15.00
Fee 18 Holes: Weekday: $23.00
Twilight Rates: Wkds after 3pm
Cart Rental: $24.00/18 $12.00/9
Lessons: Yes **Schools:** No
Clinics: No **Day Camps:** No
Other: Restaurant / Bar-lounge

Tees	Holes	Yards	Par	USGA	Slope
BACK	18	6220	71	69.3	120
MIDDLE	18	5871	71	67.7	117
FRONT	18	5151	72	72.3	116

Weekend: $15.00 after 3:00pm
Weekend: $30.00.$15 after 3pm
All Day Play: No
Discounts: Senior & Junior
Junior Golf: Yes **Membership:** Yes
Driving Range: No

Improvements include better drainage. Noted for plush greens.

	1	2	3	4	5	6	7	8	9
PAR	5	4	4	3	4	4	3	4	4
YARDS	454	342	312	158	386	404	187	354	301
HDCP	9	5	15	13	3	1	7	11	17

	10	11	12	13	14	15	16	17	18
PAR	4	3	5	4	4	5	3	4	4
YARDS	356	158	441	418	310	482	138	405	265
HDCP	8	16	10	4	12	6	18	2	14

Directions: 495 to Exit 47, Route 213. Take Exit 3 off Route 213. At lights at end of exit ramp, go left. Club is 3/4 mile on left.

Middleton Golf Course   ✪✪✪

Middleton, MA (978) 774-4075
www.middletongolf.com

Club Pro: David Nyman
Pro Shop: Full inventory
Payment: Major cards, cash
Tee Times: No
Fee 9 Holes: Weekday: $18.00
Fee 18 Holes: Weekday: $28.00
Twilight Rates: Yes, after 3:30 pm
Cart Rental: $20.00/18, $10.00/9; Reserve!
Lessons: Yes **Schools:** Yes
Clinics: Free Saturday **Day Camps:** Yes
Other: Clubhouse / Bar (beer & wine only) / Greenside Cafe / Club Fitting Center

Tees	Holes	Yards	Par	USGA	Slope
BACK	18	3215	54	57.0	83
MIDDLE	18	3000	54	53.9	75
FRONT	18	2280	54	52.1	71

Weekend: $18.00
Weekend: $30.00
All Day Play: No
Discounts: Senior & Junior
Junior Golf: Yes **Membership:** No
Driving Range: Lessons Only

COUPON

Players' Comments: "Extremely well maintained, friendly staff, and excellent pro shop." "Great greens." Cornish design. Open year round.

	1	2	3	4	5	6	7	8	9
PAR	3	3	3	3	3	3	3	3	3
YARDS	170	160	185	170	150	170	145	215	190
HDCP	13	9	5	11	15	7	17	1	3

	10	11	12	13	14	15	16	17	18
PAR	3	3	3	3	3	3	3	3	3
YARDS	135	110	195	160	155	240	215	225	225
HDCP	16	18	10	14	12	2	8	6	4

Directions: From Route 1 or Route 95 go approx. 2.5 miles west on Route 114. Parking lot entrance on the left.

Monoosnock CC

Leominster, MA (978) 537-1872

Tees	Holes	Yards	Par	USGA	Slope
BACK					
MIDDLE	9	6102	70	69.5	120
FRONT	9	5645	72	71.0	115

Club Pro: John M. Novak
Pro Shop: Full inventory
Payment: Cash
Tee Times: No
Fee 9 Holes: Weekday: $16.00   **Weekend:** No
Fee 18 Holes: Weekday: $26.00   **Weekend:** No
Twilight Rates: No   **All Day Play:** No
Cart Rental: $12pp/18 $7pp/9   **Discounts:** None
Lessons: $35/45 min. **Schools:** Night classes   **Junior Golf:** Yes **Membership:** Yes
Clinics: Yes **Day Camps:** No   **Driving Range:** $5.00/bucket
Other: Clubhouse / Restaurant / Bar-lounge

Course is open to public play on Monday - Friday until 3 pm (but not on holidays). The fairways are narrow and brooks cross through 5 holes. Full practice area. Open April 1 - November 30.

	1	2	3	4	5	6	7	8	9
PAR	4	5	4	3	3	5	4	3	4
YARDS	335	515	378	158	235	450	387	214	379
HDCP	11	1	7	17	13	9	3	15	5
	10	11	12	13	14	15	16	17	18
PAR	4	5	4	3	3	5	4	3	4
YARDS	335	515	378	158	235	450	387	214	379
HDCP	12	2	8	18	14	10	4	16	6

Directions: Route 2 East or West to Route 13 North. Go north 1 mile and take right onto Monoosnock Ave. Follow to pro shop.

Murphy's Garrison Par 3 Golf Center

Haverhill, MA (978) 374-9380
www.murphysgarrisongolf.com

Tees	Holes	Yards	Par	USGA	Slope
BACK					
MIDDLE	9	1005	27		
FRONT					

Club Pro: Ted Murphy
Pro Shop: Full inventory
Payment: Visa, MC, Disc.
Tee Times: N/A
Fee 9 Holes: Weekday: $8.00   **Weekend:** $9.00
Fee 18 Holes: Weekday: $15.00   **Weekend:** $17.00
Twilight Rates: No   **All Day Play:** No
Cart Rental: $1.00/9   **Discounts:** Senior
Lessons: $40.00/session **Schools:** Yes   **Junior Golf:** Yes **Membership:** N/R
Clinics: 3/ $65.00 **Day Camps:** Yes   **Driving Range:** $5.00
Other: Bar/Lounge/Snack Bar

COUPON

A short testing 9 hole par 3 with beautiful Vesper Velvet greens. Designed in 1966 by legendary Manuel Francis. Great course for women and juniors.

	1	2	3	4	5	6	7	8	9
PAR	3	3	3	3	3	3	3	3	3
YARDS	105	100	130	75	100	130	130	135	100
HDCP	N/A								
	10	11	12	13	14	15	16	17	18
PAR									
YARDS									
HDCP									

Directions: 495 N toward Haverhill at Exit 50. Straight across to stop sign. Straight across to next stop, take a left on Hilldale Ave. Course is 1/4 mile on left.

New Meadows GC

Topsfield, MA (978) 887-9307

Club Pro: No
Pro Shop: Limited inventory
Payment: Cash only
Tee Times: No
Fee 9 Holes: Weekday: $16.00
Fee 18 Holes: Weekday: $30.00
Twilight Rates: No
Cart Rental: $24.00/18 $12.00/9
Lessons: No **Schools:** No
Clinics: No **Day Camps:** No
Other: Clubhouse / Snack Bar

Tees	Holes	Yards	Par	USGA	Slope
BACK					
MIDDLE	9	2883	35	64.8	117
FRONT					

Weekend: $18.00
Weekend: $34.00
All Day Play: No
Discounts: None
Junior Golf: No **Membership:** No
Driving Range: No

Dress code - shirts with sleeves.

	1	2	3	4	5	6	7	8	9
PAR	4	4	3	4	4	4	5	3	4
YARDS	352	365	160	348	345	368	459	128	358
HDCP	13	3	15	11	5	7	1	17	9
	10	11	12	13	14	15	16	17	18
PAR									
YARDS									
HDCP									

Directions: Take I-95 to old Route 1 past Topsfield fairgrounds on right about 3 miles.

Olde Salem Greens

Salem, MA (978) 744-2149
www.htmlbob.com/golf

Club Pro: No
Pro Shop: No
Payment: Cash only
Tee Times: M-F 1day S/S 2 days
Fee 9 Holes: Weekday: $18.00
Fee 18 Holes: Weekday: $33.00
Twilight Rates: Yes, after 7 pm
Cart Rental: $26.00/18 $13.00/9
Lessons: Residents only **Schools:** N/R
Clinics: No **Day Camps:** No
Other: Snack Bar / Bar-lounge

Tees	Holes	Yards	Par	USGA	Slope
BACK	9	7292	70	68.4	116
MIDDLE	9	6056	70	68.5	116
FRONT	9	4966	70	68.4	112

Weekend: $19.00
Weekend: N/A
All Day Play: No
Discounts: Sr & Jr (with restrictions)
Junior Golf: No **Membership:** Resident Passes
Driving Range: No

Resident's rate. New putting green.

	1	2	3	4	5	6	7	8	9
PAR	4	3	4	5	4	4	4	3	4
YARDS	374	253	367	545	345	398	291	153	304
HDCP	7	5	9	1	11	3	13	15	17
	10	11	12	13	14	15	16	17	18
PAR	4	3	4	5	4	4	4	3	4
YARDS	374	253	367	545	345	398	291	153	304
HDCP	8	6	10	2	12	4	14	16	18

Directions: Route 128 to Route 114 toward Salem. Take Essex Street to Highland Avenue. Take a left on Wilson Street to course.

Ould Newbury GC

Newburyport, MA (978) 465-9888

Tees	Holes	Yards	Par	USGA	Slope
BACK					
MIDDLE	9	6184	70	69.6	120
FRONT	9	5700	75	70.4	115

Club Pro: James Hilton
Pro Shop: Full inventory
Payment: Cash, Disc, MC, Visa
Tee Times: No
Fee 9 Holes: Weekday: $17.00
Fee 18 Holes: Weekday: $30.00
Twilight Rates: No
Cart Rental: $26.00/18 $16.00/9
Lessons: $30.00/half hour **Schools:** No
Clinics: No **Day Camps:** No
Other: Clubhouse / Lockers / Showers / Snack bar

Weekend: N/A
Weekend: N/A
All Day Play: No
Discounts: None
Junior Golf: No **Membership:** Yes
Driving Range: No

Sig. Hole: #9 is a 207 yard par 3 up hill that requires a shot over a 50' Hickory tree. Not available to public on weekends.

	1	2	3	4	5	6	7	8	9
PAR	4	5	4	4	4	3	4	4	3
YARDS	423	457	380	442	324	152	390	317	207
HDCP	3	15	9	1	11	17	5	13	7
	10	11	12	13	14	15	16	17	18
PAR	4	5	4	4	4	3	4	4	3
YARDS	423	457	380	442	324	152	390	317	207
HDCP	4	16	10	2	12	18	6	14	8

Directions: Take Route 1 toward Newbury. Course is a sand wedge shot from Governor Dummer Academy.

Pakachoag Golf Course

Upland St., Auburn, MA (508) 755-3291

Tees	Holes	Yards	Par	USGA	Slope
BACK					
MIDDLE	9	6510	72	70.0	119
FRONT					

Club Pro: No
Pro Shop: Limited inventory
Payment: Cash only
Tee Times: Weekends & holidays
Fee 9 Holes: Weekday: $12.00
Fee 18 Holes: Weekday: $20.00
Twilight Rates: No
Cart Rental: $15.00/9
Lessons: Yes **Schools:** No
Clinics: Yes **Day Camps:** No
Other: Snack Bar

Weekend: $14.00
Weekend: $26.00
All Day Play: No
Discounts: Senior & Junior
Junior Golf: Yes **Membership:** Yes
Driving Range: No

Sig. Hole: #9, a dogleg left, has three ways to play. Short hitters - right of pond! Medium hitters - 180 yard carry over! Big hitters - 270 yards over stone wall!

	1	2	3	4	5	6	7	8	9
PAR	4	4	4	3	5	4	4	3	5
YARDS	376	329	395	143	563	372	377	189	511
HDCP	5	9	1	9	2	4	6	7	3
	10	11	12	13	14	15	16	17	18
PAR	4	4	4	3	5	4	4	3	5
YARDS	376	329	395	143	563	372	377	189	511
HDCP	6	8	2	9	1	4	7	5	3

Directions: From Route 20 to Greenwood St. to Upland St. From I-290 use Auburn St. Exit to Route 12 (Southbridge St.). Left at lights. 1/4 mile right, take Burnap St. up hill to Pakachoag St. and go left. 2 miles to Upland St.

Pine Ridge Country Club

Pleasant St., N. Oxford, MA (508) 892-9188
www.pineridgecc.com

Club Pro: Betty Donovan, LPGA
Pro Shop: Full inventory
Payment: Visa, MC, Amex, cash
Tee Times: 5 days adv.
Fee 9 Holes: Weekday: $16.00 M-F
Fee 18 Holes: Weekday: $25.00 M-F
Twilight Rates: Yes, after 3 pm
Cart Rental: $13pp/18 $8pp/9
Lessons: $50/hour **Schools:** Yes
Clinics: No **Day Camps:** No
Other: Clubhouse / Lockers / Showers / Snack bar / Restaurant / Bar-lounge

Tees	Holes	Yards	Par	USGA	Slope
BACK	18	6002	71	69.7	120
MIDDLE	18	5763	71	68.3	117
FRONT	18	5307	72	69.6	117

Weekend: $20.00
Weekend: $34.00
All Day Play: No
Discounts: Senior & Junior
Junior Golf: No **Membership:** No
Driving Range: No

COUPON

Sig. Hole: #18 requires a solid tee shot that then allows an option to lay up in front of pond, go left of it or go for the green in two. Bunkers rebuilt.

	1	2	3	4	5	6	7	8	9
PAR	4	3	4	3	4	5	4	4	3
YARDS	295	144	437	161	382	390	330	358	148
HDCP	13	17	1	11	3	9	5	7	15

	10	11	12	13	14	15	16	17	18
PAR	4	3	5	4	5	3	4	4	5
YARDS	270	188	431	403	482	166	354	344	480
HDCP	18	14	8	2	6	16	12	10	4

Directions: Exit 10 off Mass Pike or Exit 6B off Route 290. Route 20 West to Route 56 North, go right. Take Route 56 North for 1 mile, club on left.

Quaboag Country Club

Monson, MA (413) 267-5294
www.quaboagcountryclub.com

Club Pro: Arvid Hill, PGA
Pro Shop: Full inventory
Payment: Cash, Charge
Tee Times: 2 days adv
Fee 9 Holes: Weekday: $15.00
Fee 18 Holes: Weekday: $22.00
Twilight Rates: No
Cart Rental: $7pp/9
Lessons: $30.00/30 min. **Schools:** no
Clinics: Yes **Day Camps:** Yes
Other: Bar-Lounge / Banquet / Snack bar / Lockers / Showers

Tees	Holes	Yards	Par	USGA	Slope
BACK					
MIDDLE	9	5760	68	67.2	116
FRONT	9	5220	70	69.2	113

Weekend: $17.00
Weekend: $27.00
All Day Play: No
Discounts: None
Junior Golf: Yes **Membership:** Yes, $875/year
Driving Range: No

COUPON

Sig. Hole: #3, 435 yd. par 4 is a gem combining length with a fairway outlined by trees and well placed bunkers. Course is over 100 years old.

	1	2	3	4	5	6	7	8	9
PAR	4	3	4	4	4	4	4	3	4
YARDS	350	225	435	430	360	350	250	130	350
HDCP	5	11	1	3	9	13	15	17	7

	10	11	12	13	14	15	16	17	18
PAR	4	3	4	4	4	4	4	3	4
YARDS	350	225	435	430	360	350	250	130	350
HDCP	6	12	2	4	10	14	16	18	8

Directions: Take I-90 to Exit 8 in Palmer. Turn right onto Route 32 South. Go 2 lights, turn left. Go 3 miles to golf course on right.

NE/ CTRL MA

4✪ =Excellent **3✪** =Very Good **2✪** =Good   **Boston's North Shore & Central MA 105**

Quail Hollow Golf & CC

51

Old Turnpike Rd., Oakham, MA (508) 882-5516

Club Pro: K.Norcross, GM/Golf Professional
Pro Shop: Full inventory
Payment: Visa, MC, cash
Tee Times: Recommended

Tees	Holes	Yards	Par	USGA	Slope
BACK	18	5896	70	68.6	123
MIDDLE	18	5567	70	67.0	120
FRONT	18	4839	71	68.9	120

Fee 9 Holes: Weekday: $13.00   **Weekend:** $15.00
Fee 18 Holes: Weekday: $23.00   **Weekend:** $25.00
Twilight Rates: No   **All Day Play:** No
Cart Rental: $14pp/18, $7pp/9   **Discounts:** Senior & Junior
Lessons: $50.00/30 min **Schools:** No   **Junior Golf:** Yes **Membership:** Yes
Clinics: Yes **Day Camps:** Junior Camp   **Driving Range:** $7/lg $5/md $3/sm
Other: Clubhouse / Restaurant/ Bar-lounge / Snack Bar

COUPON

Beautiful view. Hole #10 voted best hole in Worcester County.

	1	2	3	4	5	6	7	8	9
PAR	4	4	4	3	5	3	4	4	4
YARDS	296	290	230	174	500	140	415	299	310
HDCP	17	13	15	5	3	7	1	11	9
	10	**11**	**12**	**13**	**14**	**15**	**16**	**17**	**18**
PAR	4	3	4	4	4	4	5	3	4
YARDS	324	178	361	340	347	408	511	115	320
HDCP	2	4	10	8	16	12	14	18	6

Directions: Route 290 to Worcester to Route 122 North to Oakham to Old Turnpike Road. Course is 3.5 miles off Route 122.

Red Tail Golf Club

✪✪✪✪ **52**

Devens, MA (978) 772-3273
www.redtailgolf.net

Club Pro: Jim Pavlik, PGA
Pro Shop: Yes
Payment: Visa, MC, Amex, Disc, checks
Tee Times: Yes

Tees	Holes	Yards	Par	USGA	Slope
BACK	18	7006	72	73.9	138
MIDDLE	18	6379	72	70.5	130
FRONT	18	5049	72	69.4	120

Fee 9 Holes: Weekday: N/A   **Weekend:** N/A
Fee 18 Holes: Weekday: $70.00 Mon-Thur **Weekend:** $80.00 F/S/S Cart inc.
Twilight Rates: Yes   **All Day Play:** No
Cart Rental: Yes   **Discounts:** None
Lessons: Yes **Schools:** Sr. & Jr.   **Junior Golf:** Yes **Membership:** Yes
Clinics: Yes **Day Camps:**   **Driving Range:** Yes
Other: Bar-Lounge "A top ten you can play." Golf Magazine

Players' Comments: Played 3 times in 2003, found to be tough but fun" "Layout exquisite." "Friendly personnel. " "#14,a par 4 with a scooped out two-tiered green. #18, a true par 5 down hill with a pond in front. " R.W.

	1	2	3	4	5	6	7	8	9
PAR	4	5	3	5	3	4	4	4	4
YARDS	354	516	170	512	161	331	425	306	417
HDCP	12	4	16	8	18	14	2	10	6
	10	**11**	**12**	**13**	**14**	**15**	**16**	**17**	**18**
PAR	5	3	4	4	4	3	4	4	5
YARDS	507	154	352	342	399	181	368	385	499
HDCP	1	17	11	13	5	15	7	9	3

Directions: Route 2 to Jackson Road, Devens Exit. North on Jackson Road to Patton Road. Right on Patton Road to Bulge Road. Left on Bulge to clubhouse.

Rockport Golf Course ✪✪ 53

Rockport, MA (978) 546-3340

Club Pro: Stephen Clayton
Pro Shop: Full inventory
Payment: Visa, MC
Tee Times: 1 day in advance
Fee 9 Holes: Weekday: $27.00
Fee 18 Holes: Weekday: $38.00
Twilight Rates: No
Cart Rental: $32/18 $20/9
Lessons: $30.00/halfhour **Schools:** No
Clinics: No **Day Camps:** No
Other:

Weekend: $17.00, after 3:30 pm
Weekend: $26.00, after 3:30 pm
All Day Play: No
Discounts: None
Junior Golf: Yes **Membership:** Waiting List
Driving Range: Practice Area

Tees	Holes	Yards	Par	USGA	Slope
BACK					
MIDDLE	9	5938	72	68.8	120
FRONT	9	5434	74	71.2	115

Semi-private challenging 9 hole course. Traps and brooks thru course. Closed to the public on weekends until 3:30.

	1	2	3	4	5	6	7	8	9
PAR	3	4	4	5	5	4	3	4	4
YARDS	163	338	353	489	489	421	136	395	355
HDCP	15	11	1	5	7	5	17	3	7

	10	11	12	13	14	15	16	17	18
PAR	3	4	4	5	4	5	3	4	4
YARDS	163	338	353	489	409	455	136	395	355
HDCP	16	12	2	6	4	10	18	4	8

Directions: Route 128N to 1st set of lights . Left to Rockport approximately 4 miles; at end turn right onto Pleasant St. Follow about 3 miles. Course is on right.

Rolling Green GC 54

911 Lowell St., Andover, MA (978) 475-4066

Club Pro: Tim Kilcoyne, PGA
Pro Shop: Full inventory
Payment: Visa, MC
Tee Times: No
Fee 9 Holes: Weekday: $15.00
Fee 18 Holes: Weekday: $22.00
Twilight Rates: No
Cart Rental: $2.00/9 pull carts
Lessons: Yes **Schools:** No
Clinics: Yes **Day Camps:** No
Other: Snack bar / Restaurant / Bar-lounge

Weekend: $16.00
Weekend: $23.00
All Day Play: No
Discounts: Senior & Junior
Junior Golf: No **Membership:** No
Driving Range: $4/5/6/10

Tees	Holes	Yards	Par	USGA	Slope
BACK					
MIDDLE	9	1500	27		
FRONT					

The course is a short par 3 that offers a challenge to the average golfer.

	1	2	3	4	5	6	7	8	9
PAR	3	3	3	3	3	3	3	3	3
YARDS	180	195	105	170	240	120	175	170	145
HDCP	5	2	9	6	1	8	3	4	7

	10	11	12	13	14	15	16	17	18
PAR									
YARDS									
HDCP									

Directions: Take I-93 to Exit 43. Right onto Route 133 East.

Rowley Country Club

Rowley, MA (978) 948-2731
www.rowleygolf.com

Club Pro: James Falco, PGA
Pro Shop: Full inventory
Payment: Visa, MC
Tee Times: 1 week in adv.
Fee 9 Holes: Weekday: $17.00
Fee 18 Holes: Weekday: $32.00
Twilight Rates: After 5 pm
Cart Rental: $24.00/18 $12.00/9
Lessons: $45/30 min. **Schools:** Yes
Clinics: Yes **Day Camps:** Yes
Other: Clubhouse / Restaurant / Bar-lounge

Tees	Holes	Yards	Par	USGA	Slope
BACK					
MIDDLE	9	6380	72	70.7	127
FRONT	9	4940	70	67.5	109

Weekend: $19.00
Weekend: $36.00
All Day Play: N/R
Discounts: Senior
Junior Golf: Yes **Membership:** Yes
Driving Range: $8/lg. $5/med. $3/sm.

COUPON

"Voted best 9 hole course on the North Shore!" J.F. (PGA)

	1	2	3	4	5	6	7	8	9
PAR	4	3	4	5	4	4	3	5	4
YARDS	360	190	360	480	350	325	205	475	310
HDCP	7	11	1	3	15	17	13	5	9
	10	11	12	13	14	15	16	17	18
PAR	4	3	4	5	4	4	3	5	4
YARDS	390	210	435	480	360	360	225	500	365
HDCP	8	12	2	4	16	18	14	6	10

Directions: I-95 to Exit 54 A (Rowley/Georgetown). 2 miles to Rowley CC sign and make left. Follow for 1 mile, club is on right.

Royal Oaks Country Club

Southbridge, MA (508) 764-GOLF (4653)

Club Pro:
Pro Shop: Yes
Payment: Visa, MC, Amex
Tee Times: 5 days adv.
Fee 9 Holes: Weekday: $12.00
Fee 18 Holes: Weekday: $20.00
Twilight Rates: No
Cart Rental: $8pp
Lessons: No **Schools:** No
Clinics: N/R **Day Camps:** No
Other: Clubhouse / Bar-Lounge / Snack Bar / Outings / Leagues

Tees	Holes	Yards	Par	USGA	Slope
BACK	18	6451	72		
MIDDLE	18	6109	72	66.9	104
FRONT	18	5786	72		

Weekend: $15.00
Weekend: $24.00
All Day Play: No
Discounts: Senior & Junior
Junior Golf: No **Membership:** No
Driving Range: No

Leagues and outings encouraged.

	1	2	3	4	5	6	7	8	9
PAR	4	5	3	4	4	3	5	4	4
YARDS	264	492	186	344	285	156	466	240	284
HDCP	13	2	15	5	11	14	4	16	12
	10	11	12	13	14	15	16	17	18
PAR	4	5	4	3	5	4	4	3	4
YARDS	393	529	329	182	499	419	329	181	425
HDCP	8	1	10	18	3	7	9	17	6

Directions: Mass Pike, Sturbridge Exit to Route 20 West to Route 131 to Main St. Southbridge (Route 131) at Gold Star Circle rotary, bear right take first right onto Morris St. (at blue building) to top of hill on left.

Sagamore Spring GC

Lynnfield, MA (781) 334-3151
www.sagamorespring.com

Club Pro: Steven Vaughn, PGA
Pro Shop: Full inventory
Payment: Cash, Credit
Tee Times: 4 Days advance
Fee 9 Holes: Weekday: $20.00
Fee 18 Holes: Weekday: $34.00
Twilight Rates: No
Cart Rental: $26.00/18 $13.00/9
Lessons: $40/30 min. **Schools:** No
Clinics: Yes **Day Camps:** No
Other: Clubhouse / Showers / Snack bar

Tees	Holes	Yards	Par	USGA	Slope
BACK	18	5936	70	68.6	119
MIDDLE	18	5505	70	66.5	114
FRONT	18	4784	70	66.5	112

Weekend: $23.00
Weekend: $44.00
All Day Play: No
Discounts: Senior.Spring or Fall
Junior Golf: Yes **Membership:** No
Driving Range: $5.00/lg. bucket

COUPON

Sig. Hole: #9 is a 210 yard, par 3 with elevated tee to an elevated green. Must hit a solid long iron or fairway wood over a large pond to reach this green.

	1	2	3	4	5	6	7	8	9
PAR	5	4	5	4	4	3	4	3	3
YARDS	465	344	473	364	276	146	336	179	198
HDCP	10	4	6	2	16	18	12	14	8

	10	11	12	13	14	15	16	17	18
PAR	4	5	5	4	3	4	4	3	3
YARDS	247	499	431	398	137	330	317	185	180
HDCP	13	5	7	1	17	3	9	15	11

Directions: Exit 41 off I-95 (Route 128). Turn right off exit ramp onto Main Street. Three miles.

Scottish Meadow Golf Club

NEW 2003

Warren, MA (413) 436-5108,

Club Pro: Patrick Hinchey, PGA
Pro Shop: Yes
Payment: Cash or Charge
Tee Times: Yes, 7 days
Fee 9 Holes: Weekday: $14.00
Fee 18 Holes: Weekday: $26.00
Twilight Rates: No
Cart Rental: Yes
Lessons: Yes **Schools:** No
Clinics: **Day Camps:** No
Other: Clubhouse / Snack bar

Tees	Holes	Yards	Par	USGA	Slope
BACK	18	6668	72		
MIDDLE	9	3400	72		
FRONT	18	5114	72		

Weekend: $18.00
Weekend: $33.00 F/S/S/H
All Day Play: No
Discounts: Senior
Junior Golf: Yes **Membership:** Yes
Driving Range: Yes

COUPON

2003 Entry Links- style. Viewable from MA Pike, between Palmer and Sturbridge. Front 9 opened in 2003, back nine planned for 2005. Mark Mungheam design., "Difficult for all levels." R.W.

	1	2	3	4	5	6	7	8	9
PAR	4	3	4	4	3	5	4	4	5
YARDS	396	170	419	346	155	492	300	340	500
HDCP	3	7	1	5	9	2	8	6	4

	10	11	12	13	14	15	16	17	18
PAR	4	3	4	4	3	5	4	4	5
YARDS	408	194	385	332	135	470	320	326	515
HDCP	6	14	2	10	18	4	16	12	8

Directions: I-90 W to Exit 9 (Sturbridge, I-84). Take first exit onto Route 20 W. Go 7 miles to Brimfield Center, turn right onto Route 19 N for 2.5 miles, turn right just after the Entering Warren sign, onto Walkeen Kozial Road. Course is on left.

4❂ =Excellent 3❂ = Very Good 2❂ = Good   **Boston's North Shore & Central MA 109**

Shaker Hills Golf Club ✪✪✪✪

Harvard, MA (978) 772-2227
www.shakerhills.com

Club Pro: Michael G. Herrick, PGA
Pro Shop: Full Inventory
Payment: MC ,Visa, cash
Tee Times: 7 days adv.

Tees	Holes	Yards	Par	USGA	Slope
BACK	18	6850	71	74	137
MIDDLE	18	6394	71	71.2	129
FRONT	18	5914	71	69.4	124

Fee 9 Holes: Weekday: No   **Weekend:** No
Fee 18 Holes: Weekday: $70.00 M-Th   **Weekend:** $75.00 F/S/S/H
Twilight Rates: Seasonal   **All Day Play:** No
Cart Rental: Included   **Discounts:** None
Lessons: $40-$45/half hour   **Schools:** Yes   **Junior Golf:** Yes **Membership:** Call golf shop
Clinics: Adult/Jr **Day Camps:** No   **Driving Range:** included in fee
Other: Clubhouse / Snack bar / Function Rooms

Player's Comments: "Great conditions. Challenging but fair. Friendly staff. Great price for what you get."
Selected by Business Week as one of the "18 Greatest Country Clubs for a day" in the U.S.

	1	2	3	4	5	6	7	8	9
PAR	4	5	3	4	5	3	4	4	4
YARDS	342	507	186	449	558	172	333	390	347
HDCP	13	7	15	5	1	17	9	3	11
	10	11	12	13	14	15	16	17	18
PAR	4	4	4	3	4	5	3	4	4
YARDS	396	378	380	149	300	538	224	315	430
HDCP	10	6	8	18	12	2	14	16	4

Directions: Route 495 to Exit 30 (Route 2A West). Four miles to Shaker Road on left. Course is 1/2 mile on left.

Sheraton Hotel & Colonial Golf Club

Lynnfield, MA (781) 876-6031

Club Pro: Bob Jacobs, PGA
Pro Shop: Full inventory
Payment: Most major
Tee Times: 3 days in adv.

Tees	Holes	Yards	Par	USGA	Slope
BACK	18	6565	70	72.8	130
MIDDLE	18	6187	70	71.1	129
FRONT	18	5580	72	70.5	119

Fee 9 Holes: Weekday: N/A   **Weekend:** N/A
Fee 18 Holes: Weekday: $50.00 M-Th   **Weekend:** $60.00 F-S
Twilight Rates: Yes, after 3:30 pm   **All Day Play:** Yes
Cart Rental: Included   **Discounts:** None
Lessons: $50.00/45min. **Schools:** No   **Junior Golf:** No **Membership:** No
Clinics: Yes **Day Camps:** No   **Driving Range:** Yes
Other: Restaurant / Clubhouse / Hotel / Bar-lounge / Lockers / Snack Bar / Showers

COUPON

Sig. Hole: #14, 169 par 3, length is deceptive. Open April 1 - December 15.

	1	2	3	4	5	6	7	8	9
PAR	4	4	3	4	3	5	4	5	4
YARDS	419	345	136	422	195	531	339	537	315
HDCP	3	13	17	1	9	5	11	7	15
	10	11	12	13	14	15	16	17	18
PAR	4	4	4	4	3	4	4	3	4
YARDS	398	333	356	390	169	411	330	171	390
HDCP	8	10	12	2	18	4	14	16	6

Directions: Course is located off I-95 at Exit 43, 12 miles north of Boston.

Shining Rock Golf Community

Northbridge, MA (508) 234-1746
www.shiningrockgc.com

Club Pro: TBA
Pro Shop:
Payment:
Tee Times:
Fee 9 Holes: Weekday: TBA
Fee 18 Holes: Weekday:
Twilight Rates:
Cart Rental: TBA
Lessons: Schools:
Clinics: Day Camps:
Other:

Tees	Holes	Yards	Par	USGA	Slope
BACK					
MIDDLE	18	7010			
FRONT					

Weekend:
Weekend:
All Day Play:
Discounts:
Junior Golf: Membership:
Driving Range:

New Entry 2004

	1	2	3	4	5	6	7	8	9
PAR									
YARDS									
HDCP									
	10	11	12	13	14	15	16	17	18
PAR									
YARDS									
HDCP									

Directions: I-90 W to I-495 S, Take Exit 21 (Upton). Go right off ramp onto West Main St. (Hopkinton). Go about 5 miles to traffic light at intersection of Route 140. Go straight through light at Maple St. Turn right onto Pleasant St., right onto School St. Entrance 1/4 mile on right.

St. Mark's Golf Course

Southborough, MA (508) 460-0946

Club Pro:
Pro Shop: Limited inventory
Payment: Cash,checks
Tee Times: Weekends
Fee 9 Holes: Weekday: $16.00
Fee 18 Holes: Weekday: $30.00
Twilight Rates: No
Cart Rental: $28.00/18 $15.00/9
Lessons: Yes **Schools:** No
Clinics: Yes **Day Camps:** No
Other: No

Tees	Holes	Yards	Par	USGA	Slope
BACK					
MIDDLE	9	5810	70	67.1	117
FRONT					

Weekend: $19.00
Weekend: $32.00
All Day Play: Yes
Discounts: None
Junior Golf: No **Membership:** Yes
Driving Range: Practice area

Open to public. Large landing areas where drivers can be used on most par 4's and 5's. Good for beginners. Challenging, small greens. Inquire about ongoing weekday specials.

	1	2	3	4	5	6	7	8	9
PAR	4	3	5	4	4	4	3	4	4
YARDS	325	155	445	345	375	335	195	320	410
HDCP	7	17	13	5	1	15	11	9	3
	10	11	12	13	14	15	16	17	18
PAR	4	3	5	4	4	4	3	4	4
YARDS	325	155	445	345	375	335	195	320	410
HDCP	8	18	14	6	2	16	12	10	4

Directions: Take Route 9 West, to Route 85 North. Course is 1 mile after intersection.

Stony Brook Golf Course

Southboro, MA (508) 485-3151
www.stonybrook.com

Club Pro: Jack Hester, PGA
Pro Shop: No
Payment: Visa, MC
Tee Times: No

Tees	Holes	Yards	Par	USGA	Slope
BACK					
MIDDLE	9	1287	27		
FRONT					

Fee 9 Holes: Weekday: $12.00   **Weekend:** $13.00
Fee 18 Holes: Weekday: $17.00   **Weekend:** N/A
Twilight Rates: No   **All Day Play:** No
Cart Rental: Pull Carts, $2.00   **Discounts:** Seniors (M-F)
Lessons: $45.00/ 4 lessons **Schools:** No   **Junior Golf:** No **Membership:** No
Clinics: No **Day Camps:** No   **Driving Range:** No
Other: Snack bar, accessories.

Good for beginners and experienced golfers. "No frills course but always improving. Plays fair. Greens are beautiful, honest but must be read right. Need accurate iron play." R & C A (senior players)

	1	2	3	4	5	6	7	8	9
PAR	3	3	3	3	3	3	3	3	3
YARDS	145	103	210	125	125	165	163	106	145
HDCP									
	10	11	12	13	14	15	16	17	18
PAR									
YARDS									
HDCP									

Directions: Accessible from Routes I-90, I-495 and Route 9. Located in Southboro off of Route 30 on Valley Road.

Swanson Meadows

Billerica, MA, (978) 670-7777
www.swansonmeadows.com

Club Pro: Mike Gaffney
Pro Shop:
Payment: Visa, MC
Tee Times: Yes, 7 days

Tees	Holes	Yards	Par	USGA	Slope
BACK					
MIDDLE	9	2178	32		
FRONT	9	1829	32		

Fee 9 Holes: Weekday: $18.00   **Weekend:** $22.00
Fee 18 Holes: Weekday: $30.00   **Weekend:** $40.00
Twilight Rates: No   **All Day Play:** No
Cart Rental: $6.00pp   **Discounts:** Senior
Lessons: Schools: N/A   **Junior Golf: Membership:** Yes, Season Passes
Clinics: N/A **Day Camps:** N/A   **Driving Range:** No
Other: Snack Bar

COUPON

2003 Entry. The Divine Nine." "Layout squeezed onto a moderate space." R.W. **Player's comment:'** Quick hike after work."

	1	2	3	4	5	6	7	8	9
PAR	4	4	4	3	3	4	3	3	4
YARDS	360	287	345	163	119	296	121	143	344
HDCP	4	6	1	5	9	8	7	3	2
	10	11	12	13	14	15	16	17	18
PAR									
YARDS									
HDCP									

Directions: Route 3, Exit 29. Turn left off ramp. Go 1 mile. Take right on to Rangeway Road. Course is 1 mile on left.

Templewood Golf Course

Templeton, MA (978) 939-5031

Club Pro: John Ross
Pro Shop: Full inventory
Payment: Visa, MC, Cash
Tee Times: No.
Fee 9 Holes: Weekday: $12.00
Fee 18 Holes: Weekday: $20.00
Twilight Rates: No
Cart Rental: $24/18 $16/9 Wknds
Lessons: Yes **Schools:** NRHS
Clinics: Yes **Day Camps:** No
Other: Clubhouse / Lounge

Tees	Holes	Yards	Par	USGA	Slope
BACK	9	2941	35		
MIDDLE	9	2745	35		
FRONT	9	2441	35		

Weekend: $15.00 S/S/H
Weekend: $22.00 S/S/H
All Day Play: No
Discounts: Senior & Junior: $10.00
Junior Golf: Yes **Membership:** No
Driving Range: Practice Net

COUPON

Player's Comment: "Inspiring panoramic view of Mt. Monadnock. Friendly staff seek input after play" "Lots of up and down hill shots. Magnificent setting." R.W. New 9 holes under construction. Carts reduced wkdys.

	1	2	3	4	5	6	7	8	9
PAR	5	3	4	3	5	4	3	4	4
YARDS	515	135	375	135	455	405	135	245	345
HDCP	2	8	3	9	1	4	7	6	5
	10	**11**	**12**	**13**	**14**	**15**	**16**	**17**	**18**
PAR									
YARDS									
HDCP									

Directions: Route 2, Exit 20. Follow Trailblazing Signs.

Tewksbury CC

Tewksbury, MA (978) 640-0033
www.tewksburycountryclub.com

Club Pro: Mike Rogers, PGA
Pro Shop: Full inventory
Payment: Visa, MC
Tee Times: Friday/Saturday/Sunday
Fee 9 Holes: Weekday: $16.00
Fee 18 Holes: Weekday: $32.00
Twilight Rates: No
Cart Rental: $12pp/18 $6.00pp/9
Lessons: $35.00/30 minutes **Schools:** Junior
Clinics: Junior **Day Camps:** Yes
Other:

Tees	Holes	Yards	Par	USGA	Slope
BACK	9	2701	33	33.3	114
MIDDLE	9	2529	33	32.2	112
FRONT	9	1971	33	31.4	107

Weekend: $20.00
Weekend: $40.00
All Day Play: No
Discounts: Senior & Junior
Junior Golf: Yes **Membership:** Yes
Driving Range:

All new proshop and clubhouse opened August 2003. 4 sets of tees challenge all. **Player's Comments:** "Nice nine holes, great staff, and great pro. Seems you can always get a good tee time. Nice layout "

	1	2	3	4	5	6	7	8	9
PAR	4	3	3	4	4	5	4	3	3
YARDS	350	179	148	397	336	475	330	161	136
HDCP	11	3	15	5	7	17	1	13	9
	10	**11**	**12**	**13**	**14**	**15**	**16**	**17**	**18**
PAR									
YARDS									
HDCP									

Directions: I-93 to Exit 42 (Dascomb Road) towards Tewksbury. Turn left onto Shawsheen St. Follow Shawsheen to Route 38. Turn right onto Livingston St. From Route 128, take Route 38 N to Livingston St.

4✪ =Excellent **3✪** =Very Good **2✪** = Good **Boston's North Shore & Central MA 113**

The Meadow at Peabody ✪✪ ▸ 67

Peabody, MA (978) 532-9390
www.peabodymeadowgolf.com

Tees	Holes	Yards	Par	USGA	Slope
BACK	18	6708	71	72.4	128
MIDDLE	18	5869	71	69.4	121
FRONT	18	5136	71	70.8	123

Club Pro: Richard W. Nagle, PGA
Pro Shop: Full inventory
Payment: Visa, MC, Amex
Tee Times: 3 days adv.
Fee 9 Holes: Weekday: $17.00   **Weekend:** $18.00
Fee 18 Holes: Weekday: $32.00   **Weekend:** $34.00
Twilight Rates: No   **All Day Play:** No
Cart Rental: Yes   **Discounts:** Sr. & Jr. before noon (M-F)
Lessons: $40/45 min. **Schools:** No   **Junior Golf:** Yes **Membership:** No
Clinics: Junior **Day Camps:** No   **Driving Range:** No
Other: Restaurant / Showers / Beverage Cart

Players Comments: "Back side target golf." "Blind shots on many holes. Fun layout, hilly, but fair course." Dress code. Lodging available at nearby Marriott. "A must visit." F.P.

	1	2	3	4	5	6	7	8	9
PAR	5	4	4	4	4	3	5	3	4
YARDS	526	343	312	324	388	110	437	146	372
HDCP									
	10	11	12	13	14	15	16	17	18
PAR	4	5	3	4	4	4	3	4	4
YARDS	360	457	153	389	319	329	143	341	420
HDCP									

Directions: From Route 128 N, take Exit 28 (Forest St/Centennial Dr.) Keep right at end of ramp. Stay straight onto Centennial Dr. Right onto Summit. Left onto Lynnfield St. Left onto Washington St. Immediate right onto Granite St. Street deadends to course.

Townsend Ridge Country Club ✪✪ ▸ 68

Townsend, MA (978) 597-8400
www.townsendridge.com

Tees	Holes	Yards	Par	USGA	Slope
BACK	18	6188	70	70.2	125
MIDDLE	18	5814	70	68.5	123
FRONT	18	4709	71	68.3	115

Club Pro: Corey Mansfield
Pro Shop: Full inventory
Payment: Visa, MC, Amex
Tee Times: 7 days advance
Fee 9 Holes: Weekday: $15.00   **Weekend:** $15.00
Fee 18 Holes: Weekday: $30.00   **Weekend:** $42, cart req. before 2pm
Twilight Rates: Yes, after 3 pm   **All Day Play:** No
Cart Rental: $16.00   **Discounts:** Senior & Junior
Lessons: $40/30 min. **Schools:** Jr.   **Junior Golf:** Yes **Membership:** Yes
Clinics: Yes **Day Camps:** Yes   **Driving Range:** $4.00
Other: Clubhouse / 19th hole lounge / Full bar / Outings encouraged!

Course noted for condition and target golf. Challenging popular course.

	1	2	3	4	5	6	7	8	9
PAR	4	4	3	4	5	4	3	4	4
YARDS	312	375	126	383	457	308	156	349	351
HDCP	13	5	17	1	11	7	15	3	9
	10	11	12	13	14	15	16	17	18
PAR	4	4	5	4	4	3	4	3	4
YARDS	375	377	460	328	429	135	359	170	364
HDCP	6	2	10	4	8	18	12	16	14

Directions: Exit 31 off Route 495. Go West on Route 119 for 15 miles. Take first left after Townsend Ford on to Scales Lane.

Trull Brook Golf Course ○○

N. Tewksbury, MA (978) 851-6731

Club Pro: Al Santos, PGA
Pro Shop: Full inventory
Payment: Visa, MC
Tee Times: 1 week adv.

Tees	Holes	Yards	Par	USGA	Slope
BACK	18	6345	72	69.8	123
MIDDLE	18	6006	72	68.8	122
FRONT	18	5193	72	69.6	118

Fee 9 Holes: Weekday: $20.00 afternoons
Fee 18 Holes: Weekday: $39.00
Twilight Rates: Yes, after 5:45 pm
Cart Rental: $28.50/18 $14.50/9
Lessons: Yes **Schools:** No
Clinics: No **Day Camps:** No
Other: Clubhouse / Lockers / Showers / Snack bar

Weekend: $26.00 after 3:15
Weekend: $42.00 F/S/S/H
All Day Play: No
Discounts: Senior & Junior (M-Th)
Junior Golf: No **Membership:** No
Driving Range: No

NE/
CTRL
MA

Players' Comments: "Very well kept. Nice greens." "Challenging course. Scenic." A Geoffrey Cornish design.

	1	2	3	4	5	6	7	8	9
PAR	4	5	4	3	4	3	5	4	4
YARDS	338	498	383	123	368	138	470	353	323
HDCP	5	7	1	17	3	15	11	9	13
	10	11	12	13	14	15	16	17	18
PAR	4	3	5	4	4	3	4	5	4
YARDS	323	168	463	323	343	178	373	458	383
HDCP	12	16	10	6	2	18	8	14	4

Directions: From I-495 or I-93, take Route 133 exit, follow West toward Lowell. At Mobil station, sharp right onto River Road. Course is 1/3 mile on left.

Tyngsboro CC 70

Tyngsboro, MA (978) 649-7334

Club Pro: Allan Pottle
Pro Shop: Limited inventory
Payment: Cash only
Tee Times: Wkends 5 days

Tees	Holes	Yards	Par	USGA	Slope
BACK	9	5120	70	63.2	104
MIDDLE	9	4794	70	65.2	104
FRONT	9	4046	70	62.6	97

Fee 9 Holes: Weekday: $16.00
Fee 18 Holes: Weekday: $27.00
Twilight Rates: No
Cart Rental: $20.00/18 $12.00/9
Lessons: No **Schools:** N/R
Clinics: No **Day Camps:** No
Other: Snack bar / Bar-lounge

Weekend: $18.00
Weekend: $30.00
All Day Play: No
Discounts: Senior Wkdays $1 before 12pm
Junior Golf: No **Membership:** 7 day/5 day
Driving Range: No

Improvements include 4th hole lengthened 100 yards from all tees. The course requires accurate shots and is easy to walk. Dress code.

	1	2	3	4	5	6	7	8	9
PAR	4	4	3	5	3	5	4	4	3
YARDS	320	314	216	430	160	463	282	249	140
HDCP	7	9	5	3	11	1	15	13	17
	10	11	12	13	14	15	16	17	18
PAR	4	4	3	5	3	5	4	4	3
YARDS	321	314	216	430	160	463	282	249	140
HDCP	8	10	6	4	12	2	16	14	18

Directions: Take Route 3 to Exit 35; onto Route 113 East; approximately 2.5 miles.

Wachusett CC ✪✪ ▸ 71

W. Boylston, MA (508) 835-2264
www.wachusettcc.com

Club Pro: Tim Bishop, PGA
Pro Shop: Full inventory
Payment: Visa, MC, Amex
Tee Times: 7 days adv.
Fee 9 Holes: Weekday: N/A
Fee 18 Holes: Weekday: $35.00
Twilight Rates: After 3 pm
Cart Rental: $34.00/18
Lessons: $55/ 45 min. **Schools:** No
Clinics: Yes **Day Camps:** No
Other: Snack bar / Bar-lounge / Banquet facilities

Tees	Holes	Yards	Par	USGA	Slope
BACK	18	6608	72	71.4	124
MIDDLE	18	6206	72	71.7	123
FRONT	18	6216	73	70.0	120

Weekend: N/A
Weekend: $45.00
All Day Play: Yes
Discounts: None
Junior Golf: Yes **Membership:** Yes, wait list
Driving Range: Yes

Sig. Hole: #8 is a par 4, 436 yards with a dogleg left that narrows to a well protected green. A Donald Ross gem. Reduced rates after 1 pm on weekends.

	1	2	3	4	5	6	7	8	9
PAR	4	5	4	3	5	3	4	4	4
YARDS	388	518	380	145	507	175	360	436	426
HDCP	9	1	11	17	3	15	13	7	5
	10	**11**	**12**	**13**	**14**	**15**	**16**	**17**	**18**
PAR	5	4	4	3	4	5	4	4	3
YARDS	494	430	426	203	330	508	316	374	192
HDCP	10	2	4	8	16	6	12	14	18

Directions: Take Mass Pike 290 to 190, Exit 4 onto Route 12 North. Approximately 2 miles to Franklin Street, turn left. At end of road turn left onto Prospect.

Webster Dudley Golf Club ✪✪ ▸ 72

Dudley, MA (508) 943-4538
www.dudleyhill.homestead.com

Club Pro: Marilyn Bell
Pro Shop: Full inventory
Payment: Visa, MC
Tee Times: Weekends
Fee 9 Holes: Weekday: $15.00
Fee 18 Holes: Weekday: $25.00
Twilight Rates: No
Cart Rental: $22.00/18 $11.00/9
Lessons: $30.00/half hour **Schools:** No
Clinics: Yes **Day Camps:** No
Other: Snack bar / Bar lounge

Tees	Holes	Yards	Par	USGA	Slope
BACK					
MIDDLE	9	6482	72	71.4	123
FRONT	9	5696	72	71.3	115

Weekend: $15.00
Weekend: $25.00
All Day Play: No
Discounts: Junior
Junior Golf: No **Membership:** Yes, open to all.
Driving Range: No

New ladies tee on 9th hole. Open April - November.

	1	2	3	4	5	6	7	8	9
PAR	4	4	3	4	4	3	4	5	5
YARDS	367	384	170	399	232	323	423	509	472
HDCP	7	5	15	3	17	13	1	9	11
	10	**11**	**12**	**13**	**14**	**15**	**16**	**17**	**18**
PAR	4	4	3	4	4	3	4	5	5
YARDS	367	384	170	399	232	323	423	509	472
HDCP	8	6	16	4	18	14	2	10	12

Directions: I-395S to Exit 4B. Go to Oxford Ctr. thru lights. Go .5 mi. Take left on Dudley Rd. .5 mi to 4-way stop sign. Straight thru to next stop sign. Go left. Club is .5 mi on left.

Wenham Country Club

Wenham, MA (978) 468-4714

Club Pro: Peter Collins, PGA
Pro Shop: Full inventory
Payment: Cash only
Tee Times: Wknds only after 12 noon
Fee 9 Holes: Weekday: $18.00
Fee 18 Holes: Weekday: $30.00
Twilight Rates: After 5 pm on wknds
Cart Rental: $26.00/18 $14.00/9
Lessons: $40/half hour **Schools:** No
Clinics: Yes **Day Camps:** No
Other: Snack bar until 2pm Thursday - Sunday

Tees	Holes	Yards	Par	USGA	Slope
BACK					
MIDDLE	18	4537	65	62.6	107
FRONT	18	4315	67	65.0	106

Weekend: $20 after 5pm
Weekend: $20 after 5pm
All Day Play: No
Discounts: None
Junior Golf: Yes **Membership:** Yes, wait list
Driving Range: No

Improvements include 7th hole redone. Open April - November. Semi-private.

	1	2	3	4	5	6	7	8	9
PAR	4	3	3	4	3	4	3	4	3
YARDS	347	115	187	279	208	309	153	278	170
HDCP	6	18	10	2	12	4	16	8	14
	10	**11**	**12**	**13**	**14**	**15**	**16**	**17**	**18**
PAR	3	5	3	3	4	4	4	4	4
YARDS	216	413	186	136	357	246	395	300	272
HDCP	5	9	11	17	3	5	1	7	3

Directions: Take Route 128 to Exit 20 North, Route 1A. Course is 3 miles on right.

Westborough CC

Westboro, MA (508) 366-9947

Club Pro: Jack A. Negoshian
Pro Shop: Yes
Payment: Visa, MC, cash
Tee Times: Wknds, 1 day
Fee 9 Holes: Weekday: $15.00
Fee 18 Holes: Weekday: $25.00
Twilight Rates: No
Cart Rental: $24.00/18 $14.00/9
Lessons: Limited **Schools:** No

Clinics: No **Day Camps:** No
Other: Restaurant / Bar-lounge

Tees	Holes	Yards	Par	USGA	Slope
BACK	9	3182	36	35.5	125
MIDDLE	9	2979	36	34.7	122
FRONT	9	2816	36	34.1	121

Weekend: $18.00 after 4:00 pm
Weekend: $28.00
All Day Play: No
Discounts: Senior & Junior
Junior Golf: No **Membership:** Waiting list

Driving Range: No

Sig. Hole: #3 par 5 is a pretty uphill approach to a scenic green. Open April - November.

	1	2	3	4	5	6	7	8	9
PAR	5	4	5	4	3	4	3	4	4
YARDS	412	265	491	322	168	344	149	411	415
HDCP	12	16	2	10	14	8	18	4	6
	10	**11**	**12**	**13**	**14**	**15**	**16**	**17**	**18**
PAR									
YARDS									
HDCP									

Directions: Route 9 to Route 30 toward Westboro. Take a right at the stop sign. Course is 1 mile past center of town on the right.

Westminster CC

Westminster, MA (978) 874-5938
www.westminstercountryclub.com

Tees	Holes	Yards	Par	USGA	Slope
BACK	18	6491	71	70.9	133
MIDDLE	18	6223	71	69.5	123
FRONT	18	5453	71	70.0	115

Club Pro: Michael LeBlanc PGA
Pro Shop: Full inventory
Payment: Most major
Tee Times: 3 days in advance
Fee 9 Holes: Weekday: $14.00
Fee 18 Holes: Weekday: $28.00
Twilight Rates: No
Cart Rental: $13.00pp/18, $6.50pp/9
Lessons: Yes **Schools:** No
Clinics: No **Day Camps:** No
Other: Clubhouse / Lockers / Showers / Snack bar / Restaurant / Bar-lounge

Weekend: $17.00
Weekend: $33.00
All Day Play: No
Discounts: None
Junior Golf: Yes **Membership:** Yes, $1090.00
Driving Range: No

Player's Comment: "Moderately easy to walk. Carts not required." Open April 15 - October 31.

	1	2	3	4	5	6	7	8	9
PAR	4	4	4	4	4	4	4	4	3
YARDS	422	396	344	384	353	316	333	312	173
HDCP	1	3	7	5	9	17	11	15	13
	10	**11**	**12**	**13**	**14**	**15**	**16**	**17**	**18**
PAR	3	4	3	4	5	4	5	3	5
YARDS	131	381	224	452	532	314	548	157	451
HDCP	18	8	12	2	4	10	6	16	14

Directions: Take Route 2 to Route 140 East. Take an immediate right after bridge, through Westminster Center. Follow 2 miles. Left onto Nichols. Bear right at fork onto Ellis, Course is 1 mile on right.

Winchendon School CC

Winchendon, MA   (978) 297-9897

Tees	Holes	Yards	Par	USGA	Slope
BACK					
MIDDLE	18	5424	70	65.7	114
FRONT	18	5030	72	68.5	116

Club Pro: Tom Borden, PGA
Pro Shop: Full Inventory
Payment: All major
Tee Times: Yes, 3 days adv.
Fee 9 Holes: Weekday: $12, $19.00 ride
Fee 18 Holes: Weekday: $20, $34.00 ride
Twilight Rates: Yes, after 4 pm
Cart Rental: $14.00/18 $7.00/9
Lessons: Yes **Schools:** No
Clinics: Yes **Day Camps:** No
Other: Clubhouse / Bar-lounge / Snack bar / Banquets / Outings

Weekend: $14, $21.00 ride
Weekend: $25, $39.00 ride
All Day Play: No
Discounts: None
Junior Golf: Yes **Membership:** Yes
Driving Range: No

Improvements include a new clubhouse and proshop.

	1	2	3	4	5	6	7	8	9
PAR	3	3	4	5	4	4	4	4	4
YARDS	204	170	314	472	385	369	368	365	285
HDCP	15	11	9	3	1	7	13	5	17
	10	**11**	**12**	**13**	**14**	**15**	**16**	**17**	**18**
PAR	3	5	3	4	5	4	4	3	4
YARDS	155	502	165	278	409	238	280	237	231
HDCP	18	4	6	16	8	14	10	2	12

Directions: Route 2 to Route 140 North to Route 12. Take left onto Route 12. Go 3/4 miles. Take first left at McDonalds. Take left on to Ash St. Course is at top of hill.

Woburn Country Club

Woburn, MA (781) 933-9880

Club Pro: P.Barkhouse PGA
Pro Shop: Full inventory
Payment: Cash only
Tee Times: 2 days / weekends only
Fee 9 Holes: Weekday: $18.00
Fee 18 Holes: Weekday: $27.00
Twilight Rates: No
Cart Rental: $25.00/18 $16.00/9 Wknds
Lessons: $40.00/half hour **Schools:** No
Clinics: N/R **Day Camps:** No
Other: Restaurant / Snack bar / Function Hall

Tees	Holes	Yards	Par	USGA	Slope
BACK	N/A				
MIDDLE	9	5973	68	68.9	121
FRONT	9	2565	70	68.0	104

Weekend: $19.00
Weekend: $30.00
All Day Play: No
Discounts: Senior & Junior (Wkdays only)
Junior Golf: Yes **Membership:** Yes, Res. only
Driving Range: No

Small greens. Need a good short game to score well, every lie in the book. No tank tops.

	1	2	3	4	5	6	7	8	9
PAR	4	4	4	4	4	4	3	4	3
YARDS	373	363	359	371	410	326	190	389	215
HDCP	7	5	11	9	1	15	17	3	13

	10	11	12	13	14	15	16	17	18
PAR	4	4	4	4	4	4	3	4	3
YARDS	362	374	331	387	405	337	182	402	197
HDCP	8	6	12	10	4	14	18	2	16

Directions: I-93 to Route 128 South, Exit 33A (Winchester), straight through Woburn Four Corners, take left at first set of lights onto Country Club Road.

Woods of Westminster CC ✪✪

Westminster, MA (978) 874-0500
www.woodscc.com

Club Pro: Richard Farland, Dir. of Golf
Pro Shop: Limited inventory
Payment: Visa, MC, Amex, Disc, Checks
Tee Times: 3 days adv.
Fee 9 Holes: Weekday: $12.00
Fee 18 Holes: Weekday: $24.00
Twilight Rates: No
Cart Rental: $11.00pp/18 $7.00pp/9
Lessons: $25/30 min. **Schools:** No
Clinics: No **Day Camps:** No
Other: Full Restaurant / Clubhouse / Bar

Tees	Holes	Yards	Par	USGA	Slope
BACK	18	5830	72	67.2	121
MIDDLE	18	5725	72	65.7	117
FRONT	18	4765	72	66.6	111

Weekend: $16.00
Weekend: $32.00
All Day Play: Yes
Discounts: Senior & Junior
Junior Golf: Yes **Membership:** Yes
Driving Range: $5.00/ lg. $3.50/ sm.

COUPON

Player's comment: "Best value insider secret: Mon-Thurs. before noon, tee-time". New tees on #1, 6, 7, and 12. Magnificent mountain views. Open year round. Noted for lunch and dinner golf packages.

	1	2	3	4	5	6	7	8	9
PAR	5	4	5	4	4	3	4	3	4
YARDS	460	325	525	295	345	185	405	155	320
HDCP	5	7	3	9	11	17	1	15	13

	10	11	12	13	14	15	16	17	18
PAR	5	4	4	5	3	4	3	4	4
YARDS	415	270	330	435	145	315	160	320	340
HDCP	6	10	8	4	16	12	18	14	2

Directions: Take Exit 27 off of Route 2 onto Depot Rd. Go right to stop sign. Take right onto Route 2A to first left (S. Ashburn Rd.). Go 1.2 miles to Bean Porridge Hill Rd. on right (#90).

4✪ =Excellent **3✪** =Very Good **2✪** = Good   **Boston's North Shore & Central MA 119**

CHAPTER 3
Western Massachusetts

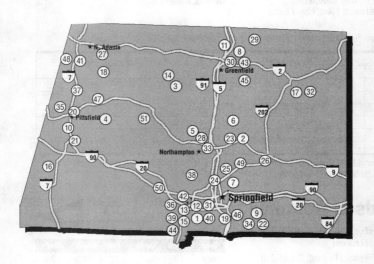

Agawam Municipal CC

Route 57, Feeding Hills, MA (413) 786-2194

Club Pro: Ron Dunn, PGA
Pro Shop: Yes
Payment: Cash only
Tee Times: 3 days adv.
Fee 9 Holes: Weekday: $10.00
Fee 18 Holes: Weekday: $15.00
Twilight Rates: Yes, after 12 pm
Cart Rental: $11pp/18 $5.50pp/9
Lessons: Private & Group **Schools:** No
Clinics: No **Day Camps:** No
Other: Snack bar / Bar-lounge

Tees	Holes	Yards	Par	USGA	Slope
BACK					
MIDDLE	18	6119	71	67.0	110
FRONT	18	5345	71	71.2	110

Weekend: $12.00
Weekend: $18.00
All Day Play: Yes
Discounts: Senior & Junior
Junior Golf: Yes **Membership:** No
Driving Range: No

A friendly course. No water holes but 1 creek and 8 sand traps. Total irrigation. The 9th hole is referred to as "Cardiac Hill," and for good reason. Weekend specials before 8 am and after 1 pm.

	1	2	3	4	5	6	7	8	9
PAR	5	4	3	4	3	4	4	5	3
YARDS	480	375	144	465	121	360	385	560	175
HDCP	13	9	15	3	17	7	11	1	5
	10	**11**	**12**	**13**	**14**	**15**	**16**	**17**	**18**
PAR	5	4	4	3	4	3	5	5	3
YARDS	475	395	348	160	322	145	554	475	180
HDCP	8	4	14	16	12	18	2	10	6

Directions: Take I-90 (Mass Pike) to I-91 to Route 57 (Agawam). Go north on Route 57, club is in the town of Feeding Hills.

Amherst Golf Club

S. Pleasant, Amherst, MA (413) 256-6894

Club Pro: Dave Twohig, PGA
Pro Shop: Full inventory
Payment: Visa, MC
Tee Times: No
Fee 9 Holes: Weekday: $25.00
Fee 18 Holes: Weekday: $25.00
Twilight Rates: No
Cart Rental: $24.00/2R,18 $15.00/2R,9
Lessons: $40.00/half hour **Schools:** No
Clinics: Yes **Day Camps:** No
Other: Clubhouse / Lockers / Showers / Snack bar

Tees	Holes	Yards	Par	USGA	Slope
BACK					
MIDDLE	9	6058	70	68.9	117
FRONT	9	5548	72	68.9	122

Weekend: $25.00
Weekend: $25.00
All Day Play: Yes
Discounts: Sr & Jr memberships
Junior Golf: No **Membership:** Wait list
Driving Range: No

Sig. Hole # 9 is a long, uphill par 3 with a sloping green. Collared shirts. Course is short in length with small greens, but always in good shape. Daily rate same for 9 or 18 holes.

	1	2	3	4	5	6	7	8	9
PAR	4	4	4	3	4	4	5	4	3
YARDS	390	375	405	160	350	340	525	310	200
HDCP	5	7	3	13	9	15	1	17	11
	10	**11**	**12**	**13**	**14**	**15**	**16**	**17**	**18**
PAR	4	4	4	3	4	4	5	4	3
YARDS	390	375	405	160	350	340	525	310	188
HDCP	6	8	4	14	10	16	2	18	12

Directions: Take Mass Pike to Route 181 to Route 9 into Amherst. Course is located by Amherst College.

W
MA

4✪ =Excellent **3✪** =Very Good **2✪** = Good

Ashfield Community Golf Club

![3]

Ashfield, MA (413) 628- 4413

Club Pro: No
Pro Shop: No
Payment: Cash or Check
Tee Times: Not needed
Fee 9 Holes: Weekday: $8.00
Fee 18 Holes: Weekday: $10.00
Twilight Rates: No
Cart Rental: None
Lessons: No **Schools:** No
Clinics: No **Day Camps:** No
Other: Clubhouse / Snack Bar

Weekend: $10.00
Weekend: $14.00
All Day Play: No
Discounts: None
Junior Golf: Yes **Membership:** Yes
Driving Range: No

Tees	Holes	Yards	Par	USGA	Slope
BACK					
MIDDLE	9	4187	66		
FRONT	9	3458	66		

COUPON

Bunkers have been redone on hole's #1, 3, 4, and 6. Honor System for play during week, instructions for payment on clubhouse door. Attendant on weekends and holidays.

	1	2	3	4	5	6	7	8	9
PAR	4	4	3	4	3	4	4	4	3
YARDS	286	289	201	317	102	200	185	341	156
HDCP	14	6	16	4	18	8	10	2	12
	10	11	12	13	14	15	16	17	18
PAR	4	4	3	4	3	4	4	4	3
YARDS	286	289	201	317	122	200	185	354	156
HDCP	13	5	15	3	17	7	9	1	11

Directions: I-91N, Exit 19. Bear right off ramp.Go staight thu intersection onto Damon Rd. Go straight thru next intersection onto Bridge Rd. At stop sign, turn right onto Rte. 9, go about 14 mi. Turn right onto Rte. 112 for 6 mi. Go right on Rte. 116E to center of Ashfield. Turn right at Norton Hill Rd.

Bas Ridge Golf Course

![4]

Plunkett St., Hinsdale, MA (413) 655-2605

Club Pro:
Pro Shop: No
Payment: Cash only
Tee Times: Weekends
Fee 9 Holes: Weekday: $10.00
Fee 18 Holes: Weekday: $15.00
Twilight Rates: Yes
Cart Rental: $20.00/18, $10.00/9
Lessons: No **Schools:** N/R
Clinics: No **Day Camps:** No
Other: Clubhouse / Bar-lounge

Weekend: $12.00
Weekend: $30.00
All Day Play: No
Discounts: Senior Wkdays
Junior Golf: No **Membership:** Limited
Driving Range: No

Tees	Holes	Yards	Par	USGA	Slope
BACK					
MIDDLE	18	5051	70	63.7	111
FRONT	18	4369	70	65.9	110

COUPON

Player's Comments: "Each hole is more beautiful and the greens are incredible." Open April 1 - Nov. 1. Senior weekday special available except during July and August.

	1	2	3	4	5	6	7	8	9
PAR	4	4	3	4	3	4	4	4	4
YARDS	335	269	193	280	170	224	233	331	276
HDCP	4	10	6	14	12	16	18	2	8
	10	11	12	13	14	15	16	17	18
PAR	4	4	3	4	5	3	5	4	4
YARDS	270	336	187	313	451	112	466	278	327
HDCP	13	1	11	9	7	15	5	17	3

Directions: Take Mass Pike to Lee exit, take left onto Route 8. Course is located off Route 8 south of Pittsfield.

Beaver Brook CC

Main St., Haydenville, MA (413) 268-7229

Club Pro: No
Pro Shop: Limited inventory
Payment: Most major
Tee Times: Anytime
Fee 9 Holes: Weekday: $12.00
Fee 18 Holes: Weekday: $18.00
Twilight Rates: After 4pm, Sun
Cart Rental: $24.00/18 $12.00/9
Lessons: No **Schools:** No
Clinics: No **Day Camps:** No
Other: Clubhouse / Snack bar / Bar-lounge

Tees	Holes	Yards	Par	USGA	Slope
BACK					
MIDDLE	9	6092	72	68.1	110
FRONT	9	4960	72	67.7	107

Weekend: $14.00
Weekend: $21.00
All Day Play: Yes
Discounts: Senior, $1.00 off
Junior Golf: Yes **Membership:** Yes
Driving Range: No

Beautifully laid out and maintained nine hole course. The course sports two brooks and four ponds. Special Mon-Sat: 2 Players w/ cart 9 holes $32, 18 holes $46 until 11 am.

	1	2	3	4	5	6	7	8	9
PAR	4	4	5	3	4	4	4	3	5
YARDS	403	323	496	146	361	370	290	167	490
HDCP	1	11	3	17	5	9	15	13	7
	10	11	12	13	14	15	16	17	18
PAR	4	4	5	3	4	4	4	3	5
YARDS	403	323	496	146	361	370	290	167	490
HDCP	2	12	4	18	6	10	16	14	8

Directions: Route 91 to Exit 19 North. Continue to end; make right. Course is 2 miles on State Rd. (Route 9 West).

Cherry Hills GC

323 Montague Rd., N. Amherst (413) 256-4071

Club Pro: No
Pro Shop: Limited inventory
Payment: Most major (not Amex)
Tee Times: No
Fee 9 Holes: Weekday: $12.00
Fee 18 Holes: Weekday: $15.00
Twilight Rates: No
Cart Rental: $23.10/18 $12.60/9
Lessons: No **Schools:** No
Clinics: No **Day Camps:** No
Other: Snack-bar

Tees	Holes	Yards	Par	USGA	Slope
BACK	9	5556	70	65.7	101
MIDDLE	9	5340	72	65.7	101
FRONT	9	4940	70	N/A	N/A

Weekend: $16.00
Weekend: $20.00
All Day Play: No
Discounts: Senior & Junior
Junior Golf: No **Membership:** Yes
Driving Range: No

Good beginner course with easy walking.

	1	2	3	4	5	6	7	8	9
PAR	5	3	4	4	4	4	5	4	3
YARDS	555	159	298	341	406	291	415	296	183
HDCP	2	15	9	5	3	18	8	13	6
	10	11	12	13	14	15	16	17	18
PAR	5	4	4	3	4	4	5	4	3
YARDS	579	270	288	165	396	300	425	290	158
HDCP	1	17	10	14	4	16	7	12	11

Directions: Take I-91 to Hadley exit, right on Route 9 into Amherst. Go North on Route 16 for 3 miles, turn right at light onto Pine St and onto Route 63. Course is 1/2 mile on right.

4⭘ =Excellent 3⭘ =Very Good 2⭘ =Good

Chicopee Municipal GC

Burnett Rd., Chicopee, MA (413) 594-9295

Club Pro: Thomas DiRico,PGA
Pro Shop: Full inventory
Payment: Cash/Credit
Tee Times: Yes
Fee 9 Holes: Weekday: $13.00
Fee 18 Holes: Weekday: $23.00
Twilight Rates:
Cart Rental: $22.00/18
Lessons: Yes **Schools:** No
Clinics: Yes **Day Camps:** No
Other: Clubhouse / Snack bar

Weekend: $16.00
Weekend: $26.00
All Day Play:
Discounts: Senior Residents
Junior Golf: No **Membership:** Yes
Driving Range: No

Tees	Holes	Yards	Par	USGA	Slope
BACK	18	6742	71	73.0	126
MIDDLE	18	6109	71	70.4	120
FRONT	18	5123	71	72.45	115

Player's Comments: Course provides the opportunity to hit every shot. A combination of 'Target and Grip-and-Rip It Golf,' it provides a solid test of your skills from tee to green. Always in excellent condition."

	1	2	3	4	5	6	7	8	9
PAR	4	5	3	4	4	4	5	3	4
YARDS	382	481	173	316	433	354	535	193	285
HDCP	7	5	17	11	1	9	3	13	15
	10	11	12	13	14	15	16	17	18
PAR	4	3	3	4	4	5	3	5	4
YARDS	362	157	160	340	391	473	173	534	367
HDCP	10	18	16	14	6	4	12	2	8

Directions: Take Mass. Pike to Exit 6, turn right at light; course is 2 1/2 miles on left.

Country Club of Greenfield

Greenfield, MA (413) 773 -7530

Club Pro: Kevin Piecuch
Pro Shop: Yes
Payment: Cash and check
Tee Times: No
Fee 9 Holes: Weekday: $15.00
Fee 18 Holes: Weekday: $30.00
Twilight Rates: Leagues
Cart Rental: $26.25/18, $13.13/9
Lessons: $30.00/30 min. **Schools:** No
Clinics: Yes **Day Camps:** Yes
Other: Full restaurant / Clubhouse / Bar-lounge / Snack Bar / Showers

Weekend: $30.00
Weekend: $30.00
All Day Play: Yes
Discounts: Senior & Junior- $25.00 fee
Junior Golf: Yes **Membership:** Yes
Driving Range: $3.50/lg

Tees	Holes	Yards	Par	USGA	Slope
BACK	18	6450	72	70.1	117
MIDDLE	18	6210	72	68.6	114
FRONT	18	5444	73	70.6	119

COUPON

Sig. Hole: #9, 362 yd. par 4 with elevated tee, brook in front of green, bunkers to the side. "A very pretty hole," James "Bucky" O'Brien, Director of Golf.

	1	2	3	4	5	6	7	8	9
PAR	4	3	4	4	3	5	4	5	4
YARDS	380	144	421	380	130	565	283	455	362
HDCP	11	15	1	7	17	3	13	9	5
	10	11	12	13	14	15	16	17	18
PAR	4	3	5	4	5	3	4	4	4
YARDS	357	185	470	280	570	145	315	387	320
HDCP	8	10	6	16	2	12	18	4	14

Directions: Route 91, take Exit 27. Turn right at Route 5 and 10. Take right at first set of lights onto Silver St.. Country Club Rd. is fourth street on right.

Country Club of Wilbraham

Wilbraham, MA (413) 596-8887

Club Pro: Todd Scarafoni, PGA
Pro Shop: Full inventory
Payment: Cash, Credit Card
Tee Times: No
Fee 9 Holes: Weekday: $35.00
Fee 18 Holes: Weekday: $35.00
Twilight Rates: Yes, after 6:30 pm
Cart Rental: $12.00, pull-no charge
Lessons: $45.00/half hour **Schools:** No
Clinics: No **Day Camps:** No
Other: Clubhouse / Practice green

Tees	Holes	Yards	Par	USGA	Slope
BACK	18	6380	72	71.2	130
MIDDLE	18	5967	72	68.9	125
FRONT	18	5168	72	65.4	115

Weekend: $40.00, $20 after 6:30
Weekend: $40.00
All Day Play: Yes
Discounts: None
Junior Golf: For residents **Membership:** Yes
Driving Range: Yes

**W
MA**

Semi-private. Residents of Wilbraham after 3:00, or as a guest with a member.

	1	2	3	4	5	6	7	8	9
PAR	4	3	4	4	3	5	4	5	4
YARDS	375	162	364	416	142	481	258	528	359
HDCP	14	12	10	2	16	8	18	4	6
	10	**11**	**12**	**13**	**14**	**15**	**16**	**17**	**18**
PAR	3	5	4	4	3	4	4	4	5
YARDS	136	445	383	304	167	327	295	350	475
HDCP	11	3	7	15	13	9	17	1	5

Directions: Take I-90 (MA. Trpke) West to Exit 7, Belchertown/Ludlow. Turn left at end of ramp. Follow signs to Wilbraham. Call for details.

Cranwell Resort, Spa and GC ✪✪✪

Lenox, MA (413) 637-2563
www.cranwell.com

Club Pro: David Strawn
Pro Shop: Full inventory
Payment: Visa, MC, Amex,Disc.
Tee Times: 1 week adv.
Fee 9 Holes: Weekday: N/A
Fee 18 Holes: Weekday: $84 w/cart summer
Twilight Rates: Yes, after 4 pm
Cart Rental: Included - $16.00pp
Lessons: $55/30 min. **Schools:** Yes
Clinics: Women/Beg **Day Camps:** No
Other: Hotel / Lockers / Showers / Snack bar / Restaurant / Bar-lounge/Major Golf School

Tees	Holes	Yards	Par	USGA	Slope
BACK	18	6346	70	70	123
MIDDLE	18	6169	70	69.4	120
FRONT	18	5602	72	70.2	121

Weekend: N/A
Weekend: $99 w/cart summer
All Day Play: No
Discounts: None
Junior Golf: No **Membership:** Yes
Driving Range: $7.00/bucket

COUPON

Scottish style course with heavy rough and panoramic mountain views. 9 hole non-twilight play offered in spring and fall only. Working on sandtraps and cart path. Extensive golf school.

	1	2	3	4	5	6	7	8	9
PAR	4	5	3	4	3	4	4	4	4
YARDS	384	463	144	373	218	370	360	340	405
HDCP	9	11	17	13	3	7	5	15	1
	10	**11**	**12**	**13**	**14**	**15**	**16**	**17**	**18**
PAR	4	4	3	4	4	5	3	4	4
YARDS	263	390	195	426	315	495	148	315	375
HDCP	10	4	6	2	12	8	14	16	18

Directions: Take Mass Pike to Exit 2, take Route 20 West. Course is 10 minutes up.

4✪ =Excellent **3✪** =Very Good **2✪** =Good

Crumpin-Fox Club ✪✪✪✪

Bernardston, MA (413) 648-9101
www.sandri.com

Club Pro: Michael Zaranek
Pro Shop: Full inventory
Payment: Visa, MC, Amex, Disc
Tee Times: 3 days adv.
Fee 9 Holes: Weekday: $32.00
Fee 18 Holes: Weekday: $64.00
Twilight Rates: No
Cart Rental: $16.00/18 $10.00/9
Lessons: $35/half hour **Schools:** Jr.& Sr.
Clinics: Yes **Day Camps:** Yes

Tees	Holes	Yards	Par	USGA	Slope
BACK	18	7007	72	73.8	141
MIDDLE	18	6508	72	71.3	136
FRONT	18	5432	72	71.5	131

Weekend: $35.00
Weekend: $69.00
All Day Play: No
Discounts: Junior
Junior Golf: Yes **Membership:** Yes
Driving Range: $5.00/Bag

COUPON

Other: Restaurant / Clubhouse / Hotel / Bar-lounge / Lockers / Snack Bar / Showers / Tennis / Pond

A *Golf Magazine* top 100 US course. **Players Comments:** " Variety of holes." "You really need to think before you hit." "Beautiful landscape" "Great staff and atmosphere." "Emmaculate." 2004 rates may change.

	1	2	3	4	5	6	7	8	9
PAR	4	4	3	4	5	4	4	5	3
YARDS	386	338	165	345	501	402	353	568	177
HDCP	5	13	15	11	7	3	9	1	17
	10	**11**	**12**	**13**	**14**	**15**	**16**	**17**	**18**
PAR	4	3	4	4	5	3	4	5	4
YARDS	394	150	374	370	506	172	410	508	389
HDCP	4	18	12	10	14	16	2	6	8

Directions: Take I-91 to Exit 28A (between Brattleboro, VT and Greenfield, MA). Follow Route 10 North for 1 mile, take left on Parmenter Road and follow signs to club.

Dunroamin CC

Gilbertville, MA (413) 477-0004

Club Pro:
Pro Shop: Full inventory
Payment: Cash or credit card
Tee Times: No
Fee 9 Holes: Weekday: $14.00
Fee 18 Holes: Weekday: $26.00
Twilight Rates: No
Cart Rental: $12.00/18; $6.00/9, per person
Lessons: Yes **Schools:** No
Clinics: N/R **Day Camps:** Yes

Tees	Holes	Yards	Par	USGA	Slope
BACK	N/A				
MIDDLE	9	5914	70	68.6	117
FRONT	9	4802	70	66.8	106

Weekend: $14.00
Weekend: $26.00
All Day Play: No
Discounts: None
Junior Golf: Yes **Membership:** Yes
Driving Range: $2.50/bucket

Other: Clubhouse / Lockers / Showers / Snack bar / Bar-lounge

The course is closed to the public on Sundays 9:00 am - 2:00 pm.

	1	2	3	4	5	6	7	8	9
PAR	3	4	4	5	4	4	4	3	4
YARDS	204	331	393	493	322	310	367	166	277
HDCP	10	12	2	6	8	14	4	18	16
	10	**11**	**12**	**13**	**14**	**15**	**16**	**17**	**18**
PAR	3	4	4	5	4	4	4	3	4
YARDS	228	349	405	549	336	318	385	182	299
HDCP	9	11	1	5	7	13	3	17	15

Directions: Take Mass Pike to Exit 8, follow Route 32 for 15 miles into Gilbertville, course is on right.

East Mountain CC

Westfield, MA (413) 568-1539
www.eastmountaincc.com

Club Pro: Ted Perez Jr., PGA
Pro Shop: Full inventory
Payment: Visa, MC, Amex, cash
Tee Times: 1 week adv.

Tees	Holes	Yards	Par	USGA	Slope
BACK	18	6118	71	67.5	107
MIDDLE	18	5819	71	66.4	105
FRONT	18	4564	71	61.7	96

Fee 9 Holes: Weekday: $14.50
Fee 18 Holes: Weekday: $21.00
Twilight Rates: Yes, after 5 pm
Cart Rental: $22.00/18 $13.00/9
Lessons: Yes **Schools:** No
Clinics: No **Day Camps:** No
Other: Clubhouse / Snack bar / Lounge

Weekend: $15.00
Weekend: $24.00
All Day Play: Yes
Discounts: Senior & Junior: $14 Wkdys
Junior Golf: Yes **Membership:** Associate
Driving Range: Yes

Sig. Hole: #18 has elevated tees. Play conservative around the pond or gamble over. Fairway slopes toward water, short but tricky.

	1	2	3	4	5	6	7	8	9
PAR	4	4	3	5	4	4	4	4	3
YARDS	305	361	149	495	372	426	319	352	175
HDCP	16	8	18	4	10	2	14	12	6
	10	**11**	**12**	**13**	**14**	**15**	**16**	**17**	**18**
PAR	3	5	5	3	4	5	4	3	4
YARDS	159	492	481	168	394	536	429	174	331
HDCP	15	5	9	13	7	3	1	17	11

Directions: Take Mass Pike to Exit 3, follow Route 202 N to East Mountain Road. Course is 1.5 miles down on right.

Edge Hill GC

Ashfield, MA (413) 625-6018

Club Pro:
Pro Shop: Limited inventory
Payment: Personal checks, Cash
Tee Times: N/A

Tees	Holes	Yards	Par	USGA	Slope
BACK	9	3250	36	69.2	123
MIDDLE	9	3110	36	67.6	119
FRONT	9	2990	36	66.0	115

Fee 9 Holes: Weekday: $12.00
Fee 18 Holes: Weekday: $17.00
Twilight Rates: N/R
Cart Rental: $20.00/18 $10.00/9
Lessons: $30.00/45 min. **Schools:** No
Clinics: No **Day Camps:** No
Other: Full restaurant / Clubhouse / Bar- Lounge

Weekend: $14.00
Weekend: $20.00
All Day Play: N/R
Discounts: None
Junior Golf: No **Membership:** Yes
Driving Range: $4.00/lg. $2.50/sm.

COUPON

Mountain course designed by Mark Graves. Very challenging course demands position. Open May-November.

	1	2	3	4	5	6	7	8	9
PAR	5	4	3	4	4	3	5	4	4
YARDS	520	300	150	320	370	160	520	370	400
HDCP	6	18	10	8	12	14	1	16	4
	10	**11**	**12**	**13**	**14**	**15**	**16**	**17**	**18**
PAR									
YARDS									
HDCP									

Directions: Take Route 116 from South Deerfield of I-91 to Conway-Ashfield. Turn right in Ashfield at Baptist Corner Rd. Follow signs.

4✪ =Excellent **3✪** =Very Good **2✪** =Good

Edgewood Golf Club

Southwick, MA (413) 569-6826

Club Pro: Mike Grigley, PGA
Pro Shop: Full inventory
Payment: Cash, check, charge
Tee Times: 4 days adv.
Fee 9 Holes: Weekday: $12.00
Fee 18 Holes: Weekday: $18.50
Twilight Rates: No
Cart Rental: $13.00pp/18 $7.50pp/9
Lessons: $30.00/half hour **Schools:** No
Clinics: Women **Day Camps:** No

Tees	Holes	Yards	Par	USGA	Slope
BACK	18	6510	71	69.1	115
MIDDLE	18	6050	71	67.6	113
FRONT	18	5580	71	71.8	109

Weekend: $15.00
Weekend: $23.00
All Day Play: No
Discounts: Senior & Junior
Junior Golf: Yes, clinics **Membership:** Yes
Driving Range: $5.00/lg. $2.50/sm.
Other: Clubhouse / Showers / Snack bar / Restaurant / Bar-lounge

Sig. Hole: #12 is a dogleg right par 4. Long iron off the tee hitting down hill to a green sloping away. Three protective grass hills are in front of green. Trees line both sides.

	1	2	3	4	5	6	7	8	9
PAR	5	4	4	5	4	3	4	3	4
YARDS	450	415	315	523	385	170	390	205	340
HDCP	10	4	16	2	6	18	12	14	8
	10	11	12	13	14	15	16	17	18
PAR	4	3	4	3	5	5	4	3	4
YARDS	295	160	375	150	545	480	355	150	340
HDCP	11	15	5	17	1	3	9	13	7

Directions: Take Mass Pike to Springfield. From Springfield take Route 57 to Southwick. Route 57 goes through Routes 10 and 202. Go through center of town. Take a left on Depot. Right onto Sheep Pasture Road, follow it around to the right.

Egremont Country Club

Great Barrington, MA (413) 528-4222
www.egremontcountryclub.com

Club Pro: Marc Levesque, PGA
Pro Shop: Full inventory
Payment: Visa, MC or cash
Tee Times: 7 days adv.
Fee 9 Holes: Weekday: $15.00
Fee 18 Holes: Weekday: $25.00
Twilight Rates: Yes, after 4 pm
Cart Rental: $26.00/18
Lessons: $35/45 min. **Schools:** No
Clinics: Yes **Day Camps:** No

Tees	Holes	Yards	Par	USGA	Slope
BACK	18	6036	71	68.7	122
MIDDLE	18	5771	71	67.5	120
FRONT	18	4894	71	68.1	113

Weekend: N/A
Weekend: $40.00
All Day Play: No
Discounts: Senior, Thurs.
Junior Golf: Yes **Membership:** Yes
Driving Range: $6.00/lg.
Other: Clubhouse / Lockers / Showers / Snack bar / Restaurant / Bar-lounge

Sig. Hole: #18 -Double tiered elevated tee area, framed by large maples. Feel of #18th hole 'chute' at Augusta. Green guarded by 2 bunkers. Accurate approach shot a must.

	1	2	3	4	5	6	7	8	9
PAR	4	4	3	4	5	3	4	4	3
YARDS	335	245	175	389	497	140	320	325	151
HDCP	7	15	5	3	1	17	11	9	13
	10	11	12	13	14	15	16	17	18
PAR	4	4	5	4	3	4	4	4	4
YARDS	338	275	532	538	152	320	325	353	361
HDCP	8	18	6	2	14	12	16	10	4

Directions: Located on Route 23 between Route 22 in NY and Route 7 in MA and CT. 3 miles west of Great Barrington, MA.

Ellinwood CC

Athol, MA (978) 249-7460
www.ellinwoodcc.com

Club Pro: Eric Sandstrum, PGA
Pro Shop: Full inventory
Payment: Visa, MC, Cash
Tee Times: Yes
Fee 9 Holes: Weekday: $14.00
Fee 18 Holes: Weekday: $24.00
Twilight Rates: Yes, after 5 pm
Cart Rental: $12.50pp
Lessons: Yes **Schools:** No
Clinics: No **Day Camps:** No
Other: Clubhouse / Snack bar / Bar-lounge / Showers / Banquet Hall

Tees	Holes	Yards	Par	USGA	Slope
BACK	18	6207	71	70.1	122
MIDDLE	18	5737	71	67.8	117
FRONT	18	5047	72	68.7	111

Weekend: $16.00
Weekend: $29.00
All Day Play: Yes, pay for carts
Discounts: Junior
Junior Golf: Yes **Membership:** Yes
Driving Range: No

COUPON

Course noted for: immaculate fast greens. No back and forth holes. Every hole offers a different challenge. 9 holes designed by Donald Ross in 1929. 9 holes designed by Geoff Cornish in 1968.

	1	2	3	4	5	6	7	8	9
PAR	4	4	3	5	5	3	4	3	4
YARDS	390	315	155	465	410	157	405	156	355
HDCP	3	11	15	5	9	13	1	17	7
	10	11	12	13	14	15	16	17	18
PAR	3	4	3	5	3	4	5	4	5
YARDS	210	282	133	445	118	356	470	425	490
HDCP	6	14	16	12	18	4	10	2	8

Directions: Take Route 2 to Exit 17. Right off exit 1/2 mile on right to Woodlawn Road. Go all the way to the end, club house is on the right.

Forest Park CC

Adams, MA (413) 743-3311

Club Pro: No
Pro Shop: Yes
Payment: Cash/check only
Tee Times: No
Fee 9 Holes: Weekday: $11.00
Fee 18 Holes: Weekday: $16.00
Twilight Rates: No
Cart Rental: $21.00/18 $10.50/9
Lessons: No **Schools:** No
Clinics: No **Day Camps:** No
Other: Clubhouse / Lockers / Showers / Snack bar / Bar-lounge/ Banquet Hall

Tees	Holes	Yards	Par	USGA	Slope
BACK	N/A				
MIDDLE	9	5183	68	63.8	110
FRONT	9	4646	68	63.8	110

Weekend: $11.00
Weekend: $16.00
All Day Play: No
Discounts: None
Junior Golf: Yes **Membership:** Yes
Driving Range: No

COUPON

Sig. Hole: #5 is a 157 yard par 3: all carry, well bunkered, small sloping green. Tricky to birdie. On going clubhouse renovations.

	1	2	3	4	5	6	7	8	9
PAR	4	4	3	4	3	4	4	4	4
YARDS	270	341	157	327	147	333	314	389	277
HDCP	15	1	17	7	9	11	3	5	13
	10	11	12	13	14	15	16	17	18
PAR	4	4	3	4	3	4	4	4	4
YARDS	280	358	162	327	147	349	330	389	286
HDCP	16	2	18	8	10	12	4	6	14

Directions: Take Mass Pike to Lee exit. Take Route 8 to Adams. Take left at statue on Park Street to Maple Street. Take first left on to Forest Park Avenue.

4❂ =Excellent **3❂** =Very Good **2❂** =Good

Franconia Muni. GC

Springfield, MA (413) 734-9334

Club Pro: Daniel DiRico, PGA
Pro Shop: Full inventory
Payment: Cash only
Tee Times: Weekends
Fee 9 Holes: Weekday: No
Fee 18 Holes: Weekday: $18.00
Twilight Rates: Yes, after 3 pm
Cart Rental: $22.00/18, $11.00/9
Lessons: $24.00/1/2 hour **Schools:** No
Clinics: Ladies/Juniors **Day Camps:** No
Other: Clubhouse / Snack bar / Restaurant / Bar-lounge

Tees	Holes	Yards	Par	USGA	Slope
BACK	18	6153	71	68.7	118
MIDDLE	18	5825	71	67.1	115
FRONT	18	5348	71	67.1	115

Weekend: No
Weekend: $20.00
All Day Play: Yes
Discounts: Sr & Jr Weekdays
Junior Golf: Yes **Membership:** Yes
Driving Range: No

Sig. Hole: #12 is a challenging par 5. A 220 yard second shot over 2 streams if you want to get to green.

	1	2	3	4	5	6	7	8	9
PAR	4	4	4	5	3	4	4	3	4
YARDS	314	307	349	557	124	412	360	162	387
HDCP	15	11	9	1	17	3	5	13	7

	10	11	12	13	14	15	16	17	18
PAR	5	4	5	4	3	4	4	3	4
YARDS	491	307	468	368	132	350	282	173	282
HDCP	6	10	4	2	18	8	12	14	16

Directions: Take Mass Pike to Route 291 West to 91 South. Take Longmeadow Exit. At 2nd light take a left onto Converge Street. At end take left onto Dwight Road. Follow to course.

GEAA Golf Club

Pittsfield, MA (413) 443-5746

Club Pro: Jay Abir, PGA
Pro Shop: Full inventory
Payment: Cash /checks only
Tee Times: Yes Weekends
Fee 9 Holes: Weekday: $11.00
Fee 18 Holes: Weekday: $18.00
Twilight Rates: No
Cart Rental: $18.00/18 $10.00/9
Lessons: Yes **Schools:** No
Clinics: Yes **Day Camps:** No
Other: Restaurant / Club House / Snack bar / Bar-lounge / Lockers / Showers

Tees	Holes	Yards	Par	USGA	Slope
BACK	9	6360	72	70.0	111
MIDDLE	9	6205	72	69.6	117
FRONT	9	5274	72	69.4	110

Weekend: $14.00
Weekend: $20.00
All Day Play: Yes
Discounts: Senior
Junior Golf: Yes **Membership:** Yes
Driving Range: For members

Gently rolling hills and windy all year round. Tree lined fairways with beautiful view of Mt. Greylock.

	1	2	3	4	5	6	7	8	9
PAR	4	3	4	3	4	4	4	5	5
YARDS	332	155	391	179	379	362	276	456	549
HDCP	15	17	1	11	5	7	13	9	3

	10	11	12	13	14	15	16	17	18
PAR	4	3	4	3	4	4	4	5	5
YARDS	332	155	391	179	379	362	276	456	549
HDCP	16	18	2	12	6	8	14	10	4

Directions: Take Mass Pike to Lee Exit, follow Route 7N through Lee, Lenox, 1/2 mile past Reed Middle School is Crane Street, take right to the course.

Greenock Country Club ✪✪✪ 21 ▶

W. Park St., Lee, MA (413) 243-3323

Club Pro: Micheal Bechard, PGA
Pro Shop: Full inventory
Payment: Visa, MC,Cash, Check
Tee Times: Sat. and Sun., Call
Fee 9 Holes: Weekday: $20.00
Fee 18 Holes: Weekday: $28.00
Twilight Rates: After 5 pm wkdys
Cart Rental: $25.00/18 $13.00/9
Lessons: $25/lesson **Schools:** No
Clinics: No **Day Camps:** No
Other: Clubhouse / Lockers / Showers / Snack bar / Restaurant / Bar-lounge

Tees	Holes	Yards	Par	USGA	Slope
BACK	9	6140	74	68.9	120
MIDDLE	9	5898	74	68.9	120
FRONT	9	5686	74	72.2	123

Weekend: $24.00
Weekend: $42.00
All Day Play: No
Discounts: None
Junior Golf: Yes **Membership:** No
Driving Range: No

W
MA

Small postage stamp greens. Ratings are for 18 holes. Donald Ross design.

	1	2	3	4	5	6	7	8	9
PAR	4	3	5	4	5	5	3	4	4
YARDS	330	158	391	300	423	453	168	360	364
HDCP	12	16	2	14	4	10	18	6	8
	10	**11**	**12**	**13**	**14**	**15**	**16**	**17**	**18**
PAR	4	3	5	4	5	5	3	4	4
YARDS	345	168	408	307	441	465	184	372	390
HDCP	11	15	1	13	3	9	17	5	7

Directions: Exit 2 on Mass. Pike. Take right on Housatonic Street to the Center of Lee. Come to the stop sign next to town park. Take West Park Street up the hill over the RR tracks. Course on right.

Hampden Country Club ✪✪ 22 ▶

Hampden, MA (413) 566-8010
www.hampdencountryclub.com

Club Pro: Bill Tragakis, PGA
Pro Shop: Full inventory
Payment: Visa, MC, Amex, Cash
Tee Times: 7 days adv.
Fee 9 Holes: Weekday: $16.00
Fee 18 Holes: Weekday: $23.00
Twilight Rates: Yes, after 3 pm
Cart Rental: $12pp
Lessons: Yes **Schools:** No
Clinics: Yes **Day Camps:** N/R
Other: Clubhouse / Bar-Lounge / Snack Bar / Lockers / Showers / Banquet Hall

Tees	Holes	Yards	Par	USGA	Slope
BACK	18	6833	72	72.5	129
MIDDLE	18	6349	72	70.1	126
FRONT	18	5283	72	72.3	113

Weekend: N/A
Weekend: $36, $22 after 3pm
All Day Play: replay/cart fee
Discounts: Junior
Junior Golf: Yes **Membership:** No
Driving Range: $6.00/large

Moderately hilly; challenging; water comes into play on seven holes. Immaculate condition.

	1	2	3	4	5	6	7	8	9
PAR	4	5	3	4	4	4	4	5	3
YARDS	323	533	201	359	364	374	368	517	150
HDCP	7	1	17	5	13	9	11	3	15
	10	**11**	**12**	**13**	**14**	**15**	**16**	**17**	**18**
PAR	4	5	3	4	5	3	4	4	4
YARDS	362	555	185	350	529	163	319	347	350
HDCP	16	2	14	6	4	18	12	10	8

Directions: I-91, Exit 1 (Longmeadow.) Second set of lights, left onto Converse Street. Follow to end, take right on Dwight Road, then immediate left at intersection onto Maple Street. 2 miles to 83 South, turn right, 1 mile. Left onto Hampden Rd. 5 miles to club on right.

4✪ =Excellent **3✪** =Very Good **2✪** =Good

Hickory Ridge CC   ✪✪✪   ▶ 23

S. Amherst, MA (413) 253-9320
www.hickoryridgecc.com

Club Pro: Rick Fleury, PGA
Pro Shop: Full inventory
Payment: Cash, Visa, Amex ,MC
Tee Times: 3 day adv.

Tees	Holes	Yards	Par	USGA	Slope
BACK	18	6794	72	72.5	129
MIDDLE	18	6427	72	71.1	128
FRONT	18	5340	74	70.4	117

Fee 9 Holes: Weekday: $27.50
Fee 18 Holes: Weekday: $55.00 inc. cart
Twilight Rates: No
Cart Rental: $25.00/18 $13.00/9
Lessons: $30.00/30 min. **Schools:** No
Clinics: No **Day Camps:** No
Weekend: $37.50
Weekend: $65.00 inc. cart
All Day Play: No
Discounts: Junior
Junior Golf: Yes **Membership:** Wait list
Driving Range: $4.00/lg. $3.00/sm.
Other: Clubhouse / Lockers / Showers / Snack bar / Restaurant / Bar-lounge

Improvements include enhanced practice facility. Last two holes rated among the top 10 in Massachusetts. Open April - October.

	1	2	3	4	5	6	7	8	9
PAR	5	4	4	4	3	5	4	3	4
YARDS	500	375	325	380	201	510	345	174	435
HDCP	5	11	13	7	15	15	3	17	1

	10	11	12	13	14	15	16	17	18
PAR	4	5	4	4	4	3	5	3	4
YARDS	365	451	410	340	352	144	481	183	444
HDCP	8	14	4	10	12	18	6	16	2

Directions: Take Route 9 East from I-91 in Northampton to Route 116 in Amherst.. Go south on Route 116 for 2.5 miles to West Pomeroy Lane. Right onto West Pomeroy for 1/2 mile.

Holyoke Country Club   ▶ 24

Holyoke, MA (413) 534-1933

Club Pro: Via Whightman, PGA
Pro Shop: Full inventory
Payment: Visa, MC
Tee Times: S/S Members

Tees	Holes	Yards	Par	USGA	Slope
BACK					
MIDDLE	9	6299	72	71	118
FRONT	9	5446	75	N/A	N/A

Fee 9 Holes: Weekday: $10.00
Fee 18 Holes: Weekday: $18.00
Twilight Rates: No
Cart Rental: $16pp/18 $8pp/9
Lessons: $30.00/45minutes **Schools:** Yes
Clinics: Ladies/Juniors **Day Camps:** N/R
Weekend: $23.00
Weekend: $23.00
All Day Play: Yes
Discounts: Junior $8/9 holes
Junior Golf: Yes **Membership:** No
Driving Range: No
Other: Clubhouse / Lockers / Showers / Snack bar / Restaurant / Bar-lounge

Second hole is difficult hole with a quick green. Hitting up to 2 layers. If on top and flag is on bottom, can bogey or double bogey.

	1	2	3	4	5	6	7	8	9
PAR	4	4	4	4	5	4	4	3	4
YARDS	343	356	409	292	472	407	323	121	347
HDCP	10	2	4	16	8	6	14	18	12

	10	11	12	13	14	15	16	17	18
PAR	4	4	4	4	5	4	4	3	4
YARDS	353	370	425	302	488	411	343	150	387
HDCP	9	1	3	15	7	5	13	17	11

Directions: From Springfield: I-91 North, Exit 17A to traffic light, turn left onto Route 5, approximately 2 1/2 miles. At the Delaney Restaurant go through entrance, past restaurant 50 yards, then turn left to country club.

Ledges Golf Club

South Hadley, MA (413) 532-2307
www.ledgesgc.com

Club Pro: Wayne Leal, PGA
Pro Shop: Full inventory
Payment: Visa, MC
Tee Times: 7 days adv.

Tees	Holes	Yards	Par	USGA	Slope
BACK	18	6507	72	72.2	133
MIDDLE	18	6110	72	70.9	129
FRONT	18	5001	72	69.5	125

Fee 9 Holes: Weekday: $14.00   **Weekend:** $18.00
Fee 18 Holes: Weekday: $22.00   **Weekend:** $35.00
Twilight Rates: Yes, after 3 pm   **All Day Play:** Seasonal
Cart Rental: $12pp/18 $8pp/9   **Discounts:** Senior & Junior
Lessons: Yes, rates TBD **Schools:** TBD   **Junior Golf:** Yes **Membership:** Yes
Clinics: TBD **Day Camps:**   **Driving Range:** NO
Other: Snack Bar / Bar

Rolling, tree-lined fairways with a few links-style holes. Resident rates. "Inexpensive. Sprawling layout with with a wide variety of difficulty. Several very short par 4"s that should produce birdies." R.W.

	1	2	3	4	5	6	7	8	9
PAR	5	4	3	4	3	4	4	4	5
YARDS	564	405	215	397	176	270	273	372	500
HDCP	7	1	5	3	13	17	15	11	9

	10	11	12	13	14	15	16	17	18
PAR	4	4	3	4	5	4	3	4	5
YARDS	386	424	96	276	456	300	123	349	528
HDCP	6	2	18	12	8	4	16	10	4

Directions: I-91 Exit 16 onto Route 202. Go through Holyoke about 5 miles. Take rotary and exit onto West Summit Rd. Go right and left on Lathrop Rd. At blinking light, Lathrop becomes Alvord. Left turn onto Mulligan. Go straight and follow signs to club on Mulligan.

Mill Valley Links

Belchertown, MA (413) 323-4079
www.millvalleygolflinks.com

Tees	Holes	Yards	Par	USGA	Slope
BACK					
MIDDLE	18	6119	72	70.5	117
FRONT	18	5279	72	69.5	110

Club Pro: None
Pro Shop: Yes
Payment: Cash, Credit Cards
Tee Times: Weekends

Fee 9 Holes: Weekday: $11.00   **Weekend:** $13.00
Fee 18 Holes: Weekday: $16.00   **Weekend:** $18.00
Twilight Rates: No   **All Day Play:** No
Cart Rental: $20.00/18 $10.00/9   **Discounts:** Senior & Junior
Lessons: No **Schools:** No   **Junior Golf:** Yes **Membership:** Yes
Clinics: No **Day Camps:** No   **Driving Range:** No
Other: Restaurant / Bar-lounge / Snack Bar / Keno / Lottery

Nine hole course has two sets of tees. Excellent greens. Placement golf. Expanding to 18 in 2005.

	1	2	3	4	5	6	7	8	9
PAR	3	4	5	5	4	4	3	4	4
YARDS	160	250	482	520	320	305	190	360	295
HDCP	17	15	5	1	13	11	9	7	3

	10	11	12	13	14	15	16	17	18
PAR	3	4	5	5	4	4	3	4	4
YARDS	212	258	512	525	360	315	240	400	415
HDCP	8	18	6	2	16	14	12	10	4

Directions: Take Mass Pike to Exit 7. Follow Route 21 (becomes Route 202) to Belchertown. Go right onto Route 181. Course is about 2 miles on right.

4✪ =Excellent 3✪ =Very Good 2✪ = Good

North Adams CC

Clarksburg, MA (413)-663-7887
nacc@adelphia.net

Club Pro: Jack Tosone, PGA
Pro Shop: Full inventory
Payment: Visa, MC, Amex
Tee Times: Weekends & Holidays
Fee 9 Holes: Weekday: $12.00
Fee 18 Holes: Weekday: $22.00
Twilight Rates: No
Cart Rental: $10pp/18 $7pp/9
Lessons: Yes **Schools:** No
Clinics: Yes **Day Camps:** No
Other: Snack bar / Bar-lounge

Tees	Holes	Yards	Par	USGA	Slope
BACK	9	2899	36	67.0	119
MIDDLE	9	2782	36	67.0	119
FRONT	9	2503	36	68.4	122

Weekend: $12.00
Weekend: $22.00
All Day Play: No
Discounts: None
Junior Golf: Yes **Membership:** Yes
Driving Range: No

COUPON

Tradition course in the midst of the Berkshires features small, fast greens requiring a good short game. Well conditioned course with a great value for the price.

	1	2	3	4	5	6	7	8	9
PAR	4	3	4	4	5	4	4	3	5
YARDS	339	143	364	257	484	360	273	143	419
HDCP	10	12	8	16	2	4	14	18	6
	10	11	12	13	14	15	16	17	18
PAR									
YARDS									
HDCP									

Directions: Take Route 2 to Route 8; go North 2 miles. Course is on left side.

Northampton CC

Leeds, MA (413) 586-1898
www.hampgolf.com

Club Pro: Tim Walko
Pro Shop: Full inventory
Payment: Cash or credit card
Tee Times: Yes
Fee 9 Holes: Weekday: $12.00
Fee 18 Holes: Weekday: $18.00
Twilight Rates: No
Cart Rental: $26/18, $15/9: for 2
Lessons: $35.00 for 30 min **Schools:** Jr.Yes
Clinics: Yes **Day Camps:** No
Other: Bar-Lounge

Tees	Holes	Yards	Par	USGA	Slope
BACK	9	3041	35	69.0	119
MIDDLE	9	2948	35	68.0	116
FRONT	9	2502	36	67.8	112

Weekend: $14.00
Weekend: $20.00
All Day Play: No
Discounts: None
Junior Golf: Yes **Membership:** Yes
Driving Range: No

COUPON

Short, but tricky. Small greens prove challenging for most players. Hit to centers of greens for a successful day. Open all year .

	1	2	3	4	5	6	7	8	9
PAR	5	4	4	4	4	4	3	3	4
YARDS	503	343	374	339	327	256	222	162	422
HDCP	13	9	7	5	3	15	11	17	1
	10	11	12	13	14	15	16	17	18
PAR									
YARDS									
HDCP									

Directions: From I 90, take 2nd Northampton Exit (Northampton/Amherst). Go through 4 sets of lights to crossing of Route 9. Take right on Route 9, 2 miles turn left on Florence St., 1st left on Arch St. follow until fork, bear left, go over bridge.

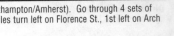

Northfield CC

East Northfield, MA (413) 498-2432

Club Pro: Bill Tenney
Pro Shop: Full inventory
Payment: Visa, MC
Tee Times: No
Fee 9 Holes: Weekday: $12.00
Fee 18 Holes: Weekday: $24.00
Twilight Rates: No
Cart Rental: $24.00/18 $12.00/9
Lessons: No **Schools:** No
Clinics: Junior **Day Camps:** Yes
Other: Snack bar

Weekend: $15.00
Weekend: $30.00
All Day Play: No
Discounts: None
Junior Golf: Yes **Membership:** Yes
Driving Range: No

Tees	Holes	Yards	Par	USGA	Slope
BACK					
MIDDLE	9	5520	72	66.2	121
FRONT	9	4810	72	68.0	121

Sig. Hole: #6, 170 yards, par 3. Expansion of clubhouse in 1999. Very difficult to shoot the course rating. Open April - November.

	1	2	3	4	5	6	7	8	9
PAR	5	4	4	4	5	3	3	4	4
YARDS	430	300	370	260	450	170	130	270	380
HDCP	5	11	3	15	1	9	17	13	7
	10	**11**	**12**	**13**	**14**	**15**	**16**	**17**	**18**
PAR	5	4	4	4	5	3	3	4	4
YARDS	430	300	370	260	450	170	130	270	380
HDCP	6	12	4	16	2	10	18	14	8

Directions: Course is on Routes 10 and 63, one mile north of the center of town. Take Holton Street, turn right into parking lot.

Oak Ridge Golf Club

W. Gill Rd, Gill, MA (413) 863-9693

Club Pro: No
Pro Shop: Limited inventory
Payment: Visa, MC
Tee Times: No
Fee 9 Holes: Weekday: $12.00
Fee 18 Holes: Weekday: $22.00
Twilight Rates: No
Cart Rental: $22.00/18 $12.00/9
Lessons: No **Schools:** No
Clinics: N/R **Day Camps:** No
Other: Snack bar / Clubhouse / Bar-lounge / New deck for patio dining

Weekend: $14.00
Weekend: $25.00
All Day Play: No
Discounts: Senior & Junior
Junior Golf: No **Membership:** Yes
Driving Range: No

COUPON

Tees	Holes	Yards	Par	USGA	Slope
BACK	9	5904	72	68.7	117
MIDDLE	9	5813	72	68.7	117
FRONT	9	5190	72	70.0	117

Scenic rolling hills, well groomed. Special rates for seniors (60+) and weekdays prior to 11:00. Open March - November. New owners.

	1	2	3	4	5	6	7	8	9
PAR	4	4	5	4	4	4	4	4	3
YARDS	290	319	481	364	300	329	410	240	128
HDCP	13	11	9	5	3	7	1	17	15
	10	**11**	**12**	**13**	**14**	**15**	**16**	**17**	**18**
PAR	4	4	5	4	4	4	4	4	3
YARDS	315	340	487	374	308	335	414	246	133
HDCP	14	12	10	6	4	8	2	18	16

Directions: From I-91 North, take Exit 27 East and follow signs to golf course. From I-91 South, take Exit 27 and follow signs to golf course.

4★ =Excellent **3★** =Very Good **2★** =Good

Oak Ridge Golf Club

Feeding Hills, MA (413) 789-7307
www.oakridgegc.com

Club Pro: E. Nelson, J. Modzelesky
Pro Shop: Full inventory
Payment: Cash, MC, Visa, AMEX
Tee Times: 1 wk / wkdys: Wed/wknds

Tees	Holes	Yards	Par	USGA	Slope
BACK	18	6702	70	72.2	124
MIDDLE	18	6390	70	70.2	121
FRONT	18	5297	70	70.8	124

Fee 9 Holes: Weekday: $16.00
Fee 18 Holes: Weekday: $29.00
Twilight Rates: No
Cart Rental: $30.00/18
Lessons: $40.00/45 min **Schools:** No
Clinics: Yes **Day Camps:** No
Other: Clubhouse / Lockers / Showers / Bar-lounge / Snack Bar

Weekend: NA
Weekend: $36.00
All Day Play: No
Discounts: Senior wkdays
Junior Golf: Yes **Membership:** Yes
Driving Range: N/A

Sig. Hole: #16, 493 yd, par 5. Excellent condition, flowers throughout course make for a real New England beauty. Open Mar.1 - Dec1. Reduced rates after 2 on weekends.

	1	2	3	4	5	6	7	8	9
PAR	4	4	4	3	4	5	4	3	4
YARDS	379	379	395	191	378	570	385	151	387
HDCP	13	3	9	15	11	1	7	17	5
	10	11	12	13	14	15	16	17	18
PAR	4	3	5	3	4	4	5	3	4
YARDS	431	195	559	176	352	363	493	200	406
HDCP	8	16	2	18	12	10	4	14	6

Directions: Take Exit 3 Agawam/Southwick off I-91. Take Route 57 West to end. Take left then first left at Oak Ridge sign. Course 1/4 mi. on right.

Petersham CC

Petersham, MA (978) 724-3388

Club Pro: Don Cross, PGA
Pro Shop: Full inventory
Payment: Cash only
Tee Times: Weekends, 2 days adv.

Tees	Holes	Yards	Par	USGA	Slope
BACK	9	6007	70	68.9	116
MIDDLE	9	5486	70	66.4	114
FRONT	9	5032	72	69.1	114

Fee 9 Holes: Weekday: $10.00
Fee 18 Holes: Weekday: $20.00
Twilight Rates: No
Cart Rental: $13.65pp/18, $7.35pp/9
Lessons: $35/lesson **Schools:** No
Clinics: Junior **Day Camps:** No
Other: Clubhouse / Lockers / Showers / Snack bar / Bar-lounge

Weekend: $13.00
Weekend: $22.00
All Day Play: No
Discounts: Junior $5
Junior Golf: Yes **Membership:** Yes
Driving Range: No

Donald Ross design from 1922.

	1	2	3	4	5	6	7	8	9
PAR	4	3	4	4	5	4	4	3	4
YARDS	328	205	344	422	475	365	376	124	316
HDCP	15	7	5	3	6	11	1	17	13
	10	11	12	13	14	15	16	17	18
PAR	4	3	4	4	5	4	4	3	4
YARDS	343	220	368	432	489	380	385	131	343
HDCP	16	8	10	4	8	12	2	18	16

Directions: Take Route 2 to Petersham/Athol Exit 17, take right onto Route 32, follow 6 miles, course is on left.

Pine Grove Golf Club

Northampton, MA (413) 584-4570

Club Pro: Ray Millette
Pro Shop: Limited inventory
Payment: Cash only
Tee Times: Yes
Fee 9 Holes: Weekday: $12.00
Fee 18 Holes: Weekday: $18.00
Twilight Rates: No
Cart Rental: $20.00/18,$10.00/9
Lessons: Yes **Schools:** No
Clinics: No **Day Camps:** No
Other: Clubhouse / Snack bar / Bar-lounge

Tees	Holes	Yards	Par	USGA	Slope
BACK					
MIDDLE	18	6115	72	68.8	121
FRONT	18	4890	72	67.3	114

Weekend: $15.00
Weekend: $21.00
All Day Play: No
Discounts: Senior
Junior Golf: No **Membership:** N/A
Driving Range: No

COUPON

Open April 1 - December 1.

	1	2	3	4	5	6	7	8	9
PAR	4	5	5	3	4	3	4	4	4
YARDS	315	475	500	140	350	165	370	385	335
HDCP	16	8	10	14	3	7	4	2	13
	10	11	12	13	14	15	16	17	18
PAR	4	3	4	4	5	3	4	5	4
YARDS	375	125	370	330	470	140	360	600	310
HDCP	12	9	5	15	11	18	6	1	17

Directions: I-91 to Exit 18. Left off exit, Route 5N about 1.5 miles to light. Left onto Route 9W to next light. Straight through light, then bear left onto Route 66 for 3 miles, and bear left onto Wilson Road.

Pine Knoll Par 3

East Longmeadow, MA (413) 525-8320

Club Pro: Robert Lake, PGA
Pro Shop: No
Payment: Cash only
Tee Times: No
Fee 9 Holes: Weekday: $8.00
Fee 18 Holes: Weekday: $8.00
Twilight Rates: No
Cart Rental: $1.50 Pull carts
Lessons: Yes **Schools:** No
Clinics: No **Day Camps:** No
$5.50/med., $3.75/sm.
Other:

Tees	Holes	Yards	Par	USGA	Slope
BACK					
MIDDLE	18	1567	54		
FRONT					

Weekend: $9.00
Weekend: $9.00
All Day Play: No
Discounts: Senior & Junior Wkdays
Junior Golf: No **Membership:** No
Driving Range: $10/jumbo, $7/Lg.,

Easy Walker. Open March- November.

	1	2	3	4	5	6	7	8	9
PAR	3	3	3	3	3	3	3	3	3
YARDS	86	64	80	92	78	60	72	60	102
HDCP									
	10	11	12	13	14	15	16	17	18
PAR	3	3	3	3	3	3	3	3	3
YARDS	74	96	48	130	114	124	115	85	87
HDCP									

Directions: I-91 to Exit 4. Go to end of Summer Ave., bear right by McDonald's. 1 1/2 mi. to Porter Road. Left turn onto Porter to course entrance on left.

4 =Excellent **3** =Very Good **2** =Good

Pontoosuc Lake CC

35

Pittsfield, MA (413) 445-4217

Club Pro: Bob Dastoli
Pro Shop: Limited inventory
Payment: Cash / Check
Tee Times: Weekends & Holidays
Fee 9 Holes: Weekday: N/A
Fee 18 Holes: Weekday: $17.00 all day
Twilight Rates: Yes, after 5 pm
Cart Rental: $21.00/18
Lessons: Yes **Schools:** No
Clinics: No **Day Camps:** No
Other: Snack bar / Bar-lounge / Grinders

Tees	Holes	Yards	Par	USGA	Slope
BACK					
MIDDLE	18	6207	70	68.1	114
FRONT					

Weekend: N/A
Weekend: $20.00 all day
All Day Play: Yes
Discounts: Junior & Senior, Weekdays only.
Junior Golf: No **Membership:** Yes
Driving Range: No

COUPON

Sig. Hole: #9 links hole with large mounds and hills leading to a highly elevated green. Considered moderately difficult. No one under 14 unless accompanied by and adult. Prices subject to change.

	1	2	3	4	5	6	7	8	9
PAR	4	4	5	3	4	4	4	3	4
YARDS	367	295	597	137	372	284	404	223	361
HDCP	11	14	1	18	3	13	5	12	8
	10	11	12	13	14	15	16	17	18
PAR	4	3	4	4	3	5	3	4	5
YARDS	411	152	386	355	173	593	196	360	541
HDCP	2	17	4	10	15	6	16	9	7

Directions: Take Route 7 to Hancock Road (left); approx. 1 mile to Ridge Ave (right), turn left on Kirkwood Dr.

Shaker Farms CC

36

Shaker Rd, Westfield, MA (413) 562-2770
www.shakerfarms.com

Club Pro: Bob Mucha, PGA
Pro Shop: Full inventory
Payment: Visa, MC
Tee Times: Yes, preferably
Fee 9 Holes: Weekday: $12.00
Fee 18 Holes: Weekday: $25.00 with cart
Twilight Rates: No
Cart Rental: $14pp/18 $7pp/9
Lessons: Yes **Schools:** No
Clinics: Yes **Day Camps:** No
Other:

Tees	Holes	Yards	Par	USGA	Slope
BACK	18	6804	72	71.9	125
MIDDLE	18	6669	72	71.9	125
FRONT	18	5212	72	71.9	125

Weekend: $15.00
Weekend: $30.00 with cart
All Day Play: Yes
Discounts: Junior
Junior Golf: Yes **Membership:** Yes
Driving Range: Yes

Semi-private, members till noon weekends. Dress code.

	1	2	3	4	5	6	7	8	9
PAR	5	4	4	5	4	5	3	4	3
YARDS	540	375	365	495	420	614	225	420	175
HDCP	11	9	15	13	5	1	7	3	17
	10	11	12	13	14	15	16	17	18
PAR	4	4	3	4	3	4	4	5	4
YARDS	325	368	165	380	167	390	405	470	370
HDCP	8	12	18	10	16	4	2	6	14

Directions: Take I-90 (MA Pike) to Exit 3 Westfield. Follow Routes 10 and 202 South to Route 20. Stay on Route 20 E passing Westfield shops, Turn right on Route 187 at blinking light. Follow to course.

Skyline Country Club

Rt. 7, Lanesborough, MA (413) 445-5584
www.skyline-cc.com

Club Pro: Jim Mitus
Pro Shop: Yes
Payment: MC, Visa, cash
Tee Times: 1 week adv.

Tees	Holes	Yards	Par	USGA	Slope
BACK	18	6250	71	68.8	117
MIDDLE	18	6100	72	66.9	113
FRONT	18	4900	71	67.5	114

Fee 9 Holes: Weekday: $13.00
Fee 18 Holes: Weekday: $22.00
Twilight Rates: Yes, after 4 pm
Cart Rental: $12pp/18 $6.25pp/9
Lessons: $40.00/half hour **Schools:** No
Clinics: No **Day Camps:** No
Other: Snack bar / Bar-lounge

Weekend: $15.00
Weekend: $25.00
All Day Play: Yes
Discounts: None
Junior Golf: Yes **Membership:** Yes
Driving Range: Yes

COUPON

Sig. Hole: #14 is a downhill 310 yard hole that overlooks mountains. The course is somewhat hilly; considered moderately difficult.

	1	2	3	4	5	6	7	8	9
PAR	4	5	3	4	4	4	3	5	4
YARDS	369	487	127	331	363	390	196	540	379
HDCP	6	4	18	8	2	12	10	16	14

	10	11	12	13	14	15	16	17	18
PAR	4	3	5	4	4	3	5	4	4
YARDS	395	167	490	343	295	167	432	362	379
HDCP	3	13	1	5	17	11	9	15	7

Directions: Take Mass Pike to Exit 2 (Lee). Go north on Route 7. Course is approximately 20 miles on right.

Southampton CC

Southampton, MA (413) 527-9815

Club Pro: John Strycharz
Pro Shop: Limited inventory
Payment: Cash, Check
Tee Times: S/S 1 wk. adv.

Tees	Holes	Yards	Par	USGA	Slope
BACK	18	6585	72	69.0	114
MIDDLE	18	6135	72	69.0	114
FRONT	18	5125	71	67.0	113

Fee 9 Holes: Weekday: $10 after 2 pm
Fee 18 Holes: Weekday: $15., $8 after 5 pm
Twilight Rates: Yes, after 4 pm
Cart Rental: $20.00/18 $10.00/9
Lessons: No **Schools:** No
Clinics: No **Day Camps:** No
Other: Snack bar / Restaurant / Bar-lounge

Weekend: $14.00 after 2 pm
Weekend: $24.00, $14 after 5 pm
All Day Play: Yes, $15wkdy/$24/wknd
Discounts: None
Junior Golf: No **Membership:** Yes
Driving Range: No

Sig. Hole: #4, 165 yard par 3. This meticulously maintained course is moderately easy with large greens, rolling hills and panoramic views. Busy course on weekends.

	1	2	3	4	5	6	7	8	9
PAR	4	3	4	3	4	5	4	4	5
YARDS	325	165	380	165	310	455	400	390	460
HDCP	13	17	8	16	14	11	1	3	5

	10	11	12	13	14	15	16	17	18
PAR	3	5	5	3	4	4	4	4	4
YARDS	140	485	460	200	340	365	405	325	365
HDCP	18	4	6	15	10	7	2	12	9

Directions: Take Mass Pike to Westfield Exit; go north on Route 10. Course is 5 miles lon right

4✪ =Excellent 3✪ =Very Good 2✪ =Good

Southwick CC

Southwick, MA (413) 569-0136

Club Pro: No
Pro Shop: Full inventory
Payment: Cash, Credit Cards
Tee Times: 1 day adv.

Tees	Holes	Yards	Par	USGA	Slope
BACK					
MIDDLE	18	6100	71	64.8	102
FRONT	18	5570	71	64.7	103

Fee 9 Holes: Weekday: $13.00
Fee 18 Holes: Weekday: $17.00
Twilight Rates: After 6 pm
Cart Rental: $24.00/18 $14.00/9
Lessons: Yes **Schools:** No
Clinics: Yes **Day Camps:** No
Other: Snack bar / Restaurant / Lounge/ Weekday Specials

Weekend: $18.00
Weekend: $23.00
All Day Play: No
Discounts: Senior & Junior (M-F)
Junior Golf: Yes **Membership:** Yes
Driving Range: No

COUPON

The course is flat and wide open; considered an easy walker. Putting green available. New watering system.

	1	2	3	4	5	6	7	8	9
PAR	4	5	3	4	4	3	4	4	4
YARDS	410	525	175	400	430	120	325	300	355
HDCP	2	5	8	6	3	16	13	15	10

	10	11	12	13	14	15	16	17	18
PAR	5	4	4	4	3	4	4	4	4
YARDS	490	290	320	315	125	450	415	310	345
HDCP	7	18	12	14	17	1	4	11	8

Directions: Take Mass Pike I-90 Exit 3, Westfield; turn right onto Route 202 . Course is approximate 4 miles South of Westfield.

St. Anne Country Club

Feeding Hills, MA (413) 786-2088
www.stannecc.com

Club Pro: Douglas Goodrich
Pro Shop: Limited inventory
Payment: Most major
Tee Times: 1 week adv.

Tees	Holes	Yards	Par	USGA	Slope
BACK	18	6608	72	70.8	120
MIDDLE	18	5927	72	69.5	118
FRONT	18	5566	72	70.0	118

Fee 9 Holes: Weekday: $13.00
Fee 18 Holes: Weekday: $17.00
Twilight Rates: Yes, after 3 pm
Cart Rental: $26.00/18 $13.00/9
Lessons: Yes **Schools:** No
Clinics: No **Day Camps:** No
Other: Snack bar / Bar-lounge

Weekend: $17.00 after 12pm
Weekend: $22.00, $35.00 ride
All Day Play: Yes
Discounts: Senior
Junior Golf: No **Membership:** Limited
Driving Range: No

Improvements also include new bag drop. Player comment: "Many renovations and a new irrigation system have really improved this course."

	1	2	3	4	5	6	7	8	9
PAR	4	4	3	4	5	4	4	5	3
YARDS	385	312	141	342	500	381	394	420	171
HDCP	11	9	15	13	1	3	5	7	17

	10	11	12	13	14	15	16	17	18
PAR	4	3	4	4	4	3	5	4	5
YARDS	310	133	315	315	273	185	467	360	523
HDCP	12	18	10	14	16	6	2	8	4

Directions: Take Route 57 west to Route 187. Turn right. First right is Shoemaker Lane, The club is 1/2 mile on the right.

Taconic Golf Club

☺☺☺☺   41

Williamstown, MA (413) 458-3997
N/A

Club Pro: Rick Pohle, PGA
Pro Shop: Full inventory
Payment: Credit cards and checks
Tee Times: 7 days adv.

Tees	Holes	Yards	Par	USGA	Slope
BACK	18	6640	71	71.7	127
MIDDLE	18	6230	71	69.9	124
FRONT	18	5202	71	69.9	123

Fee 9 Holes: Weekday: No   **Weekend:** No
Fee 18 Holes: Weekday: $140.00 (Incl. cart) **Weekend:** No
Twilight Rates: No   **All Day Play:** No
Cart Rental: Included in greens fee   **Discounts:** None
Lessons: $50.00/3/4 hour **Schools:** **Junior Golf:** Yes **Membership:** No
Clinics: Yes **Day Camps:** No   **Driving Range:** Yes
Other: Clubhouse / Lockers / Showers / Snack-bar / Bar-lounge

Player's Comment: "Outstanding course. Worth 4 star rating and the $140 price tag. Nice people. Course was in super shape. I'm glad we went."

	1	2	3	4	5	6	7	8	9
PAR	5	4	4	4	3	4	4	4	3
YARDS	475	391	409	358	172	361	402	394	188
HDCP	18	10	2	12	16	8	4	6	14

	10	11	12	13	14	15	16	17	18
PAR	5	4	4	4	3	4	4	3	5
YARDS	506	470	363	391	173	426	430	221	510
HDCP	13	1	7	9	15	5	3	11	17

Directions: Route 2 West to Williamstown; left on Route 43 South; 3rd street on right.

Tekoa Country Club

☺☺   42

Westfield, MA (413) 568-1064
www.tekoacc.com

Club Pro: E.J. Altobello, PGA & B. Crawford
Pro Shop: Full inventory
Payment: Visa, MC
Tee Times: 7 days adv.

Tees	Holes	Yards	Par	USGA	Slope
BACK	18	6002	70	69.8	119
MIDDLE	18	5655	70	68.4	117
FRONT	18	5115	74	71.0	116

Fee 9 Holes: Weekday: $13.00   **Weekend:** $16.00
Fee 18 Holes: Weekday: $21.00   **Weekend:** $27.00
Twilight Rates: Yes, after 5 pm   **All Day Play:** Yes
Cart Rental: $13pp/18 $7pp/9   **Discounts:** Senior Weekdays
Lessons: $35/30 min. **Schools:** No **Junior Golf:** Yes **Membership:** Yes
Clinics: Ladies/Juniors **Day Camps:** No **Driving Range:** No
Other: Clubhouse / Restaurant / Snack bar / Bar-lounge

COUPON

Donald Ross design, one hundred years old. Scenic views of Tekoa Mountain and Westfield River. Easy walking, short but challenging. Full banquet facilities. Course lengthened.

	1	2	3	4	5	6	7	8	9
PAR	4	4	3	5	4	3	4	4	4
YARDS	345	385	135	475	345	210	417	365	340
HDCP	11	1	17	13	7	5	15	3	9

	10	11	12	13	14	15	16	17	18
PAR	4	3	5	4	5	4	3	4	3
YARDS	345	145	470	380	465	345	130	415	200
HDCP	6	16	12	4	14	10	18	2	8

Directions: Take Mass Pike to Exit 3. Bear right onto Routes 10/202 South. Travel 2 miles into the center of Westfield. Bear right onto Route 20 West. Course is 2 miles on the right.

4☺ =Excellent **3**☺ =Very Good **2**☺ =Good

The Meadows Golf Club ✪✪ ▶ 43

Greenfield, MA (413)773-9047

Club Pro: No
Pro Shop: Limited inventory
Payment: Visa, MC
Tee Times: No
Fee 9 Holes: Weekday: $12.00
Fee 18 Holes: Weekday: $16.00
Twilight Rates: No
Cart Rental: $20.00/18, $12.00/9, $2.00 pull
Lessons: No **Schools:** No
Clinics: No **Day Camps:** No
Other: Bar-lounge / Restaurant open all year

Tees	Holes	Yards	Par	USGA	Slope
BACK	9	5716	72	66.6	106
MIDDLE	9	5600	72	66.6	106
FRONT	9	5094	72	66.6	106

Weekend: $14.00
Weekend: $19.00
All Day Play: Yes
Discounts: Senior
Junior Golf: No **Membership:** Yes
Driving Range: No

Player's Comment: "Great condition. Pretty elevation changes which also make for a challenging round. Extremely friendly and helpful staff." Rates may change.

	1	2	3	4	5	6	7	8	9
PAR	5	3	4	4	4	3	5	4	4
YARDS	475	155	320	280	255	135	470	365	345
HDCP	11	7	5	13	17	15	9	1	3
	10	**11**	**12**	**13**	**14**	**15**	**16**	**17**	**18**
PAR	5	3	4	4	4	3	5	4	4
YARDS	475	163	320	280	255	135	470	365	345
HDCP	12	8	6	14	18	16	10	2	4

Directions: From Route 2- take Route 5 South, through Greenfield center. Course is 1.5- 2 miles on right after center.

The Ranch Golf Club ✪✪✪✪ ▶ 44

Southwick, MA (413) 569-9333
www.theranchgolfclub.com

Club Pro: P.Chapman, PGA, M. Robichaud, PG
Pro Shop: Yes
Payment: Visa, MC, Amex, checks, cash
Tee Times: 14 days adv.
Fee 9 Holes: Weekday: N/A
Fee 18 Holes: Weekday: $100 TBD
Twilight Rates: Yes, after 3:30 pm
Cart Rental: Included
Lessons: $45/30 min **Schools:** Jr.
Clinics: Day Camps:
Other: Clubhouse / Lockers / Showers / Bar-lounge

Tees	Holes	Yards	Par	USGA	Slope
BACK	18	7174	72	74.1	140
MIDDLE	18	6020	72	69.4	129
FRONT	18	4983	72	69.7	122

Weekend: N/A
Weekend: $100, subject to change
All Day Play: Replay rate
Discounts: Junior $30.00 after 3pm.
Junior Golf: Membership: No
Driving Range: Yes

Noted as "3rd Best New Upscale" Golf Digest 2002. Many amenities included. "Wonderful setting. 9th hole par 5, straight downhill with green tucked to right. 17th par 3 over a pond--terrific hole!" R.W.

	1	2	3	4	5	6	7	8	9
PAR	5	4	4	4	3	4	4	3	5
YARDS	469	341	350	361	111	303	328	170	495
HDCP	13	11	5	1	17	7	9	15	3
	10	**11**	**12**	**13**	**14**	**15**	**16**	**17**	**18**
PAR	4	4	3	5	4	4	5	3	4
YARDS	361	353	145	540	375	275	539	133	371
HDCP	12	8	18	2	10	14	6	16	4

Directions: Route 91 to Route 57 W. Go right on 202 N past Chuck's Steak. Turn right on Sunnyside Dr. Club 1/2 mile on left.

Thomas Memorial Golf & CC

Turner Falls, MA (413) 863-8003 .... 45 ▶

Club Pro:
Pro Shop: Limited inventory
Payment: Visa, MC, Disc
Tee Times: No
Fee 9 Holes: Weekday: $10.00
Fee 18 Holes: Weekday: $16.00
Twilight Rates: No
Cart Rental: $20.00/18 $12.00/9
Lessons: **Schools:** No
Clinics: No **Day Camps:** No
Other: Bar-Lounge / Snack Bar

Tees	Holes	Yards	Par	USGA	Slope
BACK					
MIDDLE	9	5103	70	66.0	113
FRONT	9	4634	70	68.0	113

Weekend: $13.00
Weekend: $20.00
All Day Play: Yes
Discounts: None
Junior Golf: Yes **Membership:** Yes
Driving Range: No

W
MA

Course layout is interesting: hilly, several blind holes, narrow fairways, and some water hazards, 2 holes have 2 separate greens.

	1	2	3	4	5	6	7	8	9
PAR	4	4	4	4	5	4	3	4	3
YARDS	360	323	235	280	460	352	128	256	145
HDCP	3	7	18	11	5	1	16	9	14
	10	**11**	**12**	**13**	**14**	**15**	**16**	**17**	**18**
PAR	4	4	4	4	5	4	3	4	3
YARDS	360	323	300	240	460	352	128	256	145
HDCP	4	8	12	13	6	2	17	10	15

Directions: From Route 2 West-turn left at lights for Turners Falls. Ask for directions when arriving in town.

Veteran's Golf Club

  46 ▶

Springfield, MA (413) 783-9611

Club Pro: Robert W. Downes
Pro Shop: Full inventory
Payment: Cash only
Tee Times: Sat., Sun.
Fee 9 Holes: Weekday: N/A
Fee 18 Holes: Weekday: $18.00, $14 after 3pm
Twilight Rates: Yes, after 3 pm
Cart Rental: $22.00/18 $12.00/9
Lessons: $25/halfhour **Schools:** N/R
Clinics: Yes **Day Camps:** No
Other: Snack bar

Tees	Holes	Yards	Par	USGA	Slope
BACK	18	6350	72	69.9	116
MIDDLE	18	6115	72	69.9	116
FRONT	18	5884	72	70.2	112

Weekend: N/A
Weekend: $20.00, $16 after 3pm
All Day Play: Yes
Discounts: Senior & Junior
Junior Golf: No **Membership:** Yes
Driving Range: No

Special Monday- Thursday; $25.00pp with cart for 18.

	1	2	3	4	5	6	7	8	9
PAR	4	4	5	4	3	4	3	4	5
YARDS	290	381	496	350	200	332	143	292	498
HDCP	14	6	8	10	12	2	16	18	4
	10	**11**	**12**	**13**	**14**	**15**	**16**	**17**	**18**
PAR	4	4	5	4	5	3	4	4	3
YARDS	373	421	510	360	490	173	300	334	172
HDCP	3	1	7	9	5	17	15	11	13

Directions: Call course for directions.

4🟢 =Excellent 3🟢 =Very Good 2🟢 = Good

Wahconah CC

Dalton, MA (413) 684-2864

Tees	Holes	Yards	Par	USGA	Slope
BACK	18	6567	71	71.9	126
MIDDLE	18	6223	71	69.9	123
FRONT	18	5835	71	68.6	119

Club Pro: Paul Daniels, PGA
Pro Shop: Full inventory
Payment: Cash, Check
Tee Times: 1 week adv.
Fee 9 Holes: Weekday: N/A   **Weekend:** N/A
Fee 18 Holes: Weekday: $65.00   **Weekend:** $75.00
Twilight Rates: No   **All Day Play:** Yes
Cart Rental: $30.00/18, 2 riders   **Discounts:** None
Lessons: $35.00/halfhour **Schools:** Jr.Yes   **Junior Golf:** Yes **Membership:** 3 year wait list
Clinics: Yes **Day Camps:** No   **Driving Range:** $3/sm., $4/med. & $6/lg.
Other: Clubhouse / Restaurant / Bar-lounge / Landscaped Patio

A beautiful, very challenging, semi-private course with fast greens. Considered to be moderately difficult.
" Excellent conditions, difficult to get tee times before noon." F.P. Open Apr 15 - Nov15.

	1	2	3	4	5	6	7	8	9
PAR	4	3	4	4	4	3	5	4	4
YARDS	382	206	398	300	360	147	476	390	388
HDCP	12	10	8	14	6	16	18	4	2
	10	11	12	13	14	15	16	17	18
PAR	4	4	4	3	5	4	4	3	5
YARDS	368	340	371	203	480	349	430	177	458
HDCP	13	15	7	5	3	9	1	11	17

Directions: Take Mass Pike to Exit 2. Follow Route 9 North from Amherst into Dalton. In Dalton, take left onto Orchard Road. Course is approximately 1/2 mile on left.

Waubeeka Golf Links

So. Williamstown, MA (413) 458-8355
waubeekaGL@aol.com

Tees	Holes	Yards	Par	USGA	Slope
BACK	18	6394	72	70.6	126
MIDDLE	18	6024	72	69.5	122
FRONT	18	5023	72	69.6	119

Club Pro: Erik Tiele, PGA
Pro Shop: Full inventory
Payment: Most major
Tee Times: Yes
Fee 9 Holes: Weekday: $20, $28 w/cart   **Weekend:** $25, $33 w/cart
Fee 18 Holes: Weekday: $33, $47 w/cart   **Weekend:** $42, $56 w/cart
Twilight Rates: After 4 pm, S/S/M/T   **All Day Play:** No
Cart Rental: $11pp/9   **Discounts:** Junior Wkdays
Lessons: $30/hr., lessons **Schools:** Jr./Women   **Junior Golf:** Yes **Membership:** Yes
Clinics: Yes **Day Camps:** No   **Driving Range:** Yes
Other: Clubhouse / Lockers / Showers/ Snack bar / Restaurant / Bar-lounge

Cart paths added to every hole. Well-groomed, scenic. Audubon Society member. Open April - November. Dress code.

	1	2	3	4	5	6	7	8	9
PAR	4	4	4	4	3	5	3	5	4
YARDS	351	370	330	286	132	482	161	473	318
HDCP	9	1	5	11	15	3	7	13	17
	10	11	12	13	14	15	16	17	18
PAR	4	4	3	5	4	4	3	5	4
YARDS	348	405	167	480	410	342	169	453	347
HDCP	2	6	12	8	4	10	14	18	16

Directions: Mass Pike, Exit 2 (Lee) to Route 20 North to Route 7 North. Course is on left going north about 45 minutes from exit.

Westover Golf Course

Granby, MA (413) 547-8610

Club Pro: Bill Kubinski, PGA
Pro Shop: Full inventory
Payment: Cash/Credit Card
Tee Times: 3 days adv.
Fee 9 Holes: Weekday: No
Fee 18 Holes: Weekday: $21.00
Twilight Rates: Yes, after 4 pm
Cart Rental: $20.00/18 $12.00/9
Lessons: $35.00/45 minutes **Schools:** No
Clinics: Yes **Day Camps:** No
Other: Clubhouse/Lockers/Showers/Snack bar/Restaurant/Bar-lounge

Tees	Holes	Yards	Par	USGA	Slope
BACK	18	7025	72	74.0	131
MIDDLE	18	6610	72	71.9	129
FRONT	18	5580	72	71.9	115

Weekend: No
Weekend: $23.00
All Day Play: Yes
Discounts: Senior & Junior wkdys
Junior Golf: Yes **Membership:** Range Member.
Driving Range: $5.50/lg. bucket

**W
MA**

Player's Comments: "A great challenge for a reasonable proce." Fantastic layout, very challenging. Dress code: no cutoffs or tank tops. Lessons for all ages and abilities. Open April 1 - December.

	1	2	3	4	5	6	7	8	9
PAR	4	4	4	3	4	4	5	3	5
YARDS	390	410	335	207	396	419	489	163	532
HDCP	9	7	13	15	11	1	3	17	5
	10	11	12	13	14	15	16	17	18
PAR	3	4	5	3	4	4	4	4	5
YARDS	160	422	490	160	364	405	373	354	541
HDCP	16	2	4	18	12	8	10	14	6

Directions: I-91 to I-90 to Exit 5. Go left on Route 33 North, follow for approximately 5 miles to New Ludlow Road. Take right and go 3 miles to South Street.

Whippernon CC

Russell, MA (413) 862-3606

Club Pro: No
Pro Shop: Limited inventory
Payment: Visa, MC
Tee Times: 1 week adv.
Fee 9 Holes: Weekday: $10.00
Fee 18 Holes: Weekday: $14.00
Twilight Rates: No
Cart Rental: $18.00/18 $10.00/9
Lessons: No **Schools:** No
Clinics: No **Day Camps:** No
Other: Snack bar / Bar-lounge

Tees	Holes	Yards	Par	USGA	Slope
BACK	9	5678	68	N/A	113
MIDDLE	9	5186	68	N/A	113
FRONT	9	4012	68	N/A	113

Weekend: $12.00
Weekend: $16.00
All Day Play: No
Discounts: Senior & Junior
Junior Golf: No **Membership:** Yes
Driving Range: No

Prices subject to change.

	1	2	3	4	5	6	7	8	9
PAR	3	4	4	4	3	5	3	4	4
YARDS	185	305	310	305	170	448	160	360	350
HDCP	17	3	11	5	13	1	15	7	9
	10	11	12	13	14	15	16	17	18
PAR	3	4	4	4	3	5	3	4	4
YARDS	185	305	310	305	170	448	160	360	350
HDCP	18	4	12	6	14	2	16	8	10

Directions: Take Route 20; course is 6 miles west of Westfield.

4★ =Excellent 3★ =Very Good 2★ = Good

Worthington GC

Worthington, MA (413) 238-4464

Club Pro: Mark Duane, PGA
Pro Shop: Full inventory
Payment: Cash, Credit
Tee Times: Yes, 1 week adv.
Fee 9 Holes: Weekday: $10.00
Fee 18 Holes: Weekday: $18.00
Twilight Rates: No
Cart Rental: $23.00/18 $15.00/9
Lessons: $35.00/ 45 minutes **Schools:** No
Clinics: For members **Day Camps:** No
Other: Clubhouse / Snack bar / Restaurant / Bar-lounge

Tees	Holes	Yards	Par	USGA	Slope
BACK	N/A				
MIDDLE	9	5579	70	66.8	116
FRONT	9	5229	73	66.8	116

Weekend: $16.00
Weekend: $27.00
All Day Play: Yes
Discounts: None
Junior Golf: Yes **Membership:** Yes
Driving Range: 4.00 per bag

COUPON

Sig. Hole: #6, par 3, 2 trees guarding fairway. 2 sand traps in front and two-tiered green. Call ahead for tee times.

	1	2	3	4	5	6	7	8	9
PAR	4	4	4	4	3	3	5	5	3
YARDS	333	322	340	301	201	148	528	476	148
HDCP	7	11	5	13	9	17	1	3	15

	10	11	12	13	14	15	16	17	18
PAR	4	4	4	4	4	3	5	4	3
YARDS	351	347	340	301	240	152	464	406	181
HDCP	8	10	6	12	14	18	2	4	16

Directions: Take I-91 to Northampton. Then take Route 9 North to Route 143 and continue to Worthington Center; then take Buffinton Hill to Ridge Road.

CHAPTER 4

Southeastern Massachusetts & Rhode Island

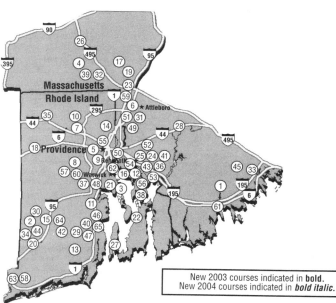

New 2003 courses indicated in **bold**.
New 2004 courses indicated in ***bold italic***.

Acushnet River Valley Golf	1	Heather Hill CC	23	Rochester Golf Club	45
Beaver River Golf Club	2	Hidden Hollow CG	24	Rolling Greens GC	46
Bristol Golf Club	3	Hillside CC	25	Rose Hill Golf Course	47
Bungay Brook Golf Club	4	Hopedale CC	26	Seaview Country Club	48
Button Hole	5	Jamestown Golf & CC	27	Shadow Brook Golf Course	49
Chemawa Golf Course	6	John F. Parker GC	28	Silver Spring Golf Club	50
Country View Golf Club	7	Laurel Lane GC	29	Stone-E-Lea Golf Course	51
Coventry Pines Golf Club	8	Lindhbrook Golf Club	30	Sun Valley CC	52
Cranston Country Club	9	Locust Valley Golf Course	31	Swansea Country Club	53
Crystal Lake GC of RI	**10**	Maplegate Country Club	32	Touisset Country Club	54
East Greenwich CC	11	Marion Golf Course	33	Triggs Memorial GC	55
Executive Par 3 at Swansea	12	Meadow Brook GC	34	Wampanoag Golf Club	56
Exeter Country Club	13	Melody Hill Golf Course	35	Washington Village GC	57
Fairlawn Golf Course	14	Middlebrook CC	36	Weekapaug Golf Club	58
Fenner Hill Golf Club	15	Midville Country Club	37	Wentworth Hills Golf & CC	59
Fire Fly Country Club	16	Montaup Country Club	38	West Warwick CC	60
Fore Kicks GC	***17***	New England CC	39	Whaling City GC	61
Foster Country Club	18	North Kingstown Muni	40	Windmill Hill Golf Course	62
Foxborough Country Club	19	Pine Valley Golf Club	41	Winnapaug Golf Course	63
Foxwoods Golf CC	20	Pinehurst CC	42	Wood River Golf	64
Goddard Park GC	21	Rehoboth Country Club	43	Woodland Greens GC	65
Green Valley CC	22	Richmond Country Club	44		

Acushnet River Valley Golf Course ✪✪ ▶ 1

Acushnet, MA 508-998-7777
www.golfacushnet.com

Club Pro: Richard LaGrasse, PGA
Pro Shop: Full inventory
Payment: All Types
Tee Times: 7 days adv.
Fee 9 Holes: Weekday: $17.00
Fee 18 Holes: Weekday: $34.00
Twilight Rates: Yes, after 3 pm
Cart Rental: $16.00pp/18 $8.00pp/9
Lessons: $35.00 **Schools:** No
Clinics: Yes **Day Camps:** No
Other: Snack bar / Clubhouse / Bar lounge

Weekend: $21.00
Weekend: $42.00
All Day Play: No
Discounts: Junior
Junior Golf: Yes **Membership:** season passes
Driving Range: $5/lg $3/sm.

Tees	Holes	Yards	Par	USGA	Slope
BACK	18	6302	72	70.0	122
MIDDLE	18	5735	72	66.9	116
FRONT	18	5099	72	68.4	115

Dick LaGrasse School of Golf- Private video, group lessons available. New customer service oriented management/ staff. Operations Manger: Dana Przybyszewski, "Regions best kept secret."

	1	2	3	4	5	6	7	8	9
PAR	4	4	4	5	4	3	4	3	5
YARDS	375	289	275	436	336	119	382	141	501
HDCP	5	7	15	11	13	17	3	9	1
	10	**11**	**12**	**13**	**14**	**15**	**16**	**17**	**18**
PAR	4	3	5	4	5	4	4	3	4
YARDS	315	113	470	388	529	257	328	145	336
HDCP	14	18	10	2	4	16	8	12	6

Directions: Route 128 to Route 24 South to Route 140 South. Take Exit 6 to Route 18 South. Stay on Route 18 South for 2 miles. At lights, turn left onto Tarkiln Hill Rd. which becomes Main St. in Acushnet. Course will be on left about 2 miles after Acushnet Town Hall.

Beaver River Golf Club ✪✪ ▶ 2

Richmond, RI (401) 539-6022
www.rigolf.com

Club Pro: No
Pro Shop: Yes
Payment: Visa, MC, Amex
Tee Times: 5 days adv.
Fee 9 Holes: Weekday: $16, $22 ride M-Th
Fee 18 Holes: Weekday: $32, $44 ride M-Th
Twilight Rates: Yes, after 3 pm
Cart Rental: $12.00pp/18, $6.00/9
Lessons: No **Schools:**
Clinics: No **Day Camps:** No
Other: Clubhouse / Bar-Lounge

Weekend: $19, $25 ride
Weekend: $37, $49 ride
All Day Play: No
Discounts: N/R
Junior Golf: Yes **Membership:** Yes
Driving Range: No

Tees	Holes	Yards	Par	USGA	Slope
BACK	18	6086	70	67.1	123
MIDDLE	18	5802	70	65.7	123
FRONT	18	5410	70	70.8	115

"Best new 18 hole course in Rhode Island," *RI Monthly*. Bent grass from tee to green. Excellent conditions and service. South County course.

	1	2	3	4	5	6	7	8	9
PAR	5	4	3	4	4	5	3	4	4
YARDS	477	334	150	326	318	485	201	411	332
HDCP	5	13	17	11	15	3	7	1	9
	10	**11**	**12**	**13**	**14**	**15**	**16**	**17**	**18**
PAR	4	3	4	4	4	3	4	4	4
YARDS	328	146	433	379	300	170	265	367	380
HDCP	8	14	2	12	16	10	18	6	4

Directions: Located on Route 138, 3 miles east from Interstate 95. (Exit 3)

Bristol Golf Club

Tupelo St., Bristol, RI (401) 253-9844

Club Pro: No
Pro Shop: No
Payment: Cash only
Tee Times: No
Fee 9 Holes: Weekday: $8.00
Fee 18 Holes: Weekday: $10.00
Twilight Rates: No
Cart Rental: $15.00/18, Pull $4.00
Lessons: No **Schools:** No
Clinics: No **Day Camps:** No
Other: Snack bar / Bar-lounge

Tees	Holes	Yards	Par	USGA	Slope
BACK					
MIDDLE	9	2273	33	69.9	118
FRONT					

Weekend: $10.00
Weekend: $12.00
All Day Play: No
Discounts: None
Junior Golf: No **Membership:** Yes
Driving Range: No

A good course for beginners.

	1	2	3	4	5	6	7	8	9
PAR	3	4	3	3	3	4	5	4	4
YARDS	137	254	148	130	167	337	480	320	300
HDCP	N/A								
	10	11	12	13	14	15	16	17	18
PAR									
YARDS									
HDCP									

Directions: Take Route 195 East to Exit 2, follow Route 136 to Tupelo Street, take right and course is on left.

Bungay Brook Golf Club

Bellingham, MA (508) 883-1600
www.bungaybrook.com

Club Pro: PGA , Teaching Pro.
Pro Shop: Yes
Payment: Visa, MC, Amex
Tee Times: 2 weeks in adv.
Fee 9 Holes: Weekday: $22.00
Fee 18 Holes: Weekday: $40.00
Twilight Rates: No
Cart Rental: $6pp/9
Lessons: Yes **Schools:**
Clinics: Yes **Day Camps:**
Other: Restaurant / Bar-Lounge

Tees	Holes	Yards	Par	USGA	Slope
BACK					
MIDDLE	9	3136	36	69.2	113
FRONT					

Weekend: $24.00
Weekend: $46.00
All Day Play: No
Discounts: Senior & Junior
Junior Golf: **Membership:** No
Driving Range: Yes

COUPON

Impeccable conditions, finest greens, fast pace. All grass driving range.

	1	2	3	4	5	6	7	8	9
PAR	4	3	4	5	3	4	5	4	4
YARDS	278	153	313	450	107	421	434	393	336
HDCP	9	4	6	3	5	1	7	2	8
	10	11	12	13	14	15	16	17	18
PAR									
YARDS									
HDCP									

Directions: Exit 16 off Route 495. 4.5 miles to Bellingham townline. First left Locust St. 1/2 mile to course.

Button Hole ✪✪ 5

Providence, RI (401) 421-1664
www.buttonhole.org

Tees	Holes	Yards	Par	USGA	Slope
BACK	9	1035	27		50.9
MIDDLE	9	780	27		48.6
FRONT					

Club Pro: Shane Drury
Pro Shop: Limited inventory
Payment: Visa, MC
Tee Times: Yes
Fee 9 Holes: Weekday: $10Adult/$8Jr/Sr
Fee 18 Holes: Weekday: $15Adult/$13Jr/Sr
Twilight Rates: No
Cart Rental: No
Lessons: Yes * **Schools:** Yes
Clinics: Adult **Day Camps:** Junior Camp

Weekend: $10 Adult / $8 Jr/Sr
Weekend: $15 Adult / $13 Jr/Sr
All Day Play: No
Discounts: Senior & Junior
Junior Golf: Yes **Membership:** Range + Course
Driving Range: Yes

Other: Clubhouse / Patio / Snacks / 16,000 sq. ft. putting green / Chipping area

Short course and teaching center designed to lower cost, provide easy access and playing time. "Not just a beginner's layout. Shots and putts have to be made to score." R.W. *Lessons priced according to age.

	1	2	3	4	5	6	7	8	9
PAR	3	3	3	3	3	3	3	3	3
YARDS	70	118	60	90	95	62	110	90	85
HDCP	9	5	1	4	6	7	3	2	8
	10	11	12	13	14	15	16	17	18
PAR									
YARDS									
HDCP									

Directions: Route 95 to Route 6 West to Route 6A West-Hartford Ave. exit. Take left (east) on Hartford Ave. Go .7 mi. and take right on Glenbridge Ave. Go .3 mi. and take left on Button Hole Dr. Facility on right.

Chemawa Golf Course ✪✪ 6

N. Attleboro, MA (508) 399-7330

Tees	Holes	Yards	Par	USGA	Slope
BACK	18	5267	68	65.1	113
MIDDLE	18	4884	68	63.5	110
FRONT	18	4351	69	64.6	109

Club Pro: Glen Bourgue
Pro Shop: No
Payment: Most major
Tee Times: Wknd. only
Fee 9 Holes: Weekday: $17.00
Fee 18 Holes: Weekday: $25.00
Twilight Rates: No
Cart Rental: $22.00/18 $11.00/9
Lessons: No **Schools:** No
Clinics: No **Day Camps:** No
Other: Snack bar / Bar-lounge

Weekend: $20.00
Weekend: $30.00
All Day Play: No
Discounts: Senior, $20/18, $15/9
Junior Golf: No **Membership:** No
Driving Range: No

Players' Comments: "Parkland layout presents water and wetlands in play on 11 holes with generous driving zones. Downhill par 3 16th offers an early version of the island green concept." "Challenging, difficult course."

	1	2	3	4	5	6	7	8	9
PAR	4	4	4	4	4	4	5	4	3
YARDS	334	286	324	321	312	236	427	265	136
HDCP	7	15	11	9	5	1	3	13	17
	10	11	12	13	14	15	16	17	18
PAR	4	3	4	3	3	4	3	4	4
YARDS	348	126	309	146	198	332	109	265	410
HDCP	2	14	10	12	16	6	18	8	4

Directions: I-95 South to I-295 toward Woonsocket, Route 1 South. Take right onto May Street, then take a right onto Cushman Road.

Country View Golf Club

7

Burrillville, RI (401) 568-7157
www.countryviewgc.com

Club Pro: Rick Finlayson
Pro Shop: Full inventory
Payment: Visa, MC
Tee Times: 7 days adv.
Fee 9 Holes: Weekday: $15.00
Fee 18 Holes: Weekday: $23.00
Twilight Rates: No
Cart Rental: $26.00/18 $13.00/9
Lessons: $35.00/half hour **Schools:** No
Clinics: Yes **Day Camps:** No

Tees	Holes	Yards	Par	USGA	Slope
BACK	18	6067	70	69.2	119
MIDDLE	18	5721	70	67.7	116
FRONT	18	5010	70	67.0	105

Weekend: $16.00 before 7am/ after 4pm
Weekend: $30.00
All Day Play: No
Discounts: Senior & Junior
Junior Golf: No **Membership:** Yes
Driving Range: No

COUPON

Other: Clubhouse / Lockers / Showers / Snack bar / Restaurant / Bar-lounge

Sig. Hole: #3 is a par 5. Long hitters have a chance to go for it in two but most players have to layup to a down hill lie for the third shot. After 4 pm on Sat. and Sun., juniors are free with one paid adult fee.

	1	2	3	4	5	6	7	8	9
PAR	4	4	5	3	4	4	4	3	4
YARDS	379	281	485	178	332	392	386	184	367
HDCP	9	11	7	15	17	1	3	13	5
	10	**11**	**12**	**13**	**14**	**15**	**16**	**17**	**18**
PAR	4	3	4	4	4	5	3	4	4
YARDS	318	126	341	347	315	461	137	344	348
HDCP	10	18	4	6	12	14	16	2	8

Directions: From I-295 take Exit 8 (Route 7 North). After 12 miles, take a left onto Tarklin Road. Then a left onto Cowell Road.

SE MA /RI

Coventry Pines Golf Club

8

Coventry, RI (401) 397-9482
www.coventrypines.com

Club Pro: No
Pro Shop: Limited inventory
Payment: Cash only
Tee Times: No
Fee 9 Holes: Weekday: $14.00
Fee 18 Holes: Weekday: $21.00
Twilight Rates: Yes, after 6 pm
Cart Rental: $24.00/18 $12.00/9
Lessons: No **Schools:** No
Clinics: No **Day Camps:** No
Other: Snack Bar

Tees	Holes	Yards	Par	USGA	Slope
BACK					
MIDDLE	9	3170	36	68.0	113
FRONT	9	3120	36	70.0	113

Weekend: $16.00
Weekend: $24.00
All Day Play: No
Discounts: Senior M-F
Junior Golf: No **Membership:** No
Driving Range: Practice Field

A very scenic course with rolling hills and tree-lined fairways. 3 water holes. Noted for their Par 5 sixth which has two different greens, men's and ladies. South County course. Open March- December.

	1	2	3	4	5	6	7	8	9
PAR	4	4	3	5	4	5	4	3	4
YARDS	375	308	169	484	408	520	357	187	362
HDCP	9	17	15	3	5	1	11	7	13
	10	**11**	**12**	**13**	**14**	**15**	**16**	**17**	**18**
PAR									
YARDS									
HDCP									

Directions: I-95 to RI exit 6 (Route 3). Continue north on Route 3 for one mile. Take a left on Harkney Hill Rd. The course is 2 mi. on the left.

Cranston Country Club ✪✪ 9

Cranston, RI (401) 826-1683
www.cranstoncc.com

Club Pro: Edward Hanley
Pro Shop: Yes
Payment: Visa, MC, Cash
Tee Times: Yes
Fee 9 Holes: Weekday: $23.00 M - Th
Fee 18 Holes: Weekday: $34.00 M - Th
Twilight Rates: Yes, after 4 pm
Cart Rental: $28.00/18 $14.00/9
Lessons: Yes **Schools:** Yes
Clinics: Yes **Day Camps:** No
Other: Clubhouse / Lockers / Showers / Snack bar / Bar / Banquet Facilities

Tees	Holes	Yards	Par	USGA	Slope
BACK	18	6914	71	72.3	125
MIDDLE	18	6493	71	69.1	122
FRONT	18	6109	71	71.9	120

Weekend: $25.00 F/S/S
Weekend: $40.00 F/S/S
All Day Play: No
Discounts: Senior
Junior Golf: Yes **Membership:** Yes
Driving Range: Grass

Championship tees added on #2, 4. 5. 7. 10, 11, 13, 14, & 17. Scenic country setting.

	1	2	3	4	5	6	7	8	9
PAR	5	4	4	3	4	4	4	3	4
YARDS	529	348	375	180	338	346	344	173	410
HDCP	1	11	17	9	7	5	13	15	3
	10	11	12	13	14	15	16	17	18
PAR	4	4	3	5	4	3	4	5	4
YARDS	345	377	125	475	349	166	369	545	355
HDCP	8	4	18	12	14	16	10	2	6

Directions: I-95 to Route 37 West (Exit 14). Go to end of Route 37, turn left. Go 0.2 mile to intersection, turn right; 0.4 mile to stop sign, bear right. Proceed 0.2 mile to crossroads and turn left (Phoenix Avenue). 2 miles to golf course.

NEW 2003

Crystal Lake Golf Course of R I 10

Burrillville, RI (401) 567-4500

Club Pro: Dan Gaughan, PGA
Pro Shop:
Payment: Yes
Tee Times: Yes
Fee 9 Holes: Weekday: $20.00
Fee 18 Holes: Weekday: $30.00
Twilight Rates: No
Cart Rental: $14.00/18, $8.00/9
Lessons: Yes **Schools:** Yes
Clinics: Yes **Day Camps:**
Other: Clubhouse / Bar-lounge / Function facility

Tees	Holes	Yards	Par	USGA	Slope
BACK	18	6365	71		
MIDDLE	18	6035	71		
FRONT	18	5165	71		

Weekend: $25.00
Weekend: $35.00
All Day Play: Yes
Discounts: Senior & Junior
Junior Golf: **Membership:** Yes
Driving Range: No

2003 New Entry. 18 hole links style course wrapped around the lake. Clubhouse sits on the lake with "fantastic views and greens" **Player's Comments.**

	1	2	3	4	5	6	7	8	9
PAR	4	3	4	4	5	5	4	3	4
YARDS	330	180	370	350	500	480	435	185	290
HDCP									
	10	11	12	13	14	15	16	17	18
PAR	4	3	4	4	5	3	4	4	4
YARDS	380	160	340	290	510	150	320	385	380
HDCP									

Directions: From Providence, Route 146 N to Route 102 W. Go about 8 miles, course is on right. From Worcester, take Route 146 South to 102 W.

East Greenwich CC

E. Greenwich, RI (401) 884-5656
www.rigolf.com/eg

Club Pro: Larry Rittmann
Pro Shop: No
Payment: Cash only
Tee Times: No

Tees	Holes	Yards	Par	USGA	Slope
BACK	9	3315	36		127
MIDDLE	9	3125	36		124
FRONT	9	2875	36		119

Fee 9 Holes: Weekday: $15.00
Fee 18 Holes: Weekday: $25.00
Twilight Rates: Yes, after 5 pm
Cart Rental: $22.00/18 $12.00./9
Lessons: Yes **Schools:** Sr.Yes
Clinics: No **Day Camps:** No
Other: Snack bar / Bar-lounge

Weekend: $18.00
Weekend: $28.00
All Day Play: No
Discounts: Senior
Junior Golf: Yes **Membership:** Yes
Driving Range: No

Rated as one of the more challenging 9-hole courses in N.E. Private country club conditions. Fantastic greens, trees, and ponds!

	1	2	3	4	5	6	7	8	9
PAR	4	4	5	4	4	3	5	4	3
YARDS	365	325	500	360	385	160	475	380	175
HDCP	6	7	4	5	2	9	3	1	8
	10	11	12	13	14	15	16	17	18
PAR									
YARDS									
HDCP									

Directions: Take I 95 North or South to East Greenwich Exit (#8). Take right off exit (Route 2). Head South for 300 yards to traffic light. Take right (Division Rd.). Course is 1/2 mile on left.

**SE
MA
/RI**

Executive Par 3 at Swansea CC ✪✪

Swansea, MA, (508) 379-9886

Club Pro: Glenn Kornasla
Pro Shop: Limited inventory
Payment: Most major cards, no checks
Tee Times: Thurs noon for wknds

Tees	Holes	Yards	Par	USGA	Slope
BACK	9	1378	27	54.8	84
MIDDLE	9	1196	27	54..8	84
FRONT	9	957	27	57.0	89

Fee 9 Holes: Weekday: $9.00
Fee 18 Holes: Weekday: $15.00
Twilight Rates: Yes, after 6 pm
Cart Rental: $20.00/18 $13.00/9
Lessons: Yes **Schools:** No
Clinics: Yes **Day Camps:** No
Other:

Weekend: $9.00
Weekend: $15.00
All Day Play: No
Discounts: Senior & Junior
Junior Golf: Yes **Membership:** Yes
Driving Range: Yes

COUPON

"A great compliment to the original 18 holes course. Interior five holes a fine track in a beautiful setting." R. W. Member rates: $600/Family, $400/Adult, $200/Junior. Single rider cart rates.

	1	2	3	4	5	6	7	8	9
PAR	3	3	3	3	3	3	3	3	3
YARDS	153	115	160	128	134	141	101	122	142
HDCP	33	13	5	15	7	9	17	11	1
	10	11	12	13	14	15	16	17	18
PAR									
YARDS									
HDCP									

Directions: MA Exit 2 off I-195. Course is one mile south of freeway.

4✪ =Excellent **3✪** =Very Good **2✪** = Good   **Southeastern MA & Rhode Island 153**

Exeter Country Club ✪✪ ▶ 13

Exeter, RI (401) 295-8212

Club Pro: No
Pro Shop: Full inventory
Payment: Visa,MC $25 minimum
Tee Times: 1 day. Call after 8 am
Fee 9 Holes: Weekday: $18 after 1 pm
Fee 18 Holes: Weekday: $30 walk, $42 ride
Twilight Rates: Yes, after 4 pm
Cart Rental: $24.00/18, $14.00/9
Lessons: No **Schools:** No
Clinics: N/R **Day Camps:** No
Other: Clubhouse / Snack bar / Lockers / Bar-lounge / Full Restaurant

Tees	Holes	Yards	Par	USGA	Slope
BACK	18	6919	72	72.3	123
MIDDLE	18	6390	72	69.9	116
FRONT	18	5733	72	72.1	115

Weekend: $20 after 4 pm,F/S/S/H
Weekend: $35 walk, $47 ride F/S/S/H
All Day Play: No
Discounts: Junior
Junior Golf: No **Membership:** Yes, waiting list
Driving Range: $8.00/lg. $5.00/med.

Sig. Hole: #13 is scenic and long, featuring a covered bridge. Course has a beautiful layout with strategically placed hazards. Open March - November. South County course

	1	2	3	4	5	6	7	8	9
PAR	4	5	3	5	3	4	4	4	4
YARDS	350	530	190	510	180	360	420	370	400
HDCP	9	3	13	5	17	11	1	15	7

	10	11	12	13	14	15	16	17	18
PAR	4	3	4	4	5	4	4	3	5
YARDS	400	150	330	310	480	350	370	200	490
HDCP	8	16	18	10	4	12	2	14	6

Directions: Take I-95 to Route 4 (Exit 9 south) into Exeter (approx. 4-5 mi.), take Route 102 North. Course is on left.

Fairlawn Golf Course ▶ 14

Lincoln, RI (401) 334-3937
www.rigolf.com/fairlawn

Club Pro: No
Pro Shop: No
Payment: Cash only
Tee Times: No
Fee 9 Holes: Weekday: $10.00
Fee 18 Holes: Weekday: $15.00
Twilight Rates: N/R
Cart Rental: Pull carts
Lessons: No **Schools:** No
Clinics: No **Day Camps:** No
Other: Clubhouse/ Beer and Wine

Tees	Holes	Yards	Par	USGA	Slope
BACK					
MIDDLE	9	2534	54	52.2	N/A
FRONT					

Weekend: $12.00
Weekend: $18.00
All Day Play: N/R
Discounts: Senior
Junior Golf: No **Membership:** Yes
Driving Range: No

COUPON

Sig. Hole: #8, 116 yd. par 3 with island green. Open April - November.

	1	2	3	4	5	6	7	8	9
PAR	3	3	3	3	3	3	3	3	3
YARDS	133	181	121	167	91	110	110	161	193
HDCP	14	1	11	3	17	5	15	9	7

	10	11	12	13	14	15	16	17	18
PAR	3	3	3	3	3	3	3	3	3
YARDS	133	181	121	167	91	110	110	161	193
HDCP	15	2	12	4	18	6	16	10	8

Directions: I-95 North to Route 146 North to Sherman Avenue exit. Course is on right. You can't miss it!

Fenner Hill Golf Club ✪✪ ▶15

Hope Valley, RI 401-539-8000
www.fennerhill.com

Club Pro: None
Pro Shop: Limited inventory
Payment: Visa, MC
Tee Times: 3 days adv.

Tees	Holes	Yards	Par	USGA	Slope
BACK	18	6636	72	71.8	131
MIDDLE	18	6260	72	70.1	128
FRONT	18	5112	72	68.8	117

Fee 9 Holes: Weekday: $18.00
Fee 18 Holes: Weekday: $30.00
Twilight Rates: Yes, after 3 pm
Cart Rental: $13pp/18 $9pp/9
Lessons: $30.00/half hour **Schools:** No
Clinics: No **Day Camps:** No
Weekend: $20.00
Weekend: $37.00
All Day Play: Yes
Discounts: Sr & Jr Weekdays
Junior Golf: No **Membership:** No
Driving Range: $6.00/lg $3.00/med
Other: Restaurant / Bar-Lounge / Banquet Facilities / Corporate Outings

Course captures the beauty of the landscape to please all levels of golfers and challenge the experienced. "Looks easy from the road, but watch out. Walkable." (Player) South County course.

	1	2	3	4	5	6	7	8	9
PAR	4	4	5	3	4	3	4	5	4
YARDS	366	347	486	152	352	158	394	520	355
HDCP	13	11	5	15	7	17	1	3	9

	10	11	12	13	14	15	16	17	18
PAR	5	3	4	4	5	4	3	4	4
YARDS	468	164	440	338	525	309	166	297	425
HDCP	6	14	8	12	4	16	10	18	2

Directions: I-95 South to exit 2. Bear right to stop, take right, 3/4 mile on right. I-95 North to exit 2. Left off exit to stop sign. Take a right, 3/4 mile on right.

Fire Fly Country Club ▶16

Seekonk, MA (508) 336-6622

Club Pro: Phil Fecteau, PGA
Pro Shop: Full inventory
Payment: Visa, MC
Tee Times: Yes, for weekends

Tees	Holes	Yards	Par	USGA	Slope
BACK	18	3644	59	58.0	87
MIDDLE	18	3083	59	55.4	81
FRONT	18	2786	59	58.0	86

Fee 9 Holes: Weekday: $16.50
Fee 18 Holes: Weekday: $22.00
Twilight Rates: Yes, after 7 pm
Cart Rental: $12.50pp/18
Lessons: $40/40 min. **Schools:** No
Clinics: Yes **Day Camps:** No
Weekend: $17.00
Weekend: $25.00
All Day Play: No
Discounts: Senior & Junior (M-F)
Junior Golf: Yes **Membership:** Yes
Driving Range: $5.00 per bucket
Other: Snack bar / Restaurant / Bar-lounge

2 New Holes. #13, par 3 & #5, par 4. Par 59. Executive course, great for beginners and seasoned golfers who like to practice their short game. Junior clinics available at the Golf Learning Center.

	1	2	3	4	5	6	7	8	9
PAR	3	3	3	3	4	3	4	4	3
YARDS	145	150	148	147	441	122	286	251	123
HDCP	11	9	7	5	1	17	3	13	15

	10	11	12	13	14	15	16	17	18
PAR	4	3	3	3	3	3	3	4	3
YARDS	240	146	126	87	139	155	182	240	134
HDCP	10	6	12	18	8	4	2	14	16

Directions: From Providence I-95 to I-195 E to Exit 1 MA (Seekonk /Barrington). (From Fall River 195 W to Exit 1 MA). Go north on Route 114. At fork, bear left. Take right at Firefly.

SE MA /RI

4✪ =Excellent 3✪ =Very Good 2✪ =Good **Southeastern MA & Rhode Island 155**

Fore Kicks Golf Course & Sports Complex ▶ 17

Norfolk, Ma (508) 384-4433
www.forekicks.com

Club Pro: C. Estes, J. Marston, & M. Vasalotti
Pro Shop: Yes
Payment:
Tee Times:
Fee 9 Holes: Weekday: $12/day, $15/night **Weekend:** $15.00 S/S
Fee 18 Holes: Weekday: $17/day, $20/night **Weekend:** $20.00 S/S
Twilight Rates: No **All Day Play:** Replay
Cart Rental: $3pp/pull cart **Discounts:** Senior & Junior
Lessons: Schools: **Junior Golf: Membership:**
Clinics: Day Camps: **Driving Range:** Indoors
Other: Lounge / Indoor soccer / Basketball courts

Tees	Holes	Yards	Par	USGA	Slope
BACK					
MIDDLE	9	1003	27		
FRONT					

2004 New Entry. Silky smooth greens, artificial turf tees and lights for night play. Links-style. "Impressive multi-sport complex." A.P.

	1	2	3	4	5	6	7	8	9
PAR	3	3	3	3	3	3	3	3	3
YARDS	115	112	81	78	118	93	122	127	157
HDCP	4	5	8	9	3	7	6	2	1
	10	11	12	13	14	15	16	17	18
PAR									
YARDS									
HDCP									

Directions:

Foster Country Club ▶ 18

Foster, RI (401) 397-7750
www.fostercountryclub.com

Club Pro: Brian Benson
Pro Shop: Full inventory
Payment: Visa, MC
Tee Times: 7 days adv.
Fee 9 Holes: Weekday: $17.00 **Weekend:** $23 after 3 pm
Fee 18 Holes: Weekday: $26.00 **Weekend:** $33.00
Twilight Rates: After 3 pm **All Day Play:** Yes
Cart Rental: $24.00/18 $14.00/9 **Discounts:** Junior weekdays
Lessons: Yes **Schools:** No **Junior Golf:** No **Membership:** Yes
Clinics: Yes **Day Camps:** No **Driving Range:** Practice Nets
Other: Clubhouse / Snack bar / Restaurant / Bar-lounge / 180-seat Banquet hall

Tees	Holes	Yards	Par	USGA	Slope
BACK					
MIDDLE	18	6187	72	71.5	117
FRONT	18	5499	72	70.0	112

Discover golf's best kept secret in Western Rhode Island. Open April - November.

	1	2	3	4	5	6	7	8	9
PAR	4	4	3	5	4	4	3	5	4
YARDS	356	340	241	595	295	425	130	485	310
HDCP	5	11	9	3	13	1	17	7	15
	10	11	12	13	14	15	16	17	18
PAR	4	4	5	4	5	4	4	3	3
YARDS	405	310	495	375	450	295	315	170	195
HDCP	4	16	10	2	8	12	6	18	14

Directions: Take I-95 to Route 102 North to Route 14. Left on Route 14 to Moosup Valley Road (on right) to Johnson Road (on right.) Follow to course.

Foxborough Country Club ✪✪ 19

Foxborough, MA (508) 543-4661

Club Pro: Bob Day, PGA
Pro Shop: Full inventory
Payment: Visa, MC, Amex
Tee Times: Call
Fee 9 Holes: Weekday: N/A
Fee 18 Holes: Weekday: $40.00 (M-Th)
Twilight Rates: No
Cart Rental: $24.00/18
Lessons: Yes **Schools:** No
Clinics: Junior **Day Camps:** No
Other: Restaurant/ Bar- Lounge/

Weekend: N/A
Weekend: $50.00
All Day Play: No
Discounts: None
Junior Golf: No **Membership:** Yes
Driving Range: Yes

Tees	Holes	Yards	Par	USGA	Slope
BACK	18	6850	72	72.2	126
MIDDLE	18	6607	72	70.9	123
FRONT	18	5627	72	73.4	122

Player's Comment: "Excellent golf course, tough but fair. Great greens." Be sure to call for tee times. Dress code. Semi-Private.

	1	2	3	4	5	6	7	8	9
PAR	4	4	3	5	4	3	4	4	5
YARDS	385	390	190	500	325	185	318	425	531
HDCP	3	9	13	7	5	17	15	1	11

	10	11	12	13	14	15	16	17	18
PAR	4	5	3	4	4	4	4	3	5
YARDS	385	551	165	325	320	410	425	157	475
HDCP	4	8	14	12	18	6	2	16	10

Directions: I -95 to Exit 7B (140 N) towards Foxborough. Take first left onto Walnut Street. Club will be on left after stop sign.

Foxwoods Golf CC ✪✪ 20

Route 138, Richmond, RI 02898 (401) 539-4653)
www.foxwoods.golf

Club Pro: Dick Johnson, PGA
Pro Shop: Full inventory
Payment: Visa, MC, Amex, Checks
Tee Times: 7 days adv.
Fee 9 Holes: Weekday: N/A
Fee 18 Holes: Weekday: $41.00 cart included
Twilight Rates: Yes, after 3 pm
Cart Rental: Included
Lessons: $40.00/30 min. **Schools:** No
Clinics: Yes **Day Camps:** No
Other: Restaurant / Clubhouse / Bar / Lockers / Snack bar / Showers / Banquet facilities

Weekend: N/A
Weekend: $53.00 cart included
All Day Play: No
Discounts: Senior & Junior
Junior Golf: Yes **Membership:** Yes
Driving Range: Yes

Tees	Holes	Yards	Par	USGA	Slope
BACK	18	6004	70	69.1	131
MIDDLE	18	5627	70	67.7	126
FRONT	18	4881	70	70.9	123

COUPON

Championship course with 18 very distinct holes, beautiful vistas. Affiliated with Foxwoods Casino. Playing lessons available. South County course.

	1	2	3	4	5	6	7	8	9
PAR	3	4	4	5	4	3	5	3	4
YARDS	120	290	410	465	380	107	448	137	333
HDCP	15	9	1	5	3	17	7	13	11

	10	11	12	13	14	15	16	17	18
PAR	4	4	3	4	4	5	4	4	3
YARDS	368	344	167	331	398	430	415	331	153
HDCP	2	6	18	10	4	14	8	12	16

Directions: From I-95, take RI Exit 3A. Take Route 138 East off highway. Golf course is 3/4 mile on the right.

4✪ =Excellent 3✪ =Very Good 2✪ =Good **Southeastern MA & Rhode Island 157**

Goddard State Park GC

Warwick, RI (401) 884-9834
www.riparks.com

Tees	Holes	Yards	Par	USGA	Slope
BACK	18	6234	72	68.4	111
MIDDLE	18	6054	72	67.6	109
FRONT					

Club Pro: No
Pro Shop: Limited inventory
Payment: Cash only
Tee Times: No
Fee 9 Holes: Weekday: $12.00   **Weekend:** $14.00
Fee 18 Holes: Weekday: $24.00   **Weekend:** $28.00
Twilight Rates: No   **All Day Play:** No
Cart Rental: $24/18 $12/9   **Discounts:** Senior 1/2 price
Lessons: No **Schools:** No   **Junior Golf:** No **Membership:** No
Clinics: No **Day Camps:** No   **Driving Range:** No
Other: Clubhouse / Snack Bar / Picnic Facilities / Beach / Showers

The course, located inside Goddard State Park, is open and very walkable. Horse paths and jogging trails are also available.

	1	2	3	4	5	6	7	8	9
PAR	5	4	3	4	5	4	3	4	4
YARDS	503	377	180	292	500	301	168	390	321
HDCP									
	10	**11**	**12**	**13**	**14**	**15**	**16**	**17**	**18**
PAR	5	4	3	4	5	4	3	4	4
YARDS	500	375	185	286	496	300	168	390	324
HDCP									

Directions: Take I-95 South to Route 4 cutoff, take first exit (East Greenwich). Take Route 401 and follow signs to course.

Green Valley CC

Portsmouth, RI (401) 847-9543
www.greenvalleyccofri.com

Tees	Holes	Yards	Par	USGA	Slope
BACK	18	6830	71	72.1	125
MIDDLE	18	6721	71	71.6	122
FRONT	18	5459	71	69.5	120

Club Pro: Gary P. Dorsi
Pro Shop: Full inventory
Payment: Visa, MC, Amex
Tee Times: 3 days adv.
Fee 9 Holes: Weekday: No   **Weekend:** No
Fee 18 Holes: Weekday: $42.00 M-Th   **Weekend:** $57.00 F/S/S, Inc. Cart
Twilight Rates: Yes, after 4 pm, $22   **All Day Play:** No
Cart Rental: $13pp/18   **Discounts:** Junior
Lessons: $30/30 min. **Schools:** Yes   **Junior Golf:** Yes **Membership:** Yes, Junior
Clinics: Yes **Day Camps:** No   **Driving Range:** $3.00/bucket
Other: Snack bar / Clubhouse / Outings

Hosted the USGA Qualifiers, RI Amateur, RI Open. May book large or small outings. Challenging course rated by *Golf Digest*. Walking rates available in pm.

	1	2	3	4	5	6	7	8	9
PAR	4	4	4	5	3	4	4	3	4
YARDS	361	454	386	541	175	392	354	201	424
HDCP	15	3	7	1	11	9	13	17	5
	10	**11**	**12**	**13**	**14**	**15**	**16**	**17**	**18**
PAR	5	3	3	4	4	4	4	5	4
YARDS	605	220	125	327	440	334	394	540	368
HDCP	2	12	18	6	10	8	16	4	14

Directions: Take Route 195 to Route 24 South, follow Route 114 South, Raytheon Corp is on right. Take left on Union St. (a few mi. past Raytheon Corp.), club is on left 1/2 mile.

Heather Hill CC

Plainville, MA (508) 695-0309

Club Pro: Mike Cosentino, PGA
Pro Shop: Full inventory
Payment: Cash, checks
Tee Times: 1 week adv.

Tees	Holes	Yards	Par	USGA	Slope
BACK	27/18	6005	72	67.8	117
MIDDLE	27/18	5724	72	66.5	115
FRONT	27/18	4736	70	67.1	111

Fee 9 Holes: Weekday: $15.00
Fee 18 Holes: Weekday: $23.00
Twilight Rates: No
Cart Rental: $24.00/18 $12.00/9
Lessons: Yes **Schools:** No
Clinics: No **Day Camps:** No
Other: Clubhouse / Snack bar / Bar-lounge

Weekend: $18.00
Weekend: $30.00
All Day Play: No
Discounts: None
Junior Golf: No **Membership:** No
Driving Range: Yes

27 hole course: Middle and South courses play for 18. North course is 9 holes, 3368 yards. Open year round.

	1	2	3	4	5	6	7	8	9
PAR	3	4	4	5	4	4	5	3	4
YARDS	340	397	489	373	274	419	197	173	339
HDCP	7	3	11	5	13	1	15	17	9

	10	11	12	13	14	15	16	17	18
PAR	3	4	4	5	4	4	5	3	4
YARDS	388	169	518	334	317	367	183	413	315
HDCP	6	16	8	10	18	4	14	2	12

Directions: Take I-495 to Exit 15, follow Route 1A South to Route 106, take right on Route 106 (West Bacon St.) in Plainville Center. Course is on right.

Hidden Hollow Country Club

Rehoboth, MA (508) 252-9392

Club Pro: No
Pro Shop: No
Payment: Cash only
Tee Times: No

Tees	Holes	Yards	Par	USGA	Slope
BACK					
MIDDLE	9	2905	35		
FRONT					

Fee 9 Holes: Weekday: No
Fee 18 Holes: Weekday: $16.00
Twilight Rates: No
Cart Rental: $21.00/18 $13.00/9
Lessons: No **Schools:** No
Clinics: No **Day Camps:**
Other: Snack Bar / Bar-lounge / Clubhouse (1735)

Weekend: No
Weekend: $20.00
All Day Play: No
Discounts: None
Junior Golf: **Membership:** No
Driving Range: No

Old-style, picturesque short course. Popular preference of female golfers. Rates subject to change.

	1	2	3	4	5	6	7	8	9
PAR	4	4	3	4	4	5	4	3	4
YARDS	341	307	187	382	400	481	313	233	261
HDCP	7	11	17	5	3	1	9	15	13

	10	11	12	13	14	15	16	17	18
PAR									
YARDS									
HDCP									

Directions: I-195 to MA Exit 2. North off exit to Davis St. Left on Pleasant. Course is one mile on left.

4☺ =Excellent **3☺** =Very Good **2☺** =Good   **Southeastern MA & Rhode Island 159**

Hillside CC

Rehoboth, MA (508) 252-9761
www.rigolf.com/hillside

Club Pro: Ron Kapp, Golf Dir.
Pro Shop: Full inventory
Payment: Visa, MC, Disc., Cash
Tee Times: 7 days advance
Fee 9 Holes: Weekday: $16.00
Fee 18 Holes: Weekday: $25.00
Twilight Rates: No
Cart Rental: $12.00 pp/18 $6.00 pp/9
Lessons: No **Schools:** No
Clinics: No **Day Camps:** No
Other: Full food and beverage / Functions

Tees	Holes	Yards	Par	USGA	Slope
BACK	18	5780	71	69.5	126
MIDDLE	18	5575	71	68.4	122
FRONT	18	4825	72	68.4	122

Weekend: $18.00
Weekend: $30.00
All Day Play: No
Discounts: Senior & Junior
Junior Golf: No **Membership:** Yes
Driving Range: No

Sig. Hole: #16-Great view from elevated tee on this 165 yard par 3 to undulating green protected by a giant oak left front of green.

	1	2	3	4	5	6	7	8	9
PAR	4	3	5	3	4	4	5	4	4
YARDS	417	175	476	183	312	338	468	331	369
HDCP	1	11	9	17	15	5	7	13	3
	10	**11**	**12**	**13**	**14**	**15**	**16**	**17**	**18**
PAR	4	4	3	4	4	4	3	5	4
YARDS	325	277	130	377	355	315	162	448	322
HDCP	12	16	18	4	2	8	14	10	6

Directions: Take Route 24 S. Off at Route 44 West Taunton. Right onto Danforth Street. 1 mile west of intersection of Routes 118 & 44, Take first left onto River Street and first right onto Hillside Ave.

Hopedale CC

⊙⊙

Hill St., Hopedale, MA (508) 473-9876
www.hopedalecc.com

Club Pro: Donald Groft, PGA
Pro Shop: Full inventory
Payment: Visa, MC, Cash
Tee Times: No
Fee 9 Holes: Weekday: $20 bef. 3pm, $40 F
Fee 18 Holes: Weekday: $35 bef. 1pm, $40 F
Twilight Rates: No
Cart Rental: $20.00/18 $10.00/9
Lessons: $30/half hour **Schools:** No
Clinics: Junior **Day Camps:** No
Other: Clubhouse/Bar-lounge/Snack Bar

Tees	Holes	Yards	Par	USGA	Slope
BACK	9	6099	70	69	125
MIDDLE	9	6068	70	69	118
FRONT	9	5482	70	70.8	121

Weekend: No public play
Weekend: No public play
All Day Play: No
Discounts: None
Junior Golf: Yes **Membership:** Yes
Driving Range: No

New clubhouse. Water on first, third and sixth holes. Specified times for public play.

	1	2	3	4	5	6	7	8	9
PAR	4	5	3	4	4	4	4	4	3
YARDS	374	508	140	371	362	316	304	381	216
HDCP	2	6	18	10	12	14	16	4	8
	10	**11**	**12**	**13**	**14**	**15**	**16**	**17**	**18**
PAR	4	5	3	4	4	4	4	4	3
YARDS	383	508	172	400	393	334	312	396	229
HDCP	1	5	15	9	11	13	17	3	7

Directions: I -495 onto Route 85 Milford. Turn right onto Route 85 and right onto Route 16 thru center of Milford to Hopedale. At lights go left onto Hopedale St to end. Take right onto Green St to course.

Jamestown Golf & CC

Jamestown, RI (401) 423-9930

Club Pro: No
Pro Shop: Limited inventory
Payment: All Types
Tee Times: No
Fee 9 Holes: Weekday: $15.00
Fee 18 Holes: Weekday: $23.00
Twilight Rates: No
Cart Rental: $20.00/18 $12.00/9
Lessons: No **Schools:** No
Clinics: No **Day Camps:** No
Other: Clubhouse / Snack bar / Bar-lounge

Tees	Holes	Yards	Par	USGA	Slope
BACK	9	3048	36	69.7	110
MIDDLE	9	2751	36	69.7	110
FRONT	9	2421	38		

Weekend: $16.00
Weekend: $24.00
All Day Play: Yes
Discounts: None
Junior Golf: Yes **Membership:** No
Driving Range: No

Course is completely watered by irrigation. Open April - Nov.

	1	2	3	4	5	6	7	8	9
PAR	4	5	4	4	3	5	3	4	4
YARDS	270	484	279	375	114	379	141	368	328
HDCP	13	3	11	7	17	1	15	5	9
	10	**11**	**12**	**13**	**14**	**15**	**16**	**17**	**18**
PAR									
YARDS									
HDCP									

SE MA /RI

Directions: Take I-95 to Route 138 East. Go over Jamestown Bridge. Cross the island and follow signs to the Newport Bridge. When toll booths are in sight, stay to the right. Course is located just south of the Newport Bridge.

John F. Parker Municipal GC

Taunton, MA (508) 822-1797
www.ci.taunton.ma.us/ParkergolfIndex.htm

Club Pro: Phil Shuster
Pro Shop: Balls&Gloves
Payment: Cash only
Tee Times: No
Fee 9 Holes: Weekday: $16.00
Fee 18 Holes: Weekday: $19.00
Twilight Rates: No
Cart Rental: $20.00/18 $10.00/9
Lessons: Yes **Schools:**
Clinics: Yes **Day Camps:** No
Other: Snack bar / Bar-lounge

Tees	Holes	Yards	Par	USGA	Slope
BACK					
MIDDLE	9	3068	35	69.8	117
FRONT					

Weekend: $19.00
Weekend: $22.00
All Day Play: No
Discounts: Senior & Junior
Junior Golf: Yes **Membership:** Yes
Driving Range: $4.00/lg bucket

Reseeded fairways.

	1	2	3	4	5	6	7	8	9
PAR	4	4	4	5	4	3	4	4	3
YARDS	360	412	350	478	345	168	330	390	235
HDCP	9	1	8	2	3	5	6	4	7
	10	**11**	**12**	**13**	**14**	**15**	**16**	**17**	**18**
PAR									
YARDS									
HDCP									

Directions: From Providence, take Route 44 East into Taunton, left at Highland Street. From center of Taunton, go West on Route 44. Go to second set of lights. Turn right at Highland Street.

4✪ =Excellent 3✪ =Very Good 2✪ =Good   **Southeastern MA & Rhode Island 161**

Laurel Lane GC

◆◆

W. Kingston, RI (401) 783-3844

Club Pro: Ralph Lenihan
Pro Shop: Full inventory
Payment: Visa, MC
Tee Times: Yes
Fee 9 Holes: Weekday: $18.00
Fee 18 Holes: Weekday: $28.00
Twilight Rates: N/R
Cart Rental: $26/18, $13/9
Lessons: Yes **Schools:** No
Clinics: Yes **Day Camps:** No
Other: Clubhouse / Snack Bar / Bar-lounge

Tees	Holes	Yards	Par	USGA	Slope
BACK					120
MIDDLE	18	5806	71	68.1	114
FRONT	18	5381	70	70.8	115

Weekend: NA
Weekend: $35.00, $28 w/cart after 2pm
All Day Play:
Discounts: Junior
Junior Golf: No **Membership:** Yes
Driving Range: Yes

Home course for URI and Narragansett. Open Mar. - Dec. New clubhouse completed fall of 2003. South County course.

	1	2	3	4	5	6	7	8	9
PAR	4	5	3	4	4	4	3	4	4
YARDS	389	480	147	363	315	245	206	320	303
HDCP	1	9	17	11	5	13	3	15	7
	10	11	12	13	14	15	16	17	18
PAR	3	5	3	5	4	4	4	4	4
YARDS	143	472	161	538	392	317	311	323	381
HDCP	18	10	14	2	4	12	16	6	8

Directions: From I-95 N: Exit 3A to Route 138 E. approx. 7 mi. on right. From I-95 S: Exit 9, Exit 5B - Route 2 S to red light (Junction Route 138 W.) Turn right. Course is 0.1 miles on left.

Lindhbrook GC

Hope Valley, RI (401) 539-8700

Club Pro: No
Pro Shop: Full inventory
Payment: Visa, MC, Amex
Tee Times: Yes
Fee 9 Holes: Weekday: $13.00
Fee 18 Holes: Weekday: $18.00
Twilight Rates: Yes, after 6 pm
Cart Rental: $16pp/18
Lessons: Yes **Schools:** No
Clinics: Yes **Day Camps:** No
Other: Snack bar / Restaurant / Bar-lounge

Tees	Holes	Yards	Par	USGA	Slope
BACK	18	3000	54		
MIDDLE	18	2869	54		
FRONT	18	2600	54		

Weekend: $13.00
Weekend: $20.00
All Day Play: No
Discounts: Senior & Junior
Junior Golf: Yes **Membership:** Yes
Driving Range: No

South County course.

	1	2	3	4	5	6	7	8	9
PAR	3	3	3	3	3	3	3	3	3
YARDS	132	146	171	172	150	168	158	175	125
HDCP	16	14	4	10	12	6	8	2	12
	10	11	12	13	14	15	16	17	18
PAR	3	3	3	3	3	3	3	3	3
YARDS	139	143	127	180	181	192	143	183	184
HDCP	15	17	11	3	9	7	13	5	1

Directions: Take I-95 to Exit 2. If Northbound - bear right; if Southbound - turn left. Course 800 yards from I-95 on right.

Locust Valley Golf Course

.... 31

Attleboro, MA (508) 222-1500

Club Pro: No
Pro Shop: Limited inventory
Payment: Visa, MC
Tee Times: No
Fee 9 Holes: Weekday: $10.00
Fee 18 Holes: Weekday: $10.00
Twilight Rates: Yes, after 3 pm
Cart Rental: $20.00/18 10.00/9
Lessons: No **Schools:** No
Clinics: No **Day Camps:** No
Other: Snack bar / Bar-lounge

Tees	Holes	Yards	Par	USGA	Slope
BACK					
MIDDLE	9	6130	71	69.8	124
FRONT	9	5230	72	NA	NA

Weekend: $13.00
Weekend: $13.00
All Day Play: Yes
Discounts: Senior & Junior (M-F)
Junior Golf: No **Membership:** Yes
Driving Range: No

Special $7.50 weekday fee: Monday, Juniors and Wednesday, Ladies. Wide open and an easy walker.

	1	2	3	4	5	6	7	8	9
PAR	5	5	4	4	4	3	4	3	4
YARDS	465	485	360	335	375	150	373	160	362
HDCP	5	15	7	1	3	17	9	13	11
	10	11	12	13	14	15	16	17	18
PAR	5	4	4	4	4	3	4	3	4
YARDS	475	440	370	342	380	180	350	174	372
HDCP	8	4	10	12	6	18	12	16	14

Directions: Take I-95 South, take Route 123A Exit, follow to end, take right, quick left onto Tylor Street, ends at course.

SE MA /RI

Maplegate Country Club ✪✪

.... 32

Bellingham, MA (508) 966-4040
www.maplegate.com

Club Pro: D. Munroe
Pro Shop: Limited Inventory
Payment: Cash , MC, Visa
Tee Times: 6 days adv.
Fee 9 Holes: Weekday: $37 before 7am
Fee 18 Holes: Weekday: $46, $60 w/cart
Twilight Rates: Yes, after 2 pm
Cart Rental: $10 wk, $14 wknd
Lessons: Yes **Schools:** Jr. & Sr.
Clinics: Yes **Day Camps:** N/R
Other: Snack Bar

Tees	Holes	Yards	Par	USGA	Slope
BACK	18	6815	72	74.2	133
MIDDLE	18	5837	72	69.5	122
FRONT	18	4852	72	70.2	124

Weekend: $37 before 7am
Weekend: $56, $70 w/cart
All Day Play: Replays
Discounts: Jr., Early Bird (M-TH)
Junior Golf: Yes **Membership:** No
Driving Range: Yes

COUPON

Player's Comments: "Must be straight shooter. Tee boxes need work, but great layout." Landing area design allows use of drivers for all par 4's and 5's. Carts required weekends, holidays before noon.

	1	2	3	4	5	6	7	8	9
PAR	5	4	3	5	4	4	4	3	4
YARDS	515	335	173	522	431	435	417	145	434
HDCP	7	13	15	1	5	9	3	17	11
	10	11	12	13	14	15	16	17	18
PAR	4	4	3	4	5	3	5	4	4
YARDS	376	382	191	388	510	227	530	357	447
HDCP	14	10	18	8	4	16	2	12	6

Directions: I-495 to Exit 18. Bear right off exit and take first right ot Maple St. Course will be 1 mile on left.

4✪ =Excellent **3✪** =Very Good **2✪** =Good   **Southeastern MA & Rhode Island 163**

Marion Golf Course

South Dr., Marion, MA (508) 748-0199

Club Pro: No
Pro Shop: Limited inventory
Payment: Cash only
Tee Times: No
Fee 9 Holes: Weekday: $11.00
Fee 18 Holes: Weekday: $18.00
Twilight Rates: N/R
Cart Rental: No
Lessons: No **Schools:** No
Clinics: No **Day Camps:** No
Other: Club Rentals

Tees	Holes	Yards	Par	USGA	Slope
BACK	9	2695	34	67.1	121
MIDDLE	9	2695	34	67.1	121
FRONT	9	2089	35	66.0	117

Weekend: $13.00
Weekend: $20.00
All Day Play: N/R
Discounts: Senior & Junior
Junior Golf: No **Membership:** Yes
Driving Range: No

Sig. Hole: #9, 115 yard, very challenging par 3. European Links. Open year round. "Several greens are defended by stonewalls and cross bunkers. A must play for the golf purist." A.P.

	1	2	3	4	5	6	7	8	9
PAR	4	4	3	5	4	4	4	3	3
YARDS	315	290	175	460	365	430	365	180	115
HDCP	8	6	4	7	5	1	2	3	9
	10	11	12	13	14	15	16	17	18
PAR									
YARDS									
HDCP									

Directions: Take I-495 South to I-195 East. Go to Exit 20. Bear right off exit onto Route 105. Follow to lights, bear left onto Route 6. Follow to next set of lights, bear right onto Point Rd. Follow approx. 1.5 mi. Course on right.

Meadow Brook GC

Richmond, RI (401) 539-8491

Club Pro: No
Pro Shop: Yes
Payment: Cash only
Tee Times: No
Fee 9 Holes: Weekday: No
Fee 18 Holes: Weekday: $16.00
Twilight Rates: Yes, after 5 pm
Cart Rental: $18.00/18 $10.00/9
Lessons: No **Schools:** No
Clinics: No **Day Camps:** No
Other: Clubhouse / Snack bar

Tees	Holes	Yards	Par	USGA	Slope
BACK					
MIDDLE	18	6075	71	70.1	118
FRONT	18	5605	73	N/A	N/A

Weekend: No
Weekend: $20.00
All Day Play: Yes
Discounts: None
Junior Golf: No **Membership:** No
Driving Range: No

New tees. The course is very level and well laid out. Carts only available for 18 hole play on weekends. Children and non-golfers must be paid for. South County course

	1	2	3	4	5	6	7	8	9
PAR	4	3	4	4	3	5	4	4	5
YARDS	300	175	350	335	155	535	300	365	505
HDCP	13	15	7	9	17	1	11	5	3
	10	11	12	13	14	15	16	17	18
PAR	3	4	4	5	4	4	4	4	3
YARDS	180	385	350	485	395	385	340	395	140
HDCP	16	8	14	2	6	10	12	4	18

Directions: I-95 to Exit 3A in RI. Continue on Route 138 East. Course is 1 mile East of I-95.

Melody Hill Golf Course

Harmony, RI (401) 949-9851

Club Pro: Lynn Molhan
Pro Shop: Full inventory
Payment: Cash only
Tee Times: No
Fee 9 Holes: Weekday: $15.00
Fee 18 Holes: Weekday: $21.00
Twilight Rates: Yes
Cart Rental: $24.00/18 $12.00/9
Lessons: Yes **Schools:** No
Clinics: No **Day Camps:** No
Other: Clubhouse / Snack bar / Bar-lounge

Tees	Holes	Yards	Par	USGA	Slope
BACK					
MIDDLE	18	6185	71	69.0	113
FRONT					

Weekend: $16.00
Weekend: $25.00
All Day Play: No
Discounts: Sr,$18/18 $14/9, M-F
Junior Golf: Yes **Membership:** No
Driving Range: No

Sig. Hole: #8, 500 yard par 5. Challenging sloping fairway, hit straight to avoid woods. Lessons by certified teacher of golf. Twilight rates: 9 holes only $12 after 5 weekdays, $15 after 4 weekends

	1	2	3	4	5	6	7	8	9
PAR	4	4	4	3	4	3	4	5	4
YARDS	360	315	385	95	465	145	425	500	235
HDCP	10	13	8	18	3	17	5	1	14

	10	11	12	13	14	15	16	17	18
PAR	5	4	5	3	4	3	4	4	4
YARDS	445	405	535	185	360	165	355	400	410
HDCP	2	6	4	15	11	16	12	7	9

Directions: Take Route 44 West toward CT, take first left after fire station in Harmony Center onto Saw Mill Road.

Middlebrook CC

Rehoboth, MA (508) 252-9395

Club Pro: No
Pro Shop: Limited inventory
Payment: Cash only
Tee Times: Weekends
Fee 9 Holes: Weekday: $13.00
Fee 18 Holes: Weekday: $17.00
Twilight Rates: No
Cart Rental: $20.00/18 $12.00/9
Lessons: No **Schools:** No
Clinics: No **Day Camps:** No
Other: Snack bar / Bar-lounge / Clubhouse

Tees	Holes	Yards	Par	USGA	Slope
BACK	N/A				
MIDDLE	9	5592	70	67.0	122
FRONT	9	5018	70	N/A	108

Weekend: $16.00
Weekend: $21.00
All Day Play: No
Discounts: Senior
Junior Golf: No **Membership:** Yes, Full.
Driving Range: No

Sig. Hole: #5. Par 5 plays 530 yards from the back markers. Creek runs across the fairway 100 yards from green. Green is tiered and bunkered. Open April 1-Nov. 30. Beautiful gardens.

	1	2	3	4	5	6	7	8	9
PAR	4	4	4	4	5	3	3	4	4
YARDS	340	360	301	350	500	213	130	300	290
HDCP	9	5	15	3	1	7	17	13	11

	10	11	12	13	14	15	16	17	18
PAR	4	4	4	4	5	3	3	4	4
YARDS	353	340	320	340	530	180	145	280	300
HDCP	10	6	16	4	2	8	18	14	12

Directions: Take I-195 to MA Exit 2. North off exit to Davis St. Right on Davis to Pleasant St. Left on Pleasant. Course is one mi. on right.

Midville Country Club

W. Warwick, RI (401) 828-9215

Club Pro: No
Pro Shop: Limited inventory
Payment: Cash only
Tee Times: No
Fee 9 Holes: Weekday: $20.00
Fee 18 Holes: Weekday: $29.00
Twilight Rates: No
Cart Rental: $28.00/18 $14.00/9
Lessons: No **Schools:** No
Clinics: No **Day Camps:** No
Other: Clubhouse / Snack bar / Bar-lounge

Tees	Holes	Yards	Par	USGA	Slope
BACK	9	2970	35	68.3	115
MIDDLE	9	2779	70	68.2	114
FRONT	9	2340	35		

Weekend: $21.00
Weekend: $33.00
All Day Play: No
Discounts: Senior
Junior Golf: No **Membership:** No
Driving Range: No

Scenic nine hole layout. One of the best conditioned public courses in N.E. Open April - December.

	1	2	3	4	5	6	7	8	9
PAR	4	4	4	4	3	5	3	4	4
YARDS	334	314	327	346	145	523	145	309	336
HDCP	7	5	3	9	17	1	15	13	11
	10	11	12	13	14	15	16	17	18
PAR	4	4	4	4	3	5	3	4	4
YARDS	359	321	343	378	171	540	168	346	344
HDCP									

Directions: Take I-95 to Route 113 West Exit. Go straight through 3 sets of lights. Cross bridge, bear right and then straight through the fourth light. Course is 1 mi. on left.

Montaup Country Club

Portsmouth, RI (401) 683-0955

Club Pro: Stephen Diemoz
Pro Shop: Full inventory
Payment: Cash, Credit Card, Check
Tee Times: 1 day adv.
Fee 9 Holes: Weekday: N/A
Fee 18 Holes: Weekday: $44.00
Twilight Rates: No
Cart Rental: $32.00/18
Lessons: $30.00/half hour **Schools:** No
Clinics: No **Day Camps:** No
Other: Clubhouse Snack bar / Restaurant / Bar-lounge

Tees	Holes	Yards	Par	USGA	Slope
BACK	18	6446	71	71.7	126
MIDDLE	18	6010	71	69.6	123
FRONT	18	5432	73	71.5	120

Weekend: N/A
Weekend: $44.00
All Day Play: No
Discounts: None
Junior Golf: Yes **Membership:** Yes
Driving Range: No

Player's Comment: "Always in excellent shape and great to walk. Very golfer friendly." Open April - Dec.

	1	2	3	4	5	6	7	8	9
PAR	4	4	3	4	5	4	5	3	4
YARDS	413	399	219	391	527	360	561	152	334
HDCP	3	7	9	11	1	13	5	15	17
	10	11	12	13	14	15	16	17	18
PAR	3	4	3	5	3	4	5	4	4
YARDS	159	408	187	513	166	431	518	404	304
HDCP	12	6	14	10	16	2	8	4	18

Directions: Take Route 24 to Anthony Rd. Exit, right off ramp; course is visible from ramp.

New England CC

★★ 39

Bellingham, MA (508) 883-2300
www.newenglandcountryclub.com

Tees	Holes	Yards	Par	USGA	Slope
BACK	18	6430	71	70.8	130
MIDDLE	18	5867	71	67.2	122
FRONT	18	4908	71	68.7	121

Club Pro: Mark Copithorne
Pro Shop: Full Inventory
Payment: MC/Visa
Tee Times: 3 dys/Wknd, 5 dys/Wkday
Fee 9 Holes: Weekday: None
Fee 18 Holes: Weekday: $56 ride Mon-Th
Twilight Rates: Yes, after 2 pm
Cart Rental: Carts Included F/S/S/H
Lessons: $45/45 min **Schools:** clinics
Clinics: Yes **Day Camps:** No
Other: Clubhouse / Restaurant / Pub / Outdoor Deck / Tent

Weekend: None
Weekend: $69 F, $71 S/S/H
All Day Play: No
Discounts: None
Junior Golf: No **Membership:** weekday/ 7-day.
Driving Range: All Grass

COUPON

Sig. Hole: #18, 397 yard, downhill par 4 is a spectacular finishing hole. Voted "One of the Best 18" by the Boston Globe. New amenities include GPS in cart and added new set of tees.

	1	2	3	4	5	6	7	8	9
PAR	5	4	4	3	5	3	4	4	4
YARDS	497	357	314	145	490	122	386	320	352
HDCP	5	9	13	15	1	17	7	11	3

	10	11	12	13	14	15	16	17	18
PAR	4	5	3	4	4	4	3	4	4
YARDS	355	501	145	382	327	297	140	340	397
HDCP	6	2	16	8	10	18	14	12	4

Directions: Route 495 to Exit 16 (King St.) Continue West on King St. for 6 mi. At light make a left onto Wrentham St. Bear right at the fire station onto Paine St. Course is .25 mi. on left.

North Kingstown Muni.

★★ 40

N. Kingstown, RI (401) 294-0684

Tees	Holes	Yards	Par	USGA	Slope
BACK	18	6161	70	69.3	123
MIDDLE	18	5848	70	67.8	121
FRONT	18	5227	70	69.5	115

Club Pro: John Rainone, Head Pro
Pro Shop: Full inventory
Payment: Cash
Tee Times: 2 days adv.
Fee 9 Holes: Weekday: $18.00
Fee 18 Holes: Weekday: $28.00
Twilight Rates: Yes, after 4 pm
Cart Rental: $24.00/18 $13.00/9
Lessons: Yes **Schools:** Jr.
Clinics: Yes **Day Camps:** No
Other: Restaurant / Lounge / Clubhouse

Weekend: $20.00
Weekend: $35.00
All Day Play: No
Discounts: Senior & Junior
Junior Golf: Yes **Membership:** Yes. Residents
Driving Range: $5/lg. $3/sm.

COUPON

Players' Comments: "Just plain enjoyable. Cannot believe it is a muncipal course." Links style overlooking Narragansett Bay. South County course

	1	2	3	4	5	6	7	8	9
PAR	4	4	3	5	4	4	5	3	4
YARDS	369	411	185	499	375	353	545	197	283
HDCP	11	1	15	9	7	5	3	13	17

	10	11	12	13	14	15	16	17	18
PAR	3	5	4	4	3	4	4	4	3
YARDS	171	559	333	403	194	413	398	315	158
HDCP	16	6	10	8	14	2	4	12	18

Directions: Route 95 to Route 4 S. (Exit 7). Take Route 403 (Quonset Point). 3 miles take right at light. 1 mile Left at light. Follow to end, take right, club is 1/2 mile on right.

Pine Valley Golf Course

Rehoboth, MA (508) 336-9815

Club Pro: Bob Tacheco
Pro Shop: Yes
Payment: Visa, MC
Tee Times: No
Fee 9 Holes: Weekday: $17.00
Fee 18 Holes: Weekday: $17.00
Twilight Rates: After 3:30 wkdys, 2:30 wknds
Cart Rental: $20.00/18, $12.00/9
Lessons: no **Schools:** No
Clinics: No **Day Camps:** No
Other: Snack bar / Bar-lounge

Tees	Holes	Yards	Par	USGA	Slope
BACK					
MIDDLE	9	3015	35		118
FRONT	9	2375	35		113

Weekend: $19.00
Weekend: $19.00
All Day Play: Yes
Discounts: Senior wkdys $13
Junior Golf: No **Membership:** No
Driving Range: No

Players' Comments: "Short course. Need to be creative. Big greens. Two practice greens." "Narrow and challenging fairways." "In good repair. I liked the course."

	1	2	3	4	5	6	7	8	9
PAR	4	3	4	5	4	3	4	4	4
YARDS	387	172	397	568	306	218	383	301	283
HDCP	3	9	2	1	5	8	4	7	6
	10	11	12	13	14	15	16	17	18
PAR									
YARDS									
HDCP									

Directions: I-95 to I-195 East, take Exit 2 Route 136 North, left onto Davis, turn right at end of road.

Pinehurst CC

✪✪

Carolina, RI (401) 364-8600
www.pinehurstgolfri.com

Club Pro: David McBride
Pro Shop: Limited inventory
Payment: Cash only
Tee Times: 1 day
Fee 9 Holes: Weekday: $17.00
Fee 18 Holes: Weekday: $25.00
Twilight Rates: Yes, after 5 pm
Cart Rental: $12.00
Lessons: **Schools:**
Clinics: **Day Camps:**
Other: Snack Bar / Restaurant / Bar-lounge

Tees	Holes	Yards	Par	USGA	Slope
BACK	9	2900	35	67.7	131
MIDDLE	9	2611	35	66.2	123
FRONT	9	2309	35		

Weekend: $19.00
Weekend: $27.00
All Day Play: No
Discounts: Senior & Junior
Junior Golf: **Membership:** Yes
Driving Range:

"Short 9 holes with one par 5. Very playable for all levels of golfing ability. 9th is the signature hole." R.W. Beakman-Wermy / Intergolf Design.

	1	2	3	4	5	6	7	8	9
PAR	4	5	3	4	4	3	4	4	4
YARDS	348	540	129	382	337	145	314	320	385
HDCP	7	3	17	5	11	9	15	13	1
	10	11	12	13	14	15	16	17	18
PAR									
YARDS									
HDCP									

Directions: Route I-95, Exit 3 to Route138 East to Route 112. 2.4 miles to Pinehurst Drive on left.

Rehoboth Country Club

Rehoboth, MA (508) 252-6259
www.rehobothgolfcourse.com

Club Pro: No
Pro Shop: Full inventory
Payment: Visa, MC
Tee Times: 5 days adv.

Tees	Holes	Yards	Par	USGA	Slope
BACK	18	6760	72	71.4	124
MIDDLE	18	6340	72	69.3	121
FRONT	18	5490	72	70.6	114

Fee 9 Holes: Weekday: $18.00   **Weekend:** $20.00
Fee 18 Holes: Weekday: $27.00   **Weekend:** $32.00
Twilight Rates: Yes, after 3 pm   **All Day Play:** No
Cart Rental: $24.00/18, $12.00/9   **Discounts:** Senior & Junior
Lessons: No **Schools:** Yes   **Junior Golf:** No **Membership:** Yes
Clinics: No **Day Camps:** No   **Driving Range:** Yes
Other: Snack bar / Clubhouse / Restaurant / Bar-lounge

Driving range to open mid 2004. Bunkers being redone. Noted for large true greens and use of every club in bag.

	1	2	3	4	5	6	7	8	9
PAR	4	5	3	5	4	4	4	3	4
YARDS	380	500	155	550	400	310	300	155	410
HDCP	4	5	3	5	4	4	4	3	4

	10	11	12	13	14	15	16	17	18
PAR	5	4	3	4	4	4	3	5	4
YARDS	500	345	205	380	330	270	170	540	440
HDCP	5	4	3	4	4	4	3	5	4

Directions: From Providence: East on Route 44 to Route 118, turn left and 1st left to course. From Taunton: West on Route 44 to Route 118. Turn right, 1st left to course. From Attleboro: East on Route 118, right on Fairview to Homestead. Right, then 1st left onto Perryville.

Richmond Country Club   ✪✪✪

Richmond, RI (401) 364-9200

Club Pro: No
Pro Shop: Full inventory
Payment: Visa, MC
Tee Times: 2 days adv.

Tees	Holes	Yards	Par	USGA	Slope
BACK	18	6515	71	69.9	117
MIDDLE	18	5827	71	68.5	114
FRONT	18	4974	71	70.4	113

Fee 9 Holes: Weekday: $15 after 3:00 pm   **Weekend:** $18.00 after 3:00 pm
Fee 18 Holes: Weekday: $30.00   **Weekend:** $35.00
Twilight Rates: Yes   **All Day Play:**
Cart Rental: $12pp/18   **Discounts:** None
Lessons: No **Schools:** No   **Junior Golf:** No **Membership:** No
Clinics: No **Day Camps:** No   **Driving Range:** Yes
Other: Restaurant / Clubhouse / Bar-Lounge / Banquet facilities

Players' Comments: "Plush fairways. Pure greens. Aesthetically pleasant." "Just like North Carolina." South County course.

	1	2	3	4	5	6	7	8	9
PAR	4	4	3	5	3	4	5	4	4
YARDS	318	353	204	504	165	428	450	277	285
HDCP	9	5	13	1	17	3	7	15	11

	10	11	12	13	14	15	16	17	18
PAR	4	5	3	4	4	3	5	3	4
YARDS	320	431	184	408	368	176	474	154	328
HDCP	14	10	16	2	6	8	4	18	12

Directions: I-95, Exit 3B; follow 2 miles. Left at flashing light onto Mechanic Street. 2.5 miles, turn right onto Sandy Pond Road.

4✪ =Excellent **3✪** =Very Good **2✪** =Good   **Southeastern MA & Rhode Island 169**

Rochester Golf Club

Rochester, MA (508) 763-5155

Club Pro: Herb Giffen
Pro Shop: Yes
Payment: Cash only
Tee Times: Sat, Sun, & holidays
Fee 9 Holes: Weekday: $15.00
Fee 18 Holes: Weekday: $25.00
Twilight Rates: No
Cart Rental: Limited, $20/18 $10/9
Lessons: Private **Schools:** No
Clinics: No **Day Camps:** Yes
Other: Snack bar

Tees	Holes	Yards	Par	USGA	Slope
BACK	18	5250	69	66	115
MIDDLE	18	4830	69	64	107
FRONT	18	4032	69	58	100

Weekend: $15.00
Weekend: $25.00
All Day Play: No
Discounts: None
Junior Golf: Yes **Membership:** No
Driving Range: No

Course is challenging with beautiful scenery. Accuracy at premium, not long but tight. " Heavy forest and water on 14 holes define the challenge. Think twice about pulling out the big dawg." A.P.

	1	2	3	4	5	6	7	8	9
PAR	3	4	4	4	3	5	4	4	3
YARDS	156	386	258	252	128	435	250	312	116
HDCP	14	2	9	15	16	11	18	6	13
	10	11	12	13	14	15	16	17	18
PAR	4	3	4	4	3	4	4	4	5
YARDS	280	110	272	290	180	260	280	373	492
HDCP	10	17	12	7	3	8	4	1	5

Directions: Take I-195 to Rochester Exit, follow Route 105 approximately 4 miles north on right.

Rolling Greens GC

N. Kingstown, RI (401) 294-9859

Club Pro: No
Pro Shop: Limited inventory
Payment: Cash only
Tee Times: No
Fee 9 Holes: Weekday: $15.00
Fee 18 Holes: Weekday: $21.00
Twilight Rates: No
Cart Rental: $20.00/18 $12.00/9
Lessons: No **Schools:** No
Clinics: No **Day Camps:** No
Other: Clubhouse / Snack bar / Restaurant / Bar-lounge

Tees	Holes	Yards	Par	USGA	Slope
BACK					
MIDDLE	9	3072	35		
FRONT					

Weekend: $17.00
Weekend: $24.00
All Day Play: No
Discounts: None
Junior Golf: No **Membership:** Yes
Driving Range: No

The course is hilly and has just one water hole. The remodeled 7th hole has a new green. South County course

	1	2	3	4	5	6	7	8	9
PAR	4	4	4	3	5	4	4	3	4
YARDS	339	353	383	147	550	325	315	220	440
HDCP	13	5	7	17	3	9	11	15	1
	10	11	12	13	14	15	16	17	18
PAR									
YARDS									
HDCP									

Directions: Take I-95 South to Route 4, N. Kingston. Get onto Route 102 West toward Exeter. Course is 1.25 mi. on right.

Rose Hill Golf Course

South Kingston, RI (401) 788-1088
www.rosehillgolfclub.com

Club Pro: Dave McBride
Pro Shop: Limited inventory
Payment:
Tee Times: 1 days adv.
Fee 9 Holes: Weekday: $13.00
Fee 18 Holes: Weekday: $18.00
Twilight Rates: After 4 pm
Cart Rental: $12/9, $20/18
Lessons: Yes **Schools:** Sr. & Jr.
Clinics: Yes **Day Camps:**
Other: New Bistro / Restaurant / Clubhouse / League play

Tees	Holes	Yards	Par	USGA	Slope
BACK	9	1206	27		
MIDDLE					
FRONT	9	981	27		

Weekend: $13.00
Weekend: $18.00
All Day Play: No
Discounts: Senior
Junior Golf: **Membership:** No
Driving Range: No

COUPON

"Sophisticated design for a 9 holer that circles a pond situated in the middle of the course. Excellent greens." R.W. Family friendly environment. South County course

	1	2	3	4	5	6	7	8	9
PAR	3	3	3	3	3	3	3	3	3
YARDS	144	140	74	101	143	168	129	178	129
HDCP									

	10	11	12	13	14	15	16	17	18
PAR									
YARDS									
HDCP									

Directions: From Route 1 North or South, take Route 138 West 2.5 miles and turn left onto Rose Hill Road. Course is 9/10 mile on right.

Seaview Country Club

Warwick, RI (401) 739-6311

Club Pro: Bill D'Angelos, PGA
Pro Shop: Full inventory
Payment: Visa, MC, Amex
Tee Times: Weekends
Fee 9 Holes: Weekday: $16.00
Fee 18 Holes: Weekday: $23.00
Twilight Rates: Yes, after 6 pm
Cart Rental: $24.00/18 $12.00/9
Lessons: $20/halfhour **Schools:** No
Clinics: Yes **Day Camps:** No
Other: Clubhouse / Lockers / Showers / Restaurant / Bar-lounge

Tees	Holes	Yards	Par	USGA	Slope
BACK					
MIDDLE	9	5646	72	67.7	119
FRONT	9	5054	72	66.8	117

Weekend: $18.00
Weekend: $27.00
All Day Play: No
Discounts: Senior
Junior Golf: Yes **Membership:** Yes
Driving Range: $6/lg. $4/sm.

Set on Narrangansett Bay, the course provides a challenge for all levels of golfers. Short and very challenging with many water hazards and bunkers.

	1	2	3	4	5	6	7	8	9
PAR	4	4	4	5	3	3	4	4	5
YARDS	305	274	242	551	143	201	302	310	495
HDCP	7	13	15	1	17	3	9	5	11

	10	11	12	13	14	15	16	17	18
PAR	4	4	4	5	3	3	4	4	5
YARDS	305	274	242	551	143	201	302	310	495
HDCP	8	14	16	2	18	4	10	6	12

Directions: Take I-95 to Route 117 East, continue for 5 mi. Take right onto Warwick Neck Ave., right onto Meadow View Ave., Follow signs 1 mile to club.

4✪ =Excellent 3✪ =Very Good 2✪ =Good   **Southeastern MA & Rhode Island 171**

Shadow Brook Golf Course

So. Attleboro, MA (508) 399-8400

Club Pro: Al Vallente, PGA
Pro Shop: Full inventory
Payment: Most major
Tee Times: 7 days adv.
Fee 9 Holes: Weekday: $10.00
Fee 18 Holes: Weekday: $14.00
Twilight Rates: No
Cart Rental: No
Lessons: Yes **Schools:** Jr./Sr.
Clinics: Yes **Day Camps:** Yes
Other: Vending machines

Weekend: $10.00
Weekend: $14.00
All Day Play: No
Discounts: None
Junior Golf: Yes **Membership:** Value cards
Driving Range: $10/jumbo $6/lg. $4/med.

Tees	Holes	Yards	Par	USGA	Slope
BACK					
MIDDLE	9	752	27		
FRONT					

COUPON

"Perfect for all level players to practice wedge game." R. W.

	1	2	3	4	5	6	7	8	9
PAR	3	3	3	3	3	3	3	3	3
YARDS	82	62	70	81	75	64	65	95	83
HDCP									
	10	11	12	13	14	15	16	17	18
PAR									
YARDS									
HDCP									

Directions: From 95 N or S, take Exit 2B. Course is one mile on right.

Silver Spring Golf Club

50

E. Providence, RI (401) 434-9697

Club Pro: No
Pro Shop: No
Payment: Cash only
Tee Times: No
Fee 9 Holes: Weekday:
Fee 18 Holes: Weekday: $6/6, $12/12, $15/18
Twilight Rates:
Cart Rental: No
Lessons: No **Schools:** No
Clinics: No **Day Camps:** No
Other: No

Weekend:
Weekend: $7/6, $13/12, $18/18
All Day Play:
Discounts: None
Junior Golf: No **Membership:** Yes
Driving Range: No

Tees	Holes	Yards	Par	USGA	Slope
BACK					
MIDDLE	4	1668	23	N/A	N/A
FRONT					

6 hole course, fairly hilly with tree-lined fairways. Good practice course. *Can play 6, 12 or 18 holes at various rates. Open May - Dec.

	1	2	3	4	5	6	7	8	9
PAR	4	5	3	3	5	3			
YARDS	315	433	173	123	411	122			
HDCP									
	10	11	12	13	14	15	16	17	18
PAR									
YARDS									
HDCP									

Directions: Take I-195 to RI Exit 4. Go south on Veterans Memorial Parkway. Course is 3 mi. on Route 103 South.

Stone-E-Lea Golf Course

Attleboro, MA (508) 222-9735

Tees	Holes	Yards	Par	USGA	Slope
BACK	18	6251	69	69.5	116
MIDDLE	18	6030	69	67.8	112
FRONT					

Club Pro: No
Pro Shop: No
Payment: Cash only
Tee Times: No
Fee 9 Holes: Weekday: $13.00
Fee 18 Holes: Weekday: $20.00
Twilight Rates: No
Cart Rental: $20.00/18 $10.00/9
Lessons: No **Schools:** No
Clinics: No **Day Camps:** No
Other: Snack bar / Bar

Weekend: $17.00
Weekend: $28.00
All Day Play: Yes
Discounts: Senior M-F before 2
Junior Golf: No **Membership:** No
Driving Range: No

Discounts for seniors over 62. Open year round.

	1	2	3	4	5	6	7	8	9
PAR	4	4	4	3	4	4	3	4	4
YARDS	360	350	310	185	330	420	175	380	430
HDCP	9	5	11	13	17	1	15	3	7

	10	11	12	13	14	15	16	17	18
PAR	5	4	4	4	4	3	4	4	3
YARDS	490	390	410	390	265	190	390	325	240
HDCP	14	12	4	8	18	6	2	16	10

Directions: Take I-95 to Exit PA (Newport Avenue South). At first light take left onto Cottage Street. Course is 2 miles on left.From R.I. take I-95 N to Exit 2A, remaining directions same.

Sun Valley CC

Rehoboth, MA (508) 336-8686

Tees	Holes	Yards	Par	USGA	Slope
BACK	18	6734	71	71.0	118
MIDDLE	18	6383	71	71.0	118
FRONT	18	5654	71	71.0	N/A

Club Pro: No
Pro Shop: Limited inventory
Payment: Cash only
Tee Times: No
Fee 9 Holes: Weekday: $18.00
Fee 18 Holes: Weekday: $23.00
Twilight Rates: No
Cart Rental: $22.00/18, $12.00/9
Lessons: No **Schools:** No
Clinics: No **Day Camps:** No
Other: Restaurant / Clubhouse / Bar-lounge / Lockers / Snack Bar / Showers

Weekend: N/A
Weekend: $28.00, $21 after 2 pm
All Day Play:
Discounts: Senior. Weekdays.
Junior Golf: No **Membership:** No
Driving Range:

COUPON

Sig. Hole: #12, dogleg right, green to the left, brook runs through it. Championship course, flat, willow tree lined, large fairways (wide), some brooks, greens excellent, shirts required. Open March - Nov.

	1	2	3	4	5	6	7	8	9
PAR	4	4	5	3	4	3	5	4	4
YARDS	345	336	475	180	380	155	510	415	400
HDCP	13	11	5	15	9	17	3	1	7

	10	11	12	13	14	15	16	17	18
PAR	4	5	4	3	4	4	3	4	4
YARDS	365	450	425	172	380	400	195	385	415
HDCP	14	4	2	18	10	8	16	12	6

Directions: Route I-195 West to Route 114A to Route 44 East for 3 miles. Take right on Lake Street. Go 1 mile to course.

4✪ =Excellent **3✪** =Very Good **2✪** =Good

Swansea Country Club ✪✪ 53 ▶

Swansea, MA (508) 379-9886

Club Pro: Glenn Kornasla
Pro Shop: Limited inventory
Payment: Most major cards, no checks
Tee Times: Thurs noon for following wkdys

Tees	Holes	Yards	Par	USGA	Slope
BACK	18	6840	72	72.8	126
MIDDLE	18	6429	72	70.9	125
FRONT	18	5598	72	69.4	113

Fee 9 Holes: Weekday: $21.00
Fee 18 Holes: Weekday: $30.00
Twilight Rates: Yes, after 6 pm
Cart Rental: $12pp/18, $7pp/9
Lessons: $30/ half hour, $120/5 **Schools:** No
Clinics: Yes **Day Camps:** No

Weekend: $25.00
Weekend: $39, $30 after 2 pm
All Day Play: No
Discounts: Sr & Jr.18 hole wkdy spec
Junior Golf: Yes **Membership:** Yes
Driving Range: Yes - grass tees

COUPON

Other: Clubhouse / Snack bar / Restaurant / Bar-lounge / Outdoor patio & tent seating 200

Players' Comments: "Fastest public greens in S.E. MA and RI." "Challenging; but fair." Improvements include new bunkers on holes 2, 10, 18, and drainage work. Open year round, weather permitting. Walkable.

	1	2	3	4	5	6	7	8	9
PAR	4	5	4	3	4	3	4	5	4
YARDS	331	496	415	206	353	118	366	475	419
HDCP	11	13	3	7	5	17	9	15	1
	10	11	12	13	14	15	16	17	18
PAR	4	3	4	5	4	3	4	5	4
YARDS	323	170	366	615	291	203	368	478	436
HDCP	16	12	10	4	14	8	6	18	2

Directions: I-195 East or West to Exit #2 (Massachusetts). South on Route 136 for 1 mile. Golf course on right.

Touisset Country Club ✪✪ 54 ▶

Swansea, MA (508) 679-9577
www.touissetcountryclub.com

Club Pro: Les Brigham
Pro Shop: Full inventory
Payment: Cash,Visa, MC, DSC
Tee Times: No

Tees	Holes	Yards	Par	USGA	Slope
BACK	N/A					
MIDDLE	9	6206	71	69.1	111
FRONT	9	5551	72	71.1	114

Fee 9 Holes: Weekday: $16.00
Fee 18 Holes: Weekday: $17.50
Twilight Rates: Yes
Cart Rental: $26.00/18 $13.50/9
Lessons: $18.00/half hour **Schools:** Yes
Clinics: Yes **Day Camps:** N/R

Weekend: $18.50
Weekend: $22.00
All Day Play: No
Discounts: Senior & Junior
Junior Golf: Yes **Membership:** Yes
Driving Range: No

Other: Snack bar / Restaurant / Bar-lounge / Clubhouse / Lockers / Practice area and putting greens.

Nine hole course with four sets of tees. Fairly flat but challenging. Open year round if possible.

	1	2	3	4	5	6	7	8	9
PAR	4	4	4	4	3	4	3	5	4
YARDS	324	291	373	388	118	448	160	534	388
HDCP	11	13	9	3	17	1	15	5	7
	10	11	12	13	14	15	16	17	18
PAR	4	4	4	4	3	5	3	5	4
YARDS	324	305	383	405	140	514	164	547	400
HDCP	12	14	8	4	18	10	16	6	2

Directions: Exit 3 off I-195, Route 6 West. Left at first traffic light onto Maple Street. Straight 3/4 mile to 221 Pearse Road.

Triggs Memorial GC

Providence, RI (401) 521-8460

○○ 55 ▶

Club Pro: Mike Ryan
Pro Shop: Limited inventory
Payment: Visa, MC, Cash
Tee Times: 1 week adv.
Fee 9 Holes: Weekday: $19.50
Fee 18 Holes: Weekday: $33.00
Twilight Rates: No
Cart Rental: $28.00/18
Lessons: Yes **Schools:** No
Clinics: Yes **Day Camps:** No
Other: Clubhouse / Lockers / Showers / Snack bar / Restaurant / Bar-lounge

Tees	Holes	Yards	Par	USGA	Slope
BACK	18	6522	72	72.8	128
MIDDLE	18	6302	72	71.7	125
FRONT	18	5392	72	73.1	123

Weekend: $20.00
Weekend: $35.00
All Day Play: No
Discounts: Senior & Junior
Junior Golf: Yes **Membership:** Yes
Driving Range: No

Classic Ross: subtle, tough, enjoyable,long open fairways, many green side bunkers. **Player's Comment:** "Solid layout. No easy holes, quick greens, very challenging. Course maintenance has improved."

	1	2	3	4	5	6	7	8	9
PAR	4	4	4	3	4	5	3	4	4
YARDS	379	411	445	184	316	437	185	332	391
HDCP	9	3	1	17	11	7	15	13	5

	10	11	12	13	14	15	16	17	18
PAR	5	4	3	5	3	5	4	4	4
YARDS	502	340	195	447	140	496	302	401	399
HDCP	8	10	16	12	18	4	14	2	6

Directions: 95N to Exit 23.Go right at exit.Right on Douglas Ave. First red light is Chalkstone, turn left. Go 2 miles. 95 S take Exit 21. Right onto Atwell at light, right at Dean St., at 5th light, take left ontoChalkstone.Go 1.5 miles.

Wampanoag Golf Club

N. Swansea, MA (508) 379-9832

▶ 56 ▶

Club Pro: No
Pro Shop: Yes
Payment: Cash only
Tee Times: No
Fee 9 Holes: Weekday: $14.00
Fee 18 Holes: Weekday: $18.00
Twilight Rates: No
Cart Rental: $20.00/18 $15.00/9
Lessons: No **Schools:** No
Clinics: No **Day Camps:** No
Other: Snack bar / Bar-lounge

Tees	Holes	Yards	Par	USGA	Slope
BACK	9	2930	35	69.5	112
MIDDLE	9	2831	35	69.5	112
FRONT	9	2500	37	69.5	112

Weekend: $16.00
Weekend: $20.00
All Day Play: No
Discounts: Senior $12/9, $15/18
Junior Golf: No **Membership:** No
Driving Range: No

This course has a good mix of long par threes and short par fives. Long ball hitters have a definite advantage. Open year round. Play front and back for an enjoyable 18 holes.

	1	2	3	4	5	6	7	8	9
PAR	4	4	4	3	5	4	4	4	3
YARDS	355	400	400	150	450	301	355	300	120
HDCP	8	2	4	16	6	14	10	12	18

	10	11	12	13	14	15	16	17	18
PAR									
YARDS									
HDCP									

Directions: Take I-95 to Exit 2 (Warren/Newport), turn right onto Route 6. Turn left at Mason Street. At stop sign turn right on Old Providence Road.

Washington Village Golf Course

Coventry, RI (401) 823-0010

Tees	Holes	Yards	Par	USGA	Slope
BACK					
MIDDLE	9	2525	33	N/A	N/A
FRONT	9	1993	33		

Club Pro: Richard Tambone, PGA
Pro Shop: Limited inventory
Payment: Visa, MC
Tee Times: No
Fee 9 Holes: Weekday: $13.00 (M-F)
Fee 18 Holes: Weekday: $18.00 (M-F)
Twilight Rates: After 3:30 pm
Cart Rental: $21.00/18 $10.50/9
Lessons: $25.00/30 min. **Schools:** No
Clinics: No **Day Camps:** No
Other: Bar-lounge / Snack Bar

Weekend: $14.00 (S/S)
Weekend: $19.00 (S/S/H)
All Day Play: Yes
Discounts: Senior & Junior
Junior Golf: Yes **Membership:** Yes
Driving Range: No

COUPON

Course is well kept and is easy to walk. South County course

	1	2	3	4	5	6	7	8	9
PAR	3	4	3	4	5	3	4	3	4
YARDS	175	360	150	310	470	200	360	200	300
HDCP	15	1	17	5	9	13	3	11	7
	10	11	12	13	14	15	16	17	18
PAR									
YARDS									
HDCP									

Directions: Take I-95 to Route 117 West, follow 5 miles into Coventry; follow signs.

Weekapaug Golf Club

Westerly, RI (401) 322-7870
www.weekapauggolfclub.com

Tees	Holes	Yards	Par	USGA	Slope
BACK	9	3253	36	69.9	114
MIDDLE	9	3181	36	67.6	109
FRONT	9	2674	36	66.0	107

Club Pro: Susan Bond, PGA
Pro Shop: Full inventory
Payment: Visa, MC, Disc, Check
Tee Times: 2 day adv.
Fee 9 Holes: Weekday: TBD
Fee 18 Holes: Weekday: TBD
Twilight Rates: Yes, after 6 pm
Cart Rental: $26/18 $16/9
Lessons: $35.00/half hour **Schools:** Jr. & Sr.
Clinics: Yes **Day Camps:** No
Other: Full Restaurant / Clubhouse / Bar-Lounge

Weekend: TBD
Weekend: TBD
All Day Play: No
Discounts: Junior
Junior Golf: Yes **Membership:** Yes
Driving Range: $9/lg $6/med $3/sm

Sig. Hole: #4, 342 yd par 4, beautiful and challenging, runs along the water. Open year round. South County course. Available for off season play. Members only June 21- Sep. 8.

	1	2	3	4	5	6	7	8	9
PAR	4	4	3	4	5	4	4	3	5
YARDS	410	336	176	342	466	417	371	151	512
HDCP	3	15	9	5	13	1	11	17	7
	10	11	12	13	14	15	16	17	18
PAR									
YARDS									
HDCP									

Directions: Take Exit 1 from I-95. Bear right off ramp to Route 3 for 3-4 miles to Route 78 East. Take Route 1, turn left. Go 2 miles to light, turn right. At Route 1A turn right. Course is 1/2 mile on left.

Wentworth Hills Golf & Country Club

59

Plainville, MA (508) 699-9406
www.wentworthhillsgolf.com

Club Pro: Tom Rooney, PGA
Pro Shop: Limited inventory
Payment: Visa, MC, Amex, Disc
Tee Times: 3 days adv.

Tees	Holes	Yards	Par	USGA	Slope
BACK	18	5718	71	67.2	115
MIDDLE	18	5252	71	64.7	112
FRONT	18	4630	71	66.4	114

Fee 9 Holes: Weekday: $22 M, $24 (T-Thu) **Weekend:** $25.00 F/S/S
Fee 18 Holes: Weekday: $35 M, $38 (T-Thu) **Weekend:** $44.00 F/S/S
Twilight Rates: No **All Day Play:** No
Cart Rental: $13.65pp/18 $7.35pp/9 **Discounts:** Junior
Lessons: $30/30 min **Schools:** No **Junior Golf:** Yes **Membership:** Yes
Clinics: Junior **Day Camps:** No **Driving Range:** Yes
Other: Restaurant / Clubhouse / Bar-lounge

COUPON

Player comment: "Several interesting holes, immaculate conditioning, flawless greens, and friendly staff make this a must play" (A.P) Back 9 opened 2002. Now a par 71.

	1	2	3	4	5	6	7	8	9
PAR	4	3	4	4	5	3	4	4	4
YARDS	334	88	368	264	430	366	282	134	328
HDCP	9	17	1	7	13	5	11	15	3

	10	11	12	13	14	15	16	17	18
PAR	4	4	5	4	4	5	3	3	4
YARDS	396	320	448	244	268	460	136	130	256
HDCP	4	8	10	18	14	6	16	12	2

SE MA /RI

Directions: From Route 495 - Route 1A/Wrentham-Plainville exit. Follow 1A South for .7 miles, right onto Green St. Follow .3 miles, left onto High St. Follow 1 mile, right onto Hancock St. Follow .4 miles, left onto Bow St. Follow Bow to entrance.

West Warwick Country Club, The

60

West Warwick, RI (401) 821-9789

Club Pro: No
Pro Shop: Limited inventory
Payment: Most major
Tee Times: No

Tees	Holes	Yards	Par	USGA	Slope
BACK					
MIDDLE	9	6030	70	67.6	120
FRONT					

Fee 9 Holes: Weekday: $24.00 **Weekend:** $24.00
Fee 18 Holes: Weekday: $36.00 **Weekend:** $36.00
Twilight Rates: No **All Day Play:** No
Cart Rental: $12.00,2r/9 **Discounts:** Sr & Jr memberships
Lessons: No **Schools:** No **Junior Golf:** No **Membership:** Yes
Clinics: No **Day Camps:** No **Driving Range:** No
Other: Bar-lounge / Snacks / Restaurant / Banquet Facilities

Road divides course: First four holes are hilly, back five are parallel and flat. Public play limited to weekends after 2:30.

	1	2	3	4	5	6	7	8	9
PAR	4	4	3	4	4	4	4	3	5
YARDS	419	338	140	390	360	363	333	162	510
HDCP	1	13	15	3	7	9	11	17	5

	10	11	12	13	14	15	16	17	18
PAR	4	4	3	4	4	4	4	3	5
YARDS	419	338	140	390	360	363	333	162	510
HDCP	2	14	16	4	8	10	12	18	6

Directions: From I-95, take Route 113W. for 1 mile. At intersection of Route 2. go straight through, onto East Ave. for 1/2 mile. Turn right onto River St.for 1/4 mile. River St. becomes Wakefield St. at light. Club is 1.5 miles up on top of hill.

4✪ =Excellent **3✪** =Very Good **2✪** =Good

Whaling City GC

New Bedford, MA (508) 996-9393

Club Pro: No
Pro Shop: Yes
Payment: Cash only
Tee Times: 7 days adv.
Fee 9 Holes: Weekday: $16.00
Fee 18 Holes: Weekday: $28.00
Twilight Rates: Yes, after 5 pm
Cart Rental: $27.00/18 $15.00/9
Lessons: Yes **Schools:** No
Clinics: Yes **Day Camps:** No
Other: Snack bar / Restaurant / Bar-lounge

Tees	Holes	Yards	Par	USGA	Slope
BACK	18	6780	72	73	131
MIDDLE	18	6527	72	70.2	126
FRONT	18	6457	74	70.1	118

Weekend: $19.00
Weekend: $33.00
All Day Play: No
Discounts: Junior
Junior Golf: No **Membership:** Yes
Driving Range: No

New tees. Municipal course. Managed by Johnson Management Company.

	1	2	3	4	5	6	7	8	9
PAR	4	4	4	4	3	4	5	3	5
YARDS	448	382	409	343	190	381	530	140	453
HDCP	5	3	1	13	15	9	7	17	11
	10	**11**	**12**	**13**	**14**	**15**	**16**	**17**	**18**
PAR	5	4	4	3	5	4	4	3	4
YARDS	535	379	436	163	499	333	356	179	331
HDCP	6	12	2	18	4	10	16	16	14

Directions: Take Route 140 in New Bedford to Exit 3. Bear right.

Windmill Hill Golf Course

Warren, RI (401) 245-1463

Club Pro: No
Pro Shop: Limited inventory
Payment: Most major
Tee Times: 6 days adv.
Fee 9 Holes: Weekday: $12.00
Fee 18 Holes: Weekday: $17.00
Twilight Rates: No
Cart Rental: $24.00/18 $12.00/9
Lessons: Available **Schools:** No
Clinics: No **Day Camps:** No
Other: Clubhouse / Showers / Restaurant / Bar-lounge / Banquet Facilities / Decks

Tees	Holes	Yards	Par	USGA	Slope
BACK	9	1432	27		
MIDDLE	9	1191	27		
FRONT	9	891	27		

Weekend: $15.00
Weekend: $20.00
All Day Play: $20
Discounts: Senior & Junior
Junior Golf: No **Membership:** Yes
Driving Range: No

COUPON

Pleasant challenge for all levels that makes you use all your clubs. Lush greens and fairways.

	1	2	3	4	5	6	7	8	9
PAR	3	3	3	3	3	3	3	3	3
YARDS	91	129	167	120	136	150	162	125	111
HDCP	9	6	1	4	3	5	2	7	8
	10	**11**	**12**	**13**	**14**	**15**	**16**	**17**	**18**
PAR									
YARDS									
HDCP									

Directions: I-195 to Exit 2. Follow signs for Route 136 South, 2 miles. Turn left on to Schoolhouse Rd. Entrance is .3 miles on right.

Winnapaug Golf Course

✪✪

Westerly, RI (401) 596-1237

Club Pro: Jeff Beaupre, PGA
Pro Shop: Yes
Payment: Cash/check/charge
Tee Times: 1 week adv.
Fee 9 Holes: Weekday: $18.00
Fee 18 Holes: Weekday: $35.00
Twilight Rates: Yes, after 4 pm
Cart Rental: $13pp/18
Lessons: Yes **Schools:** Yes
Clinics: Yes **Day Camps:** Yes
Other: Clubhouse / Restaurant / Bar-lounge / Beverage cart

Tees	Holes	Yards	Par	USGA	Slope
BACK	18	6361	72	70.6	124
MIDDLE	18	5914	72	68.6	119
FRONT	18	5153	73	69.2	118

Weekend: $18.00
Weekend: $35.00
All Day Play: No
Discounts: Senior & Junior
Junior Golf: No **Membership:** Yes
Driving Range: Practice range

Donald Ross design with tight, short fairways with demanding greens. Open year round. South County course

	1	2	3	4	5	6	7	8	9
PAR	4	5	3	4	4	3	4	4	5
YARDS	319	484	156	402	270	106	344	322	508
HDCP	13	6	8	2	15	18	10	12	4

	10	11	12	13	14	15	16	17	18
PAR	4	4	3	5	4	5	3	4	4
YARDS	395	348	141	472	383	451	140	376	302
HDCP	3	11	17	9	1	7	15	5	13

Directions: Take Route 95 North to Exit 92, take right onto Route 2, follow to Route 78, follow signs for beaches. Turn left onto Route 1A, course is 1 mile on left.

Wood River Golf

Hope Valley, RI (401) 364-0700
www.woodrivergolf.com

Club Pro: Harold Russell, PGA
Pro Shop: Limited inventory
Payment: Cash, Checks & Credit Cards
Tee Times: No
Fee 9 Holes: Weekday: $12.00 (11)
Fee 18 Holes: Weekday: $20.00
Twilight Rates: Yes, after 3 pm
Cart Rental: $12.00
Lessons: N/R **Schools:** N/R
Clinics: **Day Camps:** No
Other: Pub and Restaurant / Clubhouse

Tees	Holes	Yards	Par	USGA	Slope
BACK					
MIDDLE	18	5273	69		
FRONT	18	4452	69		

Weekend: $12.00 (11)
Weekend: $20.00
All Day Play: $25 M-F
Discounts: None
Junior Golf: No **Membership:** No
Driving Range: No

COUPON

Full 18 holes opened September 2002. Natural setting links style course. South county course. Noted for 11 hole rate of $12.00. "A nice polite course for beginners and intermediate players." R.W.

	1	2	3	4	5	6	7	8	9
PAR	5	3	4	3	5	4	3	4	4
YARDS	453	152	332	185	445	315	217	331	315
HDCP									

	10	11	12	13	14	15	16	17	18
PAR	3	4	4	4	4	4	4	4	3
YARDS	153	305	315	300	265	400	330	305	155
HDCP									

Directions: Exit 2 off Route 95. Turn left of ramp. Follow Woodville Alton Rd. for 3 miles. Once through 4 corner stop sign, course will be 1/4 mile on your left.

Woodland Greens GC

N. Kingstown, RI (401) 294-2872

Tees	Holes	Yards	Par	USGA	Slope
BACK					
MIDDLE	9	6046	70	69.2	126
FRONT	9	5744	70	68.3	124

Club Pro: No
Pro Shop: Full inventory
Payment: Cash only
Tee Times: No
Fee 9 Holes: Weekday: $19.00   **Weekend:** $21.00
Fee 18 Holes: Weekday: $26.00   **Weekend:** $29.00
Twilight Rates: No   **All Day Play:** No
Cart Rental: $14.00pp/9   **Discounts:** Senior M-F, 7-11
Lessons: Yes **Schools:** No   **Junior Golf:** Yes **Membership:** Yes
Clinics: Yes **Day Camps:** No   **Driving Range:** No
Other: Snack bar / Bar-lounge

Player's Comment: "Private country club conditions." The course has tight fairways and fast greens.
Open March - December. South County course.

	1	2	3	4	5	6	7	8	9
PAR	4	5	3	5	3	4	4	3	4
YARDS	360	413	198	505	152	330	297	203	414
HDCP	7	5	11	3	15	9	17	13	1

	10	11	12	13	14	15	16	17	18
PAR	4	5	3	5	3	4	4	3	4
YARDS	360	413	198	505	152	330	297	203	414
HDCP	8	6	12	4	16	10	18	14	2

Directions: Take I-95 South to Route 4 South. Take left at 2nd light onto Stony Lane. At 1st intersection take left onto Old Baptist Road. Course is 1/8 mile on left.

CHAPTER 5
New Hampshire

New 2003 courses indicated in **bold**.

Alpine Ridge

▶ **1**

Hollis, NH (603) 594-4260

Club Pro: Bill Robes, USGA
Pro Shop: Limited inventory
Payment: Yes
Tee Times: No
Fee 9 Holes: Weekday: $10.00
Fee 18 Holes: Weekday: $18.00
Twilight Rates: No
Cart Rental: Pullcarts @ $1.50
Lessons: $25.00/ 1 hour **Schools:**
Clinics: Day Camps:
Other:

Tees	Holes	Yards	Par	USGA	Slope
BACK					
MIDDLE	9	950	27		
FRONT					

Weekend: $10.00
Weekend: $18.00
All Day Play: No
Discounts: Senior & Junior
Junior Golf: Membership: No
Driving Range:

Glow golf Friday nights. Good learning experience. "Fun par 3. All straight putts." R.W. "Impeccably maintained. Attack the pins as all the greens hold extremely well." A.P.

	1	2	3	4	5	6	7	8	9
PAR	3	3	3	3	3	3	3	3	3
YARDS	84	114	93	125	105	98	130	94	107
HDCP									
	10	11	12	13	14	15	16	17	18
PAR									
YARDS									
HDCP									

Directions: Route 3 North, Exit 5 West (Route 111). 1 mile to Hollis. Course is 1/4 mile on left.

Amherst Country Club

✪✪ ▶ **2**

Ponemah Rd., Amherst, NH (603) 673-9908
www.amherstcountryclub.com

Club Pro: Dan Diskin, PGA
Pro Shop: Full inventory
Payment: Visa, MC, Cash, Check
Tee Times: 5 day adv.
Fee 9 Holes: Weekday: $23.00
Fee 18 Holes: Weekday: $35.00
Twilight Rates: Yes, after 6 pm
Cart Rental: $14 per person
Lessons: Yes **Schools:** No
Clinics: No **Day Camps:** No
Other: Lounge / Cafe / Outings / Functions

Tees	Holes	Yards	Par	USGA	Slope
BACK	18	6543	72	70.7	123
MIDDLE	18	6036	72	68.4	117
FRONT	18	5615	74	71.7	118

Weekend: N/A
Weekend: $45.00
All Day Play: N/R
Discounts: Senior
Junior Golf: No **Membership:** No
Driving Range: No

New layout of back nine. Souhegan River meanders through course affecting six holes; the course sits in River Valley. Flat terrain; penncross greens with variety of contours.

	1	2	3	4	5	6	7	8	9
PAR	4	5	3	5	4	4	3	4	4
YARDS	300	475	188	460	370	338	183	412	373
HDCP	17	3	7	5	11	13	9	1	15
	10	11	12	13	14	15	16	17	18
PAR	4	4	4	3	5	3	5	4	4
YARDS	350	260	344	135	455	135	508	391	359
HDCP	12	18	2	14	10	16	8	4	6

Directions: Take I-93 to I-293 in Manchester, NH. Then take Route 101 West to Amherst and Route 122 South. The club is located on Route 122, 3 miles on left.

Androscoggin Valley CC ✪✪

Route. 2, Gorham, NH (603) 466-9468

Club Pro: Gary A. Riff
Pro Shop: Full inventory
Payment: Visa, MC, Amex, Disc
Tee Times: 1 day adv.
Fee 9 Holes: Weekday: $15.00
Fee 18 Holes: Weekday: $25.00
Twilight Rates: Yes, after 2 pm
Cart Rental: $25.00/18 $15.00/9
Lessons: $50.00/hour **Schools:** N/R
Clinics: Yes **Day Camps:** No
Other: Clubhouse / Snack bar / Bar-lounge / Lockers / Showers

Tees	Holes	Yards	Par	USGA	Slope
BACK	18	5764	70	67	114
MIDDLE	18	5499	70	67.0	114
FRONT	N/A				

Weekend: $20.00
Weekend: $30.00
All Day Play: No
Discounts: Junior
Junior Golf: Yes **Membership:** N/R
Driving Range: $5.00/lg. $3.00/sm.

COUPON

Flat course with a scenery of the mountains. Some holes border the Androscoggin River. Open May 1 - October 31.

	1	2	3	4	5	6	7	8	9
PAR	5	4	3	5	4	3	3	4	3
YARDS	453	365	157	451	287	178	146	284	189
HDCP	4	2	16	6	12	8	18	10	14
	10	11	12	13	14	15	16	17	18
PAR	4	4	4	3	5	3	4	5	4
YARDS	359	347	230	206	524	134	336	507	346
HDCP	7	5	15	11	1	17	13	3	9

Directions: From I-93 take Route 3 through Twin Mountain to Route 115 East to Route 2. Take Route 2 to Gorham. At light, take a right through town. Cross bridge, club is on left.

Angus Lea Golf Course

West Main St., Hillsboro, NH (603) 464-5404
www.angusleagolf.com

Club Pro: Curtis R. Niven, PGA
Pro Shop: Full inventory
Payment: Visa, MC
Tee Times: Wknds/Hldys
Fee 9 Holes: Weekday: $15.00
Fee 18 Holes: Weekday: $25.00
Twilight Rates: No
Cart Rental: $25.00/18 $13.00/9
Lessons: $35.00/ hour **Schools:** No
Clinics: Yes **Day Camps:** No
Other: Snack bar / Bar-lounge / Tennis courts

Tees	Holes	Yards	Par	USGA	Slope
BACK					
MIDDLE	9	4638	66	60.0	94
FRONT	9	4194	66	65.6	101

Weekend: $15.00
Weekend: $25.00
All Day Play: No
Discounts: None
Junior Golf: Yes **Membership:** Yes
Driving Range: No

Sig. Hole: #5. 310 yd. par 4. Bordered by the Contoocook River, the course is watered and wooded. Beautiful view from large screened porch.

	1	2	3	4	5	6	7	8	9
PAR	4	3	3	4	4	4	4	3	4
YARDS	283	150	160	300	310	435	245	161	275
HDCP	10	18	16	6	4	2	12	14	8
	10	11	12	13	14	15	16	17	18
PAR	4	3	3	4	4	4	4	3	4
YARDS	283	150	160	300	310	435	245	161	275
HDCP	9	17	15	5	3	1	11	13	7

Directions: Located on Main St. (Route 202/9) in Hillsboro, just off Routes 202/9 bypass. Follow the signs.

4✪ =Excellent 3✪ =Very Good 2✪ =Good

Apple Hill Golf Club

5 ▶

E. Kingston, NH (603) 642-4414

Club Pro: Steve Lundquist
Pro Shop: Yes
Payment: Visa, MC, Checks
Tee Times: 1 week adv.
Fee 9 Holes: Weekday: $17.00
Fee 18 Holes: Weekday: $27.00
Twilight Rates: No
Cart Rental: $13pp/18 $7.00pp/9
Lessons: Yes **Schools:** No
Clinics: Junior **Day Camps:** No
Other: Clubhouse / Snack bar / Bar-lounge

Weekend: $19.00
Weekend: $34.00
All Day Play: No
Discounts: Senior & Junior
Junior Golf: Yes **Membership:** No
Driving Range: No

COUPON

Tees	Holes	Yards	Par	USGA	Slope
BACK	18	6311	70	70.4	134
MIDDLE	18	6003	70	69.1	131
FRONT	18	5006	70	69..8	122

Now 27 holes. Apple Hill 9 Hole Par 3 course, 715 yards is also now opened. Rates $10.00 every day. Both courses are well maintained.

	1	2	3	4	5	6	7	8	9
PAR	4	3	4	3	5	4	4	4	4
YARDS	365	145	377	165	479	415	368	358	357
HDCP	10	18	2	11	12	7	4	15	5
	10	**11**	**12**	**13**	**14**	**15**	**16**	**17**	**18**
PAR	5	4	4	4	3	4	4	3	4
YARDS	458	374	363	414	169	294	356	136	410
HDCP	1	8	3	9	17	13	14	16	6

Directions: Take I-95 Exit 1 in New Hampshire (Route 107). The course is 6 miles on right. From Route 125 Kingston, take Route 107 East, 3 1/2 miles.

Applewood Golf Links ●●

6 ▶

Range Rd., Windham, NH (603) 898-6793
www.heavyhittersgolf.com

Club Pro: Ed Whalley, PGA
Pro Shop: Full inventory
Payment: Cash, MC, Visa
Tee Times: No
Fee 9 Holes: Weekday: $12.00
Fee 18 Holes: Weekday: $20.00
Twilight Rates: No
Cart Rental: $20.00/18 $10.00/9
Lessons: $30.00/half hour **Schools:** Jr. & Sr.
Clinics: Yes **Day Camps:** Yes
Other:

Weekend: $14.00
Weekend: $20.00
All Day Play: No
Discounts: Senior
Junior Golf: Yes **Membership:** Jr. & Sr.
Driving Range: $8.00/lg. bucket

COUPON

Tees	Holes	Yards	Par	USGA	Slope
BACK	9	1867	27	56.0	82
MIDDLE	9	1367	27	56.0	82
FRONT					

Player's comment: "An impeccably maintained par 3 that's pure fun to play." Noted improvement: driving range has heated bays for winter usage. Attention given to senior and women golfers. Open April 1 - Dec 1.

	1	2	3	4	5	6	7	8	9
PAR	3	3	3	3	3	3	3	3	3
YARDS	179	150	136	170	123	129	158	147	175
HDCP	5	15	11	3	17	13	9	7	1
	10	**11**	**12**	**13**	**14**	**15**	**16**	**17**	**18**
PAR									
YARDS									
HDCP									

Directions: I-93 to Exit 3 in NH. Right at end of ramp onto Route 111. 500 yards to course and range.

Atkinson Resort and Country Club ✪✪✪   7▶

Atkinson, NH (603)-362-5681
www.atkinsoncc.com

Club Pro: Joe Healey, PGA
Pro Shop: Full inventory
Payment: Visa, MC, Amex, Checks
Tee Times: 5 days adv.

Tees	Holes	Yards	Par	USGA	Slope
BACK	18	6564	72	72.0	140
MIDDLE	18	6087	72	69.6	137
FRONT	18	4847	72	67.6	115

Fee 9 Holes: Weekday: $25.00 **Weekend:** $30.00
Fee 18 Holes: Weekday: $45.00 **Weekend:** $55.00
Twilight Rates: Yes, after 6 pm **All Day Play:** No
Cart Rental: $15pp/18 $8pp/9 **Discounts:** Senior & Junior
Lessons: Yes **Schools:** No **Junior Golf:** Yes **Membership:** Yes, Inner Club
Clinics: Yes **Day Camps:** Yes **Driving Range:** Yes
Other: Snack bar / New clubhouse / Restaurant / Function facility

Upscale public golf with resort. GPS system on carts. Spectacular views. 16 guest rooms.
Player's Comment: "A demanding difficult course without being unfair." "Priced very well, affordable." F.P.

	1	2	3	4	5	6	7	8	9
PAR	4	5	3	4	4	5	4	3	4
YARDS	310	485	180	350	400	481	366	185	380
HDCP	17	3	13	9	5	15	1	11	7

	10	11	12	13	14	15	16	17	18
PAR	4	3	5	4	3	4	5	4	4
YARDS	346	144	477	317	127	354	481	370	334
HDCP	16	12	4	8	18	10	2	6	14

Directions: From I-495, take Exit 50. Go straight at light, left at 4-way stop. Follow to the end, left on Sawyer Ave. Course is 1 mile on left. Call for directions from I-93.

Balsams Panorama GC, The   ✪✪✪   8▶

Dixville Notch, NH (603) 255-4961
www.thebalsams.com

Club Pro: Bill Hamblen
Pro Shop: Full inventory
Payment: Visa, MC, Amex, Discover
Tee Times: 3 days adv.

Tees	Holes	Yards	Par	USGA	Slope
BACK	18	6804	72	72.8	130
MIDDLE	18	6097	72	69.1	122
FRONT	18	5069	72	67.8	115

Fee 9 Holes: Weekday: No **Weekend:** No
Fee 18 Holes: Weekday: $60.00 **Weekend:** $60.00
Twilight Rates: Yes, after 2 pm **All Day Play:** Yes
Cart Rental: $35.00/18 $23.00/9 **Discounts:** None
Lessons: $85.00 hour **Schools:** Yes **Junior Golf:** No **Membership:** Yes
Clinics: N/R **Day Camps:** No **Driving Range:** $5.00/lg.
Other: Clubhouse / Restaurant / Bar-lounge / Resort Hotel

Players' Comments: "Resort and golf! Donald Ross design." "Great view. Friendly staff. Always interesting. No flat hills."

	1	2	3	4	5	6	7	8	9
PAR	4	5	4	4	3	5	3	4	4
YARDS	366	457	376	363	175	463	157	346	316
HDCP	9	5	3	13	17	1	15	11	7

	10	11	12	13	14	15	16	17	18
PAR	4	4	4	4	3	5	3	4	5
YARDS	320	302	323	423	191	501	173	365	480
HDCP	12	10	6	2	8	18	16	14	4

Directions: 1) Take I-93 N to Exit 35, Route 3 N to Colebrook, east on Route 26 for 10 miles, or 2) Take I-91 to exit at St. Johnsbury, Route 2. Go east on Route 2 to Lancaster, take Route 3 N to Colebrook, and east on Route 26 for 10 miles.

4✪ =Excellent 3✪ =Very Good 2✪ =Good

Balsams-Coashaukee Golf Course ▶ 9

Dixville Notch, NH (603) 255-4961
www.thebalsams.com

Club Pro: Bill Hamblen
Pro Shop: Full inventory
Payment: MC, Visa, Discover, Amex
Tee Times: None required
Fee 9 Holes: Weekday:
Fee 18 Holes: Weekday: $25.00
Twilight Rates: No
Cart Rental: $25.00/18 $17.00/9
Lessons: Yes **Schools:** Sr.
Clinics: N/R **Day Camps:** No
Other:

Tees	Holes	Yards	Par	USGA	Slope
BACK					
MIDDLE	9	3834	64	59.1	87
FRONT					

Weekend:
Weekend: $25.00
All Day Play: Yes
Discounts: None
Junior Golf: No **Membership:** Yes
Driving Range: No

A 9 hole executive layout adjacent the Balsams resort hotel.

	1	2	3	4	5	6	7	8	9
PAR	4	3	3	4	4	4	3	4	3
YARDS	304	147	174	223	265	236	145	313	110
HDCP	9	17	1	13	5	11	15	3	7

	10	11	12	13	14	15	16	17	18
PAR	4	3	3	4	4	4	3	4	3
YARDS	304	147	174	223	265	236	145	313	110
HDCP	10	18	2	14	6	12	16	4	8

Directions: 1) Take I-93 N to Exit 35, Route 3 N to Colebrook, east on Route 26 for 10 miles,or 2) Take I-91 to Exit at St. Johnbury, Route 2. Go east on Route 2 to Lancaster, take Route 3 N to Colebrook, and east on Route 26 for 10 miles.

Beaver Meadow GC ⊙⊙ ▶ 10

Concord, NH (603) 228-8954

Club Pro: E. Deshaies, K. Gagnon
Pro Shop: Full inventory
Payment: Visa, MC
Tee Times: Weekends, 2 days adv.
Fee 9 Holes: Weekday: $18.00
Fee 18 Holes: Weekday: $29.00
Twilight Rates: After 3 pm
Cart Rental: $26.00/18
Lessons: $50.00/45 minutes **Schools:** No
Clinics: Junior **Day Camps:** Yes
Other: Clubhouse / Snack bar / Bar-lounge

Tees	Holes	Yards	Par	USGA	Slope
BACK	18	6356	72	70.8	127
MIDDLE	18	6034	72	69.2	121
FRONT	18	6519	72	71.8	123

Weekend: $18.00 after 12pm
Weekend: $35.00
All Day Play: No
Discounts: Srs. on annual basis
Junior Golf: City Rec. Dept. **Membership:** Yes
Driving Range: $5.00- $7.00

Player's comment: "Good for high handicaps. Easy to walk. Carts not required. Friendly staff." Improvements include remodeled driving range.

	1	2	3	4	5	6	7	8	9
PAR	4	5	3	5	4	3	4	4	4
YARDS	341	480	153	474	336	138	366	414	315
HDCP	9	5	15	1	13	17	7	3	11

	10	11	12	13	14	15	16	17	18
PAR	5	4	4	3	4	4	5	3	4
YARDS	527	320	301	130	347	400	560	156	276
HDCP	6	10	14	18	8	4	2	16	12

Directions: Take I-93 to Exit 15 West (North Main St.). At second light take right onto Route 3 North. Course is 3.1 miles on right.

Bethlehem CC

Bethlehem, NH (603) 869-5745
www.bethlehemccnhgolf.com

Club Pro: Jon Wood
Pro Shop: Full inventory
Payment: Visa, MC, Cash
Tee Times: Required
Fee 9 Holes: Weekday: $20.00
Fee 18 Holes: Weekday: $28.00
Twilight Rates: Yes, after 4 pm
Cart Rental: $14.00 pp/18
Lessons: $35.00/half hour **Schools:** No
Clinics: Yes **Day Camps:** No
Other: Club repair service / Snack Bar / Retail

Tees	Holes	Yards	Par	USGA	Slope
BACK	18	5808	70	68.2	114
MIDDLE	18	5619	70	68.2	114
FRONT	18	5008	70	63.0	98

Weekend: $25.00
Weekend: $33.00
All Day Play: No
Discounts: Junior
Junior Golf: Yes **Membership:** Yes
Driving Range: No

COUPON

Leader in North County public golf. "Generous fairways and light rough will have you blasting your driver on all long holes. Accuracy is required on the four par 3 holes. " A.P.

	1	2	3	4	5	6	7	8	9
PAR	4	4	3	4	4	4	3	4	4
YARDS	413	319	210	264	402	399	157	328	288
HDCP	3	11	7	17	5	1	15	9	13
	10	11	12	13	14	15	16	17	18
PAR	3	5	3	4	4	5	4	4	4
YARDS	95	487	153	417	260	501	270	296	360
HDCP	18	6	12	2	16	4	14	10	8

Directions: Exit 40 from I-93. 2.5 miles on Route 302.

Blackmount Country Club

N Haverhill, NH (603) 787-6564
www.blackmountcountryclub.com

Club Pro: Bill Grimes
Pro Shop: Yes
Payment: Cash or Check
Tee Times: No
Fee 9 Holes: Weekday: $10.00
Fee 18 Holes: Weekday: $15.00
Twilight Rates: No
Cart Rental: $18.00/18, $12.00/9
Lessons: Yes **Schools:** No
Clinics: No **Day Camps:** No
Other: Clubhouse / Snack bar / Gazebo

Tees	Holes	Yards	Par	USGA	Slope
BACK	9	2995	36	34.4	124
MIDDLE	9	2658	36	32.9	121
FRONT	9	2316	36		

Weekend: $15.00
Weekend: $20.00
All Day Play: No
Discounts: Senior, Junior, Ladies
Junior Golf: No **Membership:** Yes
Driving Range: Yes, $3 and $5

COUPON

2 new sand traps added to guard greens. A challenging, scenic delight with excellent greens!

	1	2	3	4	5	6	7	8	9
PAR	3	5	4	5	4	4	4	3	4
YARDS	150	400	333	383	217	317	350	142	366
HDCP	13	7	1	11	15	9	3	17	5
	10	11	12	13	14	15	16	17	18
PAR									
YARDS									
HDCP									

Directions: From I-91, take Bradford ,Vt. exit to NH Route 10 to village of North Haverhill,NH. Turn onto Clark Pond Rd., across from Aldrich's General Store. Bear right for 1.5 miles.

4✪ =Excellent **3✪** =Very Good **2✪** =Good

Bramber Valley Golf Course

13

Greenland, NH 03840 (603) 436-4288
www.seacoastonline\BramberValley.com

Club Pro: John Stacy, PGA
Pro Shop: Limited inventory
Payment: Cash, Check
Tee Times: No
Fee 9 Holes: Weekday: $14.00
Fee 18 Holes: Weekday: $24.00
Twilight Rates: Fall only, after 2pm
Cart Rental: $20.00/18 $12.00/9
Lessons: Yes **Schools:** Jr.
Clinics: Yes **Day Camps:** No
Other: Clubhouse / Bar-Lounge

Tees	Holes	Yards	Par	USGA	Slope
BACK					
MIDDLE	9	4228	64	61.4	103
FRONT					

Weekend: $14.00
Weekend: $24.00
All Day Play: No
Discounts: Senior & Junior
Junior Golf: Yes **Membership:** No
Driving Range: Yes 3.00 per token

COUPON

Great playing surfaces, friendly staff, wonderful practice facility, and low prices make this course a winner. Improvements on going.

	1	2	3	4	5	6	7	8	9
PAR	3	4	3	4	3	4	4	3	4
YARDS	133	333	107	312	160	260	315	180	314
HDCP	13	1	17	7	15	9	5	11	3
	10	11	12	13	14	15	16	17	18
PAR	3	4	3	4	3	4	4	3	4
YARDS	133	333	107	312	160	260	315	180	314
HDCP	14	2	18	8	16	10	5	12	4

Directions: I-95 North or South, take Exit 3A. Go west on Route 33 for about 3 miles. Blue sign for club is after Golf & Ski Warehouse.

Breakfast Hill Golf Club

⊙⊙ **14**

Greenland, NH (603) 436-5001
www.breakfasthill.com

Club Pro: Steve Chandler
Pro Shop: Full inventory
Payment: Visa, MC, Amex, Disc
Tee Times: 5 days adv.
Fee 9 Holes: Weekday: $30.00
Fee 18 Holes: Weekday: $39.00
Twilight Rates: Yes, after 5 pm
Cart Rental: $14pp/18 $7pp/9
Lessons: $35.00 / 30 min. **Schools:** Yes
Clinics: Yes **Day Camps:** No
Other: Restaurant / Clubhouse / Bar-lounge

Tees	Holes	Yards	Par	USGA	Slope
BACK	18	6493	71	70.5	133
MIDDLE	18	5981	71	68.4	126
FRONT	18	4994	72	68.6	120

Weekend: $30.00
Weekend: $49.00
All Day Play: No
Discounts: None
Junior Golf: Yes **Membership:** Season pass
Driving Range: $4.00/bucket

COUPON

18 unique holes with rolling fairways and countoured greens. Brian Silva design. " A fun challenge, pay close attention to the handout sheet. Give it a try, a nice N.H. visit." F.P.

	1	2	3	4	5	6	7	8	9
PAR	4	5	4	3	5	3	4	4	4
YARDS	350	465	365	149	489	124	364	332	350
HDCP	12	10	4	18	8	16	2	6	14
	10	11	12	13	14	15	16	17	18
PAR	4	4	5	4	3	4	4	3	4
YARDS	309	460	526	296	165	322	378	143	394
HDCP	7	1	5	15	9	13	11	17	3

Directions: I-95, Exit 3 (Greenland/Portsmouth). Left onto Route 33. Left onto Route 151 South for 1.4 miles. Go left onto Breakfast Hill Road. Course is 1 mile on left.

Bretwood Golf Course (North) ✪✪ ▶ 15

Keene, NH (603) 352-7626
www.bretwoodgolf.com

Club Pro: Matt Barrett, PGA
Pro Shop: Full inventory
Payment: Visa, MC, Disc.
Tee Times: Weekends, 3 days adv.
Fee 9 Holes: Weekday: $16.00
Fee 18 Holes: Weekday: $30.00
Twilight Rates: No
Cart Rental: $24.00/18 $14.00/9
Lessons: $30/30 min. **Schools:** No
Clinics: No **Day Camps:** No
Other: Clubhouse / Snack bar

Tees	Holes	Yards	Par	USGA	Slope
BACK	18	6974	72	73.7	136
MIDDLE	18	6434	72	71.5	131
FRONT	18	5822	72	68.9	125

Weekend: $20.00
Weekend: $36.00
All Day Play: $43, Wkday
Discounts: None
Junior Golf: Yes **Membership:** Yes
Driving Range: $6/lg. $5/med. $4/sm.

Players' comments: "Gets better every year. Favorite hole # 13 island green." "Scenic. Great layouts."

	1	2	3	4	5	6	7	8	9
PAR	4	5	3	4	5	4	5	3	4
YARDS	413	552	187	340	505	390	480	138	400
HDCP	9	1	15	13	11	3	7	17	5

	10	11	12	13	14	15	16	17	18
PAR	4	4	4	3	4	4	3	5	4
YARDS	400	340	372	130	380	379	154	501	373
HDCP	2	12	10	16	4	6	18	8	14

Directions: Take I-91 North to Route 9 East to Keene. Follow hospital signs to Court St. East Surry Rd. is off Upper Court St. 1.5 mi. to course.

NH

Bretwood Golf Course (South) ✪✪ ▶ 16

Keene, NH (603) 352-7626
www.bretwoodgolf.com

Club Pro: Matt Barrett, PGA
Pro Shop: Full inventory
Payment: Visa,MC, Disc.
Tee Times: Weekends, 3 days adv.
Fee 9 Holes: Weekday: $16.00
Fee 18 Holes: Weekday: $30.00
Twilight Rates: No
Cart Rental: $24.00/18 $14.00/9
Lessons: $30/30 min. **Schools:** No
Clinics: No **Day Camps:** No
Other: Clubhouse / Snack bar

Tees	Holes	Yards	Par	USGA	Slope
BACK	18	6952	72	73.2	133
MIDDLE	18	6345	72	70.7	124
FRONT	18	5645	70	68.0	119

Weekend: $20.00
Weekend: $36.00
All Day Play: $43, Wkday
Discounts: None
Junior Golf: Yes **Membership:** Yes
Driving Range: $6/lg. $5/med $4/sm.

Sig. Hole: #16, 176 yard par 3. Elevated tee into green well-guarded by bunkers. Water on front and left. Wetland hazard to right and back. Bunkers left and right. Challenging course.

	1	2	3	4	5	6	7	8	9
PAR	5	5	3	4	4	4	3	4	4
YARDS	477	530	168	364	288	305	181	394	383
HDCP	15	3	13	7	17	11	9	1	5

	10	11	12	13	14	15	16	17	18
PAR	5	4	3	5	4	4	3	4	4
YARDS	472	372	133	536	371	340	176	410	445
HDCP	18	12	16	4	14	2	10	8	6

Directions: Take I-91 North to Route 9 East to Keene. Follow hospital signs to Court St. East Surry Rd. is off Upper Court St. 1.5 mi. to course.

Buckmeadow Golf Club

Amherst, NH (603) 673-7077

Tees	Holes	Yards	Par	USGA	Slope
BACK	9	4850	66	61.8	101
MIDDLE	9	4680	66	60.9	100
FRONT	9	4560	68	66.2	103

Club Pro: No
Pro Shop: Limited inventory
Payment: Cash, Check
Tee Times: Public/ Members
Fee 9 Holes: Weekday: $12.00
Fee 18 Holes: Weekday: $22.00
Twilight Rates: No
Cart Rental: $20.00/18 $10.00/9
Lessons: Yes **Schools:** No
Clinics: Yes **Day Camps:** No
Other: Bar-Lounge / Snack Bar

Weekend: $15.00
Weekend: $26.00
All Day Play: No
Discounts: None
Junior Golf: No **Membership:** Limited/100 max.
Driving Range: No

"Six dogleg par fours and three interesting one-shot holes make for a challenging round on this nicely maintained venue." A.P.

	1	2	3	4	5	6	7	8	9
PAR	4	3	4	4	4	3	4	3	4
YARDS	320	120	190	335	345	175	330	185	340
HDCP	1	17	15	9	5	13	7	11	3

	10	11	12	13	14	15	16	17	18
PAR	4	3	4	4	4	3	4	3	4
YARDS	320	120	190	335	345	175	330	185	340
HDCP	2	18	16	10	6	14	8	12	4

Directions: Course is 1.5 miles off Route 101 outside of Milford.

Campbell's Scottish Highlands ✪✪

Brady Ave., Salem, NH (603) 894-4653

Tees	Holes	Yards	Par	USGA	Slope
BACK	18	6249	71	69.3	124
MIDDLE	18	5746	71	67.6	116
FRONT	18	5056	71	68.4	114

Club Pro: Tony Zdunko
Pro Shop: Yes
Payment: Visa, MC
Tee Times: 5 days adv.
Fee 9 Holes: Weekday: $20.00
Fee 18 Holes: Weekday: $35.00
Twilight Rates: Yes
Cart Rental: $30.00/18 $20.00/9
Lessons: $40.00/30 **Schools:** N/A
Clinics: Yes **Day Camps:** No
Other: Clubhouse / Bar-Lounge / Lockers / Shower / Snack Bar

Weekend: $25.00
Weekend: $45.00
All Day Play: No
Discounts: Senior & Junior
Junior Golf: Yes **Membership:** No
Driving Range: Yes

Noted for friendly staff, well maintained turf, and it is "player-friendly." Open , rolling fairways and "true rolling" velvet greens. Links style course with well-placed hazards, very challenging.

	1	2	3	4	5	6	7	8	9
PAR	4	5	3	4	5	4	3	4	4
YARDS	341	454	185	418	482	358	167	260	352
HDCP	13	5	15	3	1	7	17	9	11

	10	11	12	13	14	15	16	17	18
PAR	4	3	4	4	4	3	4	4	5
YARDS	295	162	330	322	395	125	303	305	492
HDCP	10	16	12	8	2	18	6	14	4

Directions: I-93 to Exit 2. Bear right off ramp. Right at first set of lights, right onto South Policy Street. Next light, right on to Route 38. Straight through next set of lights, left on to Brady Ave for .5 mi.

Candia Woods

Candia, NH (603) 483-2307
www.candiawoods.com

Club Pro: Geoffrey Williams, PGA
Pro Shop: Full inventory
Payment: Visa, MC, Disc
Tee Times: 5 days adv.
Fee 9 Holes: Weekday: $23.00 (M-F)
Fee 18 Holes: Weekday: $40.00 (M-F)
Twilight Rates: Yes, after 6 pm
Cart Rental: $15pp/18 $8pp/9
Lessons: $50/30 min. **Schools:** No
Clinics: Yes **Day Camps:** Yes
Other: Restaurant / Bar-lounge / Lockers / Showers / Snack bar / Pavilion / Outings

Tees	Holes	Yards	Par	USGA	Slope
BACK	18	6540	71	70.9	118
MIDDLE	18	6317	71	69.8	117
FRONT	18	5367	71	69.8	116

Weekend: $28.00
Weekend: $50.00
All Day Play: No
Discounts: Senior & Junior
Junior Golf: Yes **Membership:** Yes
Driving Range: $6.00/bucket

COUPON

Multiple tees allow for all skill levels, user friendly layout. Private club conditions and service.

	1	2	3	4	5	6	7	8	9
PAR	4	4	4	4	3	4	4	3	5
YARDS	409	359	355	389	183	357	382	195	521
HDCP	5	13	17	1	15	3	9	11	7
	10	**11**	**12**	**13**	**14**	**15**	**16**	**17**	**18**
PAR	5	4	4	4	4	3	5	3	4
YARDS	464	443	394	309	308	158	540	146	405
HDCP	14	2	4	10	12	16	6	18	8

Directions: Take I-93, Exit 7 to Route 101 East. Take Exit 3. Straight at stop sign, right at next stop sign. Club is 1/8 mile on left at top of hill.

NH

Canterbury Woods CC ✪✪

NEW 2003

Canterbury, NH (603) 783-9400
www.canterburywoodscc.com

Club Pro: Wayne Natti, PGA
Pro Shop: Limited inventory
Payment: Visa, MC
Tee Times: 5 days
Fee 9 Holes: Weekday: $18.00
Fee 18 Holes: Weekday: $32.00
Twilight Rates: Yes
Cart Rental: $13pp/18, $8pp/9
Lessons: $35/30-40 min **Schools:**
Clinics: **Day Camps:** Yes
Other: Restaurant / Clubhouse/ Snack bar / Bar-Lounge

Tees	Holes	Yards	Par	USGA	Slope
BACK	18	6650	72	71.7	136
MIDDLE	18	6134	72	69.2	130
FRONT	18	5535	72	66.1	118

Weekend: $22.00
Weekend: $38.00
All Day Play: No
Discounts: Junior
Junior Golf: Clinics **Membership:** Yes
Driving Range: Yes

2003 Entry. Newest 18 hole championship public course. Site of 2006 NH State Amateur Championshop. Bent grass greens, tees, & fairways. Outstanding playing conditions. "Fair, challenging." R.W.

	1	2	3	4	5	6	7	8	9
PAR	4	5	4	5	4	3	4	3	4
YARDS	394	488	364	518	264	128	353	208	347
HDCP									
	10	**11**	**12**	**13**	**14**	**15**	**16**	**17**	**18**
PAR	5	3	4	3	4	5	5	3	4
YARDS	456	180	381	176	340	516	474	138	409
HDCP									

Directions: From I 93 North or South, take Exit 18. Turn left on to West Road. Continue left at fork 1/2 mile from exit ramp. Course entrance is on the left just beyond Sloping Acres Farm (approx. 1/2 mile) from fork.

4✪=Excellent 3✪ =Very Good 2✪ =Good

Carter Country Club

Lebanon, NH (603) 448-4483
www.cartercountryclub.com

Tees	Holes	Yards	Par	USGA	Slope
BACK	9	5600	72	68.1	116
MIDDLE	9	5450	72	66.1	114
FRONT	9	5130	72	71.7	127

Club Pro: Rich Parker, PGA
Pro Shop: Full inventory
Payment: Most major
Tee Times: No
Fee 9 Holes: Weekday: $12.00
Fee 18 Holes: Weekday: $22.00
Twilight Rates: No
Cart Rental: $24.00/18 $14.00/9
Lessons: Yes **Schools:** No
Clinics: Junior **Day Camps:** No
Other: Restaurant / Clubhouse / Bar-lounge

Weekend: $14.00
Weekend: $24.00
All Day Play: N/R
Discounts: None
Junior Golf: Yes **Membership:** Yes
Driving Range: No

COUPON

Established in 1920. Semi-hilly course, very scenic, especially nice in the fall, small greens, very sloped! Open April - November.

	1	2	3	4	5	6	7	8	9
PAR	4	3	5	4	4	5	4	4	3
YARDS	350	155	470	365	280	480	265	285	75
HDCP	2	3	5	1	7	4	6	8	9
	10	11	12	13	14	15	16	17	18
PAR	4	3	5	4	4	5	4	4	3
YARDS	350	155	470	365	280	480	265	285	75
HDCP	2	3	5	1	7	4	6	8	9

Directions: Just a short pitch off I-89, Exit 19.

CC of New Hampshire ●● 22

N. Sutton, NH (603) 927-4246

Tees	Holes	Yards	Par	USGA	Slope
BACK	18	6743	72	72.5	134
MIDDLE	18	6256	72	70.3	126
FRONT	18	5416	72	71.7	127

Club Pro: Kevin Gibson
Pro Shop: Full inventory
Payment: Visa, MC, Amex, Disc
Tee Times: 1 week adv.
Fee 9 Holes: Weekday: $18.00
Fee 18 Holes: Weekday: $31.00
Twilight Rates: Yes, after 3 pm
Cart Rental: $26.00/18 $16.00/9
Lessons: $30.00/half hour **Schools:** No
Clinics: Yes **Day Camps:** No
Other: Clubhouse / Showers / Snack bar / Restaurant / Bar-lounge / Hotel

Weekend: $25.00
Weekend: $39.00
All Day Play: No
Discounts: None
Junior Golf: No **Membership:** No
Driving Range: $12/lg., $6/sm.

COUPON

The front nine is level, the back is hilly. Rated one of the top 5 golf courses in New Hampshire by *Golf Digest*. Home of the N.E. Senior Open. Golf Management LLC Company.

	1	2	3	4	5	6	7	8	9
PAR	4	3	5	4	4	3	4	5	4
YARDS	380	160	495	330	346	169	376	452	380
HDCP	8	18	6	12	14	16	10	2	4
	10	11	12	13	14	15	16	17	18
PAR	4	3	4	5	4	3	4	4	5
YARDS	410	124	351	471	366	169	412	400	465
HDCP	5	17	13	7	11	15	1	3	9

Directions: One mile off I-89 at Exit 10. Follow signs to Winslow State Park.

Claremont CC

Maple Ave., Claremont, NH (603) 542-9550

Club Pro:
Pro Shop: Limited inventory
Payment: Cash,Check
Tee Times: No
Fee 9 Holes: Weekday: $16.00
Fee 18 Holes: Weekday: $25.00
Twilight Rates: No
Cart Rental: $25.00/18 $15.00/9
Lessons: Schools: No
Clinics: Yes **Day Camps:** No
Other: Clubhouse / Bar-Lounge / Snack Bar / Lockers / Showers

Tees	Holes	Yards	Par	USGA	Slope
BACK					
MIDDLE	9	5418	68	64.7	104
FRONT	9	4830	72	N/R	113

Weekend: $18.00
Weekend: $28.00
All Day Play: No
Discounts: None
Junior Golf: Yes **Membership:** Yes
Driving Range: Practice Area

Old style course. Established 1914. Small greens, hilly with woods.

	1	2	3	4	5	6	7	8	9
PAR	4	4	4	4	4	3	4	3	4
YARDS	420	328	273	262	275	174	434	169	312
HDCP	4	12	14	10	16	6	2	18	8
	10	11	12	13	14	15	16	17	18
PAR	4	4	4	4	4	3	4	3	4
YARDS	428	336	286	277	284	215	446	177	322
HDCP	3	11	13	9	15	5	1	17	7

Directions: Claremont exit off I-91 to downtown. Follow Pleasant Street to Maple Avenue. Make right turn. About 1/2 mile on left.

Colebrook CC

Colebrook, NH (603) 237-5566
www.colebrookcountryclub.com

Club Pro: No
Pro Shop: Limited inventory
Payment: Visa, MC, Disc.
Tee Times: No
Fee 9 Holes: Weekday: $18.00
Fee 18 Holes: Weekday: $18.00
Twilight Rates: Yes, after 5 pm
Cart Rental: $25.00/18 $20.00/9
Lessons: No **Schools:**
Clinics: Yes **Day Camps:** No
Other: Restaurant / Bar-lounge / Motel

Tees	Holes	Yards	Par	USGA	Slope
BACK	N/A				
MIDDLE	9	5893	72	67.5	114
FRONT	9	4368	73	72.3	114

Weekend: $22.00
Weekend: $22.00
All Day Play: Yes
Discounts: Senior/Junior/Women
Junior Golf: Yes **Membership:** Yes
Driving Range: No

COUPON

Beautifully maintained. Hole #5 is 612 yards. Open May 1 - October 31 (weather permitting). Discounts after 5 pm everyday and on Mondays and Wednesdays.

	1	2	3	4	5	6	7	8	9
PAR	4	4	3	4	6	3	5	3	4
YARDS	345	328	191	289	612	186	518	122	300
HDCP	11	6	4	13	7	9	2	17	14
	10	11	12	13	14	15	16	17	18
PAR	4	4	3	4	6	3	5	3	4
YARDS	345	350	134	376	612	186	518	181	300
HDCP	12	5	16	1	8	10	3	18	15

Directions: From I-93 or I-91, take Route 3 North from Littleton, NH. When in Colebrook, take right onto Route 26 East about 1/2 mile. Club is on left.

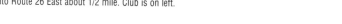

Countryside Golf Club

25

Dunbarton, NH (603) 774-5031

Club Pro: Chuck Urwin, PGA
Pro Shop: Full inventory
Payment: Visa, MC
Tee Times: Weekends, 1 week adv.
Fee 9 Holes: Weekday: $16.00
Fee 18 Holes: Weekday: $25.00
Twilight Rates: After 3pm wknds, 2pm wkdys
Cart Rental: $26.00/18 16.00/9
Lessons: $50/45 min. **Schools:** No
Clinics: Yes **Day Camps:** No
Other: Clubhouse / Snack bar / Bar-lounge / Function Room

Tees	Holes	Yards	Par	USGA	Slope
BACK	9	6314	72	69.6	129
MIDDLE	9	6002	72	69.2	126
FRONT	9	5516	72	69.2	126

Weekend: $18.00
Weekend: $28.00
All Day Play: Yes
Discounts: None
Junior Golf: Yes **Membership:** No
Driving Range: $3.50/lg., $2.00/sm bucket

Improvements include: automatic irrigation system, added deck and renovated snack bar and pro shop.

	1	2	3	4	5	6	7	8	9
PAR	4	4	3	5	4	4	4	3	5
YARDS	305	369	138	483	386	365	344	143	466
HDCP	17	11	13	1	9	3	7	15	5
	10	**11**	**12**	**13**	**14**	**15**	**16**	**17**	**18**
PAR	4	4	3	5	4	4	4	3	5
YARDS	305	369	138	485	386	365	344	143	466
HDCP	18	12	14	2	10	4	8	16	6

Directions: Take Route 101 to Route 114 toward Goffstown. Take Route 13 N at Sully's Superette. 4 miles. Club on left.

Den Brae Golf Course

26

Sanbornton, NH (603) 934-9818
www.denbrae.com

Club Pro: Tom Gilley
Pro Shop: Full inventory
Payment: Visa, MC
Tee Times: Weekends, Holidays
Fee 9 Holes: Weekday: $14.00
Fee 18 Holes: Weekday: $22.00
Twilight Rates: Yes, after 3 pm
Cart Rental: $22.00/18 $14.00/9
Lessons: $28/one hour **Schools:** No
Clinics: Yes **Day Camps:** No
Other: Clubhouse / Snack bar / Bar-lounge

Tees	Holes	Yards	Par	USGA	Slope
BACK					
MIDDLE	9	6040	72	67.0	112
FRONT	9	5326	72	70.0	123

Weekend: $15.00
Weekend: $24.00
All Day Play: No
Discounts: None
Junior Golf: Yes **Membership:** Yes
Driving Range: $6.50/lg., grass tees

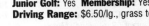

New 6,500 square foot 7th green is pure putting purgatory! Open April - October.

	1	2	3	4	5	6	7	8	9
PAR	4	4	3	5	4	4	4	4	4
YARDS	380	241	170	490	270	370	288	355	395
HDCP	7	17	11	5	15	1	13	9	3
	10	**11**	**12**	**13**	**14**	**15**	**16**	**17**	**18**
PAR	4	4	3	5	4	4	4	4	4
YARDS	385	247	175	500	275	388	339	390	410
HDCP	8	18	12	6	16	2	14	10	4

Directions: Take I-93 to Exit 22, go south on Route 127 for 1.5 miles, right on Prescott Road, .3 mile on right.

Derryfield CC

Manchester, NH (603) 669-0235
www.derryfieldgolf.com

Club Pro: Mike Ryan, PGA
Pro Shop: Full inventory
Payment: Cash/charge
Tee Times: S/S/H

Tees	Holes	Yards	Par	USGA	Slope
BACK	18	6144	70	68.0	113
MIDDLE	18	5714	70	67.9	116
FRONT	18	5524	71	71.0	125

Fee 9 Holes: Weekday: $20.00
Fee 18 Holes: Weekday: $34.00
Twilight Rates: No
Cart Rental: $25.00/18 $15.00/9
Lessons: $30.00/half hour **Schools:** No
Clinics: Yes **Day Camps:** No
Other: Snack bar / Restaurant / Bar-lounge

Weekend: $20.00
Weekend: $34.00
All Day Play: No
Discounts: None
Junior Golf: Yes **Membership:** Yes
Driving Range: No

Sig. Hole: #11, 434 yard par 4. Tough driving hole. Keep ball to left-center. Because course is hilly with small greens, approach shots are key. Wide open fairways let you open up.

	1	2	3	4	5	6	7	8	9
PAR	4	4	3	4	4	4	4	3	4
YARDS	302	386	176	349	361	363	349	159	313
HDCP	15	5	9	7	11	3	1	13	17
	10	**11**	**12**	**13**	**14**	**15**	**16**	**17**	**18**
PAR	4	4	3	4	4	4	4	5	4
YARDS	312	409	146	238	327	327	320	504	374
HDCP	14	2	18	16	10	6	12	8	4

Directions: Route I-93 North to Exit 8. Bear right at the bottom of the ramp. At second set of lights, take a left. Course is on the left.

Duston Country Club

Hopkinton, NH (603) 746-4234

Club Pro: Ken Hamel
Pro Shop: Full inventory
Payment: Visa, MC
Tee Times: Weekends & holidays

Tees	Holes	Yards	Par	USGA	Slope
BACK	N/A				
MIDDLE	9	2109	32	59.9	99
FRONT	9	2083	33	63.8	107

Fee 9 Holes: Weekday: $12.00
Fee 18 Holes: Weekday: $18.00
Twilight Rates: No
Cart Rental: $20.00/18, $13.00/9
Lessons: Yes **Schools:** No
Clinics: Yes **Day Camps:** No
Other: Clubhouse / Snack bar / Bar-lounge

Weekend: $13.00
Weekend: $20.00
All Day Play: No
Discounts: Senior & Junior
Junior Golf: Yes **Membership:** Yes
Driving Range: No

A family run scenic nine hole course built in 1926. Scottish style bunkers and lush greens. Some hills. Greens are small to medium in size. Open April - Nov.

	1	2	3	4	5	6	7	8	9
PAR	4	3	4	3	4	4	3	4	3
YARDS	295	117	353	133	265	299	194	273	180
HDCP	7	17	3	15	13	9	1	11	5
	10	**11**	**12**	**13**	**14**	**15**	**16**	**17**	**18**
PAR									
YARDS									
HDCP									

Directions: Take I-89 North to Exit 5 onto Routes 202 & 9 for 3 1/2 miles. Exit Country Club Road.

4❂ =Excellent **3❂** =Very Good **2❂** =Good

Eagle Mountain House

Jackson, NH (603) 383-9090
www.eaglemt.com

Club Pro: No
Pro Shop: Full inventory
Payment: Visa, MC, Amex, Dis
Tee Times: 1 week adv.
Fee 9 Holes: Weekday: $14.00
Fee 18 Holes: Weekday: $20.00
Twilight Rates: Yes, after 4 pm
Cart Rental: $22.00/18 $16.00/9
Lessons: Yes **Schools:** No
Clinics: Yes **Day Camps:** No
Other: Hotel / Lockers / Showers / Snack bar / Restaurant / Bar-lounge

Tees	Holes	Yards	Par	USGA	Slope
BACK					
MIDDLE	9	2154	32	61.0	102
FRONT	9	1620	32		

Weekend: $22.00
Weekend: $28.00
All Day Play: No
Discounts: Junior 1/2 price
Junior Golf: Yes **Membership:** Yes
Driving Range: Full

Breathtaking views of mountains and river. Grass driving range. Open late May - late October.

	1	2	3	4	5	6	7	8	9
PAR	4	3	4	5	3	3	3	3	4
YARDS	255	190	310	395	146	192	170	208	228
HDCP	7	13	5	1	17	11	15	9	3
	10	11	12	13	14	15	16	17	18
PAR									
YARDS									
HDCP									

Directions: I-95 North to Route 16 North. 9 miles North of North Conway. Continue through covered bridge into Jackson, 1/2 mile up Carter Notch Road.

Eastman Golf Links

Grantham, NH (603) 863-4500
www.eastmannh.com

Club Pro: Dick Tuxbury, PGA
Pro Shop: Full inventory
Payment: Visa, MC, Amex
Tee Times: 2 days adv.
Fee 9 Holes: Weekday: $31.00
Fee 18 Holes: Weekday: $52.00
Twilight Rates: Yes, after 4 pm
Cart Rental: $17.50pp/18 $12.50pp/9
Lessons: $30.00/half hour **Schools:** No
Clinics: Yes **Day Camps:** No
Other: Clubhouse / Snack bar / Restaurant / Bar-lounge

Tees	Holes	Yards	Par	USGA	Slope
BACK	18	6731	71	73.5	131
MIDDLE	18	6338	71	71.7	128
FRONT	18	5499	73	71.9	128

Weekend: $31.00
Weekend: $52.00
All Day Play: No
Discounts: Junior After 4 pm
Junior Golf: Yes **Membership:** Yes
Driving Range: $2.50/bucket

Pro's Comment: "Fantastic shape!" DT. Guaranteed a spot from 9 am on Saturdays and Sundays with credit card and foursome. Carts required Friday, Saturday, and Sunday until 3:00.

	1	2	3	4	5	6	7	8	9
PAR	4	5	3	4	4	4	3	5	4
YARDS	354	544	167	353	389	409	189	493	395
HDCP	11	5	17	13	3	9	15	7	1
	10	11	12	13	14	15	16	17	18
PAR	4	4	4	3	4	3	5	4	4
YARDS	322	384	443	189	384	113	441	385	384
HDCP	12	6	4	16	2	18	14	8	10

Directions: Take I-89 to Exit 13; course is right off exit ramp.

Exeter Country Club

31

Exeter, NH (603) 772-4752
www.exetercountryclub.com

Club Pro: Donald R. Folsom
Pro Shop: Full inventory
Payment: Visa, MC
Tee Times: Yes
Fee 9 Holes: Weekday: $17.00
Fee 18 Holes: Weekday: $27.00
Twilight Rates: After 4 pm
Cart Rental: $24.00/18 $12.00/9
Lessons: $40/ half hour   **Schools:** No
Clinics: Yes   **Day Camps:** No
Other: Restaurant / Clubhouse / Snack Bar / Showers / Bar-lounge

Tees	Holes	Yards	Par	USGA	Slope
BACK	N/A				
MIDDLE	9	5522	70	67.8	115
FRONT	9	5157	74	70.5	125

Weekend: $18.00
Weekend: $30.00
All Day Play: No
Discounts: None
Junior Golf: Yes **Membership:** Yes
Driving Range: yes

COUPON

Player's comment: "A placement course. Makes you think about each shot." Rolling terrain with a variety of challenges. Not overly difficult. Open April 1 - December 1.

	1	2	3	4	5	6	7	8	9
PAR	4	3	5	4	4	4	4	3	4
YARDS	379	160	460	361	365	250	281	165	300
HDCP	5	17	9	3	1	15	11	7	13

	10	11	12	13	14	15	16	17	18
PAR	4	3	5	4	4	4	4	3	4
YARDS	381	170	473	366	370	260	286	180	315
HDCP	6	18	10	4	2	16	12	8	14

Directions: Take I 95 to Hampton, NH exit to Route 101 West, Exit to Route 108 to Stratham, Exeter. Bear left. Go right at 3rd light, take 1st left, then the next right. Go right at end of street. Course is on left.

Farmington CC

32

Farmington, NH (603) 755-2412

Club Pro: Bert Prenaveau,PGA
Pro Shop: Full inventory
Payment: Cash only
Tee Times: Weekends
Fee 9 Holes: Weekday: No
Fee 18 Holes: Weekday: $22.00
Twilight Rates: N/R
Cart Rental: $20.00/18 $14.00/9
Lessons: $35.00/half hour   **Schools:** Yes
Clinics: Yes   **Day Camps:** No
Other: Clubhouse / Snack bar/ Bar-lounge

Tees	Holes	Yards	Par	USGA	Slope
BACK					
MIDDLE	9	6279	72	70.0	127
FRONT	9	5506	72	70.8	116

Weekend: No
Weekend: $28.00
All Day Play: N/R
Discounts: None
Junior Golf: Yes **Membership:** Yes
Driving Range: No

Challenging redesigned course.

	1	2	3	4	5	6	7	8	9
PAR	4	4	3	5	4	3	5	4	4
YARDS	350	350	140	491	375	135	516	406	345
HDCP	13	7	17	5	9	15	3	1	11

	10	11	12	13	14	15	16	17	18
PAR	4	4	3	5	4	3	5	4	4
YARDS	335	394	128	500	335	196	484	435	330
HDCP	14	8	18	6	10	16	4	2	12

Directions: From Route I-95 take Spaulding Turnpike to Exit 15. Then take Route 11 North to Route 153. About 1 mile.

NH

4✪ =Excellent 3✪ =Very Good 2✪ =Good

Fore-U-Golf Center

West Lebanon,NH (603) 298-9702

Tees	Holes	Yards	Par	USGA	Slope
BACK					
MIDDLE	9	1031	27		
FRONT	9	907	27		

Club Pro:
Pro Shop: No
Payment: Cash only
Tee Times: No
Fee 9 Holes: Weekday: $7.50, $5 for Jrs.   **Weekend:** $7.50, $5 for Jrs.
Fee 18 Holes: Weekday: $10.50, $8 for Jrs.   **Weekend:** $10.50, $8 for Jrs.
Twilight Rates: No   **All Day Play:** Am, 15.00
Cart Rental: None   **Discounts:** Junior
Lessons: TBA **Schools:** No   **Junior Golf:** Yes **Membership:** No
Clinics: Yes **Day Camps:** No   **Driving Range:** $7/lg., $6/med., $5/sm.
Other: Miniature Golf / Share parking lot with Golf and Ski Warehouse

COUPON

Lighted for night play. Fun, challenging par 3 golf course. Open March-November.

	1	2	3	4	5	6	7	8	9
PAR	3	3	3	3	3	3	3	3	3
YARDS	130	78	96	65	193	138	124	111	96
HDCP									
	10	11	12	13	14	15	16	17	18
PAR									
YARDS									
HDCP									

Directions: I-89 Exit 20 to Route 12A South. Approximately 1 mile on right.

Green Meadow GC #1, The Prairie ✪✪

Steele Rd., Hudson, NH (603) 889-1555

Tees	Holes	Yards	Par	USGA	Slope
BACK	18	6160	70	68.2	112
MIDDLE	18	5809	70	66.5	108
FRONT	18	4877	70	66.6	106

Club Pro: Brain Doyle, PGA
Pro Shop: Yes
Payment: Visa, MC, Disc, Cash
Tee Times: Weekends, 1 week adv.
Fee 9 Holes: Weekday: $20.00 after 2pm   **Weekend:** N/A
Fee 18 Holes: Weekday: $33.00   **Weekend:** $43.00
Twilight Rates: Yes, after 2 pm   **All Day Play:** Yes
Cart Rental: $26.00/18, $16.00/9.   **Discounts:** Senior & Junior
Lessons: $35.00/30 min **Schools:** No   **Junior Golf:** Yes **Membership:** No
Clinics: Yes **Day Camps:** Yes   **Driving Range:** $5.00/lg.
Other: Snack bar / Bar-lounge / Showers

Course set along the Merrimac River. Junior discounts S/S after 3 pm. Senior playbook available.

	1	2	3	4	5	6	7	8	9
PAR	4	4	3	4	4	3	5	4	4
YARDS	334	328	141	376	341	169	471	411	364
HDCP	12	14	18	6	10	16	2	4	8
	10	11	12	13	14	15	16	17	18
PAR	4	3	4	3	4	4	4	4	5
YARDS	353	157	324	153	329	410	313	329	506
HDCP	5	17	9	15	7	3	13	11	1

Directions: Take Route 3 to Exit 34. Take right off ramp. Left at first light. Bear left as you cross Tyngsboro Bridge. Follow Route 3A 2.5 miles. Take a left on Steele Rd . to course.

Green Meadow GC # 2, The Jungle ⭕⭕ ▶ 35

Steele Rd., Hudson, NH (603) 889-1555

Club Pro: Brian Doyle, PGA
Pro Shop: Yes
Payment: Cash, MC, Visa, Disc, Amex
Tee Times: Weekends, 1 week adv.
Fee 9 Holes: Weekday: $20.00 after 2pm
Fee 18 Holes: Weekday: $33.00
Twilight Rates: Yes, after 2 pm
Cart Rental: $26.00/18 $14.00/9
Lessons: $35.00/30 min **Schools:** No
Clinics: Yes **Day Camps:** Yes
Other: Snack bar / Bar-lounge / Showers

Tees	Holes	Yards	Par	USGA	Slope
BACK	18	6940	72	71.4	122
MIDDLE	18	6394	72	69.1	120
FRONT	18	5352	72	69.7	114

Weekend: N/A
Weekend: $43.00
All Day Play: Yes
Discounts: Senior & Junior
Junior Golf: Yes **Membership:** No
Driving Range: $5.00/lg.

Junior discounts on weekends after 3 pm. Senior playbook available. "Good dollar value on weekdays." F.P.

	1	2	3	4	5	6	7	8	9
PAR	4	4	5	3	4	4	4	3	5
YARDS	368	341	513	164	351	405	366	185	479
HDCP	12	14	2	18	10	8	6	16	4
	10	**11**	**12**	**13**	**14**	**15**	**16**	**17**	**18**
PAR	4	3	4	5	4	4	3	4	5
YARDS	358	137	370	358	382	368	142	415	512
HDCP	13	17	11	1	7	9	15	5	3

Directions: Take Route 3 to Exit 34. Take right off ramp. Left at first light. Bear left as you cross Tyngsboro Bridge. Follow Route 3A 2.5 miles. Take a left on Steele Rd. to course.

Groton Road CC ▶ 36 NEW 2003

Nashua, NH (603) 598- 8454

Club Pro: Kelly-Yong Collins
Pro Shop: Limited inventory
Payment: Visa, MC, Amex
Tee Times: Preferred
Fee 9 Holes: Weekday: $18.00
Fee 18 Holes: Weekday: $25.00
Twilight Rates: Yes
Cart Rental: $12pp/9
Lessons: Yes **Schools:**
Clinics: **Day Camps:**
Other: Clubhouse / Snackbar

Tees	Holes	Yards	Par	USGA	Slope
BACK	9	6242	70	69.4	117
MIDDLE	9	5676	72	69.4	117
FRONT	9	4476	72		

Weekend: $22.00
Weekend: $29.00
All Day Play:
Discounts: Senior
Junior Golf: **Membership:** Yes
Driving Range: Yes

2003 Entry. Opened 2002. A challenging regulation 9 hole course that requires 'course mangement play.' "A work in progress. Several blind shots required." R.W.

	1	2	3	4	5	6	7	8	9
PAR	4	3	4	3	5	4	4	5	4
YARDS	362	153	297	141	418	400	350	464	253
HDCP	3	17	13	7	5	1	9	11	15
	10	**11**	**12**	**13**	**14**	**15**	**16**	**17**	**18**
PAR	4	3	4	3	5	4	4	5	4
YARDS	362	153	297	141	418	400	350	464	253
HDCP	4	18	14	8	6	2	10	12	16

Directions: Route 3 to Exit 5 then Exit 5 West. Follow signs to Route 111, Pepperell, MA. Stay on Route 111 for 2 miles. Look for sign to Groton Road CC, Left at traffic light onto Route 111A. Course is 3/4 of a mile on left.

4⭕ =Excellent **3⭕** =Very Good **2⭕** =Good

Hales Location Golf Course ⊙⊙

North Conway, NH (603) 356-2140
www.jonathansgolf.com

Club Pro: Jonathan Rivers
Pro Shop: Full inventory
Payment: All major cards,
Tee Times: May 1st for season
Fee 9 Holes: Weekday: $28.00
Fee 18 Holes: Weekday: $39.00
Twilight Rates: Yes, after 3:30 pm
Cart Rental: $14pp/18 $8pp/9
Lessons: Yes **Schools:** Yes
Clinics: Yes **Day Camps:** Yes
Other: Clubhouse / Hotel / Restaurant / Bar-lounge / Snack bar / Lockers / Showers

Weekend: $31.00
Weekend: $42.00
All Day Play: Yes
Discounts: None
Junior Golf: No **Membership:** Yes
Driving Range: No

Tees	Holes	Yards	Par	USGA	Slope
BACK	9	6050	72	68.8	122
MIDDLE	9	5632	72	66.8	115
FRONT	9	5016	72	67.4	113

COUPON

Special holes: #1 and #9. Great 9 hole layout with breath taking views of the White Mts. Bent grass fairways and greens. Golf rates vary seasonally. Open May-Nov.

	1	2	3	4	5	6	7	8	9
PAR	5	4	3	4	5	3	4	4	4
YARDS	458	312	148	256	468	130	334	368	342
HDCP	1	5	15	13	3	17	11	7	9
	10	**11**	**12**	**13**	**14**	**15**	**16**	**17**	**18**
PAR	5	4	3	4	5	3	4	4	4
YARDS	458	312	148	256	468	130	334	368	342
HDCP	2	6	16	14	4	18	12	8	10

Directions: Take Route 16 to traffic light in Conway. Turn on to Washington St., then right on to West Side Road; 5 miles on left.

Hanover Country Club ⊙⊙

Hanover, NH (603) 646-2000
www.dartmouth.edu/~hccweb

Club Pro: J. Calhoun, PGA & C. Phillips, PGA
Pro Shop: Full inventory
Payment: Visa, MC, Amex
Tee Times: 3 days adv.
Fee 9 Holes: Weekday: N/A
Fee 18 Holes: Weekday: $45.00 M-F
Twilight Rates: Yes, after 4 pm
Cart Rental: $18pp/18
Lessons: $35.00/half hour **Schools:** No
Clinics: Yes **Day Camps:** No
Other: Clubhouse / Lockers / Showers / Snack bar

Weekend: N/A
Weekend: $55.00
All Day Play: No
Discounts: None
Junior Golf: Yes **Membership:** Yes
Driving Range: Yes

Tees	Holes	Yards	Par	USGA	Slope
BACK	18	6515	71	70.9	130
MIDDLE	18	6031	71	68.8	128
FRONT	18	4972	72	65.1	118

Home of Dartmouth Golf. Practice area (4 holes) and driving range only open to students and members.

	1	2	3	4	5	6	7	8	9
PAR	4	4	4	3	3	4	4	4	5
YARDS	400	408	290	115	183	341	405	283	572
HDCP	6	10	18	16	12	14	8	2	4
	10	**11**	**12**	**13**	**14**	**15**	**16**	**17**	**18**
PAR	4	4	3	4	3	4	4	5	5
YARDS	385	315	177	308	142	425	358	467	457
HDCP	15	7	9	11	13	3	1	5	17

Directions: Hanover / Dartmouth Exit on both I-89 and I-91 to center of town. North on Main Street. Extension on north side of campus.

Hickory Pond Inn and Golf Course

Durham, NH (603) 659-7642
www.hickorypond.com

Club Pro: No
Pro Shop: Limited inventory
Payment: Most major
Tee Times: No
Fee 9 Holes: Weekday: $9.00   **Weekend:** $10.00
Fee 18 Holes: Weekday: $15.00   **Weekend:** $16.00
Twilight Rates: No   **All Day Play:** No
Cart Rental: No   **Discounts:** Senior & Junior
Lessons: Yes **Schools:** No   **Junior Golf:** Yes **Membership:** Yes
Clinics: Yes **Day Camps:** No   **Driving Range:** Putting green
Other: Bed & Breakfast-20 luxurious rooms / Banquet Room / Snacks / Inn

Tees	Holes	Yards	Par	USGA	Slope
BACK					
MIDDLE	9	1006	27		
FRONT					

Front 9 are golf holes, back 9 are "chain baskets on poles perfect for Frisbee or disc golf. Great family fun." A.P. Renovated 2002.

	1	2	3	4	5	6	7	8	9
PAR	3	3	3	3	3	3	3	3	3
YARDS	89	80	77	110	80	140	130	145	155
HDCP									

	10	11	12	13	14	15	16	17	18
PAR									
YARDS									
HDCP									

Directions: Take I-95 to Route 16(Spaulding Turnpike). Take Exit 6W (Route 4). Continue on Route 4 to Route 108 South. Go 4 miles to intersection of Route 108 and Stagecoach Rd.

Hidden Valley R.V. and Golf Park

Derry, NH (603) 887-PUTT
www.ucampnh.com/hiddenvalley

Club Pro: No
Pro Shop: Yes
Payment: Visa, MC, Cash
Tee Times: 5 days adv.
Fee 9 Holes: Weekday: $14.00   **Weekend:** $16.00
Fee 18 Holes: Weekday: $25.00   **Weekend:** $30.00
Twilight Rates: Yes, after 5 pm   **All Day Play:** No
Cart Rental: Yes   **Discounts:** Senior
Lessons: No **Schools:** No   **Junior Golf:** No **Membership:** Yes
Clinics: No **Day Camps:** No   **Driving Range:** No
Other: RV campsites

Tees	Holes	Yards	Par	USGA	Slope
BACK	18	6310	72	71	127
MIDDLE	18	5838	72	68.2	120
FRONT	18	5200	72	64.5	119

COUPON

Scenic, well maintained. R.V. sites at course. Nice big greens. Added 9 holes.

	1	2	3	4	5	6	7	8	9
PAR	3	4	3	5	4	4	4	5	4
YARDS	150	310	155	420	355	345	345	505	275
HDCP	15	11	17	3	7	13	5	1	9

	10	11	12	13	14	15	16	17	18
PAR	5	4	3	5	4	4	3	4	4
YARDS	420	325	190	530	365	308	155	355	330
HDCP	6	17	15	4	2	18	10	12	8

Directions: Route 93 to Exit 4 to rotary. Take E. Derry Rd. for 4 1/2 miles. Sign on left- 1 mile to park.

Highlands Links GC

41

Plymouth, NH (603) 536-3452
www.highlandlinks.net

Club Pro: Joe Clark, Sr.,PGA Master
Pro Shop: Full inventory
Payment: Cash, Credit
Tee Times: No
Fee 9 Holes: Weekday: $12.00
Fee 18 Holes: Weekday: $18.00
Twilight Rates: No
Cart Rental: $22.00/18 $12.00/9
Lessons: Yes, Inquire! **Schools:** Yes
Clinics: Yes **Day Camps:** Yes
Other: Clubhouse / Custom clubfitting

Tees	Holes	Yards	Par	USGA	Slope
BACK					
MIDDLE	9	2970	54	59.0	97
FRONT	9	2710	64		

Weekend: $12.00
Weekend: $18.00
All Day Play: No
Discounts: Senior & Junior
Junior Golf: Yes **Membership:** Yes
Driving Range: No

COUPON

Sig. Hole: #8, 190 yd. par 3 called "Ballybunion". Elevated tee with rolling fairway- outstanding southwest view! Improved conditions.

	1	2	3	4	5	6	7	8	9
PAR	3	3	3	3	3	3	3	3	3
YARDS	210	185	140	165	145	130	165	190	155
HDCP	3	9	11	15	13	17	5	1	7
	10	**11**	**12**	**13**	**14**	**15**	**16**	**17**	**18**
PAR	3	3	3	3	3	3	3	3	3
YARDS	210	185	140	165	145	130	165	190	155
HDCP	4	10	12	16	14	18	6	2	8

Directions: Rte. 93 to Exit 25, turn left at end of ramp. Follow 1/4 mi. to Route 175 South, at stop sign. Opposite Holderness Prep School, take left onto Mt. Prospect Rd., follow 1.5 mi. to GC.

Hoodkroft CC

42

Derry, NH (603) 434-0651
www.hoodkroft.com

Club Pro: R. Berberian, PGA & L. Ward, PGA
Pro Shop: Full inventory
Payment: Visa, MC, Disc
Tee Times: Tues for weekend
Fee 9 Holes: Weekday: $19.00
Fee 18 Holes: Weekday: $31.00
Twilight Rates: Yes, after 4 pm
Cart Rental: $14.00pp/18 $7.00pp/9
Lessons: $30/30 min. **Schools:** No
Clinics: No **Day Camps:** No
Other: Clubhouse / Bar-lounge / Snack bar / Showers

Tees	Holes	Yards	Par	USGA	Slope
BACK	9	6471	72	35.5	128
MIDDLE	9	6466	72	35.7	128
FRONT	9	4984	72	63.8	109

Weekend: $20.00
Weekend: $31.00
All Day Play: No
Discounts: Senior. Wkdays only.
Junior Golf: Yes **Membership:** Waiting List
Driving Range: No

Noted for excellent conditions. Mostly flat, open fairways, lots of water. Large open greens. Open April 1 - November 30 (or snow).

	1	2	3	4	5	6	7	8	9
PAR	4	4	3	5	4	4	4	3	4
YARDS	335	430	187	555	355	400	340	175	426
HDCP	13	3	11	1	9	5	15	17	7
	10	**11**	**12**	**13**	**14**	**15**	**16**	**17**	**18**
PAR	4	4	3	5	4	4	4	4	5
YARDS	355	420	224	538	375	380	360	155	456
HDCP	14	10	16	2	4	12	6	18	8

Directions: Take Exit 4 in N.H. off I-193, head east on Route 102. Go about 2 miles. Golf course is on right hand side.

Hooper Golf Club ✪✪ 43

Walpole, NH (603) 756-4020

Tees	Holes	Yards	Par	USGA	Slope
BACK					
MIDDLE	9	6028	71	68.5	122
FRONT	9	5418	72	71.2	121

Club Pro: Jay Clace
Pro Shop: Full inventory
Payment: Visa, MC
Tee Times: No
Fee 9 Holes: Weekday: $25.00 **Weekend:** $25.00
Fee 18 Holes: Weekday: $25.00 **Weekend:** $25.00
Twilight Rates: After 4 pm on wknds. **All Day Play:** Yes
Cart Rental: $25.00/18 $15.00/9 for 2 **Discounts:** Sat - Sun. after 4
Lessons: No **Schools:** No **Junior Golf:** Yes **Membership:** $460/Adult
Clinics: N/R **Day Camps:** No **Driving Range:** No
Other: Full Restaurant / Clubhouse/ Bed and breakfast hotel- $75/ night for 2

Noted for great conditions, historic clubhouse and Bed & breakfast. Improved irrigation. Call ahead to this busy course. Open April- October.

	1	2	3	4	5	6	7	8	9
PAR	5	4	4	3	5	3	4	4	4
YARDS	456	427	285	155	474	194	311	381	350
HDCP	9	1	7	17	5	15	13	11	3
	10	11	12	13	14	15	16	17	18
PAR	4	4	4	3	5	3	4	4	4
YARDS	435	427	275	155	481	194	311	381	336
HDCP	2	4	10	18	8	16	14	12	6

Directions: I-91 to Exit 5- Route 5 South to Route 12 South. After 1/2 mile, take first left onto South Street. Go to the end of South Street to Prospect Hill. 5 miles from I-91.

NH

Indian Mound GC 44

Center Ossipee, NH (603) 539-7733
www.indianmoundgc.com

Tees	Holes	Yards	Par	USGA	Slope
BACK	18	5675	70	67.1	118
MIDDLE	18	5360	70	67.1	118
FRONT	18	4713	70	67.5	117

Club Pro: Wendy Simmons
Pro Shop: Full inventory
Payment: Visa, MC
Tee Times: Yes
Fee 9 Holes: Weekday: N/A **Weekend:** N/A
Fee 18 Holes: Weekday: $35.00 **Weekend:** $40.00
Twilight Rates: Yes, after 3 pm **All Day Play:** No
Cart Rental: $24.00/18 **Discounts:** None
Lessons: Yes **Schools:** No **Junior Golf:** No **Membership:** Yes
Clinics: Yes **Day Camps:** No **Driving Range:** No
Other: Clubhouse / Restaurant / Bar-lounge

COUPON

Manchester Union Leader Review 2002, "This course is a gem... Expensive feel at reasonable rates".

	1	2	3	4	5	6	7	8	9
PAR	4	5	4	3	4	4	4	3	4
YARDS	295	465	355	118	288	276	295	170	365
HDCP	10	14	2	16	6	18	12	8	4
	10	11	12	13	14	15	16	17	18
PAR	4	3	4	4	5	4	3	5	3
YARDS	340	113	303	400	433	360	104	495	185
HDCP	7	17	11	1	9	3	15	13	5

Directions: From south or north, take Route 16 to Center Ossipee exit. From west or east, Route 25 or Route 28 to Route 16 to Center Osspipee exit. Course is .5 mile on left.

4✪ =Excellent 3✪ =Very Good 2✪ =Good

Intervale Country Club

Manchester, NH (603) 647-6811
www.intervalecc.com

Club Pro: Matt Thibeault, PGA
Pro Shop: Full inventory
Payment: Cash or Personal check
Tee Times: No
Fee 9 Holes: Weekday: $20.00
Fee 18 Holes: Weekday: $28.00
Twilight Rates: No
Cart Rental: $22.00/18 $12.00/9
Lessons: $50.00/hour **Schools:** No
Clinics: No **Day Camps:** No
Other: Restaurant / Bar-lounge

Tees	Holes	Yards	Par	USGA	Slope
BACK					
MIDDLE	9	3077	36	68.2	108
FRONT	9	2774	37	71..7	120

Weekend: $20.00
Weekend: $28.00
All Day Play: Yes
Discounts: None
Junior Golf: Yes **Membership:** Yes
Driving Range: No

Sig. Hole: #1, Right out of gate you face a par 3 of over 220 yards that plays over and along water to a small elevated green. Semi-private. Call for details. Open April-November

	1	2	3	4	5	6	7	8	9
PAR	3	4	4	5	4	4	4	3	5
YARDS	222	338	334	385	425	342	284	137	516
HDCP	7	15	13	5	1	9	11	17	3
	10	**11**	**12**	**13**	**14**	**15**	**16**	**17**	**18**
PAR									
YARDS									
HDCP									

Directions: Exit 7 off 293 North. Course is 1/2 mile on right. Exit 10 off 93, left and course is 2 mi. on left.

Jack O'Lantern Resort

Woodstock, NH (603) 745-3636
www.jackolanternresort.com

Club Pro: Fletcher Ivey
Pro Shop: Full inventory
Payment: Visa, MC, Amex, Disc.
Tee Times: 24 hrs. adv.
Fee 9 Holes: Weekday: $23.00
Fee 18 Holes: Weekday: $39.00
Twilight Rates: Yes, after 2 pm
Cart Rental: $27.00/18 $16.00/9
Lessons: $30.00/half hour **Schools:** No
Clinics: N/R **Day Camps:** No
Other: Restaurant / Hotel / Bar-lounge / Snack bar

Tees	Holes	Yards	Par	USGA	Slope
BACK					
MIDDLE	18	6003	70	68.6	117
FRONT	18	4917	71	67.0	113

Weekend: $28.00
Weekend: $44.00
All Day Play: No
Discounts: None
Junior Golf: No **Membership:** No
Driving Range: No

Players' Comments: "Short but fair course." "Great resort for golf and fun." "Good golf package." Open May - October. Carts required on Friday, Saturday, and Sunday.

	1	2	3	4	5	6	7	8	9
PAR	4	4	4	4	3	4	4	3	4
YARDS	370	365	414	362	175	421	320	175	325
HDCP	10	12	1	5	17	4	16	14	8
	10	**11**	**12**	**13**	**14**	**15**	**16**	**17**	**18**
PAR	4	4	3	5	4	4	3	4	5
YARDS	335	395	160	519	292	305	140	410	520
HDCP	13	3	11	9	6	15	18	2	7

Directions: Exit 30 off I-93.

Kingston Fairways

Kingston, NH (603) 642-7722

Club Pro: Mike Andersen
Pro Shop: Full inventory
Payment: Visa, MC
Tee Times: No
Fee 9 Holes: Weekday: $16.00
Fee 18 Holes: Weekday: $27.00
Twilight Rates: Yes, after 6 pm
Cart Rental: $24.00/18 $12.00/9
Lessons: No **Schools:** No
Clinics: Yes **Day Camps:** No
Other: Clubhouse / Snack bar

Tees	Holes	Yards	Par	USGA	Slope
BACK					
MIDDLE	18	5710	72	33.2	113
FRONT	9	2669	36		

Weekend: $19.00
Weekend: $33.00
All Day Play: No
Discounts: Senior -$2 & Junior -$2 weekdays
Junior Golf: Yes **Membership:** No
Driving Range: No

Now18 holes. Additional 9 opened in 2002.

	1	2	3	4	5	6	7	8	9
PAR	3	5	4	4	4	4	4	4	4
YARDS	125	505	315	329	347	300	300	330	381
HDCP	17	3	13	11	10	12	7	8	6
	10	11	12	13	14	15	16	17	18
PAR	3	4	4	3	4	4	5	4	4
YARDS	154	429	300	135	280	380	470	252	378
HDCP	16	2	5	18	14	4	9	15	1

Directions: Route 107 off Route 125 in Kingston, 1/4 of a mile. Or Exit 1 in Seabrook off of Route 95. Go 10 miles.

NH

Kingswood Golf Club

Wolfeboro, NH (603) 569-3569

Club Pro: David Pollini, PGA
Pro Shop: Full inventory
Payment: Visa, MC
Tee Times: 3 days adv.
Fee 9 Holes: Weekday: No
Fee 18 Holes: Weekday: $55.00 inc. cart
Twilight Rates: Yes, after 4:30 pm
Cart Rental: Included
Lessons: $50/hr., $35/30 min. **Schools:** No
Clinics: Yes **Day Camps:** No
Other: Snack bar / Bar-lounge

Tees	Holes	Yards	Par	USGA	Slope
BACK	18	6360	72	71.1	125
MIDDLE	18	5860	72	68.8	122
FRONT	18	5300	72	73.1	130

Weekend: No
Weekend: $60 inc. cart F/S/S
All Day Play: No
Discounts: None
Junior Golf: Yes **Membership:** Yes
Driving Range: $5.00/lg., $2.50/sm.

The course is hilly with five ponds. Has an excellent iron practice range with a green to hit with short irons (190 yard range). Reduced fees after 2 pm without cart. Open April - Oct. 31.

	1	2	3	4	5	6	7	8	9
PAR	4	5	3	4	4	3	4	4	4
YARDS	405	455	175	380	335	150	375	315	375
HDCP	7	6	15	1	11	17	9	13	3
	10	11	12	13	14	15	16	17	18
PAR	4	5	4	3	4	4	5	4	4
YARDS	360	490	410	205	360	300	495	405	370
HDCP	12	16	2	14	8	18	6	4	10

Directions: Take Route 28 North 1/4 mile past Kingswood High School. Turn left onto Kingswood Road.

Kona Mansion Inn

Moultonboro, NH (603) 253-4900
www.konamansioninn.com

Club Pro:
Pro Shop: No
Payment: Visa, MC
Tee Times: No
Fee 9 Holes: Weekday: $15.00
Fee 18 Holes: Weekday: $15.00
Twilight Rates: Yes, after 4 pm
Cart Rental: Pull $3.00
Lessons: No **Schools:** No
Clinics: No **Day Camps:** No
Other: Hotel / Full Service Restaurant

Tees	Holes	Yards	Par	USGA	Slope
BACK					
MIDDLE	9	1170	27		
FRONT					

Weekend: $15.00
Weekend: $15.00
All Day Play: No
Discounts: None
Junior Golf: No **Membership:** Yes-seasonal
Driving Range: Yes, Nova grass tees

A resort on Lake Winnipesaukee. Par 3 course.

	1	2	3	4	5	6	7	8	9
PAR	3	3	3	3	3	3	3	3	3
YARDS	105	150	130	135	128	150	162	125	85
HDCP									
	10	11	12	13	14	15	16	17	18
PAR									
YARDS									
HDCP									

Directions: From I-93 take Exit 23 and follow to the end in Meredith 11 miles, left on Route 3 to lights, right on Route 25. 9 miles to Moultonboro Neck Road on right. Go right, 2.5 miles to Kona Road on right. Follow signs.

Laconia Country Club

✪✪✪

Lakeport, NH (603) 524-1273

Club Pro: Dan Wilkins, PGA
Pro Shop: Full inventory
Payment: Visa, MC, Amex
Tee Times: 2 days in adv.
Fee 9 Holes: Weekday: N/A
Fee 18 Holes: Weekday: $75
Twilight Rates: No
Cart Rental: Included
Lessons: $35.00/half hour **Schools:** No
Clinics: Junior **Day Camps:** No
Other: Clubhouse / Lockers / Showers / Snack bar / Restaurant / Bar-lounge / Tennis Courts

Tees	Holes	Yards	Par	USGA	Slope
BACK	18	6789	72	72.5	139
MIDDLE	18	6348	72	70.4	135
FRONT	18	5595	72	67.5	117

Weekend: N/A
Weekend: $100
All Day Play: Yes
Discounts: None
Junior Golf: Yes **Membership:** Yes
Driving Range: Yes

Major renovations completed 2002, plays like a new course. New tees, fairways and greens. Semi-private. Open April 15 - Nov. 15. "Well worth playing." R.W.

	1	2	3	4	5	6	7	8	9
PAR	4	5	4	3	5	4	3	4	4
YARDS	349	540	385	155	496	350	173	370	379
HDCP	13	1	5	17	3	11	15	9	7
	10	11	12	13	14	15	16	17	18
PAR	4	4	4	5	3	4	3	5	4
YARDS	388	380	336	504	130	371	187	476	379
HDCP	6	8	14	2	18	12	16	4	10

Directions: Take I-93N to Exit 20, Route 3 into Laconia. Take left on Elm St. (Lakeport). Clubhouse is a mile on the right.

Lakeview Golf Club

Ladd Hill Road, Belmont, NH 03220 (603-524-2220)

Club Pro: No
Pro Shop: Full inventory
Payment: Cash only
Tee Times: No
Fee 9 Holes: Weekday: $14.00
Fee 18 Holes: Weekday: $20.00
Twilight Rates: Yes, after 3 pm and 5 pm
Cart Rental: $20.00/18,$12.00/9
Lessons: No **Schools:** No
Clinics: N/R **Day Camps:** No
Other:

Tees	Holes	Yards	Par	USGA	Slope
BACK					
MIDDLE	9	6220	70	69	
FRONT	9	4540	74	72.0	

Weekend: $14.00
Weekend: $20.00
All Day Play: N/R
Discounts: None
Junior Golf: No **Membership:** Yes
Driving Range: No

COUPON

Beautiful nine hole golf course overlooks a panorama of lakes and mountains. Good walking course. Dress code. Twilight rates for 9 holes after 3pm - $12; after 5pm - $10.

	1	2	3	4	5	6	7	8	9
PAR	5	4	4	4	3	4	3	5	3
YARDS	505	315	290	425	220	435	175	550	195
HDCP	3	13	15	5	9	11	17	1	7
	10	11	12	13	14	15	16	17	18
PAR	5	4	4	4	3	4	3	5	3
YARDS	505	315	290	425	220	435	175	550	195
HDCP	4	14	15	6	10	12	18	2	8

Directions: I-93 North to Exit 20, then east towards Laconia on Routes 3 & 11. Cross Winnisquam bridge and up 1 mile to set of lights. Take right-across from Belknap Mall.

Lisbon Village Country Club

Bishop Road, Lisbon, NH (603) 838-6004

Club Pro: Gary Roy
Pro Shop: Limited inventory
Payment: Cash or Check
Tee Times: Suggested
Fee 9 Holes: Weekday: $12.00
Fee 18 Holes: Weekday: $24.00
Twilight Rates: Yes, after 4 pm
Cart Rental: $24.00/18, $12.00/9
Lessons: Yes **Schools:** No
Clinics: Yes **Day Camps:** No
Other: Full restaurant/ Club House/ Bar-lounge / Snack bar

Tees	Holes	Yards	Par	USGA	Slope
BACK					
MIDDLE	9	5801	72	69.7	126
FRONT	9	4931	72	70.6	127

Weekend: $15.00
Weekend: $28.00
All Day Play: No
Discounts: Junior
Junior Golf: Yes **Membership:** Yes
Driving Range: $3.50/Lge, $2.50/Sm

COUPON

Scenic White Mt. course that is the epitome of target golf, noted for elevated tees and greens. Requires a deft touch with irons and woods. Juniors under 7 play for free. Open May through October.

	1	2	3	4	5	6	7	8	9
PAR	4	5	4	4	3	4	5	4	3
YARDS	255	535	310	397	211	248	440	350	148
HDCP	15	1	11	5	7	13	3	9	17
	10	11	12	13	14	15	16	17	18
PAR	4	5	4	5	3	4	4	4	3
YARDS	265	518	369	435	172	272	366	352	158
HDCP	16	2	8	6	12	14	4	10	18

Directions: From I-93, Exit 42, go west on Route 302 for 7 miles. Go right on Lyman Rd. for 3/4 mile, then left on Bishop Rd. for 3/4 mile to course.

4✪ =Excellent **3✪** =Very Good **2✪** = Good

Lochmere Golf & CC

53

Rt. 3, Tilton, NH (603) 528-4653
www.lochmeregolf.com

Tees	Holes	Yards	Par	USGA	Slope
BACK	18	6600	72	72.2	131
MIDDLE	18	6190	72	69.5	123
FRONT	18	5227	72	68.9	126

Club Pro: Vic Stanfield, PGA
Pro Shop: Full inventory
Payment: Visa, MC
Tee Times: 7 days adv.
Fee 9 Holes: Weekday: $16.00
Fee 18 Holes: Weekday: $32.00
Twilight Rates: Yes, after 3 pm wkdys
Cart Rental: $24.00/18 $14.00/9
Lessons: $25.00/half hour **Schools:** No
Clinics: Yes **Day Camps:** No
Other: Restaurant / Clubhouse / Bar-Lounge / Snack Bar / Function Room

Weekend: $20.00
Weekend: $40.00
All Day Play: No
Discounts: Seasonal specials
Junior Golf: Yes **Membership:** Yes
Driving Range: $4.00/bucket

COUPON

Player's comment: "Great challenging course, friendly staff."

	1	2	3	4	5	6	7	8	9
PAR	4	4	3	4	4	4	5	3	4
YARDS	330	340	140	350	368	363	480	163	390
HDCP	9	15	17	3	7	5	1	13	11
	10	**11**	**12**	**13**	**14**	**15**	**16**	**17**	**18**
PAR	4	5	4	4	3	4	4	4	5
YARDS	350	500	310	373	160	401	377	323	472
HDCP	4	14	6	2	18	8	12	10	16

Directions: I-93 Exit 20 (Laconia/Tilton). Go 1.5 miles east on Route 3. Course is on left.

Londonderry CC

54

Londonderry, NH (603) 432-9789

Tees	Holes	Yards	Par	USGA	Slope
BACK					
MIDDLE	18	3805	62	60.5	100
FRONT	18	3203	62	58.4	91

Club Pro: Peter Dupuis, PGA
Pro Shop: Yes
Payment: Cash only
Tee Times: Thur. AM for weekend
Fee 9 Holes: Weekday: $15.00
Fee 18 Holes: Weekday: $23.00
Twilight Rates: No
Cart Rental: $18.00/18 $10.00/9
Lessons: Yes **Schools:** No
Clinics: Yes **Day Camps:** No
Other: Nuttfield Lounge and snackbar

Weekend: $17.00
Weekend: $26.00
All Day Play: No
Discounts: Senior
Junior Golf: Yes **Membership:** No
Driving Range: Netted Area

Sig. Hole: #17, 345 yd. challenging and picturesque par 4. You must hit your tee shot over a pond to a tree lined fairway, a true test.

	1	2	3	4	5	6	7	8	9
PAR	3	3	4	4	3	3	3	3	3
YARDS	210	165	235	215	135	135	145	95	165
HDCP	2	4	10	18	16	12	6	14	8
	10	**11**	**12**	**13**	**14**	**15**	**16**	**17**	**18**
PAR	3	3	4	4	4	4	4	4	3
YARDS	155	115	300	310	340	235	370	345	135
HDCP	11	15	7	3	13	9	1	5	17

Directions: Take I-93 to Exit 4, left onto Route 102 West, follow to Route 128, take right onto Route 128 North, follow 4 miles to blinking light. Left on Litchfield Rd. Go 1.7 mi., take left onto Kimball Rd., Club is 1 mi. on right.

Loudon Country Club

Loudon, NH 03301 (603) 783-3372

Club Pro: Lionel Dupuis, PGA
Pro Shop: Limited inventory
Payment: Visa, MC
Tee Times: Wknds/Hldys

Tees	Holes	Yards	Par	USGA	Slope
BACK	18	6232	70	70.4	120
MIDDLE	18	5777	72	68.7	115
FRONT	18	4702	72	67.0	112

Fee 9 Holes: Weekday: $18.00
Fee 18 Holes: Weekday: $29.00
Twilight Rates: Yes, after 5:30 pm wkdys
Cart Rental: $24.00/18, $14.00/9
Lessons: Yes **Schools:** No
Clinics: No **Day Camps:** No
Other: Full restuarant / Bar-lounge / Clubhouse

Weekend: $18.00
Weekend: $35.00
All Day Play: No
Discounts: Senior weekdays
Junior Golf: No **Membership:** Yes
Driving Range: $6/Lg.,$4/Sm.

Challenging for all abilities and all ages.

	1	2	3	4	5	6	7	8	9
PAR	4	5	4	3	4	5	4	3	4
YARDS	256	490	298	158	358	455	363	145	375
HDCP	13	3	11	15	5	1	9	17	7
	10	11	12	13	14	15	16	17	18
PAR	4	3	5	3	4	4	5	4	4
YARDS	326	191	471	133	238	336	460	363	361
HDCP	10	16	2	18	14	8	4	6	12

Directions: I-93 to I-393. Take Exit 3 from 393, left at lights toRoute 106 North for 7.5 miles. Course is on left.

Maplewood Casino & CC

Bethlehem, NH (603) 869-3335
www.maplewoodgolfresort.com

Club Pro: Trevor Howard, Golf Dir.
Pro Shop: Full inventory
Payment: Visa, MC, Disc, Cash
Tee Times: Yes

Tees	Holes	Yards	Par	USGA	Slope
BACK	18	6200	72	68.0	115
MIDDLE	18	6001	72	67.4	113
FRONT	18	5013	71	68.8	113

Fee 9 Holes: Weekday: $20.00
Fee 18 Holes: Weekday: $31.00
Twilight Rates: After 4pm wkdy, after 5pm wknd
Cart Rental: $14pp/18, $10pp/9
Lessons: No **Schools:** No
Clinics: No **Day Camps:** No
Other: 1890 restored Clubhouse / Showers / Lockers / Bar-lounge / Hotel

Weekend: $24.00
Weekend: $36.00
All Day Play: No
Discounts: None
Junior Golf: No **Membership:** Yes
Driving Range: N/A

COUPON

Sig. Hole: #16 unique par 6, 651 yards. Stay and Play packages. Cart required 8 am - 2 pm on weekends. Packages include 2 players and cart for $56 on M + T.

	1	2	3	4	5	6	7	8	9
PAR	5	4	4	4	4	4	4	3	4
YARDS	445	399	277	388	367	373	319	150	355
HDCP	3	1	15	7	9	5	13	17	11
	10	11	12	13	14	15	16	17	18
PAR	4	3	3	4	4	5	6	4	3
YARDS	355	163	201	321	279	527	651	287	144
HDCP	6	14	16	8	10	4	2	12	18

Directions: I-93 Exit 40 onto Route 302 East. Approx. 5 miles.

4 =Excellent 3 =Very Good 2 =Good

Mojalaki Golf Club

Franklin, NH (603) 934-3033
www.mojalaki.com

Tees	Holes	Yards	Par	USGA	Slope
BACK	18	6236	71	70.9	119
MIDDLE	18	5030	71	65.4	108
FRONT	18	4300	71	65.0	105

Club Pro: Rick Amidon
Pro Shop: Full inventory
Payment: Visa, MC, Disc
Tee Times: 5 days in advance
Fee 9 Holes: Weekday: $16.00   **Weekend:** $16.00
Fee 18 Holes: Weekday: $28.00   **Weekend:** $28.00
Twilight Rates: Yes, after 3 pm   **All Day Play:** No
Cart Rental: $24.00/18 $14.00/9   **Discounts:** Senior & Junior
Lessons: Yes **Schools:** No   **Junior Golf:** Yes **Membership:** Yes
Clinics: Yes **Day Camps:** No   **Driving Range:** No
Other: Complete Function Facility holds 180 / Snackbar / Large outings welcome

COUPON

Beautiful views and a combination of contemporary and traditional design with tees to compliment every skill level. Rebuilt 16th green. Formerly Franklin Greens Golf & CC.

	1	2	3	4	5	6	7	8	9
PAR	4	4	4	4	5	4	3	4	4
YARDS	352	250	274	296	418	271	91	246	255
HDCP	2	8	16	12	4	10	18	6	14
	10	**11**	**12**	**13**	**14**	**15**	**16**	**17**	**18**
PAR	4	4	3	5	4	4	4	3	4
YARDS	247	283	109	410	376	285	390	147	330
HDCP	17	13	15	7	5	9	1	11	3

Directions: I-93 Exit 19 traveling north, Exit 20 traveling south. Route 3 South to downtown Franklin, left onto Prospect Street. Golf course 1 mile on left.

Monadnock CC

Peterborough, NH (603) 924-7769

Tees	Holes	Yards	Par	USGA	Slope
BACK					
MIDDLE	9	1576	29	54.0	76
FRONT	9	1576	32	54.0	76

Club Pro: Dana Hennessey
Pro Shop: Limited inventory
Payment: Cash or checks
Tee Times: No
Fee 9 Holes: Weekday: $12.00   **Weekend:** $12.00
Fee 18 Holes: Weekday: $20.00   **Weekend:** $20.00
Twilight Rates: Yes, after 3:30 pm   **All Day Play:** N/R
Cart Rental: $22/18, $12/9, $4/pull cart   **Discounts:** None
Lessons: Yes **Schools:** No   **Junior Golf:** Yes **Membership:** Yes
Clinics: N/R **Day Camps:** No   **Driving Range:** Cage, $2.50/bucket
Other: Clubhouse / Snack bar / Bar-lounge / 2 Tennis Courts / Banquet facility

While the men's Par is 29 and the women's 32, don't be fooled. This course can be challenging for both veterans and beginners. The scenic beauty alone is worth the trip!

	1	2	3	4	5	6	7	8	9
PAR	4	3	3	3	3	4	3	3	3
YARDS	241	108	205	150	166	257	134	162	153
HDCP	9	17	1	13	3	7	15	5	11
	10	**11**	**12**	**13**	**14**	**15**	**16**	**17**	**18**
PAR									
YARDS									
HDCP									

Directions: From East or West Route 101. From North or South Route 202. Located on High Street.

Mountain View Grand Resort & Spa

59 ▶

Whitefield,NH (800) 438-3017
www.mountainviewgrand.com

Tees	Holes	Yards	Par	USGA	Slope
BACK	9	2930	35	66	112
MIDDLE	9	2873	35	66	112
FRONT	9			71.9	112

Club Pro: TBA
Pro Shop: Yes
Payment: Visa, MC, Amex
Tee Times: 1 day
Fee 9 Holes: Weekday: $18.00
Fee 18 Holes: Weekday: $27.00
Twilight Rates: Yes, after 3 pm
Cart Rental: $10pp/9
Lessons: Schools:
Clinics: Day Camps:
Other: Restaurant / Clubhouse / Hotel / Bar/Lounge / Tennis

Weekend: $24.00
Weekend: $32.00
All Day Play:
Discounts: Junior
Junior Golf: Membership: Yes
Driving Range: No

COUPON

2003 Entry. Challenging course in the heart of the White Mountains. Historic 9 holes completely renovated in 1998. Additional holes being constructed, hope to open 2004 as full 18.

	1	2	3	4	5	6	7	8	9
PAR	4	4	5	4	4	3	4	3	4
YARDS	449	398	472	326	316	126	342	123	321
HDCP	3	1	5	11	7	17	9	15	13
	10	11	12	13	14	15	16	17	18
PAR									
YARDS									
HDCP									

Directions: Exit 35 (I-93). 21 miles North on Route 3.

NH

Mt. Washington Hotel G.C.

60 ▶

Bretton Woods, NH (603) 278-4653
www.mountwashington.com

Tees	Holes	Yards	Par	USGA	Slope
BACK	27	6638	71	70.6	118
MIDDLE	27	6154	71	68.0	113
FRONT	27	5336	71	69.7	116

Club Pro: Andrew R. Craig
Pro Shop: Full inventory
Payment: Visa, MC, Amex,Disc.
Tee Times: 1 wk in adv.
Fee 9 Holes: Weekday: $41.00 w/ cart
Fee 18 Holes: Weekday: $75.00 w/ cart
Twilight Rates: Yes, after 2 pm
Cart Rental: Included
Lessons: Private and Group **Schools:** Yes
Clinics: Yes **Day Camps:** Yes
Other: Resort / Golf packages / Restaurant / Clubhouse / Bar-lounge / Lockers / Showers

Weekend: $41.00 w/ cart
Weekend: $75.00 w/ cart
All Day Play: Yes, $100
Discounts: None
Junior Golf: Yes **Membership:** Yes
Driving Range: Yes

COUPON

GPS in call carts! 27 holes: Mt. Pleasant, 9 holes 3125 yds designed by Cornish & Silva. **Player's Comments:** "Good layout. Very accomodating."

	1	2	3	4	5	6	7	8	9
PAR	3	4	4	4	3	5	4	4	4
YARDS	194	360	420	385	132	510	305	410	380
HDCP	15	11	1	7	17	5	13	3	9
	10	11	12	13	14	15	16	17	18
PAR	5	5	4	4	3	4	3	4	4
YARDS	515	475	300	383	190	290	175	375	355
HDCP	2	8	18	4	14	12	16	6	10

Directions: Take I-93, Exit 35 to Route 302 to Bretton Woods.

4⊙ =Excellent **3⊙** =Very Good **2⊙** =Good

Newport Country Club

Newport, NH (603) 863-7787
www.newport-golf.com

Club Pro: Chris Pollard, PGA
Pro Shop: Full inventory
Payment: Visa, MC, Cash
Tee Times: 3 days adv.

Tees	Holes	Yards	Par	USGA	Slope
BACK	18	6415	71	71.4	133
MIDDLE	18	6005	71	68.3	127
FRONT	18	4738	71	63.8	112

Fee 9 Holes: Weekday: $18.00
Fee 18 Holes: Weekday: $32.00
Twilight Rates: Yes, after 4 pm
Cart Rental: $14pp/18 $9pp/9
Lessons: $30.00/ 30min **Schools:** No
Clinics: Jr/Ladies **Day Camps:** Yes
Other: Clubhouse / Snack bar / Bar-lounge / Lockers

Weekend: $24.00
Weekend: $40.00
All Day Play: No
Discounts: Junior
Junior Golf: Yes **Membership:** Yes
Driving Range: $3.50/med. bucket

Variety of weekday passes which include unlimited golf. New ownership.

	1	2	3	4	5	6	7	8	9
PAR	5	4	4	3	4	4	3	4	4
YARDS	511	321	315	179	373	375	145	269	369
HDCP	8	4	6	14	2	12	16	18	10
	10	**11**	**12**	**13**	**14**	**15**	**16**	**17**	**18**
PAR	5	3	4	4	4	4	3	4	5
YARDS	477	138	387	379	375	341	169	375	507
HDCP	15	17	3	1	13	9	11	5	7

Directions: I-89 North to Exit 9 . Follow Route 103 to Newport. Take Unity Rd. (on left) 1 mile to golf course . Can be seen from Unity Road.

Nippo Lake Golf Club

Barrington, NH (603) 664-7616
www.nippolake.com

Club Pro: Rick Rogers
Pro Shop: Full inventory
Payment: Visa, MC
Tee Times: Recommended

Tees	Holes	Yards	Par	USGA	Slope
BACK	18	5613	70	66.9	123
MIDDLE	18	5313	70	65.4	119
FRONT	18	4527	70	65.9	110

Fee 9 Holes: Weekday: $18.00
Fee 18 Holes: Weekday: $30.00
Twilight Rates: No
Cart Rental: $14pp/18 $7pp/9
Lessons: $45/45 min. **Schools:** Jr.Yes
Clinics: Adult **Day Camps:** Yes
Other: Clubhouse / Snack bar / Restaurant / Bar-lounge / Video instruction

Weekend: $22.00
Weekend: $35.00
All Day Play: No
Discounts: Junior
Junior Golf: Yes **Membership:** Yes
Driving Range: $2.50-5.00/bucket

COUPON

Course is noted for scenic mountain views and friendly atmosphere. Rates subject to change.

	1	2	3	4	5	6	7	8	9
PAR	4	5	3	5	4	3	4	4	3
YARDS	314	515	145	473	358	121	316	332	135
HDCP	6	4	14	6	12	2	16	8	18
	10	**11**	**12**	**13**	**14**	**15**	**16**	**17**	**18**
PAR	5	4	3	4	4	4	4	3	4
YARDS	452	312	151	293	305	347	331	166	253
HDCP	11	1	9	13	7	3	5	15	17

Directions: Take Spaulding Turnpike North. Take Exit 13 (Route 202 North). Take right onto Route 126. Go 1/4 mile, then take a left onto Province Road.

North Conway CC

N. Conway, NH (603) 356-9391

Club Pro: Larry Gallagher, PGA
Pro Shop: Full inventory
Payment: Visa, MC, Amex
Tee Times: 5 days adv.

Tees	Holes	Yards	Par	USGA	Slope
BACK	18	6659	71	71.9	125
MIDDLE	18	6281	71	70.3	121
FRONT	18	5530	71	70.7	118

Fee 9 Holes: Weekday: N/A
Fee 18 Holes: Weekday: $40 walk, $53 ride
Twilight Rates: Yes, after 4 pm
Cart Rental: $26.00/18
Lessons: By appointment **Schools:** Junior
Clinics: Yes **Day Camps:** No
Other: Restaurant / Bar-Lounge / Public Dining

Weekend: N/A
Weekend: $65 inc. cart F/S/S/H
All Day Play: No
Discounts: Senior after 12pm
Junior Golf: Yes **Membership:** Yes
Driving Range: Yes, natural grass

Player's comment: "Outstanding condition and layout! Scenic views everywhere you look! Well worth the greens fees!" Hosted NH PGA Championship, State Amateur, and NH Open. 2001 Pro of the Year.

	1	2	3	4	5	6	7	8	9
PAR	4	4	4	3	4	4	3	5	4
YARDS	395	400	351	126	318	361	198	497	375
HDCP	1	5	11	17	7	13	9	15	3

	10	11	12	13	14	15	16	17	18
PAR	4	5	4	3	4	3	4	5	4
YARDS	349	475	385	150	420	147	357	528	337
HDCP	10	8	4	16	2	18	12	6	14

Directions: Take Route 16 to Main Street North Conway. Next to scenic Rail Road Station.

Oak Hill Golf Course

Meredith, NH (603) 279-4438

Club Pro: No
Pro Shop: Full inventory
Payment: Cash, Visa, MC
Tee Times: No

Tees	Holes	Yards	Par	USGA	Slope
BACK	9	4694	68	62.2	98
MIDDLE	9	4420	68	60.7	96
FRONT	9	3780	68	62.8	108

Fee 9 Holes: Weekday: $13.00
Fee 18 Holes: Weekday: $21.00
Twilight Rates: Yes, after 3 pm
Cart Rental: $22.00/18 $14.00/9
Lessons: No **Schools:** No
Clinics: No **Day Camps:** No
Other: Snack bar / Bar-lounge

Weekend: $13.00
Weekend: $21.00
All Day Play: $21.00
Discounts: None
Junior Golf: No **Membership:** Yes
Driving Range: No

COUPON

New tees, redesigned #7 with #6 in progress. Short regulation New England course with five greens blind from tee. Good challenge for your irons. Wooded and scenic. No tank tops. Open late April to November.

	1	2	3	4	5	6	7	8	9
PAR	4	3	4	4	3	4	3	4	5
YARDS	255	136	258	298	159	229	118	300	457
HDCP	9	15	7	5	13	11	17	3	1

	10	11	12	13	14	15	16	17	18
PAR	4	3	4	4	3	4	3	4	5
YARDS	252	136	257	281	169	239	135	300	465
HDCP	10	16	8	6	14	12	18	4	2

Directions: Take I-93, Exit 23 Route 104 East, 8.5 miles to double blinking light. Turns right onto Pease Road 1.5 miles. Parking on left.

Overlook GC ✪✪ ▶ 65

Hollis, NH (603) 465-2909
www.overlookgolfclub.com

Club Pro: No
Pro Shop: Full Inventory
Payment: MC, Visa, Dis.
Tee Times: 7 days adv.

Tees	Holes	Yards	Par	USGA	Slope
BACK	18	6539	71	70.2	127
MIDDLE	18	6051	71	68.2	124
FRONT	18	5230	72	68.2	124

Fee 9 Holes: Weekday: N/A
Fee 18 Holes: Weekday: $35.00
Twilight Rates: After 3 pm, then 5 pm
Cart Rental: $26.00/18, $16.00/18 after 5
Lessons: No **Schools:** Yes, group rates
Clinics: Yes **Day Camps:** No
Other: Clubhouse / Showers / Snack bar / Bar-lounge

Weekend: N/A
Weekend: $46.00
All Day Play: Yes
Discounts: Jr. after 5 pm
Junior Golf: Yes **Membership:** Inner Club
Driving Range: No

Player's comments: "Good for all abilities." "Use all clubs in bag." The front 9 are fairly hilly, back 9 are somewhat flat.

	1	2	3	4	5	6	7	8	9
PAR	5	4	4	4	3	4	4	3	4
YARDS	535	299	433	390	177	345	292	167	326
HDCP	3	11	1	5	9	13	17	15	9
	10	**11**	**12**	**13**	**14**	**15**	**16**	**17**	**18**
PAR	5	4	4	4	3	4	4	3	5
YARDS	522	350	346	390	164	341	320	138	516
HDCP	4	10	18	8	12	6	14	16	2

Directions: Take Route 3 to Exit 5W (Route 111 West). Continue 4 miles. Course is on the right.

Owl's Nest Golf Club ✪✪✪ ▶ 66

Campton,NH (603) 726-3076
www.owlsnestgolf.com

Club Pro: Charles Wheeler
Pro Shop: Full inventory
Payment: Visa, MC, Amex
Tee Times: 7 days, 1-888-OWL-NEST

Tees	Holes	Yards	Par	USGA	Slope
BACK	18	6818	72	74.0	133
MIDDLE	18	6110	72	69.7	124
FRONT	18	5174	72	67.8	117

Fee 9 Holes: Weekday: $40.00
Fee 18 Holes: Weekday: $70.00
Twilight Rates: Yes, after 4 pm
Cart Rental: $16pp/18
Lessons: $50.00/half hour **Schools:** Jr. & Sr.
Clinics: Yes **Day Camps:** Yes
Other: Full Restaurant / Clubhouse / Bar-Lounge

Weekend: $40.00
Weekend: $75.00
All Day Play: Yes
Discounts: Senior & Junior
Junior Golf: Yes **Membership:** Yes
Driving Range: $6/lg. $4/sm.

COUPON

"A true DESTINATION course." A.P. **Player's Comments:** "Great greens" "Nice layout, well maintained, courteous staff." "Excellent customer service."

	1	2	3	4	5	6	7	8	9
PAR	4	4	4	5	3	4	3	4	5
YARDS	370	366	395	503	160	311	174	335	483
HDCP	9	7	5	1	17	13	15	11	3
	10	**11**	**12**	**13**	**14**	**15**	**16**	**17**	**18**
PAR	3	4	4	5	3	4	4	5	4
YARDS	127	316	391	489	160	259	435	488	348
HDCP	18	10	8	2	16	13	4	6	12

Directions: I-93, Exit 28, west on Route 49. North on Owl Street.

Passaconaway CC ✪✪✪ 67 ▶

Litchfield, NH (603) 424-4653

Club Pro: Michael Ozog, PGA
Pro Shop: Full Inventory
Payment: Cash , Visa, MC
Tee Times: 5 days adv.
Fee 9 Holes: Weekday: $22.00
Fee 18 Holes: Weekday: $34.00
Twilight Rates: Yes, after 6 pm
Cart Rental: $28.00/18 $18.00/9
Lessons: $40/30 min. **Schools:** No
Clinics: Yes **Day Camps:** Yes
Other: Restaurant / Showers

Tees	Holes	Yards	Par	USGA	Slope
BACK	18	6855	71	73.0	132
MIDDLE	18	6462	71	71.0	128
FRONT	18	5369	71	70.3	118

Weekend: $30.00 after 2:30pm   ᶜᵒᵁᴾᴼᴺ
Weekend: $45.00
All Day Play: No
Discounts: Sr., Jr., & Ladies wkdys
Junior Golf: Yes **Membership:** Yes, Inner Club
Driving Range: No

Player's comment: "Clubhouse very friendly. Course is well maintained, very plush, greens outstanding and true. Plenty of water on the course. Bring the driver long par 4's."

	1	2	3	4	5	6	7	8	9
PAR	5	3	4	3	5	4	4	4	4
YARDS	532	150	424	172	556	454	443	379	307
HDCP	10	16	6	12	8	2	4	14	18
	10	**11**	**12**	**13**	**14**	**15**	**16**	**17**	**18**
PAR	4	4	4	3	5	4	4	3	4
YARDS	352	327	395	203	502	348	321	169	428
HDCP	13	15	1	7	5	17	11	9	3

Directions: Route 93 North to Exit 4. Left on Route 102 for 5.5 miles to yellow blinking light. Take right on West Road, for 3 miles to the end. Left on Hillcrest for 3 miles, the course is straight ahead.

Pease Golf Course ✪✪ 68 ▶

Portsmouth, NH (603) 433-1331
www.peasedev.org

Club Pro: PGA: S. DeVito, D. DeVito, T. Riese
Pro Shop: Full inventory
Payment: Visa, MC, Amex, Cash
Tee Times: 3 days adv.
Fee 9 Holes: Weekday: $18.00
Fee 18 Holes: Weekday: $36.00
Twilight Rates: No
Cart Rental: $12.00pp/18, $6.00pp/9
Lessons: $25-$40.00/half hour **Schools:** Jr.
Clinics: Yes **Day Camps:** Yes
Other: Clubhouse / Bar-Lounge / Snack Bar / Showers / Lockers

Tees	Holes	Yards	Par	USGA	Slope
BACK	18	6346	71	70.8	128
MIDDLE	18	5901	71	69.0	125
FRONT	18	5243	71	69.9	120

Weekend: $18.00
Weekend: $36.00
All Day Play: No
Discounts: None
Junior Golf: Yes **Membership:** Yes
Driving Range: $6.00/lg. $4.00/sm.

27 holes available. New Blue course demanding for all levels: rating/35.0/, slope/120. Carts mandatory only for new 9. Scorecard below from the middle tees Red and White courses.

	1	2	3	4	5	6	7	8	9
PAR	5	5	3	4	4	4	4	4	3
YARDS	465	471	160	315	343	310	370	364	150
HDCP	3	1	17	11	7	13	9	5	15
	10	**11**	**12**	**13**	**14**	**15**	**16**	**17**	**18**
PAR	4	3	4	5	4	5	3	4	4
YARDS	322	185	385	535	143	481	162	365	375
HDCP	12	16	6	2	14	4	18	10	8

Directions: From Route I-95 N- take Exit 3, at light turn left, take 1st right. From Route I-95 S- take exit 3A, at stop sign turn right.

NH

4✪ =Excellent 3✪ =Very Good 2✪ = Good   **New Hampshire 215**

Pheasant Ridge CC

69 ▶

Gilford, NH (603) 524-7808
www.pheasantridgecc.com

Club Pro: Jim Swarthout
Pro Shop: Full inventory
Payment: Visa, MC,Disc, Amex
Tee Times: 7 days adv.
Fee 9 Holes: Weekday: $18.00
Fee 18 Holes: Weekday: $31.00
Twilight Rates: Yes, after 3 pm
Cart Rental: $26.00
Lessons: $50.00/Hour **Schools:** No
Clinics: No **Day Camps:** No
Other: Snack bar / Bar-lounge / 400 seat function hall

Tees	Holes	Yards	Par	USGA	Slope
BACK	18	6402	70	69.7	116
MIDDLE	18	6004	70	67.4	113
FRONT	9	5147	70	67.8	110

Weekend: $25.00
Weekend: $39.00
All Day Play:
Discounts: None
Junior Golf: No **Membership:** No
Driving Range: Yes, grass tee

COUPON

Sig. Hole: #8, 163 yard par 3 over water, elevated tee to green framed by the lakes. "Course reflects both the late Phil Friel's skill as golfer and as a developer." - Paul Harber. A Golf Management Company.

	1	2	3	4	5	6	7	8	9
PAR	4	3	4	4	4	5	4	3	4
YARDS	340	150	370	410	290	535	329	163	370
HDCP	13	7	11	3	15	1	17	9	5

	10	11	12	13	14	15	16	17	18
PAR	5	4	4	3	4	4	4	4	3
YARDS	480	385	380	190	340	360	360	376	176
HDCP	6	2	8	14	12	18	10	4	16

Directions: Take I-93 to Exit 20 (3 North), follow 9 miles onto Laconia Bypass. Take 2nd exit, right off ramp then next right onto Country Club Rd. Course is 1/2 mile up hill on left.

Pine Grove Springs CC

70 ▶

Rt. 9A, Spofford, NH (603) 363-4433

Club Pro:
Pro Shop: Yes
Payment: Discover, Visa, MC, Cash
Tee Times: No
Fee 9 Holes: Weekday: $12.00
Fee 18 Holes: Weekday: $20.00
Twilight Rates: Yes, after 5 pm
Cart Rental: $26.00/18 $14.00/9
Lessons: No **Schools:** No
Clinics: No **Day Camps:** No
Other: Snack bar / Bar-lounge

Tees	Holes	Yards	Par	USGA	Slope
BACK					
MIDDLE	9	6003	72	69.7	128
FRONT	9	5259	72	72.2	120

Weekend: $18.00
Weekend: $26.00
All Day Play: Yes
Discounts: Srs. and Jrs. Weekdays
Junior Golf: Yes **Membership:** Yes
Driving Range: No

COUPON

Sig. Hole: #3 is a par 5 with 3 water hazards, dogleg right, rolling fairways, and elevated green. Open April - October. Practice area. 9 hole Pitch 'n' Putt.

	1	2	3	4	5	6	7	8	9
PAR	4	4	5	4	3	4	5	4	3
YARDS	269	368	541	345	148	347	420	318	168
HDCP	14	4	2	6	18	8	12	10	16

	10	11	12	13	14	15	16	17	18
PAR	4	4	5	4	3	4	5	4	3
YARDS	277	378	578	357	166	374	436	330	183
HDCP	13	3	1	5	17	7	11	9	15

Directions: Located on Route 9A 6 miles west of Keene, NH

Pine Valley Golf Links

246 Old Gage Rd., Pelham, NH (603) 635-7979, (603) 635-8305

Club Pro: Todd Madden
Pro Shop: Yes
Payment: Cash, Visa, MC
Tee Times: Wkdys,Hldys before 12 pm
Fee 9 Holes: Weekday: $16.00
Fee 18 Holes: Weekday: $22.00
Twilight Rates: Yes, after 3 pm
Cart Rental: $22.00/18 $14.00/9
Lessons: No **Schools:** No
Clinics: No   **Day Camps:** No
Other: Snack bar / Bar-lounge

Tees	Holes	Yards	Par	USGA	Slope
BACK	9	6030	70	90	128
MIDDLE	9	5820	70	66.8	113
FRONT	9	5410	72	70	125

Weekend: $18.00
Weekend: $28.00
All Day Play: $18 hole rate
Discounts: None
Junior Golf: Yes **Membership:** Yes
Driving Range: No

Course is well-trapped and wooded. Easy to walk. Soft spikes or sneakers only. Must have sleeves or a collar in order to play. Inquire about rates for twilight and all day play.

	1	2	3	4	5	6	7	8	9
PAR	4	3	5	4	4	4	4	4	3
YARDS	290	200	510	295	335	410	320	320	125
HDCP	16	6	4	12	8	2	10	14	18
	10	11	12	13	14	15	16	17	18
PAR	4	3	5	4	4	4	4	4	3
YARDS	310	230	530	315	360	450	350	330	140
HDCP	15	5	3	11	7	1	9	13	17

Directions: I-93 N/S to Exit 1 (Rockingham Park). Follow signs to Route 38 S (Pelham) Course is located 4 miles up on left.

NH

Ponemah Green

Amherst, NH (603) 672-4732
www.amherstcountryclub.com

Club Pro: Duglas. Smith, PGA
Pro Shop: Limited inventory
Payment: Visa, MC
Tee Times: 1 week adv.
Fee 9 Holes: Weekday: $13.00
Fee 18 Holes: Weekday: $26.00
Twilight Rates: After 4pm, wknds only
Cart Rental: $12.00/18 $6.00/9
Lessons: $69/hr $40/1/2 hr **Schools:** Yes
Clinics: Yes **Day Camps:** Yes
Other: Clubhouse / Snack Shop

Tees	Holes	Yards	Par	USGA	Slope
BACK	9	4420	68	62.4	110
MIDDLE	9	4320	68	61.4	107
FRONT	9	3608	68	71.0	106

Weekend: $15.00
Weekend: $30.00
All Day Play: N/R
Discounts: Senior & Junior
Junior Golf: Yes **Membership:** Yes
Driving Range: Grass, Mat, Lighted

Executive 9 hole golf course with small undulating greens. Accuracy a must. Open April until first snow.

	1	2	3	4	5	6	7	8	9
PAR	3	3	4	4	4	4	4	4	4
YARDS	111	129	252	238	394	251	292	229	314
HDCP	17	15	13	11	1	9	5	3	7
	10	11	12	13	14	15	16	17	18
PAR	3	3	4	4	4	4	4	4	4
YARDS	111	129	252	238	394	251	292	229	314
HDCP	18	16	14	12	2	10	6	4	8

Directions: From I-293, take Route 101 west to Amherst. Then take Route 122 to the course located 1/2 mile past Amherst Country Club.

4✪ =Excellent **3✪** =Very Good **2✪** =Good

Portsmouth CC

✪✪✪ ▶ **73**

Greenland, NH (603) 436-9719
www.portsmouthcc.net

Club Pro: Bill Andrews, PGA
Pro Shop: Full inventory
Payment: Visa, MC, Disc, cash
Tee Times: 3 day adv.

Tees	Holes	Yards	Par	USGA	Slope
BACK	18	7050	72	72.0	127
MIDDLE	18	6609	72	71.5	123
FRONT	18	5478	76	70.3	135

Fee 9 Holes: Weekday: No
Fee 18 Holes: Weekday: $90 cart included
Twilight Rates: Yes, after 5 pm
Cart Rental: Included
Lessons: $80/hr. **Schools:** No
Clinics: No **Day Camps:** No
Other: Clubhouse / Snack bar / Bar-lounge

Weekend: No
Weekend: $90 cart included
All Day Play: No
Discounts: None
Junior Golf: No **Membership:** Yes, waiting list
Driving Range: $5.00/lg. $3.00/sm.

Hosted State Amateur. Architect, Robert Trent Jones, Jr., designed course to be open with gently rolling hills, nice bunkers and large fast greens. Constant sea breeze creates a challenge.

	1	2	3	4	5	6	7	8	9
PAR	4	4	4	5	3	4	5	3	4
YARDS	386	425	365	494	157	412	504	219	371
HDCP	13	5	15	1	17	7	3	11	9
	10	11	12	13	14	15	16	17	18
PAR	4	5	4	3	5	4	3	4	4
YARDS	418	511	447	152	455	329	143	401	420
HDCP	10	8	2	18	4	14	16	12	6

Directions: I-95 to Route 33 West (Greenland Exit). Follow (tiny) signs. Course is approximately 2 miles from I-95.

Ragged Mountain Golf Club

▶ **74**

Danbury, NH, (603) 768-3600
www.ragged-mt.com

Club Pro: Mike Haggis, PGA
Pro Shop: Yes
Payment: Visa, MC
Tee Times: 14 days adv.

Tees	Holes	Yards	Par	USGA	Slope
BACK	18	6482	72	72.5	136
MIDDLE	18	5762	72	69.3	125
FRONT	18	4963	72	65.1	118

Fee 9 Holes: Weekday: $33 w/ cart M-Th.
Fee 18 Holes: Weekday: $49 w/ cart M-Th.
Twilight Rates: Yes, after 3 pm
Cart Rental: Included
Lessons: $30/30 min. **Schools:** No
Clinics: Junior & Senior **Day Camps:** No
Other: Full restaurant/ Clubhouse/ Lockers/ Showers/ Bar Lounge

Weekend: $33.00 after noon
Weekend: $59.00 w/ cart
All Day Play: No
Discounts: None
Junior Golf: No **Membership:** Yes
Driving Range: $4.50

COUPON

Player's comment: "Great mountain course. Beautiful setting." Spectacular views under two hours from Boston. 4 sets of tees.

	1	2	3	4	5	6	7	8	9
PAR	4	5	4	4	3	4	3	5	4
YARDS	305	432	377	290	143	302	112	497	302
HDCP	12	10	2	8	16	14	18	6	4
	10	11	12	13	14	15	16	17	18
PAR	4	5	4	3	4	3	4	5	4
YARDS	342	438	307	136	349	188	412	500	330
HDCP	11	7	15	17	3	13	1	5	9

Directions: Route 93 N to Exit 23. Take Route 104 W for 20 minutes, through town of Bristol. Follow signs for Ragged Mountain access road on left. Follow road for 2 miles to course.

Ridgewood Country Club

Moultonborough, NH 603-476-5930
www.golfridgewood.com

Club Pro: Ken Brown, USGA
Pro Shop: Full inventory
Payment: Visa, MC
Tee Times: 3 days adv.
Fee 9 Holes: Weekday: $20.00
Fee 18 Holes: Weekday: $32.00
Twilight Rates: Yes, after 3 pm
Cart Rental: $13pp/18 $8pp/9
Lessons: $30/40 min. **Schools:** Jr. & Sr.
Clinics: Yes **Day Camps:** No
Other: Bar-Lounge

Tees	Holes	Yards	Par	USGA	Slope
BACK	9	3252	36	36.2	137
MIDDLE	9	2878	36	34.9	127
FRONT	9	2355	36	34.0	110

Weekend: $22.00
Weekend: $35.00
All Day Play: No
Discounts: Senior & Junior
Junior Golf: Yes **Membership:** Yes
Driving Range: $5.75/lg. $3.75/sm.

Additional 9 holes to open '04. New aqua range, only one in area. "Excellent greens. Some inexplicably different holes." R.W.

	1	2	3	4	5	6	7	8	9
PAR	4	4	5	4	3	4	3	4	5
YARDS	335	325	464	340	145	338	165	301	465
HDCP	6	7	5	4	9	2	3	8	1

	10	11	12	13	14	15	16	17	18
PAR									
YARDS									
HDCP									

Directions: Route I-93, exit 23 to Route 104. Left at Route 3 in Meredith to Route 25 East Moultonboro to Route 109 South. 1 1/2 mile on right. Please see website.

Rockingham CC

Newmarket, NH (603) 659-9956

Club Pro: No
Pro Shop: Basic
Payment: Visa, MC, Disc., Cash
Tee Times: 7 days adv. (non-members)
Fee 9 Holes: Weekday: $15.00
Fee 18 Holes: Weekday: $23.00
Twilight Rates: No
Cart Rental: $24.00/18 $12.00/9
Lessons: No **Schools:** No
Clinics: No **Day Camps:** Yes
Other: Clubhouse / Snack bar / Bar-lounge

Tees	Holes	Yards	Par	USGA	Slope
BACK					
MIDDLE	9	2875	35	65.3	104
FRONT	9	2622	37	69.4	104

Weekend: $16.00
Weekend: $25.00
All Day Play: No
Discounts: Senior & Juniors Wkdys
Junior Golf: No **Membership:** Jr. $400
Driving Range: No

The course is level and well kept with only 2 water holes.

	1	2	3	4	5	6	7	8	9
PAR	4	4	3	4	4	4	3	4	5
YARDS	386	315	175	393	315	380	125	306	480
HDCP	2	10	14	6	16	4	18	12	8

	10	11	12	13	14	15	16	17	18
PAR									
YARDS									
HDCP									

Directions: Take I-95 to Hampton Exit (Route 101 West) to Route 108. North to course.

4✪ =Excellent 3✪ =Very Good 2✪ =Good

Sagamore-Hampton GC

N. Hampton, NH (603) 964-5341
www.sagamoregolf.com

Club Pro: Maria Brooks
Pro Shop: Yes
Payment: Visa, MC, Amex
Tee Times: 1 week advance
Fee 9 Holes: Weekday: $17.00
Fee 18 Holes: Weekday: $30.00
Twilight Rates: Yes, after 5:30 pm
Cart Rental: $13.00pp/18 $7.00pp/9
Lessons: Yes **Schools:** No
Clinics: Yes **Day Camps:** No
Other: Frequent player discounts / USGA Handicap services / Snack bar/ Bar-lounge

Weekend: $20.00
Weekend: $36.00
All Day Play: No
Discounts: Senior & Junior
Junior Golf: Yes **Membership:** No
Driving Range: Yes, off course.

Tees	Holes	Yards	Par	USGA	Slope
BACK	18	6058	71	68.0	119
MIDDLE	18	5647	71	68.0	119
FRONT	18	5008	71	67.5	112

COUPON

One of the seacoast's most popular and well-maintained courses. Offering an enjoyable layout for all abilities at affordable prices. Redesigned practice facility only a mile away.

	1	2	3	4	5	6	7	8	9
PAR	4	4	4	3	4	5	3	5	3
YARDS	291	325	352	135	300	463	192	424	166
HDCP	16	15	6	12	13	14	3	9	11

	10	11	12	13	14	15	16	17	18
PAR	5	3	4	5	3	4	5	3	4
YARDS	527	172	380	446	125	284	456	190	419
HDCP	2	4	5	8	17	18	7	10	1

Directions: Take I-95 to Exit 2. Take right onto Route 101 W, follow 1.2 miles. Take right onto Route 111, follow 2.5 miles. Take left onto Route 151 N, follow 1.1 miles. Course is on right.

Shattuck GC, The   ⊗⊗

Jaffrey, NH (603) 532-4300
www.sterlinggolf.com

Club Pro: Mark Trantanella
Pro Shop: Full Inventory
Payment: MC, Visa, Amex, Cash
Tee Times: 14 days adv.
Fee 9 Holes: Weekday: $25 w/cart(M-Th)
Fee 18 Holes: Weekday: $44 w/cart (M-Th)
Twilight Rates: Yes, after 3 pm
Cart Rental: Included
Lessons: Yes **Schools:** No
Clinics: Yes **Day Camps:** No
Other: Bar-Lounge / Snack bar

Weekend: $25 w/cart (F/S/S) after 3pm
Weekend: $54.00 with cart (F/S/S)
All Day Play: Yes, $10.00 extra
Discounts: None
Junior Golf: Yes **Membership:** Yes
Driving Range: $4.00/lg

Tees	Holes	Yards	Par	USGA	Slope
BACK	18	6701	71	74.1	145
MIDDLE	18	6077	71	71.0	140
FRONT	18	4632	71	73.1	139

COUPON

Player's comment: "Every club in the bag course. Very challenging. Helpful Player's Guide on website. Uncrowded." Under Sterling Management. Brian Silva course.

	1	2	3	4	5	6	7	8	9
PAR	4	3	4	4	5	5	3	4	4
YARDS	357	146	343	312	551	508	183	373	356
HDCP	5	17	9	13	1	3	15	7	11

	10	11	12	13	14	15	16	17	18
PAR	4	4	3	4	3	5	4	4	4
YARDS	394	407	155	303	121	508	367	313	380
HDCP	6	4	16	14	18	2	10	12	8

Directions: Mass Pike Route 90 to 495 N to Route 2 W. Take Exit 24B Route 140 N to Route 12 N. Take a left, Go .9 mile. Go right, Route 202 N to Jaffery NH. Go left on Route 124. Follow west 2.2 miles. Go right at Mount Monadnock sign. Club is on the left

Souhegan Woods GC

Amherst, NH (603) 673-0200

Club Pro: Bill Meier, PGA
Pro Shop: Full inventory discount shop
Payment: Most major
Tee Times: 7 days adv.
Fee 9 Holes: Weekday: $25.00
Fee 18 Holes: Weekday: $35.00
Twilight Rates: Yes, after 3 pm
Cart Rental: $26.00/18 $17.00/9
Lessons: $70.00/ hour **Schools:** No
Clinics: No **Day Camps:** No
Other: Clubhouse / Bar-Lounge / Snack Bar / Showers

Tees	Holes	Yards	Par	USGA	Slope
BACK	18	6507	72	70	118
MIDDLE	18	6122	72	68.3	1115
FRONT	18	5286	71/69	70.6	123

Weekend: N/A
Weekend: $46.00
All Day Play: If Available.
Discounts: Senior, M/T/W
Junior Golf: No **Membership:** No
Driving Range: $6.00/lg. bucket

Designed to challenge all golfers. In superb condition and well spread out. Open April - November. A Golf Management Company.

	1	2	3	4	5	6	7	8	9
PAR	4	4	3	5	4	5	4	3	4
YARDS	375	312	168	445	402	501	337	149	355
HDCP	8	14	16	6	4	2	12	18	10
	10	11	12	13	14	15	16	17	18
PAR	4	3	4	4	5	4	4	3	5
YARDS	312	153	343	368	510	349	406	166	469
HDCP	13	17	9	7	1	11	3	15	5

Directions: Route 3 (Everett Tpike) to Exit 11. Left off of exit from south, turn right at Burger King past White Hen 4.3 miles.

Stonebridge Country Club

Goffstown, NH 603-497-T-OFF (8633)
www.golfstonebridge.com

Club Pro: Yes
Pro Shop: Full inventory
Payment: Visa, MC, Amex, Disc.
Tee Times: 5 days adv.
Fee 9 Holes: Weekday: $27.00
Fee 18 Holes: Weekday: $37.00
Twilight Rates: Yes, after 4 pm
Cart Rental: $15 pp
Lessons: $40.00/half hour **Schools:** No
Clinics: Yes **Day Camps:** No
Other: Full Restaurant / Clubhouse / Lockers / Showers / Bar-Lounge

Tees	Holes	Yards	Par	USGA	Slope
BACK	18	6808	72	73.0	138
MIDDLE	18	6388	72	71.4	134
FRONT	18	4747	72	67.6	116

Weekend: N/A
Weekend: $49.00
All Day Play: No
Discounts: Jr., M-Th before 3 pm
Junior Golf: Yes **Membership:** Yes
Driving Range: $4.00 per token

Players' comment: "Tough greens. Beautiful landscape." Hole #6 reminds many of #12 at Augusta.

	1	2	3	4	5	6	7	8	9
PAR	5	4	4	3	4	3	4	4	4
YARDS	480	398	370	152	366	136	332	408	417
HDCP	10	8	14	18	6	16	2	4	12
	10	11	12	13	14	15	16	17	18
PAR	5	4	4	3	5	4	3	5	4
YARDS	496	325	349	193	526	369	150	521	400
HDCP	11	15	13	9	1	5	17	7	3

Directions: From Route 93 take Route 101 West to Route 114 North for 9 miles, through Goffstown center. After Sully's Superette go 1/2 mile and take right onto Parker Station Rd. Immediate right onto Gorham Pond Rd. Course is 3/4 mile on left.

4✪ =Excellent 3✪ =Very Good 2✪ =Good

Sunningdale GC

81

Somersworth, NH (603) 742-8056

Tees	Holes	Yards	Par	USGA	Slope
BACK	9	3505	36	71.8	125
MIDDLE	9	3170	36	71.8	125
FRONT	9	3170	36	71.8	125

Club Pro:
Pro Shop: Full inventory
Payment: Visa, MC, Cash, Check
Tee Times: Yes
Fee 9 Holes: Weekday: $14.00
Fee 18 Holes: Weekday: $24.00
Twilight Rates: No
Cart Rental: $24.00/18 $12.00/9
Lessons: Schools: No
Clinics: Yes **Day Camps:** No
Other: Clubhouse / Bar-Lounge / Lockers

Weekend: $16.00
Weekend: $26.00
All Day Play: No
Discounts: Senior & Junior
Junior Golf: Yes **Membership:** Yes
Driving Range: $6/lg., $4/sm.

Hilly and fairly narrow. Tee times required. No tank tops. Open April - Nov.

	1	2	3	4	5	6	7	8	9
PAR	4	4	3	5	4	5	3	4	4
YARDS	385	335	200	500	325	470	185	350	420
HDCP	7	15	9	5	7	3	1	13	11
	10	11	12	13	14	15	16	17	18
PAR									
YARDS									
HDCP									

Directions: Exit 9 off Spaulding Turnpike. Straight through intersection on Route 9. Right on Stackpole Rd. just past Walmart. Right onto Green St. 1/3 mi. on right.

Sunset Hill Golf Course

82

Sugar Hill, NH (603) 823-7244

Tees	Holes	Yards	Par	USGA	Slope
BACK					
MIDDLE	9	1953	33	58.2	81
FRONT					

Club Pro: Gary Roy
Pro Shop: Yes
Payment: Cash, check, credit card
Tee Times: Yes
Fee 9 Holes: Weekday: $10.00
Fee 18 Holes: Weekday: $18.00
Twilight Rates: Yes, after 4 pm
Cart Rental: $20.00/18 $10.00/9
Lessons: $18.00/half hour privite **Schools:** Yes
Clinics: Yes **Day Camps:** No
Other: Snack bar / Restaurant / Hotel along 1st hole

Weekend: $15.00
Weekend: $25.00
All Day Play: Yes
Discounts: Senior & Junior
Junior Golf: Yes **Membership:** Yes
Driving Range: No

Popular old historic resort course build in 1900. "Turn-of-the-century" layout. Beautiful panoramic views. Great for the beginner; challenging for the good players.

	1	2	3	4	5	6	7	8	9
PAR	4	4	4	4	3	4	3	4	3
YARDS	233	286	231	229	169	210	157	260	178
HDCP	5	3	7	9	15	11	17	1	13
	10	11	12	13	14	15	16	17	18
PAR									
YARDS									
HDCP									

Directions: Take I-93 to Exit 38. Take Route 117 for 2.5 miles. Turn left onto Sunset Hill Road. 1/2 mile up on right.

Tory Pines Resort

●● **83** ▶

Rt. 47, Francestown, NH (603) 588-2923
www.torypinesresort.com

Club Pro:
Pro Shop: No
Payment: Visa, MC, Amex
Tee Times: 5 days adv.
Fee 9 Holes: Weekday: $15.00
Fee 18 Holes: Weekday: $28.00
Twilight Rates: Yes, after 3 pm
Cart Rental: $14pp/18 $7.50pp/9
Lessons: Schools: No
Clinics: N/R **Day Camps:** No
Other: Restaurant / Clubhouse / Hotel-Inn / Bar-Lounge / Snack bar

Tees	Holes	Yards	Par	USGA	Slope
BACK	18	6100	71	70.3	128
MIDDLE	18	5437	71	67.5	121
FRONT	18	4639	71	68.4	121

Weekend: $20.00
Weekend: $38.00
All Day Play: No
Discounts: Junior wkday pass
Junior Golf: Yes **Membership:** Yes
Driving Range: $5.00/lg. $3.00/sm.

COUPON

Sig. Hole: #4, 486 yard par 5. If you can carry pond in front of green, possible eagle. Narrow fairways, very small greens.

	1	**2**	**3**	**4**	**5**	**6**	**7**	**8**	**9**
PAR	4	4	3	5	4	3	5	4	4
YARDS	306	325	144	486	328	181	410	311	346
HDCP	11	9	17	1	7	15	3	13	5
	10	**11**	**12**	**13**	**14**	**15**	**16**	**17**	**18**
PAR	4	4	4	5	4	4	3	4	3
YARDS	339	285	333	389	320	315	168	288	163
HDCP	6	14	4	2	8	12	16	10	18

Directions: Take Route 3 North to Route 101A West; follow into Milford; turn right onto Route 13 to New Boston. Take Route 136 to Francestown Center; take right onto Route 47. Course is 4 miles on right.

NH

Twin Lake Villa Golf Course

84 ▶

New London, NH (603)526-2034
www.twinlakevillage.com

Club Pro: N/A
Pro Shop: Limited inventory
Payment: Personal checks
Tee Times: 3days in adv.
Fee 9 Holes: Weekday: $12.00
Fee 18 Holes: Weekday: $16.00
Twilight Rates: No
Cart Rental: No Carts
Lessons: Arranged off site **Schools:** No
Clinics: No **Day Camps:** No
Other:

Tees	Holes	Yards	Par	USGA	Slope
BACK	9	1515	27		
MIDDLE	9	1356	27		
FRONT	9	1149	27		

Weekend: $12.00
Weekend: $16.00
All Day Play: $10 pre and post season
Discounts: Senior, $2 off
Junior Golf: No **Membership:** Yes
Driving Range: No

Open May 1 - Oct. 31.

	1	**2**	**3**	**4**	**5**	**6**	**7**	**8**	**9**
PAR	3	3	3	3	3	3	3	3	3
YARDS	141	113	118	109	190	197	180	177	131
HDCP									
	10	**11**	**12**	**13**	**14**	**15**	**16**	**17**	**18**
PAR									
YARDS									
HDCP									

Directions: I-89 to Exit 12. Go east 2 mi. to New London. At blinking light, turn left onto Country Rd. At first stop sign, turn left onto Little Sunapee Rd. for 1 mi. Bear right onto Twin Lake Villa Rd and follow up hill to Hotel and Golf Shop.

4● =Excellent **3**● =Very Good **2**● = Good

Waterville Valley

Waterville, NH (603) 236-4805
www.waterville.com

Club Pro: Bill Baker, PGA
Pro Shop: Full inventory
Payment: Visa, MC, Amex, Dis
Tee Times: 48 hours adv.
Fee 9 Holes: Weekday: $19.00
Fee 18 Holes: Weekday: $25.00
Twilight Rates: No
Cart Rental: $24.00/18 $17.00/9
Lessons: $45/30 min. **Schools:** No
Clinics: Yes **Day Camps:** No
Other: Clubhouse / Snack bar / Club storage / Resort

Weekend: $19.00
Weekend: $25.00
All Day Play: No
Discounts: None
Junior Golf: Yes **Membership:** Yes
Driving Range: No

Tees	Holes	Yards	Par	USGA	Slope
BACK					
MIDDLE	9	4716	64	63	105
FRONT					

The course is short but sweet. Mountain resort. Open May 27 - October 15. Junior clinic Tues., Thurs. morning.

	1	2	3	4	5	6	7	8	9
PAR	4	3	3	4	3	3	4	4	4
YARDS	371	124	150	410	220	150	251	377	351
HDCP	5	17	15	1	3	11	13	9	7
	10	11	12	13	14	15	16	17	18
PAR	4	3	3	4	3	3	4	4	4
YARDS	371	124	150	353	220	115	251	377	351
HDCP	6	18	16	2	4	12	14	10	8

Directions: Take I-93 to Exit 28; follow Route 49 for 12 miles.

Waukewan Golf Club

Meredith, NH (603) 279-6661

Club Pro: Dexter Hale
Pro Shop: Full inventory
Payment: Cash or credit card
Tee Times: Yes (Upto 7 days).
Fee 9 Holes: Weekday: $20, $28 ride
Fee 18 Holes: Weekday: $35, $48 ride
Twilight Rates: After 3 pm
Cart Rental: $26.00/18 $16.00/9
Lessons: Available **Schools:** Yes
Clinics: Yes **Day Camps:** Junior Academies
Other: Clubhouse / Snack bar / Bar-lounge

Weekend: $25, $33 ride
Weekend: $40, $53 ride
All Day Play: No
Discounts: None
Junior Golf: Yes **Membership:** Yes
Driving Range: $5.00/lg. $3.00/sm.

Tees	Holes	Yards	Par	USGA	Slope
BACK					
MIDDLE	18	5828	72	67.4	117
FRONT	18	5020	72	67.8	112

Significant improvements include additional 3rd set of tees, and better drainage.

	1	2	3	4	5	6	7	8	9
PAR	4	4	3	4	4	5	3	5	4
YARDS	390	330	143	275	255	550	170	470	395
HDCP	6	12	18	16	14	4	10	8	2
	10	11	12	13	14	15	16	17	18
PAR	4	3	4	4	4	5	3	5	4
YARDS	270	190	250	410	330	470	210	490	230
HDCP	11	13	17	1	7	9	5	3	15

Directions: Take Exit 23 from I-93 North, Route 104 to Meredith, Route 3 North toward Plymouth 3 miles from Meredith traffic junction, left turn onto Waukewan Road.

Waumbek CC, The

Jefferson, NH (603) 586-7777

Tees	Holes	Yards	Par	USGA	Slope
BACK	18	6128	71	67.0	117
MIDDLE	18	5874	71	65	111
FRONT	18	4772	71	69.9	107

Club Pro: Larry Fellows
Pro Shop: Full inventory
Payment: Visa, MC, Amex
Tee Times: Wknds
Fee 9 Holes: Weekday: $14.00
Fee 18 Holes: Weekday: $23.00
Twilight Rates: Yes, after 3 pm
Cart Rental: $12 pp
Lessons: Yes **Schools:** Yes
Clinics: Yes **Day Camps:** Yes
Other: Snack Bar

Weekend: $17.00
Weekend: $29.00
All Day Play: N/R
Discounts: Junior
Junior Golf: Yes **Membership:** No
Driving Range:

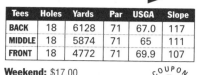

Challenging course in great shape. The oldest 18 hole course in New Hampshire. Ball magnetizes toward Cherry Mountain — don't aim for the hole, aim for the mountain. A Golf Management Company.

	1	2	3	4	5	6	7	8	9
PAR	4	4	5	4	4	4	4	3	3
YARDS	333	370	500	310	320	390	290	200	195
HDCP	11	1	5	7	13	3	9	15	17

	10	11	12	13	14	15	16	17	18
PAR	4	5	4	4	3	4	4	5	3
YARDS	310	465	387	280	110	340	335	490	170
HDCP	12	10	2	16	18	8	6	4	14

Directions: I-93 to Exit 35 (Route 3 North). Follow Route 3 for 12 miles, then take a right onto 115 North. Follow 115 North for 6.7 miles. Take a left onto 115A. Golf course is 4 miles down on the right.

Wentworth Resort GC

Rt. 16, Jackson, NH (603) 383-9641
www.wentworthgolf.com

Tees	Holes	Yards	Par	USGA	Slope
BACK					
MIDDLE	18	5581	69	66.0	115
FRONT	18	5087	70	66.7	114

Club Pro: Ed LaPierre, PGA
Pro Shop: Full inventory
Payment: MC, Visa, Amex, Disc.
Tee Times: 5 days adv.
Fee 9 Holes: Weekday: N/A
Fee 18 Holes: Weekday: $33, $25 after 1 pm
Twilight Rates: Reduced
Cart Rental: $12.50pp/18 $7.00pp/9
Lessons: $35/30 min., $60/ hr **Schools:** No
Clinics: Yes **Day Camps:** No
Other: Snack bar / Restaurant / Bar-lounge / Tent / Hotel

Weekend: N/A
Weekend: $45.00, $25 after 3 pm
All Day Play: No
Discounts: Junior
Junior Golf: Yes **Membership:** Yes
Driving Range: No

Challenging course situated in Jackson Village. Enjoy the rolling hills and the covered bridge crossing the Ellis River on the White Mt's 2nd oldest course. New restaurant among the improvements.

	1	2	3	4	5	6	7	8	9
PAR	4	4	4	3	3	4	4	4	5
YARDS	305	337	349	304	147	411	291	307	479
HDCP	15	7	5	17	9	1	11	13	3

	10	11	12	13	14	15	16	17	18
PAR	4	4	4	4	3	5	3	3	4
YARDS	333	359	336	365	185	454	180	144	295
HDCP	10	4	14	6	8	2	12	16	18

Directions: I-95 to Spaulding Turnpike. Take Route 16 North to Jackson Village. OR I-93 to Route 25 to Route 16 North to Jackson Village.

4✪ =Excellent **3✪** = Very Good **2✪** =Good   **New Hampshire 225**

Whip-Poor-Will GC

Hudson, NH (603) 889-9706

Tees	Holes	Yards	Par	USGA	Slope
BACK	9	6030	72	67.8	120
MIDDLE	9	5980	72	67.8	120
FRONT	9	5094	72	69.9	119

Club Pro: Jeff Wirbal
Pro Shop: Full inventory
Payment: Visa, MC, Amex, Disc
Tee Times: Yes, 7 days in advance
Fee 9 Holes: Weekday: $19.00   **Weekend:** $22.00
Fee 18 Holes: Weekday: $27.00   **Weekend:** $33.00
Twilight Rates: Yes, after 3 pm wknds   **All Day Play:** No
Cart Rental: $25.00/18 $16.00/9   **Discounts:** Senior
Lessons: $50/hour **Schools:** No   **Junior Golf:** No **Membership:** No
Clinics: No **Day Camps:** No   **Driving Range:** No
Other: Clubhouse / Snack Bar / Bar Lounge

COUPON

An enjoyable well maintained 9 hole course, perfect for an early afternoon off. A Golf Management Company.

	1	2	3	4	5	6	7	8	9
PAR	4	3	4	4	5	4	4	5	3
YARDS	330	170	345	315	485	402	280	498	165
HDCP	11	17	5	9	7	3	13	1	15
	10	11	12	13	14	15	16	17	18
PAR	4	3	4	4	5	4	4	5	3
YARDS	330	170	345	315	485	402	280	498	165
HDCP	12	18	6	10	8	4	14	2	16

Directions: From I-93, take Exit 4 to Route 102 west approx 7 miles. Course in on left at Marsh Road just after Alverine High School.

White Mountain CC

N. Ashland Rd., Ashland, NH (603) 536-2227

Tees	Holes	Yards	Par	USGA	Slope
BACK	18	6428	71	70.4	122
MIDDLE	18	5963	71	67.9	119
FRONT	18	5350	72	69.6	118

Club Pro: Gregg Sufat
Pro Shop: Full inventory
Payment: Visa, MC
Tee Times: 1 week adv.
Fee 9 Holes: Weekday: $18, $26 ride   **Weekend:** after 2 pm
Fee 18 Holes: Weekday: $31, $44 ride   **Weekend:** $39, $52 ride
Twilight Rates: After 3 pm   **All Day Play:** No
Cart Rental: $13pp/18, $8pp/9   **Discounts:** None
Lessons: $25.00/half hour **Schools:** No   **Junior Golf:** No **Membership:** No
Clinics: No **Day Camps:** No   **Driving Range:** $5.00/lg. bucket
Other: Bar-lounge / Snack Bar / Townhouse Rentals

COUPON

Manicured fairways, soft velvet greens, challenging yet "golfer friendly." Stay and Play packages available.
Player's Comments: "Great course in the Fall". A Golf Management Company.

	1	2	3	4	5	6	7	8	9
PAR	4	4	4	3	5	4	3	5	4
YARDS	327	334	325	174	524	300	172	508	312
HDCP	9	13	15	17	1	7	11	5	3
	10	11	12	13	14	15	16	17	18
PAR	4	3	4	4	4	4	4	4	4
YARDS	356	154	356	374	321	301	359	410	356
HDCP	12	18	8	4	14	16	6	2	10

Directions: I-93 North, Exit 24, left off ramp for 1 mile. Right onto North Ashland Road, 2.5 miles on left.

Windham Country Club ✪✪

91

1 Country Club Rd., Windham, NH, 603-434-2093
www.windhamcc.com

Club Pro: Joanne Flynn, PGA
Pro Shop: Full inventory
Payment: Visa, MC
Tee Times: 7 days a week, 5 days in adv.
Fee 9 Holes: Weekday: $20.00
Fee 18 Holes: Weekday: $39.00
Twilight Rates: Yes, after 4 pm
Cart Rental: $14 pp/18,$7 pp/9
Lessons: $45/40 min. **Schools:** Yes
Clinics: Yes **Day Camps:** Yes
Other: Full Restaurant / Club house / Bar-Lounge / Snack Bar

Tees	Holes	Yards	Par	USGA	Slope
BACK	18	6442	72	71.2	135
MIDDLE	18	6033	72	69.1	129
FRONT	18	5584	72	69.1	123

Weekend: $28.00
Weekend: $48.00
All Day Play: Yes, $60 weekdays only.
Discounts: Junior
Junior Golf: Yes **Membership:** No
Driving Range: $8.00/Lg., $5.00/Sm.

COUPON

Voted in top 10 by *Golf Digest*. Noted for condition and challenging layout. Open year round (when possible).

	1	2	3	4	5	6	7	8	9
PAR	5	4	3	4	5	3	4	4	3
YARDS	5	351	138	353	454	111	364	351	148
HDCP	5	7	13	11	3	17	9	1	15
	10	11	12	13	14	15	16	17	18
PAR	4	4	5	4	3	5	4	4	4
YARDS	255	340	435	207	157	424	370	317	287
HDCP	14	6	4	18	16	8	2	10	12

Directions: I-93 North to Exit 3. Take Route 111 West 1 1/2 miles. Then right on Church St. to fire station, then right on to N. Lowell for 1 mile. Left onto Londonderry Rd. 1/2 mile and left on Country Club Rd.

NH

Woodbound Inn GC

92

Woodbound Rd., Jaffrey, NH (603) 532-8341
www.woodbound.com

Club Pro: No
Pro Shop: No
Payment: Visa, MC, Amex, Cash
Tee Times: No
Fee 9 Holes: Weekday: $12.00
Fee 18 Holes: Weekday: $12.00
Twilight Rates: Yes, after 6 pm
Cart Rental: Pull carts
Lessons: No **Schools:** No
Clinics: No **Day Camps:** No
Other: Snack bar / Restaurant / Gift Shop / Bar-Lounge

Tees	Holes	Yards	Par	USGA	Slope
BACK					
MIDDLE	9	1956	54		
FRONT					

Weekend: $12.00
Weekend: $12.00
All Day Play: Yes
Discounts: Senior
Junior Golf: No **Membership:** Yes
Driving Range: No

COUPON

A course that is great for families, seniors, beginners, corporate outings or short game. 18 different tee boxes.

	1	2	3	4	5	6	7	8	9
PAR	3	3	3	3	3	3	3	3	3
YARDS	114	138	94	128	109	79	142	117	131
HDCP	N/A								
	10	11	12	13	14	15	16	17	18
PAR	3	3	3	3	3	3	3	3	3
YARDS	100	125	78	100	112	79	122	101	87
HDCP	N/A								

Directions: Take I-495 to Route 119 West 10 miles from NH border. Follow signs to course.

4✪ =Excellent **3✪** = Very Good **2✪** = Good

CHAPTER 6

Southern Maine

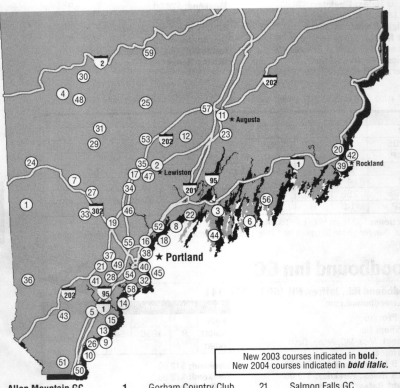

New 2003 courses indicated in **bold**.
New 2004 courses indicated in ***bold italic***.

Allen Mountain GC	**1**	Gorham Country Club	21	Salmon Falls GC	41
Apple Valley GC	2	***Highland Green GC***	***22***	Samoset Resort GC	42
Bath Country Club	3	Kennebec Heights CC	23	Sanford Country Club	43
Bethel Inn & CC	4	Lake Kezar CC	24	Sebasco Harbor GC	44
Biddeford & Saco CC	5	Maple Lane Inn & GC	25	South Portland Muni	45
Boothbay Region CC	6	Merriland Farm Par 3 GC	26	Spring Meadows GC	46
Bridgton Highlands CC	7	Naples Golf and CC	27	Spring Brook GC	47
Brunswick Golf Club	8	Nonesuch River GC	28	***Sunday River Resort GC***	***48***
Cape Arundel Golf Club	9	Norway Country Club	29	Sunset Ridge	49
Cape Neddick CC	**10**	Oakdale CC	30	The Ledges Golf Club	50
Capitol City GC	11	Paris Hill Country Club	31	The Links at Outlook	51
Cobbossee Colony GC	12	Pleasant Hill CC	32	***Toddy Brook GC***	***52***
Deep Brook Golf Course	**13**	Point Sebago Golf Club	33	Turner Highland GC	53
Dunegrass Golf Club	14	Poland Spring CC	34	Twin Falls Golf Course	54
Dutch Elm Golf Course	15	Prospect Hill GC	35	Val Halla Golf Course	55
Fairlawn Golf Club	16	Province Lake Golf Club	36	Wawenock CC	56
Fox Ridge Golf Club	17	River Meadow GC	37	Western View Golf Club	57
Freeport Country Club	18	Riverside Municipal GC	38	Willowdale Golf Club	58
Frye Island Golf Course	19	Rockland Golf Club	39	Wilson Lake CC	59
Goose River GC	20	Sable Oaks Golf Club	40		

Allen Mountain Golf Course

NEW
2003

Denmark, ME (207) 452-2282
www.allenmt@pivot.net

Club Pro:
Pro Shop:
Payment: Cash only
Tee Times: No
Fee 9 Holes: Weekday: $12.00
Fee 18 Holes: Weekday: $17.00
Twilight Rates: No
Cart Rental: $6pp/9
Lessons: Schools:
Clinics: Day Camps:
Other:

Tees	Holes	Yards	Par	USGA	Slope
BACK	9	2553	35	65.7	114
MIDDLE	9	2508	35	65.7	114
FRONT	9	2095	35	66.7	114

Weekend: $17.00
Weekend: $22.00
All Day Play: Yes
Discounts: None
Junior Golf: Membership: Yes
Driving Range: None

2003 Entry. Challenging 9 hole course with spectacular views of the White Mountains. Low pressure family golf at its best.

	1	2	3	4	5	6	7	8	9
PAR	4	4	5	4	3	5	3	4	3
YARDS	278	358	417	315	168	424	146	287	115
HDCP	11	9	3	7	13	1	15	5	17
	10	11	12	13	14	15	16	17	18
PAR									
YARDS									
HDCP									

Directions: Exit 8 from Maine Turnpike. Turn right onto Riverside Street. 3 miles to Route 302, left on Route 302 for 35 mles. Turn left on 117 to Penmark Village. Left on Burnrow Road to end (2 1/2 miles).

Apple Valley GC

S
ME

Lewiston, ME (207) 784-9773

Club Pro: No
Pro Shop: Full inventory
Payment: Cash only
Tee Times: No
Fee 9 Holes: Weekday: $14.00
Fee 18 Holes: Weekday: $21.00
Twilight Rates: Yes, after 4 pm
Cart Rental: $20.00/18 $10.00/9
Lessons: No **Schools:**
Clinics: Day Camps:
Other: Clubhouse / Snack bar

Tees	Holes	Yards	Par	USGA	Slope
BACK					
MIDDLE	18	5035	70	64.3	108
FRONT					

Weekend: $14.00
Weekend: $21.00
All Day Play:
Discounts:
Junior Golf: Membership:
Driving Range: No

Open April 15 - November 15.

	1	2	3	4	5	6	7	8	9
PAR	4	4	3	5	3	4	4	4	4
YARDS	239	258	147	445	108	333	312	300	350
HDCP	13	7	15	5	17	3	11	9	1
	10	11	12	13	14	15	16	17	18
PAR	4	4	3	5	3	4	4	4	4
YARDS	235	256	177	450	115	343	299	310	360
HDCP	14	8	16	6	18	4	12	10	2

Directions: ME Turnpike to Exit 13 (Route 196 East) for 4 mi. Right onto Dyer Road. Left onto Pinewoods Road. Course is 2 miles on left.

Bath Country Club

▶ 3

Bath, ME (207) 442-8411
www.harrisgolfonline.com

Club Pro: Shawn Arsenault, PGA
Pro Shop: Full inventory
Payment: Cash and credit cards
Tee Times: Yes
Fee 9 Holes: Weekday: $18.00
Fee 18 Holes: Weekday: $30.00
Twilight Rates: Yes, after 4 pm
Cart Rental: $26.00/18 $14.00/9
Lessons: $25/30 min **Schools:** No
Clinics: Yes **Day Camps:** No
Other: Clubhouse / Restaurant / Lounge / Lockers

Tees	Holes	Yards	Par	USGA	Slope
BACK	18	6216	70	70.2	128
MIDDLE	18	5751	70	67.8	123
FRONT	18	4708	70	67.0	115

Weekend: $18.00
Weekend: $30.00
All Day Play: Yes
Discounts: None
Junior Golf: Yes **Membership:** Yes
Driving Range: No

COUPON

Fairways are tight and tree-lined. 8th hole is an outstanding par 4. College scholarship offered for juniors. Series of lessons offered. Open year round for virtual indoor golf.

	1	2	3	4	5	6	7	8	9
PAR	4	4	5	4	4	3	4	4	3
YARDS	356	375	504	393	354	173	417	432	203
HDCP	11	5	13	7	17	9	3	1	15
	10	11	12	13	14	15	16	17	18
PAR	4	4	4	3	4	4	3	5	4
YARDS	298	358	303	132	393	356	186	528	393
HDCP	14	8	16	18	2	4	10	6	4

Directions: From I-95, take Route 1N. From 1N take New Meadows Rd. Exit. Go right at stop sign. Go 1 1/4 miles to next stop sign. Go straight through on to Ridge Road for 1 1/4 miles to 18th tee. Go right.

Bethel Inn & Country Club ⊙⊙

▶ 4

Bethel, ME (207) 824-6276
www.bethelinn.com

Club Pro: Jason Hurd, PGA
Pro Shop: Full inventory
Payment: MC, Visa, Amex, Cash
Tee Times: 2 days adv.
Fee 9 Holes: Weekday: $25.00
Fee 18 Holes: Weekday: $50.00
Twilight Rates: No
Cart Rental: $34.00/18 $24.00/9
Lessons: $40/30 min. **Schools:** Yes
Clinics: N/R **Day Camps:** Yes
Other: Clubhouse / Showers / Snack bar / Restaurant / Bar / Lodging

Tees	Holes	Yards	Par	USGA	Slope
BACK	18	6663	72	72.3	133
MIDDLE	18	6029	72	69.1	127
FRONT	18	5280	72	71.4	129

Weekend: $25.00
Weekend: $50.00 walk
All Day Play: No
Discounts: None
Junior Golf: Yes **Membership:** Yes
Driving Range: $4.00/lg. bucket

COUPON

The Guaranteed Performance School of Golf at this Cornish designed course highlights the summer season. **Player's Comment:** "Great views. Treated very well."

	1	2	3	4	5	6	7	8	9
PAR	4	4	3	4	5	3	4	5	4
YARDS	340	262	130	370	492	141	361	500	292
HDCP	11	13	17	1	7	15	3	5	9
	10	11	12	13	14	15	16	17	18
PAR	4	5	3	4	4	4	3	5	4
YARDS	325	546	179	294	397	400	151	506	343
HDCP	18	4	14	16	2	6	10	8	12

Directions: Maine Turnpike to Exit 11, Gray. Take Route 26 North to Bethel. Route 26 becomes Main Street in Bethel. Follow Main Street to the top. Course is on left behind Main Inn.

Biddeford & Saco CC

Old Orchard Rd., Saco, ME (207) 282-5883
www.biddefordsacocountryclub.com

Club Pro: Tim Angis, PGA
Pro Shop: Full inventory
Payment: All major
Tee Times: 3 days,June-Sept.

Tees	Holes	Yards	Par	USGA	Slope
BACK	18	6196	71	69.6	123
MIDDLE	18	5744	71	68.6	114
FRONT	18	5433	72	71.4	117

Fee 9 Holes: Weekday: No
Fee 18 Holes: Weekday: $40.00
Twilight Rates: No
Cart Rental: $15pp
Lessons: $30.00/half hour **Schools:** No
Clinics: Yes **Day Camps:** No
Other: Restaurant / Snack bar / Bar-lounge / Lockers / Showers

Weekend: No
Weekend: $45.00
All Day Play: Yes
Discounts: None
Junior Golf: Yes **Membership:** No
Driving Range: $3 per token

Player's Comment: "Two great layouts. Front nine is classic past (Donald Ross) and back nine is future (Brian Silva). Very enjoyable." New practice facility and driving range. Rated by *Golf Digest* in top 500.

	1	2	3	4	5	6	7	8	9
PAR	4	3	5	4	4	4	4	3	4
YARDS	347	181	496	343	391	242	340	153	425
HDCP	9	17	3	7	5	11	13	15	1
	10	11	12	13	14	15	16	17	18
PAR	3	4	5	4	4	3	4	5	4
YARDS	145	438	467	317	316	129	317	412	285
HDCP	16	2	4	14	8	18	12	6	10

Directions: Take I-95 to Exit 5 Maine Turnpike. Straight to American Motorcycle on right. Take right on Old Orchard Road, course is 1/2 mile on left.

Boothbay Region CC

Boothbay, ME (207) 633-6085
www.boothbaycountryclub.com

Club Pro: Dick Harris, PGA
Pro Shop: Full inventory
Payment: Visa, MC, Amex, Disc
Tee Times: Required

Tees	Holes	Yards	Par	USGA	Slope
BACK	18	6306	71	68.3	133
MIDDLE	18	5845	71	66.3	124
FRONT	18	5084	71	67.2	120

Fee 9 Holes: Weekday: $40.00
Fee 18 Holes: Weekday: $65.00
Twilight Rates: Yes, after 5 pm
Cart Rental: Included
Lessons: $35.00/half hour **Schools:** No
Clinics: No **Day Camps:** No
Other: Restaurant / Clubhouse / Functions

Weekend: $40.00
Weekend: $65.00
All Day Play: No
Discounts: Junior
Junior Golf: Yes **Membership:** Yes
Driving Range: $4/sm $6/med $8/lg

COUPON

Player's Comment: "Top notch facility. Excellent conditions and service. Scenic. Fun golf experience." Women friendly tees. Every hole has unique features. Non-member cart required. Open April - November.

	1	2	3	4	5	6	7	8	9
PAR	4	3	4	4	4	5	3	4	5
YARDS	342	182	340	291	349	525	184	378	446
HDCP	13	7	15	17	9	1	11	5	3
	10	11	12	13	14	15	16	17	18
PAR	4	4	4	4	4	3	4	3	5
YARDS	310	333	400	342	314	133	337	127	512
HDCP	14	12	2	6	10	16	8	18	4

Directions: I-95 to Route 1, to Route 27 South. 10 miles, take left across from Texaco station onto Country Club Road. Course at top of hill on right.

4☺ =Excellent **3☺** =Very Good **2☺** =Good

Bridgton Highlands CC

7

Bridgton, ME (207) 647-3491
www.bridgtonhighlands.com

Club Pro: Wayne Hill, PGA
Pro Shop: Full inventory
Payment: Cash, Check, Credit
Tee Times: 3 days adv.
Fee 9 Holes: Weekday: $18.00
Fee 18 Holes: Weekday: $32.00
Twilight Rates: Yes, after 3 pm
Cart Rental: $12pp/18 $6pp/9
Lessons: $25.00/half hour **Schools:** No
Clinics: Yes **Day Camps:** No
Other: Snack bar / Restaurant / Bar-lounge / Clubhouse

Tees	Holes	Yards	Par	USGA	Slope
BACK	18	6059	72	70.2	126
MIDDLE	18	5820	72	69.3	123
FRONT	18	5428	74	70.0	119

Weekend: $18.00
Weekend: $36.00
All Day Play: No
Discounts: Junior
Junior Golf: Yes **Membership:** Yes
Driving Range: No

COUPON

New tees constructed holes #6 and #16, cart paths completed 2003. The course is fully irrigated. Noted for scenery and challenging design.

	1	2	3	4	5	6	7	8	9
PAR	4	3	4	5	4	4	5	3	4
YARDS	440	145	376	440	345	304	434	150	320
HDCP	1	17	3	9	13	5	7	11	15
	10	**11**	**12**	**13**	**14**	**15**	**16**	**17**	**18**
PAR	3	4	4	3	4	5	4	4	5
YARDS	156	320	379	150	350	444	275	297	495
HDCP	12	14	4	18	10	6	2	8	16

Directions: Take Route 302 in Bridgton to Highland Rd. Course is 1.9 miles on the right.

Brunswick Golf Club

●● 8

River Rd., Brunswick, ME (207) 725-8224
www.brunswickgolfclub.com

Club Pro: Chris J. Doyle
Pro Shop: Full inventory
Payment: Visa, MC
Tee Times: 3 days everyday
Fee 9 Holes: Weekday: $21.00
Fee 18 Holes: Weekday: $42.00
Twilight Rates: No
Cart Rental: $26.00/18 $13.00/9
Lessons: $30.00/half hour **Schools:** No
Clinics: No **Day Camps:** No
Other: Clubhouse / Snack bar / Bar-lounge / Lockers

Tees	Holes	Yards	Par	USGA	Slope
BACK	18	6609	72	69.9	126
MIDDLE	18	6251	72	70	123
FRONT	18	5772	74	71.6	123

Weekend: $21.00
Weekend: $42.00
All Day Play: No
Discounts: None
Junior Golf: No **Membership:** Yes
Driving Range: Yes

Player's Comment: "Never a wait, light winter and early spring equal great summer conditions." Suited for players of all abilities. Seasonal rates. Easy walking.

	1	2	3	4	5	6	7	8	9
PAR	4	5	5	3	3	4	4	4	5
YARDS	355	547	485	179	110	440	332	364	494
HDCP	15	3	11	5	17	1	9	13	7
	10	**11**	**12**	**13**	**14**	**15**	**16**	**17**	**18**
PAR	4	3	4	4	4	3	5	4	4
YARDS	353	172	297	363	430	145	490	300	395
HDCP	6	12	16	8	2	18	10	14	4

Directions: Take I-295 to Brunswick; at 2nd light take left onto River Rd. Follow to course.

Cape Arundel Golf Club ✪✪ 9

Kennebunkport, ME (207) 967-3494

Club Pro: Ken Raynor
Pro Shop: Full inventory
Payment: Cash and credit card
Tee Times: 24 hours adv.
Fee 9 Holes: Weekday: N/A
Fee 18 Holes: Weekday: $50.00
Twilight Rates: Yes, after 5 pm
Cart Rental: $12pp/18
Lessons: $80.00/hour **Schools:** Call
Clinics: Yes, call **Day Camps:** Yes, call
Other: Clubhouse / Lockers

Tees	Holes	Yards	Par	USGA	Slope
BACK	18	5869	69	67.1	118
MIDDLE	18	5681	69	67.4	110
FRONT	18	5134	70	68.4	116

Weekend: N/A
Weekend: $50.00
All Day Play: If available
Discounts: None
Junior Golf: Yes **Membership:** Yes, waiting list.
Driving Range: No

Known as the Presidents Bush home course. Members only 11:00 am - 2:30 pm daily. Twilight rates not available during July and August.

	1	2	3	4	5	6	7	8	9
PAR	4	4	3	4	4	3	4	4	5
YARDS	375	311	154	398	350	118	381	370	480
HDCP	7	13	15	1	11	17	5	3	9

	10	11	12	13	14	15	16	17	18
PAR	4	4	4	3	4	4	3	4	4
YARDS	345	320	415	165	386	322	220	365	394
HDCP	8	16	2	14	4	18	12	10	6

Directions: Take I-95 to Biddeford Exit, take left off ramp. At 1st light take hairpin right turn at a 5-way intersection; follow 5 miles; at flashing yellow turn left onto Log Cabin Rd. Follow 4 miles; take 2nd right onto Old River Rd. to course.

Cape Neddick Country Club ✪✪ 10

Ogunquit, ME (207) 361-2011
www.capeneddickgolf.com

Club Pro: David Perroni, PGA
Pro Shop: Full inventory
Payment: Visa, MC, Amex
Tee Times: Yes, 2 days
Fee 9 Holes: Weekday: $30.00
Fee 18 Holes: Weekday: $48.00
Twilight Rates: No
Cart Rental: $15.00/18 $10.00/9
Lessons: $35/30 min **Schools:** Junior
Clinics: Junior **Day Camps:** No
Other: Restaurant / Clubhouse / Lockers / Bar-lounge

Tees	Holes	Yards	Par	USGA	Slope
BACK	18	6052	70	66.6	112
MIDDLE	18	5682	70	66.6	110
FRONT	18	4922	71	67.8	114

Weekend: $35.00
Weekend: $55.00
All Day Play: No
Discounts: None
Junior Golf: Yes **Membership:** Yes
Driving Range: Yes

 COUPON

Players' Comments: "Challenging back 9, Donald Ross flavor. Fun for all skills." "Good summer vacation course. Nice ocean setting." F.P. Semi- private, available to the public. Located one hour north of Boston!

	1	2	3	4	5	6	7	8	9
PAR	4	3	5	4	4	3	4	3	4
YARDS	345	170	574	302	301	118	304	144	329
HDCP	3	13	1	11	7	17	9	15	5

	10	11	12	13	14	15	16	17	18
PAR	4	3	5	4	3	5	4	4	4
YARDS	430	150	517	382	171	438	330	263	314
HDCP	2	14	4	8	16	6	10	18	12

Directions: From the south: I-95 to Exit 4 (York), go east .5 mile to US 1, Go north for 3.4 miles to River Rd. East on River Rd.for 1 mile to Shore Rd. Club is 2.8 miles north on Shore Rd.

S ME

4✪ =Excellent 3✪ =Very Good 2✪ = Good

Capitol City GC

Augusta, ME (207) 623-0504

Club Pro: No
Pro Shop: Limited inventory
Payment: No
Tee Times: No
Fee 9 Holes: Weekday: $9.00
Fee 18 Holes: Weekday: $16.00
Twilight Rates: No
Cart Rental: $10pp/ 9
Lessons: Schools: No
Clinics: Yes **Day Camps:** No
Other: Snack bar, club house facilities.

Tees	Holes	Yards	Par	USGA	Slope
BACK	18	2790	36	N/A	N/A
MIDDLE	18	3881	63	N/A	N/A
FRONT	18	2297	36	N/A	N/A

Weekend: $9.00
Weekend: $16.00
All Day Play: Yes
Discounts: None
Junior Golf: No **Membership:** Yes
Driving Range: No

This unique 18 hole course is the combination of a par 27 front nine and a recently renovated par 36 back nine. Fun course, good for families and beginners.

	1	2	3	4	5	6	7	8	9
PAR	3	3	3	3	3	3	3	3	3
YARDS	100	103	110	101	147	162	124	125	119
HDCP	N/A								
	10	11	12	13	14	15	16	17	18
PAR	3	4	4	5	5	4	3	4	4
YARDS	153	350	274	479	520	306	183	262	263
HDCP									

Directions: From I-95 take second exit in Augusta to Route 27. Take first right (at video store onto Old Belgrade Road, then dog leg to right to course.

Cobbossee Colony GC

Monmouth, ME (207) 268-4182
www.cobbosseegolf.com

Club Pro: No
Pro Shop: Yes
Payment: Cash, Check, Visa, MC
Tee Times: No
Fee 9 Holes: Weekday: $11.00
Fee 18 Holes: Weekday: $16.00
Twilight Rates: Yes, after 5 pm
Cart Rental: $17.00/18 $10.00/9
Lessons: No **Schools:** No
Clinics: No **Day Camps:** No
Other: Snack bar/ Clubhouse

Tees	Holes	Yards	Par	USGA	Slope
BACK					
MIDDLE	9	2417	34	63.0	108
FRONT					

Weekend: $12.00
Weekend: $17.00
All Day Play: No
Discounts: None
Junior Golf: Yes **Membership:** Yes
Driving Range: Yes

It's an easy walk, and fun. Excellent shape.

	1	2	3	4	5	6	7	8	9
PAR	5	3	4	4	3	4	3	4	4
YARDS	514	138	270	303	212	340	110	275	255
HDCP	3	7	8	5	2	4	9	1	6
	10	11	12	13	14	15	16	17	18
PAR									
YARDS									
HDCP									

Directions: Exit 28 off 95 Gardiner - Litchfield. Go approximately 5 miles west on Route 126. Right onto Hallowell Road for 1.5 miles. Left onto Cobbossee Road. Course is about 1.5 miles on both sides of the road.

Deep Brook Golf Course

NEW 2003

Saco, ME (207) 283-3500

Tees	Holes	Yards	Par	USGA	Slope
BACK	9	3076	36	69.6	127
MIDDLE	9	2831	36	67.0	125
FRONT	9	2312	36	67.6	110

Club Pro:
Pro Shop: Limited inventory
Payment: Cash or Charge
Tee Times: 1 day adv.
Fee 9 Holes: Weekday: $19.00
Fee 18 Holes: Weekday: $29.00
Twilight Rates: Yes, after 5 pm
Cart Rental: $15pp/18, $10pp/9
Lessons: Yes **Schools:**
Clinics: Day Camps:
Other: Clubhouse / Snackbar

Weekend: $19.00
Weekend: $29.00
All Day Play: Yes
Discounts: Senior & Junior
Junior Golf: Membership:
Driving Range: No

2003 Entry. Opened June 1, 2002. Challenging course, geographicaly accessible for daily play. Open April - Snow "A work in progress. Nice finishing hole." R.W.

	1	2	3	4	5	6	7	8	9
PAR	4	4	3	4	5	3	5	4	4
YARDS	363	357	138	240	520	92	462	337	321
HDCP	9	5	15	13	3	17	1	11	7
	10	**11**	**12**	**13**	**14**	**15**	**16**	**17**	**18**
PAR									
YARDS									
HDCP									

Directions: Exit 5 from Maine Turnpike, left at traffic light onto Industrial Park Road to first light, left at light. Next light go right then first left onto Garfield Street to end at light onto Route 5. Course is 1 mile on left.

Dunegrass Golf Club

◐◐ 14

S ME

Old Orchard Beach, ME (207) 934-4513
www.dunegrass.com

Tees	Holes	Yards	Par	USGA	Slope
BACK	18	6644	71	71.6	134
MIDDLE	18	6240	71	68.8	125
FRONT	18	4920	71	68.0	113

Club Pro: N/A
Pro Shop: Full inventory
Payment: Visa, MC, Amex, Cash
Tee Times: 7 days adv.
Fee 9 Holes: Weekday: N/A
Fee 18 Holes: Weekday: $80 incl. cart
Twilight Rates: Yes, after 3 pm
Cart Rental: Included
Lessons: Yes **Schools:** Yes
Clinics: Yes **Day Camps:** No
Other: New Clubhouse / Restaurant / Lockers-Showers / Bar-Lounge / Hotel / Inn

Weekend: N/A
Weekend: $80.00 incl. cart
All Day Play: Yes, Wknds.
Discounts: None
Junior Golf: Yes **Membership:** Yes
Driving Range: Yes

COUPON

Players' Comments: "Great staff, fine conditions. Good layout, not punishing fair." Vacation packages. Sporty 2953 yard 9 hole course, Old Orchard Beach is also available.

	1	2	3	4	5	6	7	8	9
PAR	5	3	4	4	4	4	5	3	4
YARDS	539	159	387	301	368	348	530	175	333
HDCP	3	17	9	11	7	1	5	15	13
	10	**11**	**12**	**13**	**14**	**15**	**16**	**17**	**18**
PAR	4	3	4	3	4	5	4	3	5
YARDS	357	177	417	189	404	443	410	179	524
HDCP	12	18	8	16	10	4	6	14	2

Directions: From I-95 take Exit 5 toExit 2 B (Route 1 North). Travel about .1 mile on Route 1 to Ross Road on right. Take Ross Rd. for about 2 miles. See Wild Dunes Way and golf course on right.

4◐ =Excellent **3◐** =Very Good **2◐** =Good

Dutch Elm Golf Course

Arundel, ME (207) 282-9850
www.dutchelmgolf.com

Club Pro: Norm Hevey
Pro Shop: Full inventory
Payment: Cash, Visa and MC
Tee Times: Yes

Tees	Holes	Yards	Par	USGA	Slope
BACK	18	6314	72	69.7	122
MIDDLE	18	5934	72	68.3	118
FRONT	18	5304	72	70.9	120

Fee 9 Holes: Weekday: $25.00 M-Thurs **Weekend:** $20.00 after 12:00
Fee 18 Holes: Weekday: $35.00 M-Thurs **Weekend:** $40.00 F/S/S/H
Twilight Rates: Yes, after 4 pm **All Day Play:** No
Cart Rental: $28.00/18 $16.00/9 **Discounts:** Senior
Lessons: $20/30 min. **Schools:** No **Junior Golf:** No **Membership:** Waiting list
Clinics: No **Day Camps:** No **Driving Range:** Yes
Other: Bar-lounge / Snack bar

"The best manicured course in southern Maine." N.H. Redid 17th green.

	1	2	3	4	5	6	7	8	9
PAR	4	5	4	4	4	5	3	3	4
YARDS	300	494	276	347	326	493	202	182	357
HDCP	13	1	9	7	11	3	15	17	5
	10	**11**	**12**	**13**	**14**	**15**	**16**	**17**	**18**
PAR	4	3	3	5	5	4	4	4	4
YARDS	356	156	150	440	486	411	300	342	357
HDCP	6	18	16	12	4	2	14	10	8

Directions: Off Maine Turnpike, take Exit 4 (Biddeford). Turn right on Route 111, go 1 mile to Texaco station. Bear left across from Agway store, go 1 mile to stop sign. Turn right, course is on left.

Fairlawn Golf Club

Poland , ME (207) 998-4277

Club Pro: David Bartasius, PGA
Pro Shop: Limited inventory
Payment: Visa, MC
Tee Times: No

Tees	Holes	Yards	Par	USGA	Slope
BACK					
MIDDLE	18	6300	72	68.6	118
FRONT	18	5379	72	70.7	112

Fee 9 Holes: Weekday: **Weekend:**
Fee 18 Holes: Weekday: $20.00 all day **Weekend:** $22.00 all day
Twilight Rates: Yes **All Day Play:** Yes
Cart Rental: $12.00/18 or $6.00/pp **Discounts:** None
Lessons: $30.00/half hour **Schools:** No **Junior Golf:** Yes **Membership:** N/A
Clinics: No **Day Camps:** Yes **Driving Range:** $3 lg./ $2 sm. bucket
Other: Clubhouse / Lockers / Showers / Snack bar / Bar-lounge

Condominiums available for monthly rent overlooking 18th green. Twilight fees after 5:00 pm. Open May 1 - until it snows.

	1	2	3	4	5	6	7	8	9
PAR	4	3	5	4	4	4	5	3	4
YARDS	323	205	544	409	364	357	497	182	317
HDCP	13	9	7	1	5	3	11	15	17
	10	**11**	**12**	**13**	**14**	**15**	**16**	**17**	**18**
PAR	4	3	5	3	4	4	5	4	4
YARDS	394	133	491	154	358	363	535	341	333
HDCP	2	18	12	14	6	4	8	10	16

Directions: From Maine Turnpike, Exit 12, take right off exit; take first right (Kittyhawk.) Go to end of road and take left (Lewiston Junction Road.) At first stop sign take right. Course on left. From West, take Route 26 South to Route 122. Take right onto Route 122 and follow signs.

Fox Ridge Golf Club

17

Auburn, ME (207) 777-GOLF(4653)
www.foxridgegolfclub.com

Club Pro: Bob Darling
Pro Shop: Full inventory
Payment: Visa, MC
Tee Times: Call anytime
Fee 9 Holes: Weekday: $20.00
Fee 18 Holes: Weekday: $30.00
Twilight Rates: Yes, after 3 pm
Cart Rental: $12pp/18 $6pp/9
Lessons: $30/30 min **Schools:** Jr.
Clinics: Yes **Day Camps:**
Other: Restaurant / Clubhouse / Bar-lounge / Showers / Lockers

Tees	Holes	Yards	Par	USGA	Slope
BACK	18	6814	72	72.0	132
MIDDLE	18	6297	72	70.1	126
FRONT	18	5832	72	68.2	116

Weekend: $22.00
Weekend: $38.00
All Day Play:
Discounts: Junior
Junior Golf: Membership:
Driving Range: Yes

COUPON

A blend of St. Andrews and the Maine Seacoast, stonewalls, stone bridges, and island greens. "Layout aesthetically magnificent, but severe on both greens and fairways." R.W.

	1	2	3	4	5	6	7	8	9
PAR	4	4	3	5	3	4	4	4	5
YARDS	322	387	167	529	191	349	360	300	489
HDCP	11	9	17	1	5	13	3	15	7

	10	11	12	13	14	15	16	17	18
PAR	4	5	4	3	4	4	3	5	4
YARDS	383	551	378	113	322	344	203	518	391
HDCP	10	2	4	18	14	12	16	6	8

Directions: Exit 12 off I-495. Follow signs.

Freeport Country Club

18

Freeport, ME (207) 865-4922

Club Pro: No
Pro Shop: Yes
Payment: MC, Visa
Tee Times: Weekends
Fee 9 Holes: Weekday: $15.00
Fee 18 Holes: Weekday: $18.00
Twilight Rates: Yes, after 5 pm
Cart Rental: $20.00/18 $10.00/9
Lessons: No **Schools:** No
Clinics: Yes **Day Camps:** No
Other: Clubhouse / Snack bar

Tees	Holes	Yards	Par	USGA	Slope
BACK					
MIDDLE	9	5900	72	69.0	116
FRONT	9	5088	72	69.1	108

Weekend: $18.00
Weekend: $22.00
All Day Play: No
Discounts: Junior
Junior Golf: No **Membership:** Yes
Driving Range: No

Good condition. New signs up on tees. Located within 5 minutes of L.L. Bean, excellent alternative to shopping in Freeport. Links-style layout with open fairways. A great value.

	1	2	3	4	5	6	7	8	9
PAR	4	4	4	4	5	3	4	3	5
YARDS	378	321	403	260	418	177	306	156	531
HDCP	3	15	1	17	13	5	7	9	11

	10	11	12	13	14	15	16	17	18
PAR	4	4	4	4	5	3	4	3	5
YARDS	388	390	353	250	453	197	316	148	460
HDCP	4	2	14	18	10	6	8	12	16

Directions: I-95 North to Exit 17, US Route 1. Look for a big wooden Indian on right. Continue 1 mile and turn left on Old County Road. Continue to course.

S ME

Frye Island Golf Course

Raymond, ME (207) 655-3551
www.fryeisland.com

Club Pro: No
Pro Shop: Yes
Payment: Cash, Credit Cards
Tee Times: Weekends
Fee 9 Holes: Weekday: $18.00
Fee 18 Holes: Weekday: $18.00
Twilight Rates: Yes, after 5 pm
Cart Rental: $26.00/18 $16.00/9
Lessons: Yes **Schools:** No
Clinics: Yes **Day Camps:** No
Other: Snack bar / Lounge

Tees	Holes	Yards	Par	USGA	Slope
BACK	9	6278	72	70.0	123
MIDDLE	9	6046	72	69.4	121
FRONT	9	5302	72	72.4	126

Weekend: $28.00
Weekend: $28.00
All Day Play: No
Discounts: Junior
Junior Golf: No **Membership:** Yes
Driving Range: No

COUPON

This course is narrow with water holes and tree-lined fairways. Open May 1 - November 1. Off season rates. Continuous improvement.

	1	**2**	**3**	**4**	**5**	**6**	**7**	**8**	**9**
PAR	4	5	4	3	4	4	5	3	4
YARDS	378	481	391	160	358	293	456	155	351
HDCP	7	5	1	13	11	17	9	15	3
	10	**11**	**12**	**13**	**14**	**15**	**16**	**17**	**18**
PAR	4	5	4	3	4	4	5	3	4
YARDS	378	481	391	160	358	293	456	155	351
HDCP	8	6	2	14	12	18	10	16	4

Directions: Take Exit 8 (Westbrook) to Route 302 (2 mi.) to Raymond Cape Rd. (20 mi.) to Frye Island Ferry Landing (5 mi.).

Goose River GC

Rockport, ME (207) 236-8488
www.gooserivergolf.com

Club Pro: Karl Enroth, PGA
Pro Shop: Full inventory
Payment: Cash, MC, Visa
Tee Times: Yes
Fee 9 Holes: Weekday: $25.00
Fee 18 Holes: Weekday: $35.00
Twilight Rates: No
Cart Rental: $25.00/18 $15.00/9
Lessons: $35.00/1 hour **Schools:** No
Clinics: Yes **Day Camps:** No
Other: Snack bar

Tees	Holes	Yards	Par	USGA	Slope
BACK					
MIDDLE	9	6056	71	68.5	119
FRONT	9	5208	72	68.5	119

Weekend: $25.00
Weekend: $35.00
All Day Play: No
Discounts: Junior
Junior Golf: Yes **Membership:** Yes
Driving Range: No

A challenging course, Goose River comes into play on four holes. There are only nine greens but eighteen different tees. Open May - October 31.

	1	**2**	**3**	**4**	**5**	**6**	**7**	**8**	**9**
PAR	5	4	4	4	5	3	4	3	3
YARDS	581	341	372	403	495	163	326	189	179
HDCP	1	11	7	5	3	17	9	13	15
	10	**11**	**12**	**13**	**14**	**15**	**16**	**17**	**18**
PAR	5	4	4	4	5	3	4	3	4
YARDS	540	338	295	336	422	190	349	231	306
HDCP	2	8	16	6	4	18	10	14	12

Directions: North on I-95, north on Route 1. Follow Route 1 into Camden and follow signs.

Gorham Country Club

....

McLellan Rd., Gorham, ME (207) 839-3490

Club Pro: Mark Fogg, PGA
Pro Shop: Yes
Payment: Cash, Check, Credit
Tee Times: Wknds/ Hldys
Fee 9 Holes: Weekday: $15.00
Fee 18 Holes: Weekday: $26.00
Twilight Rates: Yes, after 5 pm
Cart Rental: $24.00/18 $12.00/9
Lessons: Yes **Schools:** No
Clinics: Yes **Day Camps:** No
Other: Lockers / Showers / Snack bar / Restaurant

Tees	Holes	Yards	Par	USGA	Slope
BACK	18	6552	71	69.0	118
MIDDLE	18	5884	71	68.2	117
FRONT	18	5426	72	70.5	117

Weekend: $15.00
Weekend: $26.00
All Day Play: Yes
Discounts: None
Junior Golf: Yes **Membership:** Yes
Driving Range: Yes

A championship 18-hole layout located on a Game Preserve. A beautiful and challenging course for all abilities.

	1	2	3	4	5	6	7	8	9
PAR	4	4	4	3	4	3	4	4	5
YARDS	324	344	369	160	406	141	391	378	488
HDCP	18	7	5	9	2	16	6	4	15
	10	**11**	**12**	**13**	**14**	**15**	**16**	**17**	**18**
PAR	5	4	4	3	4	3	4	4	5
YARDS	561	427	365	155	424	168	358	375	500
HDCP	12	3	14	13	1	8	11	10	17

Directions: Take I-95 to Exit 7. Follow Route 114 to Gorham. Take right onto McLellan Road.

Highland Green Golf Club

....

**S
ME**

Topsham, ME (207) 725-6318, Winter
www.highlandgreenmaine.com

Club Pro: TBA
Pro Shop: Full inventory
Payment:
Tee Times: Yes
Fee 9 Holes: Weekday: TBA
Fee 18 Holes: Weekday: TBA
Twilight Rates: Yes
Cart Rental: TBA
Lessons: Yes **Schools:** Yes
Clinics: **Day Camps:**
Other: Restaurant / Clubhouse / Lockers / Showers / Bar Lounge

Tees	Holes	Yards	Par	USGA	Slope
BACK	9	2917	35		
MIDDLE	9	2518	35		
FRONT	9	2263	35		

**NEW
2004**

Weekend: TBA
Weekend: TBA
All Day Play: No
Discounts: Senior
Junior Golf: Yes **Membership:** Yes
Driving Range: Yes

COUPON

New Entry 2004.. Impeccably maintained. Traditional style golf course on the coast of Maine. Proper attire required.

	1	2	3	4	5	6	7	8	9
PAR	4	4	5	4	4	3	4	4	3
YARDS	330	335	410	295	300	150	365	400	180
HDCP	10	8	2	16	12	18	14	4	6
	10	**11**	**12**	**13**	**14**	**15**	**16**	**17**	**18**
PAR									
YARDS									
HDCP									

Directions: One minute from I-95 and Route 1, on the Coastal Connector in Topsham Maine.

4✪ =Excellent 3✪ =Very Good 2✪ =Good

Kennebec Heights Country Club

Rt. 201, Farmingdale, ME (207) 582-2000
www.kennebecheights.com

Club Pro: Ryan Madore
Pro Shop: Full inventory
Payment: Visa, MC
Tee Times: Required

Tees	Holes	Yards	Par	USGA	Slope
BACK	18	6003	70	69.0	129
MIDDLE	18	5525	70	67.1	123
FRONT	18	4800	70	67.7	119

Fee 9 Holes: Weekday: $20.00 M-Th
Fee 18 Holes: Weekday: $30.00 M-Th
Twilight Rates: Yes, after 4:30 pm
Cart Rental: $10pp M-Th, $12pp F/S/S
Lessons: Yes **Schools:** Jr. & Sr.
Clinics: No **Day Camps:** N/R
Other: Snack bar

Weekend: $20.00 F/S/S/H
Weekend: $35.00 F/S/S/H
All Day Play: Yes
Discounts: Senior & Junior
Junior Golf: Yes **Membership:** Yes
Driving Range: $3.50/lg., $2.50/sm. bucket

Great Central location. Very walkable and well manicured. Impressive and very attractive. Back nine, a
Cornish & Silva design.

	1	2	3	4	5	6	7	8	9
PAR	4	4	3	5	4	3	4	3	4
YARDS	274	297	105	461	381	185	210	162	330
HDCP	16	10	14	2	8	18	6	12	4
	10	11	12	13	14	15	16	17	18
PAR	4	4	3	4	5	3	4	4	5
YARDS	241	300	136	279	502	145	336	392	489
HDCP	11	15	13	5	1	17	7	9	3

Directions: Take I-95 to Augusta Exit; follow Route 202. Take Route 201 South to course.

Lake Kezar CC

Lovell, ME (207) 925-2462

Club Pro: Richard Dennison, PGA
Pro Shop: Limited inventory
Payment: Cash only
Tee Times: 7 days adv. members,

Tees	Holes	Yards	Par	USGA	Slope
BACK	18	5961	72	63.3	117
MIDDLE	18	5585	72	65.7	111
FRONT	18	5088	72	68.8	114

Fee 9 Holes: Weekday: $16.00
Fee 18 Holes: Weekday: $24.00
Twilight Rates: Yes, after 4 pm
Cart Rental: $20.00/18 $11.00/9
Lessons: $25.00/half hour **Schools:** No
Clinics: Yes **Day Camps:** No
Other: Snack bar / Bar-lounge

Weekend: $18.00
Weekend: $28.00
All Day Play: Yes
Discounts: None
Junior Golf: Yes **Membership:** Yes
Driving Range: No

Very scenic, pine trees, mountains, meandering brook, quiet. Design by Ross. Clubhouse was one room
school house.

	1	2	3	4	5	6	7	8	9
PAR	4	4	4	4	3	4	3	5	4
YARDS	292	305	299	291	136	383	201	498	272
HDCP	7	9	11	15	17	1	3	5	13
	10	11	12	13	14	15	16	17	18
PAR	5	4	3	4	5	4	3	4	5
YARDS	450	278	123	334	481	326	153	282	526
HDCP	12	10	18	6	4	8	16	14	2

Directions: Take I-95 to Route 302. At the base of Pleasant Mountain, take right onto Knights Hill
Rd., follow to Lovell Village. Go north on Route 5. Course is 2 miles up on Route 5.

Maple Lane Inn and Golf Club

▸ 25

Livermore, ME (207) 897-6666
www.maplelaneinn.com

Club Pro: Kevin Cullen
Pro Shop: Full inventory
Payment: Visa, MC
Tee Times: Yes
Fee 9 Holes: Weekday: $14.00
Fee 18 Holes: Weekday: $21.00
Twilight Rates: Yes, after 4 pm
Cart Rental: Yes
Lessons: Yes **Schools:** Jr. & Sr.Yes
Clinics: Yes **Day Camps:** Yes
Other: Snack bar/ Dining room and patio/ Hotel

Tees	Holes	Yards	Par	USGA	Slope
BACK	9	6038	70	65	118
MIDDLE	9	5594	70	62.8	114
FRONT	9	5330	70	65.8	118

Weekend: $14.00
Weekend: $21.00
All Day Play: $25.00
Discounts: Senior
Junior Golf: Yes **Membership:** Yes
Driving Range: To open

COUPON

New driving range and 2 new holes to open Sept. '04. 5 bedroom inn, affordable golf, Stay and Play packages.

	1	2	3	4	5	6	7	8	9
PAR	4	5	3	4	5	4	4	3	3
YARDS	356	347	555	370	155	170	348	540	168
HDCP	11	9	5	1	17	15	3	7	13

	10	11	12	13	14	15	16	17	18
PAR	4	4	5	4	3	3	4	5	3
YARDS	356	347	555	370	155	170	358	540	168
HDCP	12	10	6	2	18	16	4	8	14

Directions: Take I-95 to Auburn Exit. Take Route 4 to Livermore- Livermore Falls town line. Take a right before bridge onto River Rd. (From Augusta, take Route 17 S to 133 N.)

Merriland Farm Par 3 Golf

⚫⚫ ▸ 26

Wells, ME (207) 646-0508
www.merrilandfarm.com

Club Pro: No
Pro Shop: No
Payment: Cash only
Tee Times: No
Fee 9 Holes: Weekday: $11.00
Fee 18 Holes: Weekday: $16.00
Twilight Rates: No
Cart Rental: No
Lessons: No **Schools:** No
Clinics: N/R **Day Camps:** Yes
Other: Cafe serving breakfast & lunch. Raspberry, blueberry baked specialties.

Tees	Holes	Yards	Par	USGA	Slope
BACK					
MIDDLE	9	838	27		
FRONT					

Weekend: $11.00
Weekend: $16.00
All Day Play: No
Discounts: None
Junior Golf: Yes **Membership:** Yes
Driving Range: No

COUPON

Player's Comment: "A par 3 that let's you and the family enjoy the outing. Pleasant staff. Great muffins."

	1	2	3	4	5	6	7	8	9
PAR	3	3	3	3	3	3	3	3	3
YARDS	83	96	119	111	67	86	63	109	104
HDCP									

	10	11	12	13	14	15	16	17	18
PAR									
YARDS									
HDCP									

Directions: I-95 to Exit 2 (Wells). Left onto Route 109, left onto Route 1 about 1.5 miles to Coles Hill Road on left. 1.5 Miles up Coles Hill Road to Course on right.

4⚫ =Excellent **3⚫** =Very Good **2⚫** =Good

Naplеs Golf and Country Club ✪✪

Route 114, Naples, ME. 207-693-6424
www.naplesgolfcourse.com

Club Pro: Harry W. Andrews, PGA
Pro Shop: Full inventory
Payment: Visa, MC
Tee Times: Required.
Fee 9 Holes: Weekday: $18.00 after 1pm
Fee 18 Holes: Weekday: $28.00
Twilight Rates: Yes, after 5 pm
Cart Rental: $12pp/18 $6pp/9
Lessons: $30/30 minutes **Schools:** No
Clinics: Yes **Day Camps:** Yes
Other: Full restaurant / Clubhouse / Bar-lounge

Tees	Holes	Yards	Par	USGA	Slope
BACK	18	6039	72	67.8	121
MIDDLE	18	5617	72	71.9	126
FRONT	18	5498	72	N/A	N/A

Weekend: $18.00 after 1pm
Weekend: $32.00
All Day Play: No
Discounts: None
Junior Golf: Yes **Membership:** Yes
Driving Range: Yes

COUPON

Sig. Hole: #14 is a 500 yard par 5 downhill off ledges, large pine center of fairway at 225 yds, pond in front of elevated green. Back nine opened 2001.

	1	2	3	4	5	6	7	8	9
PAR	5	4	4	4	4	4	4	4	3
YARDS	465	305	345	405	340	340	375	340	130
HDCP	14	15	3	1	4	13	6	17	18
	10	11	12	13	14	15	16	17	18
PAR	4	3	4	4	5	4	3	4	5
YARDS	280	125	320	325	400	280	155	262	425
HDCP	12	16	11	2	7	9	10	5	8

Directions: Exit 8 from Maine Turnpike. Turn right on Riverside St.. 3 Miles to Route 302. Left on Route 302 for 30 miles to Naples. Take left on Route 114 in Naples Village. Course is 1 mile.

Nonesuch River Golf Club ✪✪

Scarborough, ME (207) 883-0007
www.nonesuchgolf.com

Club Pro: Jim Fairbanks
Pro Shop: Yes
Payment: Visa, MC, Amex
Tee Times: 7 days adv.
Fee 9 Holes: Weekday: $20.00
Fee 18 Holes: Weekday: $29.00-34.00
Twilight Rates: Yes, after 3 pm
Cart Rental: $13.00pp/18
Lessons: Yes **Schools:** Yes
Clinics: Yes **Day Camps:** Yes
Other: Clubhouse / Food and beverage, full service

Tees	Holes	Yards	Par	USGA	Slope
BACK	18	6300	70	68.8	119
MIDDLE	18	6218	70	66.9	116
FRONT	18	5248	70	68.8	109

Weekend: N/A
Weekend: $36.00-$40.00
All Day Play: No
Discounts: None
Junior Golf: Yes **Membership:** Yes
Driving Range: $5.00 per bucket

COUPON

Player's Comment: "Great shape, well run, good package deal." Stay and play partner is Sheraton Hotel. Off season rates in spring and fall. Course noted for conditions and great layout.

	1	2	3	4	5	6	7	8	9
PAR	4	3	5	3	4	3	4	4	4
YARDS	389	180	539	214	362	173	348	413	431
HDCP	13	17	1	11	15	7	9	5	3
	10	11	12	13	14	15	16	17	18
PAR	5	4	4	4	4	3	5	3	4
YARDS	492	375	341	397	381	160	496	174	435
HDCP	12	4	10	14	8	18	2	16	6

Directions: Maine Turnpike to Exit 6. Turn left out of toll. Turn left at 2nd set of lights on to Route 114. Course is .5 miles on left.

Norway Country Club

Norway, ME (207) 743-9840

Club Pro: Dave Mazzeo, PGA
Pro Shop: Full inventory
Payment: Cash, Checks
Tee Times: No
Fee 9 Holes: Weekday: $16.00
Fee 18 Holes: Weekday: $22.00
Twilight Rates: After 4 pm W/Th
Cart Rental: $20.00/18 $10.00/9
Lessons: $35/30 min. **Schools:** Clinics
Clinics: Yes **Day Camps:** No
Other: Restaurant / Clubhouse / Snack bar / Bar-lounge

Tees	Holes	Yards	Par	USGA	Slope
BACK					
MIDDLE	9	5808	70	66.6	107
FRONT					

Weekend: $16.00
Weekend: $25.00
All Day Play: No
Discounts: None
Junior Golf: Yes **Membership:** Yes
Driving Range: $4.00

Greens in excellent condition. "Most scenic 9 hole course in Maine." D.M., Pro

	1	2	3	4	5	6	7	8	9
PAR	4	3	4	4	4	3	5	4	4
YARDS	375	187	327	300	430	167	450	420	253
HDCP	9	7	11	13	1	15	5	3	17
	10	11	12	13	14	15	16	17	18
PAR	4	3	4	4	4	3	5	4	4
YARDS	375	187	327	300	430	167	465	420	233
HDCP	10	8	12	14	2	16	6	4	18

Directions: Take I-95 to Exit 11 (North Portland). Take Route 26 North to Norway, course is 1 mile past lake.

Oakdale CC

River Road, Mexico, ME (207) 364-3951

Club Pro: Steve Hodgkins, PGA
Pro Shop: Full inventory
Payment: Visa, MC, Dis
Tee Times: No
Fee 9 Holes: Weekday: $15.00
Fee 18 Holes: Weekday: $20.00
Twilight Rates: Yes, after 5 pm
Cart Rental: $24.00/18, $12.00/9
Lessons: $20.00/ 30 min. **Schools:** No
Clinics: Yes **Day Camps:** No
Other: Club house / Snack bar / Cocktails

Tees	Holes	Yards	Par	USGA	Slope
BACK	N/A				
MIDDLE	18	6133	72	68.4	121
FRONT	18	5486	74	73.6	125

Weekend: $15.00
Weekend: $20.00
All Day Play: No
Discounts: None
Junior Golf: Yes **Membership:** Yes
Driving Range: No

Course is noted for playability. Hilly fairways and challenging greens.

	1	2	3	4	5	6	7	8	9
PAR	4	5	4	3	4	4	4	4	4
YARDS	327	476	339	160	423	390	339	228	362
HDCP	11	13	9	7	1	3	15	17	5
	10	11	12	13	14	15	16	17	18
PAR	4	5	4	3	5	4	4	3	4
YARDS	336	456	354	144	430	380	391	206	392
HDCP	10	18	14	8	16	6	10	4	2

Directions: I-95 to Exit 12, Route 4 North to Route 108 towards Rumford. Then to Route 2 West to course.

Paris Hill Country Club

31

Paris Hill Rd., Paris, ME (207) 743-2371

Tees	Holes	Yards	Par	USGA	Slope
BACK					
MIDDLE	9	4637	66	62.1	102
FRONT					

Club Pro:
Pro Shop: Full inventory
Payment: Cash or check
Tee Times: No
Fee 9 Holes: Weekday: $15.00 Daily Rate **Weekend:** $15.00
Fee 18 Holes: Weekday: $15.00 **Weekend:** $15.00
Twilight Rates: Yes, after 4 pm **All Day Play:**
Cart Rental: $18.00/18 $10.00/9 **Discounts:** None
Lessons: $50 + $35/half hour **Schools:** Yes **Junior Golf:** N/R **Membership:** Yes
Clinics: Yes **Day Camps:** N/R **Driving Range:** No
Other: Clubhouse / Luncheonette / Bar / Dining Room

COUPON

Overlooks beautiful Oxford Hills and mountains. Open May - October.

	1	2	3	4	5	6	7	8	9
PAR	4	4	4	3	4	3	4	3	4
YARDS	350	260	231	194	352	125	309	129	355
HDCP	5	11	13	9	1	17	7	15	3
	10	11	12	13	14	15	16	17	18
PAR	4	4	4	3	4	3	4	3	4
YARDS	350	260	231	221	352	125	309	129	355
HDCP	6	12	14	10	2	18	8	16	4

Directions: Off Route 26 South Paris.

Pleasant Hill CC

32

Scarborough, ME (207) 883-4425

Tees	Holes	Yards	Par	USGA	Slope
BACK					
MIDDLE	9	2271	34	62.3	87
FRONT					

Club Pro: No
Pro Shop: Limited inventory
Payment: Cash only
Tee Times: No
Fee 9 Holes: Weekday: $14.00 **Weekend:** $16.00
Fee 18 Holes: Weekday: $14.00 **Weekend:** $16.00
Twilight Rates: No **All Day Play:** Yes
Cart Rental: Pull Carts, $1 **Discounts:** None
Lessons: $18.00/hour **Schools:** No **Junior Golf:** No **Membership:** No
Clinics: No **Day Camps:** No **Driving Range:** No
Other: Snack bar

The course is well conditioned, very level and considered an easy walker. Popular with senior citizens who do not use auto carts.

	1	2	3	4	5	6	7	8	9
PAR	4	4	4	4	3	3	4	4	4
YARDS	296	336	303	216	126	175	355	258	206
HDCP	N/A								
	10	11	12	13	14	15	16	17	18
PAR									
YARDS									
HDCP									

Directions: Take I-95 to Route 1 South Portland Exit. Follow Route 1 South. Turn left at Pleasant Hill; right onto Chamberlain Road to course.

Point Sebago Golf Club ✪✪✪

Route 302, Casco, ME (207) 655-2747
www.pointsebago.com

Club Pro: Sean Kicker, PGA
Pro Shop: Full inventory
Payment: Visa, MC, Disc.
Tee Times: 7 days in adv.
Fee 9 Holes: Weekday: N/A 8am-2pm
Fee 18 Holes: Weekday: $57.00
Twilight Rates: Yes, after 3 pm
Cart Rental: Included
Lessons: $75.00/hour **Schools:** Yes
Clinics: Yes **Day Camps:** Yes
Other: Resort / Restaurant / Snack Bar

Tees	Holes	Yards	Par	USGA	Slope
BACK	18	7002	72	73.7	135
MIDDLE	18	6474	72	71.3	130
FRONT	18	5645	72	67.5	122

Weekend: $35.00
Weekend: $57.00
All Day Play: No
Discounts: Senior & Junior
Junior Golf: Yes **Membership:** Yes
Driving Range: Yes

COUPON

A Golf and Beach Resort with an 18 hole championship course, tennis courts, beaches & boat slips. Discounts include: Point Sebago Club Cards, ME residents and early bird specials bef. 8 am & after 2 for 9 holes.

	1	2	3	4	5	6	7	8	9
PAR	5	3	4	4	4	4	5	3	4
YARDS	502	154	388	375	335	383	549	181	418
HDCP	7	17	5	11	9	15	1	13	3

	10	11	12	13	14	15	16	17	18
PAR	4	5	4	4	3	4	4	3	5
YARDS	390	533	380	370	163	302	361	183	507
HDCP	12	2	6	8	18	14	10	16	4

Directions: Turn off Maine Turnpike at Exit 8 and follow signs to Route 302 West for approximately 22.5. Look for Chute's Cafe in Casco. Take next left at church.

Poland Spring CC

Rt. 26, Poland Spring, ME (207) 998-6002
www.polandspringinns.com

Club Pro: No
Pro Shop: Full inventory
Payment: Cash or credit card
Tee Times: Yes
Fee 9 Holes: Weekday: N/A
Fee 18 Holes: Weekday: $22.00
Twilight Rates: Yes, after 3 pm
Cart Rental: $22.00/18
Lessons: No **Schools:** No
Clinics: No **Day Camps:** No
Other: Clubhouse / Lockers / Showers / Pool / Snack bar / Restaurant / Bar-lounge / Hotel

Tees	Holes	Yards	Par	USGA	Slope
BACK	18	6254	71	68.8	117
MIDDLE	18	5917	71	67.0	116
FRONT	18	5261	73	71.6	117

Weekend: N/A
Weekend: $24.00
All Day Play: Yes
Discounts: None
Junior Golf: No **Membership:** Yes
Driving Range: No

Oldest eighteen hole resort course in U.S (1893) designed by Donald Ross. Played by sports legends as well as many U.S. Presidents. Link-style course. Open May 1-Nov. 1.

	1	2	3	4	5	6	7	8	9
PAR	4	4	4	4	4	3	4	3	4
YARDS	337	306	388	410	305	132	378	184	322
HDCP	12	18	8	2	16	14	6	10	4

	10	11	12	13	14	15	16	17	18
PAR	4	5	4	3	4	4	5	4	4
YARDS	293	446	292	169	399	404	531	292	329
HDCP	17	13	9	5	3	1	11	15	7

Directions: Take Maine Turnpike Exit 11 (Gray) to Route 26, approx. 10 miles to course.

Prospect Hill GC

So. Main St., Auburn, ME (207) 782-9220

Club Pro: Ron Vaillancourt, PGA
Pro Shop: Full inventory
Payment: Visa, MC, Disc
Tee Times: No

Tees	Holes	Yards	Par	USGA	Slope
BACK					
MIDDLE	18	5846	71	69.9	110
FRONT	18	5227	71	69.9	111

Fee 9 Holes: Weekday: $13.00
Fee 18 Holes: Weekday: $22.00
Twilight Rates: Yes, after 4 pm
Cart Rental: $20.00/18 $12.00/9
Lessons: $35.00/half hour **Schools:** Yes
Clinics: Yes **Day Camps:** No
Other: Snack bar / Bar-lounge

Weekend: $13.00
Weekend: $22.00
All Day Play: Yes, $22
Discounts: None
Junior Golf: Yes **Membership:** Yes
Driving Range: No

The front nine are wide open with a few small creeks, while the back nine have four ponds and tree-lined fairways. Spikeless course, proper dress required.

	1	2	3	4	5	6	7	8	9
PAR	5	4	3	4	3	4	4	4	4
YARDS	460	350	210	230	225	395	370	260	290
HDCP	5	9	17	16	14	8	4	12	13
	10	11	12	13	14	15	16	17	18
PAR	4	4	5	4	4	3	4	4	4
YARDS	412	290	510	276	357	138	366	311	396
HDCP	1	11	6	10	3	18	2	15	7

Directions: Take I-95 to Exit 12, left off ramp, look for signs.

Province Lake Golf Club

Parsonfield, ME Route 153 (800) 325-4434
www.provincelakegolf.com

Club Pro: Edward Chamberlain
Pro Shop: Full inventory
Payment: Most major
Tee Times: 7 days advance

Tees	Holes	Yards	Par	USGA	Slope
BACK	18	6240	71	70.1	127
MIDDLE	18	5877	71	73.8	124
FRONT	18	4168	71	63.8	109

Fee 9 Holes: Weekday: $26 after 12 pm
Fee 18 Holes: Weekday: $36, $28 after 12
Twilight Rates: Yes, after 3 pm
Cart Rental: $13pp
Lessons: $35.00/half hour **Schools:** No
Clinics: Yes **Day Camps:** No
Other: Clubhouse / Snack bar / Restaurant / Bar-lounge / Function Room / Patio / 2 Decks / Childcare

Weekend: $18after 3 pm
Weekend: $40, $34 after 12 pm
All Day Play: No
Discounts: Senior & Junior
Junior Golf: Yes **Membership:** No
Driving Range: Mats and Turf

4 sets of tees: 4200 to 6200. Playable for all. Stay & Play at 5 inns, call course. **Player's Comment:** "A diamond in the rough. Superbly manicured. Amazing back 9. Great staff."

	1	2	3	4	5	6	7	8	9
PAR	4	5	3	4	3	5	4	4	4
YARDS	392	438	201	378	129	525	369	376	309
HDCP	7	11	15	3	17	1	9	5	13
	10	11	12	13	14	15	16	17	18
PAR	4	3	4	4	3	5	4	4	4
YARDS	338	146	295	337	142	483	383	331	305
HDCP	10	16	14	6	18	2	4	8	12

Directions: I-95 to Route 16 (Spaulding Tpk.) to Route 153 North. Course is 15 miles north. OR access Route 153 South from Route 25.

River Meadow GC

Lincoln St., Westbrook, ME (207) 854-1625

Club Pro: No
Pro Shop: Full inventory
Payment: Cash, Credit cards
Tee Times: Weekends & Holidays
Fee 9 Holes: Weekday: $14.00
Fee 18 Holes: Weekday: $20.00
Twilight Rates: No
Cart Rental: $22.00/18 $12.00/9
Lessons: No **Schools:** Yes
Clinics: Yes **Day Camps:** No
Other: New Grill Room and Bar / Clubhouse / Snack bar / Restaurant

Tees	Holes	Yards	Par	USGA	Slope
BACK	9	5830	70	67.0	112
MIDDLE	9	5518	70	67.0	112
FRONT	9	5210	72	67.0	112

Weekend: $16.00
Weekend: $22.00
All Day Play: No
Discounts: None
Junior Golf: Yes **Membership:** Yes
Driving Range: No

COUPON

Current rates could change. 2004 will see conversion of two holes. Open April- November 15th.

	1	2	3	4	5	6	7	8	9
PAR	4	4	4	3	4	4	4	3	5
YARDS	371	411	248	139	350	350	295	150	445
HDCP	7	1	11	15	3	9	13	17	5

	10	11	12	13	14	15	16	17	18
PAR	4	4	4	3	4	4	4	3	5
YARDS	371	411	248	139	350	350	295	150	445
HDCP	8	2	12	16	6	10	14	18	6

Directions: Maine Turnpike (Route 95), Exit 8 to Route 25 West into Westbrook (approx. 2 miles). Rght turn onto Bridge St. (approx. 1/4 mile). Left onto Lincoln St. to course.

Riverside Municipal Golf Course

Riverside St., Portland, ME (207) 797-3524

Club Pro: Bill May, PGA
Pro Shop: Full inventory
Payment: Visa, MC, Cash
Tee Times: Weekends
Fee 9 Holes: Weekday: $20.00
Fee 18 Holes: Weekday: $27.00
Twilight Rates: No
Cart Rental: $15pp/18 $8pp/9
Lessons: $30-$35/30 min **Schools:** No
Clinics: Yes **Day Camps:** No
Other: Clubhouse / Lockers / Showers / Snack bar / Restaurant / Bar-lounge

Tees	Holes	Yards	Par	USGA	Slope
BACK	18	6370	72	69.2	115
MIDDLE	18	6052	72	67.5	112
FRONT	18	5630	73	70.7	112

Weekend: $21.00
Weekend: $30.00
All Day Play: No
Discounts: Senior & Junior Wkdays
Junior Golf: Yes **Membership:** Yes
Driving Range: $7.00/lg. bucket

27 holes available. South course is an additional 9 hole regulation course with 3102 yards. Wide fairways, medium speed greens, only a little hilly. Open April 15 - November 10.

	1	2	3	4	5	6	7	8	9
PAR	5	4	3	5	4	3	4	4	4
YARDS	450	365	202	488	322	197	314	324	396
HDCP	5	7	15	3	9	17	11	13	1

	10	11	12	13	14	15	16	17	18
PAR	5	4	4	3	4	4	4	4	4
YARDS	540	384	414	167	346	338	334	374	382
HDCP	6	8	2	18	10	16	14	12	4

Directions: Maine Turnpike to Exit 8. Follow signs to course.

Rockland Golf Club

Old County Rd, Rockland, ME (207) 594-9322
www.rocklandgolf.com

Tees	Holes	Yards	Par	USGA	Slope
BACK	18	6041	70	67.6	122
MIDDLE	18	5831	70	66.9	120
FRONT	18	5457	73	71.8	119

Club Pro: Keenan Flanagan, PGA
Pro Shop: Full inventory
Payment: Most major
Tee Times: 3 days adv.
Fee 9 Holes: Weekday: $25.00   **Weekend:** $25.00
Fee 18 Holes: Weekday: $35.00   **Weekend:** $35.00
Twilight Rates: No   **All Day Play:** No
Cart Rental: $15pp/18 $10pp/9   **Discounts:** Junior
Lessons: $35/30 min   **Schools:** No   **Junior Golf:** Yes **Membership:** Yes
Clinics: Ladies/Juniors   **Day Camps:** No   **Driving Range:** No
Other: Clubhouse / Bar-lounge / Snack Bar / Showers

COUPON

Player's comment: "Courteous, friendly staff." New irrigation system and new tee markers. Views of ocean and Rockland Harbor.

	1	2	3	4	5	6	7	8	9
PAR	5	4	4	4	3	4	5	4	3
YARDS	521	378	268	359	136	303	485	398	215
HDCP	2	14	12	10	18	8	6	4	15
	10	11	12	13	14	15	16	17	18
PAR	3	3	4	4	4	5	4	4	3
YARDS	176	210	282	425	357	582	341	232	163
HDCP	17	15	11	3	7	1	5	9	13

Directions: I-95 to Coastal Route 1 through Thomaston. Left onto old Country Road to course 3.5 miles on left.

Sable Oaks Golf Club

❀❀❀

S. Portland, ME (207) 775-6257
www.sableoaks.com

Tees	Holes	Yards	Par	USGA	Slope
BACK	18	6359	70	71.8	138
MIDDLE	18	6056	70	70.4	134
FRONT	18	4786	72	69.4	116

Club Pro: Patrick Badcock, PGA
Pro Shop: Full inventory
Payment: Visa, MC, Disc, Amex
Tee Times: Recommended/7 days
Fee 9 Holes: Weekday: $25 after 12 M-Th   **Weekend:** $30 after 3:00 F/S/S/H
Fee 18 Holes: Weekday: $40 walk M-Th   **Weekend:** $45 walkF/S/S
Twilight Rates: Yes, after 3 pm   **All Day Play:** No
Cart Rental: $15pp/18, $10pp/9   **Discounts:** None
Lessons: $65.00/60 min.   **Schools:** No   **Junior Golf:** Yes **Membership:** Yes
Clinics: Yes   **Day Camps:** No   **Driving Range:** No
Other: Snack bar / Bar-lounge / Function Hall / Showers / Locker room / Lodging

COUPON

Challenging championship course. Improved 12th hole, all grass throughout. Noted for fast and soft greens. Sister course to Samoset Resort. Off season rates, inquire.

	1	2	3	4	5	6	7	8	9
PAR	4	5	4	4	5	3	4	3	4
YARDS	389	460	419	398	442	170	319	138	394
HDCP	8	16	2	4	12	14	10	18	6
	10	11	12	13	14	15	16	17	18
PAR	4	3	4	3	5	4	4	3	4
YARDS	378	159	437	171	443	384	383	164	408
HDCP	15	13	1	7	11	3	9	17	5

Directions: Take I-95 to Exit 7 (Maine Mall) Go right at light. At 4th light, go left on Running Hill Rd. Take the second right onto Country Club Drive.

Salmon Falls GC

Hollis, ME (207) 929-5233 or 1-800-734-1616
www.salmonfalls-resort.com

Club Pro: John Barber, PGA
Pro Shop: Full inventory
Payment: Visa, MC, Amex, Disc
Tee Times: Daily
Fee 9 Holes: Weekday: $15.00
Fee 18 Holes: Weekday: $20.00
Twilight Rates: Yes, after 5 pm
Cart Rental: $20/18, $15/9
Lessons: $35/30 $50/hour **Schools:** Jr.
Clinics: N/R **Day Camps:** N/R
Other: Clubhouse / Snack bar / Restaurant / Bar-lounge / Hotel

Tees	Holes	Yards	Par	USGA	Slope
BACK					
MIDDLE	18	5848	72	67.6	122
FRONT	18	5193	70	69.5	112

Weekend: $15.00
Weekend: $20.00
All Day Play: No
Discounts: Sr. 65 & over $18/18
Junior Golf: Yes **Membership:** Yes
Driving Range: $3.50/med bucket

Certified for Henry Griffitts Custom Club Fitting. Suggest beginners come after 1 p.m. on weekends. Add $5.00 for 2 riders for cart rental. Open Mar-Oct. Noted for beauty of Maine.

	1	2	3	4	5	6	7	8	9
PAR	4	4	3	5	5	3	4	4	4
YARDS	365	250	190	500	455	165	303	251	404
HDCP	4	18	8	6	10	12	14	16	2
	10	**11**	**12**	**13**	**14**	**15**	**16**	**17**	**18**
PAR	4	4	3	5	5	3	4	4	4
YARDS	380	245	235	510	460	165	310	265	395
HDCP	5	17	1	7	9	11	13	15	3

Directions: I-95 to Exit 5 (Saco), follow Route 112 North. Follow signs.

Samoset Resort GC   ❂❂❂

220 Warrenton St., Rockport, ME (207) 594-1431
www.samoset.com

Club Pro: Chris Christie
Pro Shop: Full inventory
Payment: All major cards, checks
Tee Times: Yes
Fee 9 Holes: Weekday: $45.00-$70.00
Fee 18 Holes: Weekday: $68.00-$125.00
Twilight Rates: Yes, after 3 pm
Cart Rental: Included
Lessons: $40-$50/half hour **Schools:** Yes
Clinics: Yes **Day Camps:** Yes
Other: Clubhouse / Snack bar / Restaurant / Bar-lounge / Resort / Indoor golf center

Tees	Holes	Yards	Par	USGA	Slope
BACK	18	6617	70	70.7	130
MIDDLE	18	5615	70	68.9	124
FRONT	18	5145	72	71.2	125

Weekend: $45.00-$70.00
Weekend: $68.00-$125.00
All Day Play: No
Discounts: None
Junior Golf: Yes **Membership:** Yes
Driving Range: $5/30 min, $10/1 Hr.

$3 million renovation. New 18th hole. Noted for ocean views and spectacular condition. Range use included in greens fee.

	1	2	3	4	5	6	7	8	9
PAR	4	4	3	5	3	4	3	4	4
YARDS	360	388	190	481	165	380	176	330	312
HDCP	4	10	18	2	16	6	12	8	14
	10	**11**	**12**	**13**	**14**	**15**	**16**	**17**	**18**
PAR	4	3	5	3	5	4	4	4	4
YARDS	338	120	494	190	500	355	375	400	446
HDCP	9	17	5	15	7	13	3	11	1

Directions: Maine Turnpike to Exit 9, Route 95 to Exit 22, Route 1 North through Rockland. Turn right onto Waldo Avenue.

4❂ =Excellent **3❂** =Very Good **2❂** =Good

Sanford Country Club

Rt. 4, Sanford, ME (207) 324-5462
www.sanfordcountryclub.com

Club Pro: John Eliis, PGA
Pro Shop: Full inventory
Payment: Cash, Visa, MC
Tee Times: Yes
Fee 9 Holes: Weekday: $30.00
Fee 18 Holes: Weekday: $40.00
Twilight Rates: Yes, after 5 pm
Cart Rental: $24.00/18 $12.00/9
Lessons: $30/45 min. **Schools:** Jr.
Clinics: Yes **Day Camps:** No
Other: Restaurant / Clubhouse / Bar-lounge / Snack bar

Tees	Holes	Yards	Par	USGA	Slope
BACK	18	6726	72	73.2	128
MIDDLE	18	6217	72	70.5	122
FRONT	18	5320	74	66.5	114

Weekend: $35.00
Weekend: $45.00
All Day Play: Yes
Discounts: None
Junior Golf: Yes **Membership:** Yes
Driving Range: $4.00/bucket

COUPON

18 hole championship layout. Full irrigation. Home of the 2004 Maine Amateur. Noted for playability. Stay and play packages available.

	1	2	3	4	5	6	7	8	9
PAR	4	4	5	3	4	4	3	4	5
YARDS	342	313	488	100	323	373	186	389	557
HDCP	11	13	1	17	9	7	15	5	3
	10	11	12	13	14	15	16	17	18
PAR	4	4	3	5	5	4	4	3	4
YARDS	417	308	185	440	488	429	326	130	423
HDCP	10	14	16	6	2	8	12	18	4

Directions: From I-95 Exit 2 head north on Route 109 for approx. 10 miles to Route 4 Intersection. Take left off 109 to Route 4 South for 2.5 miles. Located on left.

Sebasco Harbor Resort Golf Club

Sebasco Estates, ME 800-225-3819
www.sebasco.com

Club Pro: Lewis A. Kingsbury
Pro Shop: Limited inventory
Payment: Visa, MC, Amex, Disc.
Tee Times: Yes
Fee 9 Holes: Weekday: $26.00
Fee 18 Holes: Weekday: $39.00
Twilight Rates: Yes, after 4 pm
Cart Rental: $10.00/9
Lessons: $35/45 min. **Schools:** Clinics
Clinics: Yes **Day Camps:** No
Other: Full Restaurant / Clubhouse / Hotel / Inn / Lockers / Showers / Bar-Lounge

Tees	Holes	Yards	Par	USGA	Slope
BACK	9	3112	36	69.1	125
MIDDLE	9	2987	36	67.3	122
FRONT	9	2664	36	68.2	127

Weekend: $26.00
Weekend: $39.00
All Day Play: No
Discounts: None
Junior Golf: No **Membership:** Yes
Driving Range: Practice course

COUPON

Sig. Hole: #2, 113 yd. par 3 is the diamond of the newly renovated course. Eighty yards of carry over Round Cove to a two tiered, challenging green. New 3 hole practice course.

	1	2	3	4	5	6	7	8	9
PAR	4	3	5	4	4	3	4	4	5
YARDS	370	140	467	309	339	179	387	316	480
HDCP									
	10	11	12	13	14	15	16	17	18
PAR									
YARDS									
HDCP									

Directions: South of Bath on Route 209 for 10 miles. Follow the Sebasco signs.

South Portland Muni.

Wescott Rd., S. Portland, ME (207) 775-0005

Club Pro: No
Pro Shop: Limited inventory
Payment: Cash/Check only
Tee Times: No
Fee 9 Holes: Weekday: $10.00
Fee 18 Holes: Weekday: $10.00
Twilight Rates: No
Cart Rental: Pull Carts, $2.00
Lessons: Group lessons **Schools:** No
Clinics: No **Day Camps:** No
Other: Snack bar

Tees	Holes	Yards	Par	USGA	Slope
BACK					
MIDDLE	9	2071	33	59.0	92
FRONT					

Weekend: $11.00
Weekend: $11.00
All Day Play: Yes
Discounts: None
Junior Golf: No **Membership:** Yes, residents
Driving Range: No

Well maintained! Polite staff! Carts are not required. Pay once, play for 3 rounds. Clinics offered by rec center.

	1	2	3	4	5	6	7	8	9
PAR	4	3	4	3	5	3	3	4	4
YARDS	340	140	238	132	372	167	122	285	275
HDCP									
	10	11	12	13	14	15	16	17	18
PAR									
YARDS									
HDCP									

Directions: Take I 95 to Exit 3 (Westbrook Street). Go East on Westbrook Street (about 3/10 of a mile). Take a left onto Wescott Street. The clubhouse is on the left under Bradts Memorial Library.

Spring Meadows GC

◐◐

Gray, ME (207) 657-2586
www.colefarms.com

Club Pro: Nicholas E. Glicos
Pro Shop: Full inventory
Payment: Most major
Tee Times: Up to 7 days
Fee 9 Holes: Weekday: $20.00
Fee 18 Holes: Weekday: $33.00
Twilight Rates: Yes, after 4 pm
Cart Rental: $13pp/18 $7pp/9
Lessons: $45/30 min **Schools:** Junior
Clinics: Jr., Beg., & Adv. **Day Camps:** Yes
Other: Refurbished barn with banquet facilities seating 220 / Player's Lounge

Tees	Holes	Yards	Par	USGA	Slope
BACK	18	6071	71	71.7	125
MIDDLE	18	5459	71	68.5	119
FRONT	18	4906	71	65.0	108

Weekend: $23.00
Weekend: $36.00
All Day Play: No
Discounts: None
Junior Golf: No **Membership:** Yes
Driving Range: Yes

COUPON

"Excellent greens - a very fair course from tee to green." R.W. 4 sets of tees. Continuous improvement.

	1	2	3	4	5	6	7	8	9
PAR	4	4	5	3	4	3	4	4	4
YARDS	367	283	500	148	341	135	280	367	303
HDCP	5	13	1	15	9	11	17	3	7
	10	11	12	13	14	15	16	17	18
PAR	5	4	4	3	4	5	3	4	4
YARDS	464	340	263	97	268	464	100	388	351
HDCP	6	10	14	16	12	2	18	4	8

Directions: 1 mile from exit 11 off ME Tpk.

4◐ =Excellent 3◐ =Very Good 2◐ =Good

Springbrook GC

Rt. 202, Leeds, ME (207) 946-5900
www.springbrookgolfclub.com

Club Pro: Al Biondi
Pro Shop: Full inventory
Payment: Visa, MC
Tee Times: Weekends, Holidays

Tees	Holes	Yards	Par	USGA	Slope
BACK	18	6408	71	68.1	119
MIDDLE	18	6163	71	64.7	111
FRONT	18	4989	74	61.4	96

Fee 9 Holes: Weekday: $15.00
Fee 18 Holes: Weekday: $22.00 all day
Twilight Rates: Yes, after 5 pm
Cart Rental: $24.00/18 $12.00/9
Lessons: $35.00/30 min **Schools:** No
Clinics: Yes **Day Camps:** No
Weekend: $15.00 after 2pm
Weekend: $25.00 all day
All Day Play: Yes
Discounts: Jrs., Srs., Ladies
Junior Golf: Yes **Membership:** Yes
Driving Range: $2.00 bucket
Other: Clubhouse / Lockers / Showers / Snack bar / Bar-lounge / Discount game cards

Sig. Hole: #15 is a 219 yard, uphill par 3. Very difficult hole. Course has many blind shots. Rolling hills and rough reminiscent of a Scottish style course.

	1	2	3	4	5	6	7	8	9
PAR	4	3	4	4	4	4	5	3	4
YARDS	415	160	410	350	335	385	520	168	340
HDCP	7	17	1	9	13	5	3	15	11

	10	11	12	13	14	15	16	17	18
PAR	4	4	5	3	4	3	5	4	4
YARDS	420	290	460	180	350	210	480	325	365
HDCP	4	18	12	16	14	2	6	10	8

Directions: Maine Turnpike to Lewiston Exit to Route 202 East. Course is 10 miles outside of Lewiston-Auburn.

Sunday River Resort Golf Course

NEW 2004

Bethel, ME (207) 824-4653
www.sundayriver.com

Club Pro: TBA
Pro Shop:
Payment: Visa, MC, Amex, Disc
Tee Times: 7 days adv.

Tees	Holes	Yards	Par	USGA	Slope
BACK	18	6535	72		
MIDDLE	18	6065	72		
FRONT	18	5320	72		

Fee 9 Holes: Weekday: TBA
Fee 18 Holes: Weekday: TBA
Twilight Rates:
Cart Rental:
Lessons: Yes **Schools:** Yes
Clinics: **Day Camps:**
Weekend: TBA
Weekend: TBA
All Day Play:
Discounts: Yes
Junior Golf: **Membership:** Yes
Driving Range: Yes
Other: Log Cabin Clubhouse / Pub / Full Banquet at resort

New Entry 2004. Opening late 2004. Course motto: Beneath the mountains, above the rest. Robert Trent Jones, Jr. design. Each hole has 4 tee boxes. Yardage below is from the champion tees.

	1	2	3	4	5	6	7	8	9
PAR	5	4	4	3	4	3	5	4	4
YARDS	530	410	405	165	465	180	520	440	385
HDCP									

	10	11	12	13	14	15	16	17	18
PAR	4	5	4	4	3	5	3	4	4
YARDS	395	575	450	355	205	520	150	475	435
HDCP									

Directions: Take Route 1 North to I-95N to Maine Turnpike (I-495). Take Maine Tpke (I-495) to exit 11 (Gray). Take Route 26N to Bethel. Follow Route 2E for 2.6 miles. Take Left onto Sunday River Rd. Follow to the fork with Sunday River Ski Resort sign.

Sunset Ridge

Westbrook, ME (207) 854-9463
www.golfmaine.com

Club Pro: Mark Luthe
Pro Shop: Limited inventory
Payment: Visa, MC, Amex, Disc
Tee Times: Yes

Tees	Holes	Yards	Par	USGA	Slope
BACK	9	3100	35	68.6	129
MIDDLE	9	2642	35	64.5	116
FRONT	9	2277	35	64.4	102

Fee 9 Holes: Weekday: $14, $20 w/cart
Fee 18 Holes: Weekday: $20, $31 w/cart
Twilight Rates: No
Cart Rental: $11pp/18 $6pp/9
Lessons: $35.00/half hour **Schools:** Yes
Clinics: Yes **Day Camps:** Yes
Other: Snack Bar / Tennis Courts / Sports / Full Catering & Function Service

Weekend: $16, $22 w/cart, F/S/S
Weekend: $22, $33 w/cart, F/S/S
All Day Play: No
Discounts: 10 Days Play
Junior Golf: Yes **Membership:** Yes
Driving Range: $8/xlg. $6/lg. $5/sm.

COUPON

Sig.Hole: #9, 490 yd. par 5, with two forced carries. Hole can be stretched to almost 600 yards. Construction underway on back nine, opening 2005. Affiliated with sports park, Westerly Winds.

	1	2	3	4	5	6	7	8	9
PAR	4	4	4	3	4	4	3	4	5
YARDS	257	273	287	172	307	312	162	388	490
HDCP	13	7	5	11	9	15	17	3	1
	10	**11**	**12**	**13**	**14**	**15**	**16**	**17**	**18**
PAR									
YARDS									
HDCP									

Directions: Take I-95 to Exit 8. Approximately 5 minutes from Exit 8. Follow signs to course.

The Ledges Golf Club ✪✪✪

York, ME (207) 351-3000
www.ledgesgolf.com

Club Pro: Jack Sullivan, PGA
Pro Shop: Full inventory
Payment: Visa, MC
Tee Times: 7dys. 207-351-3000

Tees	Holes	Yards	Par	USGA	Slope
BACK	18	6981	72	74.0	137
MIDDLE	18	6357	72	71.2	131
FRONT	18	5960	72	69.2	130

Fee 9 Holes: Weekday: N/A
Fee 18 Holes: Weekday: $60.00
Twilight Rates: Yes, after 3 pm
Cart Rental: $15.00 pp
Lessons: Yes **Schools:** No
Clinics: Yes **Day Camps:** No
Other: Bar-Lounge / Lodging partner

Weekend: N/A
Weekend: $65.00
All Day Play: No
Discounts: None
Junior Golf: No **Membership:** Yes
Driving Range: $5.00/lg. $3.00/sm.

Players' Comments: " A difficult beautiful course." " Great staff" "Well manicured." " None better in Southern Maine." "Annual stop." Takes full advantage of natural terrain.

	1	2	3	4	5	6	7	8	9
PAR	4	4	4	5	3	4	5	3	4
YARDS	405	313	344	542	148	391	493	196	333
HDCP	4	14	8	6	18	2	10	16	12
	10	**11**	**12**	**13**	**14**	**15**	**16**	**17**	**18**
PAR	4	3	5	4	3	4	4	4	5
YARDS	388	179	470	356	131	315	377	429	547
HDCP	9	15	5	11	17	13	7	3	1

Directions: Take Route 95 North to Exit 4 in Maine. Take right to Route 1S. In 1 mile take Route 91 for 5.1 miles Club on right. Call for directions from Route 95 South.

4✪ =Excellent **3✪** =Very Good **2✪** =Good

The Links at Outlook

co ▶ 51

South Berwick, ME (207) 384-4653
www.outlookgolf.com

Tees	Holes	Yards	Par	USGA	Slope
BACK	18	6425	71	70.2	125
MIDDLE	18	6004	71	68.3	121
FRONT	18	5492	71	68.3	115

Club Pro: Dave Paskowski
Pro Shop: Yes
Payment: Cash, Visa, MC
Tee Times: 7 days adv.
Fee 9 Holes: Weekday: $25.00 (M-Thur)
Fee 18 Holes: Weekday: $43.00 (M-Thur)
Twilight Rates: Yes, after 3 pm, $40 w/cart
Cart Rental: $13pp
Lessons: $40/30min **Schools:** Adult
Clinics: Junior **Day Camps:** No
Other: The Medalist Golf School & The Grille Room

Weekend: $30 after 2pm (9Holes)
Weekend: $50.00
All Day Play: Yes
Discounts: Sr. Mon. & Tues. only
Junior Golf: Yes **Membership:** Yes
Driving Range: grass tees w/ target greens

COUPON

Player's Comment: "Challenges beginners to perform better. Great staff." "Golf In The Scottish Tradition." New bunkers added on 3 holes.

	1	2	3	4	5	6	7	8	9
PAR	5	4	3	5	4	4	4	3	4
YARDS	481	396	162	453	316	317	310	190	314
HDCP	3	1	9	7	17	13	15	5	11

	10	11	12	13	14	15	16	17	18
PAR	4	3	4	4	3	4	4	5	4
YARDS	331	138	224	322	123	344	340	415	316
HDCP	4	14	16	12	18	6	8	2	10

Directions: From Boston: I-95 N to Exit 3, S. Berwick. Right on Rte. 236. Follow 11 mi. to end and take right. After 1/4 mi., take right onto Rte. 4. Course is 1 mi. up on right. From Portland: I-95 S to Exit 2, Wells/Sanford. Take right past toll booths. Take next left onto Rte. 9. Follow Rte. 4 into S. Berwick. Course on left.

NEW 2004

Toddy Brook Golf Course

▶ 52

North Yarmouth, ME (207) 829-5100

Tees	Holes	Yards	Par	USGA	Slope
BACK	9	3003	36	69.1	133
MIDDLE	9	2717	36	67.0	124
FRONT	9	2179	36	65.0	119

Club Pro: N/A
Pro Shop: Full inventory
Payment: Visa, MC, Amex, Disc
Tee Times:
Fee 9 Holes: Weekday: $17.00
Fee 18 Holes: Weekday: $28.00
Twilight Rates: After 5:30 pm
Cart Rental: $12/18, $8/9
Lessons: Schools:
Clinics: Day Camps:
Other: Restaurant / Clubhouse / Lockers / Showers / Bar-Lounge

Weekend: $22.00
Weekend: $32.00
All Day Play: No
Discounts: SR. & JR (Tue/Thur)
Junior Golf: Membership:
Driving Range: Yes

COUPON

New Entry 2004. Beautiful layout with challenging tees. Each hole has unique design with plenty of sand & water to test your skills. Combination of back, middle and front for 18 hole play.

	1	2	3	4	5	6	7	8	9
PAR	4	4	4	4	3	5	3	4	5
YARDS	320	275	360	320	125	427	155	280	455
HDCP	12	16	4	2	18	6	10	14	8

	10	11	12	13	14	15	16	17	18
PAR									
YARDS									
HDCP									

Directions: Take I-95 to Yarmouth Exit. Follow ____ Route 1 to RT-115 Exit. Take 115 West about 1/4 mile to Sligo Road on Right. Go Approx. 3 1/8 mi. WE are on the right side of the road.

Turner Highland Golf Course

Turner, ME (207) 224-7060

Club Pro: Ron Bibeau
Pro Shop: Full inventory
Payment: Yes
Tee Times: Yes
Fee 9 Holes: Weekday: $15.00
Fee 18 Holes: Weekday: $25.00
Twilight Rates: No
Cart Rental: $20/18, $12/9
Lessons: $60/ 1 hour **Schools:** No
Clinics: No **Day Camps:** No
Other: Lockers, showers, snack bar, restaurant.

Tees	Holes	Yards	Par	USGA	Slope
BACK					
MIDDLE	18	6033	71	68.6	115
FRONT	18	4705	71	67.5	113

Weekend: $15.00
Weekend: $25.00
All Day Play:
Discounts: None
Junior Golf: No **Membership:** Yes
Driving Range: $2/bucket

COUPON

Now 18 holes. A scenic golf course situated high on a hill. "A well maintained local popular favorite." S.R.

	1	2	3	4	5	6	7	8	9
PAR	4	5	4	3	4	5	4	3	4
YARDS	280	442	282	149	365	452	372	204	376
HDCP	14	12	16	18	2	4	10	6	8
	10	11	12	13	14	15	16	17	18
PAR	3	4	4	4	5	3	5	4	3
YARDS	135	365	370	430	592	125	500	387	182
HDCP	17	7	13	1	3	15	11	5	9

Directions: Exit 12 from I-95 towards Auburn. Get onto Route 4 North. Turn right onto Route 117. Stay on Route 117 for 8.5 miles. Course is on the right.

Twin Falls Golf Course

364 Spring St., Westbrook, ME (207) 854-5397

Club Pro: No
Pro Shop: Limited inventory
Payment: Cash, Credit, Debit
Tee Times: No
Fee 9 Holes: Weekday: $15.00
Fee 18 Holes: Weekday: $15.00
Twilight Rates: Yes, after 5 pm
Cart Rental: $18.00/18 $10.00/9
Lessons: No **Schools:** No
Clinics: No **Day Camps:** No
Other: Clubhouse / Snack bar

Tees	Holes	Yards	Par	USGA	Slope
BACK					
MIDDLE	18	4880	66	61.3	90
FRONT					

Weekend: $18.00
Weekend: $18.00
All Day Play: No
Discounts: Senior Wkdays
Junior Golf: No **Membership:** Yes
Driving Range: No

Redesign with 3 new holes, 2 new par 4 and 1 par 5 opened 2003. "Fine public course for beginners... Keep your drive on #1 to the left of center as the brook hidden from view will come into play." A.P.

	1	2	3	4	5	6	7	8	9
PAR	4	3	3	4	4	3	4	4	4
YARDS	364	165	137	374	408	185	248	301	258
HDCP	1	15	17	3	5	13	11	7	9
	10	11	12	13	14	15	16	17	18
PAR	4	3	3	4	4	3	4	4	4
YARDS	364	165	137	374	408	185	248	301	258
HDCP	2	16	18	4	6	14	12	8	10

Directions: Take I-95 to Exit 7, follow Maine Mall Rd. to Spring Street to course.

S
ME

4🟢 =Excellent 3🟢 =Very Good 2🟢 =Good

Val Halla Golf Course

Cumberland, ME (207) 829-2225
www.valhallagolf.com

Club Pro: Jim Nickerson, Head Pro.
Pro Shop: Full inventory
Payment: Visa, MC
Tee Times: Yes
Fee 9 Holes: Weekday: $18.00
Fee 18 Holes: Weekday: $27.00
Twilight Rates: Wknds after 4 pm
Cart Rental: $15/18 $8.75/9
Lessons: $30.00/30 minutes **Schools:** No
Clinics: Yes **Day Camps:** No
Other: Snack bar / Lounge

Tees	Holes	Yards	Par	USGA	Slope
BACK	18	6567	72	71.1	126
MIDDLE	18	6201	72	69.3	122
FRONT	18	5437	72	71.4	120

Weekend: $20.00 after 4 pm
Weekend: $30.00
All Day Play: N/R
Discounts: Senior & Junior
Junior Golf: Yes **Membership:** Yes
Driving Range: $3.00/ bucket

Consistently rated one of Maine's best public championship 18 holes. Bent grass, good shape, wooded, hilly, scenic, brooks and streams, excellent layout. Open April 15 - November 1.

	1	2	3	4	5	6	7	8	9
PAR	4	3	5	4	4	4	4	3	5
YARDS	350	142	553	383	394	340	369	175	484
HDCP	16	18	2	4	6	12	10	14	8
	10	**11**	**12**	**13**	**14**	**15**	**16**	**17**	**18**
PAR	4	4	3	5	5	4	4	3	4
YARDS	376	347	148	465	440	388	294	155	398
HDCP	7	11	13	9	5	1	15	17	3

Directions: From Portland take 295 N to Exit 10. Follow Route 9 to Cumberland Center. The course is off Greely Road on Val Halla Road.

Wawenock CC

Rt. 129, Walpole, ME (207) 563-3938

Club Pro: Leon Oliver, PGA
Pro Shop: Yes
Payment: MC, Visa
Tee Times: July - August
Fee 9 Holes: Weekday: $22.00
Fee 18 Holes: Weekday: $32.00
Twilight Rates: No
Cart Rental: $25.00/18 $20.00/9
Lessons: $35/half hour **Schools:** No
Clinics: Ladies/Juniors **Day Camps:** No
Other: Clubhouse / Bar-Lounge / Snack bar / Showers

Tees	Holes	Yards	Par	USGA	Slope
BACK					
MIDDLE	9	6112	70	69.0	120
FRONT					

Weekend: $22.00
Weekend: $32.00
All Day Play: No
Discounts: Jrs. 1/2 price
Junior Golf: Yes **Membership:** Yes
Driving Range: Yes, Irons only

A fine nine hole tract in the Boothbay Region. Fairly open, but challenging with small greens and hills. Open May - October. Seasonal and non-seasonal rates.

	1	2	3	4	5	6	7	8	9
PAR	4	4	3	5	4	4	4	3	4
YARDS	330	339	235	527	412	294	357	134	368
HDCP	13	3	5	7	1	15	11	17	9
	10	**11**	**12**	**13**	**14**	**15**	**16**	**17**	**18**
PAR	4	4	3	5	4	4	4	3	4
YARDS	330	399	235	527	412	294	357	134	368
HDCP	14	4	6	8	2	16	12	18	10

Directions: Take Route 1 to Route 129; follow for 7 miles.

Western View Golf Club

Augusta, ME (207) 622-5309

Club Pro: Peter Matthews, PGA
Pro Shop: Full inventory
Payment: Visa, MC, Amex, Disc
Tee Times: No
Fee 9 Holes: Weekday: $12.00
Fee 18 Holes: Weekday: $20.00
Twilight Rates: No
Cart Rental: $10pp/18 $7pp/9
Lessons: $25/30 min. **Schools:** No
Clinics: Yes **Day Camps:** No
Other: Snack bar / Clubhouse / Lounge / Restaurant

Tees	Holes	Yards	Par	USGA	Slope
BACK					
MIDDLE	9	5410	70	64.5	107
FRONT	9	5012	72	68.0	110

Weekend: $12.00
Weekend: $20.00
All Day Play: Yes
Discounts: Junior Membership
Junior Golf: Yes **Membership:** Yes
Driving Range: $3.00/bucket

COUPON

Now fully irrigated: tees, greens, fairways

	1	2	3	4	5	6	7	8	9
PAR	4	3	4	3	5	4	4	4	4
YARDS	305	180	260	150	445	315	285	385	375
HDCP	7	15	13	17	1	11	9	3	5
	10	11	12	13	14	15	16	17	18
PAR	4	3	4	3	5	4	4	4	4
YARDS	305	180	260	150	445	315	285	385	375
HDCP	8	16	14	18	2	12	10	4	6

Directions: Located 4 miles from Augusta on Route 3. From Route 95, take Exit 30 East. Go to rotary, follow signs to Route 3. At 2nd rotary follow signs to Route 3. Take Route 3 for about 4 miles to Bolton Hill Road.

Willowdale Golf Club

Scarborough, ME (207)883-9351
www.willowdalegolf.com

Club Pro:
Pro Shop: Limited inventory
Payment: Visa, Amex, MC, Disc, Checks
Tee Times: 3 days prior for wknds.
Fee 9 Holes: Weekday: $17.00
Fee 18 Holes: Weekday: $28.00
Twilight Rates: After 4 pm
Cart Rental: $24.00/18, $14.00/9
Lessons: Schools: No
Clinics: No **Day Camps:** No
Other: Clubhouse / Snack Bar / Showers

Tees	Holes	Yards	Par	USGA	Slope
BACK	18	5881	70	67.7	115
MIDDLE					
FRONT	18	5049	70	68.9	116

Weekend: $19.00
Weekend: $30.00
All Day Play: No
Discounts: Junior Memberships
Junior Golf: No **Membership:** Yes
Driving Range: No

Sig. Hole: #5 is a beautiful, 195 yard par 3. Water on one side, tree-lined on the other. Difficult shot for a par 3. Twilight rates offered 7 days a week. Pitching and putting green available.

	1	2	3	4	5	6	7	8	9
PAR	4	5	4	4	3	4	3	4	4
YARDS	357	487	386	349	197	367	163	342	325
HDCP	8	10	2	4	6	12	14	16	18
	10	11	12	13	14	15	16	17	18
PAR	4	3	4	4	4	3	4	4	5
YARDS	393	185	367	382	280	150	374	288	489
HDCP	1	9	5	3	15	13	7	17	11

Directions: Exit 6 off Maine Turnpike. US 95 to Route1. Turn left onto Route. 1 North,. First light turn right. 1/4 mi.

4❂ =Excellent **3❂** = Very Good **2❂** = Good

Wilson Lake CC

Weld Rd., Wilton, ME (207) 645-2016
golf@wlcc.com

Club Pro: Gavin Kane, PGA
Pro Shop: Limited inventory
Payment: Visa, MC
Tee Times: Weekends
Fee 9 Holes: Weekday: $12.00
Fee 18 Holes: Weekday: $20.00
Twilight Rates: 4 pm wkdays
Cart Rental: $20/18 $12/9
Lessons: Yes **Schools:** No
Clinics: Ladies/Juniors **Day Camps:** Yes
Other: Clubhouse / Bar-Lounge / Snack bar / Lockers / Showers

Tees	Holes	Yards	Par	USGA	Slope
BACK	9	6159	70	68.8	117
MIDDLE	9	6044	70	68.8	117
FRONT	9	5614	74	71.9	119

Weekend: $12.00
Weekend: $20.00
All Day Play: Yes
Discounts: None
Junior Golf: Yes **Membership:** Yes
Driving Range: No

Noted for having some of the best greens in the state. Hole #11, 210 yards is one of the toughest par 3's in the state.

	1	2	3	4	5	6	7	8	9
PAR	4	3	5	4	4	4	3	4	4
YARDS	399	159	501	406	364	379	135	327	352
HDCP	10	16	4	2	8	6	18	14	12

	10	11	12	13	14	15	16	17	18
PAR	4	3	5	4	4	4	3	4	4
YARDS	399	210	501	406	364	379	135	327	352
HDCP	9	15	3	1	7	5	17	13	11

Directions: Take Route 4 to Route 2 to Route 156 into Wilton. Course is on Weld Rd. in Wilton.

CHAPTER 7

Northern Maine

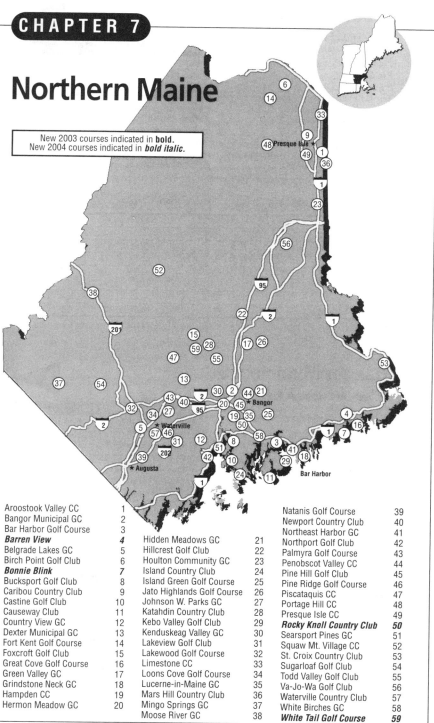

New 2003 courses indicated in **bold**.
New 2004 courses indicated in ***bold italic***.

Aroostook Valley CC	1
Bangor Municipal GC	2
Bar Harbor Golf Course	3
Barren View	***4***
Belgrade Lakes GC	5
Birch Point Golf Club	6
Bonnie Blink	***7***
Bucksport Golf Club	8
Caribou Country Club	9
Castine Golf Club	10
Causeway Club	11
Country View GC	12
Dexter Municipal GC	13
Fort Kent Golf Course	14
Foxcroft Golf Club	15
Great Cove Golf Course	16
Green Valley GC	17
Grindstone Neck GC	18
Hampden CC	19
Hermon Meadow GC	20

Hidden Meadows GC	21
Hillcrest Golf Club	22
Houlton Community GC	23
Island Country Club	24
Island Green Golf Course	25
Jato Highlands Golf Course	26
Johnson W. Parks GC	27
Katahdin Country Club	28
Kebo Valley Golf Club	29
Kenduskeag Valley GC	30
Lakeview Golf Club	31
Lakewood Golf Course	32
Limestone CC	33
Loons Cove Golf Course	34
Lucerne-in-Maine GC	35
Mars Hill Country Club	36
Mingo Springs GC	37
Moose River GC	38

Natanis Golf Course	39
Newport Country Club	40
Northeast Harbor GC	41
Northport Golf Club	42
Palmyra Golf Course	43
Penobscot Valley CC	44
Pine Hill Golf Club	45
Pine Ridge Golf Course	46
Piscataquis CC	47
Portage Hill CC	48
Presque Isle CC	49
Rocky Knoll Country Club	***50***
Searsport Pines GC	51
Squaw Mt. Village CC	52
St. Croix Country Club	53
Sugarloaf Golf Club	54
Todd Valley Golf Club	55
Va-Jo-Wa Golf Club	56
Waterville Country Club	57
White Birches GC	58
White Tail Golf Course	***59***

Aroostook Valley CC

Russell Rd., Ft. Fairfield, ME (207) 476-8083
www.intellis.net/avcc

Club Pro: Steven Leitch, PGA
Pro Shop: Yes
Payment: Visa, MC
Tee Times: Weekends, 2 days adv.

Tees	Holes	Yards	Par	USGA	Slope
BACK	18	6304	72	69.6	117
MIDDLE	18	5957	72	68.4	113
FRONT	18	5373	72	74.1	119

Fee 9 Holes: Weekday: $16.00
Fee 18 Holes: Weekday: $30.00
Twilight Rates: No
Cart Rental: $24.00/18 $13.00/9
Lessons: $20.00/half hour **Schools:** No
Clinics: Yes **Day Camps:** No
Other: Clubhouse / Snack bar / Bar-lounge / Lockers / Showers

Weekend: $16.00
Weekend: $30.00
All Day Play: Yes
Discounts: Junior
Junior Golf: Yes **Membership:** Yes
Driving Range: $2.00/sm. bucket

Rated 3 & 1/2 stars by *Golf Digest*. Very beautiful course; difficult inclines on back 9 make it challenging.

	1	2	3	4	5	6	7	8	9
PAR	4	4	5	3	5	4	4	3	4
YARDS	375	327	478	132	440	308	334	139	365
HDCP	1	13	7	15	3	9	11	17	5
	10	11	12	13	14	15	16	17	18
PAR	4	4	5	3	5	3	4	3	5
YARDS	382	322	489	189	510	156	383	134	494
HDCP	6	16	4	12	8	14	2	18	10

Directions: Take I-95 to last exit; take right onto Route 1 to Ft. Fairfield, cross bridge. Take first right. Follow Russell Road to course.

Bangor Municipal GC

Webster Ave., Bangor, ME (207) 941-0232

Club Pro: Brian Enman
Pro Shop: Full inventory
Payment: Cash, Visa, MC
Tee Times: Weekends, Holidays

Tees	Holes	Yards	Par	USGA	Slope
BACK	18	6345	71	69.2	115
MIDDLE	18	6150	71	67.9	112
FRONT	18	5172	71	69.1	111

Fee 9 Holes: Weekday: $12.00
Fee 18 Holes: Weekday: $24.00
Twilight Rates: Yes, after 4 pm
Cart Rental: $22.00/18 $11.00/9
Lessons: $40.00/45 minutes **Schools:** Yes
Clinics: Yes **Day Camps:** Yes
Other: Restaurant / Clubhouse / Bar-Lounge

Weekend: $13.00
Weekend: $27.00
All Day Play: No
Discounts: Yes
Junior Golf: Yes **Membership:** Yes
Driving Range: $3.50/lg. bucket

27 holes includes a 9 hole course with 3215 yards, par 36, USGA rating 69.6 / slope, 128. New sand in all bunkers. Hosted USGA Public Links Championship,.

	1	2	3	4	5	6	7	8	9
PAR	4	4	3	5	4	3	4	4	4
YARDS	335	395	165	530	330	200	400	410	415
HDCP	11	7	17	9	13	15	3	1	5
	10	11	12	13	14	15	16	17	18
PAR	4	3	4	4	4	5	3	4	5
YARDS	400	200	400	315	410	470	165	340	480
HDCP	6	16	2	10	4	14	18	8	12

Directions: Take I-95 North to Exit 46 (Hammond St.). Follow highway signs. Course is on left.

Bar Harbor Golf Course ✪✪ ▶ 3

Rt. 204, Trenton, ME (207) 667-7505
www.barharborgolfcourse.com

Club Pro: No
Pro Shop: Full inventory
Payment: Visa, MC
Tee Times: No
Fee 9 Holes: Weekday: $28.00
Fee 18 Holes: Weekday: $50.00
Twilight Rates: 5 pm, Wed./ Thu.
Cart Rental: $30.00/18 $15.00/9
Lessons: $20.00/half hour **Schools:** No
Clinics: Yes **Day Camps:** No
Other: Clubhouse / Snack bar / Bar-lounge

Weekend: $28.00
Weekend: $50.00
All Day Play: No
Discounts: None
Junior Golf: No **Membership:** $595
Driving Range: Yes

Tees	Holes	Yards	Par	USGA	Slope
BACK	18	6680	71	71.1	125
MIDDLE	18	6450	71	69.8	121
FRONT	18	5428	73	70.4	115

COUPON

One of the best kept secrets in the state. Links-style tract was designed by Phil Wogan. Located adjacent to the ocean, it is very challenging.

	1	2	3	4	5	6	7	8	9
PAR	4	3	4	5	4	4	4	3	5
YARDS	428	155	295	589	374	318	405	158	544
HDCP	7	17	16	6	9	18	3	14	2

	10	11	12	13	14	15	16	17	18
PAR	4	4	5	3	4	4	4	3	4
YARDS	427	388	520	156	402	408	368	172	343
HDCP	1	5	11	13	4	8	12	10	15

Directions: Take Route 3 to Bar Harbor. Course is located at intersection of Route 3 and Route 204 in Trenton.

Barren View ▶ 4 NEW 2004

Rt. 1, Jonesboro, ME (207) 734-6531
www.barrenview.com

Club Pro: No
Pro Shop: Limited inventory
Payment:
Tee Times: Open
Fee 9 Holes: Weekday: $10.00, M-Th
Fee 18 Holes: Weekday: $18.00
Twilight Rates:
Cart Rental: $20/18, $12/9
Lessons: Yes **Schools:**
Clinics: **Day Camps:**
Other:

Weekend: $12.00 F/S/S/H
Weekend: $20.00
All Day Play: $23 M-Th
Discounts:
Junior Golf: **Membership:** Yes
Driving Range: $3.00/ bucket

Tees	Holes	Yards	Par	USGA	Slope
BACK	9	2741	34	64.9	112
MIDDLE	9	2613	34	64.9	112
FRONT	9	2321	34	64.9	112

COUPON

N ME

New Entry 2004. Links style course for all levels. Opened June, 2003.

	1	2	3	4	5	6	7	8	9
PAR	4	3	5	3	3	4	4	4	4
YARDS	369	129	406	201	143	280	292	361	430
HDCP	5	17	1	13	15	11	9	7	3

	10	11	12	13	14	15	16	17	18
PAR									
YARDS									
HDCP									

Directions: I-95N to I-395E to Route 1A . Exit towards Bar Harbor/ Ellsworth. Take Route 1 out of Ellsworth towards Machais. Course is on right.

Belgrade Lakes GC ✪✪✪✪ ▶ 5

Belgrade Lakes, ME 207-495-GOLF
www.belgradelakesgolf.com

Tees	Holes	Yards	Par	USGA	Slope
BACK	18	6640	71	71.6	142
MIDDLE	18	6138	71	68.4	133
FRONT	18	4881	71	67.6	117

Club Pro: No
Pro Shop: Yes
Payment: Visa, MC, Amex
Tee Times: 7 days adv.
Fee 9 Holes: Weekday:
Fee 18 Holes: Weekday: $100.00 in season
Twilight Rates: No
Cart Rental: $20pp/18
Lessons: Yes **Schools:** No
Clinics: Yes **Day Camps:** No
Other: Snack Bar

Weekend:
Weekend: $100.00 in season
All Day Play: Replay policy
Discounts: Junior
Junior Golf: Yes **Membership:** No
Driving Range: Hitting Net

2003 Top 100 Public Courses noted by *Golf Digest*. **Player's Comment:** "Every hole different and spectacularly beautiful." Improvements: enlarged and lengthened several tees. Walking encouraged. Caddies available.

	1	2	3	4	5	6	7	8	9
PAR	4	3	5	4	3	5	4	3	4
YARDS	413	152	470	372	156	476	370	175	366
HDCP	16	18	10	6	8	4	12	14	2
	10	**11**	**12**	**13**	**14**	**15**	**16**	**17**	**18**
PAR	4	4	5	3	4	4	5	3	4
YARDS	350	397	519	190	335	312	530	160	361
HDCP	15	9	1	7	13	17	3	11	5

Directions: 95 North. Take Exit 31B. Turn right on to Route 27. Go for 12 miles to town of Belgrade Lakes. Turn left at the Sunset Grille onto West Road. Course is 1/4 mile on left.

Birch Point Golf Club ▶ 6

Madawaska, ME (207) 895-6957

Tees	Holes	Yards	Par	USGA	Slope
BACK	9	2955	35		
MIDDLE	9	2760	35		
FRONT	9	2565	36		

Club Pro: Larry Plourde
Pro Shop: Full inventory
Payment: Credit card, check, cash
Tee Times: No
Fee 9 Holes: Weekday: $12.00
Fee 18 Holes: Weekday: $18.00
Twilight Rates: N/R
Cart Rental: $15.00/18 $10.00/9
Lessons: Yes **Schools:** N/R
Clinics: No **Day Camps:** No
Other: Bar-lounge / Restaurant / Indoor Simulator

Weekend: $12.00
Weekend: $18.00
All Day Play: N/R
Discounts: Junior
Junior Golf: No **Membership:** Yes
Driving Range: $2.00/bucket

COUPON

Very pretty course located next to Long Lake.

	1	2	3	4	5	6	7	8	9
PAR	4	4	4	4	3	4	5	4	3
YARDS	265	345	395	290	160	385	475	290	155
HDCP	9	2	1	5	4	6	7	8	3
	10	**11**	**12**	**13**	**14**	**15**	**16**	**17**	**18**
PAR									
YARDS									
HDCP									

Directions: Take Route 1 North to Madawaska. Left on Beauliew Rd. Take Birch Point Rd. to course.

Bonnie Blink

7 ▶

Sorrento, ME (207) 422-3930
www.groupstart.msn.com/sorrentoyachtclub

Club Pro: None
Pro Shop: No
Payment:
Tee Times:
Fee 9 Holes: Weekday: $18 M-F All Day
Fee 18 Holes: Weekday:
Twilight Rates: No
Cart Rental: None
Lessons: Schools:
Clinics: Day Camps:
Other:

Weekend:
Weekend: $25
All Day Play: Yes
Discounts:
Junior Golf: Membership: Yes
Driving Range:

Tees	Holes	Yards	Par	USGA	Slope
BACK					
MIDDLE	9	2520	36	65	112
FRONT					

New Entry 2004. **Player's comment:** "Undiscovered gem.Breath taking views, right on the ocean." Sorrento VIA Yacht Club members onlyFri. morn. until noon and Wed. twilight members' league at 5pm.

	1	2	3	4	5	6	7	8	9
PAR	4	4	3	5	5	4	3	4	4
YARDS	350	270	180	510	490	310	120	290	330
HDCP									
	10	11	12	13	14	15	16	17	18
PAR									
YARDS									
HDCP									

Directions: 48 miles from Bangor, Route alt.1 to Ellsworth (23 miles). Stay on Route 1 to Hancock, then in Sullivan. Go right at convenience store. Turn left at next intersection. Golf Course is on left.

Bucksport Golf Club

8 ▶

Rt. 49, Bucksport, ME (207) 469-7612

Club Pro: Wayne Hand, PGA
Pro Shop: Full inventory
Payment: Visa, MC
Tee Times: No
Fee 9 Holes: Weekday: $15.00
Fee 18 Holes: Weekday: $20.00 all day
Twilight Rates: No
Cart Rental: $26.00/18 $13.00/9
Lessons: Yes **Schools:** No
Clinics: Yes **Day Camps:** Yes
Other: Bar-Lounge / Snack bar / Lockers / Showers

Weekend: $15.00 all day
Weekend: $20.00 all day
All Day Play: Yes
Discounts: Junior
Junior Golf: Yes **Membership:** Yes
Driving Range: $4.00/lg. $3.00/sm.

Tees	Holes	Yards	Par	USGA	Slope
BACK	9	7200	74	72.5	
MIDDLE	9	6600	74	72.5	136
FRONT	9	5972	74	72.2	128

N
ME

Improvements include tee to green irrigation. Nine holes with two sets of tees. Natural state of land emphasized in redesign.

	1	2	3	4	5	6	7	8	9
PAR	4	5	3	4	5	3	4	4	5
YARDS	330	500	147	407	504	163	408	354	560
HDCP	13	7	17	9	3	15	5	11	1
	10	11	12	13	14	15	16	17	18
PAR	4	5	3	4	5	3	4	4	5
YARDS	360	454	161	397	495	200	400	340	600
HDCP	14	8	18	10	4	16	6	12	2

Directions: From Augusta: Route 3 to Belfast. Route 1 North to Bucksport. From Bangor: Take Route 46 to Route 1 or 1A. Course is 3 miles from Down town Bucksport.

4✪ =Excellent 3✪ =Very Good 2✪ =Good

Caribou Country Club

9

Caribou, ME (207) 493-3933

Club Pro: Ron Matlock
Pro Shop: Full inventory
Payment: Visa, MC, Amex, Disc
Tee Times: No
Fee 9 Holes: Weekday: $12.00
Fee 18 Holes: Weekday: $18.00
Twilight Rates: No
Cart Rental: $20.00/18 $15.00/9
Lessons: Yes **Schools:** No
Clinics: No **Day Camps:** No
Other: Restaurant / Clubhouse / Bar-lounge / Snack Bar / Lockers / Showers

Weekend: $12.00
Weekend: $18.00
All Day Play: No
Discounts: Junior memberships
Junior Golf: Yes **Membership:** Yes
Driving Range: $4/lg $2.50/sm

Tees	Holes	Yards	Par	USGA	Slope
BACK					
MIDDLE	9	6429	72	69.0	124
FRONT	9	5631	72	69.6	116

COUPON

The course has a beautiful log cabin clubhouse. 9 hole layout with two sets of tees. Rates may change. Open May 1 - October 15.

	1	2	3	4	5	6	7	8	9
PAR	4	5	3	4	4	4	3	5	4
YARDS	340	515	195	330	360	340	150	530	400
HDCP	14	4	16	12	9	10	18	2	6
	10	11	12	13	14	15	16	17	18
PAR	4	4	3	4	4	4	3	5	5
YARDS	360	408	215	345	411	330	170	550	480
HDCP	13	3	15	11	8	7	17	17	5

Directions: Take Route 161 North; follow 1 1/2 miles outside Caribou; course is on right side.

Castine Golf Club

10

Battle Ave., Castine, ME (207) 326-8844

Club Pro: Paul Dailey, PGA
Pro Shop: Full inventory
Payment: Cash only
Tee Times: No
Fee 9 Holes: Weekday: $18.00
Fee 18 Holes: Weekday: $30.00
Twilight Rates: Yes, after 4 pm
Cart Rental: $25.00/18 $15.00/9
Lessons: $50/45 min. **Schools:** No
Clinics: Yes **Day Camps:** No
Other: Clubhouse - Members only

Weekend: $18.00
Weekend: $30.00
All Day Play: $30
Discounts: Junior
Junior Golf: Yes **Membership:** Yes
Driving Range: No

Tees	Holes	Yards	Par	USGA	Slope
BACK	N/A				
MIDDLE	9	5954	70	68.1	116
FRONT	9	5458	72	71.4	122

Semi private. Small greens, hilly terrain and contour mowed rough challenge all levels of players.

	1	2	3	4	5	6	7	8	9
PAR	4	3	4	3	4	4	5	4	4
YARDS	400	175	397	146	376	344	465	316	358
HDCP	3	15	1	17	5	9	7	13	11
	10	11	12	13	14	15	16	17	18
PAR	4	3	4	3	4	4	5	4	4
YARDS	400	175	397	146	376	344	465	316	358
HDCP	4	16	2	18	6	10	8	14	12

Directions: Route 1 & 3 through Bucksport. Turn right onto Route 175 to Route 166. Course is on right.

Causeway Club

Fernald Rd., S.W. Harbor, ME (207) 244-3780

Club Pro: Dan Granholm
Pro Shop: Full inventory
Payment: Visa, MC
Tee Times: No
Fee 9 Holes: Weekday: $40.00
Fee 18 Holes: Weekday: $40.00
Twilight Rates: Yes, after 4:30 pm
Cart Rental: $25.00/18 $13.00/9
Lessons: $25/45 min. **Schools:** No
Clinics: Yes **Day Camps:** Yes
Other: Clubhouse / Lockers / Snacks

Tees	Holes	Yards	Par	USGA	Slope
BACK					
MIDDLE	9	4718	65	60.9	95
FRONT	9	4170	64	63.9	102

Weekend: $40.00
Weekend: $41.00
All Day Play: Yes
Discounts: Junior
Junior Golf: Yes **Membership:** Yes
Driving Range: No

Located on S.W. Harbor with scenic views. Closed to public after 6:30 p.m.

	1	2	3	4	5	6	7	8	9
PAR	4	4	4	4	4	3	3	3	3
YARDS	390	270	298	278	390	140	228	175	133
HDCP	4	12	11	17	2	16	5	7	15
	10	11	12	13	14	15	16	17	18
PAR	4	4	4	4	4	3	4	3	3
YARDS	402	305	310	262	392	158	266	178	143
HDCP	3	9	10	18	1	13	8	6	14

Directions: Take I-95 to ALT Route 1 to Ellsworth. Follow Route 3 to Mt. Desert Island. Take Route 102 to Southwest Harbor.

Country View GC

Rt. 7, Brooks, ME (207) 722-3161
www.countryviewgc.com

Club Pro: No
Pro Shop: Yes
Payment: Most major
Tee Times: No
Fee 9 Holes: Weekday: $15.00
Fee 18 Holes: Weekday: $22.00
Twilight Rates: No
Cart Rental: $10.00/9
Lessons: Yes **Schools:** Yes
Clinics: No **Day Camps:** No
Other: Snack bar

Tees	Holes	Yards	Par	USGA	Slope
BACK	9	3000	36		115
MIDDLE	9	2885	36		115
FRONT	9	2480	36		105

Weekend: $15.00
Weekend: $22.00
All Day Play: Yes, $30.00
Discounts: None
Junior Golf: No **Membership:** Yes
Driving Range: Yes

COUPON

Sig. Hole: #6, par 4, 500 yards, high elevated tee, beautiful view, dog leg water on left and right.

	1	2	3	4	5	6	7	8	9
PAR	4	4	5	3	4	5	4	4	3
YARDS	330	335	450	125	345	480	340	335	145
HDCP	3	13	9	15	7	5	11	1	17
	10	11	12	13	14	15	16	17	18
PAR									
YARDS									
HDCP									

Directions: Take Route 1 to Route 137 North, take right onto Route 7. Course is 1 mile north of Brooks, on Route 7.

4✪ =Excellent 3✪ =Very Good 2✪ =Good

Dexter Municipal GC ●● ▶13

Sunrise Ave., Dexter, ME (207) 924-6477

Tees	Holes	Yards	Par	USGA	Slope
BACK	9	5281	70	65.7	115
MIDDLE	9	5241	70	65.7	115
FRONT	9	4784	70		

Club Pro: Gary R. Rees, PGA
Pro Shop: Full inventory
Payment: Cash or checks only
Tee Times: No
Fee 9 Holes: Weekday: $12.00 all day
Fee 18 Holes: Weekday: $12.00 all day
Twilight Rates: Yes, after 5 pm
Cart Rental: $19.00/18 $11.00/9
Lessons: Yes **Schools:** Yes
Clinics: Yes **Day Camps:** No
Other: Clubhouse / Snack bar

Weekend: $15.00 all day
Weekend: $15.00 all day
All Day Play: Yes
Discounts: Junior
Junior Golf: Yes **Membership:** Yes
Driving Range: Yes

Not too long, but full of challenges. Lots of hills and ponds - fun course to play. High School Golf State Champions 2001 and 2002. Open April 15 - October 15.

	1	2	3	4	5	6	7	8	9
PAR	4	4	4	4	3	4	4	3	5
YARDS	275	285	338	242	173	260	390	179	444
HDCP	17	9	11	7	13	5	1	3	5

	10	11	12	13	14	15	16	17	18
PAR	4	4	4	4	3	4	4	3	5
YARDS	305	290	340	248	180	265	395	184	448
HDCP	12	14	10	8	16	6	2	4	18

Directions: From I-95 Exit 39, take Route 7 to Dexter (14 miles.) Left at Liberty Street, follow to end. Go left, course is second driveway on right.

Fort Kent Golf Course ▶14

Fort Kent, ME (207) 834-3149

Tees	Holes	Yards	Par	USGA	Slope
BACK					
MIDDLE	9	6367	71	69.0	111
FRONT	9	5361	72	69.0	111

Club Pro: Kelly O'Leary, PGA
Pro Shop: Full inventory
Payment: Visa, MC
Tee Times: No
Fee 9 Holes: Weekday: $14.00
Fee 18 Holes: Weekday: $20.00
Twilight Rates: No
Cart Rental: $20.00/18 $14.00/9
Lessons: $20/lesson **Schools:** No
Clinics: Yes **Day Camps:** No
Other: Restaurant / Clubhouse / Bar-lounge / Lockers / Showers

Weekend: $14.00
Weekend: $20.00
All Day Play: No
Discounts: Sr & Jr memberships
Junior Golf: Yes **Membership:** Yes
Driving Range: $2.00/bucket

The course, located a chip shot from the Canadian border, sports many challenges: bunkers, water hazards, and hills.

	1	2	3	4	5	6	7	8	9
PAR	4	4	3	4	3	4	4	4	5
YARDS	406	302	160	322	151	390	412	437	542
HDCP	1	15	13	17	9	7	5	3	11

	10	11	12	13	14	15	16	17	18
PAR	4	4	3	4	3	4	5	4	5
YARDS	412	310	181	328	159	398	460	449	548
HDCP	2	16	8	18	10	6	14	4	12

Directions: Take Route 161 to Fort Kent; follow 3 miles to course.

Foxcroft Golf Club

15

Dover Foxcroft (207) 564-8887

Club Pro: Louis G. Thibeault, PGA
Pro Shop: Yes
Payment: Personal checks, Cash
Tee Times: No
Fee 9 Holes: Weekday: $12.00
Fee 18 Holes: Weekday: $20.00
Twilight Rates: Yes, after 5 pm
Cart Rental: $20.00/18 $12.00/9
Lessons: Yes **Schools:** No
Clinics: No **Day Camps:** No
Other: Snack Bar / Clubhouse

Tees	Holes	Yards	Par	USGA	Slope
BACK	9	3136	36	66.1	109
MIDDLE	9	2968	36	66.1	107
FRONT	9	2753	37	67.0	101

Weekend: $12.00
Weekend: $20.00
All Day Play: No
Discounts: None
Junior Golf: No **Membership:** N/A
Driving Range: No

Sig. Hole: #4, 110 yd. par 3 is the hole you may most remember, long after your visit.

	1	2	3	4	5	6	7	8	9
PAR	5	4	4	3	4	4	3	4	5
YARDS	468	430	380	102	330	267	138	381	472
HDCP	5	1	3	17	11	13	15	9	7
	10	**11**	**12**	**13**	**14**	**15**	**16**	**17**	**18**
PAR									
YARDS									
HDCP									

Directions: From I-95, take Exit 39 (Newport Exit). Follow Route 7 into Dover-Foxcroft. Turn left. Go right at traffic light. Take 2nd right, Route 16. Take Route 16 from the Post Office 1.3 miles to Foxcroft Center Rd. Sign is at corner of Milo Rd.

Great Cove Golf Course

16

Rogue Bluffs, ME (207) 434-7200

Club Pro: No
Pro Shop: No
Payment: Cash only
Tee Times: No
Fee 9 Holes: Weekday: $8.00
Fee 18 Holes: Weekday: $14.00
Twilight Rates: No
Cart Rental: $12.00/18 $8.00/9
Lessons: No **Schools:** No
Clinics: No **Day Camps:** No
Other: Clubhouse / Snack bar

Tees	Holes	Yards	Par	USGA	Slope
BACK					
MIDDLE	9	1709	30	59.1	100
FRONT					

Weekend: $8.00
Weekend: $14.00
All Day Play: No
Discounts: None
Junior Golf: Yes **Membership:** Yes
Driving Range: $4/lg, $2.75/sm

**N
ME**

Three tricky par 3's with natural hazards.

	1	2	3	4	5	6	7	8	9
PAR	4	3	4	3	4	3	3	3	3
YARDS	304	185	245	193	228	103	137	177	137
HDCP	2	8	1	7	3	9	6	4	5
	10	**11**	**12**	**13**	**14**	**15**	**16**	**17**	**18**
PAR									
YARDS									
HDCP									

Directions: 3 miles off Route 1 from Jonesboro. Located on Great Cove Road.

4☺ =Excellent **3☺** =Very Good **2☺** = Good

Green Valley GC

Rt. 2, Lincoln, ME (207) 732-3006

Tees	Holes	Yards	Par	USGA	Slope
BACK					
MIDDLE	9	2824	35	65.8	112
FRONT					

Club Pro: No
Pro Shop: Limited inventory
Payment: Visa, MC, Disc
Tee Times: No
Fee 9 Holes: Weekday: $9.00
Fee 18 Holes: Weekday: $13.00 All Day
Twilight Rates: No
Cart Rental: $16.00/18 $8.00/9
Lessons: $15/lesson **Schools:** No
Clinics: Yes **Day Camps:** No
Other: Clubhouse / Snack Bar

Weekend: $9.00
Weekend: $13.00 All Day
All Day Play: $13.00
Discounts: None
Junior Golf: Yes **Membership:** Yes
Driving Range: $3.00/bucket

Small greens. The course is relatively easy to walk and well maintained. New irrigation system 2002. Open May - November.

	1	2	3	4	5	6	7	8	9
PAR	5	3	4	4	4	4	3	4	4
YARDS	497	185	291	242	363	367	159	356	364
HDCP	9	6	7	8	1	2	3	4	9
	10	11	12	13	14	15	16	17	18
PAR									
YARDS									
HDCP									

Directions: Take I-95 to Howland Exit; follow Route 2 into Lincoln town center. Course is located off of Route 2.

Grindstone Neck GC

Winter Harbor, ME (207) 963-7760

Tees	Holes	Yards	Par	USGA	Slope
BACK					
MIDDLE	9	6190	72		
FRONT	9	5100	72		

Club Pro: Kevin Conley
Pro Shop: Full inventory
Payment: Cash only
Tee Times: No
Fee 9 Holes: Weekday: $22.00
Fee 18 Holes: Weekday: $35.00
Twilight Rates: Yes, after 4:30 pm
Cart Rental: $25.00/18 $15.00/9
Lessons: $10/30 min. **Schools:** No
Clinics: No **Day Camps:** No
Other: No

Weekend: $28.00
Weekend: $45.00
All Day Play: Yes
Discounts: College & Juniors
Junior Golf: No **Membership:** Yes
Driving Range: No

Player's Comment: "Could not be more beautiful." Semi-private, members tee time from 9-10:30am. Located on Frenchman's Bay. Enjoy cool sea breezes, spectacular ocean views, while challenging your skills.

	1	2	3	4	5	6	7	8	9
PAR	4	4	4	3	4	4	5	4	4
YARDS	345	340	317	138	413	335	457	343	407
HDCP	5	14	9	18	7	16	1	10	6
	10	11	12	13	14	15	16	17	18
PAR	4	4	4	3	4	4	5	4	4
YARDS	345	340	317	138	413	335	457	343	407
HDCP	15	8	17	2	11	3	12	4	13

Directions: Take Route 1 North to Route 186. Follow 6 miles to the course.

Hampden CC

Hampden, ME (207) 862-9999

Club Pro: No
Pro Shop: Limited inventory
Payment: Cash, Checks
Tee Times: No
Fee 9 Holes: Weekday: $10.00
Fee 18 Holes: Weekday: $15.00
Twilight Rates: Yes, after 5 pm
Cart Rental: $15.00/18 $10.00/9
Lessons: No **Schools:** No
Clinics: No **Day Camps:** No
Other: Snack bar

Weekend: $10.00
Weekend: $15.00
All Day Play: N/R
Discounts: Sr. Thurs - $5
Junior Golf: No **Membership:** Yes
Driving Range: No

Tees	Holes	Yards	Par	USGA	Slope
BACK	9	2570	36		
MIDDLE	9	2737	36	66.0	108
FRONT	9	2550	36		112

The course is fairly wide open, friendly for beginners and seniors. Considered an easy walker. Tuesday is Ladies Day 8:30 am - 12 pm for $5.

	1	2	3	4	5	6	7	8	9
PAR	4	3	4	4	4	3	5	4	5
YARDS	320	170	330	295	257	195	450	310	410
HDCP									
	10	11	12	13	14	15	16	17	18
PAR									
YARDS									
HDCP									

Directions: Take I-95 to Exit 43, follow Route 69 East for 1 1/2 miles, take Route 9 East for 2 miles, course in on right

Hermon Meadow GC

Bangor, ME (207) 848-3741
www.hermonmeadow.com

Club Pro: Thea Davis
Pro Shop: Full inventory
Payment: Most major
Tee Times: No
Fee 9 Holes: Weekday: $14.00
Fee 18 Holes: Weekday: $25.00 all day
Twilight Rates: Yes, after 3 pm
Cart Rental: Yes
Lessons: Yes **Schools:** Jr.
Clinics: Yes **Day Camps:** No
Other: Clubhouse / Snack bar / Bar-lounge

Weekend: $14.00
Weekend: $25.00 all day
All Day Play: $25
Discounts: Junior
Junior Golf: Yes **Membership:** $200
Driving Range: $4.00/bucket

Tees	Holes	Yards	Par	USGA	Slope
BACK	18	6329	72	69.4	117
MIDDLE	18	5895	72	67.7	113
FRONT	18	5395	72	70.9	120

COUPON

N
ME

The greens are small and fast; back nine are heavily wooded. Driving range has largest bent grass tees in Maine. Call for daily specials.

	1	2	3	4	5	6	7	8	9
PAR	4	4	3	5	4	5	4	3	4
YARDS	350	385	130	460	270	545	350	165	350
HDCP	7	9	17	3	15	1	11	5	13
	10	11	12	13	14	15	16	17	18
PAR	4	4	3	5	4	5	3	4	4
YARDS	265	310	160	430	320	510	135	370	390
HDCP	16	14	10	6	8	4	18	12	2

Directions: Take Union Street 4 miles past airport in Bangor, take left on Billings Road, course is 2 miles on left.

4 =Excellent **3** =Very Good **2** =Good

Hidden Meadows Golf Course

Old Town, ME (207) 827-4779
www.oldtowngolf.com

Tees	Holes	Yards	Par	USGA	Slope
BACK					
MIDDLE	9	2974	35	66.5	112
FRONT	9	2481	35	66.4	109

Club Pro: Marv Tolson
Pro Shop: Limited inventory
Payment: Cash only
Tee Times: No
Fee 9 Holes: Weekday: $10.00   **Weekend:** $15.00
Fee 18 Holes: Weekday: $12.00   **Weekend:** $18.00
Twilight Rates: No   **All Day Play:** $20.00
Cart Rental: $15.00/18 $10.00/9   **Discounts:** Yes
Lessons: Yes **Schools:** Yes   **Junior Golf:** Yes **Membership:** Yes
Clinics: No **Day Camps:** No   **Driving Range:** No
Other: Open from May to October

Sig. Hole: #7, scenic par 5, double dogleg. Plays well for both novice and advanced players. New tees, traps & layout in September, 2001. Family owned and operated.

	1	2	3	4	5	6	7	8	9
PAR	4	4	4	3	5	4	4	3	4
YARDS	389	323	339	148	547	335	394	167	332
HDCP	4	9	8	7	2	5	1	3	6
	10	**11**	**12**	**13**	**14**	**15**	**16**	**17**	**18**
PAR									
YARDS									
HDCP									

Directions: I-95 to Exit 52. West on Route 43 towards Hudson. Golf course is 1/2 mile from interstate on left.

Hillcrest Golf Club

Millinocket, ME (207) 723-8410

Tees	Holes	Yards	Par	USGA	Slope
BACK					
MIDDLE	9	2477	33	63.2	104
FRONT					

Club Pro: Stanley Glidden
Pro Shop: Full inventory
Payment: Visa, MC
Tee Times: No
Fee 9 Holes: Weekday: $12.00   **Weekend:** $12.00
Fee 18 Holes: Weekday: $18.00, All day   **Weekend:** $18.00, All day
Twilight Rates: No   **All Day Play:** Yes
Cart Rental: $20.00/18 $10.00/9   **Discounts:** None
Lessons: Yes **Schools:** No   **Junior Golf:** Yes **Membership:** Yes
Clinics: Yes **Day Camps:** No   **Driving Range:** No
Other: Clubhouse / Snack bar / Bar-lounge

Sits on bottom of Mt. Katahdin. Very nice short course, very tight with narrow, tree-lined fairways. Open April - October.

	1	2	3	4	5	6	7	8	9
PAR	4	3	4	4	4	4	3	3	4
YARDS	359	152	364	287	265	401	221	153	275
HDCP	5	9	3	11	13	1	7	17	15
	10	**11**	**12**	**13**	**14**	**15**	**16**	**17**	**18**
PAR									
YARDS									
HDCP									

Directions: I-95 to Medway Exit 56, left off ramp onto Route 157. Follow 12 miles to Millinocket. Past McDonald's to bottom of hill. Follow signs at right.

Houlton Community GC

Houlton, ME (207) 532-2662

Club Pro: Nathan Dewitt
Pro Shop: Yes
Payment: Cash, Check
Tee Times: No
Fee 9 Holes: Weekday: $14.00
Fee 18 Holes: Weekday: $20.00
Twilight Rates: League play
Cart Rental: $10.00pp
Lessons: $25/30 min. **Schools:** No
Clinics: Yes **Day Camps:** No
Other: Clubhouse / Snack bar / Bar-lounge

Weekend: $16.00
Weekend: $22.00
All Day Play: No
Discounts: None
Junior Golf: Yes **Membership:** Yes
Driving Range: Yes

COUPON

Tees	Holes	Yards	Par	USGA	Slope
BACK					
MIDDLE	9	6103	72	68.9	117
FRONT	9	5410	76	73.6	109

The course is adjacent to beautiful Nickerson Lake. Hilly, but other than a scenic view of the lake, has few water hazards. 2 sets of tees. Open May - September.

	1	2	3	4	5	6	7	8	9
PAR	4	5	3	4	4	5	4	3	4
YARDS	325	475	150	260	425	455	345	175	383
HDCP	15	5	13	17	1	11	9	3	7

	10	11	12	13	14	15	16	17	18
PAR	4	4	3	4	4	5	4	4	4
YARDS	390	375	170	285	385	475	365	285	380
HDCP	2	4	14	16	12	8	10	18	6

Directions: Take I-95 to Houlton Exit (last US Exit on I-95 North), follow signs to course.

Island Country Club

Sunset, ME (207) 348-2379

Club Pro: David Klopfenstein
Pro Shop: Limited inventory
Payment: Visa, MC
Tee Times: No
Fee 9 Holes: Weekday: $15.00
Fee 18 Holes: Weekday: $22.00
Twilight Rates: No
Cart Rental: $20.00pp/18 $10.00pp/9
Lessons: Yes **Schools:** No
Clinics: No **Day Camps:** No
Other: Clubhouse / Snack bar

Weekend: $15.00
Weekend: $25.00
All Day Play: Yes
Discounts: Junior
Junior Golf: No **Membership:** Yes
Driving Range: No

Tees	Holes	Yards	Par	USGA	Slope
BACK					
MIDDLE	9	1930	62	58.8	97
FRONT					

Hilly, greens fast. Contoured fairways, fully irrigated. No alcohol on course.

	1	2	3	4	5	6	7	8	9
PAR	4	4	3	3	3	3	3	4	4
YARDS	309	251	116	145	155	114	199	318	323
HDCP	9	7	15	13	11	17	5	1	3

	10	11	12	13	14	15	16	17	18
PAR	4	4	3	3	3	3	3	4	4
YARDS	309	297	116	145	155	114	199	277	323
HDCP	8	2	16	14	12	18	6	10	4

Directions: Route 15 to Deer Isle then Route 15A to Sunset. Club is about 3 miles on the left.

4❂ =Excellent 3❂ =Very Good 2❂ =Good

Island Green Golf Course

Holden, ME 207-989-9909

Club Pro: Brian Lawton, Mark Hall
Pro Shop: Full inventory
Payment: Visa, MC, Amex
Tee Times: Preferred
Fee 9 Holes: Weekday: $11.00
Fee 18 Holes: Weekday: $19.00
Twilight Rates: Early Bird
Cart Rental: $10pp/18 $6pp/9
Lessons: Yes **Schools:** Yes
Clinics: No **Day Camps:** No
Other: Restaurant / Lounge / Night lit driving range

Tees	Holes	Yards	Par	USGA	Slope
BACK	9	4922	70		
MIDDLE	9	4522	70		
FRONT	9	3334	66		

Weekend: $11.00
Weekend: $19.00
All Day Play: Yes
Discounts: Senior & Junior
Junior Golf: Yes **Membership:** Yes
Driving Range: $7/lg $5.50/med $4/sm

COUPON

Sig. Hole: #5, 240 yard, par 4 to island green. Great risk/reward course. Although a short course, the greens are regulation size. A challenge for all levels. Easy walker. Formerly Felt Brook GC.

	1	2	3	4	5	6	7	8	9
PAR	4	4	4	4	4	5	3	3	4
YARDS	255	190	305	345	185	447	109	129	296
HDCP	9	13	5	1	11	7	17	15	3
	10	**11**	**12**	**13**	**14**	**15**	**16**	**17**	**18**
PAR	4	4	4	4	4	5	3	3	4
YARDS	255	190	305	345	185	447	109	129	296
HDCP	10	14	6	2	12	8	18	16	4

Directions: Take Holden Exit from 395 to Route 1A.

Jato Highlands Golf Course

Town Farm Rd. Lincoln, ME (207) 794-2433
www.jatohighlands.com

Club Pro: Eric Dubay
Pro Shop: Limited inventory
Payment: Visa, MC
Tee Times: 1 day adv.
Fee 9 Holes: Weekday: $12.00
Fee 18 Holes: Weekday: $25.00
Twilight Rates: No
Cart Rental: $20/18 $12/9
Lessons: $20.00/30min. **Schools:** Junior
Clinics: Yes **Day Camps:** No
Other: Restaurant / Clubhouse / Bar-lounge

Tees	Holes	Yards	Par	USGA	Slope
BACK	18	5647	72	67.7	113
MIDDLE	18	5444	72	66.6	111
FRONT	18	4739	72	66.3	107

Weekend: $12.00
Weekend: $25.00
All Day Play: No
Discounts: Junior
Junior Golf: Yes **Membership:** Yes
Driving Range: 3.00/bucket

Sig. Hole: #10, 183 yd. par 3 includes a 100' vertical drop with beautiful views of rolling hills and surrounding ponds. **Player's Comment:** "A hidden gem. Well maintained."

	1	2	3	4	5	6	7	8	9
PAR	4	4	3	5	4	4	4	3	5
YARDS	332	325	175	403	267	305	296	114	416
HDCP	4	9	12	5	15	11	8	18	3
	10	**11**	**12**	**13**	**14**	**15**	**16**	**17**	**18**
PAR	3	5	4	4	3	5	3	4	5
YARDS	183	435	381	374	160	432	139	296	411
HDCP	13	6	2	10	16	1	17	14	7

Directions: Exit 55 off I-95. Right off ramp, at blinking light turn left onto Route 2 for 6 miles. Right onto Town Farm Road. 1 mile.

Johnson W. Parks GC

Pittsfield, ME (207) 487-5545
www.jwparksgolf.com

Club Pro: Michael Dugas, PGA
Pro Shop: Full inventory
Payment: Most major
Tee Times: No
Fee 9 Holes: Weekday: $14.00
Fee 18 Holes: Weekday: $18.00
Twilight Rates: Yes, after 5 pm
Cart Rental: $22.00/18 $11.00/9
Lessons: $20/30 min. **Schools:** No
Clinics: Yes **Day Camps:** No
Other: Clubhouse / Sports Bar

Tees	Holes	Yards	Par	USGA	Slope
BACK	9	2927	35	34.1	120
MIDDLE	9	2678	35	35.1	120
FRONT	9	2554	35	35.0	120

Weekend: $16.00
Weekend: $22.00
All Day Play: No
Discounts: Junior- 1/2 price
Junior Golf: Yes **Membership:** Yes
Driving Range: Yes

COUPON

Sig. Hole: #3. Tall pines, narrow fairways and series of streams add to the challenge at one of central Maine's most popular courses. Open April 25 - October 31.

	1	2	3	4	5	6	7	8	9
PAR	4	4	5	3	4	4	4	3	4
YARDS	375	405	531	227	308	268	322	160	331
HDCP	5	3	1	7	11	17	9	15	13
	10	11	12	13	14	15	16	17	18
PAR									
YARDS									
HDCP									

Directions: Take I-95 to Pittsfield Exit 38, go east off ramp. Take a left on to Route 152. 1/2 mile on the left.

Katahdin Country Club

Milo, ME (207) 943-8734

Club Pro: No
Pro Shop: Limited nventory
Payment: Cash only
Tee Times: No
Fee 9 Holes: Weekday: $12.00
Fee 18 Holes: Weekday: $12.00
Twilight Rates: No
Cart Rental: $16.00/18 $8.00/9
Lessons: No **Schools:** N/R
Clinics: Yes **Day Camps:** N/R
Other: Clubhouse / Snack bar

Tees	Holes	Yards	Par	USGA	Slope
BACK					
MIDDLE	9	5936	72	65.8	103
FRONT					

Weekend: $12.00
Weekend: $12.00
All Day Play: $12.00 per day
Discounts: None
Junior Golf: Yes **Membership:** Yes, $150.00
Driving Range: No

Wide open fairways, short cut rough and no water hazards. Largest sand trap around. Open April 15 - November.

	1	2	3	4	5	6	7	8	9
PAR	4	3	4	4	3	5	5	4	4
YARDS	327	150	322	257	180	485	519	447	281
HDCP	11	5	13	17	3	9	7	1	15
	10	11	12	13	14	15	16	17	18
PAR	4	3	4	4	3	5	5	4	4
YARDS	327	150	322	257	180	485	519	447	281
HDCP	12	6	14	18	4	10	8	2	16

Directions: Take I-95 North to LaGrange-Milo Exit, follow signs to course.

4✪ =Excellent 3✪ =Very Good 2✪ = Good

Kebo Valley Golf Club

Bar Harbor, ME (207) 288-3000
www.kebovalleyclub.com

Tees	Holes	Yards	Par	USGA	Slope
BACK	18	6131	70	69.0	124
MIDDLE	18	5933	70	69.0	122
FRONT	18	5440	72	72	121

Club Pro: Pieter K. DeVos
Pro Shop: Full inventory
Payment: Cash, Visa, MC
Tee Times: 6 days adv.
Fee 9 Holes: Weekday: $45.00   **Weekend:** $45.00
Fee 18 Holes: Weekday: $76.00   **Weekend:** $76.00
Twilight Rates: No   **All Day Play:** No
Cart Rental: $18.00pp/18   **Discounts:** None
Lessons: $35.00/45 min. **Schools:** No   **Junior Golf:** Yes **Membership:** Yes
Clinics: Yes **Day Camps:** No   **Driving Range:** No
Other: Restaurant / Bar-lounge / Lockers

8th oldest club in the country. Majestic views of Acadia National Park. Improvements include holes #8, #13, and refurbished fame hole #17. President Taft made 27 on it. Lodging partner available.

	1	2	3	4	5	6	7	8	9
PAR	4	4	4	3	5	3	4	4	3
YARDS	388	438	336	143	500	165	322	413	194
HDCP	7	3	11	17	9	13	15	1	5
	10	**11**	**12**	**13**	**14**	**15**	**16**	**17**	**18**
PAR	4	4	4	4	5	3	4	4	4
YARDS	338	400	283	390	530	146	258	349	340
HDCP	10	8	12	2	4	16	18	6	14

Directions: Take I 95 to Bangor, 395 to Route1A, Route 1A to Route 3, Route 3 to Route 233. Look for signs to course.

Kenduskeag Valley GC

Kenduskeag, ME (207) 884-7330

Tees	Holes	Yards	Par	USGA	Slope
BACK	9	2610	35	63.9	108
MIDDLE	9	2573	35	68	98
FRONT	9	2416	35	67.4	108

Club Pro: No
Pro Shop: Limited inventory
Payment: Cash, Check
Tee Times: No
Fee 9 Holes: Weekday: $9.00   **Weekend:** $9.00
Fee 18 Holes: Weekday: $13.00   **Weekend:** $13.00
Twilight Rates: No   **All Day Play:** No
Cart Rental: Yes   **Discounts:** Senior & Junior
Lessons: No **Schools:** No   **Junior Golf:** Yes **Membership:** Yes
Clinics: No **Day Camps:** No   **Driving Range:** No
Other: Clubhouse / Snack bar

COUPON

Under new ownership. An easy, but pretty course. Rolling, wooded and stream scenery. Appropriate dress. Open May 1- October 31.

	1	2	3	4	5	6	7	8	9
PAR	4	4	5	3	4	3	5	3	4
YARDS	320	343	483	107	285	143	465	154	310
HDCP	5	3	2	9	6	8	1	7	4
	10	**11**	**12**	**13**	**14**	**15**	**16**	**17**	**18**
PAR									
YARDS									
HDCP									

Directions: From I-95, take Exit 48. Right to Route 15 Broadway North, 12 miles to course. Left onto Grant Rd.

Lakeview Golf Club

Burnham, ME (207) 948-5414

Club Pro: Joe Berry, PGA
Pro Shop: Limited inventory
Payment: Cash only
Tee Times: No
Fee 9 Holes: Weekday: $11.00
Fee 18 Holes: Weekday: $15.00
Twilight Rates: No
Cart Rental: $20.00/18 $10.00/9
Lessons: Yes **Schools:** No
Clinics: Yes **Day Camps:** No
Other: Snack bar / Clubhouse / Lockers

Tees	Holes	Yards	Par	USGA	Slope
BACK	9	6032	72	68.0	116
MIDDLE	9	5396	72	69.9	114
FRONT	9	5090	72	65.9	114

Weekend: $12.00
Weekend: $18.00
All Day Play: Yes
Discounts: Junior
Junior Golf: No **Membership:** Yes
Driving Range: No

An excellent walking course with level fairways. Highly recommended for senior citizens. All day specials $22.00 during the week and $24.00 on weekends.

	1	2	3	4	5	6	7	8	9
PAR	4	4	3	3	4	5	5	4	4
YARDS	387	305	124	169	339	514	491	354	333
HDCP	7	13	17	15	9	1	3	5	11

	10	11	12	13	14	15	16	17	18
PAR	4	4	3	3	4	5	5	4	4
YARDS	387	305	124	169	339	514	491	354	333
HDCP	8	14	18	16	10	2	4	6	12

Directions: Take Route 139 from Fairfield to Burnham West. Course is on the left.

Lakewood Golf Course

Madison, ME (207) 474-5955

Club Pro: No
Pro Shop: Limited inventory
Payment: Cash only
Tee Times: Wknds & Hldys Only
Fee 9 Holes: Weekday: $16.00
Fee 18 Holes: Weekday: $25.00
Twilight Rates: Yes, after 5 pm
Cart Rental: $26.00/18 $14.00/9
Lessons: Yes **Schools:** No
Clinics: Sometimes **Day Camps:** No
Other: Snack bar / Bar-Lounge / Hall Rental

Tees	Holes	Yards	Par	USGA	Slope
BACK					
MIDDLE	18	6278	72	70.1	128
FRONT	18	5490	74	71.9	120

Weekend: $16.00
Weekend: $25.00
All Day Play: Yes
Discounts: Junior
Junior Golf: No **Membership:** Yes
Driving Range: No

Practice, chipping, and putting areas. Open May - November.

	1	2	3	4	5	6	7	8	9
PAR	4	4	3	5	4	3	4	4	5
YARDS	365	435	160	471	285	141	325	410	510
HDCP	6	3	10	12	17	14	16	4	8

	10	11	12	13	14	15	16	17	18
PAR	3	4	6	4	4	4	4	4	3
YARDS	130	350	660	410	370	350	360	394	152
HDCP	18	13	1	2	7	11	5	15	9

Directions: Take Route 201; 6 miles past Shawhegan toward Bingham.

4✪ =Excellent **3✪** =Very Good **2✪** = Good

Limestone CC

◘◘ ▸ 33

Limestone, ME (207) 328-7277
www.limestonecountryclub.com

Club Pro: C. Phair & P. Weatherhead
Pro Shop: Full inventory
Payment: Visa, MC, Amex, Personal checks
Tee Times: No
Fee 9 Holes: Weekday: $12.00
Fee 18 Holes: Weekday: $18.00
Twilight Rates: Yes, after 5 pm
Cart Rental: $15.00/18 $10.00/9
Lessons: $15/30 min **Schools:** No
Clinics: No **Day Camps:** No
Other: Clubhouse / Bar / Lounge / Snack Bar / Lodging- 2 bedroom condos

Weekend: $12.00
Weekend: $18.00
All Day Play: No
Discounts: Senior & Junior
Junior Golf: No **Membership:** Yes
Driving Range: Yes

Tees	Holes	Yards	Par	USGA	Slope
BACK					
MIDDLE	9	3355	36	70.4	114
FRONT	9	2870	36	71.4	116

COUPON

Course is sited to capture the wind. Fairways lined with evergreens and hardwoods. Elevated greens at different angles. Long and short term accomodations are available. Golf packages.

	1	2	3	4	5	6	7	8	9
PAR	4	5	3	4	4	3	4	5	4
YARDS	415	525	160	370	355	225	390	515	400
HDCP	1	3	17	15	11	9	13	5	7
	10	11	12	13	14	15	16	17	18
PAR									
YARDS									
HDCP									

Directions: I-95 North to Holton then Route 1 North to Caribou. From Caribou take Route 89 East to Loring- Limestone. Take a left on West Gate Rd. for 2.5 miles and club is located on the right.

Loons Cove Golf Course

▸ 34

Skowhegan, ME (207) 474-9550

Club Pro: No
Pro Shop: Limited inventory
Payment: Cash only
Tee Times: No
Fee 9 Holes: Weekday: $7.00
Fee 18 Holes: Weekday: $11.00
Twilight Rates: No
Cart Rental: $20pp/18 $10pp/9
Lessons: Yes **Schools:** No
Clinics: Yes **Day Camps:** No
Other: Snacks / Beverages / Lunch Counter

Weekend: $7.00
Weekend: $11.00
All Day Play: Yes, $15
Discounts: For members
Junior Golf: Yes **Membership:** Yes
Driving Range: Yes

Tees	Holes	Yards	Par	USGA	Slope
BACK					
MIDDLE	9	1214	27		
FRONT					

Host for Central Maine Junior Program.

	1	2	3	4	5	6	7	8	9
PAR	3	3	3	3	3	3	3	3	3
YARDS	142	162	125	160	110	125	128	115	147
HDCP									
	10	11	12	13	14	15	16	17	18
PAR									
YARDS									
HDCP									

Directions: 6 miles from I 95 on Route 201 in Skowhegan

Lucerne-in-Maine Golf Course

Dedham, ME (207) 843-6282
www.lucernegolf.com

Club Pro: No
Pro Shop: Full inventory
Payment: Cash, Check, Visa, MC
Tee Times: 7 dys. adv.
Fee 9 Holes: Weekday: $15.00
Fee 18 Holes: Weekday: $25.00
Twilight Rates: Yes, after 3 pm
Cart Rental: $12.00pp/18 $6.00pp/9
Lessons: Yes **Schools:**
Clinics: Yes **Day Camps:** No
Other: Snackbar / Lodging available at Lucerne Inn

Tees	Holes	Yards	Par	USGA	Slope
BACK	9	3205	36	70.6	119
MIDDLE	9	2880	36	67.4	119
FRONT	9	2650	36	69.5	116

Weekend: $15.00
Weekend: $25.00
All Day Play: No
Discounts: None
Junior Golf: No **Membership:** Yes
Driving Range: Yes

1926 Donald Ross course features tree-lined fairways, ample landing areas and small greens guarded by pot bunkers. Spectacular views of Lucerne Inn, Phillips Lake and Bald Mtn. New owners, manager.

	1	2	3	4	5	6	7	8	9
PAR	5	3	4	4	4	3	4	5	4
YARDS	450	155	235	360	305	150	340	485	365
HDCP	5	13	17	11	1	15	3	7	9
	10	11	12	13	14	15	16	17	18
PAR									
YARDS									
HDCP									

Directions: Take Route I-95 to Exit 45A (Route I-395). Course is 8 miles on left, halfway between Bangor and Ellsworth on Route 1A.

Mars Hill Country Club

Mars Hill, ME (207) 425-4802
www.mainerec.com/mhcc

Club Pro: No
Pro Shop: Yes
Payment: Visa, MC
Tee Times: No
Fee 9 Holes: Weekday: $10.00
Fee 18 Holes: Weekday: $20.00
Twilight Rates: No
Cart Rental: $15pp/18, $7.50pp/9
Lessons: $20.00/hour **Schools:** No
Clinics: No **Day Camps:** No
Other: Clubhouse / Full restaurant / Beer

Tees	Holes	Yards	Par	USGA	Slope
BACK	18	6043	72		
MIDDLE	18	5742	72	68.7	125
FRONT	18	5159	72		

Weekend: $10.00
Weekend: $20.00
All Day Play: No
Discounts: None
Junior Golf: Yes **Membership:** Yes
Driving Range: $2.00/sm bucket

162 foot vertical drop on the #6 par 3. Maine Lung Card Participant.

	1	2	3	4	5	6	7	8	9
PAR	4	5	4	5	4	3	4	3	4
YARDS	350	481	257	470	326	145	313	130	300
HDCP	11	1	5	9	13	7	3	15	17
	10	11	12	13	14	15	16	17	18
PAR	4	4	5	3	4	3	4	5	4
YARDS	398	380	470	163	363	125	309	447	315
HDCP	4	2	8	6	14	18	10	12	16

Directions: I-95 to Route US1 to Mars Hill. Then north 2 miles onRoute 1A. Turn right onto East Ridge Road. See sign to golf course.

4✪ =Excellent 3✪ =Very Good 2✪ =Good

Mingo Springs GC

Rangeley, ME (207) 864-5021

Club Pro: Tom Cockcroft, PGA
Pro Shop: Yes
Payment: Visa, MC, Cash
Tee Times: Yes
Fee 9 Holes: Weekday: $22 (M-Th)
Fee 18 Holes: Weekday: $30 (M-Th) All Day
Twilight Rates: No
Cart Rental: $14pp/18 $9pp/9
Lessons: $25.00/30 min. **Schools:** No
Clinics: Yes **Day Camps:** No
Other: Snack bar / Bar-lounge

Weekend: $23.00
Weekend: $34.00 All Day
All Day Play: Yes
Discounts: None
Junior Golf: Yes **Membership:** Yes
Driving Range: Irons Only

Tees	Holes	Yards	Par	USGA	Slope
BACK					
MIDDLE	18	6014	70	65.5	114
FRONT	18	5158	70	67.4	110

Improvements include shaped holes and new tees. Noted for being a challenging old-fashioned course, yet family and beginner friendly. Exceptionally scenic views of Rangeley Mountains.

	1	2	3	4	5	6	7	8	9
PAR	4	4	4	3	4	4	3	4	5
YARDS	350	375	378	173	360	391	177	318	470
HDCP	9	7	5	17	11	1	15	13	3
	10	11	12	13	14	15	16	17	18
PAR	3	5	3	4	4	4	4	4	4
YARDS	152	522	133	400	360	277	419	363	396
HDCP	16	2	18	8	12	14	4	10	6

Directions: Take I-95 to Exit 12 (Auburn). Pick up Route 4. Go throughFarmington to Rangley Village. 2 miles to Oquossoc, left on Mingo Loop Road. Follow signs to course.

Moose River GC

Rt. 201, Moose River, ME (207) 668-4841
www.jackman.com

Club Pro: No
Pro Shop: No
Payment: Cash only
Tee Times: No
Fee 9 Holes: Weekday: $10.00
Fee 18 Holes: Weekday: $16.00
Twilight Rates: No
Cart Rental: $12.00/18 $8.00/9
Lessons: No **Schools:** No
Clinics: No **Day Camps:** No
Other:

Weekend: $10.00
Weekend: $16.00
All Day Play: No
Discounts: None
Junior Golf: No **Membership:** Yes
Driving Range: No

Tees	Holes	Yards	Par	USGA	Slope
BACK					
MIDDLE	9	1976	31		
FRONT					

Open May 15 - October 15. Rate subject to change.

	1	2	3	4	5	6	7	8	9
PAR	3	3	4	4	4	3	3	3	4
YARDS	204	168	213	248	259	168	171	169	376
HDCP	1	15	17	9	11	5	7	13	3
	10	11	12	13	14	15	16	17	18
PAR									
YARDS									
HDCP									

Directions: Take I-95 to Fairfield Exit, follow Route 201 North about 85 miles to Moose River.

Natanis Golf Course ✪✪ 39 ▶

Vassalboro, ME (207) 622-3561
www.natanisgc.com

Club Pro: Richard Browne
Pro Shop: Full inventory
Payment: Visa, MC, cash
Tee Times: 1 week adv.

Tees	Holes	Yards	Par	USGA	Slope
BACK	18	6607	72	70.6	132
MIDDLE	18	6060	72	67.3	132
FRONT	18	5034	72	63.8	104

Fee 9 Holes: Weekday: $18.00
Fee 18 Holes: Weekday: $32 Arrow.\$30 Tom.
Twilight Rates: Yes, after 4 pm
Cart Rental: $26.00/18 $15.00/9
Lessons: Yes **Schools:** No
Clinics: Yes **Day Camps:** No
Other: Clubhouse / Lockers / Snack bar

Weekend: $18.00
Weekend: $32 Arrowhead\$30 Tomahawk
All Day Play: No
Discounts: None
Junior Golf: Yes **Membership:** Yes
Driving Range: $3.50/lg. $2.50/sm.

Player's Comment: "36 holes for top notch golf. Good conditions. Challenging yet fair. Visually pleasing." Tomahawk scorecard below. Arrowhead: 5847 yards, 72 par, USGA 67.8, slope 116.

	1	2	3	4	5	6	7	8	9
PAR	5	4	5	3	4	4	3	4	4
YARDS	490	342	526	124	358	362	121	354	359
HDCP	6	11	10	18	14	2	9	15	5
	10	11	12	13	14	15	16	17	18
PAR	3	4	4	3	5	5	4	4	4
YARDS	130	320	373	163	481	503	311	365	378
HDCP	17	4	1	12	3	7	16	13	8

Directions: Route 295 to Augusta / Winthrop Exit onto Route 201 to Webber Pond Road. Follow signs.

Newport CC 40 ▶

Newport, ME (207) 368-5600

Club Pro: Jeff Peabody, PGA
Pro Shop: Yes
Payment: Cash only
Tee Times: Yes

Tees	Holes	Yards	Par	USGA	Slope
BACK					
MIDDLE	9	4995	69		
FRONT					

Fee 9 Holes: Weekday: $10.00
Fee 18 Holes: Weekday: $18.00
Twilight Rates: No
Cart Rental: $10.00/9
Lessons: Yes **Schools:** Yes
Clinics: Yes **Day Camps:** Yes
Other: Clubhouse / Snack bar

Weekend: $10.00
Weekend: $18.00
All Day Play: No
Discounts: Senior & Junior
Junior Golf: Yes **Membership:** Yes
Driving Range: Yes

N
ME

	1	2	3	4	5	6	7	8	9
PAR	3	3	5	4	4	5	4	3	4
YARDS	155	135	430	380	255	450	290	190	235
HDCP									
	10	11	12	13	14	15	16	17	18
PAR	3	3	5	4	3	5	4	4	3
YARDS	140	165	430	380	210	450	260	250	190
HDCP									

Directions: Take I-95 to Exit 39 to Route 7 to right turn on Golf Course road in Newport.

Northeast Harbor GC ●●● ▶ 41

N.E. Harbor, ME (207) 276-5335

Club Pro: R.Gardner, PGA, B. Haynes Ass't.
Pro Shop: Full inventory
Payment: Visa, MC, Amex, Disc
Tee Times: No
Fee 9 Holes: Weekday: N/A
Fee 18 Holes: Weekday: $80.00
Twilight Rates: No
Cart Rental: $18pp/18
Lessons: Private, Group, Jr. . **Schools:** Yes
Clinics: Junior **Day Camps:** No
Other: Clubhouse/ Lockers

Weekend: N/A
Weekend: $80.00
All Day Play: Yes, $80.00
Discounts: None
Junior Golf: Yes **Membership:** Yes
Driving Range: Members

COUPON

Tees	Holes	Yards	Par	USGA	Slope
BACK	18	5505	69	66.7	128
MIDDLE	18	5324	69	65.9	124
FRONT	18	4602	71	66.9	124

Classic Donald Ross design. Added irrigation and fairway water. Located on Mt. Desert Island.

	1	2	3	4	5	6	7	8	9
PAR	4	4	3	4	4	3	4	3	5
YARDS	325	320	149	425	305	127	284	155	457
HDCP	9	13	11	1	5	17	7	15	3
	10	**11**	**12**	**13**	**14**	**15**	**16**	**17**	**18**
PAR	5	4	3	4	3	4	4	4	4
YARDS	495	310	175	337	187	415	281	338	239
HDCP	4	10	16	12	18	2	14	6	8

Directions: Take I-95 to Bangor Exit (Route 1A), follow to Ellsworth, take Rte 3 to Mt. Desert Island. Right at light at head of island on Rte 198. Left at next light (still198), right on Sargent Drive. NEHGC on left.

Northport Golf Club ▶ 42

Belfast, ME (207) 338-2270

Club Pro: Peter Hodgkins, PGA
Pro Shop: Full inventory
Payment: Visa, MC
Tee Times: Weekends & Holidays
Fee 9 Holes: Weekday: $22.00
Fee 18 Holes: Weekday: $30.00
Twilight Rates: No
Cart Rental: $25.00/18 $15.00/9
Lessons: $40/30 minutes **Schools:** No
Clinics: Sometimes **Day Camps:** No
Other: Clubhouse / Snack bar

Weekend: $22.00
Weekend: $30.00
All Day Play: No
Discounts: Spring/Fall
Junior Golf: Yes **Membership:** Yes
Driving Range: Yes

Tees	Holes	Yards	Par	USGA	Slope
BACK					
MIDDLE	9	6094	72	34.2	112
FRONT	9	5494	74	35.7	113

Sig. Hole: #7 is a 530 yard, par 5. Slight dogleg left to a two tiered uphill green. Bunkered on both sides. Good three shot hole. Fully irrigated.

	1	2	3	4	5	6	7	8	9
PAR	4	4	3	4	5	4	5	4	3
YARDS	290	377	157	310	483	412	530	338	150
HDCP	15	5	11	13	7	3	1	9	17
	10	**11**	**12**	**13**	**14**	**15**	**16**	**17**	**18**
PAR	4	4	3	4	5	4	5	4	3
YARDS	290	377	157	310	483	412	530	338	150
HDCP	16	6	12	14	8	4	2	10	18

Directions: Turn East off Route 1 at Bayside Store. 20 minutes North of Camden Rockport or 5 minutes South of Belfast.

Palmyra Golf Course

✪✪ ▶ 43

Palmyra, ME (207)938-4947
www.palmyra-me.com

Club Pro: None
Pro Shop: Full inventory
Payment: Visa, MC, Disc.
Tee Times: Fri,Sat,Sun
Fee 9 Holes: Weekday: $10.00
Fee 18 Holes: Weekday: $20.00
Twilight Rates: Yes, after 6 pm
Cart Rental: $20.00 /18 $10.00/9
Lessons: No **Schools:** No
Clinics: No **Day Camps:** No
Other: Snack Bar / RV facility with 100 full hookup sites

Tees	Holes	Yards	Par	USGA	Slope
BACK	18	6617	72	70.1	120
MIDDLE	18	6367	72	69.0	118
FRONT	18	5464	72	69.0	118

Weekend: $10.00
Weekend: $20.00
All Day Play: Yes
Discounts: None
Junior Golf: Yes **Membership:** Yes
Driving Range: $3.00 token/30 balls

COUPON

Complete renovation and extensive changes. Course noted for excellent value and high quality.

	1	2	3	4	5	6	7	8	9
PAR	4	4	5	3	4	4	4	3	5
YARDS	430	281	575	153	400	407	400	129	476
HDCP	11	13	1	15	7	5	3	17	9
	10	11	12	13	14	15	16	17	18
PAR	4	3	4	4	5	4	4	3	5
YARDS	386	150	350	387	487	373	304	198	481
HDCP	4	18	12	2	16	10	14	6	8

Directions: I-95 to Exit 39 (Newport). Route 2 West, approx. 5 miles. Right at white church, Course is on top of hill.

Penobscot Valley CC

▶ 44

Maine St., Orono, ME (207) 866-2423
www.penobscotvalleycc.com

Club Pro: Colin Gillies, PGA
Pro Shop: Full inventory
Payment: MC, Visa
Tee Times: No
Fee 9 Holes: Weekday: $30.00
Fee 18 Holes: Weekday: $60.00
Twilight Rates: No
Cart Rental: $15pp
Lessons: $25.00/half hour **Schools:** Yes
Clinics: Junior **Day Camps:** Yes
Other: Clubhouse / Lockers / Showers / Snack bar / Restaurant / Bar-lounge

Tees	Holes	Yards	Par	USGA	Slope
BACK	18	6445	72	71.2	128
MIDDLE	18	6301	72	70.5	126
FRONT	18	5796	74	73.9	128

Weekend: $30.00
Weekend: $60.00
All Day Play: Yes
Discounts: None
Junior Golf: Yes **Membership:** Yes
Driving Range: $3.00/Lg

N
ME

This Donald Ross course holds many amateur tournaments. A shot maker's course, it is in great shape. The course is very challenging and hilly with scenic views.

	1	2	3	4	5	6	7	8	9
PAR	4	4	5	3	4	3	5	4	4
YARDS	396	396	471	143	354	163	443	337	384
HDCP	11	3	5	17	9	15	7	13	1
	10	11	12	13	14	15	16	17	18
PAR	5	4	4	4	3	5	3	4	4
YARDS	490	390	371	424	143	455	193	323	425
HDCP	6	14	12	10	18	8	4	16	2

Directions: Take I-95 to Kelly Rd. Exit 50, take right to US Route 2. Turn right. Follow to course.

4✪ =Excellent 3✪ =Very Good 2✪ =Good

Pine Hill Golf Club

Outer Mill St., Brewer, ME (207) 989-3824

Club Pro: Buck Gagnier, PGA
Pro Shop: Limited inventory
Payment: Visa, MC
Tee Times: No
Fee 9 Holes: Weekday: $12.50
Fee 18 Holes: Weekday: $15.00 All day
Twilight Rates: No
Cart Rental: $18.00/18 $10.00/9
Lessons: Yes **Schools:** No
Clinics: No **Day Camps:** No
Other: Clubhouse / Snack bar

Tees	Holes	Yards	Par	USGA	Slope
BACK	9	2979	36	66	100
MIDDLE	9	2749	36	66	100
FRONT	9	2580	36	67	99

Weekend: $13.50
Weekend: $15.00 All day
All Day Play: Yes
Discounts: Ladies Monday
Junior Golf: No **Membership:** Yes
Driving Range: $3.50/med.

COUPON

Mostly level. Very scenic. Good course for beginners and intermediates. Open April - October.

	1	2	3	4	5	6	7	8	9
PAR	4	4	4	4	3	5	4	5	3
YARDS	292	333	326	339	166	498	320	495	210
HDCP	11	13	7	1	17	3	9	5	15
	10	11	12	13	14	15	16	17	18
PAR									
YARDS									
HDCP									

Directions: Take I-395 to South Main St./Brewer Exit, follow signs to course.

Pine Ridge Golf Course

W. River Rd., Waterville, ME (207) 873-0474

Club Pro: N/A
Pro Shop: Limited inventory
Payment: Cash only
Tee Times: No
Fee 9 Holes: Weekday: $7.00
Fee 18 Holes: Weekday: $7.00
Twilight Rates: No
Cart Rental: Pull cart $3.00
Lessons: No **Schools:** No
Clinics: No **Day Camps:** No
Other: Restaurant / Bar-lounge

Tees	Holes	Yards	Par	USGA	Slope
BACK					
MIDDLE	9	2570	27		
FRONT					

Weekend: $8.00
Weekend: $8.00
All Day Play: Yes
Discounts: Sr & Jr memberships
Junior Golf: No **Membership:** Yes
Driving Range: No

Well built and maintained par 3. Great for beginners, seniors and people with little time.

	1	2	3	4	5	6	7	8	9
PAR	3	3	3	3	3	3	3	3	3
YARDS	160	135	110	125	220	100	125	175	135
HDCP	5	9	15	13	1	17	11	3	7
	10	11	12	13	14	15	16	17	18
PAR									
YARDS									
HDCP									

Directions: I-95 (Maine Turnpike) to Waterville Exit. Follow signs for Thomas College.

Piscataquis CC

✪✪ 47 ▶

Dover Rd., Guilford, ME (207) 876-3203

Club Pro: No
Pro Shop: Full inventory
Payment: Cash only
Tee Times: No
Fee 9 Holes: Weekday: $12.00
Fee 18 Holes: Weekday: $18.00
Twilight Rates: After 1 pm (M-F)
Cart Rental: $20.00/18 $10.00/9
Lessons: N/A **Schools:** No
Clinics: No **Day Camps:** No
Other: Clubhouse / Snack bar / Showers

Tees	Holes	Yards	Par	USGA	Slope
BACK					
MIDDLE	9	5414	69	64.6	112
FRONT	9	4846	72	67.5	109

Weekend: $15.00
Weekend: $20.00
All Day Play:
Discounts: Junior
Junior Golf: Yes **Membership:** Yes
Driving Range: No

COUPON

Renovations on holes 2, 3, 5, and 9 completed. Open April 15 - October 15. Student all day rate: $5 weekdays, $7 weekends.

	1	2	3	4	5	6	7	8	9
PAR	4	4	4	4	4	3	4	4	4
YARDS	352	324	251	290	370	164	268	348	377
HDCP	5	13	15	17	1	9	11	3	7
	10	11	12	13	14	15	16	17	18
PAR	4	4	3	4	4	3	4	4	4
YARDS	352	344	209	270	320	170	298	348	359
HDCP	6	14	2	18	8	16	12	4	10

Directions: Newport Exit Route 7 to Route 23 North. 25 miles from Newport.

Portage Hill CC

48 ▶

Rt. 11, Portage, ME (207) 435-8221

Club Pro: N/A
Pro Shop: No
Payment: Cash only
Tee Times: No
Fee 9 Holes: Weekday: $12.00
Fee 18 Holes: Weekday: $18.00 All Day
Twilight Rates: No
Cart Rental: $18.00/18 $12.00/9
Lessons: No **Schools:** N/R
Clinics: No **Day Camps:** No
Other: Clubhouse / Snack bar / Bar-lounge.

Tees	Holes	Yards	Par	USGA	Slope
BACK					
MIDDLE	9	3109	36	69.5	110
FRONT	9	2796	37	71.5	113

Weekend: $12.00
Weekend: $18.00
All Day Play: Wkdys
Discounts: Senior & Junior
Junior Golf: No **Membership:** Yes
Driving Range: No

**N
ME**

The course is well maintained, hilly and scenic. Open from mid May to mid Sept. Rates subject to change.

	1	2	3	4	5	6	7	8	9
PAR	4	4	4	4	5	3	4	5	3
YARDS	432	323	321	343	478	128	388	504	165
HDCP	1	13	16	6	11	18	4	8	15
	10	11	12	13	14	15	16	17	18
PAR									
YARDS									
HDCP									

Directions: Take I-95 to Sherman/Patton Exit (Route 11). Follow Route 11 North into Portage (60 mi.).

Presque Isle CC

49

Presque Isle, ME (207) 764-0430
www.picountryclub.com

Club Pro: Barry Madore
Pro Shop: Full inventory
Payment: Visa, MC, Cash
Tee Times: No
Fee 9 Holes: Weekday: $14.00
Fee 18 Holes: Weekday: $25.00
Twilight Rates: No
Cart Rental: $12pp/18 $7pp/9
Lessons: $20/35 min. **Schools:** No
Clinics: Yes **Day Camps:** No
Other: Clubhouse / Lockers / Showers / Restaurant/Lounge

Tees	Holes	Yards	Par	USGA	Slope
BACK	18	6730	72	71.4	122
MIDDLE	18	6326	72	69.1	117
FRONT	18	5600	72	72.5	119

Weekend: $14.00
Weekend: $25.00
All Day Play: No
Discounts: None
Junior Golf: Yes **Membership:** Yes
Driving Range: $3.00 /bucket.

A very picturesque golf course. Front 9 designed by Architect Ben Gray. More recent back 9 designed by Geoffrey Cornish and Rick Hobbs.

	1	2	3	4	5	6	7	8	9
PAR	4	4	4	3	4	4	5	3	5
YARDS	343	400	363	167	423	389	463	146	465
HDCP	13	5	9	15	1	3	11	17	7
	10	11	12	13	14	15	16	17	18
PAR	4	4	5	4	4	5	3	3	4
YARDS	381	387	525	359	396	473	103	202	341
HDCP	12	10	4	8	6	2	18	16	14

Directions: From Presque Isle, take Route 167 to Route 205. You can't miss it, but if you do, call course for directions.

NEW 2004 Rocky Knoll Country Club

50

River Rd., Orrington, ME (207) 989-0109
www.rockyknoll.com

Club Pro: B. Curtis & M. Clendenning
Pro Shop: Yes
Payment: Visa, MC, Amex, Checks
Tee Times: No
Fee 9 Holes: Weekday: $10.00
Fee 18 Holes: Weekday: $15.00
Twilight Rates: No
Cart Rental: $15/18, $10/9
Lessons: $35/60 min. **Schools:** No
Clinics: **Day Camps:** No
Other: Restaurant / Clubhouse

Tees	Holes	Yards	Par	USGA	Slope
BACK					
MIDDLE	9	3055	36	65.9	94
FRONT	9	2653	36		

Weekend: $13.00
Weekend: $18.00
All Day Play: $15 wkday/ $18 wknd
Discounts: Senior, Wed./ Junior
Junior Golf: No **Membership:** Yes
Driving Range: Yes

New Entry 2004. Easy to walk. Water comes into play only on two holes. The signature hole is # 5. From off this tee golfers can see picturesque view of the course and clubhouse.

	1	2	3	4	5	6	7	8	9
PAR	5	4	4	5	3	4	3	4	4
YARDS	490	350	425	475	160	410	154	280	311
HDCP	5	13	1	9	11	3	7	15	17
	10	11	12	13	14	15	16	17	18
PAR									
YARDS									
HDCP									

Directions: I-395 Exit South Main Street, Brewer. Turn left onto Route 15 for about 3 miles. Course is on left.

NEW ENGLAND GOLFGUIDE

Searsport Pines Golf Course

Searsport, ME (207) 548-2854

51

Club Pro: N/A
Pro Shop: Limited inventory
Payment: Visa, MC
Tee Times: recommended for weekends
Fee 9 Holes: Weekday: $15.00
Fee 18 Holes: Weekday: $23.00
Twilight Rates: No
Cart Rental: $22.00/18 $7.50pp/9
Lessons: No **Schools:** No
Clinics: No **Day Camps:** No
Other: Food concession / Beer / Wine

Tees	Holes	Yards	Par	USGA	Slope
BACK					
MIDDLE	9	2695	36	66.1	116
FRONT	9	2366	35/36	68.7	116

Weekend: $15.00
Weekend: $23.00
All Day Play: No
Discounts: Sr & Jr memberships only
Junior Golf: No **Membership:** Yes
Driving Range: Yes

COUPON

Many new tees and traps added. Juniors must be over 12 to play alone.

	1	2	3	4	5	6	7	8	9
PAR	4	4	4	4	5	3	4	5	3
YARDS	285	353	313	316	390	150	295	464	129
HDCP	15	1	9	13	3	7	17	5	11
	10	**11**	**12**	**13**	**14**	**15**	**16**	**17**	**18**
PAR									
YARDS									
HDCP									

Directions: I 95 to Route 3 on the Maine coast. Pick up Route 1 in Belfast. In center of Searsport turn left onto Mt. Ephraim Road. Course is 2 miles on left.

Squaw Mt. Village CC

Greenville Junction, ME (207) 695-3609

52

Club Pro: No
Pro Shop: No
Payment: Cash only
Tee Times: No
Fee 9 Holes: Weekday: $15.00
Fee 18 Holes: Weekday: $22.00
Twilight Rates: No
Cart Rental: $18.00/18 $12.00/9
Lessons: **Schools:** No
Clinics: Yes **Day Camps:** No
Other:

Tees	Holes	Yards	Par	USGA	Slope
BACK					
MIDDLE	9	2463	34	N/A	N/A
FRONT					

Weekend: $15.00
Weekend: $22.00
All Day Play: Yes
Discounts: None
Junior Golf: Yes **Membership:** Yes
Driving Range: No

**N
ME**

Discount on membership for juniors, seniors, and families.

	1	2	3	4	5	6	7	8	9
PAR	4	3	5	4	4	3	4	3	4
YARDS	310	126	455	295	330	120	360	117	350
HDCP	9	15	1	11	7	13	3	17	5
	10	**11**	**12**	**13**	**14**	**15**	**16**	**17**	**18**
PAR									
YARDS									
HDCP									

Directions: 95 N take Newport exit. Left on Route 57 til Dexter. After traffic light, take left onto Route 23 until Route 15, go left. Course is 3.2 miles on right. 95 S, Exit 15 Bangor, Stay on Route 15. At blinking light in Greenville, go left on Route 15. Course is 33.2 miles on right.

4✪ =Excellent **3✪** =Very Good **2✪** =Good

St. Croix Country Club

Calais, ME (207) 454-8875

Tees	Holes	Yards	Par	USGA	Slope
BACK					
MIDDLE	9	2797	35	65.2	107
FRONT	9	2647	36	64.8	119

Club Pro: Duane Ellis
Pro Shop: Full inventory
Payment: Visa, MC
Tee Times: No
Fee 9 Holes: Weekday: $15.00   **Weekend:** $15.00
Fee 18 Holes: Weekday: $25.00   **Weekend:** $25.00
Twilight Rates: No   **All Day Play:** Yes, $25.00
Cart Rental: $22.00/18 $14.00/9   **Discounts:** None
Lessons: $20.00/half hour   **Schools:** No   **Junior Golf:** Yes **Membership:** Yes
Clinics: N/R   **Day Camps:** No   **Driving Range:** No
Other: Clubhouse / Showers / Bar-Lounge

Sig. Hole: #7 on river with eagle's nest. Watch eagles train the young.   Call ahead for league or tournament times. Reduced cart rate for members. Open May 1 - October 31.

	1	2	3	4	5	6	7	8	9
PAR	3	5	4	4	5	3	4	3	4
YARDS	162	495	319	405	495	126	295	188	312
HDCP	15	1	7	3	5	17	11	13	9
	10	11	12	13	14	15	16	17	18
PAR									
YARDS									
HDCP									

Directions: Head east on Route 1. 2 miles outside of Calais.

Sugarloaf Golf Club

✪✪✪

Carrabassett Valley, ME (207) 237-2000
www.sugarloaf.com

Tees	Holes	Yards	Par	USGA	Slope
BACK	18	6910	72	74.4	151
MIDDLE	18	5946	72	72.3	146
FRONT	18	5309	72	73.7	136

Club Pro: J. Scott Hoisington
Pro Shop: Full inventory
Payment: Cash or credit card
Tee Times: 14 days adv.
Fee 9 Holes: Weekday: $50.00   **Weekend:** $50.00
Fee 18 Holes: Weekday: $82.00   **Weekend:** $88.00
Twilight Rates: Yes, after 3 pm   **All Day Play:**
Cart Rental: $18.00/18 $10.00/9   **Discounts:** Junior 50%
Lessons: $35.00/half/hour   **Schools:** Jr. & Sr.   **Junior Golf:** Yes **Membership:** Yes
Clinics: Yes   **Day Camps:** No   **Driving Range:** $3.00-6.00/bag
Other: Snack bar / Restaurant / Bar-lounge / Health club / Hotel

COUPON

Rated among the best resort courses in U.S. by *Golf Digest*. Discounted rates for guests.
Players' Comments: "Breathtaking resort course, I wish it were closer." "Challenging and picturesque."

	1	2	3	4	5	6	7	8	9
PAR	4	5	3	5	4	4	4	3	4
YARDS	372	510	168	466	358	337	331	153	363
HDCP	11	9	15	7	1	5	13	17	3
	10	11	12	13	14	15	16	17	18
PAR	4	3	5	4	4	3	5	4	4
YARDS	255	166	495	359	333	132	458	339	351
HDCP	18	12	8	14	4	16	10	6	2

Directions: Located 36 miles north of Farmington on Route 27 at Sugarloaf Mountain Ski Resort.

Todd Valley Golf Club

Charleston, ME (207) 285-7725

Club Pro: Kenneth J. Young
Pro Shop: Limited inventory
Payment: Cash, Check
Tee Times: No
Fee 9 Holes: Weekday: $9.00
Fee 18 Holes: Weekday: $14.00
Twilight Rates: No
Cart Rental: $16.00/18 $10.00/9
Lessons: Yes **Schools:** No
Clinics: No **Day Camps:** No
Other: Snack Bar

Weekend: $9.00
Weekend: $14.00
All Day Play: No
Discounts: None
Junior Golf: No **Membership:** No
Driving Range: $3.00/lg

Tees	Holes	Yards	Par	USGA	Slope
BACK					
MIDDLE	9	4672	68	61.1	93
FRONT	9	4042	66	61.1	93

Holes 1 & 9 now Par 4. The 6th hole is compared to a Coney Island roller coaster. After the first run, each run is half price for the rest of the day. Open from snow melt to snow fall.

	1	2	3	4	5	6	7	8	9
PAR	4	4	4	5	3	3	4	4	4
YARDS	183	255	315	487	120	150	250	280	196
HDCP	11	17	3	1	13	15	7	9	5

	10	11	12	13	14	15	16	17	18
PAR	3	4	4	5	3	3	4	4	3
YARDS	183	255	315	487	120	150	250	280	196
HDCP	12	18	4	2	14	16	8	10	6

Directions: From 95 Bangor west on Route 15. 20 miles to Charleston (1 mile after E. Corinth). Turn left on to Bacon Rd. Course is 1 mile on left.

Va-Jo-Wa Golf Club

Walker Settlement Road, Island Falls, ME (207) 463-2128
www.vajowa.com

Club Pro: Warren Walker
Pro Shop: Full inventory
Payment: MC, Visa, Dis.
Tee Times: Suggested
Fee 9 Holes: Weekday: $18.00
Fee 18 Holes: Weekday: $30.00
Twilight Rates: N/R
Cart Rental: $30/18, $20/9
Lessons: $25/30 min. by appt. **Schools:** No
Clinics: Junior **Day Camps:** No
Other: Clubhouse / Snack bar / Restaurant / Bar-lounge / Condos / Bag Storage

Weekend: $18.00
Weekend: $30.00
All Day Play: Yes
Discounts: Junior
Junior Golf: July **Membership:** Yes
Driving Range: Yes

COUPON

Tees	Holes	Yards	Par	USGA	Slope
BACK	18	6223	72	70.4	125
MIDDLE	18	5862	72	69.1	121
FRONT	18	5065	72	69.6	115

Only 18 hole course in 80 mile radius. Noted for scenic value and quality layout. Open May 1 - Oct 31.

	1	2	3	4	5	6	7	8	9
PAR	4	4	4	3	4	3	5	4	5
YARDS	308	445	283	207	378	116	517	354	531
HDCP	9	1	3	13	7	17	3	11	5

	10	11	12	13	14	15	16	17	18
PAR	4	3	4	4	4	5	3	4	5
YARDS	315	138	381	458	387	478	161	371	524
HDCP	12	18	14	2	6	8	16	10	4

Directions: Take I-95 to Island Falls Exit (#59); follow Route 2 East 3 miles; look for signs to VA-JO-WA.

4✪ =Excellent 3✪ =Very Good 2✪ =Good

Waterville Country Club ✪✪ ▶ 57

Oakland, ME (207) 465-9861

Club Pro: Don Roberts, PGA
Pro Shop: Full inventory
Payment: Cash only
Tee Times: Yes

Tees	Holes	Yards	Par	USGA	Slope
BACK	18	6427	70	70.1	123
MIDDLE	18	6108	70	68.6	118
FRONT	18	5381	70	71.3	119

Fee 9 Holes: Weekday: No
Fee 18 Holes: Weekday: $48.00
Twilight Rates: No
Cart Rental: $28.00/18
Lessons: $30/30 min. **Schools:** No
Clinics: Yes **Day Camps:** No
Other: Snack bar / Restaurant / Bar-lounge

Weekend: No
Weekend: $48.00
All Day Play: Yes
Discounts: None
Junior Golf: Yes **Membership:** Yes
Driving Range: $3.00/bucket

Sig. Hole: #7, 325 yard short par 4. Green surrounded by pond. Ranked 4th in ME by *Golf Digest*.
Excellent for all golfers. Semi-private.

	1	2	3	4	5	6	7	8	9
PAR	4	3	5	4	4	3	4	4	5
YARDS	350	140	455	378	430	170	300	385	505
HDCP	15	13	17	3	1	9	7	5	11
	10	11	12	13	14	15	16	17	18
PAR	4	4	4	3	4	4	3	4	4
YARDS	435	410	370	200	355	330	185	370	340
HDCP	2	4	6	8	14	16	10	12	18

Directions: I-95 North to Exit 33 to Oakland. Waterville Country Club is 1 1/2 miles on left.

White Birches GC ▶ 58

Ellsworth, ME (207) 667-3621
www.wbirches.com

Club Pro: No
Pro Shop: Full inventory
Payment: Visa, MC, Amex
Tee Times: No

Tees	Holes	Yards	Par	USGA	Slope
BACK					
MIDDLE	18	1922	54		
FRONT					

Fee 9 Holes: Weekday: $15.00 all day
Fee 18 Holes: Weekday: $15.00 all day
Twilight Rates: No
Cart Rental: $18.00/18 $10.00/9
Lessons: **Schools:** NR
Clinics: No **Day Camps:** No
Other: Clubhouse / Bar-lounge / Restaurant / Motel

Weekend: $15.00 all day
Weekend: $15.00 all day
All Day Play: Yes
Discounts: None
Junior Golf: No **Membership:** Yes
Driving Range: No

The course has been converted into a lighted 18 hole par 3 course.

	1	2	3	4	5	6	7	8	9
PAR	3	3	3	3	3	3	3	3	3
YARDS	123	84	129	92	113	104	74	87	142
HDCP	1	17	5	11	13	7	9	15	3
	10	11	12	13	14	15	16	17	18
PAR	3	3	3	3	3	3	3	3	3
YARDS	111	83	120	144	134	119	77	81	105
HDCP	18	2	10	8	6	4	14	12	16

Directions: Take I-95 to Route 45A Exit, follow to Ellsworth on Route 1 East; course is 1 1/2 miles on left.

White Tail Golf Course

Charleston, ME (207) 285-7730

Club Pro: Scott Duthie
Pro Shop: Limited inventory
Payment: Cash and checks
Tee Times: No
Fee 9 Holes: Weekday: $8.00
Fee 18 Holes: Weekday: $10.00
Twilight Rates: No
Cart Rental: $14.00/18 $9.00/9
Lessons: No **Schools:** No
Clinics: **Day Camps:**
Other: Restaurant / Clubhouse

Weekend: $8.00
Weekend: $10.00
All Day Play: Yes
Discounts: None
Junior Golf: **Membership:**
Driving Range: No

Tees	Holes	Yards	Par	USGA	Slope
BACK	9	2780	34	64.2	109
MIDDLE	9	2577	34	64.2	109
FRONT	9	4716	34	64.2	109

New Entry 2004. Scenic 9 hole course, country setting. Variety of short and long holes. Sig.Hole, #4 short downhill par 4 requires accurate tee shot. Opened in 1997.

	1	2	3	4	5	6	7	8	9
PAR	5	3	3	4	3	4	4	4	4
YARDS	494	136	176	235	150	329	330	370	357
HDCP	2	9	6	8	7	4	3	1	5
	10	**11**	**12**	**13**	**14**	**15**	**16**	**17**	**18**
PAR									
YARDS									
HDCP									

Directions: From I-95 Bangor, exit north on Route 15. Go approximately 30 miles. Course is at the corner of Route 15 and School Road in Charleston. Turn left.

N
ME

4✪ =Excellent 3✪ =Very Good 2✪ =Good

CHAPTER 8
Vermont

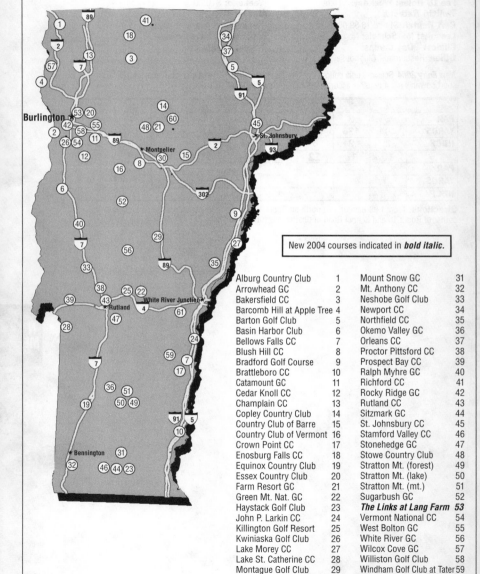

New 2004 courses indicated in **_bold italic._**

Alburg Country Club

Rt. 79, Alburg, VT (802) 796-3586
www.alburg.com

1

Club Pro: No
Pro Shop: Limited inventory
Payment: Cash, Check
Tee Times: Call
Fee 9 Holes: Weekday: N/A
Fee 18 Holes: Weekday: $25.00
Twilight Rates: After 2 pm, 4 pm
Cart Rental: $25/18
Lessons: No **Schools:** No
Clinics: No **Day Camps:** No
Other: Clubhouse / Snack bar / Bar-lounge / 10 play discount card

Tees	Holes	Yards	Par	USGA	Slope
BACK	18	6434	72	70.2	119
MIDDLE	18	5776	72	67.4	116
FRONT	18	5536	75	71.2	120

Weekend: N/A
Weekend: $25.00
All Day Play: No
Discounts: None
Junior Golf: Yes **Membership:** Yes
Driving Range: $4.00/bucket

A good vacation course. A moderate challenge for a good time. Reduced rates after 2:00 pm. Canadian money accepted.

	1	2	3	4	5	6	7	8	9
PAR	4	4	4	4	3	4	5	4	3
YARDS	315	317	387	310	120	362	459	143	344
HDCP	15	7	1	11	9	5	13	17	3

	10	11	12	13	14	15	16	17	18
PAR	5	3	4	5	4	4	3	5	4
YARDS	467	167	404	488	296	286	140	447	322
HDCP	4	18	2	6	16	14	12	8	10

Directions: Take I-89 to Exit 17; take Route 2 to Champlain Islands North to Alburg; take Route 129 to course.

Arrowhead Golf Course

Milton, VT (802) 893-0234

2

Club Pro: Holly Reynolds
Pro Shop: Limited inventory
Payment: Cash, Check, Credit
Tee Times: No
Fee 9 Holes: Weekday: $13.00
Fee 18 Holes: Weekday: $14.00
Twilight Rates: Yes, after 5 pm
Cart Rental: Yes
Lessons: Yes **Schools:** No
Clinics: Yes **Day Camps:** Yes
Other: Club House

Tees	Holes	Yards	Par	USGA	Slope
BACK	9	1542	27	56.6	80
MIDDLE	9	1330	27	56.0	79
FRONT	9	1005	27	48.8	55

Weekend: $15.00
Weekend: $16.00
All Day Play: No
Discounts: None
Junior Golf: No **Membership:** Yes
Driving Range: $5.00/lg. $3.00/sm.

VT

This 9 hole, par 3 golf course consists of gently rolling fairways, unique design characteristics, excellent greens, sand bunkers, water hazards, and natural hazards. 3rd hole is very challenging.

	1	2	3	4	5	6	7	8	9
PAR	3	3	3	3	3	3	3	3	3
YARDS	165	148	195	90	119	195	136	104	178
HDCP									

	10	11	12	13	14	15	16	17	18
PAR									
YARDS									
HDCP									

Directions: Exit 18 from I-89. Go south on Route 7 approximately 1/2 mile. Turn right onto Ballard Rd. for 1/2 mile, take left onto Old Stage Rd. for 1 mile, then right onto Murray Ave for 1.6 miles. Course is on left.

4✪ =Excellent 3✪ =Very Good 2✪ =Good

Bakersfield CC

3

Rt. 108, Bakersfield, VT (802) 933-5100

Tees	Holes	Yards	Par	USGA	Slope
BACK	18	6222	72		
MIDDLE	18	5881	72	69.0	115
FRONT	18	5006	72	68.7	108

Club Pro:
Pro Shop: Limited inventory
Payment: Visa, MC, Amex
Tee Times: Yes
Fee 9 Holes: Weekday: N/A
Fee 18 Holes: Weekday: $20.00 all day
Twilight Rates: Yes, after 6 pm
Cart Rental: $20.00/18
Lessons: Yes **Schools:** No
Clinics: Yes **Day Camps:** No
Other: Snack bar / Restaurant / Bar-lounge

Weekend: N/A
Weekend: $21.00 all day
All Day Play: Yes
Discounts: None
Junior Golf: No **Membership:** Junior
Driving Range: No

COUPON

Expanded to 18 holes.

	1	2	3	4	5	6	7	8	9
PAR	4	4	5	3	4	3	4	5	4
YARDS	273	357	424	128	445	155	350	460	375
HDCP	18	12	11	17	4	5	14	6	3

	10	11	12	13	14	15	16	17	18
PAR	4	3	4	4	5	3	5	3	5
YARDS	360	155	345	290	468	150	392	155	599
HDCP	10	15	16	7	2	13	8	9	1

Directions: Take Route 108 through Bakersfield. Take right onto Boston Post Road. Follow signs.

Barcomb Hill At Apple Tree Bay Resort

4

South Hero, VT (802) 372-4135

Tees	Holes	Yards	Par	USGA	Slope
BACK					
MIDDLE	9	1108	27		
FRONT					

Club Pro: No
Pro Shop: Limited inventory
Payment: Cash, Checks
Tee Times: No
Fee 9 Holes: Weekday: $10.50
Fee 18 Holes: Weekday: $10.50
Twilight Rates: Yes, after 5 pm
Cart Rental: Pull $2.00
Lessons: No **Schools:** No
Clinics: No **Day Camps:** No
Other: Resort

Weekend: $12.60
Weekend: $12.60
All Day Play: No
Discounts: None
Junior Golf: No **Membership:** Yes
Driving Range: No

Course in great shape and all tees have been redone. No one under 5 years allowed. Open May 1 - October 20.

	1	2	3	4	5	6	7	8	9
PAR	3	3	3	3	3	3	3	3	3
YARDS	100	90	158	184	158	108	84	96	130
HDCP									

	10	11	12	13	14	15	16	17	18
PAR									
YARDS									
HDCP									

Directions: Exit 17 off I 89. 6 miles on left. Must drive through campground to reach.

Barton Golf Club

Barton, VT (802) 525-1126

Club Pro: Bill King
Pro Shop: Yes
Payment: Visa, MC
Tee Times: Yes
Fee 9 Holes: Weekday: $10.00
Fee 18 Holes: Weekday: $15.00
Twilight Rates: Yes, after 6 pm
Cart Rental: $10.00/9
Lessons: No **Schools:** No
Clinics: **Day Camps:** No
Other: Light fare menu.

Tees	Holes	Yards	Par	USGA	Slope
BACK	18	5500	70	66.3	107
MIDDLE	18	5304	70	65.3	104
FRONT	18	4500	69		

Weekend: $10.00
Weekend: $15.00
All Day Play: No
Discounts: None
Junior Golf: No **Membership:** Yes
Driving Range: No

COUPON

Scenic 18 holes in the heart of Vermont's Northeast Kingdom.

	1	2	3	4	5	6	7	8	9
PAR	4	5	4	3	4	4	3	5	4
YARDS	256	465	303	120	304	396	160	440	365
HDCP	17	5	9	15	113	3	1	13	7

	10	11	12	13	14	15	16	17	18
PAR	4	3	5	4	3	3	5	3	4
YARDS	268	130	450	385	140	150	502	135	335
HDCP	18	8	6	2	10	14	16	12	4

Directions: Exit 25 off I-91. Take Route 16 into Barton. Go right on Water St. Cross Route 5. Left on High St. Club is one mile on right.

Basin Harbor Club

Vergennes, VT (802) 475-2309
www.basinharbor.com

Club Pro: Steve Gonsalves, PGA
Pro Shop: Full inventory
Payment: Visa, MC
Tee Times: 3 days adv.
Fee 9 Holes: Weekday: $25 before 2pm
Fee 18 Holes: Weekday: $47 before 1pm
Twilight Rates: No
Cart Rental: $17.50pp/18 $10pp/9
Lessons: $40/30 min **Schools:** Yes
Clinics: Yes **Day Camps:** No
Other: Clubhouse / Snack bar / Restaurant / Bar-lounge / Hotel

Tees	Holes	Yards	Par	USGA	Slope
BACK	18	6513	72	71.5	122
MIDDLE	18	6232	72	70.4	120
FRONT	18	5745	72	68.1	116

Weekend: $25 before 2pm
Weekend: $47 before 1pm
All Day Play: Yes
Discounts: None
Junior Golf: Yes **Membership:** Yes
Driving Range: $7.00 bucket

Fairly flat, located on Lake Champlain. Collared shirt required. No cutoffs. Open May 1 - mid October. 18 hole rate reduced after 1 pm, 9 hole after 2 pm.

	1	2	3	4	5	6	7	8	9
PAR	4	4	4	4	3	4	3	5	5
YARDS	360	361	398	328	103	323	150	458	475
HDCP	9	7	1	11	17	13	15	3	5

	10	11	12	13	14	15	16	17	18
PAR	4	4	5	3	4	4	3	5	4
YARDS	387	376	500	181	324	414	175	510	409
HDCP	16	10	6	18	8	2	14	4	12

Directions: Take Route 7 to Vergennes Exit. Straight through town on Route 22A. Cross over bridge, take right at sign to Basin Harbor. 1 mile to Basin Harbor Road, take right, 6 miles to course.

Bellows Falls CC

Rt. 103, Rockingham, VT (802) 463-9809

Club Pro:
Pro Shop: Full inventory
Payment: Visa, MC, Cash
Tee Times: No
Fee 9 Holes: Weekday: $14.00
Fee 18 Holes: Weekday: $22.00
Twilight Rates: After 4 pm
Cart Rental: $24.00/18 $16.00/9
Lessons: Yes **Schools:** No
Clinics: No **Day Camps:** No
Other: Restaurant / Bar

Tees	Holes	Yards	Par	USGA	Slope
BACK					
MIDDLE	9	5928	70	65.8	117
FRONT	9	5138	70	65.8	110

Weekend: $17.00
Weekend: $25.00
All Day Play: No
Discounts: None
Junior Golf: No **Membership:** Yes
Driving Range: No

In the process of completing new irrigation system and paving of cart paths while maintaining playability. Open May 1 - November 1.

	1	2	3	4	5	6	7	8	9
PAR	4	5	3	3	4	4	4	3	5
YARDS	389	513	178	155	381	370	320	158	428
HDCP	4	8	10	16	6	2	12	18	14
	10	11	12	13	14	15	16	17	18
PAR	4	5	3	3	4	4	4	3	5
YARDS	402	529	194	177	391	380	355	170	438
HDCP	3	7	9	15	5	1	11	17	13

Directions: I-91 to Route 103 North. Appx. 3 miles, turn right onto Rockingham Road. Across from VT Country Store.

Blush Hill CC

Waterbury, VT (802) 244-8974

Club Pro: Jon Milne, PGA
Pro Shop: Full inventory
Payment: Visa, MC
Tee Times: F-Sun
Fee 9 Holes: Weekday: $18.00 M-Th
Fee 18 Holes: Weekday: $24.00 M-Th
Twilight Rates: No
Cart Rental: $24.00/18 $16.00/9
Lessons: $30/30 min. **Schools:** No
Clinics: No **Day Camps:** Yes
Other: Clubhouse / Lockers / Showers / Snack bar / Restaurant / Bar-lounge

Tees	Holes	Yards	Par	USGA	Slope
BACK					
MIDDLE	9	4831	66	62.7	113
FRONT	9	4550	67	66.2	114

Weekend: $21.00 F/S/S
Weekend: $27.00 F/S/S
All Day Play:
Discounts: None
Junior Golf: Yes **Membership:** Yes
Driving Range: $5.00/lg. $4.00/sm.

One of the most extraordinary scenic views in Vermont. Course kept in excellent shape.   Open May 1 to October 15.

	1	2	3	4	5	6	7	8	9
PAR	4	4	4	3	4	3	3	4	4
YARDS	377	350	206	171	266	146	157	377	302
HDCP	4	2	14	16	8	18	12	6	10
	10	11	12	13	14	15	16	17	18
PAR	4	4	4	3	4	3	3	4	4
YARDS	391	358	222	191	276	160	166	392	316
HDCP	3	1	13	15	7	17	11	5	9

Directions: 1/2 mile off I-89 North on Route 100. 1000 feet left on Blush Hill Road, 1/2 mile behind Holiday Inn.

Bradford Golf Course

Bradford, VT (802) 222-5207

Club Pro: No
Pro Shop: Limited inventory
Payment: Cash, Visa, MC
Tee Times: No
Fee 9 Holes: Weekday: $14.00
Fee 18 Holes: Weekday: $18.00
Twilight Rates: Yes, after 5 pm
Cart Rental: $12pp/18 $9pp/9
Lessons: No **Schools:** No
Clinics: No **Day Camps:** No
Other: Snacks

Tees	Holes	Yards	Par	USGA	Slope
BACK	9	2155	32		
MIDDLE	9	2052	32		
FRONT					

Weekend: $14.00
Weekend: $20.00
All Day Play: No
Discounts: None
Junior Golf: No **Membership:** Yes
Driving Range: No

Par 32, 18 sets of tees.

	1	2	3	4	5	6	7	8	9
PAR	3	4	3	3	4	3	5	4	3
YARDS	174	239	160	115	304	185	431	294	150
HDCP									
	10	11	12	13	14	15	16	17	18
PAR									
YARDS									
HDCP									

Directions: From I-91, take Exit 16, turn right and go 3/4 of a mile. Turn left, go 1 mile north. Turn right, go by Bradford Academy to bottom of hill.

Brattleboro CC

Rt. 30, Brattleboro, VT (802) 257-7380
www.brattleborogolf.com

Club Pro: Bill Tooley, PGA
Pro Shop: Full inventory
Payment: Visa, MC, Amex
Tee Times: 3 days adv.
Fee 9 Holes: Weekday: $20.00
Fee 18 Holes: Weekday: $40.00
Twilight Rates: No
Cart Rental: $18pp/18 $10pp/9
Lessons: Yes **Schools:** Yes
Clinics: Yes **Day Camps:** No
Other: Restaurant / Bar-lounge

Tees	Holes	Yards	Par	USGA	Slope
BACK	18	6508	71	71.0	123
MIDDLE	18	6073	71	69.3	118
FRONT	18	5059	71	70.0	116

Weekend: $25.00
Weekend: $50.00
All Day Play: No
Discounts: Senior
Junior Golf: Yes **Membership:** Yes
Driving Range: Yes

Expansion to 18 holes completed. Inquire about special offers.

	1	2	3	4	5	6	7	8	9
PAR	4	5	4	3	4	4	5	3	4
YARDS	405	504	359	155	397	243	455	155	363
HDCP	3	1	7	17	5	13	11	15	9
	10	11	12	13	14	15	16	17	18
PAR	5	4	4	3	4	4	3	4	4
YARDS	492	378	376	172	346	386	152	346	389
HDCP	8	2	6	16	12	4	18	14	10

Directions: I-91 N or S to Exit 2. Left off exit, go 1/2 mile to Cedar St. Turn left, follow to bottom of hill. Left on Route 30. Left at Upper Dumerston Rd. Club 1/2 mile on left.

4🟢 =Excellent 3🟢 =Very Good 2🟢 =Good

Catamount Golf Course

11

Williston, VT. 802-878-7227

Club Pro:
Pro Shop: Full inventory
Payment: Visa, MC, Disc, Check
Tee Times:
Fee 9 Holes: Weekday: $13.00
Fee 18 Holes: Weekday: $22.00
Twilight Rates: No
Cart Rental: $6pp/9
Lessons: Schools: No
Clinics: Adult/Jr **Day Camps:** Yes
Other: Snackbar

Weekend: $13.00
Weekend: $22.00
All Day Play: No
Discounts: None
Junior Golf: Yes **Membership:** No
Driving Range: $6/lg. $4/sm. Double-decker

Tees	Holes	Yards	Par	USGA	Slope
BACK					
MIDDLE	9	3040	35		
FRONT					

$100 discount card available for ten 9 hole rounds. Course landscaped to provide visual depiction of the route to play this links style course.

	1	2	3	4	5	6	7	8	9
PAR	4	3	4	3	5	3	5	4	4
YARDS	385	160	380	185	520	170	485	365	390
HDCP	6	9	5	8	1	7	4	3	2
	10	11	12	13	14	15	16	17	18
PAR									
YARDS									
HDCP									

Directions: Take I-89 to Exit 12 (Route 2A). Go north on Route 2A for about 1 mile. Turn right on Williston Rd. for 1 1/2 miles. Course will be on your right.

Cedar Knoll CC

12

Hinesburg, VT (802) 482-3186
cedarknollgolf.com

Club Pro: Barry Churchill
Pro Shop: Limited inventory
Payment: Visa, MC, Amex
Tee Times: Yes
Fee 9 Holes: Weekday: $16.50
Fee 18 Holes: Weekday: $26.00
Twilight Rates: Yes, after 5 pm
Cart Rental: $26.00/18
Lessons: Yes **Schools:** No
Clinics: Yes **Day Camps:** No
Other: Restaurant / Clubhouse / Bar-Lounge / Lockers / Showers / Snack Bar

Weekend: $16.50
Weekend: $26.00
All Day Play: $26.00
Discounts: Senior
Junior Golf: No **Membership:** Yes
Driving Range: $2.00-$5.00/bucket

Tees	Holes	Yards	Par	USGA	Slope
BACK	27/18	6541	72	72.5	117
MIDDLE	27/18	6144	72	72.5	117
FRONT	27/18	5360	72	69.5	108

COUPON

Now 27 holes. Rolling hills. 250 acres allows for much spacing of holes. Beautiful scenery. Cedar Knoll South 9 hole addition is also open. 9 hole rate, $16.50.

	1	2	3	4	5	6	7	8	9
PAR	5	3	4	4	5	3	4	4	4
YARDS	500	156	315	358	505	170	392	313	438
HDCP	3	17	5	11	7	15	9	13	1
	10	11	12	13	14	15	16	17	18
PAR	5	3	4	4	3	4	4	4	5
YARDS	494	169	298	333	156	291	341	315	536
HDCP	4	16	12	6	18	14	10	8	2

Directions: I-89, Exit 12; follow 5 miles to intersection of Routes 2A and 116. Take left and go 5 miles on 116. Course on right.

Champlain CC

Swanton, VT (802) 527-1187
www.champlaincountryclub.com

Club Pro: Michael Swim, PGA
Pro Shop: Full inventory
Payment: MC, Visa, Discover
Tee Times: Weekends, Holidays
Fee 9 Holes: Weekday: $20.00
Fee 18 Holes: Weekday: $30.00
Twilight Rates: Yes, after 4 pm
Cart Rental: $30.00/18 $20.00/9
Lessons: $25.00/half hour **Schools:**
Clinics: Yes **Day Camps:** No
Other: Clubhouse / Lockers / Showers / Snack bar / Restaurant / Bar-lounge

Tees	Holes	Yards	Par	USGA	Slope
BACK	18	6237	70	69.9	123
MIDDLE	18	5959	70	68.8	121
FRONT	18	5266	70	70.4	117

Weekend: $25.00
Weekend: $35.00
All Day Play: Yes
Discounts: None
Junior Golf: Yes **Membership:** Yes
Driving Range: No

Sig. Hole: #7 is a raised tee overlooking Lake Champlain. Hit to lower plateau green with pond on left.

	1	2	3	4	5	6	7	8	9
PAR	4	5	3	4	4	4	3	4	4
YARDS	359	472	157	377	355	360	135	350	342
HDCP	1	7	15	3	13	9	17	5	11

	10	11	12	13	14	15	16	17	18
PAR	4	4	3	4	3	5	4	4	4
YARDS	303	444	142	370	167	558	338	415	315
HDCP	16	2	18	8	14	4	10	6	12

Directions: Take I-89 to Exit 20; take Route 7 North 1/2 mile to course.

Copley Country Club

Maple Rd., Morrisville, VT (802) 888-3013

Club Pro: No
Pro Shop: Full inventory
Payment: Visa, MC
Tee Times: Required
Fee 9 Holes: Weekday: $18.00
Fee 18 Holes: Weekday: $26.00
Twilight Rates: Yes, after 3 pm
Cart Rental: $24.00/18 $12/9
Lessons: No **Schools:** No
Clinics: No **Day Camps:** No
Other: Clubhouse / Lockers / Snack bar / Restaurant / Bar-lounge

Tees	Holes	Yards	Par	USGA	Slope
BACK	9	6000	70	67.4	112
MIDDLE	9	5549	70	67.4	112
FRONT	9	5020	70	68.0	104

Weekend: $18.00
Weekend: $26.00
All Day Play: No
Discounts: None
Junior Golf: Yes **Membership:** Yes
Driving Range: No

VT

Ideal conditions. The course is level with a handful of tree-lined holes.

	1	2	3	4	5	6	7	8	9
PAR	4	3	4	4	3	5	4	4	4
YARDS	310	218	326	296	171	526	395	270	262
HDCP	7	15	5	13	17	1	3	11	9

	10	11	12	13	14	15	16	17	18
PAR	4	3	4	4	3	5	4	4	4
YARDS	310	218	326	296	171	526	396	270	262
HDCP	8	16	6	14	18	2	4	12	10

Directions: Take I-89 to Waterbury Exit, follow 18 miles to Morrisville.

4❂ =Excellent **3❂** =Very Good **2❂** =Good

Country Club of Barre

15

Plainsfield Rd., Barre, VT (802) 476-7658

Tees	Holes	Yards	Par	USGA	Slope
BACK	18	6250	71	70.2	123
MIDDLE	18	5938	71	69.2	119
FRONT	18	5126	71	70.3	121

Club Pro: Roger King, PGA
Pro Shop: Full inventory
Payment: Visa, MC
Tee Times: 1 week adv.
Fee 9 Holes: Weekday: $25.00   **Weekend:** $25.00
Fee 18 Holes: Weekday: $45.00   **Weekend:** $45.00
Twilight Rates: No   **All Day Play:** No
Cart Rental: $18pp/18 $10pp/9   **Discounts:** None
Lessons: $30-$35/30 min. **Schools:** No   **Junior Golf:** For members **Membership:** Yes
Clinics: For members **Day Camps:** No   **Driving Range:** $3.00/lg.
Other: Clubhouse / Lockers / Showers / Snack bar / Restaurant / Bar-lounge

"One of the hidden gems in Vermont." Reviewed by *Vermont Golf Magazine*. Semi-private, call for tee times.

	1	2	3	4	5	6	7	8	9
PAR	4	4	4	3	5	4	3	4	4
YARDS	368	383	285	190	455	339	142	370	368
HDCP	11	1	13	15	7	5	17	9	3

	10	11	12	13	14	15	16	17	18
PAR	5	4	4	3	4	5	3	4	4
YARDS	492	372	314	170	431	439	125	343	352
HDCP	4	6	12	16	2	10	18	14	8

Directions: Take I-89 to Exit 7 (to Barre), follow Route 14 3.9 miles. Follow signs.

Country Club of Vermont ✪✪✪ **16**

Waterbury Center, Vt (802) 244-1800
www.countryclubvt.com

Tees	Holes	Yards	Par	USGA	Slope
BACK	18	6788	72	72.6	130
MIDDLE	18	5965	72	69.1	121
FRONT	18	5243	72	69.7	121

Club Pro: Ron Philo
Pro Shop:
Payment: Credit Cards only
Tee Times: Yes, 3 days
Fee 9 Holes: Weekday: No   **Weekend:** No
Fee 18 Holes: Weekday: $125   **Weekend:** $125
Twilight Rates: No   **All Day Play:** Yes
Cart Rental: $16.00pp/18   **Discounts:** None
Lessons: $100/60min **Schools:**   **Junior Golf:** **Membership:** Yes
Clinics: **Day Camps:**   **Driving Range:** Included in daily fee
Other:

Vermont's newest upscale facility, semi-private. Member introduction or PGA reciprocal. Designed by Graham Cooke: front 9, links style; back 9, into the woods.

	1	2	3	4	5	6	7	8	9
PAR	4	4	5	3	4	4	4	3	5
YARDS	328	378	415	143	339	356	374	150	523
HDCP	15	1	5	17	7	11	3	13	9

	10	11	12	13	14	15	16	17	18
PAR	4	3	5	4	3	5	3	4	5
YARDS	341	167	457	386	150	495	156	260	547
HDCP	10	14	6	2	16	12	8	18	4

Directions: Exit 10 off I-89. 2 miles from center of town.

Crown Point CC

⊙⊙ ▶ 17

Springfield, VT (802) 885-1010
www.crownpointcc.com

Club Pro: Paul Politano, PGA
Pro Shop: Full inventory
Payment: Visa, MC, cash
Tee Times: Recommended
Fee 9 Holes: Weekday: $28.00
Fee 18 Holes: Weekday: $45.00
Twilight Rates: Yes, after 5 pm
Cart Rental: Yes
Lessons: Yes **Schools:** No
Clinics: Yes **Day Camps:** No
Other: Clubhouse / Showers / Restaurant / Bar-lounge

Tees	Holes	Yards	Par	USGA	Slope
BACK	18	6602	72	71.2	123
MIDDLE	18	6120	72	69.1	119
FRONT	18	5542	72	71.3	117

Weekend: $28.00
Weekend: $55.00
All Day Play: No
Discounts: Senior & Junior
Junior Golf: Yes **Membership:** Yes
Driving Range: Yes

COUPON

Course noted for smooth fast greens. Great views. Open April 15 - November 1 (weather permitting.)

	1	2	3	4	5	6	7	8	9
PAR	4	5	4	4	3	4	5	4	3
YARDS	370	426	344	337	168	365	487	376	154
HDCP	13	7	11	9	15	3	1	5	17

	10	11	12	13	14	15	16	17	18
PAR	4	5	4	3	4	5	4	4	3
YARDS	344	463	390	158	344	459	381	371	183
HDCP	12	10	8	16	4	2	14	6	18

Directions: From I-91 North, Exit 7: turn right and follow to center of Springfield. Turn right onto Valley Street. Course 3 miles on left.

Enosburg Falls CC

▶ 18

Enosburg Falls, VT (802) 933-2296
Search "Enosburg Falls"

Club Pro: Pepper Sweeney
Pro Shop: Full inventory
Payment: MC, Visa
Tee Times: Yes
Fee 9 Holes: Weekday: $13.00 + tax
Fee 18 Holes: Weekday: $20.00 + tax
Twilight Rates: No
Cart Rental: $25.00/18, $15.00/9
Lessons: Yes **Schools:** No
Clinics: Yes **Day Camps:** No
Other: Restaurant / Clubhouse / Lockers / Showers

Tees	Holes	Yards	Par	USGA	Slope
BACK	18	5580	72	67.4	116
MIDDLE	18	5418	72	66.8	115
FRONT	18	4633	72	63.4	108

Weekend: $15.00 + tax
Weekend: $23.00 + tax
All Day Play: No
Discounts: Junior
Junior Golf: Yes **Membership:** Yes
Driving Range: Irons range

COUPON

VT

Sig. Hole: #7, 331 yd. par 4 has a long beautiful view. Course has some great birdie opportunities. Variety of rates for special memberships. Inquire. Open May - October.

	1	2	3	4	5	6	7	8	9
PAR	4	5	4	4	4	3	4	5	3
YARDS	249	498	337	251	350	115	331	552	119
HDCP	13	5	9	17	1	11	7	3	15

	10	11	12	13	14	15	16	17	18
PAR	4	3	4	5	5	3	4	4	4
YARDS	272	140	335	490	478	112	267	255	267
HDCP	12	14	10	4	2	18	6	8	16

Directions: Exit at St. Albans to Route 105 North; follow to Enosberg Falls. Take left at Jct. of Routes 108 and 105 to course.

4⊙ =Excellent **3**⊙ =Very Good **2**⊙ =Good

Equinox Country Club

Rt. 7A, Manchester, VT (802) 362-3223
www.equinoxresort.com

Club Pro: Steven Shepardson
Pro Shop: Full inventory
Payment: MC, Visa, Amex, Dis.
Tee Times: 7 days adv.
Fee 9 Holes: Weekday: N/A
Fee 18 Holes: Weekday: $110.00
Twilight Rates: Yes, after 3 pm
Cart Rental: $22.50pp
Lessons: $50.00/half hour **Schools:** No
Clinics: Yes **Day Camps:** No
Other: Restaurant / Clubhouse / Snack bar / Bar-lounge / Hotel / Lockers / Showers

Tees	Holes	Yards	Par	USGA	Slope
BACK	18	6423	71	70.8	129
MIDDLE	18	6069	71	69.2	125
FRONT	18	5082	71	64.3	113

Weekend: N/A
Weekend: $125.00
All Day Play: No
Discounts: None
Junior Golf: No **Membership:** Yes
Driving Range: No

Players' Comments: "A great place to stay and play while on a New England vacation." "Wonderful challenge." "Elegant surroundings, impeccable fairways. The views make you forget the score."

	1	2	3	4	5	6	7	8	9
PAR	4	4	4	3	4	4	5	4	4
YARDS	334	385	346	141	316	323	502	380	344
HDCP	15	1	9	17	13	11	7	3	5

	10	11	12	13	14	15	16	17	18
PAR	4	4	4	4	3	5	3	4	4
YARDS	336	361	347	401	112	462	181	403	395
HDCP	16	12	10	4	18	8	14	6	2

Directions: Located on Route 7A in Manchester.

Essex Country Club

20

Essex Junction, VT (802) 879-3232

Club Pro: Lou Jarvis, PGA
Pro Shop: Limited inventory
Payment: Visa, MC, Amex
Tee Times: Weekends
Fee 9 Holes: Weekday: N/A
Fee 18 Holes: Weekday: $25.00
Twilight Rates: Yes, after 5 pm
Cart Rental: $24.00/18 $13.00/9
Lessons: Yes **Schools:** No
Clinics: Yes **Day Camps:** N/R
Other:

Tees	Holes	Yards	Par	USGA	Slope
BACK	18	6475	72	70.0	117
MIDDLE	18	6315	72	70.4	117
FRONT	18	5500	72	69.1	112

Weekend: N/A
Weekend: $25.00
All Day Play: Yes
Discounts: None
Junior Golf: Yes **Membership:** No
Driving Range: No

Ongoing improvements. Monday and Wednesday specials.

	1	2	3	4	5	6	7	8	9
PAR	4	3	4	4	5	4	5	4	3
YARDS	365	155	400	330	450	335	530	315	190
HDCP	7	17	1	11	15	5	9	4	3

	10	11	12	13	14	15	16	17	18
PAR	5	4	4	3	4	5	3	4	4
YARDS	580	320	355	130	360	530	170	350	450
HDCP	2	6	10	18	4	8	14	16	12

Directions: I-89 Exit - Williston Exit Route 2A to Essex 5 corner; then take Route 15 to Old Stage Road 3 miles north to course.

Farm Resort GC

Rt. 100, Morrisville, VT (802) 888-3525
www.farmresortgolf.com

Club Pro: Frank McCullough, PGA
Pro Shop: Full inventory
Payment: Visa, MC, Dis.
Tee Times: Yes
Fee 9 Holes: Weekday: $18.00
Fee 18 Holes: Weekday: $26.00
Twilight Rates: Yes, after 4:30 pm
Cart Rental: Yes
Lessons: Yes **Schools:** Yes
Clinics: Yes **Day Camps:** Yes
Other: Camp

Tees	Holes	Yards	Par	USGA	Slope
BACK	9	6038	72	69.4	108
MIDDLE	9	5798	72	68.3	108
FRONT	9	5198	72	68.9	113

Weekend: $18.00
Weekend: $27.00
All Day Play: No
Discounts: Junior
Junior Golf: Yes **Membership:** Yes
Driving Range: $7.00/lg., $4.00/med.

COUPON

Sig. Hole: #7, 391 yd. par 4. Water comes into play twice- both off the tee and on the approach. Great course for golfers of all abilities. Play & Stay at one location. Open May - October.

	1	2	3	4	5	6	7	8	9
PAR	4	4	5	3	3	5	4	3	5
YARDS	331	290	460	147	142	556	391	142	450
HDCP	9	11	3	15	17	1	7	13	5
	10	**11**	**12**	**13**	**14**	**15**	**16**	**17**	**18**
PAR	4	4	5	3	3	5	4	3	5
YARDS	331	290	460	147	142	556	391	142	450
HDCP	10	12	4	16	18	2	8	14	6

Directions: 5 1/2 miles North of Stowe, VT on Route 100.

Green Mountain National GC ✪✪✪

Barrows Town Rd., Sherburne, VT (802) 422-GOLF
www.gmngc.com

Club Pro: Jeff Hadley, PGA, Head Pro
Pro Shop: Full inventory
Payment: Visa, MC, AMEX, Dis
Tee Times: 7 days in adv.
Fee 9 Holes: Weekday: $45 cart inc. M-Th
Fee 18 Holes: Weekday: $69 cart inc. M-Th
Twilight Rates: After 3:30 pm
Cart Rental: Included
Lessons: $60.00/hour **Schools:** Adult
Clinics: Adult, Fri **Day Camps:** Yes
Other: Bar / Lounge / Snack Bar

Tees	Holes	Yards	Par	USGA	Slope
BACK	18	6589	71	72.1	138
MIDDLE	18	6164	71	70.2	133
FRONT	18	4740	71	68.9	118

Weekend: $45 after 1pm F/S/S/H
Weekend: $87.00 cart inc. F/S/S/H
All Day Play: Replay/ Space
Discounts: Junior
Junior Golf: Yes **Membership:** Res. / Non-Res.
Driving Range: $8.00/lg. $5.00/sm.

COUPON

Voted # 1 public course in Vermont by *Golf Digest.* Several stay and play partners.
Player's Comments: "Unbelievable in the fall. Incredibly challenging. Great layout, condition & friendly "

	1	2	3	4	5	6	7	8	9
PAR	5	4	4	4	3	5	3	4	4
YARDS	494	387	381	406	152	492	145	348	419
HDCP	7	9	11	1	15	5	17	13	3
	10	**11**	**12**	**13**	**14**	**15**	**16**	**17**	**18**
PAR	4	4	4	3	4	5	4	3	4
YARDS	396	350	375	157	326	437	359	169	371
HDCP	2	6	4	18	16	10	14	12	8

Directions: Exit 6 from I-91. Turn left onto Route 103 North for about 30 minutes. Take right on to Route 100 North. Go by Killington Mountain Road. Course is 2 miles on left. Travel time from I-91 is about 1 hour.

VT

4✪ =Excellent **3✪** =Very Good **2✪** =Good

Haystack Golf Club ✪✪ ▶ 23

Mann Rd., Wilmington, VT (802) 464-8301
www.haystackgolf.com

Tees	Holes	Yards	Par	USGA	Slope
BACK	18	6549	72	71.7	128
MIDDLE	18	6164	72	69.3	125
FRONT	18	5396	74	71.4	122

Club Pro: Chuck Deedman
Pro Shop: Full inventory
Payment: Visa, MC, Amex, Disc
Tee Times: Call
Fee 9 Holes: Weekday: $30.00 M-Th
Fee 18 Holes: Weekday: $30.00 M-Th
Twilight Rates: Yes, after 2 pm
Cart Rental: $12/9, $17pp/18 req.
Lessons: Yes **Schools:** Junior
Clinics: Yes **Day Camps:** No
Other: Clubhouse / Lockers / Showers / Restaurant / Bar-lounge / Snack Bar/ Hotel

Weekend: N/A
Weekend: $50 F/S/S, $60 Holiday
All Day Play: Yes
Discounts: Junior
Junior Golf: Yes **Membership:** Yes
Driving Range: $4.00/lg. Irons only

Scottish architect Desmond Muirhead design. Hole #11 has an elevation drop of over 150 ft. with spectacular views. Seasonal rates.

	1	2	3	4	5	6	7	8	9
PAR	4	4	5	3	4	4	3	5	4
YARDS	348	389	460	181	347	291	166	505	380
HDCP	9	1	7	13	11	15	17	3	5
	10	**11**	**12**	**13**	**14**	**15**	**16**	**17**	**18**
PAR	4	5	4	3	5	4	3	4	4
YARDS	328	509	352	160	516	343	165	301	423
HDCP	6	10	12	18	2	8	16	14	4

Directions: I-91 to Brattleboro, take Route 9 W to Wilmington. At light head north on Route 100 (3 miles.) Look for signs, turn left on Coldbrook Road (2 miles.) Take left on Mann Road (1.5 miles) to gate.

John P. Larkin Country Club ▶ 24

Rt. 5, Windsor, VT (802) 674-6491

Tees	Holes	Yards	Par	USGA	Slope
BACK					
MIDDLE	9	5382	68	65.1	105
FRONT	9	4924	72	68.2	109

Club Pro: Ken St. Onge
Pro Shop: Limited inventory
Payment: Visa, MC
Tee Times: Wknds/M/T/Hldy
Fee 9 Holes: Weekday: $16.00
Fee 18 Holes: Weekday: $23.00
Twilight Rates: No
Cart Rental: $21.00/18 $13.00/9
Lessons: Yes **Schools:** No
Clinics: No **Day Camps:** No
Other: Restaurant / Clubhouse / Snack bar / Bar-lounge / Lockers / Showers

Weekend: $19.00
Weekend: $27.00
All Day Play: No
Discounts: None
Junior Golf: Yes **Membership:** Yes
Driving Range: No

Course has views of Mt. Ascutney and Connecticut River. New Hampshire is out of bounds. Formerly Windsor Country Club.

	1	2	3	4	5	6	7	8	9
PAR	4	3	4	4	4	3	3	5	4
YARDS	332	215	333	309	383	176	140	442	340
HDCP	13	1	3	15	5	9	17	11	7
	10	**11**	**12**	**13**	**14**	**15**	**16**	**17**	**18**
PAR	4	3	4	4	4	3	3	5	4
YARDS	338	188	342	318	386	185	145	453	357
HDCP	14	2	4	16	6	10	18	12	8

Directions: Take I-91 to Exit 9, left on Route 5, course is 3.5 miles down.

Killington Golf Resort

Killington, VT (802) 422-6700
www.killingtongolf.com

Club Pro: Dave Pfannenstein, PGA
Pro Shop: Full inventory
Payment: Most major
Tee Times: Recommended

Tees	Holes	Yards	Par	USGA	Slope
BACK	18	6326	72	70.6	126
MIDDLE	18	5876	72	69.6	123
FRONT	18	4833	72	68.3	119

Fee 9 Holes: Weekday: Call
Fee 18 Holes: Weekday: Call
Twilight Rates: Yes, after 3 pm
Cart Rental: Call
Lessons: $60.00/hour **Schools:** Jr. & Sr.
Clinics: No **Day Camps:** N/R
Other: Hotel / Clubhouse / Snack bar / Restaurant / Bar-lounge

Weekend: Call
Weekend: Call
All Day Play: No
Discounts: Junior
Junior Golf: No **Membership:** Yes
Driving Range: $3.00/bucket

COUPON

Sig. Hole: #13, 355 yard par 4 makes great use of natural slope. **Players' Comments:** "Great mountain course." "Beautiful setting."

	1	2	3	4	5	6	7	8	9
PAR	4	5	3	4	5	3	5	4	4
YARDS	354	485	163	395	452	138	480	321	270
HDCP	9	7	11	3	1	17	5	13	15
	10	11	12	13	14	15	16	17	18
PAR	4	5	4	4	3	4	4	3	4
YARDS	334	485	300	355	174	370	360	150	290
HDCP	14	4	12	8	16	2	6	18	10

Directions: From I-89 take Exit 1 onto Route 4 West to the Killington Road. Turn left onto Killington Road. Go 3.5 miles and look for signs.

Kwiniaska Golf Club

Shelburne, VT (802) 985-3672
www.kwiniaska.com

Club Pro: Michael Bailey
Pro Shop: Full inventory
Payment: MC, Visa, Cash
Tee Times: Weekends & Holidays

Tees	Holes	Yards	Par	USGA	Slope
BACK	18	6848	72	72.7	129
MIDDLE	18	6601	72	71.7	126
FRONT	18	5246	72	70.6	115

Fee 9 Holes: Weekday: N/A
Fee 18 Holes: Weekday: $33.00
Twilight Rates: Yes, after 4 pm
Cart Rental: $24.00
Lessons: Yes **Schools:** No
Clinics: Yes **Day Camps:** No
Other: Clubhouse / Locker room facilities / Showers / Snack bar

Weekend: N/A
Weekend: $33.00
All Day Play: Yes
Discounts: None
Junior Golf: Yes **Membership:** Yes
Driving Range: Yes.

VT

Sig Hole: #17 is a beautiful, short, par 4, framed w/ trees that are especially spectacular during foliage season. A large maple tree on the left puts a premium on driving.

	1	2	3	4	5	6	7	8	9
PAR	4	3	5	3	4	4	4	4	5
YARDS	425	186	467	181	446	375	407	374	541
HDCP	5	15	11	17	1	9	7	13	3
	10	11	12	13	14	15	16	17	18
PAR	4	4	3	5	4	3	5	4	4
YARDS	367	341	169	495	399	193	490	328	417
HDCP	18	6	16	8	10	12	2	14	4

Directions: Exit 14W from I-89. Follow signs to Spear Street then 5 miles south.

4✪ =Excellent 3✪ =Very Good 2✪ =Good

Lake Morey CC

Fairlee, VT (802) 333-4800
www.lakemoreyresort.com

Tees	Holes	Yards	Par	USGA	Slope
BACK	18	6024	70	69.4	120
MIDDLE	18	5807	70	68.4	118
FRONT	18	4942	70	68.0	116

Club Pro: B. Ross, Jr. Golf Dir., B. Hanlon
Pro Shop: Full inventory
Payment: Visa, MC, Disc
Tee Times: 4 days adv.
Fee 9 Holes: Weekday: $22.00   **Weekend:** $22.00
Fee 18 Holes: Weekday: $33.00   **Weekend:** $40.00
Twilight Rates: After 3 pm   **All Day Play:** Yes
Cart Rental: $16.00pp/18   **Discounts:** Senior, M-Tu.
Lessons: $45.00/45 minutes **Schools:** No   **Junior Golf:** Yes **Membership:** Yes
Clinics: Yes **Day Camps:** No   **Driving Range:** $3.00/bucket
Other: Clubhouse / Showers / Snack bar / Restaurant / Bar-lounge / Hotel

COUPON

Player Comment: "Good package for golfers and family." Home of Vermont Open for 50 years.

	1	2	3	4	5	6	7	8	9
PAR	3	5	4	4	4	3	3	4	4
YARDS	213	460	356	337	334	158	114	395	321
HDCP	4	16	6	12	14	8	18	2	10
	10	11	12	13	14	15	16	17	18
PAR	4	4	5	5	4	3	4	3	4
YARDS	324	369	504	517	373	188	371	160	313
HDCP	15	5	1	7	3	9	11	17	13

Directions: Take I-91 North to Exit 15, take left off ramp and follow signs. 25 minutes north of White River Junction.

Lake St. Catherine CC

Poultney, VT (802) 287-9341

Tees	Holes	Yards	Par	USGA	Slope
BACK	18	6293	72	70.9	127
MIDDLE	18	5971	72	69.1	123
FRONT	18	4940	72	68.2	116

Club Pro: Brett Toon, PGA
Pro Shop: Full inventory
Payment: Visa, MC, Cash
Tee Times: Weekends and Holidays
Fee 9 Holes: Weekday: $14.00   **Weekend:** $17.00
Fee 18 Holes: Weekday: $25.00   **Weekend:** $32.00
Twilight Rates: No   **All Day Play:** No
Cart Rental: $14/18pp $8pp/9   **Discounts:** None
Lessons: $30/30 min. **Schools:** Yes   **Junior Golf:** Yes **Membership:** Yes
Clinics: Yes **Day Camps:** No   **Driving Range:** Yes
Other: Snack bar / Bar-lounge

Player's Comments: "15th and 16th holes most scenic in state." Specials after 1pm weekday and 2pm weekends. New tee boxes. Open April- October.

	1	2	3	4	5	6	7	8	9
PAR	4	4	3	4	4	4	5	3	5
YARDS	402	308	147	425	360	333	488	185	414
HDCP	5	15	11	3	13	9	7	17	2
	10	11	12	13	14	15	16	17	18
PAR	5	4	4	4	3	4	3	4	5
YARDS	508	359	317	301	102	355	147	351	469
HDCP	4	14	10	1	12	8	6	16	18

Directions: Take Route 149 to Route 4 North, take Route 30 North to course. Between Rutland and Manchester, Vermont and Lake George, New York.

Montague Golf Club

Randolph, VT (802) 728-3806
www.montaguegolf.com

Club Pro: Bob Allen, Pro - Manager
Pro Shop: Full inventory
Payment: Visa, MC
Tee Times: Yes
Fee 9 Holes: Weekday: $17.00
Fee 18 Holes: Weekday: $25.00
Twilight Rates: Yes, after 4 pm
Cart Rental: $27.00/18 $14.25/9
Lessons: Yes, PGA **Schools:** No
Clinics: Yes **Day Camps:** No
Other: Clubhouse / Snack bar / Putting green

Tees	Holes	Yards	Par	USGA	Slope
BACK	18	5741	69	66.9	116
MIDDLE	18	5438	69	65.5	114
FRONT	18	5025	71	63.3	108

Weekend: $19.00
Weekend: $30.00
All Day Play: Yes, $25 Wkdys
Discounts: Sr (Mon), Jr (w/ adult)
Junior Golf: Yes **Membership:** Yes
Driving Range: Yes

COUPON

Sig. Hole: #5, 415 yd. par 4 is a beautiful hole looking over the 5,6, and 7th holes. A good drive is needed to reach the green on your second shot with a swamp to the right. Links style course.

	1	2	3	4	5	6	7	8	9
PAR	4	4	4	3	4	4	3	4	3
YARDS	312	365	332	196	415	368	140	317	97
HDCP	10	6	12	14	4	2	16	8	18

	10	11	12	13	14	15	16	17	18
PAR	3	5	4	4	4	4	4	4	4
YARDS	198	486	298	300	340	276	335	376	307
HDCP	11	5	15	13	7	17	7	1	3

Directions: Take I-89 North to Exit 4. Follow Route 66 into downtown Randolph on Route 12 South. Take left on Merchant Rd. Go straight onto Randolph Avenue - end of road take left.

Montpelier CC

Montpelier, VT (802) 223-7457

Club Pro: Brian M. Haley, PGA
Pro Shop: Full inventory
Payment: Cash, Credit
Tee Times: Weekends, 1 day adv.
Fee 9 Holes: Weekday: $18.00
Fee 18 Holes: Weekday: $25.00
Twilight Rates: No
Cart Rental: $25.00/18 $16.00/9
Lessons: Private and Group **Schools:** No
Clinics: Yes **Day Camps:** No
Other: Clubhouse / Lockers / Showers / Snack bar / Restaurant / Bar-lounge

Tees	Holes	Yards	Par	USGA	Slope
BACK	9	2564	35	67.0	117
MIDDLE	9	2739	35	66.6	114
FRONT	9	2383	35	67.9	112

Weekend: $20.00
Weekend: $30.00
All Day Play: Yes
Discounts: None
Junior Golf: Yes **Membership:** Yes
Driving Range: No

VT

The course is relatively short but made challenging by the hilly terrain. Open April 1 - October 31.

	1	2	3	4	5	6	7	8	9
PAR	4	3	5	5	4	3	4	3	4
YARDS	358	155	422	459	226	149	325	191	279
HDCP	5	15	1	3	11	17	7	13	9

	10	11	12	13	14	15	16	17	18
PAR									
YARDS									
HDCP									

Directions: Take I-89 to Route 2 Exit, follow signs for Montpelier.

4🟡 =Excellent 3🟡 =Very Good 2🟡 =Good

Mount Snow Golf Club ✪✪ ▶ 31

Mount Snow, VT (802) 464-4254
www.mountsnow.com

Tees	Holes	Yards	Par	USGA	Slope
BACK	18	6894	72	73.3	133
MIDDLE	18	6443	72	70.7	126
FRONT	18	5436	72	72.8	121

Club Pro: Jay Morelli, PGA
Pro Shop: Full inventory
Payment: Visa, MC, Amex, Disc
Tee Times: Yes
Fee 9 Holes: Weekday: $34.00 after 4:00 **Weekend:** $39.00
Fee 18 Holes: Weekday: $39-$59 power lunch **Weekend:** $59.00
Twilight Rates: After 4 pm   **All Day Play:** No
Cart Rental: $17pp/18, $12pp/9   **Discounts:** Senior & Junior
Lessons: $39/30 min. **Schools:** Yes   **Junior Golf:** Yes **Membership:** Yes
Clinics: Yes **Day Camps:** Yes   **Driving Range:** Yes
Other: Clubhouse / Snack bar / Restaurant / Bar-lounge / Hotel

COUPON

Noted for variety of instruction at The Original Golf School, headed by Jay Morelli. Inquire about specials and seasonal rates.

	1	2	3	4	5	6	7	8	9
PAR	4	4	3	4	5	3	5	4	4
YARDS	394	364	143	344	479	187	532	318	363
HDCP	11	3	17	15	7	9	1	13	5

	10	11	12	13	14	15	16	17	18
PAR	4	5	3	4	4	3	5	4	4
YARDS	372	577	147	403	420	142	474	388	396
HDCP	14	2	16	6	10	18	12	4	8

Directions: Take Exit 2 off I-91 in Brattleboro to Route 9 W. 20 miles to Wilmington, VT. Turn right at the stop light onto Route 100 N. About 6 miles, take a left on CrosstownRoad. At top of hill on left.

Mt. Anthony CC ✪✪ ▶ 32

Bennington, VT (802) 447-7079

Tees	Holes	Yards	Par	USGA	Slope
BACK	18	6200	71	75.0	125
MIDDLE	18	6000	71	69.2	125
FRONT	18	5200	71	67.7	106

Club Pro: David Soucy, PGA
Pro Shop: Full inventory
Payment: Visa, MC, Amex
Tee Times: Yes
Fee 9 Holes: Weekday: $17.00   **Weekend:** $20.00
Fee 18 Holes: Weekday: $33.00   **Weekend:** $38.00
Twilight Rates: No   **All Day Play:** Yes
Cart Rental: $13pp/18 $8pp/9   **Discounts:** Junior
Lessons: $35.00/half hour **Schools:** Junior   **Junior Golf:** Yes **Membership:** Yes
Clinics: Ladies/Juniors **Day Camps:** No   **Driving Range:** $5.00/lg. $3.00/sm.
Other: Snack bar / Restaurant / Bar-lounge / Lockers / Showers

"Good price. Scenic. Great services. Well maintained." AMH (player) Open April - October.

	1	2	3	4	5	6	7	8	9
PAR	4	3	5	3	5	4	4	4	4
YARDS	366	182	474	104	538	369	338	331	304
HDCP	11	7	13	17	1	3	9	5	15

	10	11	12	13	14	15	16	17	18
PAR	4	4	4	3	3	4	5	4	4
YARDS	344	368	348	156	182	304	435	406	351
HDCP	6	4	8	18	10	14	16	2	12

Directions: From Route 7 go to Bennington Center. Turn onto West Main St. (Rt. 9 West), 1/4 mile after Paradise Motel take first right onto Convent Ave. Follow to end and take left. Course is down on the right.

Neshobe Golf Club

Brandon, VT (802) 247-3611
www.neshobe.com

Club Pro: Dennis Blank, Head Pro, PGA
Pro Shop: Full inventory
Payment: MC, Visa
Tee Times: Yes
Fee 9 Holes: Weekday: N/A
Fee 18 Holes: Weekday: $32.00
Twilight Rates: After 4 pm
Cart Rental: $16.00pp
Lessons: $30.00/half hour **Schools:** No
Clinics: Jr./Beg. **Day Camps:** No
Other: Clubhouse / Lockers / Showers / Snack bar / Restaurant / Bar-lounge / Horseshoes / Billiards / Card room.

Tees	Holes	Yards	Par	USGA	Slope
BACK	18	6362	72	71.6	125
MIDDLE	18	5865	72	68.7	122
FRONT	18	5046	71	64.9	115

Weekend: N/A
Weekend: $39.00
All Day Play: Yes
Discounts: None
Junior Golf: Yes **Membership:** Yes
Driving Range: $6/lg., $4.50/med., $3/sm.

Player's Comments: "Best buy in the area."

	1	2	3	4	5	6	7	8	9
PAR	4	4	4	4	5	3	4	5	4
YARDS	309	317	339	389	508	132	384	458	272
HDCP	11	17	5	1	7	15	3	9	13
	10	**11**	**12**	**13**	**14**	**15**	**16**	**17**	**18**
PAR	3	5	3	4	5	4	4	3	4
YARDS	192	491	148	343	522	357	243	117	344
HDCP	14	8	16	4	2	6	12	18	10

Directions: From Route 7, take Route 73 East. Follow for 1 1/2 miles east of Brandon Center.

Newport CC

Newport, VT (802) 334-2391
www.newportcountryclub.com

Club Pro: Mike Santa Maria
Pro Shop: Full inventory
Payment: MC, Visa
Tee Times: 1 day adv.
Fee 9 Holes: Weekday: $15.00
Fee 18 Holes: Weekday: $25.00
Twilight Rates: Yes, after 5 pm
Cart Rental: $24.00/18 $15.00/9
Lessons: $30.00/half hour **Schools:** N/A
Clinics: Junior **Day Camps:** No
Other: Restaurant / Clubhouse / Bar-Lounge / Lockers / Showers / Snack Bar

Tees	Holes	Yards	Par	USGA	Slope
BACK	18	6491	72	70.4	117
MIDDLE	18	6228	72	68.6	114
FRONT	18	5274	72	64.4	108

Weekend: $15.00
Weekend: $25.00
All Day Play: Yes
Discounts: None
Junior Golf: Yes **Membership:** Yes
Driving Range: $5.00/bucket

Clubhouse rated top 5 in state by *VT Golf Magazine*. Very Friendly!! Improvements continuing. Series of 5 thirty minute lessons for $120.00

	1	2	3	4	5	6	7	8	9
PAR	4	3	4	5	4	3	4	4	5
YARDS	354	172	356	484	326	150	397	335	469
HDCP	9	15	3	7	11	17	1	5	13
	10	**11**	**12**	**13**	**14**	**15**	**16**	**17**	**18**
PAR	5	4	4	3	4	4	4	3	5
YARDS	479	374	387	144	375	395	314	142	464
HDCP	12	6	8	18	4	2	10	16	14

Directions: Exit 27 off I-91. Head toward Newport about 1/2 mile. Take left and follow signs.

VT

4🌑 =Excellent 3🌑 =Very Good 2🌑 =Good

Northfield CC

Northfield, VT (802) 485-4515

Tees	Holes	Yards	Par	USGA	Slope
BACK	18	5972	70	69.0	122
MIDDLE	18	5768	70	68.0	120
FRONT	18	5140	70	63.1	119

Club Pro: Joseph Dingledine, PGA Apprentice
Pro Shop: Limited inventory
Payment: Visa, MC, cash, checks
Tee Times: Required
Fee 9 Holes: Weekday: $18.00
Fee 18 Holes: Weekday: $26.00
Twilight Rates: No
Cart Rental: $26.00/18 $14.00/9
Lessons: Private and Group **Schools:** No
Clinics: No **Day Camps:** No
Other: Restaurant / Bar / Clubhouse / Showers

Weekend: $18.00
Weekend: $26.00
All Day Play: No
Discounts: None
Junior Golf: Yes **Membership:** Yes
Driving Range: No

Player's Comment: "Old fashioned, wonderful and friendly." Known for 'The Volcano' hole #4.

	1	2	3	4	5	6	7	8	9
PAR	4	4	4	3	4	5	4	3	4
YARDS	348	314	276	148	377	532	336	183	367
HDCP	9	13	17	7	5	1	11	15	3
	10	11	12	13	14	15	16	17	18
PAR	4	4	3	3	5	5	4	3	4
YARDS	340	352	175	148	465	532	325	183	367
HDCP	10	8	12	6	18	2	16	14	4

Directions: Take I-89 to Exit 5, follow to bottom of hill. Go straight 3/4 mi. to a T. Turn left on 12A and go 2.5 miles. Clubhouse on right.

Okemo Valley Golf Club ⚬✪

Ludlow,VT (802) 228-1396
www.okemo.com

Tees	Holes	Yards	Par	USGA	Slope
BACK	18	6400	70	71.1	130
MIDDLE	18	6104	70	69.6	128
FRONT	18	5105	70	67.6	118

Club Pro: James Remy, PGA
Pro Shop: Full inventory
Payment: Visa, MC, Amex
Tee Times: Yes, 3 days adv.
Fee 9 Holes: Weekday: $39.00
Fee 18 Holes: Weekday: $70.00
Twilight Rates: No
Cart Rental: $18pp/18 $10pp/9
Lessons: $65.00/hr privite **Schools:** Adult
Clinics: $25.00 **Day Camps:** No
Other: Full Restaurant / Clubhouse / Hotel / Inn / Lockers / Showers / Bar

Weekend: $39.00
Weekend: $70.00
All Day Play: No
Discounts: Junior
Junior Golf: No **Membership:** Waiting list
Driving Range: Yes

COUPON

"Noted among top 50 courses in America for women."JR, PGA. **Players comments:** " Challenging 18 holes layout." "Excellent club pro. Beautiful greens. Friendly people." "Fun to play, pricing fair, will be back."

	1	2	3	4	5	6	7	8	9
PAR	4	5	4	3	4	3	5	3	4
YARDS	381	522	352	175	368	167	487	173	347
HDCP	3	1	7	15	5	13	9	17	11
	10	11	12	13	14	15	16	17	18
PAR	4	5	4	4	3	4	4	3	4
YARDS	305	502	371	304	205	396	435	196	418
HDCP	18	6	10	16	14	8	2	12	4

Directions: Just North of Ludlow about 2 miles on Route 103. Right on Fox Lane (signs on highway).

Orleans Country Club

37

316 Country Club Lane, Orleans, VT (802) 754-2333

Tees	Holes	Yards	Par	USGA	Slope
BACK	18	6123	72	69.3	121
MIDDLE	18	5934	72	68.5	119
FRONT	18	5545	73	71.8	124

Club Pro: Robert Silvester, PGA
Pro Shop: Full inventory
Payment: MC, Visa
Tee Times: 1 day,after 9am
Fee 9 Holes: Weekday: $15.00 after 4:00   **Weekend:** $15.00 after 4:00
Fee 18 Holes: Weekday: $27.00   **Weekend:** $27.00
Twilight Rates: After 3pm   **All Day Play:** Yes
Cart Rental: $13.00/pp   **Discounts:** Mondays, Except Holidays
Lessons: $30/half hour **Schools:** No   **Junior Golf:** Yes **Membership:** Yes
Clinics: Yes **Day Camps:** No   **Driving Range:** $6.00/lg., $4.00 /sm.
Other: Clubhouse / Restaurant / Snackbar / Bar Lounge / Complete practice facility

The course has scenic mountain views on most holes. Considered challenging. 2004 rates TBD for weekday, weekend, and twilight play.

	1	2	3	4	5	6	7	8	9
PAR	5	4	3	5	4	4	4	3	4
YARDS	442	319	148	439	368	356	290	170	340
HDCP	11	9	17	13	3	1	7	15	5

	10	11	12	13	14	15	16	17	18
PAR	3	5	4	3	4	4	5	4	4
YARDS	202	479	359	134	426	290	495	285	392
HDCP	8	10	16	8	2	12	6	14	4

Directions: Take I-91 to Exit 26. Follow Route 58 1 1/2 miles east, turn right onto Country Club Lane.

Proctor Pittsford CC

38

Pittsford, VT (802) 483-9379

Tees	Holes	Yards	Par	USGA	Slope
BACK	18	6052	70	69.4	121
MIDDLE	18	5728	70	67.9	118
FRONT	18	5446	72	66.1	115

Club Pro: Merle Schoenfeld
Pro Shop: Full inventory
Payment: MC, Visa
Tee Times: 2 days adv.
Fee 9 Holes: Weekday: $18.00   **Weekend:** $32.00
Fee 18 Holes: Weekday: $32.00   **Weekend:** $32.00
Twilight Rates: Yes, after 5 pm   **All Day Play:** No
Cart Rental: $13.00 pp   **Discounts:** None
Lessons: Yes **Schools:** No   **Junior Golf:** Yes **Membership:** No
Clinics: No **Day Camps:** No   **Driving Range:** $3.00/lg. bucket
Other: Restaurant / Lounge

Sig. Hole: #10 409 yard par 5, slight dogleg left. 2 ponds on either right or left. Well bunkered. Beautiful views, excellent greens and fairways, good test of golf. Open April 15 to October 31.

	1	2	3	4	5	6	7	8	9
PAR	4	4	4	5	4	4	3	4	3
YARDS	325	386	308	489	370	326	133	281	219
HDCP	14	4	10	2	8	12	16	18	6

	10	11	12	13	14	15	16	17	18
PAR	4	3	5	4	4	4	4	3	4
YARDS	409	144	468	377	332	301	388	163	309
HDCP	5	13	7	1	9	17	3	11	15

Directions: Located 1 mile off Route 7. Take Route 7 for 4 miles north, take left after Nissan dealer. Go 1/2 mile, take right at "T" 3 miles on Corn Hill Road.

VT

4✪ =Excellent 3✪ =Very Good 2✪ =Good

Prospect Bay CC

Rt. 30, Bomoseen, VT (802) 468-5581

Club Pro:
Pro Shop: Limited inventory
Payment: MC, Visa
Tee Times: No
Fee 9 Holes: Weekday: $12.00
Fee 18 Holes: Weekday: $18.00
Twilight Rates: After 4 pm wkdys
Cart Rental: $24.00/18 $12.00/9
Lessons: No **Schools:** No
Clinics: Yes **Day Camps:** No
Other: Clubhouse / Snack bar

Weekend: $15.00 after 1pm
Weekend: $22.00
All Day Play: Yes
Discounts: None
Junior Golf: No **Membership:** Yes
Driving Range: No

Tees	Holes	Yards	Par	USGA	Slope
BACK	9	2635	35	65.2	115
MIDDLE	9	2557	70	64.6	114
FRONT	9	2294	35	65.4	114

The course is hilly and scenic. Great shape. Open April - October.

	1	2	3	4	5	6	7	8	9
PAR	5	3	4	4	4	4	4	4	3
YARDS	405	155	311	283	268	335	298	370	132
HDCP	2	14	12	8	16	10	4	6	18
	10	**11**	**12**	**13**	**14**	**15**	**16**	**17**	**18**
PAR	5	3	4	4	4	4	4	4	3
YARDS	410	165	326	290	270	340	303	375	156
HDCP	1	13	11	7	15	9	3	5	17

Directions: Take US Route 4 to Exit 4; follow Route 30 North for 2 miles to course entrance.

Ralph Myhre GC

Middlebury, VT (802) 443-5125
www.middlebury.edu

Club Pro: Jim Dayton
Pro Shop: Full inventory
Payment: Cash, Visa
Tee Times: Recommended
Fee 9 Holes: Weekday: $20.00
Fee 18 Holes: Weekday: $35.00
Twilight Rates: Yes, after 5 pm
Cart Rental: $15.00pp/18
Lessons: Yes **Schools:** No
Clinics: Yes **Day Camps:** Yes
Other: Clubhouse / Snack bar / Showers

Weekend: $20.00
Weekend: $35.00
All Day Play: Yes
Discounts: Student
Junior Golf: Yes **Membership:** Yes
Driving Range: Yes

Tees	Holes	Yards	Par	USGA	Slope
BACK	18	6379	71	71.3	129
MIDDLE	18	6014	71	69.6	126
FRONT	18	5337	71	66.9	120

Open fairways with moderate hills. Well kept and tees sodded. Owned by Middlebury College. Any student (any school) pays $15.00.

	1	2	3	4	5	6	7	8	9
PAR	5	4	4	3	4	4	3	4	4
YARDS	479	341	311	166	356	370	141	353	365
HDCP	18	3	16	12	6	13	15	8	7
	10	**11**	**12**	**13**	**14**	**15**	**16**	**17**	**18**
PAR	4	5	3	4	3	4	5	4	4
YARDS	404	525	152	325	126	363	512	351	377
HDCP	2	1	17	10	14	4	5	11	9

Directions: Route 7 to Route 30 South. Course is just beyond Middlebury College Field House.

Richford Country Club

Rt. 106, Richford, VT (802) 848-3527

Club Pro: No
Pro Shop: Limited inventory
Payment: Visa, MC
Tee Times: No
Fee 9 Holes: Weekday: $14.00 M-Th
Fee 18 Holes: Weekday: $14.00 M-Th
Twilight Rates: No
Cart Rental: $22.00/18, $15.70/9
Lessons: No **Schools:** No
Clinics: No **Day Camps:** No
Other: Clubhouse / Snack bar / Bar-lounge.

Tees	Holes	Yards	Par	USGA	Slope
BACK					
MIDDLE	9	2908	36	68.2	116
FRONT	9	2326	36	72.0	118

Weekend: $16.00 F/S/S
Weekend: $21.00 F/S/S
All Day Play: No
Discounts: None
Junior Golf: Yes **Membership:** Yes
Driving Range: No

Excellent views of the Green Mountains. New Clubhouse. Open April to October.

	1	2	3	4	5	6	7	8	9
PAR	4	5	3	4	5	3	4	4	4
YARDS	283	453	170	400	453	175	309	376	289
HDCP	7	9	8	1	3	5	2	6	4
	10	11	12	13	14	15	16	17	18
PAR									
YARDS									
HDCP									

Directions: Take I-89 to St. Albans Exit. Follow Route 105 North to Richford (28 miles).

Rocky Ridge Golf Club

Rt. 116, St. George, VT (802) 482-2191
www.rockyridge.com

Club Pro: Ed Coleman
Pro Shop: Full inventory
Payment: All Major
Tee Times: 48 hours in advance 7 days/week
Fee 9 Holes: Weekday:
Fee 18 Holes: Weekday: $30.00
Twilight Rates: Yes, after 5 pm
Cart Rental: $13.00pp
Lessons: Yes **Schools:** N/A
Clinics: Junior **Day Camps:** No
Other: Clubhouse / Lockers/ Restaurant / Bar-lounge

Tees	Holes	Yards	Par	USGA	Slope
BACK	18	6282	72	70.3	126
MIDDLE	18	6000	72	69.1	124
FRONT	18	5230	72	65.6	117

Weekend:
Weekend: $30.00
All Day Play: Yes
Discounts: None
Junior Golf: Yes **Membership:** Yes
Driving Range: Yes

COUPON

A challenging and very scenic country setting for all skill levels.

	1	2	3	4	5	6	7	8	9
PAR	4	5	3	5	4	4	4	3	4
YARDS	270	542	195	576	314	251	339	191	345
HDCP	17	1	11	7	5	13	9	15	3
	10	11	12	13	14	15	16	17	18
PAR	4	4	4	4	3	4	5	3	5
YARDS	395	289	312	367	156	315	460	163	513
HDCP	10	14	12	2	16	8	6	18	4

Directions: 12 miles south of Burlington. Located at the intersections of Routes 2A and 116.

4✪ =Excellent 3✪ = Very Good 2✪ = Good

Rutland Country Club

Grove St., Rutland, VT (802) 773-3254
www.rutlandcountryclub.com

Tees	Holes	Yards	Par	USGA	Slope
BACK	18	6135	70	69.7	125
MIDDLE	18	5758	70	67.9	122
FRONT	18	5368	71	71.6	125

Club Pro: Greg Nelson, PGA
Pro Shop: Full inventory
Payment: Visa, MC
Tee Times: 48 hrs. in adv.
Fee 9 Holes: Weekday: N/A
Fee 18 Holes: Weekday: $90.10, cart inc.
Twilight Rates: No
Cart Rental: Included
Lessons: Yes **Schools:** No
Clinics: Junior **Day Camps:** No
Other: Clubhouse / Lockers / Showers / Snack bar / Restaurant / Bar-lounge

Weekend: N/A
Weekend: $90.10 after 12pm
All Day Play: No
Discounts: None
Junior Golf: Yes **Membership:** Yes
Driving Range: No

Player's Comment: "Great greens and great values. Worth the money." Open May - October.

	1	2	3	4	5	6	7	8	9
PAR	4	4	3	5	3	4	4	4	4
YARDS	379	381	125	463	215	366	322	368	300
HDCP	5	7	17	1	11	9	13	3	15

	10	11	12	13	14	15	16	17	18
PAR	4	4	3	5	4	3	4	4	4
YARDS	296	316	193	513	347	121	351	326	376
HDCP	16	10	14	2	6	18	4	12	8

Directions: From I-89 Exit 1 take Route 4 West to Rutland. Take right onto Grove St. and follow signs to course.

Sitzmark Golf Course

44

Rt. 100, Wilmington, VT (802) 464-3384

Tees	Holes	Yards	Par	USGA	Slope
BACK					
MIDDLE	18	2300	54		
FRONT					

Club Pro: No
Pro Shop: Yes
Payment: Visa, MC
Tee Times: No
Fee 9 Holes: Weekday: N/A
Fee 18 Holes: Weekday: $15.00
Twilight Rates: No
Cart Rental: $17.00
Lessons: No **Schools:** Yes
Clinics: No **Day Camps:** No
Other: Snack bar / Bar-lounge

Weekend: N/A
Weekend: $15.00
All Day Play: No
Discounts: None
Junior Golf: No **Membership:** Yes
Driving Range: No

An 18 hole par 3. Generally considered an "Iron Course," it provides a challenge for the experienced golfer and an excellent introduction for the beginner.

	1	2	3	4	5	6	7	8	9
PAR	3	3	3	3	3	3	3	3	3
YARDS	105	95	105	125	155	90	115	127	115
HDCP	13	15	11	5	1	17	9	3	7

	10	11	12	13	14	15	16	17	18
PAR	3	3	3	3	3	3	3	3	3
YARDS	90	110	105	126	120	90	105	90	115
HDCP	14	8	10	2	4	18	12	16	6

Directions: Take I-91 to Brattleboro, get on Route 9 to Wilmington, take Route 100 to course (5 miles).

St. Johnsbury CC

St. Johnsbury, VT (802) 748-9894

✪✪

Club Pro: Steve Holland, PGA
Pro Shop: Full inventory
Payment: Cash, credit card
Tee Times: 3 days adv.
Fee 9 Holes: Weekday: $20.00
Fee 18 Holes: Weekday: $35.00
Twilight Rates: Yes, after 4 pm
Cart Rental: $16pp/18 $10pp/9
Lessons: 3 lessons/$125.00 **Schools:** No
Clinics: No **Day Camps:** No
Other: Clubhouse / Snack bar / Restaurant / Bar-lounge

Tees	Holes	Yards	Par	USGA	Slope
BACK	18	6373	70	70.4	129
MIDDLE	18	5860	70	68.6	125
FRONT	18	5480	70	71.3	120

Weekend: $25.00
Weekend: $40.00
All Day Play: No
Discounts: Junior
Junior Golf: Yes **Membership:** Yes
Driving Range: $7/lg $5/med $3/sm

COUPON

Rated the #1 course in VT to play for under $50 by *Golf Digest* and *USA Today*! **Player's Comment:** "Front 9, wide open. Back 9, narrow and challenging. Lot's of hills and blind shots. Not for the timid."

	1	2	3	4	5	6	7	8	9
PAR	4	4	3	4	3	5	3	5	4
YARDS	314	363	168	434	232	578	188	473	434
HDCP	11	9	17	3	13	1	15	5	7

	10	11	12	13	14	15	16	17	18
PAR	5	4	3	4	4	3	5	3	4
YARDS	496	385	176	398	395	195	575	203	366
HDCP	6	10	16	8	4	14	2	18	12

Directions: From I-91 North to Exit 23 (US Route 5); follow 3 miles. From I-91 South to Exit 22 to Route 5; follow 4 miles.

Stamford Valley CC

Rt. 9, Stamford, VT (802) 694-9144

Club Pro: No
Pro Shop: No
Payment: Cash only
Tee Times: No
Fee 9 Holes: Weekday: $9.00
Fee 18 Holes: Weekday: $16.00
Twilight Rates: No
Cart Rental: $16.00/18 $10.00/9
Lessons: No **Schools:** No
Clinics: No **Day Camps:** No
Other: Snack Bar

Tees	Holes	Yards	Par	USGA	Slope
BACK					
MIDDLE	9	2709	36	66.6	104
FRONT					

Weekend: $9.00
Weekend: $16.00
All Day Play: No
Discounts: None
Junior Golf: No **Membership:** Yes, limited
Driving Range: No

VT

The course is level and considered an easy walker. Noted for friendly atmosphere.

	1	2	3	4	5	6	7	8	9
PAR	4	4	4	5	4	4	3	4	4
YARDS	232	288	342	392	330	320	215	355	235
HDCP	N/A								

	10	11	12	13	14	15	16	17	18
PAR									
YARDS									
HDCP									

Directions: Take Route 8 North (out of North Adams) about 5 miles over Stamford line.

4✪ =Excellent **3✪** =Very Good **2✪** =Good

Stonehedge GC

North Clarendon, VT (802) 773-2666
www.stonehedgegolf.com

Club Pro: Bob Matson
Pro Shop: Yes
Payment: Cash, Check
Tee Times: Yes
Fee 9 Holes: Weekday: $10.00
Fee 18 Holes: Weekday: $13.50
Twilight Rates: No
Cart Rental: $12.50/18 $10.00/9
Lessons: No **Schools:** No
Clinics: No **Day Camps:** No
Other: Snacks and Soft drinks

Tees	Holes	Yards	Par	USGA	Slope
BACK					
MIDDLE	9	1107	27		
FRONT					

Weekend: $11.00
Weekend: $15.50
All Day Play: No
Discounts: Senior Wednesdays
Junior Golf: No **Membership:** No
Driving Range: No

Challenging Par 3 with pretty views- excellent greens, water and sand traps- easy course to walk.

	1	2	3	4	5	6	7	8	9
PAR	3	3	3	3	3	3	3	3	3
YARDS	153	84	181	152	86	77	180	93	101
HDCP									
	10	11	12	13	14	15	16	17	18
PAR									
YARDS									
HDCP									

Directions: Located 3 miles South of Rutland, VT (No interstate nearby) at the junction of Routes 7 and 103.

Stowe Country Club

✪✪

Stowe, VT (802) 253-4893
www.stowe.com

Club Pro: Tom White
Pro Shop: Full inventory
Payment: Visa, MC, Amex, Disc
Tee Times: Anytime
Fee 9 Holes: Weekday: N/A
Fee 18 Holes: Weekday: $60, $50 after 1 pm
Twilight Rates: Yes, after 4 pm
Cart Rental: $17pp/18
Lessons: Yes **Schools:** Yes
Clinics: Yes **Day Camps:** No
Other: Clubhouse / Lockers / Showers / Restaurant / Bar/ Hotel / Beverage Cart

Tees	Holes	Yards	Par	USGA	Slope
BACK	18	6213	72	69.3	117
MIDDLE	18	5851	72	67.5	114
FRONT	18	5365	74	68.5	112

Weekend: $30.00 after 4 pm
Weekend: $75.00
All Day Play: $29.00
Discounts: None
Junior Golf: Yes **Membership:** Yes
Driving Range: $5.00

Players' Comments: "Beautiful course." "Friendly staff." "Got my first par ever here." Excellent stay & play golf package. Open May-mid Oct. Rates subject to change.

	1	2	3	4	5	6	7	8	9
PAR	5	3	5	3	4	5	4	3	4
YARDS	482	152	450	153	367	472	381	135	370
HDCP	9	15	5	13	3	11	1	17	7
	10	11	12	13	14	15	16	17	18
PAR	3	5	4	4	5	3	4	4	4
YARDS	170	445	371	327	447	158	352	341	279
HDCP	12	8	4	10	14	16	2	6	18

Directions: Exit 10 off I-89. Follow Route 100 for 10 miles to blinking light in center of Stowe village, turn left onto Route 108. Turn right directly past Whiskers Restaurant onto Cape Cod Road. Course straight ahead.

Stratton Mt. (forest) ✪✪✪

Stratton Mountain, VT (802) 297-4114
www.stratton.com

Tees	Holes	Yards	Par	USGA	Slope
BACK	9	6526	72	71.2	125
MIDDLE	9	6044	72	69.4	122
FRONT	9	5155	74	69.8	123

Club Pro: Danny Caverly, PGA
Pro Shop: Full inventory
Payment: Visa, MC, Amex
Tee Times: Anytime
Fee 9 Holes: Weekday: $49 (M-Th)w/ cart   **Weekend:** $55 icl. cart
Fee 18 Holes: Weekday: $79 (M-Th) w/ cart   **Weekend:** $99 incl. cart
Twilight Rates: Yes, after 5 pm   **All Day Play:** No
Cart Rental: Cart included   **Discounts:** Junior
Lessons: $40.00/half hour   **Schools:** Yes   **Junior Golf:** No   **Membership:** Yes
Clinics: Yes   **Day Camps:** No   **Driving Range:** $7/lg. $4/sm.
Other: Clubhouse / Lockers-Showers / Snack bar / Restaurant / Bar-lounge / Hotel

COUPON

Player's Comment: "1st class services really makes a golfer feel special." The back 9 is the front 9 of "lake". Cornish design features.

	1	2	3	4	5	6	7	8	9
PAR	4	4	4	3	5	4	3	5	4
YARDS	372	387	305	129	467	295	140	504	379
HDCP	5	2	6	9	1	8	7	4	3

	10	11	12	13	14	15	16	17	18
PAR	4	4	4	3	4	5	3	4	5
YARDS	353	395	328	164	269	466	193	390	508
HDCP	6	1	8	7	9	4	5	3	2

Directions: Take I-91 to Brattleboro Exit, follow Route 30 East 30 miles to Bondville; look for signs to Stratton Mountain.

Stratton Mt. (lake) ✪✪✪

Stratton Mountain, VT (802) 297-4114
www.stratton.com

Tees	Holes	Yards	Par	USGA	Slope
BACK	9	6602	72	72.0	125
MIDDLE	9	6107	72	70.3	123
FRONT	9	5410	74	71.1	124

Club Pro: Danny Caverly, PGA
Pro Shop: Full inventory
Payment: Visa, MC, Amex, Disc, Cash, Checks
Tee Times: Anytime
Fee 9 Holes: Weekday: $49 (M-Th) w/ cart   **Weekend:** $55 incl. cart F/S/S/H
Fee 18 Holes: Weekday: $79 (M-Th) w/ cart   **Weekend:** $99incl. cart F/S/S/H
Twilight Rates: Yes, after 5 pm   **All Day Play:** No
Cart Rental: Cart included   **Discounts:** Junior
Lessons: $40.00/half hour   **Schools:** Yes   **Junior Golf:** No   **Membership:** Yes
Clinics: Yes   **Day Camps:** No   **Driving Range:** $7/lg. $4/sm.
Other: Clubhouse / Lockers / Snack bar / Restaurant / Bar-Lounge / Hotel

COUPON

Requires good shot management both off the tee and to the green. Sports center, tennis courts, horseback riding and mountain biking are available. **Player's Comment:** "Just a wonderful experience".

	1	2	3	4	5	6	7	8	9
PAR	4	4	4	3	4	5	3	4	5
YARDS	353	395	328	164	269	466	193	390	508
HDCP	6	1	8	7	9	4	5	3	2

	10	11	12	13	14	15	16	17	18
PAR	4	3	4	4	5	4	4	3	5
YARDS	323	186	372	355	545	304	358	150	448
HDCP	5	4	2	6	1	8	3	9	7

Directions: Exit 1 off I-91 in Vermont. Take Route 30 North to town off Bondville (about 40 miles from Brattleboro). Turn left on Sratton Access Rd. Go straight 2 miles.

VT

Stratton Mt. (mountain)

✪✪✪

Stratton Mountain, VT (802) 297-4114
www.stratton.com

Tees	Holes	Yards	Par	USGA	Slope
BACK	9	6478	72	71.2	126
MIDDLE	9	6019	72	69.3	123
FRONT	9	5163	74	69.9	123

Club Pro: Danny Caverly, PGA
Pro Shop: Full inventory
Payment: Visa, MC, Amex
Tee Times: Anytime
Fee 9 Holes: Weekday: $49(M-Th) w/cart
Fee 18 Holes: Weekday: $79(M-Th) w/ cart
Twilight Rates: Yes, after 5 pm
Cart Rental: Cart included
Lessons: $40.00/half hour **Schools:** Yes
Clinics: Yes **Day Camps:** No

Weekend: $55.00 incl. cart
Weekend: $99.00 incl. cart
All Day Play: No
Discounts: Junior
Junior Golf: No **Membership:** Yes
Driving Range: $7/lg. $4/sm.

Other: Clubhouse / Lockers / Showers / Snack bar / Restaurant / Bar-lounge

This outstanding course consists of three separate nine hole courses. Cornish design.

	1	2	3	4	5	6	7	8	9
PAR	4	3	4	4	5	4	4	3	5
YARDS	323	186	372	355	545	304	358	150	448
HDCP	5	4	2	6	1	8	3	9	7
	10	11	12	13	14	15	16	17	18
PAR	4	4	4	3	5	4	3	5	4
YARDS	372	387	305	129	467	295	140	504	379
HDCP	5	2	6	9	1	8	7	4	3

Directions: Take I-91 to Brattleboro Exit, follow Route 30 East 30 miles to Bondville; look for signs to Stratton Mountain.

Sugarbush Golf Club

Warren, VT (802) 583-6725
www.sugarbush.com

Tees	Holes	Yards	Par	USGA	Slope
BACK	18	6464	72	71.7	128
MIDDLE	18	5922	70	69.0	122
FRONT	18	5231	72	50.5	129

Club Pro: Jonathan Rife, PGA
Pro Shop: Full inventory
Payment: Visa, MC, Amex, Disc
Tee Times: Yes
Fee 9 Holes: Weekday: $28.00
Fee 18 Holes: Weekday: $54.00
Twilight Rates: Yes, after 2 pm
Cart Rental: $15pp
Lessons: Yes **Schools:** No
Clinics: Yes **Day Camps:** No

Weekend: $28.00
Weekend: $54.00
All Day Play: No
Discounts: Junior
Junior Golf: Yes **Membership:** Yes
Driving Range: Yes

Other: Restaurant / Clubhouse / Hotel / Bar-lounge / Lockers / Snack bar / Showers / Schools

Breathtaking views. New irrigation system all 18 holes.

	1	2	3	4	5	6	7	8	9
PAR	4	4	4	4	3	4	4	3	4
YARDS	322	372	396	355	164	374	433	166	353
HDCP	13	1	5	9	15	3	7	17	11
	10	11	12	13	14	15	16	17	18
PAR	5	3	4	4	5	4	3	4	4
YARDS	504	118	395	325	449	352	157	329	322
HDCP	6	18	2	14	4	8	12	16	10

Directions: From I-89 S: Exit 10 to Route 100 S to Sugarbush Access Road. From I-89 N: take Exit 9 to Route 100B S to Route 100 S.

The Links at Lang Farm ⚫⚫ ▶53 ▶

Essex VT. (802-878-0298

Club Pro: Michael Packard
Pro Shop: Yes
Payment: Cash, Visa, MC
Tee Times: 3 day adv.

Tees	Holes	Yards	Par	USGA	Slope
BACK	18	3809	60	59.8	102
MIDDLE	18	3444	60	58	96
FRONT	18	2884	60		

Fee 9 Holes: Weekday:	**Weekend:**
Fee 18 Holes: Weekday:	**Weekend:**
Twilight Rates:	**All Day Play:**
Cart Rental:	**Discounts:**
Lessons: Yes **Schools:**	**Junior Golf:** Yes **Membership:** Yes
Clinics: **Day Camps:** Yes	**Driving Range:** Yes

Other: Inn / Lodging Partner / Tournaments / Outings

New Entry 2004. Vermont's newest golf experience appealing to all levels of play. Call ahead for tee times.
"Polished, executive course. More like championship course. Excellent conditions." R.W.

	1	2	3	4	5	6	7	8	9
PAR	3	3	3	4	3	4	3	3	3
YARDS	158	167	155	295	124	307	133	180	156
HDCP	7	1	11	15	9	17	13	3	5

	10	11	12	13	14	15	16	17	18
PAR	3	3	4	3	4	3	3	4	4
YARDS	156	147	273	126	258	102	152	231	324
HDCP	4	10	12	14	8	16	2	18	6

Directions: I-89 to Exit 11. Follow Route 117 6 miles to VT-289. Exit 10, Turn Left.

Vermont National CC ⚫⚫⚫ ▶54 ▶

S. Burlington, VT. 802-864-7770
www.vnccgolf.com

Club Pro: Zach Wyman
Pro Shop: Full inventory
Payment: Most major
Tee Times: 3 days in adv.

Tees	Holes	Yards	Par	USGA	Slope
BACK	18	7035	72	73.6	133
MIDDLE	18	6211	72	69.6	126
FRONT	18	4966	72	69.2	116

Fee 9 Holes: Weekday: N/A	**Weekend:** N/A
Fee 18 Holes: Weekday: $120.00	**Weekend:** $120.00
Twilight Rates: No	**All Day Play:** No
Cart Rental: $15.00 per person	**Discounts:** Junior
Lessons: $40.00/30 min. **Schools:** N/R	**Junior Golf:** Yes **Membership:** Yes
Clinics: Yes **Day Camps:** Yes	**Driving Range:** Players only

Other: Clubhouse/ Bar Lounge

COUPON

Tour caliber designed by Jack Nicklaus & son. **Players' Comments:** "Excellent course with immaculate
conditions. Beautiful clubhouse provides a friendly staff." "Great fun and major challenge."

	1	2	3	4	5	6	7	8	9
PAR	4	5	4	3	5	4	4	3	4
YARDS	319	525	357	188	580	469	452	227	411
HDCP	17	13	11	15	3	1	5	9	7

	10	11	12	13	14	15	16	17	18
PAR	4	5	4	3	4	3	5	3	5
YARDS	441	607	400	197	409	209	495	204	554
HDCP	4	2	10	18	6	16	12	14	8

Directions: I-89 Exit 14 East to Dorset Street. South 2 miles to club on right.

VT

4⚫ =Excellent 3⚫ =Very Good 2⚫ =Good

West Bolton Golf Club

West Bolton, Jericho, VT (802) 434-4321
www.westboltongolfclub.com

Club Pro: Holly Reynolds, PGA
Pro Shop: Full inventory
Payment: Visa, MC, Disc.
Tee Times: 1 week adv.
Fee 9 Holes: Weekday: $19.00
Fee 18 Holes: Weekday: $24.00
Twilight Rates: Yes, after 3 pm
Cart Rental: $25.00/18 $12.50/9
Lessons: Yes **Schools:** Junior
Clinics: Yes **Day Camps:** Jr, M-Th
Other: Clubhouse / Snack bar

Tees	Holes	Yards	Par	USGA	Slope
BACK					
MIDDLE	18	5661	72	66.8	115
FRONT	18	5165	72	72.5	111

Weekend: $19.00
Weekend: $24.00
All Day Play: Yes
Discounts: Srs., Jrs., & Ladies
Junior Golf: Yes **Membership:** Yes
Driving Range: No

New clubhouse. Unique18 hole course nestled in the Green Mountains. The fairway trees are small, but the mountains surrounding the course are grand.

	1	2	3	4	5	6	7	8	9
PAR	4	5	3	4	4	3	4	4	4
YARDS	303	481	149	248	353	191	329	359	295
HDCP	9	3	17	13	1	5	15	7	11
	10	11	12	13	14	15	16	17	18
PAR	3	5	4	5	3	5	4	4	4
YARDS	128	430	392	451	180	458	273	323	318
HDCP	18	8	2	4	16	6	14	10	12

Directions: I-89 to Exit 11 toward Richmond. Left at light (Four Corners). Go about 7 mi. and take a right at the West Bolton Golf Course sign. Continue for 4 miles.

White River Golf Club

Rt. 100, Rochester, VT (802) 767-4653
www.whiterivergolf.com

Club Pro: Bruce Munch
Pro Shop: Limited inventory
Payment: Cash, MC, Visa
Tee Times: Required
Fee 9 Holes: Weekday: $17.50
Fee 18 Holes: Weekday: $25.00
Twilight Rates: Thurs. & Fri.
Cart Rental: $21.00/18 $16.00/9
Lessons: Yes **Schools:** Yes
Clinics: Yes **Day Camps:** Yes
Other: Clubhouse / Bar-lounge / Snack Bar

Tees	Holes	Yards	Par	USGA	Slope
BACK	9	5314	68	65.6	115
MIDDLE	9	5038	68	62.6	112
FRONT	9	4068	68	64.6	104

Weekend: $17.50
Weekend: $25.00
All Day Play: No
Discounts: None
Junior Golf: Yes **Membership:** Yes
Driving Range: Yes

COUPON

9 hole panoramic from every hole. recent design changes have made a true test of skill for the experienced golfer while still appealing to the novice golfer. Open May - October.

	1	2	3	4	5	6	7	8	9
PAR	3	5	4	3	3	4	4	4	4
YARDS	185	545	255	115	157	430	273	355	320
HDCP	7	3	17	9	5	1	15	13	11
	10	11	12	13	14	15	16	17	18
PAR	3	5	4	3	3	4	4	4	4
YARDS	185	545	255	115	157	430	273	355	320
HDCP	8	4	18	10	6	2	16	14	12

Directions: I-89 to Route 107 West to Route 100 North. Course is 10 miles north on Route 100. Approx. halfway between Killington and Sugarbush.

Wilcox Cove GC

Hgwy. 314, Grand Isle, VT (802) 372-8343

Club Pro: No
Pro Shop: No
Payment: Cash, Check
Tee Times: No
Fee 9 Holes: Weekday: $13.00
Fee 18 Holes: Weekday: $13.00
Twilight Rates: Yes, after 6 pm
Cart Rental: Handcarts
Lessons: No **Schools:** No
Clinics: N/R **Day Camps:** N/R
Other: No

Tees	Holes	Yards	Par	USGA	Slope
BACK					
MIDDLE	9	1732	32		
FRONT					

Weekend: $15.00
Weekend: $15.00
All Day Play: Yes
Discounts: None
Junior Golf: N/R **Membership:** Yes
Driving Range: No

COUPON

An executive type course on the West shore of Grand Isle, looking over Lake Champlain to the Adirondack Mountains of New York. A fairly level course. Twilight weekend rates.

	1	2	3	4	5	6	7	8	9
PAR	4	4	4	3	4	3	4	3	3
YARDS	240	210	254	120	245	190	185	193	95
HDCP									

	10	11	12	13	14	15	16	17	18
PAR									
YARDS									
HDCP									

Directions: Take I-89 to Exit 17 (Route 2 North.) Take Route 314 past Grand Isle Ferry.

Williston Golf Club

◐◐

Williston, VT (802) 878-3747

Club Pro: Todd Trono
Pro Shop: Full inventory
Payment: Visa, MC
Tee Times: Wknds+ Hldys
Fee 9 Holes: Weekday: No
Fee 18 Holes: Weekday: $26.00
Twilight Rates: Yes, after 5 pm
Cart Rental: $12.50pp/9
Lessons: Yes **Schools:** No
Clinics: Yes **Day Camps:** No
Other: 19th hole resturant

Tees	Holes	Yards	Par	USGA	Slope
BACK	18	6621	69	N/R	N/R
MIDDLE	18	5262	69	66.6	113
FRONT	18	4716	71	64	106

Weekend: No
Weekend: $26.00
All Day Play: N/R
Discounts: None
Junior Golf: Yes **Membership:** Yes
Driving Range: Nearby

VT

Player's Comment: "Play it at least twice a season. Very well kept. Always friendly." Voted area's favorite choice. Fully irrigated. Rated 3 stars by *Golf Digest.* Open May-Nov. 1.

	1	2	3	4	5	6	7	8	9
PAR	4	4	4	4	4	3	4	4	5
YARDS	316	390	289	272	260	184	267	382	445
HDCP	13	1	5	9	17	7	15	3	11

	10	11	12	13	14	15	16	17	18
PAR	4	3	3	4	4	3	3	4	5
YARDS	325	160	212	254	395	151	90	360	510
HDCP	10	12	4	16	2	14	18	6	8

Directions: I-89 to Exit 11 or 12; Route 2 East to North Williston Rd. Course is 1/2 mile on right. 7 miles east of Burlington, Vermont.

4◐ =Excellent **3◐** =Very Good **2◐** = Good

Windham Golf Club at Tater Hill

North Windham, VT (802) 875-2517
www.windhamgolf.com

Club Pro: John Pawlak
Pro Shop: Full inventory
Payment: Visa, MC, Amex
Tee Times: 1 wk adv.

Tees	Holes	Yards	Par	USGA	Slope
BACK	18	6048	70	68.0	111
MIDDLE	18	5426	72	65.8	105
FRONT	18	4475	70	66.2	108

Fee 9 Holes: Weekday: $52, $42 after 12pm **Weekend:** $75, $57 after 12pm
Fee 18 Holes: Weekday: $52, $42 after 12pm **Weekend:** $75, $57 after 12pm
Twilight Rates: Yes, after 3 pm   **All Day Play:** No
Cart Rental: Included in fee   **Discounts:** Junior
Lessons: $30.00/half hour **Schools:** No   **Junior Golf:** Yes **Membership:** Yes
Clinics: Yes **Day Camps:** No   **Driving Range:** $6/lg. $4/sm.
Other: Clubhouse / Bar-lounge / Restaurant

18-hole championship course offers over 6800 yards of play and was designed to optimize your golf experience by blending the natural beauty of VT with the dynamic layout.

	1	2	3	4	5	6	7	8	9
PAR	5	3	3	4	3	5	4	4	5
YARDS	473	133	193	352	160	470	397	305	450
HDCP	5	15	17	3	9	11	1	13	7
	10	11	12	13	14	15	16	17	18
PAR	3	4	4	4	4	3	5	4	5
YARDS	168	388	414	373	324	148	462	295	530
HDCP	16	6	4	12	8	18	2	10	14

Directions: Take I-91 to Exit 6; take left onto Route 103, turns into 11 West; 7 miles outside Chester look for signs to course.

NEW 2004 Woodbury Golf Course

Woodbury, VT (802) 456-1250

Club Pro: Darwin Thompson
Pro Shop: Limited inventory
Payment: Visa, MC, Checks
Tee Times: No, (802) 456-1250

Tees	Holes	Yards	Par	USGA	Slope
BACK					
MIDDLE	9	1264	27		
FRONT					

Fee 9 Holes: Weekday: $10.00   **Weekend:** $10.00
Fee 18 Holes: Weekday: $15.00   **Weekend:** $15.00
Twilight Rates: No   **All Day Play:** No
Cart Rental: $10/18, $5/9   **Discounts:** Senior & Junior
Lessons: No **Schools:** No   **Junior Golf: Membership:** Yes
Clinics: No **Day Camps:** No   **Driving Range:** No
Other: Snack bar

New Entry 2004. Family owned, family run, family fun.

	1	2	3	4	5	6	7	8	9
PAR	3	3	3	3	3	3	3	3	3
YARDS	120	145	128	185	147	118	125	129	167
HDCP	9	3	6	2	8	5	7	4	1
	10	11	12	13	14	15	16	17	18
PAR									
YARDS									
HDCP									

Directions: Exit 8 North on Route 302, North on Route 2, North on Route. 14. Right onto Easthill Rd. in South Woodbury. 2 Miles on Right.

Woodstock Inn & Resort ✪✪

Woodstock, VT (802) 457-6674
www.woodstockinn.com

Club Pro: Jim Gunnare
Pro Shop: Full inventory
Payment: Cash, MC,Visa,Amex
Tee Times: Yes
Fee 9 Holes: Weekday: N/A
Fee 18 Holes: Weekday: $74.00
Twilight Rates: Yes, after 4 pm
Cart Rental: $36.00/18
Lessons: $40.00/half hour **Schools:** Jr. & Sr.
Clinics: Yes **Day Camps:** No

Tees	Holes	Yards	Par	USGA	Slope
BACK	18	6053	70	69.7	123
MIDDLE	18	5619	70	68.0	117
FRONT	18	4924	71	69.0	113

Weekend: N/A
Weekend: $85.00
All Day Play: No
Discounts: None
Junior Golf: Yes **Membership:** Yes
Driving Range: $4.00/lg. bucket

COUPON

Other: Clubhouse / Lockers / Showers / Restaurant / Bar-lounge/ Hotel / Snack Bar

Robert Trent Jones Jr. design championship resort course. Friendly staff, wonderful amenities.

	1	2	3	4	5	6	7	8	9
PAR	5	3	4	4	3	5	3	4	4
YARDS	465	162	346	382	134	503	162	356	386
HDCP	9	13	5	1	15	3	17	11	7
	10	11	12	13	14	15	16	17	18
PAR	5	3	4	3	4	3	5	4	4
YARDS	465	131	381	150	272	144	520	315	396
HDCP	4	16	2	10	14	18	6	12	8

Directions: Take Route 4 West off I-89 to Woodstock.

VT

4✪ =Excellent 3✪ =Very Good 2✪ =Good

CHAPTER 9

Northern/Eastern Connecticut

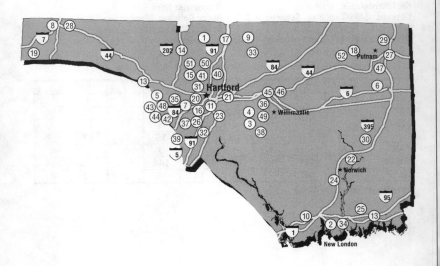

New 2003 courses indicated in **bold**.
New 2004 courses indicated in ***bold italic***.

Airways Golf Course	1	Hotchkiss School GC	19	Stanley Golf Club	37
Birch Plain Golf Course	2	Keney Park Golf Club	20	Tallwood Country Club	38
Blackledge CC - Anderson's	3	Manchester CC	21	Timberlin Golf Club	39
Blackledge CC - Gilead	4	Mile View Par 3	22	Topstone Golf Course	40
Blue Fox Run	5	Minnechaug GC	23	Tradition Golf Course	41
Brooklyn Hill GC	6	Norwich Golf Course	24	Tunxis Plantation CC (G)	42
Buena Vista GC	7	Pequot Golf Club	25	Tunxis Plantation CC (W)	43
Canaan Country Club	8	Pistol Creek Golf Club	26	Tunxis Plantation GC (R)	44
Cedar Knob GC	9	Putnam Country Club	27	Twin Hills CC	45
Cedar Ridge GC	10	**Quarryview Golf Course**	**28**	Villa Hills Golf Course	46
East Hartford GC	11	Raceway Golf Club	29	Vineyard Valley Golf Club	47
Elmridge Golf Course	12	River Ridge GC	30	Westwoods GC	48
Fairview Farm Golf Course	13	Rockledge CC	31	Willimantic CC	49
Fox Run at Copper Hill	14	Rolling Greens GC	32	**Willow Brook**	**50**
Gillette Ridge	***15***	Rolling Meadows CC	33	***Wintonbury Hills GC***	***51***
Goodwin Golf Course	16	Shennecosset GC	34	Woodstock GC	52
Grassmere CC	17	Simsbury Farms GC	35		
Harrisville GC	18	Skungamaug River GC	36		

Airways Golf Course

1070 S. Grand, West Suffield, CT (860) 668-4973
www.airwaysgolf.com

Club Pro: No
Pro Shop: Limited inventory
Payment: Visa, MC, Cash
Tee Times: 1 week adv.

Tees	Holes	Yards	Par	USGA	Slope
BACK	18	5914	71	66.0	106
MIDDLE	18	5528	71	65.0	103
FRONT	18	5134	72	65.0	103

Fee 9 Holes: Weekday: $12.00   **Weekend:** $13.00
Fee 18 Holes: Weekday: $20.00   **Weekend:** $24.00
Twilight Rates: No   **All Day Play:** No
Cart Rental: $10pp/18 $5pp/9   **Discounts:** Senior
Lessons: No   **Schools:** No   **Junior Golf:** No   **Membership:** No
Clinics: No   **Day Camps:** No   **Driving Range:** No
Other: Clubhouse / Snack bar

COUPON

Noted for great value. Easy to walk, beautiful challenging course.

	1	2	3	4	5	6	7	8	9
PAR	4	4	4	5	4	4	3	4	4
YARDS	336	351	351	487	301	302	147	320	273
HDCP	9	5	1	3	11	13	17	7	15
	10	11	12	13	14	15	16	17	18
PAR	3	5	4	3	4	3	5	4	4
YARDS	127	451	369	133	346	132	451	388	263
HDCP	18	8	10	14	6	16	4	2	12

Directions: Take I-91 to Exit 40, Exit for Route 20 West, At 4th light turn right, course 2 miles on the right.

Birch Plain Golf Course

High Rock Rd., Groton, CT (860) 445-9918

Club Pro: Jeff Doerr
Pro Shop: Limited inventory
Payment: Cash only
Tee Times: No

Tees	Holes	Yards	Par	USGA	Slope
BACK					
MIDDLE	18	2666	54		
FRONT					

Fee 9 Holes: Weekday: No   **Weekend:** No
Fee 18 Holes: Weekday: $18.00   **Weekend:** $20.00
Twilight Rates: Yes, after 5:30 pm   **All Day Play:** No
Cart Rental: $18.00/18, Pull cart $2   **Discounts:** Senior, Junior,Military
Lessons: No   **Schools:** N/R   **Junior Golf:** N/R   **Membership:** Yes
Clinics: Yes   **Day Camps:** No   **Driving Range:** $6.00/lg., $5.00/sm
Other: Snacks

On going renovations. Formerly Trumbull Golf Course. A pleasant par 3 golf course. Good for beginners.

	1	2	3	4	5	6	7	8	9
PAR	3	3	3	3	3	3	3	3	3
YARDS	107	170	148	228	206	124	113	137	129
HDCP	17	5	7	1	3	14	15	6	13
	10	11	12	13	14	15	16	17	18
PAR	3	3	3	3	3	3	3	3	3
YARDS	105	187	108	147	136	164	150	155	156
HDCP	18	2	16	9	12	4	8	10	11

Directions: I-95 S, take Route 349   (Clarence Sharp Highway.) At second light, go left. At next light, go right. Follow signs for Groton/New London Airport. Course on right.

NE CT

4⊙ =Excellent   3⊙ =Very Good   2⊙ =Good

Blackledge CC - Anderson's Glen ☉☉

180 West St., Hebron, CT (860) 228-0250
www.blackledgecc.com

Club Pro: K. J. Higgins, PGA & C. Morris
Pro Shop: Full inventory
Payment: Visa, MC
Tee Times: 1 week adv.
Fee 9 Holes: Weekday: $17.00
Fee 18 Holes: Weekday: $33.00
Twilight Rates: Yes, after 1 pm
Cart Rental: $24.00/18 $12.00/9
Lessons: $30.00/half hour **Schools:** No
Clinics: No **Day Camps:** No
Other: Clubhouse / Snack bar / Restaurant / Bar-lounge

Tees	Holes	Yards	Par	USGA	Slope
BACK	18	6787	72	72.0	128
MIDDLE	18	6137	72	68.9	122
FRONT	18	5458	72	71.7	123

Weekend: $19.00
Weekend: $38.00
All Day Play:
Discounts: Senior & Junior
Junior Golf: No **Membership:** Yes
Driving Range: No

COUPON

Good walking course that tests every shot in your game. Fairways are in great shape. Greens are on the fast side. Open March - Dec. "Tight and tree-lined." **Player's Comments.**

	1	2	3	4	5	6	7	8	9
PAR	4	4	4	5	4	3	4	3	5
YARDS	375	365	389	480	350	153	318	170	485
HDCP	11	13	1	3	7	17	9	15	5

	10	11	12	13	14	15	16	17	18
PAR	4	4	5	3	4	4	3	5	4
YARDS	316	408	465	142	383	369	179	425	365
HDCP	16	2	4	18	8	10	14	6	12

Directions: Take Route 2 East to Exit 8. Left off ramp, go 9 miles. Take a right onto West Street. Course is on the right.

Blackledge CC - Gilead Highlands

Hebron, CT (860) 228-0250
www.blackledgecc.com

Club Pro: K. J. Higgins, PGA & C. Morris
Pro Shop: Full inventory
Payment: Visa, MC
Tee Times: 1 week adv.
Fee 9 Holes: Weekday: $17.00
Fee 18 Holes: Weekday: $33.00
Twilight Rates: Yes, after 1 pm
Cart Rental: $24.00/18 $12.00/9
Lessons: $30.00/half hour **Schools:** No
Clinics: No **Day Camps:** No
Other: Clubhouse / Snack bar / Restaurant / Bar-lounge

Tees	Holes	Yards	Par	USGA	Slope
BACK	18	6129	72	69.8	121
MIDDLE	18	5714	72	68.0	116
FRONT	18	4951	72		

Weekend: $19.00
Weekend: $38.00
All Day Play: No
Discounts: Senior & Junior
Junior Golf: No **Membership:** Yes
Driving Range: No

COUPON

Open March - Dec.

	1	2	3	4	5	6	7	8	9
PAR	4	3	5	4	4	4	5	3	4
YARDS	369	133	436	275	359	325	455	142	366
HDCP	5	15	3	13	7	11	1	17	9

	10	11	12	13	14	15	16	17	18
PAR	5	3	5	3	4	4	4	4	4
YARDS	464	142	454	148	358	346	301	320	327
HDCP	4	18	2	16	12	6	14	8	10

Directions: Take Route 2 East to Exit 8. Left off ramp, go 9 miles. Take a right onto West Street. Course is on the right.

Blue Fox Run

5

Nod Rd., Avon, CT (860) 678-1679
www.bluefoxent.com

Club Pro: Bob Ellison, PGA
Pro Shop: Full inventory
Payment: Visa, MC, Amex
Tee Times: 7 days a week

Tees	Holes	Yards	Par	USGA	Slope
BACK	18	6116	71	69.4	116
MIDDLE	18	5782	71	67.9	113
FRONT	18	5213	72	70.2	124

Fee 9 Holes: Weekday: $18.00 M-Th   **Weekend:** $19.00 F/S/S/H
Fee 18 Holes: Weekday: $29.00 M-Th   **Weekend:** $35.00 F/S/S/H
Twilight Rates: No   **All Day Play:** No
Cart Rental: $15.00pp/18 $9.00pp/9   **Discounts:** Senior & Junior
Lessons: $50/half hour $100/hr. **Schools:** Yes **Junior Golf:** Yes **Membership:** No
Clinics: Yes **Day Camps:** Yes   **Driving Range:** $5.00 token
Other: Restaurant / Bar-lounge/ Banquet facilities / Child Care

COUPON

Sig. Hole: #17, 189 yds. par 3 with an island green requires a precise tee shot. Par is a great score. Open March 1 - December 15. "Course is in good shape. Very Pretty in fall." **Player's Comments.**

	1	2	3	4	5	6	7	8	9
PAR	4	4	3	4	5	4	3	5	3
YARDS	326	291	134	319	470	361	177	486	150
HDCP	13	15	17	7	3	1	9	5	11
	10	**11**	**12**	**13**	**14**	**15**	**16**	**17**	**18**
PAR	4	4	5	4	5	3	4	3	4
YARDS	357	372	494	389	483	125	340	138	358
HDCP	10	12	14	2	4	16	6	18	8

Directions: I-84 Exit 39. to Route 4, Farmington Center, turn right onto Waterville Rd. ,(Route 10 North). Go 5 miles., cross over Route 44 intersection to Nod Road. Club 1/2 mile on left.

Brooklyn Golf Course

6

South St., Brooklyn, CT (860) 774-1926

Club Pro: Raymond Carignan
Pro Shop: Limited inventory
Payment: Cash, Check
Tee Times: Wkends 7 days adv.

Tees	Holes	Yards	Par	USGA	Slope
BACK	9	5760	70		
MIDDLE	9	5566	70		
FRONT					

Fee 9 Holes: Weekday: $9.00   **Weekend:** $11.00
Fee 18 Holes: Weekday: $15.00   **Weekend:** $17.00
Twilight Rates: No   **All Day Play:** No
Cart Rental: $24.00/18 $12.00/9   **Discounts:** None
Lessons: $35.00/half hour **Schools:** No **Junior Golf:** No **Membership:** Yes
Clinics: N/R **Day Camps:** No   **Driving Range:** $5/lg. $3/sm.
Other: Clubhouse / Snack bar / Bar-lounge

Prices subject to change.

	1	2	3	4	5	6	7	8	9
PAR	4	4	4	4	5	3	4	3	4
YARDS	385	350	340	410	460	130	420	135	250
HDCP	9	7	11	3	5	15	1	17	13
	10	**11**	**12**	**13**	**14**	**15**	**16**	**17**	**18**
PAR	4	4	4	4	5	3	4	3	4
YARDS	385	350	340	410	460	130	420	135	250
HDCP	10	8	12	4	6	16	2	18	14

Directions: Take I-395 to Route 6 West Exit; take left onto Allen Hill Rd. Take first left onto South St.; course is 1/2 mile on left.

4✪ =Excellent **3✪** =Very Good **2✪** = Good

Buena Vista GC

W. Hartford, CT (860) 521-7359
www.west-hartford.com

Club Pro: Richard Crow, PGA
Pro Shop: Limited inventory
Payment: Cash only
Tee Times: No
Fee 9 Holes: Weekday: $11.25
Fee 18 Holes: Weekday: $20.50
Twilight Rates: No
Cart Rental: $20.00/18 $10.00/9
Lessons: No **Schools:** No
Clinics: No **Day Camps:** No
Other: Putting green

Tees	Holes	Yards	Par	USGA	Slope
BACK					
MIDDLE	9	1977	31		
FRONT	9	1653	30		

Weekend: $12.00
Weekend: $22.00
All Day Play: No
Discounts: Sr & Jr/only W. Hartford residents.
Junior Golf: No **Membership:** W. Hartford res.
Driving Range: No

A good mix of holes. Great for all levels of golfers. Renovations include additional sand traps on the third hole. Open April-December.

	1	2	3	4	5	6	7	8	9
PAR	4	4	4	3	3	3	3	3	4
YARDS	263	344	295	171	130	98	223	214	239
HDCP	4	1	3	7	8	9	5	2	6
	10	11	12	13	14	15	16	17	18
PAR									
YARDS									
HDCP									

Directions: Take I-84 to Exit 43 (Park Rd.); left off ramp; go through 3 lights, take left onto Buena Vista Road. Course on left. Parking lot shared with Cornerstone Pool.

Canaan Country Club

S. Canaan Rd., Canaan, CT (860) 824-7683

Club Pro: Paul Julian
Pro Shop: Full inventory
Payment: Cash only
Tee Times: No
Fee 9 Holes: Weekday: $12.00
Fee 18 Holes: Weekday: $22.00
Twilight Rates: No
Cart Rental: $20.00/18 $10.00/9
Lessons: Private Call **Schools:** No
Clinics: No **Day Camps:** No
Other: Snack bar / Restaurant / Function rooms

Tees	Holes	Yards	Par	USGA	Slope
BACK					
MIDDLE	9	3007	35	68 .2	108
FRONT					

Weekend: $15.00
Weekend: $28.00
All Day Play: No
Discounts: None
Junior Golf: No **Membership:** Yes
Driving Range: No

The course is mostly flat with a few rolling hills. Considered a good walking course.

	1	2	3	4	5	6	7	8	9
PAR	4	5	3	5	4	4	3	3	4
YARDS	320	520	180	545	402	382	125	210	323
HDCP	11	1	15	3	5	7	17	13	9
	10	11	12	13	14	15	16	17	18
PAR									
YARDS									
HDCP									

Directions: Take Route 7 to Canaan. The course is on South Canaan Road across from Greet Memorial Hospital.

Cedar Knob GC

Billings Rd., Somers, CT (860) 749-3550

Club Pro: Jeffrey Swanson
Pro Shop: Full inventory
Payment: Cash or check
Tee Times: 3 dy/wknd, 7 dy/wk
Fee 9 Holes: Weekday: $16.50
Fee 18 Holes: Weekday: $29.00
Twilight Rates: No
Cart Rental: $6.00pp/9
Lessons: $30/30 min. **Schools:** No
Clinics: No **Day Camps:** N/R
Other: Clubhouse / Snack bar / Restaurant / Bar-lounge

Tees	Holes	Yards	Par	USGA	Slope
BACK	18	6734	72	72.4	126
MIDDLE	18	6298	72	70.5	122
FRONT	18	5784	74	73.9	129

Weekend: $18.50
Weekend: $32.00
All Day Play: No
Discounts: Sr & Jr Weekdays
Junior Golf: Yes **Membership:** No
Driving Range: Yes - must use own balls

Dress code. Open year round (weather permitting). Call about specials.

	1	2	3	4	5	6	7	8	9
PAR	4	3	5	4	3	4	5	4	4
YARDS	384	154	482	397	209	319	478	327	328
HDCP	5	15	11	1	7	17	3	9	13

	10	11	12	13	14	15	16	17	18
PAR	5	4	4	4	3	4	3	5	4
YARDS	490	370	410	350	170	350	210	470	400
HDCP	6	10	2	14	18	12	8	16	4

Directions: Take Route 91 to Exit 47 (East toward Somers). Right onto Route 83; right on Billings Rd. Course is 1/2 mi. on left.

Cedar Ridge GC

E. Lyme, CT (860) 691-4568
www.cedarridgegolf.com

Club Pro: No
Pro Shop: Full inventory
Payment: Most major
Tee Times: 7 days adv.
Fee 9 Holes: Weekday: $14.00
Fee 18 Holes: Weekday: $18.50
Twilight Rates: Wknds only, after 4 pm
Cart Rental: Yes
Lessons: Yes **Schools:** No
Clinics: No **Day Camps:** N/R
Other: Snacks only

Tees	Holes	Yards	Par	USGA	Slope
BACK					
MIDDLE	18	3025	54		
FRONT					

Weekend: $18.00
Weekend: $24.00
All Day Play: N/R
Discounts: Senior & Junior
Junior Golf: Yes **Membership:** N/R
Driving Range: No

Very challenging for the serious and pleasant for the amateur. Course in excellent condition, rolling hills, water hazards. Takes around two hours. Dress is casual. Open April - November.

	1	2	3	4	5	6	7	8	9
PAR	3	3	3	3	3	3	3	3	3
YARDS	157	160	177	103	191	160	122	150	166
HDCP	9	8	7	18	6	10	17	13	11

	10	11	12	13	14	15	16	17	18
PAR	3	3	3	3	3	3	3	3	3
YARDS	155	130	250	145	196	218	215	203	127
HDCP	12	15	1	14	3	2	5	4	16

Directions: I-95 Exit 74, left on Route 161 North. 1 mile to Drabik Road on left.

NE CT

East Hartford GC

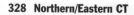

11

Long Hill St., E. Hartford, CT (860) 528-5082

Club Pro: Kevin Tierney, PGA
Pro Shop: Full inventory
Payment: Cash only
Tee Times: Weekends, 1 week adv.
Fee 9 Holes: Weekday: $15.00
Fee 18 Holes: Weekday: $24.00
Twilight Rates: No
Cart Rental: $22.00/18 $13.00/9
Lessons: $35.00/half hour **Schools:** No
Clinics: Yes **Day Camps:** No
Other: Restaurant

Tees	Holes	Yards	Par	USGA	Slope
BACK	18	6186	71	69.1	124
MIDDLE	18	6076	71	68.6	124
FRONT	18	5072	72	68.9	113

Weekend: $16.50
Weekend: $26.75
All Day Play: No
Discounts: Sr & Jr Weekdays
Junior Golf: Yes **Membership:** No
Driving Range: No

COUPON

Relatively short but challenging course which will require a player to use all the clubs in his or her bag. Dress code: no tank tops or cutoffs.

	1	2	3	4	5	6	7	8	9
PAR	4	4	4	3	5	4	4	3	4
YARDS	305	397	322	123	508	415	308	127	385
HDCP	9	7	11	17	1	5	13	15	3
	10	11	12	13	14	15	16	17	18
PAR	5	3	4	4	4	3	4	4	5
YARDS	512	188	308	330	356	150	457	384	500
HDCP	2	16	12	14	8	18	4	6	10

Directions: I-84 to Exit 60, onto Burnside Avenue towards East Hartford. Enter East Hartford, take a right a second traffic light onto Long Hill Street. Proceed through three stop signs, course on right.

Elmridge Golf Course

12 ▶

Elmridge Rd., Pawcatuck, CT (860)599-2248
www.elmridgegolf.com

Club Pro: Thomas Jones, PGA
Pro Shop: Full inventory
Payment: Visa, MC, Amex
Tee Times: Mon/wknd, Fri/wkdys
Fee 9 Holes: Weekday: $19.00
Fee 18 Holes: Weekday: $33.00 (M-TH)
Twilight Rates: Yes, after 2 pm
Cart Rental: $14.00pp/9
Lessons: $40/45 min. **Schools:** No
Clinics: Yes **Day Camps:** No
Other: Clubhouse / Snack bar / Restaurant / Bar-lounge / Outings

Tees	Holes	Yards	Par	USGA	Slope
BACK	18	6347	71	70.8	115
MIDDLE	18	6014	71	69.3	112
FRONT	18	5430	71	69.0	109

Weekend: $18.00 after 3 pm
Weekend: $38.00 after 2pm
All Day Play: No
Discounts: None
Junior Golf: No **Membership:** Yes
Driving Range: Yes

27 holes allow variety of play : Red South, White West, and Blue North courses. Scorecard presented is Red South-White West. Located 7 miles from Foxwoods Casino. Improvements include addition to clubhouse.

	1	2	3	4	5	6	7	8	9
PAR	4	4	4	5	4	3	4	3	4
YARDS	366	335	360	462	149	324	167	385	268
HDCP	3	8	2	4	5	6	7	1	9
	10	11	12	13	14	15	16	17	18
PAR	4	5	4	3	5	3	5	3	4
YARDS	365	485	342	149	576	340	365	206	370
HDCP	9	4	5	8	1	2	6	7	3

Directions: I-95 North, Exit 92 in CT. From north, go left. From south go right. Take first right on to Elmridge Road . Course is 1 mile on left.

Fairview Farm Golf Course ✪✪ 13 ▶

Harwinton, CT (860) 689-1000
www.fairviewfarmsgolfcourse.com

Club Pro: Bob Sparks, PGA
Pro Shop: Yes
Payment: Visa, MC, Amex
Tee Times: 5 days
Fee 9 Holes: Weekday: $18.00
Fee 18 Holes: Weekday: $34.00
Twilight Rates: No
Cart Rental: $15.00pp/18 $7.50pp/9
Lessons: $50.00 / 1 hour **Schools:**
Clinics: Yes **Day Camps:** No
Other: Clubhouse / Restaurant / Bar-lounge / Snacks

Weekend: $21.00
Weekend: $40.00
All Day Play: No
Discounts: None
Junior Golf: Yes **Membership:** No
Driving Range: Yes

Tees	Holes	Yards	Par	USGA	Slope
BACK	18	6539	72	71.7	128
MIDDLE	18	6149	72	69.8	122
FRONT	18	4780	72	67.6	118

Challenging scenic layout. Fabulous views with scenic par 3's. Upscale public course.
"First class design..." R. W. **Players' Comments:** "Well kept. Well laid out. Course is still young."

	1	2	3	4	5	6	7	8	9
PAR	4	4	5	3	4	5	3	4	4
YARDS	380	355	500	160	330	450	155	350	375
HDCP	9	5	1	17	7	3	15	13	11

	10	11	12	13	14	15	16	17	18
PAR	3	4	3	4	4	4	5	4	5
YARDS	187	350	175	340	320	385	520	307	510
HDCP	8	12	18	10	16	6	2	14	4

Directions: From Route 8 Exit 42 (Route 118), head east on Route 118, turn right on to Route 222. Course is 2 mi. on the left. From Route 4 West to Route 118, take left on Route 222. Club is 2 mi. on left.

Fox Run at Copper Hill 14 ▶

E. Granby, CT (860) 653-6191
www.foxrunatcopperhill.com

Club Pro: TBA
Pro Shop: Full inventory
Payment: Visa, MC, Amex
Tee Times: 7 days a week
Fee 9 Holes: Weekday: $14.00
Fee 18 Holes: Weekday: $21.00
Twilight Rates: No
Cart Rental: $13.00pp/18 $7.00pp/9
Lessons: Yes **Schools:** Jr.
Clinics: Yes **Day Camps:** No
Other: Clubhouse / Snack bar / Restaurant / Bar-lounge

Weekend: $14.00
Weekend: $22.00
All Day Play: Yes
Discounts: Senior & Junior
Junior Golf: Yes **Membership:** Yes,
Driving Range: Across street

Tees	Holes	Yards	Par	USGA	Slope
BACK					
MIDDLE	18	6004	72	68.6	116
FRONT	18	5090	72	68.1	124

COUPON

Improvements include full irrigation. Frequent Player card available. Visit our sister course, Blue Fox Run in Avon, CT.

	1	2	3	4	5	6	7	8	9
PAR	4	4	3	5	4	3	4	5	4
YARDS	331	313	163	437	241	164	308	426	376
HDCP	15	11	3	13	7	5	17	9	1

	10	11	12	13	14	15	16	17	18
PAR	4	4	3	5	4	3	4	5	4
YARDS	336	356	176	473	261	178	361	459	402
HDCP	16	4	6	14	12	10	18	8	2

Directions: Take Exit 40 off I-91 (Bradley Field Exit). Follow Route 20 west to Newgate Road (6 lights). Turn right on Newgate Road. Go past old Newgate prison to stop sign. Turn left to course.

NE CT

4✪ =Excellent 3✪ =Very Good 2✪ =Good

Gillette Ridge

15

Bloomfield Ave, Bloomfield, CT, (860) 555- 1212

Tees	Holes	Yards	Par	USGA	Slope
BACK	18	7089			
MIDDLE					
FRONT					

Club Pro: TBA
Pro Shop:
Payment:
Tee Times:
Fee 9 Holes: Weekday: TBA **Weekend:** TBA
Fee 18 Holes: Weekday: TBA **Weekend:** TBA
Twilight Rates: **All Day Play:**
Cart Rental: TBA **Discounts:**
Lessons: Schools: **Junior Golf: Membership:**
Clinics: Day Camps: **Driving Range:**
Other:

New Entry 2004. Opening summer, July 2004. Cigna sponsored. Under Kemper Sports Management. Future plans include hotel and conference center. Arnold Palmer Championship Design.

	1	2	3	4	5	6	7	8	9
PAR									
YARDS									
HDCP									
	10	11	12	13	14	15	16	17	18
PAR									
YARDS									
HDCP									

Directions: I-91, Exit 219 West for approximately 6 miles. 219 becomes Cottage Grove Rd.

Goodwin Golf Course

16

Maple Ave., Hartford, CT (860) 956-3601
www.americangolf.com

Tees	Holes	Yards	Par	USGA	Slope
BACK	18	5953	70	68.0	116
MIDDLE	18	5605	70	66.6	110
FRONT	18	5069	70	69.6	109

Club Pro: Jim Goshdigian
Pro Shop: Full inventory
Payment: Visa, MC, Amex
Tee Times: 7 days adv.
Fee 9 Holes: Weekday: $14.50 **Weekend:** $16.00
Fee 18 Holes: Weekday: $22.50 **Weekend:** $25.50
Twilight Rates: Yes, after 5 pm **All Day Play:**
Cart Rental: $23.50/18 $15.00/9 **Discounts:** Senior & Junior
Lessons: $50.00/hour **Schools:** Yes **Junior Golf:** Yes **Membership:** Yes
Clinics: Yes **Day Camps:** No **Driving Range:** Yes
Other: Banquet Facility / Snack Bar

COUPON

New banquet facilities, renovated bunkers, and cart paths. Course is noted for its playability, good contrast between open and tight holes. "Excellent for the price." **Player's Comments.**

	1	2	3	4	5	6	7	8	9
PAR	5	4	4	4	4	4	3	3	4
YARDS	486	315	367	322	370	286	127	155	332
HDCP	5	10	3	11	12	13	18	16	8
	10	11	12	13	14	15	16	17	18
PAR	4	3	5	4	4	3	4	4	4
YARDS	334	213	471	361	312	138	336	352	361
HDCP	15	2	1	9	14	17	7	4	6

Directions: I-91 to Exit 28. Take Routes15, 5 South to Exit 85 (Route 99), follow ramp to first light. Right on Joran to right on Maple.

Grassmere CC

17 ►

Enfield, CT (860) 749-7740
www.grassmerecountryclub.com

Club Pro: No
Pro Shop: Limited inventory
Payment: Cash, check, credit cards
Tee Times: 2 weeks adv.
Fee 9 Holes: Weekday: $15.00
Fee 18 Holes: Weekday: $23.00
Twilight Rates: No
Cart Rental: $6pp each 9
Lessons: No **Schools:** No
Clinics: Junior **Day Camps:** No
Other: Clubhouse / Snack bar / Banquet facility

Tees	Holes	Yards	Par	USGA	Slope
BACK					
MIDDLE	9	3065	35	69.1	111
FRONT	9	2673	70		

Weekend: $16.00
Weekend: $28.00
All Day Play: No
Discounts: Sr. & Jr. M-F until 3:30
Junior Golf: Yes **Membership:** No
Driving Range: No

A lavishly landscaped three tier tee, opens to a sloping fairway, bordered the entire length by a winding brook to the green. Open March 15 - December 31. Noted for friendly staff.

	1	2	3	4	5	6	7	8	9
PAR	4	4	4	4	3	5	4	4	3
YARDS	360	390	405	415	160	475	320	360	180
HDCP	7	4	2	1	6	9	5	8	3
	10	11	12	13	14	15	16	17	18
PAR									
YARDS									
HDCP									

Directions: From Route I-91N: Exit 45, right onto Route 140. Merge with Route 191. Stay on 191N. Left on Town Farms Road. Course on left. From Route I-91 S: Exit 45, left onto Route 140. Merge with Route 191. Stay on 191N. Left on Town Farms Road. Course on left.

Harrisville GC

18 ►

Woodstock, CT (860) 928-6098
www.harrisvillegolfcourse.com

Club Pro: Ben Riley
Pro Shop: Full inventory
Payment: Cash, Check, Credit
Tee Times: Wknd mornings
Fee 9 Holes: Weekday: $12.00
Fee 18 Holes: Weekday: $18.00
Twilight Rates: No
Cart Rental: $22.00/18 $12.00/9
Lessons: Yes **Schools:** No
Clinics: Yes **Day Camps:** NA
Other: Snackbar

Tees	Holes	Yards	Par	USGA	Slope
BACK	9	2895	36		
MIDDLE	9	2785	36		
FRONT	9	2450	35		

Weekend: $18.00
Weekend: $20.00
All Day Play: No
Discounts: Senior & Junior
Junior Golf: NA **Membership:** Yes
Driving Range: No

COUPON

Six new tees, much improved turf conditions. Enjoyable round, easy walk. Noted for small greens and rolling hills.

	1	2	3	4	5	6	7	8	9
PAR	4	3	5	4	4	5	4	4	3
YARDS	290	170	500	265	410	420	295	235	200
HDCP	15	5	2	8	1	3	6	9	4
	10	11	12	13	14	15	16	17	18
PAR									
YARDS									
HDCP									

NE CT

Directions: Route 395, Exit 97. Take right onto Route 171 West. Take left at Public Golf Course sign (Citizens Bank). Follow signs (next two rights).

4✪ =Excellent 3✪ =Very Good 2✪ =Good

Hotchkiss School GC ✪✪ ▶19

Lakeville, CT (860) 435-9033
www.marshallinthemorning.com

Club Pro: James Kennedy
Pro Shop: Limited inventory
Payment: Cash only
Tee Times: No
Fee 9 Holes: Weekday: $12.00
Fee 18 Holes: Weekday: $20.00
Twilight Rates: No
Cart Rental: $24.00/18 $12.00/9
Lessons: Yes **Schools:** Yes
Clinics: Yes **Day Camps:** No
Other: Snack Bar

Tees	Holes	Yards	Par	USGA	Slope
BACK					
MIDDLE	9	6072	70	68.8	117
FRONT					

Weekend: $15.00 after 11 am
Weekend: $25.00 after 11 am
All Day Play: No
Discounts: None
Junior Golf: No **Membership:** Yes
Driving Range: No

Seth Raynor design. Improvements include redesign of 4th hole by George Batho. While the course is long, it is still suitable for beginners. Hilly and heavily wooded.

	1	2	3	4	5	6	7	8	9
PAR	4	3	4	4	3	4	5	3	5
YARDS	420	192	401	370	128	347	500	165	520
HDCP	1	11	5	9	17	15	7	13	3
	10	11	12	13	14	15	16	17	18
PAR	4	4	4	4	3	4	4	3	5
YARDS	405	256	385	355	136	358	440	189	505
HDCP	2	16	8	10	18	14	4	12	6

Directions: Take Route 7 to 112 West to course or Route 44 to Route112 East

Keney Golf Club ▶20

Hartford, CT (860)525-3656
www.americangolf.com

Club Pro: Charles Grodovich
Pro Shop: Limited inventory
Payment: Visa, MC, Check
Tee Times: 7 days adv.
Fee 9 Holes: Weekday: $14.50
Fee 18 Holes: Weekday: $22.50
Twilight Rates: Yes, after 6 pm
Cart Rental: $15/18, $7.75/9
Lessons: Yes **Schools:** Yes
Clinics: Yes **Day Camps:** No
Other: Clubhouse / Lockers / Showers / Snack bar / Restaurant / Functions

Tees	Holes	Yards	Par	USGA	Slope
BACK	18	5969	70	68.2	118
MIDDLE	18	5678	70	67.0	115
FRONT	18	5005	70	67.2	107

Weekend: $16.00
Weekend: $25.50
All Day Play:
Discounts: Senior & Junior
Junior Golf: Yes **Membership:** Yes
Driving Range: No

True links-style. The clubhouse is reminiscent of the grand architectural style of the late 20's. Resident rate. Early bird rates. Open year round. **Players' Comments:** "Tight course. Good challenge" "A sleeper."

	1	2	3	4	5	6	7	8	9
PAR	4	5	3	4	4	3	4	4	4
YARDS	306	456	128	328	388	136	365	375	382
HDCP	13	7	17	11	1	15	9	3	5
	10	11	12	13	14	15	16	17	18
PAR	5	3	4	3	5	4	4	4	3
YARDS	518	178	287	161	438	363	366	349	154
HDCP	2	12	16	10	8	4	14	6	18

Directions: Course is 5 minutes north of downtown Hartford. Take Exit 34 from I-91 north. Left at ramp, right at light.

Manchester CC ✪✪ 21 ▶

Manchester, CT (860) 646-0226
www.mancc.com

Club Pro: Ralph DeNicolo, PGA
Pro Shop: Full inventory
Payment: MC, Visa
Tee Times: 2 days adv.
Fee 9 Holes: Weekday: $18.00
Fee 18 Holes: Weekday: $34.00
Twilight Rates: No
Cart Rental: $13.00/18 $6.50/9
Lessons: $35.00/half hour **Schools:** No
Clinics: Yes **Day Camps:** No
Other: Clubhouse / Lockers / Showers / Snack bar / Restaurant / Bar-lounge

Tees	Holes	Yards	Par	USGA	Slope
BACK	18	6285	72	70.8	125
MIDDLE	18	6167	72	69.7	123
FRONT	18	5610	73	72.0	120

Weekend: $19.00
Weekend: $37.00
All Day Play: No
Discounts: Senior & Junior
Junior Golf: Yes **Membership:** Yes
Driving Range: Yes

Old style golf course. Variety of elevation changes. Open April - December. Dress code.

	1	2	3	4	5	6	7	8	9
PAR	4	4	5	5	3	4	4	3	4
YARDS	308	333	507	500	144	406	331	143	348
HDCP	13	11	3	9	17	1	5	15	7

	10	11	12	13	14	15	16	17	18
PAR	4	4	3	4	5	5	4	4	3
YARDS	294	340	135	335	520	510	397	362	182
HDCP	12	14	18	6	10	4	2	8	16

Directions: Take I-84 to Route 384 East (Exit 3). Take left 1000 yards up onto South Main Street. Course is on the left.

Mile View Par 3 22 ▶

Preston, CT (860) 892-4992 winter: (860) 887-0252

Club Pro:
Pro Shop: Full inventory
Payment: Cash and checks only
Tee Times: No
Fee 9 Holes: Weekday: $9.00
Fee 18 Holes: Weekday: $14.00
Twilight Rates: No
Cart Rental: No
Lessons: $38.00 / 45min **Schools:** Jr.
Clinics: Yes **Day Camps:** No
Other: Snacks

Tees	Holes	Yards	Par	USGA	Slope
BACK					
MIDDLE	9	722	27		
FRONT					

Weekend: $9.00
Weekend: $14.00
All Day Play: No
Discounts: None
Junior Golf: Yes **Membership:** Yes
Driving Range: No

A challenging 9 hole par 3 golf course with holes ranging from 70 to 125 yards. Mile View has tricky sand traps and water hazards along with beautiful contouring greens.

	1	2	3	4	5	6	7	8	9
PAR	3	3	3	3	3	3	3	3	3
YARDS	75	78	73	76	120	70	83	89	74
HDCP									

	10	11	12	13	14	15	16	17	18
PAR									
YARDS									
HDCP									

NE CT

Directions: Exit 85 off Route 395 North. Take right on Route 164. Course is on the right.

4✪ =Excellent 3✪ =Very Good 2✪ =Good

Minnechaug GC

Glastonbury, CT (860) 643-9914
www.minnechauggolfclub.com

Tees	Holes	Yards	Par	USGA	Slope
BACK	9	2654	35	67.4	112
MIDDLE	9	2527	35	66.5	110
FRONT	9	2186	35	62.7	102

Club Pro: No
Pro Shop: Yes
Payment: Cash only
Tee Times: 1 week adv.
Fee 9 Holes: Weekday: $13.00
Fee 18 Holes: Weekday: $22.00
Twilight Rates: No
Cart Rental: $12.00/9
Lessons: No **Schools:** No
Clinics: N/R **Day Camps:** No
Other: Menu/ Beer/ Snacks

Weekend: $14.00
Weekend: $24.00
All Day Play: No
Discounts: Senior & Junior, Resident
Junior Golf: No **Membership:** No
Driving Range: No

Sig. Hole: #8, 116 yd. par 3 with island green. Open April - November. Reduced rates for residents.

	1	2	3	4	5	6	7	8	9
PAR	4	4	5	4	5	3	4	3	3
YARDS	311	307	464	327	437	161	269	116	135
HDCP	5	1	3	2	6	4	9	8	7
	10	11	12	13	14	15	16	17	18
PAR									
YARDS									
HDCP									

Directions: 84 East to Route 384 East, Exit 3. Left off exit on Route 83. Follow for 3 miles. Course on right.

Norwich Golf Course

Norwich, CT (860) 889-6973
www.norwichgolf.com

Tees	Holes	Yards	Par	USGA	Slope
BACK	18	6183	71	69.5	129
MIDDLE	18	5877	72	68.1	126
FRONT	18	5104	71	70.2	118

Club Pro: John Paesani, PGA
Pro Shop: Full inventory
Payment: Visa, MC
Tee Times: 3 days adv.
Fee 9 Holes: Weekday: No
Fee 18 Holes: Weekday: $33.00
Twilight Rates: Yes, after 5 pm
Cart Rental: $14pp/wknd $12pp/wkdy
Lessons: $35.00/half hour **Schools:**
Clinics: Yes **Day Camps:** Yes
Other: Clubhouse / Lockers / Showers / Restaurant / Bar-lounge

Weekend: No
Weekend: $37.00
All Day Play: No
Discounts: None
Junior Golf: Yes **Membership:** Yes
Driving Range: No

Short but tricky course: overly aggressive play could lead to disaster. Designed by Donald Ross. Open April - November. $5.00 off for residents.

	1	2	3	4	5	6	7	8	9
PAR	4	4	4	4	5	4	4	4	3
YARDS	303	276	366	410	487	330	370	300	170
HDCP	15	11	5	1	7	13	3	9	17
	10	11	12	13	14	15	16	17	18
PAR	4	4	5	3	5	4	4	4	3
YARDS	355	388	503	105	545	170	330	303	166
HDCP	6	2	8	18	4	14	10	12	16

Directions: Take I-95 to I-395 North to Exit 80E. Take right off ramp (West Main Street), follow to fifth light. Take right onto New London Turnpike. Course is 1/2 mile down on right.

Pequot Golf Club

25

Wheeler Rd., Stonington, CT (860) 535-1898
www.pequotgolf.com

Club Pro: Jon Terenzi
Pro Shop: Full inventory
Payment: Visa, MC, Cash
Tee Times: 7 days adv.
Fee 9 Holes: Weekday: $18.00
Fee 18 Holes: Weekday: $26.00
Twilight Rates: No
Cart Rental: $26/18, $19/18 sgle, $16/9, Pull $3
Lessons: $30.00/45 min. **Schools:** No
Clinics: Junior **Day Camps:** No
Other: Restaurant / Bar-lounge

Tees	Holes	Yards	Par	USGA	Slope
BACK					
MIDDLE	18	5903	70	68.7	118
FRONT	18	5246	71	69.4	112

Weekend: $19.00 after noon
Weekend: $31, $27 after 11pm
All Day Play: No
Discounts: Senior & Junior
Junior Golf: Yes **Membership:** Yes
Driving Range: No

COUPON

Player's Comment: "Beautiful course." Voted best public course greens in southeast Connecticut. Open March 1 - Dec. 15. Weekends after 3pm: $9.00 for 18 holes.

	1	2	3	4	5	6	7	8	9
PAR	4	4	4	4	4	3	4	4	3
YARDS	353	329	358	287	328	179	379	376	209
HDCP	9	13	5	15	7	17	1	3	11

	10	11	12	13	14	15	16	17	18
PAR	4	4	3	5	4	4	4	3	5
YARDS	276	361	149	469	417	336	339	193	565
HDCP	16	8	18	10	2	12	4	14	16

Directions: I-95 to Exit 91. Left off 95(S), right off 95(N). Go 1 mi. Take right onto Wheeler Rd.

Pistol Creek Golf Club

✪✪✪ **26**

Berlin, CT (860) 828-7696
www.pistolcreekgolfclub.com

Club Pro: Alex Kirk, PGA
Pro Shop: Yes
Payment: Most major
Tee Times: 7 days adv. (860) 828-7696
Fee 9 Holes: Weekday: $31.00 cart onc.
Fee 18 Holes: Weekday: $54.00 cart inc.
Twilight Rates: Yes, after 5 pm
Cart Rental: Included
Lessons: Yes **Schools:** Yes
Clinics: Yes **Day Camps:** Yes
Other: Restaurant / Log Cabin Clubhouse / Lockers / Showers / Bar / Lounge / Snack bar

Tees	Holes	Yards	Par	USGA	Slope
BACK	18	6586	72	72.2	136
MIDDLE	18	6060	72	69.6	132
FRONT	18	4522	72	67.2	112

Weekend: $36.00 cart inc.
Weekend: $64.00 cart inc.
All Day Play: No
Discounts: Senior & Junior
Junior Golf: Yes **Membership:** Yes
Driving Range: Yes

Players' Comments: "Demanding fun layout." "Greens will be a challenge for even the best with a flat stick." Winding layout. Course conditions maturing, new and improved tee boxes.

	1	2	3	4	5	6	7	8	9
PAR	4	5	4	4	3	5	4	4	3
YARDS	320	478	392	337	161	476	361	346	131
HDCP	13	5	1	11	15	7	3	9	17

	10	11	12	13	14	15	16	17	18
PAR	5	4	3	4	4	5	4	3	4
YARDS	526	284	137	336	333	491	413	176	362
HDCP	4	16	18	12	14	8	2	10	6

NE CT

Directions: I-91 to Exit 21; Right on Route 372 West. 1.5 miles to Savage Hill Rd. Left on Savage Hill Rd. to second stop sign. Right on Spruce Brook Rd. Club immediately on left.

4✪ =Excellent 3✪ =Very Good 2✪ =Good

Putnam Country Club ✪✪ 27 ▶

Putnam, CT (860) 928-7748

Tees	Holes	Yards	Par	USGA	Slope
BACK	18	6131	71	68.6	114
MIDDLE	18	5819	71	67.7	109
FRONT	18	4910	71	68.8	114

Club Pro: Eric Sarette
Pro Shop: Full inventory
Payment: Visa, MC, Disc
Tee Times: 7 days adv.

COUPON

Fee 9 Holes: Weekday: $14.00   **Weekend:** $18.00
Fee 18 Holes: Weekday: $26.00   **Weekend:** $35.00
Twilight Rates: Yes, after 1 pm   **All Day Play:** Yes
Cart Rental: $13pp/18 $8pp/9   **Discounts:** Senior & Junior Wkdays
Lessons: $25/30 **Schools:** Yes   **Junior Golf:** No **Membership:** Yes
Clinics: Yes **Day Camps:** No   **Driving Range:** $8/lg. $6/md. $4/sm.
Other: Clubhouse/ Snack Bar/ Beer & Wine

Sig. Hole: #8 Change to 8th hole, extended to 320 yards. Open April1 - November 30. **Player's Comments:** "Awesome, small, fairly priced golf course. Pro shop staff willing to help with any request."

	1	2	3	4	5	6	7	8	9
PAR	5	4	4	3	4	5	3	4	3
YARDS	436	333	380	192	304	552	160	320	111
HDCP	12	9	1	7	13	2	15	14	17
	10	11	12	13	14	15	16	17	18
PAR	4	3	5	4	4	3	4	4	5
YARDS	373	151	479	315	385	134	395	360	502
HDCP	6	18	10	12	2	16	4	8	14

Directions: Route 395Exit 97 East on Route 44. 3 1/2 mile to public course, sign on right. Right onto East Putnam Rd. At 2nd stop sign take a right (Chase Rd.) Course is 1 mile on right.

NEW 2003

Quarryview Golf Course 28 ▶

East Canaan. CT (860) 824-4252

Tees	Holes	Yards	Par	USGA	Slope
BACK	9	1626	31		
MIDDLE	9	1576	31	59.0	93
FRONT	9	1532	31	58.0	89

Club Pro: Dennis Perrone
Pro Shop: Yes
Payment: Visa, MC
Tee Times: No

Fee 9 Holes: Weekday: $10.00   **Weekend:** $12.00
Fee 18 Holes: Weekday: $16.00   **Weekend:** $20.00
Twilight Rates: No   **All Day Play:** Yes
Cart Rental: $10pp/18, $6pp/9   **Discounts:** Senior & Junior
Lessons: $40.00/hour **Schools:**   **Junior Golf: Membership:** Yes
Clinics: Junior **Day Camps:**   **Driving Range:** Yes, Grass
Other: Snackbar

2003 Entry. 9 hole executive course. A work in progress. Also has a driving range.

	1	2	3	4	5	6	7	8	9
PAR	3	3	3	3	3	3	5	4	4
YARDS	95	188	150	125	120	128	350	200	220
HDCP	7	17	9	5	13	11	1	15	3
	10	11	12	13	14	15	16	17	18
PAR									
YARDS									
HDCP									

Directions: Located on Allyndale Road off Route 44 in East Canaan.

Raceway Golf Club

Thompson, CT (860) 923-9591
www.racewaygolf.com

Club Pro: David Hall, PGA
Pro Shop: Full inventory
Payment: Visa, MC, Disc.
Tee Times: M-F 7 days S/S 4 days
Fee 9 Holes: Weekday: No
Fee 18 Holes: Weekday: $30.00 cart incl.
Twilight Rates: Yes, after 5:30 pm
Cart Rental: Included
Lessons: Call for info **Schools:**
Clinics: Junior **Day Camps:** Yes
Other: Clubhouse / Lockers / Showers / Snack bar / Restaurant / Bar-lounge

Tees	Holes	Yards	Par	USGA	Slope
BACK	18	6412	71	70.0	111
MIDDLE	18	5916	71	67.7	106
FRONT	18	5437	71	71.3	117

Weekend: No
Weekend: $38.00 cart incl.
All Day Play: No
Discounts: None
Junior Golf: Yes **Membership:**
Driving Range: 40 mats, grass $6.00

Sig. Hole: #4 is downhill with an elevated tee and water covering to front edge of green. A large oak tree to right and bunkers down left and right sides of very undulating green. A championship course.

	1	2	3	4	5	6	7	8	9
PAR	4	4	4	3	5	4	4	4	3
YARDS	277	387	304	152	536	392	350	402	174
HDCP	17	4	14	15	1	6	9	3	12
	10	**11**	**12**	**13**	**14**	**15**	**16**	**17**	**18**
PAR	5	4	4	5	3	4	4	3	4
YARDS	492	382	342	425	146	353	347	166	289
HDCP	2	7	11	5	16	8	10	13	18

Directions: Take I-395 to Exit 99; go into Thompson Center, left at blinking light onto Route 193. Follow signs to Thompson Speedway which will lead to the course.

River Ridge Golf Course

Jewitt City, Ct 860-376-3268
www.riverridgegolf.com

Club Pro: Brian Morrow
Pro Shop: Full inventory
Payment: Visa, MC, Amex
Tee Times: 24 hours a day
Fee 9 Holes: Weekday: $18.00
Fee 18 Holes: Weekday: $33, $47 w/cart
Twilight Rates: Yes, after 2 pm
Cart Rental: Above
Lessons: Yes **Schools:** No
Clinics: No **Day Camps:** No
Other: Full Restaurant / Bar-Lounge

Tees	Holes	Yards	Par	USGA	Slope
BACK	18	6812	72	71.8	124
MIDDLE	18	6415	72	69.8	122
FRONT	18	5393	72	70.4	119

Weekend: $18.00 after 2 pm
Weekend: $36.00, $50.00 w/ cart
All Day Play: No
Discounts: None
Junior Golf: No **Membership:** Yes
Driving Range: No

Challenging course cut through trees with significant elevation change. "Blind shots off the tee. Fairways very firm, lots of extra distance." R.W.

	1	2	3	4	5	6	7	8	9
PAR	4	4	5	3	5	3	4	4	5
YARDS	390	391	510	180	530	156	350	315	540
HDCP	9	7	5	13	3	17	11	15	1
	10	**11**	**12**	**13**	**14**	**15**	**16**	**17**	**18**
PAR	4	3	4	4	4	5	4	3	4
YARDS	401	122	420	326	350	530	340	185	379
HDCP	8	18	4	14	12	2	10	16	6

Directions: Route 395, Exit 85 to Route 164 South. 7/10 mile on right.

**NE
CT**

4○ =Excellent 3○ =Very Good 2○ =Good

Rockledge CC

31

W. Hartford, CT (860) 521-3156
www.rockledgegc.com

Club Pro: Richard F. Crowe, PGA
Pro Shop: Full inventory
Payment: Visa, MC
Tee Times: 3 days adv. (860) 521-6284
Fee 9 Holes: Weekday: $16.50
Fee 18 Holes: Weekday: $32.00
Twilight Rates: No
Cart Rental: $12pp/18 $7pp/9
Lessons: $35/30 min.   **Schools:** No
Clinics: Yes **Day Camps:** Yes
Other: Clubhouse / Lockers / Showers / Snack bar / Restaurant / Bar-lounge

Tees	Holes	Yards	Par	USGA	Slope
BACK	18	6436	72	71.1	129
MIDDLE	18	6069	72	69.3	125
FRONT	18	5434	72	72.7	129

Weekend: $18.50
Weekend: $36.00
All Day Play: Yes
Discounts: Senior residents M-F
Junior Golf: Yes **Membership:** Yes
Driving Range: $7.50/lg $5/md $3/sm

Player's Comment: "Challenging layout. Always in great condition." Open Apr. - Dec. Resident fees and tee times. Lottery for weekends.

	1	2	3	4	5	6	7	8	9
PAR	4	4	4	4	3	5	4	3	5
YARDS	334	286	394	395	177	450	299	181	448
HDCP	13	17	1	3	9	15	11	7	5
	10	11	12	13	14	15	16	17	18
PAR	4	4	5	3	5	4	3	4	4
YARDS	404	302	465	136	515	357	152	381	393
HDCP	2	16	10	18	8	6	14	12	4

Directions: From I-84 West or East, take Exit 41. From West take a right off the exit, from East take a left off the exit. Course is 1/4 mile on left.

Rolling Greens GC

32

Rocky Hill, CT (860) 257-9775

Club Pro: Joe DeCandia
Pro Shop: Full inventory
Payment: Visa, MC
Tee Times: No
Fee 9 Holes: Weekday: $18.00
Fee 18 Holes: Weekday: $27.00
Twilight Rates: After 5:30 pm
Cart Rental: $12pp/18 $6pp/9
Lessons: $30.00 **Schools:** No
Clinics: No **Day Camps:** No
Other: Clubhouse / Lockers / Showers / Restaurant / Bar-lounge

Tees	Holes	Yards	Par	USGA	Slope
BACK	9	6000	70	70.5	130
MIDDLE	9	5657	70	70.1	130
FRONT	9	5227	72	71.7	130

COUPON

Weekend: $20.00
Weekend: $32.00
All Day Play:
Discounts: Senior & Junior
Junior Golf: No **Membership:** Yes
Driving Range: No

Rolling hills. Dress code (no tank tops or cut-off jeans. Shot maker's course. Great Shape. Open March - November.

	1	2	3	4	5	6	7	8	9
PAR	4	5	3	4	4	4	4	3	4
YARDS	360	553	191	315	379	440	373	180	340
HDCP	9	1	15	13	5	3	7	17	11
	10	11	12	13	14	15	16	17	18
PAR	4	5	3	4	4	4	4	3	4
YARDS	374	533	160	322	363	458	354	165	352
HDCP	6	2	18	14	8	4	10	16	12

Directions: Exit 23 off I-91. Signs to Rolling Greens. Approx. 1 mile from exit.

Rolling Meadows Country Club ✪✪

Ellington, CT (860) 870-5328

Club Pro: Jeff Swanson, PGA
Pro Shop: Full inventory
Payment: Cash/check
Tee Times: 3 days adv., (860) 749-3550
Fee 9 Holes: Weekday: $16.50
Fee 18 Holes: Weekday: $29.00
Twilight Rates: No
Cart Rental: $6pp/p9
Lessons: $35/30 min. **Schools:** Yes
Clinics: No **Day Camps:** Yes
Other: Restaurant / Bar / Beverage Cart

Tees	Holes	Yards	Par	USGA	Slope
BACK	18	6818	72	72.5	128
MIDDLE	18	6269	72	70	123
FRONT	18	5331	72	70.4	122

Weekend: $18.50
Weekend: $32.00
All Day Play: No
Discounts: Sr. & Jr. (M-Th)
Junior Golf: Yes **Membership:** Yes
Driving Range: Yes

Player's Comments: " Getting better every year." Special 7am-1pm, M-F: 2 players/ 18 holes including cart. Inquire.

	1	2	3	4	5	6	7	8	9
PAR	5	4	3	5	4	4	4	3	4
YARDS	488	316	166	491	390	366	335	186	346
HDCP	5	15	11	1	7	17	3	9	13

	10	11	12	13	14	15	16	17	18
PAR	4	5	4	3	5	4	4	3	4
YARDS	383	473	366	163	490	433	345	190	342
HDCP	2	10	6	12	18	14	16	4	8

Directions: Route 91 to Route 140 or Route 84 to 83 to Route 140 (across from Brookside Park, Ellington).

Shennecosset GC

Plant St., Groton, CT (860) 445-0262

Club Pro: Todd Goodhue, PGA
Pro Shop: Full inventory
Payment: Visa, MC
Tee Times: 3 days adv.
Fee 9 Holes: Weekday: N/A
Fee 18 Holes: Weekday: $32.00
Twilight Rates: After 12
Cart Rental: $13pp/18
Lessons: $35.00/half hour **Schools:** No
Clinics: Yes **Day Camps:** Yes
Other: Clubhouse / Snack bar / Restaurant / Bar-lounge

Tees	Holes	Yards	Par	USGA	Slope
BACK	18	6562	71	71.5	122
MIDDLE	18	6088	71	69.1	121
FRONT	18	5671	74	72.4	122

Weekend: N/A
Weekend: $37.00
All Day Play: No
Discounts: Junior
Junior Golf: Yes **Membership:** Yes
Driving Range: No

Players' Comments: "Great old course. New holes are terrific along the river. " "New holes. New irrigation. Classic seaside course. Send someone to play it." Donald Ross design. Old links-style. Open year round.

	1	2	3	4	5	6	7	8	9
PAR	4	4	4	3	5	4	4	5	3
YARDS	350	368	361	195	488	145	433	367	418
HDCP	13	5	3	15	9	17	11	7	1

	10	11	12	13	14	15	16	17	18
PAR	4	4	3	4	4	3	4	4	5
YARDS	400	160	460	542	323	116	343	362	311
HDCP	2	16	10	4	8	18	12	6	14

**NE
CT**

Directions: Take I-95 to Exit 87 (Clarence Sharp Highway); take right at second light. Take left at next light, proceed past Pfizer; course is on left side.

4✪ =Excellent 3✪ =Very Good 2✪ =Good

Simsbury Farms GC

Old Farms Rd., Simsbury, CT (860) 658-6246

Club Pro: John Verrengia, PGA
Pro Shop: Full inventory
Payment: Cash, Check, MC, Visa
Tee Times: 2 days adv.

Tees	Holes	Yards	Par	USGA	Slope
BACK	18	6421	72	69.8	120
MIDDLE	18	6104	72	68.3	118
FRONT	18	5439	72	70.1	117

Fee 9 Holes: Weekday: $17.00   **Weekend:** $21.00
Fee 18 Holes: Weekday: $31.00   **Weekend:** $34.00
Twilight Rates: No   **All Day Play:** No
Cart Rental: $24.00/18 $14.00/9   **Discounts:** Senior Weekdays
Lessons: $35/ 45min. **Schools:** No   **Junior Golf:** Yes **Membership:** Residents
Clinics: Adult/Jr **Day Camps:** No   **Driving Range:** 8/ lg., $6/med, $3/sm.
Other: Restaurants / Clubhouse / Showers

Good challenge with a decent mix of holes. A nice hilly course. Open April - November.

	1	2	3	4	5	6	7	8	9
PAR	4	4	4	3	5	4	5	4	3
YARDS	341	375	361	135	487	361	528	286	178
HDCP	13	9	11	17	5	3	1	15	7

	10	11	12	13	14	15	16	17	18
PAR	4	4	5	3	5	4	3	4	4
YARDS	346	341	524	169	465	321	212	295	379
HDCP	14	12	2	16	4	10	6	18	8

Directions: Take I-84 to 44 West toward Avon. Turn right onto Route 10; 3 mi. down turn left on Stratton Brook Rd. Road becomes Old Farms at church. Course 1 mile on right.

Skungamaug River GC

Folly Ln., Coventry, CT (860) 742-9348
www.skungamauggolf.com

Club Pro: Rick Nelson
Pro Shop: Full inventory
Payment: Visa, MC
Tee Times: M-F 7 days S/S 6 days

Tees	Holes	Yards	Par	USGA	Slope
BACK	18	5785	70	69.4	123
MIDDLE	18	5624	70	68.6	120
FRONT	18	4838	71	69.3	123

Fee 9 Holes: Weekday: $16.00   **Weekend:** $18.00
Fee 18 Holes: Weekday: $31.00   **Weekend:** $34.00
Twilight Rates: Yes, after 6:30pm   **All Day Play:** No
Cart Rental: $21.00/18 $11.00/9   **Discounts:** Senior $11.50
Lessons: $30.00/half hour **Schools:** No   **Junior Golf:** Yes **Membership:** Yes
Clinics: Yes **Day Camps:** No   **Driving Range:** $5.00 large / $3.00 small
Other: Clubhouse / Snack bar / Bar-lounge

Sig. Hole: #15 is a split level hole with a small fairway on top level. River runs along right side, large tree divides upper and lower levels. No cutoffs or tank tops. Open April - December.

	1	2	3	4	5	6	7	8	9
PAR	4	3	4	5	3	4	5	3	4
YARDS	339	154	291	438	139	332	461	158	351
HDCP	8	18	10	6	16	2	4	12	14

	10	11	12	13	14	15	16	17	18
PAR	4	3	4	4	4	4	4	3	5
YARDS	376	171	363	371	395	290	323	189	483
HDCP	9	17	11	3	15	1	5	13	7

Directions: From I-84, Exit 68. South on Route 195, 1/4 mile to light. Turn right onto Goose Lane, follow yellow, triangular arrows on telephone poles. 3 miles to club.

Stanley Golf Club ✪✪

New Britain, CT (860)827-8570
www.stanleygolf.com

Club Pro: Greg Yeomans
Pro Shop: Full inventory
Payment: Cash only
Tee Times: Wknds, 3 days adv. (827-1362)

Tees	Holes	Yards	Par	USGA	Slope
BACK	27	6543	72	71.1	115
MIDDLE	27	6192	72	69.4	115
FRONT	27	5562	73	72.2	122

Fee 9 Holes: Weekday: $15.50
Fee 18 Holes: Weekday: $25.00
Twilight Rates: No
Cart Rental: $25.00/18 $14.00/9
Lessons: $27.00/45 minutes **Schools:** No
Clinics: Yes **Day Camps:** Yes
Weekend: $17.50
Weekend: $28.50
All Day Play: No
Discounts: Sr. 62+, Jr. 18 & under
Junior Golf: Yes **Membership:** Seasonal Pass
Driving Range: $8.50/lg., $6/med., $3.50/sm.
Other: Clubhouse / Lockers / Showers / Restaurant / Bar-lounge / Snack / Outings

27 holes. Blue-red score card below. Improvements include 4 redesigned holes. New frequent vistor card. New driving range. Resident rates.

	1	2	3	4	5	6	7	8	9
PAR	5	4	4	4	3	4	4	3	5
YARDS	492	347	370	387	165	296	415	136	508
HDCP	11	3	7	9	13	17	1	15	5
	10	11	12	13	14	15	16	17	18
PAR	4	3	5	4	4	4	3	4	5
YARDS	323	195	461	321	325	376	160	345	445
HDCP	8	10	14	2	12	6	18	4	16

Directions: Take I-84 to Exit 39A, then right onto route 9S to Exit 30. Take right at end of ramp. Course is 1/2 mile on left.

Tallwood Country Club ✪✪

Rt. 85, Hebron, CT (860) 646-1151
www.ctgolfer.com/tallwoodcc

Club Pro: John Nowobilski, PGA
Pro Shop: Full inventory
Payment: Visa, MC
Tee Times: M-F 7 days S/S 5 days

Tees	Holes	Yards	Par	USGA	Slope
BACK	18	6353	72	70.4	123
MIDDLE	18	6126	72	69.3	121
FRONT	18	5424	72	70.6	121

Fee 9 Holes: Weekday: $16.00
Fee 18 Holes: Weekday: $32.00
Twilight Rates: Yes, after 4 pm
Cart Rental: $24.00/18 $12.00/9
Lessons: $75.00/hour **Schools:** Jr.
Clinics: Yes **Day Camps:** Junior Camp
Other: Restaurant / Clubhouse / Snack bar
Weekend: $17.00
Weekend: $34.00
All Day Play: No
Discounts: Sr & Jr Weekdays
Junior Golf: No **Membership:** Yes
Driving Range: $7.00/lg., $4.00/sm.

Annual host of CTPGA, CSGA & USGA events. Open March - December.

	1	2	3	4	5	6	7	8	9
PAR	5	4	3	5	4	3	4	4	3
YARDS	528	287	176	483	400	158	341	359	167
HDCP	4	16	14	12	2	18	8	6	10
	10	11	12	13	14	15	16	17	18
PAR	4	5	4	4	3	4	5	4	4
YARDS	296	500	361	346	157	364	460	377	366
HDCP	15	9	5	7	17	3	13	1	11

Directions: I-84 East to I-384. Exit 5 off I-384, right off exit puts you on Route 85 South. Course is on right.

NE CT

4✪ =Excellent 3✪ =Very Good 2✪ =Good

Timberlin Golf Club

Kensington, CT (860) 828-3228
www.timberlin.com

Tees	Holes	Yards	Par	USGA	Slope
BACK	18	6733	72	72.2	129
MIDDLE	18	6342	72	70.4	126
FRONT	18	5477	72	72.0	125

Club Pro: Lindsey Hansen
Pro Shop: Full inventory
Payment: Cash or check
Tee Times: 3 days adv. Wk, 5 Wknd
Fee 9 Holes: Weekday: $18.00
Fee 18 Holes: Weekday: $28.50
Twilight Rates: Yes, after 2 pm
Cart Rental: $26.00/18 $15.00/9
Lessons: $25.00/half hour **Schools:** No
Clinics: Yes **Day Camps:** No
Other: Clubhouse / Showers / Snack bar

Weekend: $18.50
Weekend: $30.00
All Day Play: No
Discounts: Junior before 2 pm
Junior Golf: Yes **Membership:** No
Driving Range: Yes

Players' comments: "Friendly staff." "Challenging course in great shape." "Good value."Fairway roughs are thick and plush. Conservative layout with well-placed traps. Open April - November.

	1	2	3	4	5	6	7	8	9
PAR	5	4	4	3	4	5	3	4	4
YARDS	550	340	360	170	360	526	150	342	377
HDCP	3	5	11	17	9	1	15	13	7
	10	11	12	13	14	15	16	17	18
PAR	5	4	3	5	4	4	3	4	4
YARDS	492	361	160	477	362	400	163	359	393
HDCP	10	14	16	2	4	6	18	12	8

Directions: Located off Route 71 which runs between I-691 and Route 372. Course is on Route 364, .6 mile from Route 71. Left onto Kensignton Ave.

Topstone Golf Course

South Windsor, CT (860) 648-4653
www.topstonegc.com

Tees	Holes	Yards	Par	USGA	Slope
BACK	18	6549	72	70.7	124
MIDDLE	18	6199	72	69.0	121
FRONT	18	4987	72	68.2	109

Club Pro: Michael Belanger
Pro Shop: Full inventory
Payment: Visa, MC, Amex
Tee Times: 14 /wkdys; 7/wknds
Fee 9 Holes: Weekday: $17.50
Fee 18 Holes: Weekday: $34.00
Twilight Rates: No
Cart Rental: $12.00 pp/18 $6.50 pp/9
Lessons: $35/30 min. **Schools:** No
Clinics: Yes **Day Camps:** Yes
Other: Bar / Restaurant / Clubhouse

Weekend: $19.50
Weekend: $37.00
All Day Play: No
Discounts: Senior & Junior
Junior Golf: Yes **Membership:** No
Driving Range: No

Players' Comments: "A good value for your golfing dollars." "Shows a great deal of maturity. Back 9 has more distinctive holes." "Well kept course. Great greens." Challenging for all abilities with 5 sets of tees.

	1	2	3	4	5	6	7	8	9
PAR	4	5	4	3	5	4	4	3	4
YARDS	365	472	304	175	480	385	397	138	254
HDCP	10	12	8	4	14	6	2	18	16
	10	11	12	13	14	15	16	17	18
PAR	5	4	3	4	4	3	5	4	4
YARDS	482	389	167	340	399	140	471	320	336
HDCP	17	3	11	13	1	15	7	9	5

Directions: Take I-291 from either Routes 84 or 91. Take Exit 4 (Route 5) . Go north on Route 5 for 4 miles, turn right onto Route 1 94 for .5 mile. Left on to Rye St. for 1.5 miles, Turn right on to Griffin St. for 1.25 miles.

Tradition Golf Course at Windsor, The ▶ 41

Windsor, CT (860) 688-2575
www.traditionalclubs.com

Club Pro: Steve Fontanella, GM
Pro Shop: Full inventory
Payment: Visa, MC, Amex, Disc
Tee Times: 7 days adv.

Tees	Holes	Yards	Par	USGA	Slope
BACK	18	6068	71	69.8	119
MIDDLE	18	5805	71	67.9	116
FRONT	18	4877	71	68.9	117

Fee 9 Holes: Weekday: $14.50
Fee 18 Holes: Weekday: $25.00 M-Th
Twilight Rates: Yes, after 2 pm
Cart Rental: $13pp/18 $6.50pp/9
Lessons: Yes **Schools:** Call
Clinics: Call **Day Camps:** Call
Weekend: $18/W, 24.50/R
Weekend: $32/W, $45/R F/S/S
All Day Play: No
Discounts: Senior & Junior
Junior Golf: Yes **Membership:** Yes
Driving Range: Nearby
Other: Clubhouse / Snack bar / Restaurant / Patio dining / Beverage Cart / Bag Drop

Player's Comment: "Elevation changes in the front 9. Lots of decisions to make on the back 9." Expanded golf shop and restaurant overlook course. Proper attire required. Rates may change.

	1	2	3	4	5	6	7	8	9
PAR	5	4	4	4	5	3	3	4	4
YARDS	451	335	358	346	486	147	197	395	285
HDCP	5	9	15	3	7	17	11	1	13

	10	11	12	13	14	15	16	17	18
PAR	4	4	4	3	5	4	3	3	5
YARDS	399	289	325	168	451	350	140	202	481
HDCP	2	14	6	16	12	4	18	10	8

Directions: Exit 38 off I-91. Left onto Route 75, 1 mile to Pigeon Hill Road. Turn right, course 1/4 mile on left.

Tunxis Plantation CC (Green) ✪✪ ▶ 42

Farmington, CT (860) 677-1367

Club Pro: Lou Pandolfi
Pro Shop: Full inventory
Payment: Visa, MC, Amex
Tee Times: Yes, call in advance

Tees	Holes	Yards	Par	USGA	Slope
BACK	18	6354	70	70.0	120
MIDDLE	18	5958	70	68.1	117
FRONT	18	4883	70	71.0	115

Fee 9 Holes: Weekday: $17.00
Fee 18 Holes: Weekday: $30.00
Twilight Rates: No
Cart Rental: $28.00/18 $16.00/9
Lessons: $30-$32/30 min. **Schools:** No
Clinics: No **Day Camps:** No
Weekend: $19.00
Weekend: $37.00
All Day Play: No
Discounts: Sr $2 & Jr $3 Wkdays
Junior Golf: Yes **Membership:** No
Driving Range: $3.25/bucket
Other: Restaurant / Clubhouse / Bar-lounge / Lockers / Snack Bar / Showers

One of the best-kept secrets in Connecticut. Wide open fairways make for a forgiving layout. Great course for intermediate players. Open April 1 - November 20.

	1	2	3	4	5	6	7	8	9
PAR	4	5	4	4	3	4	4	3	4
YARDS	363	501	354	357	188	434	333	166	335
HDCP	5	9	1	7	11	3	15	17	13

	10	11	12	13	14	15	16	17	18
PAR	4	4	3	4	4	4	4	5	3
YARDS	348	345	165	373	342	291	397	481	185
HDCP	10	2	16	12	6	14	8	4	18

Directions: I-84 to Exit 39 (Route 4); first right over Farmington River.

NE CT

4✪ =Excellent 3✪ =Very Good 2✪ =Good

Tunxis Plantation CC (White) ✪✪ 43

Farmington, CT (860)677-1367

Club Pro: Lou Pandolfi
Pro Shop: Full inventory
Payment: Visa, MC, Amex
Tee Times: Yes, Call in advance

Tees	Holes	Yards	Par	USGA	Slope
BACK	18	6638	72	71.0	121
MIDDLE	18	6241	72	69.2	117
FRONT	18	5744	72	71.5	116

Fee 9 Holes: Weekday: $17.00   **Weekend:** $19.00
Fee 18 Holes: Weekday: $30.00   **Weekend:** $37.00
Twilight Rates: No   **All Day Play:** No
Cart Rental: $28.00/18 $16.00/9   **Discounts:** Sr $2 & Jr $3 Wkdays
Lessons: $30-$32/30 min. **Schools:** No   **Junior Golf:** Yes **Membership:** No
Clinics: No **Day Camps:** No   **Driving Range:** $3.25/bucket
Other: Restaurant / Clubhouse / Bar-lounge / Lockers / Snack Bar / Showers

Great course for intermediate players. Play from the blue tees for a real challenge. Open April 1 - November 20. "Close to Florida golf. Holes 5 & 13 really tough." AR (player)

	1	2	3	4	5	6	7	8	9
PAR	5	4	4	3	5	4	4	3	4
YARDS	526	407	343	153	476	366	358	147	332
HDCP	1	3	11	17	5	7	9	15	13
	10	**11**	**12**	**13**	**14**	**15**	**16**	**17**	**18**
PAR	4	5	4	5	3	4	3	4	4
YARDS	334	508	358	515	176	413	154	357	318
HDCP	16	2	6	4	14	8	18	10	12

Directions: I-84 to Exit 39 (Route 4); first right over Farmington River.

Tunxis Plantation GC (Red) 44

Farmington, CT (860) 677-1367

Club Pro: Lou Pandolfi
Pro Shop: Full inventory
Payment: Visa, MC, Amex
Tee Times: Yes, Call in advance

Tees	Holes	Yards	Par	USGA	Slope
BACK	9	3219	35	35.4	123
MIDDLE	9	2999	35	34.4	119
FRONT	9	2725	35	35.8	117

Fee 9 Holes: Weekday: $17.00   **Weekend:** $19.00
Fee 18 Holes: Weekday: $30.00   **Weekend:** $37.00
Twilight Rates: No   **All Day Play:** No
Cart Rental: $28.00/18 $16.00/9   **Discounts:** Sr $2 & Jr $3 Wkdays
Lessons: $30-$32/30 min. **Schools:** No   **Junior Golf:** Yes **Membership:** No
Clinics: No **Day Camps:** No   **Driving Range:** No
Other: Restaurant / Clubhouse / Bar-lounge / Lockers / Snack Bar / Showers

9 hole course in excellent condition located in Farmington Valley, next to Farmington River. Open April 1 - November 20.

	1	2	3	4	5	6	7	8	9
PAR	4	4	3	4	5	4	4	3	4
YARDS	348	395	141	322	483	396	366	177	371
HDCP	13	3	17	11	1	9	5	15	7
	10	**11**	**12**	**13**	**14**	**15**	**16**	**17**	**18**
PAR									
YARDS									
HDCP									

Directions: I-84 to Exit 39 (Route 4); first right over Farmington River.

Twin Hills CC

Coventry, CT (860) 742-9705

Club Pro: Eric DeStefano, PGA, J. Nowobilski (
Pro Shop: Limited inventory
Payment: Cash only
Tee Times: 7 days F/S/S/H

Tees	Holes	Yards	Par	USGA	Slope
BACK	18	6275	71	69.8	123
MIDDLE	18	5954	71	68.9	117
FRONT	18	5249	71	69.5	116

Fee 9 Holes: Weekday: $16.00   **Weekend:** $17.00
Fee 18 Holes: Weekday: $32.00   **Weekend:** $34.00
Twilight Rates: No   **All Day Play:** No
Cart Rental: $24.00/18 $12.00/9   **Discounts:** Senior & Junior
Lessons: No **Schools:** No   **Junior Golf:** Yes **Membership:** No
Clinics: Junior **Day Camps:** No   **Driving Range:** No
Other: Clubhouse / Snack bar / Bar-lounge / Beer & Soda

Sig. Hole; "#7 at 446 yards, is a major league par 4." R.W. Open March - December.

	1	2	3	4	5	6	7	8	9
PAR	4	4	5	3	5	4	4	3	4
YARDS	380	284	530	144	502	348	446	152	357
HDCP	9	17	2	16	6	7	1	14	11

	10	11	12	13	14	15	16	17	18
PAR	4	4	4	3	4	5	3	4	4
YARDS	320	336	311	204	374	494	144	361	267
HDCP	13	15	10	4	5	3	12	8	18

Directions: Take I-84 to Route 31 South; follow 4 miles. Course is on the right.

Villa Hills Golf Course

Storrs, CT (860) 429-6421

Club Pro: No
Pro Shop: No
Payment: Visa, MC, Cash
Tee Times:

Tees	Holes	Yards	Par	USGA	Slope
BACK					
MIDDLE	9	1158	27		
FRONT					

Fee 9 Holes: Weekday: $8.00   **Weekend:** $8.00
Fee 18 Holes: Weekday: $15.00   **Weekend:** $15.00
Twilight Rates: No   **All Day Play:** No
Cart Rental: Pull carts, $3.00   **Discounts:** Senior & Women
Lessons: **Schools:** No   **Junior Golf:** No **Membership:**
Clinics: No **Day Camps:** No   **Driving Range:**
Other: Restaurant / Snack Bar/ Bar- lounge / Dining Room

Popular par 3.

	1	2	3	4	5	6	7	8	9
PAR	3	3	3	3	3	3	3	3	3
YARDS	97	185	150	105	165	65	120	124	147
HDCP									

	10	11	12	13	14	15	16	17	18
PAR									
YARDS									
HDCP									

NE CT

Directions: Take I 384 East to Route 44. Course is on left.

4✪ =Excellent 3✪ =Very Good 2✪ = Good

Vineyard Valley Golf Club

Pomfret, CT (860) 974-2100
www.vvgolfclub.com

Tees	Holes	Yards	Par	USGA	Slope
BACK	9	3033	36	69.6	120
MIDDLE	9	2849	36	67.0	115
FRONT	9	2021	36	63.0	103

Club Pro: Dan Harder, PGA
Pro Shop: Yes
Payment: Visa, MC
Tee Times: Wknds only
Fee 9 Holes: Weekday: $18.00   **Weekend:** $22.00
Fee 18 Holes: Weekday: $30.00   **Weekend:** $35.00
Twilight Rates: No   **All Day Play:** No
Cart Rental: Included   **Discounts:**
Lessons: $20/ 30 min. **Schools:**   **Junior Golf:** Yes **Membership:**
Clinics: Yes **Day Camps:** No   **Driving Range:** Yes, grass.
Other: Restaurant / Snacks / Buford's Pub

Sig. Hole: #9, 140 yd par 3 to peninsula green, 3/4 surrounded by water. Bentgrass greens.

	1	2	3	4	5	6	7	8	9
PAR	5	3	4	4	4	5	4	4	3
YARDS	376	151	340	384	350	438	400	270	140
HDCP									
	10	11	12	13	14	15	16	17	18
PAR									
YARDS									
HDCP									

Directions: From I-395 N/S, take Exit 97. Go west on Rte. 44 to Rte. 97 S. Take to Rte. 244 W. Course is .25 mi. on left. From RI, take Rte. 44 W (same). From Hartford, I-84 E to Rte. 44 E. to Rte. 244 E, go 6 mi.

Westwoods Golf Course ✪✪

Rt.177, Farmington, CT (860) 675-2548

Tees	Holes	Yards	Par	USGA	Slope
BACK					
MIDDLE	18	4407	61	58.6	85
FRONT	18	3547	61	59.5	85

Club Pro: Jim Tennant, PGA
Pro Shop: Full inventory
Payment: Cash only
Tee Times: Weekends, 7 days adv.
Fee 9 Holes: Weekday: $14.00   **Weekend:** $16.50
Fee 18 Holes: Weekday: $21.00   **Weekend:** $24.50
Twilight Rates: League   **All Day Play:** No
Cart Rental: $28,2R/18, $16, 2R/9   **Discounts:** Senior & Junior
Lessons: $75/hr **Schools:** No   **Junior Golf:** Yes **Membership:** Yes
Clinics: Yes **Day Camps:** Yes   **Driving Range:** Yes
Other: Snack bar / Bar-lounge / Clubhouse / Restaurant

Numerous par 3's make it an easy walker. Has some challenging water holes. Reduced rates for residents. League twilight play.

	1	2	3	4	5	6	7	8	9
PAR	5	3	3	3	4	3	3	4	3
YARDS	494	164	135	187	315	204	159	344	235
HDCP	1	13	17	11	5	7	15	9	3
	10	11	12	13	14	15	16	17	18
PAR	4	3	3	4	3	4	3	3	3
YARDS	420	236	121	376	211	348	163	163	132
HDCP	2	6	18	4	8	10	14	12	16

Directions: Take I-84 to Bristol (Exit 39) Route 6; take Route 177 North. Course is 200 yards down on left.

Willimantic C. C.

◯◯ **49**

Willimantic, CT. (860) 456-1971
www.wccgolf.com

Club Pro: John Boucher, PGA
Pro Shop: Full inventory
Payment: Visa, MC, Amex, Dis, checks
Tee Times: M-Th. 7am-3pm

Tees	Holes	Yards	Par	USGA	Slope
BACK	18	6271	71	70.5	121
MIDDLE	18	6003	71	69.2	119
FRONT	18	5106	71	68.5	113

Fee 9 Holes: Weekday: N/A **Weekend:** N/A
Fee 18 Holes: Weekday: $50, $35 w/member **Weekend:** N/A
Twilight Rates: No **All Day Play:** No
Cart Rental: $12.00/cart **Discounts:** Junior, $15.00 fee
Lessons: $30.00/half hour **Schools:** No **Junior Golf:** Yes **Membership:** Yes
Clinics: Yes **Day Camps:** No **Driving Range:** No
Other: Full Restaurant / Clubhouse / Bar/Lounge / Lockers / Showers

Open to public on weekdays. Well worth the play. Play moves swiftly, long holes are compensated for by a number of short par 4's. Open April- November.

	1	2	3	4	5	6	7	8	9
PAR	4	4	4	4	4	5	3	4	4
YARDS	370	281	400	384	295	475	167	330	358
HDCP	11	15	1	3	17	13	9	7	5

	10	11	12	13	14	15	16	17	18
PAR	3	4	4	5	4	5	3	4	3
YARDS	110	388	286	485	414	483	154	417	206
HDCP	18	4	14	8	2	12	16	6	10

Directions: From Hartford, 384 East to Route 6 East. 11.6 miles to intersection of Route 6 and 66. Remain on Route 6 for 4.5 miles of Bypass Xpway. At end of bypass, turn left onto Route 66. Club is 1/2 mile on left.

Willow Brook Golf Course

50 ▶ **NEW 2003**

South Windsor, CT (860) 648-2061

Club Pro: Jim McGrath
Pro Shop: Full inventory
Payment: Visa, MC
Tee Times:

Tees	Holes	Yards	Par	USGA	Slope
BACK	18	2985	60		
MIDDLE	18	2613	60		
FRONT	18	2275	60		

Fee 9 Holes: Weekday: $12.50 **Weekend:** $14.50
Fee 18 Holes: Weekday: $24.00 **Weekend:** $26.00
Twilight Rates: **All Day Play:**
Cart Rental: $8.00/18 $4.50/9 **Discounts:** Senior & Junior
Lessons: Yes **Schools:** **Junior Golf:** **Membership:**
Clinics: **Day Camps:** **Driving Range:** Yes
Other: Restaurant / Bar / Snackbar

2003 Entry. Executive course with 6 par 4's. **Players' Comments:** "Good for beginners. Intermediate practice short game. Play 18 in 2 1/2 hours."

	1	2	3	4	5	6	7	8	9
PAR	3	3	4	3	3	4	4	3	3
YARDS	92	119	216	67	103	197	223	106	94
HDCP	10	6	12	18	14	2	4	16	8

	10	11	12	13	14	15	16	17	18
PAR	3	4	3	4	3	3	3	3	4
YARDS	100	233	83	281	137	100	86	75	301
HDCP	17	5	11	9	3	13	15	7	1

Directions: Take I-291 from Routes 84 or 91. Take Exit 4 (Route 5) towards South Windsor. Turn right onto Route 194. Go left at Troy Street, then right on to Brookfield Street. Course is on the right.

NE CT

4◯ =Excellent **3**◯ =Very Good **2**◯ =Good

Wintonbury Hills Golf Course

51

Bloomfield, CT (860) 555-1212

Tees	Holes	Yards	Par	USGA	Slope
BACK	18	6152	70		
MIDDLE	18	5734	70		
FRONT	18	5038	70		

Club Pro: D. Juhaz, Dir. of Golf
Pro Shop: Full
Payment: Credit, MC, Visa, Disc., Amex
Tee Times: 7 days
Fee 9 Holes: Weekday: TBA   **Weekend:** TBA
Fee 18 Holes: Weekday: TBA   **Weekend:** TBA
Twilight Rates: Yes, 2 pm and 5 pm   **All Day Play:**
Cart Rental: Complimentary   **Discounts:** Senior / Junior
Lessons: Yes **Schools:** Yes   **Junior Golf: Membership:** Limited
Clinics: Yes **Day Camps:** Yes   **Driving Range:** Yes
Other: Clubhouse under construction / Snack bar / Restaurant

New Entry 2004. 18 holes, stunningly beautiful, pastoral setting- built on farm land. Opened septembr '03. Pete Dye and Tom Liddy design. Managed by Billy Casper Golf. Resident discount.

	1	2	3	4	5	6	7	8	9
PAR	4	4	3	5	4	4	3	5	3
YARDS	330	357	125	467	320	355	152	489	143
HDCP	9	11	15	1	7	5	13	3	17
	10	**11**	**12**	**13**	**14**	**15**	**16**	**17**	**18**
PAR	4	4	3	5	4	4	4	3	4
YARDS	360	359	148	470	370	364	348	150	371
HDCP	16	4	18	14	2	8	10	6	12

Directions: I-91 to Exit 35B. Take Route 218 towards Bloomfield. Make right hand turn to Route 189N. Take Route 189N through Bloomfield. At light with 5 intersections, bear right onto Terry Plains Road. Course is 1 mile on right.

Woodstock Golf Course

◐◐ **52**

S. Woodstock, CT (860) 928-4130

Tees	Holes	Yards	Par	USGA	Slope
BACK	N/A				
MIDDLE	9	2413	34	32.6	107
FRONT	9	1822	34	66.8	103

Club Pro: Roland Allard, Dir. of Golf
Pro Shop: Limited inventory
Payment: Visa, MC, Amex
Tee Times: Wknd, Hol., 3 day adv.
Fee 9 Holes: Weekday: $12.00   **Weekend:** $14.00
Fee 18 Holes: Weekday: $20.00   **Weekend:** $24.00
Twilight Rates: No   **All Day Play:** No
Cart Rental: $19.00/18 $11.00/9   **Discounts:** Sr & Jr Wkdys only
Lessons: $30.00/30 min **Schools:** No   **Junior Golf:** Yes **Membership:** Yes
Clinics: Yes **Day Camps:** No   **Driving Range:** Yes
Other: Clubhouse / Snack Bar / Lockers / Showers

COUPON

Established 1896. Over one hundred and seven years old! Challenging, hilly course with small sloping greens. Target golf. Open April - November.

	1	2	3	4	5	6	7	8	9
PAR	3	4	4	4	4	4	3	4	4
YARDS	170	265	305	304	289	275	231	385	227
HDCP	6	8	3	4	7	2	5	1	9
	10	**11**	**12**	**13**	**14**	**15**	**16**	**17**	**18**
PAR									
YARDS									
HDCP									

Directions: I-395 to Route 44 (Exit 97.) West on Route 44. Take Route 171 in Putnam, continue west. Follow 4.5 miles to Roseland Park Road, take right. Course 3/4 mile on left.

CHAPTER 10

Southern/Western Connecticut

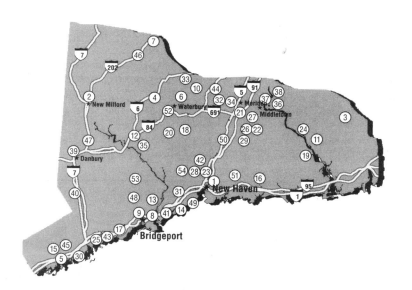

Alling Memorial GC

Eastern St., New Haven, CT (203) 946-8014

Club Pro: John Korolyshun, PGA
Pro Shop: Full inventory
Payment: Cash, Check
Tee Times: Weekends, 3 day adv.

Tees	Holes	Yards	Par	USGA	Slope
BACK	18	6241	72	71.9	127
MIDDLE	18	5884	72	69.3	120
FRONT	18	5071	72	71.0	129

Fee 9 Holes: Weekday: $16.00
Fee 18 Holes: Weekday: $24.00
Twilight Rates: Yes, after 6 pm
Cart Rental: $24.00/18 $14.00/9
Lessons: Yes **Schools:** No
Clinics: N/R **Day Camps** possible
Other: Lockers / Showers / Restaurant / Bar-lounge

Weekend: $16.00
Weekend: $27.00
All Day Play: N/R
Discounts: Senior & Junior
Junior Golf: Yes **Membership:** No
Driving Range: No

Appreciated by old, young, and new golfers alike. Excellent value for the money. Resident rates.

	1	2	3	4	5	6	7	8	9
PAR	4	4	3	5	4	4	4	4	4
YARDS	380	313	168	474	231	344	366	274	305
HDCP	3	13	11	1	17	5	9	15	7
	10	11	12	13	14	15	16	17	18
PAR	3	5	3	4	4	5	4	3	5
YARDS	148	464	174	337	408	493	331	203	471
HDCP	18	8	16	6	2	12	10	14	4

Directions: From I-91 Northbound, Exit 8, bear right to second light (Eastern Street), right 3/4 mile. Course on left.

Candlewood Valley CC

Danbury Rd., New Milford, CT (860) 354-9359
candlewoodcountryclub.com

Club Pro: Jim Alexander, PGA
Pro Shop: Full inventory
Payment: Most major
Tee Times: 4 days adv.

Tees	Holes	Yards	Par	USGA	Slope
BACK	18	6441	72	72.0	126
MIDDLE	18	6033	72	70.2	120
FRONT	18	5362	72	72.5	123

Fee 9 Holes: Weekday: NA
Fee 18 Holes: Weekday: $30.00
Twilight Rates: Yes, after 3 pm
Cart Rental: $26.00/18 $16.00/9
Lessons: $40.00/half hour **Schools:** No
Clinics: Yes **Day Camps** No
Other: Clubhouse / Lockers / Showers / Snack bar / Restaurant / Bar-lounge / Banquet facilities

Weekend: NA
Weekend: $37.00
All Day Play: No
Discounts: Senior & Junior
Junior Golf: Yes **Membership:** No
Driving Range: $5.00/lg. $2.50/sm.

Take advantage of the Wednesday special: cart, 18 holes, lunch.

	1	2	3	4	5	6	7	8	9
PAR	4	4	5	4	3	3	4	4	4
YARDS	301	315	448	370	152	160	350	447	402
HDCP	18	14	8	16	10	12	4	2	6
	10	11	12	13	14	15	16	17	18
PAR	3	4	4	4	5	5	4	4	4
YARDS	210	413	390	418	530	459	366	386	316
HDCP	13	1	5	3	7	15	11	9	17

Directions: From Route 84, take Exit 7 (Brookfield/ New Milford). Follow to end. Turn right at light onto Route 7 North. Follow 4.1 miles to CVCC on the right.

Chanticlair Golf Course

3

Colchester, CT (860) 537-3223

Club Pro: No
Pro Shop: Full inventory
Payment: Cash, Visa, MC
Tee Times: 1 week adv.
Fee 9 Holes: Weekday: $15.00
Fee 18 Holes: Weekday: $24.00
Twilight Rates: No
Cart Rental: $22.00/18 $11.00/9
Lessons: No **Schools:** No
Clinics: No **Day Camps** No
Other: Clubhouse / Snack bar

Tees	Holes	Yards	Par	USGA	Slope
BACK					
MIDDLE	9	5983	70	69.8	117
FRONT	9	5001	70	69.1	112

Weekend: $16.00
Weekend: $25.00
All Day Play: No
Discounts: Senior & Junior
Junior Golf: Yes **Membership:** Yes
Driving Range: No

The 4th hole has an elevated island green. Fairly flat; a good walking course.

	1	2	3	4	5	6	7	8	9
PAR	3	4	4	3	4	4	4	4	5
YARDS	192	385	345	138	364	362	345	350	441
HDCP	4	12	14	10	6	8	16	2	18
	10	11	12	13	14	15	16	17	18
PAR	3	4	4	3	4	4	4	4	5
YARDS	205	390	375	138	387	385	350	380	451
HDCP	7	11	9	13	3	5	15	1	17

Directions: Take Route 2 to State Police Barracks Exit; take left off ramp and go up hill. Make left onto Old Hebron Rd. at firehouse. Course 1/4 mile on right

Crestbrook Park GC

4

Watertown, CT (860) 945-5249

Club Pro: Kenneth Gemmell, PGA
Pro Shop: Full inventory
Payment: Cash only
Tee Times: Weekends, 2 days adv.
Fee 9 Holes: Weekday: $18.00
Fee 18 Holes: Weekday: $32.00
Twilight Rates: No
Cart Rental: $26.00/18 $13.00/9
Lessons: $35.00/half hour **Schools:** No
Clinics: Adult/Jr **Day Camps** No
Other: Clubhouse / Snack bar / Restaurant / Bar-lounge / Pool / Tennis / Picnic

Tees	Holes	Yards	Par	USGA	Slope
BACK	18	6915	71	73.6	128
MIDDLE	18	6098	71	69.9	121
FRONT	18	5696	75	73.8	128

Weekend: $19.00
Weekend: $34.00
All Day Play: No
Discounts: Senior & Junior
Junior Golf: Yes **Membership:** Yes
Driving Range: $6.00/lg $4.50/md $3.00/sm

Player's Comment: 'Totally different 9's, front open, back tight and angled fairways." Cornish championship layout. Resident rates.

	1	2	3	4	5	6	7	8	9
PAR	4	4	4	5	3	4	4	3	5
YARDS	370	447	411	515	152	384	405	194	536
HDCP	13	1	5	9	17	7	11	15	3
	10	11	12	13	14	15	16	17	18
PAR	4	4	3	4	4	5	3	4	4
YARDS	357	401	160	337	333	463	210	308	393
HDCP	6	4	18	12	14	8	10	16	2

Directions: Route 8 to Echo Lake Rd. (turn left). Take right at 2nd light (Buckingham); another right at stop sign (Northfield). Course is 1/4 mi. on right on Northfield Rd.

SW CT

4✪ =Excellent 3✪ =Very Good 2✪ =Good

E. Gaynor Brennan GC

Stillwater Rd., Stamford, CT (203) 324-4185

Club Pro: V. Levin, A. Aulenti, Golf Dir.
Pro Shop: Full inventory
Payment: Cash, Visa, MC
Tee Times: 7 days adv.
Fee 9 Holes: Weekday: $24.00
Fee 18 Holes: Weekday: $36.00
Twilight Rates: Yes
Cart Rental: $24.00/18 $16.00/9
Lessons: Call 324-6507 **Schools:** No
Clinics: Yes **Day Camps** No
Other: Snack bar / Restaurant / Bar-lounge / Showers

Tees	Holes	Yards	Par	USGA	Slope
BACK	18	5931	71	68.8	114
MIDDLE	18	5814	71	67.5	122
FRONT	18	5180	73	72.3	124

Weekend: N/A
Weekend: $40.00
All Day Play: N/R
Discounts: Sr. & Jr., residents only
Junior Golf: Yes **Membership:** Yes
Driving Range: No

The greens are usually in excellent condition. Course is a bit hilly. Open year round. Resident discounts and resident weekend lottery.

	1	2	3	4	5	6	7	8	9
PAR	4	4	3	5	4	5	4	4	3
YARDS	364	385	147	418	366	486	373	367	105
HDCP	7	5	13	9	3	15	1	11	17
	10	**11**	**12**	**13**	**14**	**15**	**16**	**17**	**18**
PAR	4	4	4	3	4	3	4	5	4
YARDS	301	323	341	225	385	177	278	454	319
HDCP	10	14	2	6	4	8	18	16	12

Directions: Take I-95 to Exit 7(Atlantic St.). Go straight. Right onto Washington Blvd. Left onto Broad St. Go to Still Water Rd. Course is on Right.

East Mountain GC

Waterbury, CT (203) 753-1425

Club Pro:
Pro Shop: Full inventory
Payment: Cash only
Tee Times: Weekends, 3 days adv.
Fee 9 Holes: Weekday: $16.00
Fee 18 Holes: Weekday: $25.00
Twilight Rates: No
Cart Rental: $25.00/18 $15.00/9
Lessons: Yes **Schools:** No
Clinics: No **Day Camps**
Other: Bar-Lounge

Tees	Holes	Yards	Par	USGA	Slope
BACK	18	5817	67	68.0	114
MIDDLE	18	5591	68	66.9	112
FRONT	18	5211	67	70.7	119

Weekend: $17.00
Weekend: $27.00
All Day Play: No
Discounts: Junior
Junior Golf: Yes **Membership:** Yes
Driving Range: yes

Landscaping improved throughout course. Special rate Tuesday- Thursday from 7-11am includes cart with two paid greens.

	1	2	3	4	5	6	7	8	9
PAR	4	4	4	3	4	5	4	3	4
YARDS	387	387	394	184	292	503	320	136	353
HDCP	7	3	5	15	11	1	13	17	9
	10	**11**	**12**	**13**	**14**	**15**	**16**	**17**	**18**
PAR	4	3	4	4	3	4	4	3	4
YARDS	348	221	398	355	163	356	375	183	346
HDCP	12	14	2	8	18	6	4	16	10

Directions: From Hartford: I-84 to Hamilton Avenue (Exit 23). Follow Route 69 West. Right onto East Mountain at Church.

Eastwood CC

Torrington, CT (860) 489-2630
www.eastwoodcountryclub.com

Club Pro: Skip Rotondo, PGA
Pro Shop: Limited inventory
Payment: Visa, MC, Amex, Cash, Check
Tee Times: No
Fee 9 Holes: Weekday: $16.00
Fee 18 Holes: Weekday: $26.00
Twilight Rates: No
Cart Rental: $14pp/18 $7pp/9
Lessons: No **Schools:** No
Clinics: No **Day Camps** No
Other: Restaurant / Clubhouse / Bar-lounge

Weekend: $18.00
Weekend: $28.00
All Day Play: No
Discounts: Seniors + Juniors, weekdays
Junior Golf: Yes **Membership:** Yes
Driving Range: No

Tees	Holes	Yards	Par	USGA	Slope
BACK	9	5866	72	67.8	113
MIDDLE	9	5582	72	66.5	111
FRONT	9	4718	72		

Tight greens, narrow fairways, and rough make this course challenging but enjoyable. Some hills. Pretty views. Open April - January.

	1	2	3	4	5	6	7	8	9
PAR	4	4	4	5	4	3	4	3	5
YARDS	363	309	348	411	275	131	286	137	531
HDCP	3	9	7	5	13	17	11	15	1

	10	11	12	13	14	15	16	17	18
PAR	4	4	4	5	4	3	4	3	5
YARDS	363	309	348	411	275	131	286	137	531
HDCP	4	10	8	6	14	18	12	16	2

Directions: Take Route 8 to Exit 45. Right on Winsted Road to light. Take right onto Kennedy Drive, up hill to four-way intersection. Left onto Torringford West Street. Straight until sharp corner. Course on left side.

Fairchild Wheeler GC (Black)

Fairfield, CT (203) 373-5911

Club Pro: Jack McGoldrick, PGA
Pro Shop: Full inventory
Payment: Visa, MC, Amex
Tee Times: 7 days advamce
Fee 9 Holes: Weekday: $16.00
Fee 18 Holes: Weekday: $26.00
Twilight Rates: Yes, after 5:30 pm
Cart Rental: $26/18 $18/9 $15/1 rdr
Lessons: $35.00/half hour **Schools:** Jr. & Sr.
Clinics: Ladies/Juniors **Day Camps** Yes
Other: Clubhouse / Snack bar / Restaurant / Bar-lounge / Lockers / Showers

Weekend: $22.00
Weekend: $32.00
All Day Play: No
Discounts: Senior & Junior
Junior Golf: Yes **Membership:** Yes
Driving Range: Yes

COUPON

Tees	Holes	Yards	Par	USGA	Slope
BACK	18	6559	71	72	128
MIDDLE	18	6322	71	71.0	119
FRONT	18	5234	72	70.0	119

Challenging course with some of the toughest par-fours around. Reduced rates for residents. Open year round. **Player's comments:** "Solid course at relative bargain fees." "Remarkable improvements."

	1	2	3	4	5	6	7	8	9
PAR	4	4	3	4	4	4	3	5	5
YARDS	405	377	128	367	321	432	212	431	500
HDCP	4	8	18	6	16	2	14	12	10

	10	11	12	13	14	15	16	17	18
PAR	4	3	4	4	4	4	5	3	4
YARDS	417	153	407	421	314	418	512	191	396
HDCP	11	17	7	1	15	5	9	13	3

Directions: Take Merritt Parkway (Route 15) Exit 46 to Route 59 South (Easton Turnpike.) 1/2 mile on left.

**SW
CT**

4⭐ =Excellent 3⭐ =Very Good 2⭐ =Good

Fairchild Wheeler GC (Red)

9

Fairfield, CT (203) 373-5911

Club Pro: Jack McGoldrick, PGA
Pro Shop: Full inventory
Payment: Visa, MC, Cash
Tee Times: Yes

Tees	Holes	Yards	Par	USGA	Slope
BACK	18	6568	72	72	125
MIDDLE	18	6126	72	71.3	124
FRONT	18	5330	72	68.7	117

Fee 9 Holes: Weekday: $16.00
Fee 18 Holes: Weekday: $26.00
Twilight Rates: Yes, after 5:30 pm
Cart Rental: $26/18 $18/9 $15/1rdr.
Lessons: $35.00/half hour **Schools:** Jr. & Sr.
Clinics: Ladies/Juniors **Day Camps** Yes
Other: Clubhouse / Snack bar / Restaurant / Bar-lounge / Lockers / Showers

Weekend: $22.00
Weekend: $32.00
All Day Play: No
Discounts: Senior & Junior
Junior Golf: Yes **Membership:** Yes
Driving Range: Yes

COUPON

Flat open course, good for beginners and seniors. Reduced rates for residents and other CT public course passholders. Open all year. Links style course.

	1	2	3	4	5	6	7	8	9
PAR	4	4	5	3	4	4	4	3	4
YARDS	440	402	480	127	308	412	337	190	387
HDCP	1	7	11	17	15	5	13	9	3
	10	**11**	**12**	**13**	**14**	**15**	**16**	**17**	**18**
PAR	5	4	3	4	4	3	4	5	5
YARDS	504	419	105	422	334	202	340	501	472
HDCP	2	8	18	10	12	16	14	4	6

Directions: Take Merritt Parkway (Route 15) Exit 46 to Route 59 South (Easton Turnpike.) 1/2 mile on left.

Farmingbury Hills CC

10

141 East St., Wolcott, CT (203) 879-8038

Club Pro: Craig Kealey, PGA
Pro Shop: Full inventory
Payment: Cash only
Tee Times: Weekends, 7 days adv.

Tees	Holes	Yards	Par	USGA	Slope
BACK					
MIDDLE	9	6005	71	68.7	117
FRONT	9	5355	72	71.0	120

Fee 9 Holes: Weekday: $15.00
Fee 18 Holes: Weekday: $24.00
Twilight Rates:
Cart Rental: $26.00/18 $13.00/9
Lessons: $30/30 min **Schools:** No
Clinics: N/R **Day Camps** N/R
Other: Snack bar / Bar-lounge / Restaurant

Weekend: $17.00
Weekend: $26.00
All Day Play:
Discounts: Senior & Junior
Junior Golf: Yes **Membership:** No
Driving Range: Yes

A hillside course with nice views. Easy to play. Open April 1 - Dec. 1.

	1	2	3	4	5	6	7	8	9
PAR	4	4	4	4	4	3	4	3	5
YARDS	340	419	310	373	321	102	401	190	510
HDCP	11	1	13	9	7	17	3	15	5
	10	**11**	**12**	**13**	**14**	**15**	**16**	**17**	**18**
PAR	4	4	4	4	4	3	4	4	5
YARDS	362	402	288	378	280	128	355	315	531
HDCP	10	2	14	4	12	18	8	16	6

Directions: I-84 to Cheshire Exit 28. Route 322 West, left up Southington Mountain. Right at top of hill, blinking light (East St.). Course is 1 mile on right.

Fox Hopyard Country Club ✪✪✪

East Haddam, CT (860) 434-6644
www.sandri.com

Club Pro: Ron Beck, PGA
Pro Shop: Full inventory
Payment: Visa, MC, Amex, Disc, checks, cash
Tee Times: 6 days adv.

Tees	Holes	Yards	Par	USGA	Slope
BACK	18	6512	71	72.6	131
MIDDLE	18	6109	71	70.7	124
FRONT	18	5111	71	70.7	123

Fee 9 Holes: Weekday: $45.00
Fee 18 Holes: Weekday: $85.00
Twilight Rates: Yes
Cart Rental: $18/18 $10/9
Lessons: $50/30min **Schools:** Yes
Clinics: Junior **Day Camps** No
Other: Restaurant / Bar-lounge / Clubhouse / Showers / Lockers

Weekend: $50.00
Weekend: $95.00
All Day Play: No
Discounts: Junior
Junior Golf: Yes **Membership:** Yes
Driving Range: Yes

COUPON

Player's Comment: " Great layout in unspoiled surroundings. Many memorable holes." "Sister course to Crumpin -Fox. Country club setting. Wide fairways. Shots to the greens high on risk & reward." R.W.

	1	2	3	4	5	6	7	8	9
PAR	4	4	5	3	5	4	4	3	4
YARDS	356	358	457	172	464	320	366	160	350
HDCP	11	1	7	17	9	13	3	15	5
	10	**11**	**12**	**13**	**14**	**15**	**16**	**17**	**18**
PAR	4	3	4	4	3	5	3	4	5
YARDS	382	153	372	408	188	508	189	399	507
HDCP	12	18	8	4	16	2	14	6	10

Directions: From I-95 N, take Exit 70 (Old Lyme). Go left onto Route 156 for 9 miles. Right onto Route 82 and take first left onto Hopyard. Accessible from I-91 to Route 2 to Route 11. Call for directions from I-95 S and Route 9.

Gainfield Farms GC ▶ 12

Southbury, CT (203) 262-1100

Club Pro: Bert Boyce
Pro Shop: Yes
Payment: Cash, Check
Tee Times: Yes

Tees	Holes	Yards	Par	USGA	Slope
BACK					
MIDDLE	9	1384	28		
FRONT	9	1203	27		

Fee 9 Holes: Weekday: $14.00
Fee 18 Holes: Weekday: $22.00
Twilight Rates:
Cart Rental: $22.00/18 $11.00/9
Lessons: Yes **Schools:** No
Clinics: No **Day Camps** No
Other: Snacks

Weekend: $15.00
Weekend: $24.00
All Day Play:
Discounts: Senior & Junior
Junior Golf: Yes **Membership:** N/R
Driving Range: mat and net

Sig. Hole: #3 is a narrow picturesque par 3 with a backdrop of mature hemlocks protected by 2 sand traps. Executive style, resident discounts.

	1	2	3	4	5	6	7	8	9
PAR	3	4	3	3	3	3	3	3	3
YARDS	155	261	188	123	113	94	195	127	128
HDCP	5	1	3	6	8	9	2	4	7
	10	**11**	**12**	**13**	**14**	**15**	**16**	**17**	**18**
PAR									
YARDS									
HDCP									

Directions: I-84 to Exit 15. Go north on Route 67. Turn left on Main Street. Turn right on Poverty Road. Then left on Old Field Road.

SW CT

Grassy Hill Country Club ▶ 13

Orange, CT (203)795-1422

Club Pro: Brian Fitzgibbons, PGA
Pro Shop: Limited inventory
Payment: Visa, MC
Tee Times: 7 Wkdys, 3 Wknds
Fee 9 Holes: Weekday: $20.00
Fee 18 Holes: Weekday: $34.00
Twilight Rates: No
Cart Rental: $10pp/18
Lessons: $65/1 hour **Schools:** N/A
Clinics: N/R **Day Camps** N/R
Other: Full restaurant / Clubhouse / Bar-Lounge / Lockers / Showers

Tees	Holes	Yards	Par	USGA	Slope
BACK	18	6118	70	70.5	122
MIDDLE	18	5849	70	69.4	119
FRONT	18	5209	71	71.1	118

Weekend: $29.00 w/cart
Weekend: $54.00 w/cart
All Day Play: No
Discounts: Senior (M-F)
Junior Golf: Yes **Membership:** yes
Driving Range: $5.00/lg. $3.00/sm.

New 8th green. Working to restore excellent conditions of fairways and greens.

	1	2	3	4	5	6	7	8	9
PAR	4	4	3	4	5	3	4	4	5
YARDS	385	410	158	301	563	145	363	360	432
HDCP	7	1	17	15	3	9	11	5	13

	10	11	12	13	14	15	16	17	18
PAR	3	4	4	3	4	4	5	3	4
YARDS	169	384	277	175	319	421	496	165	326
HDCP	12	4	16	10	14	2	8	18	6

Directions: From I-95: Take exit 39a. Turn right, pass Howard Johnson's . At second dual traffic light, turn right. 2-1/2 miles to Clark Lane. Turn right to Grassy Hill.

Great River Golf Club ✪✪✪ ▶ 14

Milford, CT (203) 876-8051
www.grgolfclub.com
Club Pro: Tom Rosati
Pro Shop: Full inventory
Payment: Most major
Tee Times: 5 days adv.
Fee 9 Holes: Weekday: $50.00 after 5 pm
Fee 18 Holes: Weekday: $100.00 M-TH
Twilight Rates: Yes
Cart Rental: Included
Lessons: $90.00/45 min **Schools:** No
Clinics: Yes **Day Camps** No
Other: Restaurant / Outdoor Dining / Clubhouse / Lockers / Showers / Bar-Lounge / Conf. Room

Tees	Holes	Yards	Par	USGA	Slope
BACK	18	6469	72	72.1	143
MIDDLE	18	6071	72	70.2	133
FRONT	18	4975	72	70.7	125

Weekend:
Weekend: $125.00 F/S/S/Holidays
All Day Play: No, Twilight Rate for replay
Discounts: None
Junior Golf: Yes **Membership:** Yes
Driving Range: Yes

Players' Comments: "Excellent player's course." "2 times on vacations. Everything was perfect." "Best public course in CT." "Best suited for scratch and 1-3 Hndcp. Championship tees, Slope 151/ 152." R.W.

	1	2	3	4	5	6	7	8	9
PAR	4	3	5	4	4	5	4	3	4
YARDS	330	165	470	375	355	480	380	155	360
HDCP	13	17	5	3	9	11	1	15	7

	10	11	12	13	14	15	16	17	18
PAR	3	4	4	5	4	3	4	5	4
YARDS	140	360	376	465	360	120	370	500	310
HDCP	16	6	4	14	10	18	2	8	12

Directions: I-95 S to Exit 38 bearing right, go to Wheeler Farms Rd., turn left. Turn left at Herbert St. Turn left on Coram Lane course is at end of lane. Call for directions from Hartford or NY via Wilbur Cross / Merrit Pkwy and from 95 N.

Griffith E. Harris Golf Course

Greenwich, CT, (203) 531-7261

Club Pro: Joe Felder, PGA
Pro Shop: Full inventory
Payment: Cash or check
Tee Times: Weekdays, Same day

Tees	Holes	Yards	Par	USGA	Slope
BACK	18	6512	71	70.5	120
MIDDLE	18	6093	72	68.6	115
FRONT	18	5710	73	73.6	128

Fee 9 Holes: Weekday: $48.00   **Weekend:** $48.00
Fee 18 Holes: Weekday: $48.00   **Weekend:** $48.00
Twilight Rates: No   **All Day Play:** No
Cart Rental: $24.00/18 $17.00/9   **Discounts:** Senior & Junior, wkdays only
Lessons: $55/30, J.F. **Schools:** Yes   **Junior Golf:** Yes **Membership:**
Clinics: Yes **Day Camps** No   **Driving Range:** $8.00/lg., $4.00/sm.
Other: Full Restaurant / Clubhouse / Bar / Lockers / Showers

Restaurant renovated. Open to residents of town who are members and guests only. Front side fairly open and flat. Back side narrow and hilly. Open April 1 - Dec.1.

	1	2	3	4	5	6	7	8	9
PAR	4	4	5	4	3	4	3	5	4
YARDS	407	365	503	378	169	437	138	519	323
HDCP	5	7	13	3	15	1	17	9	11
	10	11	12	13	14	15	16	17	18
PAR	4	4	5	4	3	4	3	5	4
YARDS	407	365	503	378	169	437	138	519	323
HDCP	5	7	13	3	15	1	17	9	11

Directions: Merritt Parkway South to King St. Right turn approx. 3 miles to golf course on right. Any questions call (203) 531-7200.

Guilford Lakes Golf Course   ✪✪

Guilford, CT (203) 453-8214

Club Pro: Bill Fitzhenry
Pro Shop: Limited inventory
Payment: Cash or check only
Tee Times: 3 days adv.

Tees	Holes	Yards	Par	USGA	Slope
BACK	9	1319	27		
MIDDLE	9	1165	27		
FRONT	9	739	27		

Fee 9 Holes: Weekday: $11.00   **Weekend:** $13.00
Fee 18 Holes: Weekday: $22.00   **Weekend:** $26.00
Twilight Rates: No   **All Day Play:** No
Cart Rental: Pull carts $2.00   **Discounts:** Senior & Junior
Lessons: Schools: No   **Junior Golf:** Park and Rec. **Membership:** Yes
Clinics: Yes **Day Camps** No   **Driving Range:** No
Other: Snacks / New clubhouse now open

Player's Comment: "Polished and professionally designed." R.W. Reduced resident fees. Heavily tree-lined, gentle and hilly. Challenging for both beginner and intermediate.

	1	2	3	4	5	6	7	8	9
PAR	3	3	3	3	3	3	3	3	3
YARDS	138	111	130	122	105	180	155	79	148
HDCP	6	7	3	5	9	1	2	8	4
	10	11	12	13	14	15	16	17	18
PAR									
YARDS									
HDCP									

Directions: I-95, Exit 58 onto Route 77. North on Route 77, turn right onto Stepstone Hill Rd. Straight to N. Madison Rd. Course is on the left.

4✪ =Excellent 3✪ =Very Good 2✪ =Good

H. Smith Richardson GC

Fairfield, CT (203) 255-7300

Club Pro: Sean Garrity, PGA
Pro Shop: Full inventory
Payment: Cash only
Tee Times: Weekends, 3 days adv.

Tees	Holes	Yards	Par	USGA	Slope
BACK	18	6676	72	71.0	127
MIDDLE	18	6323	72	70.2	124
FRONT	18	5764	73	73.9	127

Fee 9 Holes: Weekday: $20.00
Fee 18 Holes: Weekday: $30.00
Twilight Rates: Yes, after 5 pm (wknds only)
Cart Rental: $27,2p/18 $16,2p/9
Lessons: $50/30 min. **Schools:** No
Clinics: No **Day Camps** No
Other: Lockers / Showers / Restaurant / Bar-lounge

Weekend: $21.00 after 5pm only
Weekend: $40.00
All Day Play: No
Discounts: Senior & Junior
Junior Golf: Yes **Membership:** Yes
Driving Range: Yes

This scenic hilly course has a majestic view of Long Island Sound. Slopes on greens make putting challenging. Closed March. Single rider car and rates, inquire.

	1	2	3	4	5	6	7	8	9
PAR	4	4	3	4	4	5	4	3	5
YARDS	375	310	160	339	397	503	383	180	486
HDCP	6	14	18	12	2	4	8	16	10
	10	11	12	13	14	15	16	17	18
PAR	4	4	3	5	4	4	3	4	5
YARDS	373	351	176	502	405	350	140	373	520
HDCP	3	13	15	7	1	11	17	5	9

Directions: Take Merritt Parkway to Exit 46. Go North on Route 59. Take left on Congress, right on Morehouse Highway.

Hawk's Landing CC

Southington, CT (860) 793-6000
www.hawkslandingcc.com

Club Pro: John Vitale
Pro Shop: Full inventory
Payment: Visa, MC, Check
Tee Times: Weekends, 4 days adv.

Tees	Holes	Yards	Par	USGA	Slope
BACK	18	5650	71		
MIDDLE	18	5325	71		
FRONT	18	4285	71		

Fee 9 Holes: Weekday: $13.00 M-Th
Fee 18 Holes: Weekday: $22.00 M-Th
Twilight Rates: Yes, after 4 pm (Fri only)
Cart Rental: $24.00/18 $14.00/9
Lessons: No **Schools:** No
Clinics: No **Day Camps** No
Other: Clubhouse / Lockers / Showers / Bar-lounge / Restaurant / Snackbar

Weekend: $16.00 F/S/S
Weekend: $25.00 F/S/S
All Day Play: No
Discounts: Seniors
Junior Golf: No **Membership:** Yes
Driving Range: No

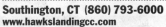

COUPON

Formerly Pattonbrook. Improvements include: lengthened and redesigned 14 holes for par 71, new tee boxes, landscaping, new ponds on holes 3, 6, 12. New irrigation system, 30 new sand bunkers.

	1	2	3	4	5	6	7	8	9
PAR	4	3	5	4	4	4	4	4	3
YARDS	265	163	420	280	310	270	230	325	220
HDCP	12	14	8	18	4	6	16	10	2
	10	11	12	13	14	15	16	17	18
PAR	4	4	3	5	4	5	3	5	3
YARDS	385	260	150	460	385	450	140	450	165
HDCP	3	17	13	1	5	15	11	7	9

Directions: Take Exit 32 from I-84. Turn South onto Queen Street (Route 10), quick left onto Laning. Left onto Flanders and first left onto Pattonwood Drive.

Highland Greens GC

Prospect, CT (203) 758-4022
www.golfatnight.com

Club Pro: No
Pro Shop: Limited inventory
Payment: Cash only
Tee Times: Same Day
Fee 9 Holes: Weekday: $12.00
Fee 18 Holes: Weekday: $20.00
Twilight Rates: Yes
Cart Rental: No
Lessons: Yes **Schools:** No
Clinics: N/R **Day Camps** N/R
Other: Snack bar / Restaurant

Tees	Holes	Yards	Par	USGA	Slope
BACK					
MIDDLE	9	1398	27		
FRONT	9	1322	27		

Weekend: $13.00
Weekend: $20.00
All Day Play: Replay
Discounts: Senior
Junior Golf: No **Membership:** N/R
Driving Range: No

Completely lighted for night play. Nightly rate after 6:30 pm $14 for nine holes. Slightly hilly. A challenging par 3 open April - First Frost.

	1	2	3	4	5	6	7	8	9
PAR	3	3	3	3	3	3	3	3	3
YARDS	132	192	115	135	188	185	157	128	166
HDCP									
	10	11	12	13	14	15	16	17	18
PAR									
YARDS									
HDCP									

Directions: Take I-84 to Exit 26 to Route 70 East to Route 68 West. At top of hill, left onto Cooke Road. Course is 1.6 miles on right.

Hillside Links LLC

Deep River, CT (860)526-9986

Club Pro: Mark Erwin
Pro Shop: Yes
Payment: Cash only
Tee Times: Wkends/Holdys
Fee 9 Holes: Weekday: $8.50
Fee 18 Holes: Weekday: $15.00
Twilight Rates: N/R
Cart Rental: Pull Carts $1.00
Lessons: Group & Private **Schools:** No
Clinics: No **Day Camps** No
Other: Golf balls/ Hats/ Candy/ Soda

Tees	Holes	Yards	Par	USGA	Slope
BACK					
MIDDLE	9	932	27		
FRONT					

Weekend: $9.50
Weekend: $17.00
All Day Play: N/R
Discounts: Senior 8-11 Wkdays
Junior Golf: No **Membership:** Multi-Play Pass
Driving Range:

COUPON

A challenging Par 3 walking course with sand and water. The feel of a full size course on a small scale. Good for family fun. Spectators not allowed.

	1	2	3	4	5	6	7	8	9
PAR	3	3	3	3	3	3	3	3	3
YARDS	73	82	97	115	96	131	164	71	103
HDCP									
	10	11	12	13	14	15	16	17	18
PAR									
YARDS									
HDCP									

Directions: From Route 9 N or S take Route 80 East and turn onto Hillside Terrace. Follow road to end.

SW CT

4✪ =Excellent 3✪ =Very Good 2✪ =Good

Hop Brook CC

Naugatuck, CT (203) 729-8013

Club Pro: No
Pro Shop: Yes
Payment: Cash, Check
Tee Times: Weekends, 2 days adv.
Fee 9 Holes: Weekday: $17.00
Fee 18 Holes: Weekday: $25.00
Twilight Rates: No
Cart Rental: $13pp/18, $8pp/9
Lessons: No **Schools:** No
Clinics: No **Day Camps** No
Other: Clubhouse / Restaurant

Tees	Holes	Yards	Par	USGA	Slope
BACK	9	3047	36	68.2	116
MIDDLE	9	2862	36	66.6	112
FRONT	9	2413	36	67.0	114

Weekend: $22.00
Weekend: $30.00
All Day Play: No
Discounts: Sr & Jr Weekdays
Junior Golf: Yes **Membership:** Yes
Driving Range: No

Nine hole course. The course is short and turns hilly near the end. Substantial discounts for residents. Open Mar - Dec. Senior tees now on every hole.

	1	2	3	4	5	6	7	8	9
PAR	5	4	4	4	3	5	3	4	4
YARDS	452	325	320	304	135	476	170	382	298
HDCP	1	9	13	5	17	7	11	3	15

	10	11	12	13	14	15	16	17	18
PAR									
YARDS									
HDCP									

Directions: Take I-84 to Exit 17 to Route 63. Course is 3 miles down on left.

Hunter Golf Club

Meriden, CT (203) 634-3366

Club Pro: Dave Cook, PGA
Pro Shop: Full inventory
Payment: Cash and Credit
Tee Times: Yes
Fee 9 Holes: Weekday: $15.00
Fee 18 Holes: Weekday: $29.00
Twilight Rates: Yes, after 7 pm
Cart Rental: No
Lessons: Yes **Schools:** No
Clinics: Yes **Day Camps** No
Other: Clubhouse / Lockers / Showers / Snack bar / Restaurant / Bar-lounge

Tees	Holes	Yards	Par	USGA	Slope
BACK	18	6604	71	71.9	124
MIDDLE	18	6198	71	70.2	121
FRONT	18	5569	72	72.7	131

Weekend: $16.00
Weekend: $32.00
All Day Play: No
Discounts: Sr & Jr Weekdays
Junior Golf: Yes **Membership:** Season Pass
Driving Range: Irons only

Sig. Hole: #5 is an uphill par 5 with a 350 year old oak tree guarding the left side of the fairway. Open year round, weather permitting. Ranked top 10 public by *Connecticut Magazine*.

	1	2	3	4	5	6	7	8	9
PAR	4	3	4	4	5	3	4	4	4
YARDS	352	183	395	326	497	147	415	400	353
HDCP	9	11	7	13	1	17	3	5	15

	10	11	12	13	14	15	16	17	18
PAR	5	3	4	4	4	4	4	3	5
YARDS	516	163	357	336	364	374	361	172	487
HDCP	2	16	6	14	4	8	12	18	10

Directions: From I-91 South: Exit 19. Right off ramp to first stop sign. Right on Bee Street, course 1/2 mile on left. From I-91 North or Merit Parkway North: Take East Main Street exit. Go straight through light onto Bee Street. Course 2 miles on left.

Indian Springs GC

Middlefield, CT (860) 349-8109 .... 23 ▶

Club Pro: Lou Wanser, PGA
Pro Shop: Yes
Payment: Cash/ Credit Cards
Tee Times: Weekends only
Fee 9 Holes: Weekday: $14.00
Fee 18 Holes: Weekday: $25.00
Twilight Rates: No
Cart Rental: $13.00pp/18 $6.50pp/9
Lessons: Variable **Schools:** Yes
Clinics: Junior **Day Camps** Yes
Other: Snack bar / Bar-lounge / Restaurant

Tees	Holes	Yards	Par	USGA	Slope
BACK	9	2961	36		
MIDDLE	9	3000	36	68.9	116
FRONT	9	2616	36	73.0	127

Weekend: $16.00
Weekend: $28.00
All Day Play: No
Discounts: Senior & Junior
Junior Golf: Yes **Membership:** Yes
Driving Range: $9/lg $5/sm

COUPON

5th is our famous "glass hill", a 560 yard par 5 with a steep drop to the green. Gorgeous views! Family-run golf course where you'll feel welcome. Jane's perennial flower gardens. Full practice facilitlies.

	1	2	3	4	5	6	7	8	9
PAR	4	5	3	4	5	4	3	4	4
YARDS	345	455	130	370	560	300	170	355	315
HDCP	7	5	17	13	3	9	15	1	11
	10	11	12	13	14	15	16	17	18
PAR									
YARDS									
HDCP									

Directions: Take I-91 North to Exit 20 (Route 66) toward Middletown. At light, take a right onto Route 147. Take 1st left onto Way Rd. Follow signs to course. Take I-91 South to Exit 19, left at stop sign. Left light. Take a right at light onto Route 147. Go 2 miles onto Way Road. Follow signs to course.

Laurel View CC

Hamden, CT (203) 287-2656 .... 24 ▶
www.laurelviewcc.com

Club Pro: Matt Menchetti, PGA
Pro Shop: Full inventory
Payment: Visa, MC
Tee Times: Weekends, 3 days adv.
Fee 9 Holes: Weekday: $18.00
Fee 18 Holes: Weekday: $26.00
Twilight Rates: No
Cart Rental: $24.00/18 $15.00/9
Lessons: $40.00/half hour **Schools:** No
Clinics: Jr/Ladies **Day Camps** No
Other: Clubhouse / Lockers / Showers / Snack bar / Restaurant / Bar-lounge

Tees	Holes	Yards	Par	USGA	Slope
BACK	18	6899	72	74.3	135
MIDDLE	18	6372	72	72.1	131
FRONT	18	5558	73	71.8	130

Weekend: $20.00
Weekend: $32.00
All Day Play: Yes
Discounts: Senior & Junior
Junior Golf: Yes **Membership:** Yes, Residents
Driving Range: $5.00/lg

This Cornish course requires maintenance, hilly terrain provides interesting challenge. Open April 1 - December 1. Many favorable comments. Greatly improved fairways, greens, bunkers and tees.

	1	2	3	4	5	6	7	8	9
PAR	4	3	4	5	4	4	3	5	4
YARDS	330	132	390	505	435	310	230	510	420
HDCP	15	17	3	5	1	13	11	7	9
	10	11	12	13	14	15	16	17	18
PAR	4	5	3	4	5	4	4	3	4
YARDS	320	560	155	280	470	380	390	160	395
HDCP	12	2	16	14	8	4	6	18	10

Directions: Take I-91 to Exit 10, take left at the end of the ramp. At first light take left, right at next light (Dixwell Avenue). Through center of town, pass Town Hall on the right. 3/4 mile, take right (Shephard Avenue) Through 5 lights, take left (W. Shephard.) Course 3/4 mile on left.

**SW
CT**

4✪ =Excellent 3✪ =Very Good 2✪ =Good

Leisure Resort At Banner Lodge

10 Banner Rd., Moodus, CT (860) 873-9075

Tees	Holes	Yards	Par	USGA	Slope
BACK					
MIDDLE	18	6015	72	68.9	118
FRONT	18	5776	74	73.7	123

Club Pro: Bill Phaneuf
Pro Shop: Complete for men and women
Payment: Cash, Check, MC, Visa, Amex, Disc.
Tee Times: Call Pro Shop
Fee 9 Holes: Weekday: $12.00
Fee 18 Holes: Weekday: $24.00
Twilight Rates: N/R
Cart Rental: $24.00/18 $12.00/9
Lessons: $30.00/30 minutes **Schools:** Yes
Clinics: Yes **Day Camps** No
Other: Clubhouse / Snack Bar / Restaurant

Weekend: $12.00
Weekend: $24.00
All Day Play: N/R
Discounts: Senior & Junior M-Th
Junior Golf: No **Membership:** Yes
Driving Range: $5.00

Improved watering on course, expanded tees, yardage markers, expanded Pro shop. New low green fees, clinics. Ladies Night-$10, cart included. All you play from 5pm til dark. Friendly, helpful staff.

	1	2	3	4	5	6	7	8	9
PAR	4	4	4	4	3	5	5	3	4
YARDS	375	320	406	324	125	477	485	154	347
HDCP	9	13	3	11	17	5	1	15	7
	10	11	12	13	14	15	16	17	18
PAR	5	4	4	4	4	3	5	3	4
YARDS	475	318	366	288	422	144	501	154	341
HDCP	6	12	8	14	4	16	2	18	10

Directions: Take CT Route 9 to Exit 7; follow Route 82 East to Route 149 North. Continue to center of Moodus. Follow signs to course.

Longshore Park

Westport, CT (203) 341-1833

Tees	Holes	Yards	Par	USGA	Slope
BACK	18	5845	69	67.4	115
MIDDLE	18	5676	69	66.7	113
FRONT	18	5227	73	69.9	119

Club Pro: John Cooper, PGA
Pro Shop: Full inventory
Payment: Cash, Check
Tee Times: 3 days adv.
Fee 9 Holes: Weekday: $27.00
Fee 18 Holes: Weekday: $38.00
Twilight Rates: No
Cart Rental: $26.00/18 $17.00/9
Lessons: Yes **Schools:** No
Clinics: Junior **Day Camps** No
Other: Snack bar / Restaurant / Bar-lounge

Weekend: N/A
Weekend: $44.00
All Day Play: No
Discounts: None
Junior Golf: Yes **Membership:** No
Driving Range: Yes

Sig. Hole: #2, 146 yard par 3. Good course for beginners. Must play with a resident with photo pass issued by Wesport Parks & Rec. Dept.

	1	2	3	4	5	6	7	8	9
PAR	4	3	4	4	4	4	5	3	4
YARDS	341	146	390	287	296	413	520	127	346
HDCP	9	13	5	15	11	1	3	17	7
	10	11	12	13	14	15	16	17	18
PAR	5	3	4	3	4	3	4	4	4
YARDS	459	192	289	189	401	166	383	344	397
HDCP	8	14	18	12	4	16	6	10	2

Directions: Take I-95 to Exit 18 to U.S. Route 1, left at 2nd light, Green Farms Road. Follow to next light, take left onto Compo. Course is on right.

Lyman Orchards GC (Jones) ⭐⭐

Middlefield, CT (860) 349-1793
www.lymanorchards.com

Club Pro: Dick Bierkan
Pro Shop: Full inventory
Payment: Visa, MC, Amex, Disc
Tee Times: 7 days adv. (888) 99Lyman

Tees	Holes	Yards	Par	USGA	Slope
BACK	18	7011	72	73.2	129
MIDDLE	18	6614	72	71.2	127
FRONT	18	6200	72	69.3	123

Fee 9 Holes: Weekday: $18 M-Th, walk   **Weekend:** $25.00
Fee 18 Holes: Weekday: $35 M-Th, walk   **Weekend:** $48.00
Twilight Rates: Yes, after 3 pm   **All Day Play:** No
Cart Rental: $14pp/18 $7pp/9   **Discounts:** Senior & Junior
Lessons: $70.00/ **Schools:** Yes   **Junior Golf:** Yes **Membership:** Yes
Clinics: Yes **Day Camps** Yes   **Driving Range:** Yes
Other: Clubhouse / Lockers / Showers / Snack bar / Restaurant / Bar-lounge

Each hole designed by Jones to be a demanding par or a comfortable bogey. Bent grass fairways and Penn Cross tees and greens. Mon-Th Early Bird before 7 am. Open Mar- Nov.

	1	2	3	4	5	6	7	8	9
PAR	4	3	4	5	4	4	3	4	5
YARDS	416	175	374	552	390	350	175	373	548
HDCP	3	17	1	9	5	13	15	11	7

	10	11	12	13	14	15	16	17	18
PAR	4	3	5	4	4	4	4	3	5
YARDS	399	152	490	370	388	382	403	162	515
HDCP	8	18	14	10	4	6	2	16	12

Directions: Take I-91 to Exit 15 (Route 68 East). Left onto Route 157. Course is 1 mile on the right.

Lyman Orchards GC (Player)

Middlefield, CT (860) 349-1793
www.lymanorchards.com

Club Pro: Dick Bierkan
Pro Shop: Full inventory
Payment: Visa, MC, Amex, Disc
Tee Times: 7 days adv. (888) 99LYMAU

Tees	Holes	Yards	Par	USGA	Slope
BACK	18	6725	71	73.1	134
MIDDLE	18	6325	71	71.3	131
FRONT	18	5763	71	68.1	129

Fee 9 Holes: Weekday: $18 M-Th walk   **Weekend:** $25.00
Fee 18 Holes: Weekday: $35 M-Th walk   **Weekend:** $48.00
Twilight Rates: Yes, after 3 pm   **All Day Play:** No
Cart Rental: $14pp/18 $7pp/9   **Discounts:** Senior & Junior
Lessons: $70.00/ hour **Schools:** Yes   **Junior Golf:** Yes **Membership:** Yes
Clinics: Yes **Day Camps** Yes   **Driving Range:** Yes
Other: Clubhouse / Lockers / Showers / Snack bar / Restaurant / Bar-lounge

Player's Comment: "Beautiful layout, stresses good shot making." Mon-Th Early Bird before 7 am. Open March - November.

	1	2	3	4	5	6	7	8	9
PAR	4	4	4	3	4	4	3	5	4
YARDS	400	367	374	173	386	342	191	578	381
HDCP	9	11	3	17	7	5	15	1	13

	10	11	12	13	14	15	16	17	18
PAR	4	3	4	3	5	4	3	5	5
YARDS	348	211	427	181	473	306	165	520	502
HDCP	2	14	4	16	12	10	18	8	6

Directions: Take I-91 to Exit 15 (Route 68 East). Left onto Route 157. Course is 1 mile on the right.

SW CT

4⭐ =Excellent 3⭐ =Very Good 2⭐ = Good

Meadowbrook CC

Hamden, CT (203) 281-4847

Club Pro: Sonny Chandler
Pro Shop: Limited inventory
Payment: Cash only
Tee Times: No
Fee 9 Holes: Weekday: $10.00
Fee 18 Holes: Weekday: $15.00
Twilight Rates: No
Cart Rental: $20.00/18 $10.00/9
Lessons: Yes **Schools:** No
Clinics: No **Day Camps** No
Other: Clubhouse / Snack bar

Tees	Holes	Yards	Par	USGA	Slope
BACK					
MIDDLE	9	2758	35		
FRONT	9	2121	35		

Weekend: $12.00
Weekend: $17.00
All Day Play: No
Discounts: Sr & Jr Weekdays
Junior Golf: No **Membership:** Yes
Driving Range: No

Good practice course. New tees added. Open year round.

	1	2	3	4	5	6	7	8	9
PAR	4	3	5	4	4	4	4	4	3
YARDS	315	103	448	390	303	333	365	324	177
HDCP	7	17	1	3	11	5	9	13	15
	10	**11**	**12**	**13**	**14**	**15**	**16**	**17**	**18**
PAR									
YARDS									
HDCP									

Directions: Take Wilbur Cross Parkway (Route 15) to Exit 60 toward center of Hamden. Course is right on Dixwell. Next to Miller Memorial Library.

Miner Hills Family Golf, LLC

Middletown, CT (860)635-0051

Club Pro: No
Pro Shop: Limited inventory
Payment: Cash, Check
Tee Times: Available
Fee 9 Holes: Weekday: $11.00
Fee 18 Holes: Weekday: $18.00
Twilight Rates: No
Cart Rental: $20.00/18 $10.00/9
Lessons: Yes **Schools:** No
Clinics: No **Day Camps** No
Other: Club house / Snack bar

Tees	Holes	Yards	Par	USGA	Slope
BACK	9	1756	30	59.1	97
MIDDLE			30		
FRONT	9	1292	30	59.5	80

Weekend: $13.00
Weekend: $23.00
All Day Play: No
Discounts: Senior & Junior
Junior Golf: No **Membership:** Season Passes
Driving Range: Yes

COUPON

"A delightful surprise with several interesting holes. A great executive layout and well-maintained" A.P. Open Mar 25 untill weather premits.

	1	2	3	4	5	6	7	8	9
PAR	3	3	4	4	3	3	4	3	3
YARDS	160	150	298	253	173	210	260	120	145
HDCP	7	8	4	9	6	5	3	2	1
	10	**11**	**12**	**13**	**14**	**15**	**16**	**17**	**18**
PAR									
YARDS									
HDCP									

Directions: Exit 20 off I-91. Westfield district of Middletown, CT.

Oak Hills Park G.C.

Fillow St., Norwalk, CT (203) 838-1015
www.oakhillsgc.com

Club Pro: Vincent Grillo, PGA
Pro Shop: Full inventory
Payment: Cash, Check
Tee Times: M-F 7 days S/S 3 days
Fee 9 Holes: Weekday: No
Fee 18 Holes: Weekday: $40.00
Twilight Rates: Yes, after 4 pm
Cart Rental: $25.00/18
Lessons: Call 853-8400 **Schools:** No
Clinics: No **Day Camps** No
Other: Snack bar

Tees	Holes	Yards	Par	USGA	Slope
BACK	18	6307	71	70.5	126
MIDDLE	18	5920	71	68.5	123
FRONT	18	5221	72	70.7	124

Weekend: No
Weekend: $45.00
All Day Play: N/R
Discounts: Sr & Jr residents M-F
Junior Golf: No **Membership:** Yes
Driving Range: No

Sig. Hole: #9, 456 yard par 4 with a well-bunkered, elevated green. Front nine hilly, woods and a lot of water. Back nine flatter and more open.

	1	2	3	4	5	6	7	8	9
PAR	4	4	3	4	3	4	4	5	4
YARDS	374	295	109	307	174	284	336	484	440
HDCP	7	11	17	9	15	13	3	5	1

	10	11	12	13	14	15	16	17	18
PAR	5	4	5	3	4	3	4	4	4
YARDS	528	365	501	154	386	205	342	336	300
HDCP	4	14	8	18	2	12	10	6	16

Directions: I-95, Exit 13. Right turn onto Route 1. Left onto Richards Avenue; right turn onto Fillow to Oak Hills Park.

Orange Hills CC

Racebrook Rd., Orange, CT (203) 795-4161
www.orangehillcountryclub.com

Club Pro:
Pro Shop: Full inventory
Payment: Visa, MC
Tee Times: M-F 7 days S/S 3 days
Fee 9 Holes: Weekday: $20.00
Fee 18 Holes: Weekday: $35.00
Twilight Rates: No
Cart Rental: $28.00/18 $14.00/9
Lessons: No **Schools:** No
Clinics: No **Day Camps** No
Other: Clubhouse / Snack bar / Bar-lounge / Restaurant

Tees	Holes	Yards	Par	USGA	Slope
BACK	18	6499	71	72.3	126
MIDDLE	18	6101	71	70.6	119
FRONT	18	5616	74	71.5	120

Weekend: $24.00
Weekend: $45.00
All Day Play: No
Discounts: None
Junior Golf: Yes **Membership:** No
Driving Range: No

Sig. Hole: #12, 365 yd. par 4, requires shot accuracy and strategic placement. Course is hilly with a tight back nine. Call for directions from Hartford. Collared shirts and soft spikes required.

	1	2	3	4	5	6	7	8	9
PAR	4	5	3	4	4	4	4	4	3
YARDS	390	481	148	435	349	365	399	300	134
HDCP	9	5	17	3	11	7	1	13	15

	10	11	12	13	14	15	16	17	18
PAR	3	5	4	3	4	4	4	4	5
YARDS	207	466	365	153	377	339	321	413	459
HDCP	16	10	2	18	12	4	8	6	14

Directions: Merrit Pkwy: Exit 57, 2 lights to Rte 114, right onto Rte 114, 1.75 miles on left. From NYC: I-95 N, Exit 41, left off ramp. 4 lights to U.S. 1. Right onto U.S. 1, one block to Racebrook Rd. Left onto Racebrook Rd. 1/4 mile on right.

**SW
CT**

4✪ =Excellent 3✪ =Very Good 2✪ =Good

Pequabuck Golf Course ✪✪ 33

School St., Pequabuck, CT (860) 583-7307
www.pequabuckgolf.com

Club Pro: Richard Toner, PGA
Pro Shop: Full inventory
Payment: Cash, Check
Tee Times: Yes

Tees	Holes	Yards	Par	USGA	Slope
BACK	18	6015	69	70.2	118
MIDDLE	18	5692	69	68.7	115
FRONT	18	5388	72	70.3	118

Fee 9 Holes: Weekday: $20.00 **Weekend:** $20.00
Fee 18 Holes: Weekday: $40.00 **Weekend:** $40.00
Twilight Rates: No **All Day Play:** No
Cart Rental: $7.50pp **Discounts:** None
Lessons: $30.00/half hour **Schools:** No **Junior Golf:** Yes **Membership:** Yes
Clinics: No **Day Camps** No **Driving Range:** Yes
Other: Restaurant / Clubhouse / Bar-Lounge / Snack Bar

Front nine open, back nine tree-lined with difficult greens. Known for perfect fairways and greens. Great corporate guest opportunities for up to 16 guests. Dress code.

	1	2	3	4	5	6	7	8	9
PAR	4	4	5	3	4	3	5	3	4
YARDS	286	424	470	169	322	155	465	174	371
HDCP	14	2	6	18	12	16	4	10	8

	10	11	12	13	14	15	16	17	18
PAR	3	4	4	4	4	4	3	4	4
YARDS	190	406	377	329	401	337	155	328	333
HDCP	9	1	5	13	3	11	17	7	15

Directions: I-84 to Route Exit 72. Follow Route 72 into Terryville. Go under railroad bridge. Take right onto School Street. Follow to club.

Pine Valley Golf Course ✪✪ 34

Welch St., Southington, CT (860) 628-0879

Club Pro: Jack McConachie
Pro Shop: Full inventory
Payment: Cash, Visa, MC
Tee Times: M-F 7 days S/S 3 days

Tees	Holes	Yards	Par	USGA	Slope
BACK	18	6325	71	70.6	123
MIDDLE	18	6043	71	70.1	117
FRONT	18	5482	73	72.0	122

Fee 9 Holes: Weekday: $17.50 **Weekend:** $20.00
Fee 18 Holes: Weekday: $31.00 **Weekend:** $36.00
Twilight Rates: No **All Day Play:** Yes
Cart Rental: $27.00/18 $14.00/9 **Discounts:** None
Lessons: $30.00/half hour **Schools:** No **Junior Golf:** Yes **Membership:** No
Clinics: Junior **Day Camps** No **Driving Range:** No
Other: Clubhouse / Lockers / Showers / Snack bar / Restaurant / Bar-lounge / Practice sand trap

Hilly front nine, while the back nine are more level with water holes and very tight greens. Accuracy is essential. Dress code. Credit cards for merchandise only.

	1	2	3	4	5	6	7	8	9
PAR	5	4	3	4	4	4	5	3	4
YARDS	497	404	125	345	345	291	505	141	405
HDCP	8	4	16	12	14	10	6	18	2

	10	11	12	13	14	15	16	17	18
PAR	3	4	5	4	4	3	5	4	3
YARDS	170	366	510	426	353	160	476	340	180
HDCP	17	5	7	1	3	9	11	15	13

Directions: Take I-84 to Exit 31 North on Route 229 1.5 miles. Left onto Welch Rd. Course is 1/2 miles on left.

Pomperaug Golf Club

Southbury, CT (203) 264-9484
www.pomperauggolf.com

Club Pro: Greg Miller
Pro Shop: Yes
Payment: Yes
Tee Times: 3 days adv.

Tees	Holes	Yards	Par	USGA	Slope
BACK	9	3025	35	68.7	111
MIDDLE	9	2750	35	67.5	105
FRONT	9	2234	36	70.0	113

Fee 9 Holes: Weekday: $25.00
Fee 18 Holes: Weekday: $37.00
Twilight Rates: No
Cart Rental: $13pp/18 $9pp/9
Lessons: $40/45 minutes **Schools:** N/R
Clinics: N/R **Day Camps** No
Other: Hotel / Cooler / Beverage cart / Stay & Play packages

Weekend: $27.00
Weekend: $40.00
All Day Play: No
Discounts: None
Junior Golf: No **Membership:** Yes
Driving Range: Practice Green

COUPON

Semi-private course. Heritage International Hotel on premises. Dress code.

	1	2	3	4	5	6	7	8	9
PAR	4	4	4	4	3	4	5	3	4
YARDS	330	356	263	411	174	316	429	166	305
HDCP	5	3	17	1	13	7	11	15	9
	10	11	12	13	14	15	16	17	18
PAR									
YARDS									
HDCP									

Directions: From Hartford take I-84 West to Route 67, Southbury, Exit 15. At 2nd light, take left onto Heritage Rd. The Heritage is 1 mile ahead on right.

Portland Golf Club

✪✪

Bartlett St., Portland, CT (860) 342-6107

Club Pro: Mark Sloan, PGA
Pro Shop: Full inventory
Payment: Cash only
Tee Times: 7 days adv.

Tees	Holes	Yards	Par	USGA	Slope
BACK	18	6213	71	70.5	127
MIDDLE	18	5802	71	68.7	123
FRONT	18	5039	71	68.6	118

Fee 9 Holes: Weekday: $17.00
Fee 18 Holes: Weekday: $33.00
Twilight Rates: No
Cart Rental: $24.00/18 $12.00/9
Lessons: $35.00/30 minutes **Schools:** No
Clinics: N/R **Day Camps** No
Other: Clubhouse / Lockers / Showers / Snack bar / Restaurant / Bar-lounge

Weekend: $20.00
Weekend: $38.00
All Day Play: No
Discounts: Senior & Junior
Junior Golf: Yes **Membership:** No
Driving Range: No

Sig. Hole: #18 tempts you with a fairway trap going full width of fairway between 180 and 210 yards from tee. Lay up or hill it one last time. March 15 - January 1.

	1	2	3	4	5	6	7	8	9
PAR	4	5	4	3	4	4	4	3	4
YARDS	365	485	350	166	270	287	351	140	301
HDCP	2	8	4	10	14	18	6	16	12
	10	11	12	13	14	15	16	17	18
PAR	4	4	5	4	3	4	5	3	4
YARDS	303	373	489	377	177	360	471	165	372
HDCP	13	5	11	1	15	7	9	17	3

Directions: Take Route 2 to 17 South (left at exit); 9.5 miles down take left on Bartlett; course is less than 1 mile.

SW CT

Portland West Golf Club ✪✪✪

Gospel Lane, Portland, CT (860) 342-6111

Tees	Holes	Yards	Par	USGA	Slope
BACK	18	4012	60	60.5	102
MIDDLE	18	3620	60	59.3	100
FRONT	18	3154	60	58.4	87

Club Pro: Gerald J. D'Amora, PGA
Pro Shop: Full inventory
Payment: Cash only
Tee Times: 7 days adv.
Fee 9 Holes: Weekday: $13.00
Fee 18 Holes: Weekday: $25.00
Twilight Rates: No
Cart Rental: $22.00/18 $12.00/9
Lessons: $40/half hour **Schools:** No
Clinics: Junior **Day Camps** No
Other: Restaurant / Bar-lounge / Snack Bar

Weekend: $15.50
Weekend: $28.00
All Day Play: No
Discounts: Senior Wkdays
Junior Golf: Yes **Membership:** No
Driving Range: Yes

Players' Comment: "Excellent greens and fairways." . The 18th hole proves to be a difficult home stretch. A challenging executive par 60 course. Nice scenery and fair prices. "

	1	2	3	4	5	6	7	8	9
PAR	3	3	3	4	3	4	3	3	4
YARDS	148	130	145	264	140	339	113	137	351
HDCP	5	9	7	15	11	1	17	13	3
	10	11	12	13	14	15	16	17	18
PAR	4	3	3	3	3	3	4	4	3
YARDS	341	135	161	114	185	122	319	293	183
HDCP	2	18	6	10	8	14	16	12	4

Directions: Take I-91 to Route 9 to Route 66; left onto Route 17 (Gospel Lane); course is 1/2 mile on right.

Quarry Ridge GC ✪✪

Rose Hill Rd., Portland, CT (860) 342-6113
www.quarryridge.com

Tees	Holes	Yards	Par	USGA	Slope
BACK	18	6369	72	70.6	121
MIDDLE	18	5900	72	68.4	114
FRONT	18	4948	72	70.268.7	117

Club Pro: John Lucas, Jr.
Pro Shop: Yes
Payment: Cash, Check, Visa, MC
Tee Times: 1 week adv.
Fee 9 Holes: Weekday: $24.00
Fee 18 Holes: Weekday: $44.00
Twilight Rates: No
Cart Rental: Included
Lessons: $45.00/half hour **Schools:** No
Clinics: No **Day Camps** No
Other: Restaurant / Clubhouse / Bar-Lounge

Weekend: $26.00
Weekend: $49.00
All Day Play: No
Discounts: Senior & Junior
Junior Golf: No **Membership:** No
Driving Range: No

Players' Comments: "Challenging, with tight fairways and small greens. Scenic views of Connecticut River Valley. ""Difficult, but popular. Well maintained." "Great layout."

	1	2	3	4	5	6	7	8	9
PAR	4	3	4	5	4	5	4	4	3
YARDS	345	144	383	463	337	448	335	343	178
HDCP	13	17	1	5	11	3	7	9	15
	10	11	12	13	14	15	16	17	18
PAR	4	5	4	4	3	4	3	5	4
YARDS	311	443	403	293	145	337	138	459	395
HDCP	12	6	2	14	16	10	18	4	8

Directions: From Hartford: Route 2 to Route 17 (left Exit 7.) Go 9 miles; take left onto Bartlett Street, go to end. Cross road to driveway of golf course.

Richter Park GC

⬭⬭⬭⬭

Danbury, CT (203) 792-2550
www.richterpark.com

Club Pro: Ralph Salito Jr., PGA
Pro Shop: Full inventory
Payment: MC, Visa, Cash
Tee Times: 3 days adv. (203) 748- 5743
Fee 9 Holes: Weekday: No
Fee 18 Holes: Weekday: $57.00
Twilight Rates: Yes, after 4 pm
Cart Rental: $26.00/18 $16.00/9
Lessons: $40.00/half hour **Schools:** Yes
Clinics: Yes **Day Camps** Yes
Other: Clubhouse / Lockers / Showers / Snack bar / Restaurant / Bar-lounge

Tees	Holes	Yards	Par	USGA	Slope
BACK	18	6744	72	73.3	134
MIDDLE	18	6304	72	71.6	128
FRONT	18	5114	72	69.8	126

Weekend: No
Weekend: $57.00
All Day Play:
Discounts: Senior & Junior
Junior Golf: Yes **Membership:** Yes
Driving Range: No

Course keeps a reputation for making even the most skillful golfers work hard: narrow fairways, approach shots require precision, water hazards on 14 fairways. "Very challenging and difficult." **Player's Comments.**

	1	2	3	4	5	6	7	8	9
PAR	4	5	3	4	3	4	5	4	4
YARDS	372	491	150	389	170	388	507	335	314
HDCP	11	9	17	3	15	1	7	5	13

	10	11	12	13	14	15	16	17	18
PAR	4	4	5	3	4	4	5	3	4
YARDS	345	360	495	142	395	324	570	152	426
HDCP	10	12	6	16	8	14	2	18	4

Directions: I-84 West to Exit 2 or I-84 East to Exit 2B. Take right off ramp (Mill Plain Rd.); take second left onto Aunt Hack Rd. to course.

Ridgefield Golf Club

Ridgefield, CT (203) 748-7008

Club Pro: Frank Sergiovanni
Pro Shop: Full inventory
Payment: Cash, Check, Visa
Tee Times: Yes
Fee 9 Holes: Weekday: N/A
Fee 18 Holes: Weekday: $40.00
Twilight Rates: After 4 pm
Cart Rental: $24.00/18
Lessons: Yes **Schools:** No
Clinics: Yes **Day Camps** No
Other: Snack bar / Bar-Lounge

Tees	Holes	Yards	Par	USGA	Slope
BACK	18	6444	71	70.9	123
MIDDLE	18	6019	71	68.9	120
FRONT	18	5124	74	70.6	119

Weekend: N/A
Weekend: $45.00
All Day Play: No
Discounts: Sr & Jr Weekdays
Junior Golf: Yes **Membership:** N/R
Driving Range: $7.00/lg. $4.00/sm.

Excellent condition. Called a "Hidden jewel" by *Golf Digest.*

	1	2	3	4	5	6	7	8	9
PAR	4	4	3	4	3	5	4	4	4
YARDS	408	411	163	344	147	542	412	411	378
HDCP	12	8	16	14	18	2	10	4	6

	10	11	12	13	14	15	16	17	18
PAR	5	4	3	4	5	4	4	3	4
YARDS	564	311	147	351	469	395	311	127	386
HDCP	3	11	15	9	7	1	13	17	5

Directions: Take Exit 1 off I-84; Saw Mill Rd. to Old Ridgebury Rd. Course is on Old Ridgebury.

SW CT

4⬭ =Excellent **3**⬭ =Very Good **2**⬭ =Good

Short Beach Par 3 Golf Course

Stratford, CT (203) 381-2070
golf@townofstafford.com

Club Pro: Michael Gaffney
Pro Shop: Limited inventory
Payment: Personal checks, cash
Tee Times: 2 days adv. wknds
Fee 9 Holes: Weekday: $10.00
Fee 18 Holes: Weekday: $15.00
Twilight Rates: No
Cart Rental: $6pp/9
Lessons: Yes **Schools:** No
Clinics: No **Day Camps** No
Other: Snack Bar/ Mini. Golf course

Tees	Holes	Yards	Par	USGA	Slope
BACK	9	1369	27		
MIDDLE	9	1270	27		
FRONT	9	1162	27		

Weekend: $12.00
Weekend: N/A
All Day Play: No
Discounts: Senior & Junior
Junior Golf: Yes **Membership:** N/A
Driving Range: No

Par 3 nine holes on beachfront. Architect - Geoffrey Cornish. Proper attire required. Resident discounts. Open March - January.

	1	2	3	4	5	6	7	8	9
PAR	3	3	3	3	3	3	3	3	3
YARDS	125	154	98	170	88	130	218	162	125
HDCP									
	10	11	12	13	14	15	16	17	18
PAR									
YARDS									
HDCP									

Directions: Call for directions.

Sleeping Giant GC

Hamden, CT (203) 281-9456

Club Pro: Carl Swanson
Pro Shop: Full inventory
Payment: Cash only
Tee Times: No
Fee 9 Holes: Weekday: $15.00
Fee 18 Holes: Weekday: $26.00
Twilight Rates: No
Cart Rental: $20.00/18,$12.00/9
Lessons: $30/half hr, $50 hr **Schools:** No
Clinics: No **Day Camps** No
Other: Restaurant nearby

Tees	Holes	Yards	Par	USGA	Slope
BACK	9	2671	36	65.4	99
MIDDLE	9	2457	36	63.4	96
FRONT	9	2216	37	64.6	104

Weekend: $17.00
Weekend: $30.00
All Day Play: No
Discounts: Sr. Weekdays
Junior Golf: No **Membership:** No
Driving Range: Yes

"A nice little well-maintained course that is pure fun. The views of Sleeping Giant Mlountain enhance the aesthetics. #3 is a nice par 3 to a punchbowl green" - A.P. Open March - Nov.

	1	2	3	4	5	6	7	8	9
PAR	3	5	3	4	5	4	4	4	4
YARDS	125	399	170	305	375	331	199	217	336
HDCP	9	2	8	4	1	5	7	6	3
	10	11	12	13	14	15	16	17	18
PAR									
YARDS									
HDCP									

Directions: Take I-91 to Exit 10. Right onto Whitney Avenue. Course is 3 miles on the right.

South Pine Creek Par 3 GC

Fairfield, CT (203) 256-3173

Club Pro: Sean Garrity, PGA
Pro Shop:
Payment: Cash only
Tee Times: 5 days adv
Fee 9 Holes: Weekday: $14.00
Fee 18 Holes: Weekday: N/A
Twilight Rates: No
Cart Rental: $2.00 pull cart
Lessons: No **Schools:** No
Clinics: No **Day Camps** No
Other: Snacks

Tees	Holes	Yards	Par	USGA	Slope
BACK					
MIDDLE	9	1240	27		
FRONT	9	1073	27		

Weekend: $18.00
Weekend: N/A
All Day Play: No
Discounts: Senior & Junior
Junior Golf: No **Membership:** No
Driving Range:

Residents half price! Great place to learn the game.

	1	2	3	4	5	6	7	8	9
PAR	3	3	3	3	3	3	3	3	3
YARDS	143	145	120	166	153	117	121	187	90
HDCP	6	5	8	3	1	7	4	2	9
	10	11	12	13	14	15	16	17	18
PAR									
YARDS									
HDCP									

Directions: I-95S to Exit 21, Mill Plain Rd, Turn Left onto Post Rd. At first set of lights take left. Course is 1/2 mile on left.

Southington CC

Savage St., Southington, CT (860) 628-7032

Club Pro: None
Pro Shop: Limited inventory
Payment: Cash only
Tee Times: Weekends, 4 days adv.
Fee 9 Holes: Weekday: $16.00
Fee 18 Holes: Weekday: $28.00
Twilight Rates: No
Cart Rental: $27.00/18 $14.00/9
Lessons: No **Schools:** No
Clinics: No **Day Camps** No
Other: Snack bar / Bar-lounge

Tees	Holes	Yards	Par	USGA	Slope
BACK					
MIDDLE	18	5675	71	67.0	123
FRONT	18	5103	73	69.8	119

Weekend: $19.00
Weekend: $32.00
All Day Play: No
Discounts: Sr & Jr Weekdays
Junior Golf: No **Membership:** Yes
Driving Range: No

The course is level and considered an easy walker. Front nine is a bit more hilly. Open March - November.

	1	2	3	4	5	6	7	8	9
PAR	4	4	3	5	4	5	3	4	4
YARDS	377	306	144	481	387	508	192	338	324
HDCP	5	14	17	3	7	1	15	9	10
	10	11	12	13	14	15	16	17	18
PAR	4	4	3	4	5	3	4	3	5
YARDS	300	316	96	323	453	202	323	160	445
HDCP	12	13	18	6	2	11	8	16	4

Directions: Take I-84 to Exit 27 (Route 691), take Exit 3; turn left, at 2nd light bear right; next light take right; next light turn left; take 1st left onto Savage Street.

SW CT

Sterling Farms GC ⚫⚫ ▶ 45

Newfield Ave., Stamford, CT (203) 461-9090
www.sterlingfarmsgc.com

Club Pro: Angela Aulenti, PGA
Pro Shop: Full inventory
Payment: Cash only
Tee Times: 1 week adv.

Tees	Holes	Yards	Par	USGA	Slope
BACK	18	6310	72	70.7	127
MIDDLE	18	6082	72	69.7	123
FRONT	18	5500	73	71.7	125

Fee 9 Holes: Weekday: $30.00 (6-7:30am)   **Weekend:** $30.00 (6-7:30am)
Fee 18 Holes: Weekday: $50.00   **Weekend:** $50.00
Twilight Rates: Yes, after 4 pm   **All Day Play:** No
Cart Rental: $24.00/18 $15.00/9   **Discounts:** Sr & Jr Weekdays
Lessons: Call 203-329-7888 **Schools:** Yes   **Junior Golf:** Yes **Membership:** No
Clinics: N/R **Day Camps** Yes   **Driving Range:** Yes
Other: Restaurant

Course has hilly front 9; more level back 9. Two of the course's five lakes come into play on the 14th hole. Resident rates.

	1	2	3	4	5	6	7	8	9
PAR	4	5	4	4	3	5	4	3	4
YARDS	331	489	316	350	191	465	382	179	326
HDCP	17	9	15	5	3	7	1	13	11
	10	**11**	**12**	**13**	**14**	**15**	**16**	**17**	**18**
PAR	4	4	4	5	4	3	4	3	5
YARDS	397	307	341	477	393	147	301	215	475
HDCP	6	14	4	10	2	18	12	8	16

Directions: Merritt Pkwy S to Exit 35. Right onto High Ridge Rd. Left onto Vine (5 lights). Left at end to Newfield Ave. Club is 1/4 mi. on right.

Stonybrook GC ▶ 46

263 Milton Rd., Litchfield, CT (860) 567-9977

Club Pro: Rich Bredice
Pro Shop: Full inventory
Payment: Visa, MC
Tee Times: Weekends

Tees	Holes	Yards	Par	USGA	Slope
BACK	9	2986	35	70.4	115
MIDDLE	9	2878	35	69.0	111
FRONT	9	2669	36	71.6	123

Fee 9 Holes: Weekday: $17.00   **Weekend:** $20.00
Fee 18 Holes: Weekday: $32.00   **Weekend:** $38.00
Twilight Rates: No   **All Day Play:** Yes
Cart Rental: $7.50pp   **Discounts:** Junior
Lessons: $35.00/half hour **Schools:** No   **Junior Golf:** Yes **Membership:** Yes
Clinics: N/R **Day Camps** No   **Driving Range:** No
Other: Clubhouse / Snack bar / Bar-lounge / Lockers

Terrain is rolling; greens contoured (medium/fast).

	1	2	3	4	5	6	7	8	9
PAR	5	4	3	4	4	4	4	4	3
YARDS	530	374	150	366	325	300	375	295	163
HDCP	2	10	18	8	6	14	4	12	16
	10	**11**	**12**	**13**	**14**	**15**	**16**	**17**	**18**
PAR									
YARDS									
HDCP									

Directions: I-84 to Route 8 N. Take Litchfield Exit 42; follow signs to Litchfield Green (8 miles.) Take Route 202 W at stop sign by green. At fourth light, take right onto Milton Road. Course 2 miles on left.

Sunset Hill GC

Brookfield, CT (203) 740-7800
www.sunsethillgolfclub.com

Club Pro:
Pro Shop: Limited inventory
Payment: Cash, Check
Tee Times: No
Fee 9 Holes: Weekday: $20.00
Fee 18 Holes: Weekday: $20.00
Twilight Rates: Yes, after 4 pm
Cart Rental: $30.00/18 $15.00/9
Lessons: No **Schools:** No
Clinics: Yes **Day Camps** Yes
Other: Clubhouse / Snack bar / Bar-lounge

Tees	Holes	Yards	Par	USGA	Slope
BACK					
MIDDLE	9	4692	69	62.6	100
FRONT	9	4692	70	66.3	100

Weekend: $26.00
Weekend: $26.00
All Day Play: No
Discounts: Senior & Junior
Junior Golf: Yes **Membership:** Yes
Driving Range: No

COUPON

Sig.Hole: #3, par 116, is a pretty hole with elevated tees with a nice view. Open April - November.

	1	2	3	4	5	6	7	8	9
PAR	5	3	3	4	4	4	5	4	3
YARDS	452	145	116	278	304	270	426	278	125
HDCP	3	12	17	9	5	11	1	7	15
	10	11	12	13	14	15	16	17	18
PAR	5	3	3	4	4	4	4	4	3
YARDS	452	145	116	278	304	250	350	278	125
HDCP	4	14	18	10	6	12	2	8	16

Directions: Take I-84 to Exit 9; follow Route 25 North 3 miles; take left onto Sunset Hill Rd. to course.

Tashua Knolls CC

⊙⊙

Trumbull, CT (203) 452-5186

Club Pro: Sammy Samson , PGA
Pro Shop: Full inventory
Payment: Cash or check
Tee Times: 3 day adv.
Fee 9 Holes: Weekday: $22.00
Fee 18 Holes: Weekday: $36.00
Twilight Rates: No
Cart Rental: $26.00/18 $17.00/9
Lessons: $35.00/half hour **Schools:** No
Clinics: Junior **Day Camps** No
Other: Snack bar / Restaurant / Bar-lounge / Lockers / Showers

Tees	Holes	Yards	Par	USGA	Slope
BACK	18	6540	72	71.9	125
MIDDLE	18	6119	72	70.0	121
FRONT	18	5454	72	71.7	124

Weekend: $26.00 F/S/S
Weekend: $40.00 F/S/S
All Day Play: Yes
Discounts: Sr & Jr residents M-F
Junior Golf: Yes **Membership:** Men's Club
Driving Range: $6.00/lg. $3.00/sm.

Changes and improvements include new pro shop, friendly customer service and new professional. Resident rates.

	1	2	3	4	5	6	7	8	9
PAR	5	4	3	4	4	3	5	4	4
YARDS	532	317	151	342	353	192	480	354	356
HDCP	3	7	17	1	11	15	5	13	9
	10	11	12	13	14	15	16	17	18
PAR	4	4	3	4	5	4	5	3	4
YARDS	349	367	154	262	495	373	506	145	391
HDCP	10	12	18	14	2	8	4	16	6

Directions: Take Merritt Parkway (Route 15) to Exit 49 (Route 25); go straight, take left onto Tashua Knolls Lane. Course at top of hill.

SW CT

4⊙ =Excellent **3**⊙ = Very Good **2**⊙ = Good

The Orchards Golf Course

Milford, CT 203-877-8200

Club Pro:
Pro Shop: Yes
Payment: Cash only
Tee Times: 7days advance
Fee 9 Holes: Weekday: $13.40
Fee 18 Holes: Weekday: $25.80
Twilight Rates: No
Cart Rental: Pull carts, $3.25
Lessons: No **Schools:** No
Clinics: No **Day Camps** No
Other: Snacks

Tees	Holes	Yards	Par	USGA	Slope
BACK					
MIDDLE	9	1625	32		
FRONT	9	1433	32		

Weekend: $14.45
Weekend: $27.90
All Day Play: No
Discounts: Senior & Junior
Junior Golf: No **Membership:** No
Driving Range: Putting Green

Resident discounts. "Perfectly maintained executive course that plays through an apple orchard" A.P. New superintendent.

	1	2	3	4	5	6	7	8	9
PAR	4	3	4	4	4	3	3	3	4
YARDS	242	93	222	207	217	120	167	91	266
HDCP									
	10	11	12	13	14	15	16	17	18
PAR									
YARDS									
HDCP									

Directions: I 95, take Exit 39. Go South on Route 1 to Route 121 North (North Street). Turn right onto Kozlowski Rd.

Tradition Golf Course at Wallingford

Wallingford, CT (203) 269-6023
www.traditionalclubs.com

Club Pro: Bill Foreman, Dir. of Golf
Pro Shop: Full inventory
Payment: Cash only
Tee Times: 7 days adv.
Fee 9 Holes: Weekday: $16 M-Th, $25 F
Fee 18 Holes: Weekday: $45 M-Th, $49 F
Twilight Rates: Yes, after 6 pm
Cart Rental: $8pp/9
Lessons: Yes **Schools:** Yes
Clinics: Yes **Day Camps** Yes
Other: Bar-Lounge / Snack Bar / Banquet facility

Tees	Holes	Yards	Par	USGA	Slope
BACK	18	5772	70	68.8	121
MIDDLE	18	5398	70	66.9	119
FRONT	18	4458	70	68.4	116

Weekend: $22 w/cart S/S/H
Weekend: $59 w/cart S/S/H
All Day Play: Yes
Discounts: Senior & Junior
Junior Golf: Yes **Membership:** Yes
Driving Range: Yes

Players comments: "Well manicured greens. Great staff. Fairly priced." Dress code. Variety of special rates.

	1	2	3	4	5	6	7	8	9
PAR	5	4	3	4	4	4	3	4	4
YARDS	518	281	152	389	347	320	106	370	342
HDCP	10	12	16	2	14	6	18	4	8
	10	11	12	13	14	15	16	17	18
PAR	4	5	3	4	5	3	4	4	3
YARDS	256	447	140	392	535	123	326	275	105
HDCP	13	5	11	3	1	17	7	9	15

Directions: Take I-91 to Exit 14. Take right onto Route 150 towards Wallingford. Take right onto Harrison Road.

Twin Lakes GC

North Branford, CT (203) 488-8778
www.executivedecisionsgolf.com

Club Pro: Larry Thornhill, PGA
Pro Shop: Limited inventory
Payment: Cash only
Tee Times: N/A
Fee 9 Holes: Weekday: $8.00
Fee 18 Holes: Weekday: $13.00
Twilight Rates: No
Cart Rental: Pull carts $1.00
Lessons: No **Schools:** No
Clinics: No **Day Camps** No
Other: Snack Bar

Tees	Holes	Yards	Par	USGA	Slope
BACK					
MIDDLE	9	835	27		
FRONT					

Weekend: $10.00
Weekend: $15.00
All Day Play:
Discounts: None
Junior Golf: Yes **Membership:** No
Driving Range: No

Open March 15- Oct. 15. This is a very short, 9 hole pare 3 course good for family fun. Season passes for unlimited play.

	1	2	3	4	5	6	7	8	9
PAR	3	3	3	3	3	3	3	3	3
YARDS	118	98	86	84	85	88	134	80	78
HDCP									

	10	11	12	13	14	15	16	17	18
PAR									
YARDS									
HDCP									

Directions: From I-95, exit 55 on left . Take a left at first light.2 miles, Twin Lakes Rd. on left.

Western Hills GC

Waterbury, CT (203) 756-1211

Club Pro: Ralph Tremaglio
Pro Shop: Full inventory
Payment: Visa, MC
Tee Times: 3 days adv for wknds, 1day for wkdys.
Fee 9 Holes: Weekday: $16.00
Fee 18 Holes: Weekday: $25.00
Twilight Rates: No
Cart Rental: $25.00/18 $15.00/9
Lessons: Yes **Schools:** No
Clinics: No **Day Camps** No
Other: Clubhouse / Snack bar / Restaurant / Bar-lounge / Banquet / Lockers / Showers

Tees	Holes	Yards	Par	USGA	Slope
BACK	18	6356	72	69.5	120
MIDDLE	18	6136	72	68.5	118
FRONT	18	5237	72	69.5	127

COUPON

Weekend: $17.00
Weekend: $27.00
All Day Play: No
Discounts: Junior
Junior Golf: Yes **Membership:** Yes
Driving Range: No

Scenic New England golf course with a variety of terrain and vistas. A good test of golf.

	1	2	3	4	5	6	7	8	9
PAR	4	5	4	4	3	4	5	4	3
YARDS	354	458	356	340	162	374	527	387	145
HDCP	7	9	5	4	17	8	11	2	16

	10	11	12	13	14	15	16	17	18
PAR	4	3	4	5	4	5	3	4	4
YARDS	363	138	305	495	391	480	153	381	327
HDCP	6	18	10	12	1	13	15	3	14

SW CT

Directions: Take I-84 to Exit 17. Follow Route 63 North to Park Road. Right on Park Road to stop sign. Left at stop sign to clubhouse.

4🟢 =Excellent 3🟢 =Very Good 2🟢 =Good

Whitney Farms

Monroe, CT (203) 268-0707

Tees	Holes	Yards	Par	USGA	Slope
BACK	18	6628	72	72.4	134
MIDDLE	18	6262	72	70.9	129
FRONT	18	5832	73	72.9	135

Club Pro: Paul McGuire
Pro Shop: Full inventory
Payment: Visa, MC, Amex
Tee Times: Yes
Fee 9 Holes: Weekday: $27.00   **Weekend:** $30.00 with cart
Fee 18 Holes: Weekday: $50.00   **Weekend:** $60.00 with cart
Twilight Rates: No   **All Day Play:** No
Cart Rental: Included   **Discounts:** Senior
Lessons: $50.00/half hour **Schools:** No   **Junior Golf:** No **Membership:** No
Clinics: No **Day Camps** No   **Driving Range:** $6.00
Other: Clubhouse / Lockers / Showers / Snack bar / Restaurant / Bar-lounge

Sig. Hole: #15, 164 yd. par 3 is the prettiest scene on the course. Awarded 4-star rating by *Golf Digest*. New senior discount Monday-Thursday is $40.00 for greens fee and cart.

	1	2	3	4	5	6	7	8	9
PAR	4	4	5	3	4	5	3	5	3
YARDS	399	381	508	161	324	533	210	469	168
HDCP	11	5	1	15	13	3	7	9	17
	10	11	12	13	14	15	16	17	18
PAR	4	5	3	4	4	3	5	4	4
YARDS	341	522	132	329	324	164	547	335	415
HDCP	14	2	18	16	8	10	6	12	4

Directions: Merritt Pkwy. Exit 49 N to Route 25. Take right on Route 111 and follow for 4 miles. Take right at intersection of Route 110. Course 1 mile on left.

Woodhaven CC

Bethany, CT (203) 393-3230

Tees	Holes	Yards	Par	USGA	Slope
BACK	9	6774	72	72.7	128
MIDDLE	9	6294	72	70.6	123
FRONT	9	5370	72	72.0	125

Club Pro: Dale Humphrey, PGA
Pro Shop: Full inventory
Payment: Cash, Check, MC, Visa
Tee Times: 7 days adv.
Fee 9 Holes: Weekday: $19.00   **Weekend:** $22.00
Fee 18 Holes: Weekday: $30.00   **Weekend:** $38.00
Twilight Rates: No   **All Day Play:** No
Cart Rental: $28.00/18 $14.00/9   **Discounts:** Sr. & Jr. Wkdays before 2pm
Lessons: Yes **Schools:** No   **Junior Golf:** Yes **Membership:** No
Clinics: Adult/Jr **Day Camps** No   **Driving Range:** Yes
Other: Snack bar / Restaurant

Rebuilt traps and added new tee on hole #4. The course is scenic, challenging and easy walking; A family owned "Labor of Love." Noted for tough greens.

	1	2	3	4	5	6	7	8	9
PAR	5	3	4	4	4	5	4	3	4
YARDS	517	156	331	375	342	542	350	152	382
HDCP	6	18	14	8	12	5	10	16	4
	10	11	12	13	14	15	16	17	18
PAR	5	3	4	4	4	5	4	3	4
YARDS	517	156	331	375	342	542	350	152	382
HDCP	7	17	9	2	11	3	15	13	1

Directions: Route 15 to Exit 59. Left to Lucy st. Left to Route 63, turn right on Route 63 to Route 67. Left to Bearhill rd. Right on Bearhill Rd. Bear left onto Miller Rd. to club.

Table of Contents
Directories & Coupons

Merchant Coupons & Directory

Adirondack Golf Shops	Route 44, Smithfield, RI, 401-233-1575
Al's Caddy Shack	16 Temby Street, Springfield, MA, 413-782-9333
Atlantic Golf Centers	734 Newport Ave., South Attleboro, MA 508-399-8400
City Golf Boston	38 Bromfield St., Boston, MA, 617-357-4653
Dave's Golf	1319 White Mt. Hwy, Rte. 16, N. Conway, NH, 800-549-9783
David Walker Golf Shop	850 Main Street, Falmouth, MA, 508-457-9333
	3090 Cranberry Highway, Wareham, MA, 508-241-8093
Drew's Back 9	73-75 Main Street, Salisbury, MA 978-465-5700
Edwin Watts Golf	200 Webster Street, Hanover, MA, 781-871-0000
	1019 Ianough Road, Hyannis, MA, 508-771-4653
	681 Falmouth Street, Mashpee, MA, 508-539-7937
	60 Winter Street, Weymouth, MA, 781-331-2600
Fairway Footprints	2075 South Willow Street, Manchester, NH, 603-642-8836
Fran Johnson's Golf & Racket	1050 Riverdale St.,W.Springfield, MA, 413-734-4444
Golf Boston Magazine	www.golfBoston.com, Lynnfield, MA, 783-592-7688
Golf Country	160 S. Main St., Middleton, MA, 978-774-4476
Golf Country	1129 Union St., Bangor, ME, 207-990-4777
Golf Club Factory	351 Turnpike St., Canton, MA, 781-828-1688
Golf Express	573 Main Street, Waltham, MA, 781-893-4177
Golf & Ski Warehouse	Route 12A, W. Lebanon, NH, 603-298-8282
	Route 33, Greenland, NH, 603-433-8585
	Route 3A, Hudson, NH, 603-595-8434
Golf Strokes	195 Hamilton Street, Leominster, MA , 978-534-4275
Golf Unlimited	15 West Union Street, Ashland, MA, 508-881-4653
Golf USA	145 Faunce Corner Rd., NO. Dartmouth, MA, 508-984-GOLF
Golf USA	470 Franklin Village Drive, Franklin, MA, 508-520-0192
Golfer's Clubhouse	Rt. 1 South, 10 Newbury St., Danvers, MA, 978-777- 4653
	2 Campanelli Dr. Braintree, MA 781-848-9777
	321D Speen Street, Natick, MA. 508-651-2582

Note: Not all rmerchants listed in the directory have offered coupons.

Golfer's Warehouse	65 Albany Turnpike, Canton, CT, 860-693-6286
	216 Murphy Rd., Hartford, CT, 860-522-6829
	190 Boston Post Road, Orange, CT, 203-799-3606
	60 Freeway Drive, Cranston, RI, 401-467-8740
Golfstarts	www.golfstarts.com, Peabody, MA, 978-535-8039
Grip and Rip-It Golf	20 Diamond Hill Avenue, Boylston, MA, 508-869-6855
Island Green	Route 1A, Bar Harbor Road, Holden, ME, 207-989-8853
Jonathan's Golf	North Conway, NH, 603-356-2140
at Hale's Location	
Juniper Hill Pro Shop	202 Brigham St., Northboro, MA, 508-393-2444
Ken & Dan's Golf Country	44 Fort Eddy Rd., Concord, NH 603-224-2299
Lady's Golf.com	50-60 Worcester Road, Natick, MA, 508-628-1748
Lancaster Golf Center	Exit 34, Route 2, Lancaster, MA, 978-537-8922
Leeder Board Golf	150 Federal Street, Boston, MA, 617-737-4075
Middleton Country Club	105 S. Main Steet, Middleton, MA, 978-774-4075
N.E. Golf Course Owners	300 Arnold Palmer Blvd., Norton, MA 774-430-9030
River Ridge GC	259 Preston Rd., Griswald, CT, 860-376-3268
Shaker Hill Golf Club	Shaker Road, Harvard, MA, 978-772-2227
Ski & Golf Outlet	1 Oak St., Westboro, MA, 508-616-0333
Stow Acres CC	58 Randall Road, Stow, MA 978-774-8180
Sun 'n Air Range	210 Conant Street, Danvers, MA, 978-774-8180
Tee Time Magazine	www.teetime-mag.com, Whitman, MA 02382, 781-447-2299
The Golf Circuit	7 New Pond Road, Groton, MA 978-448-2068
The Golf Guy	96 Route 101A, Amherst, NH, 603-881-1722.
The Tour	www.golfthetour.com, Needham MA, 800-645-TOUR
Wayland Golf Shops	890 Commonwealth Avenue, Boston, MA, 617-277-3999
	86 Cambridge Street, Burlington, MA, 781-221-0030
	Solomon Pond Mall, Marborough, MA, 508-303-8394
	28 Highland Avenue, Needham, MA, 781-444-6886
	North Shore Mall, Peabody, MA, 978-531-5155
	2121 Old Sudbury Rd, Wayland, MA, 508-358-4775
	87 Providence Highway, Westwood, MA, 781-461-5953
Whirlaway Golf Center	500 Merrimack Street, Methuen, MA, 978-688-8356
Yankee Golfworks	156 Main Street, Groveland, MA, 978-374-5230

Note: Not all rmerchants listed in the directory have offered coupons.

Merchandise Coupons

NEW ENGLAND
GOLFGUIDE

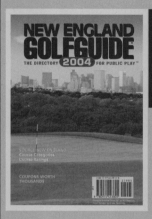

The 2004 Edition of the New England GolfGuide

It's the perfect gift for golfers of all ages and abilities. One size fits all. The book is packed with data, scorecards, fees, and directions for all 663 New England public, semi-private and resort courses. With 310 discount coupons for greens fees worth THOUSANDS of dollars, plus coupons for merchandise, driving ranges and services, the book pays for itself and is a gift that keeps on giving.

Adirondack GOLF SHOPS

375 Putnam Pike - Rte 44
Smithfield, RI
(401) 233-1575

$**10** OFF

**any purchase of $50
or more
Excludes golf balls**

Valid through Dec. 31, 2004. One coupon
per customer. Not valid on prior sales. Store
sales only. Excludes sale items. Not
combinable with any other coupon.

Al's Caddy Shack
16 Temby Street
Springfield, MA
(413) 782-9333

¹/₂ PRICE

**on a custom fitting
by appointment only
(bring driver, 5 iron and shoes)**

Valid through Dec. 31, 2004. One coupon
per customer. Not combinable with any
other coupon.

CityGolf BOSTON

38 Bromfield St.
Boston, MA
(617) 357-4653

**Free clubfitting session
with a PGA Professional**
with club purchase or

20% OFF 1st hour

on the Virtual Golf Simulator
Can only use one of the above options

Valid through Dec. 31, 2004. Not combinable
with any other coupon.

DAVE'S GOLF SHOP

1319 White Mt. Hwy, Rte. 16
North Conway, NH
800-549-9783

$**10** OFF

**any purchase
of $50 or more**

Valid through Dec. 31, 2004. One coupon
per customer. Store sales only. Not combinable with any other coupon.

NEW ENGLAND GOLFGUIDE

2 0 0 4

NEW ENGLAND GOLFGUIDE

2 0 0 4

NEW ENGLAND GOLFGUIDE

2 0 0 4

NEW ENGLAND GOLFGUIDE

2 0 0 4

Merchandise Coupons

NEW ENGLAND GOLFGUIDE

2 0 0 4

NEW ENGLAND GOLFGUIDE

2 0 0 4

NEW ENGLAND GOLFGUIDE

2 0 0 4

NEW ENGLAND GOLFGUIDE

2 0 0 4

NEW ENGLAND GOLFGUIDE

2 0 0 4

NEW ENGLAND GOLFGUIDE

2 0 0 4

NEW ENGLAND GOLFGUIDE

2 0 0 4

NEW ENGLAND GOLFGUIDE

2 0 0 4

Merchandise Coupons

NEW ENGLAND GOLFGUIDE

2 0 0 4

NEW ENGLAND GOLFGUIDE

2 0 0 4

NEW ENGLAND GOLFGUIDE

2 0 0 4

NEW ENGLAND GOLFGUIDE

2 0 0 4

Merchandise Coupons

NEW ENGLAND GOLFGUIDE

2 0 0 4

NEW ENGLAND GOLFGUIDE

2 0 0 4

NEW ENGLAND GOLFGUIDE

2 0 0 4

NEW ENGLAND GOLFGUIDE

2 0 0 4

Merchandise Coupons

NEW ENGLAND GOLFGUIDE

2 0 0 4

NEW ENGLAND GOLFGUIDE

2 0 0 4

NEW ENGLAND GOLFGUIDE

2 0 0 4

NEW ENGLAND GOLFGUIDE

2 0 0 4

Driving Range Coupons & Directory

Massachusetts

Airport Driving Range	North Attleboro, MA (508) 643-2229
Atlantic CC Driving Range	Plymouth, MA (508)888-6644
Atlantic Golf Center	South Attleboro, MA (508) 761-5484
Bill Pappas Golf School	Chelmsford, MA (978) 251-3933
Country Club of Billerica	Billerica, MA (978) 670-5396
Dartmouth Sports Dome	North Dartmouth, MA (508) 991-3663
East Coast Golf Academy	Northboro, Ma (508) 842-3311
Easton Family Golf Center	South Easton, MA (508) 230-6007
Fairway, The	Marlboro, MA (508) 624-9999
Glen Ellen CC Golf Range	Millis,MA (508) 376-2775
Golf Country	Middleton, MA (978) 774-4476
Golf Dome	The Shrewsbury, MA 508-845-1001
Golfer's Gym at Ironwood	Woburn, MA (781) 933-6657
Golftown Driving Range	Saugus, MA (781) 233-4455
Hackers Paradise Golf Range	E. Bridgewater, MA (508) 378-3441
Kimball Farm Driving Range	Westford, MA (978) 486-4944
Lakeview Driving Range	Lunenburg, MA (978) 345-7070
Lancaster Golf Center	Lancaster, MA (978) 537-8922
Rangeway Golf of Billerica	Billerica, MA (978) 439-0091
Rangeway Golf of Salisbury	Salisbury, MA (978)-462-8534
Rangeway Golf of Taunton	Taunton, MA (508) 880-9996
Sarkisian Farms Driving Range	Andover, MA (978) 688-5522
Star* Land Recreation Ctr. Inc.	Hanover, MA (781) 826-3083
Stone Meadows	Lexington, MA (781) 863-0445
Sun 'n Air Practice	Danvers, MA (978) 774-8180
Swingaway	Danvers, MA (978) 777-4774
T-Time Family Sports Center	Eastham, MA (508) 255-5697
Wayside Golf Center	Marlboro, MA (508) 480-8891
Whirlaway Golf Center	Methuen, MA (978) 688-8356

Note: Not all ranges listed in the directory have offered coupons.

Maine

College Street Driving Range	Lewiston, ME (207) 786-7818
Sonny's Driving Range	Winterport, ME (207) 223-5242
Taber's Lakeside Stand	Auburn, ME (207) 784-2521
XL Golf	Bangor, ME 207-848-5850

New Hampshire

Bedford Golfland, Inc.	Bedford, NH (603) 436-2300
Callahan's Sportech Golf	Nashua, NH (603) 888-1976
Classic Clubs Driving Range	Londonderry, NH (603) 437-9669
Fore-U-Golf Center	W. Lebanon, NH (603) 298-9702
Heavy Hitters Golf Range	Windham, NH (603) 898-6793
Legends Golf & Family Rec.	Hooksett, NH (603) 627-0099
Sugar Shack Driving Range	Campton, NH (603) 726-3867
World Cup Golf Center	Hudson, NH (603) 598-3838

Rhode Island

Eagle Quest Golf Dome	West Warwick, RI (401) 828-3663
Golf Central Driving Range	Richmond, RI (401) 539-2383
Ironwood's Golf Practice	North Smithfield, RI (401) 766-1151
Mike Harbour's Golf Learning	Exeter, RI (401) 397-2211
Mulligan's Island	Cranston, RI, (401) 464-8855

Vermont

Bomoseen Golfland	Bomoseen, VT (802) 468-2975
The Practice Tee	Manchester, VT (802) 362-3100

Connecticut

Brown's Driving Range	Windsor, CT (860) 688-1745
Burlington Golf Center	Burlington, CT (860) 675-7320
Caddy Shack	OxfordCT (203) 888-6035
Club Golf	Manchester, CT (860) 645-6363
Copper Hill Golf Acad. & DR	East Granby, CT (800) 653-7272
East Lyme Driving Range	East Lyme, CT (860) 739-1883
Glastonbury Golf Practice Center	Glastonbury, CT (860) 659-0334
Golf Quest Family Sports Centers	Brookfield , CT (203) 775-3556
Golf Quest Family Sports Centers	Southington, CT (860) 621-3663
Golf Training Center	Norwalk, CT (203) 847-8008
Great Golf Learning Center	Avon, CT (860) 676-0151
Highland Ridge Golf Range	Mansfield, CT (860) 423-9494
Lori Spielman Driving Range	East Hartford, CT (860) 282-7809
Pleasant View Golf Center	Somers,CT (860) 749-5868
Pleasant View Golf Park	Enfield, CT (860) 763-4202
Prospect Golf Driving Range	Prospect, CT (203) 758-4121
The Golf Improvement Center	Newington, CT (203) 666-4653
The Rockpile Driving Range	Winsted, CT (860) 379-5161
Toll Gate Golf Range	Litchfield, CT (860) 824-7266

Note: Not all ranges listed in the directory have offered coupons.

Bill Pappas Golf School

- **Type of Discount:**
  Purchase 1/2 hour, Get 1/2 hour free
- **Days of the Week:**
  7 days a week
- **Hours of the Day:**

Coupon expires 12/04
Can not be combined with any other offer.

55 Middlesex Street
N. Chelmsford, MA
(978) 251-3933
www.egolfschool.net

Pro: Bill Pappas
Indoor golf, Simulator, Analyzer

Clinics: Jr., Sr., Adult, & Ladies

Golf Country at Richardson's

- **Type of Discount:**
  Buy 1 Large Bucket, get 1 Free
- **Days of the Week:**
  7 days a week
- **Hours of the Day:**
  All day

Coupon expires 12/04
Can not be combined with any other offer.

160 South Main Street
Middleton, MA
(978) 774-4476
www.golfcountry114.com

Pro: Chuck Frithsen, PGA

Bucket Fees:
Small: $5.00
Large: $7.00   XL: $10.00

Open year round

Golf Country @ Easton

- **Type of Discount:**
  Buy 1 Large Bucket, get 1 Free
- **Days of the Week:**
  7 days a week
- **Hours of the Day:**
  All day

Coupon expires 12/04
Can not be combined with any other offer.

530 Turnpike St.
Easton , MA
(508) 230-8190

Pro: Lee Bader, PGA

Bucket Fees:
Small: $5.00 Med: $7.00
Large: $10.00

Open year round

Golftown Driving Range and Mini Golf

- **Type of Discount:**
  Buy 1 large, get 1 small bucket of balls free
- **Days of the Week:**
  7 days a week
- **Hours of the Day:**
  All day

Coupon expires 12/04
Can not be combined with any other offer.

860 Broadway, Route 1 North
Saugus, MA
(781) 233-4455
www.golftownsaugus.com

Pro: Lou O'Keefe

Bucket Fees:
Small: $5.00 Med: $7.75
Large: $9.75

Clinics: Junior & Adult

Open year round

Driving Range Coupons

NEW ENGLAND GOLFGUIDE

2 0 0 4

NEW ENGLAND GOLFGUIDE

2 0 0 4

NEW ENGLAND GOLFGUIDE

2 0 0 4

NEW ENGLAND GOLFGUIDE

2 0 0 4

Lakeview Driving Range & Mini Golf

- **Type of Discount:**
  $1.00 off any large or jumbo bucket/$1.00 off mini golf
- **Days of the Week:**
  7 days a week
- **Hours of the Day:**
  All day

Coupon expires 12/04
Can not be combined
with any other offer.

1 Whalom Road
Lunenburg, MA
(978) 345-7070

Pro: John Ross, USGTA
Bucket Fees:
Small: $3.00 Med: $5.00
Large: $7.00 XLarge: $11.00
Clinics: Junior

Lancaster Golf Center Driving Range and Par 3

- **Type of Discount:**
  $1.00 off any size bucket.
  $2.00 off 9 hole greens fee.
- **Days of the Week:**
  7 days a week
- **Hours of the Day:**
  All day

Coupon expires 12/04
Can not be combined
with any other offer.

Exit 34 on Route 2
Lancaster, MA
(978) 537-8922
www.lancastergolfcenter.com
Pro: J. Gordon, PGA/ E. Tulowiecki
Bucket Fees:
Sm.: $5, Lg: $8, XL: $14
Clinics: Junior & Adult

Open year round

Rangeway Golf of Billerica, Salisbury and Taunton

- **Type of Discount:**
  Get 2 rounds of miniature golf or 2 buckets of balls for the price of one
- **Days of the Week:**
  7 days a week
- **Hours of the Day:**
  All day

Coupon expires 12/04
Can not be combined
with any other offer.

44 Nashua Rd. Route 4
Billerica, MA
978-439-0091

Junction Rte. 95 and Rte 1
Salisbury, MA
(978) 462-8534

Junction Rte. 140 and Rte 24
Taunton, MA
(508) 880-9996

Bucket Fees:
Large: $6.00

Clinics: Yes
Open year round

Star Land Sports & Fun Park

- **Type of Discount:**
  Get 2 buckets of balls for the price of 1
- **Days of the Week:**
  7 days a week
- **Hours of the Day:**
  All day

Coupon expires 12/04
Can not be combined
with any other offer.

PO Box 994, 645 Washington
Street, Rte 53
Hanover, MA
(781) 826-3083
www.starland.us
Pro: No
Bucket Fees:
Med: $6.00
 XLarge: $10.00
Clinics: Junior & Adult
Open year round

Driving Range Coupons

NEW ENGLAND GOLFGUIDE

2 0 0 4

NEW ENGLAND GOLFGUIDE

2 0 0 4

NEW ENGLAND GOLFGUIDE

2 0 0 4

NEW ENGLAND GOLFGUIDE

2 0 0 4

Driving Range Coupons

NEW ENGLAND GOLFGUIDE

2 0 0 4

NEW ENGLAND GOLFGUIDE

2 0 0 4

NEW ENGLAND GOLFGUIDE

2 0 0 4

NEW ENGLAND GOLFGUIDE

2 0 0 4

Driving Range Coupons

NEW ENGLAND
GOLFGUIDE

2 0 0 4

NEW ENGLAND
GOLFGUIDE

2 0 0 4

NEW ENGLAND
GOLFGUIDE

2 0 0 4

NEW ENGLAND
GOLFGUIDE

2 0 0 4

Driving Range Coupons

NEW ENGLAND GOLFGUIDE

2 0 0 4

NEW ENGLAND GOLFGUIDE

2 0 0 4

NEW ENGLAND GOLFGUIDE

2 0 0 4

NEW ENGLAND GOLFGUIDE

2 0 0 4

Driving Range Coupons

NEW ENGLAND GOLFGUIDE

2 0 0 4

NEW ENGLAND GOLFGUIDE

2 0 0 4

NEW ENGLAND GOLFGUIDE

2 0 0 4

NEW ENGLAND GOLFGUIDE

2 0 0 4

East Lyme Driving Range

- **Type of Discount:**
  Get 2 buckets of balls for the price of 1
- **Days of the Week:**
  7 days a week
- **Hours of the Day:**
  All day

298 Flanders Road, POBox 543
East Lyme, CT
(860) 739-1883

Pro: Matt Boland, PGA

Bucket Fees:
Small: $5.00
Large: $8.00

Clinics: Yes

Coupon expires 12/04
Can not be combined
with any other offer.

Fairways on RTE 17

- **Type of Discount:**
  Get 2 buckets of balls for the price of 1
- **Days of the Week:**
  7 days a week
- **Hours of the Day:**
  All day

2015 South Main St.
Middletown, CT
(860) 346-GOLF(4653)

Pro: Dave Avery, PGA Apprentice

Bucket Fees:
Small: $5   Med: $8
Large: $10   XL: $35 (Jumbo)

Clinics: Jr., Sr., Adult, & Ladies

Open year round

Coupon expires 12/04
Can not be combined
with any other offer.

Golf Training Center, The

- **Type of Discount:**
  1 free practice session
  (unlimited time and balls)
- **Days of the Week:**
  7 days a week
- **Hours of the Day:**
  First time customers only.
  Reservations required
  Jan-March

145 Main Street
Norwalk, CT
203-847-8008
www.golftraining.com

Pro: Frank Sergiovanni, PGA

Swing analyzer, 9-hole putting green, Simulator

Clinics: Yes

Open year round

Coupon expires 12/04
Can not be combined
with any other offer.

Highland Ridge Golf Range LLC

- **Type of Discount:**
  $1.00 off medium or larger bucket
- **Days of the Week:**
  7 days a week
- **Hours of the Day:**
  9 am to dusk, noon to dusk after Labor Day

164 Stafford Road (Rte 32)
Mansfield, CT
(860) 423-9494

Pro: Bryce Waller

Bucket Fees:
Small: 3.5   Med: 6
Large: 8   XLarge:

Clinics: Junior & Adult

Coupon expires 12/04
Can not be combined
with any other offer.

Driving Range Coupons

NEW ENGLAND
GOLFGUIDE

2 0 0 4

NEW ENGLAND
GOLFGUIDE

2 0 0 4

NEW ENGLAND
GOLFGUIDE

2 0 0 4

NEW ENGLAND
GOLFGUIDE

2 0 0 4

Driving Range Coupons

Golf Course Coupons & Directory

35 of these coupons are included in the GolfGuide for the first time. They are indicated in **BOLD**.

Golf Course Coupons

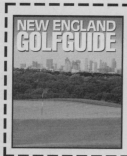

Acushnet River Valley Golf ICourse
Acushnet, MA 508-998-7777

- **Type of Discount**
  Free Golf Cart with 2 paid Greens Fees.
  Monday Free Hot Dog & Chips w/ Coupon.
- **Days of the Week**
  Weekdays only (except holidays)
- **Hours of the Day**
  All day

Coupon expires 12/04. Can not be combined with any other offer.

Ashfield Community Golf Club
Ashfield, MA (413) 628- 4413

- **Type of Discount**
  $5.00 off greens fee.
- **Days of the Week**
  Weekends and holidays only
- **Hours of the Day**
  All day

Coupon expires 12/04. Can not be combined with any other offer.

Atlantic Country Club
Plymouth, MA (508) 759-6644

- **Type of Discount**
  $5.00 off greens fee
- **Days of the Week**
  Mon. thru Thurs.
- **Hours of the Day**
  All day (Excluding Twi-light)

Coupon expires 12/04. Can not be combined with any other offer.

Bas Ridge Golf Course
Plunkett St., Hinsdale, MA (413) 655-2605

- **Type of Discount**
  Two players for the price of one
- **Days of the Week**
  Mon - Sat
- **Hours of the Day**
  All day Not valid July and August. Call ahead

Coupon expires 12/04. Can not be combined with any other offer.

NEW ENGLAND GOLFGUIDE

2 0 0 4

NEW ENGLAND GOLFGUIDE

2 0 0 4

NEW ENGLAND GOLFGUIDE

2 0 0 4

NEW ENGLAND GOLFGUIDE

2 0 0 4

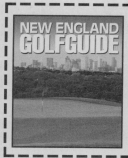

Bay Pointe CC
Onset, MA (508) 759-8802, 1-800-24T-TIME

- **Type of Discount**
  18 holes and riding cart- $35 per person up to 2 players
- **Days of the Week**
  M - Th, June 1 - Sept. 30
- **Hours of the Day**
  After 12:00

Coupon expires 12/04. Can not be combined with any other offer.

Beaver Brook CC
Main St., Haydenville, MA (413) 268-7229

- **Type of Discount**
  Two players for the price of one. Cart rental required.
- **Days of the Week**
  7 days a week
- **Hours of the Day**
  All day.

Coupon expires 12/04. Can not be combined with any other offer.

Blissful Meadows GC
Uxbridge, MA (508) 278-6113

- **Type of Discount**
  4 Greens Fees For the Price of 3
- **Days of the Week**
  Mon -Thurs only (except holidays)
- **Hours of the Day**
  7 am - 11 am

Coupon expires 12/04. Can not be combined with any other offer.

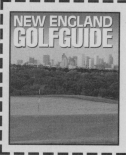

Bradford Country Club
Bradford, MA (978) 372-8587

- **Type of Discount**
  $37 for 18 holes, cart included.
- **Days of the Week**
  Weekdays before 3 pm or Weekends after 2 pm

Coupon expires 12/04. Can not be combined with any other offer.

Golf Course Coupons

NEW ENGLAND GOLFGUIDE

2 0 0 4

NEW ENGLAND GOLFGUIDE

2 0 0 4

NEW ENGLAND GOLFGUIDE

2 0 0 4

NEW ENGLAND GOLFGUIDE

2 0 0 4

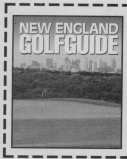

Brookline GC at Putterham
Brookline, MA (617) 730-2078

- **Type of Discount**
  $5.00 off greens fee for up to 2 players
- **Days of the Week**
  Monday thru Thursday
- **Hours of the Day**
  All day

Coupon expires 12/04. Can not be combined with any other offer.

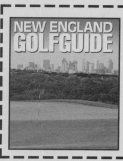

Bungay Brook Golf Club
Bellingham, MA (508) 883-1600

- **Type of Discount**
  Free Golf Cart with 2 paid greens fees. Free small pail range balls with paid greens fee.
- **Days of the Week**
  7 days a week
- **Hours of the Day**
  All day

Coupon expires 12/04. Can not be combined with any other offer.

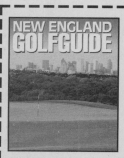

Captains GC
Brewster, MA (508) 896-1716

- **Type of Discount**
  $5.00 off each greens fee for up to 4 players
- **Days of the Week**
  Monday through Thursday only
- **Hours of the Day**
  All day

Coupon expires 12/04. Can not be combined with any other offer.

CC of Billerica
Billerica, MA (978) 667-9121 ext. 20

- **Type of Discount**
  4 to Play, 3 to Pay
- **Days of the Week**
  Weekdays only (except holidays)
- **Hours of the Day**
  9 am to 2 pm. Riding carts not included

Coupon expires 12/04. Can not be combined with any other offer.

Golf Course Coupons

NEW ENGLAND GOLFGUIDE

2 0 0 4

NEW ENGLAND GOLFGUIDE

2 0 0 4

NEW ENGLAND GOLFGUIDE

2 0 0 4

NEW ENGLAND GOLFGUIDE

2 0 0 4

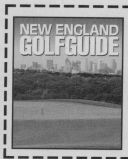

Chelmsford Country Club
66 Park Rd., Chelmsford, MA (978) 256-1818

- **Type of Discount**
  Two players for the price of one
- **Days of the Week**
  Mon-Thurs (except holidays)
- **Hours of the Day**
  Expires at 2:00 pm. With cart rental only.
  Managed by Sterling Golf Management, Inc.

Coupon expires 12/04. Can not be combined with any other offer.

Clearview Golf Course
Millbury, MA (508) 754-5654

- **Type of Discount**
  Complimentary cart with 2 paid green fees.
- **Days of the Week**
  Saturday, Sunday & Holidays
- **Hours of the Day**
  After 2 pm

Coupon expires 12/04. Can not be combined with any other offer.

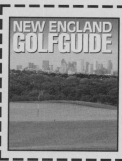

Country Club of Greenfield
Greenfield, MA (413) 773-7530

- **Type of Discount**
  $125.00 foursome w/carts
- **Days of the Week**
  7 days a week
- **Hours of the Day**
  Please call ahead

Coupon expires 12/04. Can not be combined with any other offer.

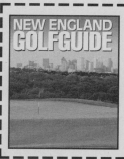

Cranwell Resort, Spa and Golf Club
Lenox, MA (413) 637-2563

- **Type of Discount**
  25% discount for 2 players for greens fees only.
- **Days of the Week**
  Weekdays only (except holidays)
- **Hours of the Day**
  All day. Based on space availability. Tee times
  required.

Coupon expires 12/04. Can not be combined with any other offer.

Golf Course Coupons

NEW ENGLAND GOLFGUIDE

2 0 0 4

NEW ENGLAND GOLFGUIDE

2 0 0 4

NEW ENGLAND GOLFGUIDE

2 0 0 4

NEW ENGLAND GOLFGUIDE

2 0 0 4

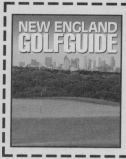

Crosswinds Golf Club
Long Pond Rd., Plymouth, MA (508) 830-1199

- **Type of Discount**
  4 Players for the price of 3
- **Days of the Week**
  Monday -Thursday (Except Holidays)
- **Hours of the Day**
  All day. Cannot be combined with other offers,
  Valid through 12/31/04

Coupon expires 12/04. Can not be combined with any other offer.

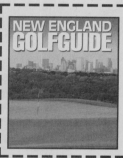

Crumpin-Fox Club
Bernardston, MA (413) 648-9101

- **Type of Discount**
  Two players for the price of one
- **Days of the Week**
  Daily
- **Hours of the Day**
  All day. Opening until May 15 and Oct. 20 until
  closing

Coupon expires 12/04. Can not be combined with any other offer.

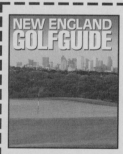

Cyprian Keyes Golf Club & Par 3
Boylston, MA (508) 869-9900

- **Type of Discount**
  4 players for the price of 3
- **Days of the Week**
  Mon-Thurs. (Except Holidays)
- **Hours of the Day**
  Before 11 am

Coupon expires 12/04. Can not be combined with any other offer.

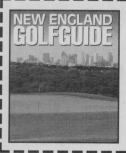

Dennis Highlands / Dennis Pines G.C.
Dennis, MA (508) 385-8347

- **Type of Discount**
  Two players for the price of one
- **Days of the Week**
  Monday - Thursday
- **Hours of the Day**
  All day. 1. Cart is mandatory 2. Not valid for
  advanced prepaid tee times.

Coupon expires 12/04. Can not be combined with any other offer.

Golf Course Coupons

NEW ENGLAND GOLFGUIDE

2 0 0 4

NEW ENGLAND GOLFGUIDE

2 0 0 4

NEW ENGLAND GOLFGUIDE

2 0 0 4

NEW ENGLAND GOLFGUIDE

2 0 0 4

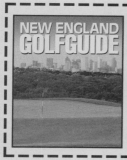

Edge Hill GC
Ashfield, MA (413) 625-6018

- **Type of Discount**
  Two players for the price of one
- **Days of the Week**
  Weekdays only (except holidays)
- **Hours of the Day**
  All day

Coupon expires 12/04. Can not be combined with any other offer.

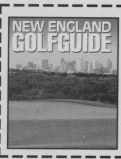

Ellinwood CC
Athol, MA (978) 249-7460

- **Type of Discount**
  Foursome with carts: $100.00
- **Days of the Week**
  Monday through Thursday only (except holidays).
- **Hours of the Day**
  All day

Coupon expires 12/04. Can not be combined with any other offer.

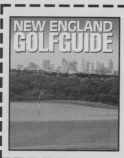

Evergreen Valley GC
Newburyport, MA (978) 463-8600

- **Type of Discount**
  Two players for the price of one for nine holes only. Cart required.
- **Days of the Week**
  Weekdays only (except holidays)
- **Hours of the Day**
  5am-7pm. Cart required.

Coupon expires 12/04. Can not be combined with any other offer.

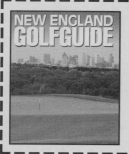

Executive Par 3 at Swansea CC, The
Swansea, MA, (508) 379-9886

- **Type of Discount**
  18 hole special: $23.50 pp, parties of 2 or 4.
  9 hole special: $15.50pp, parties of 2 or 4.
- **Days of the Week**
  Weekdays only (except holidays)
- **Hours of the Day**
  11:00 am - 1:00 pm

Coupon expires 12/04. Can not be combined with any other offer.

Golf Course Coupons

NEW ENGLAND GOLFGUIDE

2 0 0 4

NEW ENGLAND GOLFGUIDE

2 0 0 4

NEW ENGLAND GOLFGUIDE

2 0 0 4

NEW ENGLAND GOLFGUIDE

2 0 0 4

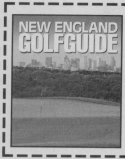

Forest Park CC
Adams, MA (413) 743-3311

- **Type of Discount**
  Two players for the price of one
- **Days of the Week**
  7 days a week
- **Hours of the Day**
  Please call ahead on weekends for availability

Coupon expires 12/04. Can not be combined with any other offer.

Franklin Park, (William J. Devine GC)
Dorchester, MA (617) 265-4084

- **Type of Discount**
  $5.00 off regular 18 hole greens fee (cart rental required).
- **Days of the Week**
  Monday-Thursday only
- **Hours of the Day**
  Before 5:00 pm

Coupon expires 12/04. Can not be combined with any other offer.

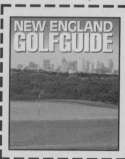

Glen Ellen CC
Rt.115, Millis, MA (508) 376-2775

- **Type of Discount**
  (1).$5.00 off greens fee for 18 holes (2). 3 range buckets for the price of 2.
- **Days of the Week**
  Mon.-Thurs. (except holidays)
- **Hours of the Day**
  Call ahead for tee times. Range offer, M-F, all day

Coupon expires 12/04. Can not be combined with any other offer.

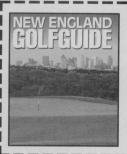

Groton Country Club
Groton, MA (978) 448-2564

- **Type of Discount**
  Two players for the price of one
- **Days of the Week**
  Weekdays only (except holidays)
- **Hours of the Day**
  Call ahead for tee times

Coupon expires 12/04. Can not be combined with any other offer.

NEW ENGLAND GOLFGUIDE

2 0 0 4

NEW ENGLAND GOLFGUIDE

2 0 0 4

NEW ENGLAND GOLFGUIDE

2 0 0 4

NEW ENGLAND GOLFGUIDE

2 0 0 4

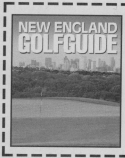

Heritage Country Club
Charlton, MA (508) 248-5111

- **Type of Discount**
  20% off Greens Fees for 1 or 2 players
- **Days of the Week**
  Monday thru Thursday
- **Hours of the Day**
  10 am - 2 pm No holidays. No tournaments.

Coupon expires 12/04. Can not be combined with any other offer.

Heritage Hill CC
Lakeville, MA (508) 947-7743

- **Type of Discount**
  Free Golf Cart with 2 paid Greens Fees
- **Days of the Week**
  Weekdays only (except holidays)
- **Hours of the Day**
  11AM-3PM

Coupon expires 12/04. Can not be combined with any other offer.

Highfields Golf & CC
Grafton,MA (508) 839-1945

- **Type of Discount**
  4 players for the price of 3
- **Days of the Week**
  Weekdays only (except holidays)
- **Hours of the Day**
  All day

Coupon expires 12/04. Can not be combined with any other offer.

Hillcrest Country Club
Leicester, MA (508) 892-0963

- **Type of Discount**
  Two players for the price of one (Must rent cart)
- **Days of the Week**
  Tues-Sat. Sun after 2:00pm if no outings. Tee time suggested
- **Hours of the Day**
  Tues- Sat: All day. Sun: after 2:00pm

Coupon expires 12/04. Can not be combined with any other offer.

Golf Course Coupons

NEW ENGLAND GOLFGUIDE

2 0 0 4

NEW ENGLAND GOLFGUIDE

2 0 0 4

NEW ENGLAND GOLFGUIDE

2 0 0 4

NEW ENGLAND GOLFGUIDE

2 0 0 4

Hillside CC
Rehoboth, MA (508) 252-9761

- **Type of Discount**
  $5.00 off greens fee for up to 2 players
- **Days of the Week**
  7 days a week
- **Hours of the Day**
  Weekdays - before noon. Weekends - after noon.

Coupon expires 12/04. Can not be combined with any other offer.

Holly Ridge Golf Club
S. Sandwich, MA (508) 428-5577

- **Type of Discount**
  $5.00 off greens fee for up to 2 players
- **Days of the Week**
  7 days a week
- **Hours of the Day**
  7am to 3:30pm

Coupon expires 12/04. Can not be combined with any other offer.

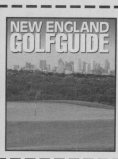

Hyannis Golf Club
Hyannis, MA (508) 362-2606

- **Type of Discount**
  Free Golf Cart with 2 paid Greens Fees
- **Days of the Week**
  Weekdays only (except holidays)
- **Hours of the Day**
  Good until 2pm.

Coupon expires 12/04. Can not be combined with any other offer.

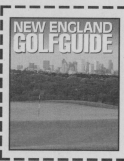

Kelley Greens By The Sea
Nahant, MA (781) 581-0840 ext. 101

- **Type of Discount**
  Two players for the price of one
- **Days of the Week**
  Weekdays only (except holidays)
- **Hours of the Day**
  Before 4 pm

Coupon expires 12/04. Can not be combined with any other offer.

Golf Course Coupons

NEW ENGLAND GOLFGUIDE

2 0 0 4

✂ -

NEW ENGLAND GOLFGUIDE

2 0 0 4

✂ -

NEW ENGLAND GOLFGUIDE

2 0 0 4

✂ -

NEW ENGLAND GOLFGUIDE

2 0 0 4

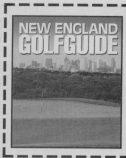

Lakeview Golf Club
Wenham, MA (978) 468-6676

- **Type of Discount**
  Two players for the price of one
- **Days of the Week**
  Weekdays only (except holidays)
- **Hours of the Day**
  Before noon

Coupon expires 12/04. Can not be combined with any other offer.

Leicester Country Club
Leicester, MA (508) 892-1390 Ext. 12

- **Type of Discount**
  Free Golf Cart with 2 paid Greens Fees
- **Days of the Week**
  Weekdays only (except holidays)
- **Hours of the Day**
  7 am until 2 pm. Must call for tee times.

Coupon expires 12/04. Can not be combined with any other offer.

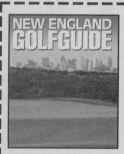

Little Harbor CC
Wareham, MA (508) 295-2617

- **Type of Discount**
  $4.00 off regular greens fee
- **Days of the Week**
  Weekdays only (except holidays and Weds.)
- **Hours of the Day**
  Before 3 pm

Coupon expires 12/04. Can not be combined with any other offer.

Maplegate Country Club
Bellingham, MA (508) 966-4040

- **Type of Discount**
  One free round of golf with three paying guests.
- **Days of the Week**
  Before noon Mon, Tues, Wed & Thurs (excuding holidays)
- **Hours of the Day**
  Valid April - October 29, 2004

Coupon expires 12/04. Can not be combined with any other offer.

Golf Course Coupons

NEW ENGLAND GOLFGUIDE

2 0 0 4

NEW ENGLAND GOLFGUIDE

2 0 0 4

NEW ENGLAND GOLFGUIDE

2 0 0 4

NEW ENGLAND GOLFGUIDE

2 0 0 4

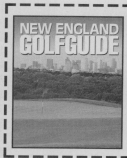

Marion Golf Course
South Dr., Marion, MA (508) 748-0199

- **Type of Discount**
  One free 18 hole greens fee with 3 paid 18 hole greens fees
- **Days of the Week**
  Weekdays only (except holidays)
- **Hours of the Day**
  With coupon only

Coupon expires 12/04. Can not be combined with any other offer.

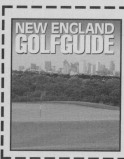

Middleton Golf Course
Middleton, MA (978) 774-4075

- **Type of Discount**
  $5.00 off each Greens Fee for up to 4 players
- **Days of the Week**
  Weekdays only (except holidays)
- **Hours of the Day**
  All day

Coupon expires 12/04. Can not be combined with any other offer.

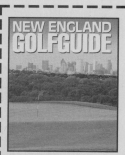

Mink Meadows GC
Vineyard Haven, MA (508) 693-0600

- **Type of Discount**
  4 players for the price of 3
- **Days of the Week**
  April 1 through June 14 only.
- **Hours of the Day**

Coupon expires 12/04. Can not be combined with any other offer.

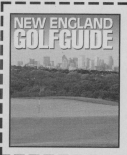

Murphy's Garrison Par 3 Golf Center
Haverhill, MA (978) 374-9380

- **Type of Discount**
  $2.00 off 9 holes when accompanied by one full paying customer.
- **Days of the Week**
  Weekdays only (except holidays)
- **Hours of the Day**
  All day

Coupon expires 12/04. Can not be combined with any other offer.

Golf Course Coupons

NEW ENGLAND GOLFGUIDE

2 0 0 4

NEW ENGLAND GOLFGUIDE

2 0 0 4

NEW ENGLAND GOLFGUIDE

2 0 0 4

NEW ENGLAND GOLFGUIDE

2 0 0 4

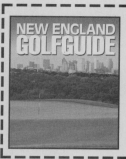

New England CC
Bellingham, MA (508) 883-2300

- **Type of Discount**
  $10.00 off greens fee with cart rate.
- **Days of the Week**
  Monday thru Thursday (except holidays)
- **Hours of the Day**
  Before 2 pm

Coupon expires 12/04. Can not be combined with any other offer.

✂

Newton Commonwealth GC
Newton, MA (617) 630-1971

- **Type of Discount**
  $5.00 off regular 18 hole greens fee (cart rental required)
- **Days of the Week**
  Monday - Thursday only
- **Hours of the Day**
  Before 5:00 pm Operated by Sterling Golf Management, Inc.

Coupon expires 12/04. Can not be combined with any other offer.

✂

North Adams CC
Clarksburg, MA (413) -663-7887

- **Type of Discount**
  Two players for the price of one
- **Days of the Week**
  Weekdays only (except holidays)
- **Hours of the Day**
  All day. Golf carts mandatory.

Coupon expires 12/04. Can not be combined with any other offer.

✂

Northampton CC
Leeds, MA (413) 586-1898

- **Type of Discount**
  2 for 1 with cart rental for 18 holes.
- **Days of the Week**
  Weekdays only (except holidays)
- **Hours of the Day**
  Weekdays before 12:00

Coupon expires 12/04. Can not be combined with any other offer.

Golf Course Coupons

NEW ENGLAND GOLFGUIDE

2 0 0 4

NEW ENGLAND GOLFGUIDE

2 0 0 4

NEW ENGLAND GOLFGUIDE

2 0 0 4

NEW ENGLAND GOLFGUIDE

2 0 0 4

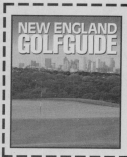

Norton Country Club
Norton, MA (508) 285-2400

- **Type of Discount**
  $49.95 Lunch Special
- **Days of the Week**
  Monday thru Thursday
- **Hours of the Day**
  All day

Coupon expires 12/04. Can not be combined with any other offer.

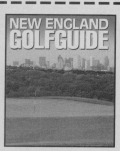

Norwood Country Club
Norwood, MA (781) 769-5880

- **Type of Discount**
  Two players for the price of one
- **Days of the Week**
  Weekdays only (except holidays)
- **Hours of the Day**
  Before Noon 18 hole power cart rental at regular weekday prices is required.

Coupon expires 12/04. Can not be combined with any other offer.

Oak Ridge Golf Club
W. Gill Rd, Gill, MA (413) 863-9693

- **Type of Discount**
  Two players for the price of one
- **Days of the Week**
  Weekdays only (except holidays)
- **Hours of the Day**
  Prior to 1 PM

Coupon expires 12/04. Can not be combined with any other offer.

Oak Ridge Golf Club
Feeding Hills, MA (413) 789-7307

- **Type of Discount**
  Two players for the price of one for 18 holes
- **Days of the Week**
  Weekdays only (except holidays)
- **Hours of the Day**
  Prior to 1:00 pm

Coupon expires 12/04. Can not be combined with any other offer.

NEW ENGLAND GOLFGUIDE

2 0 0 4

NEW ENGLAND GOLFGUIDE

2 0 0 4

NEW ENGLAND GOLFGUIDE

2 0 0 4

NEW ENGLAND GOLFGUIDE

2 0 0 4

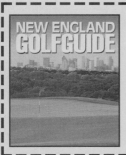

Ocean Edge GC
Brewster, MA (508) 896-5911

- **Type of Discount**
  4 player for the price of 3 for 18 holes
- **Days of the Week**
  Mon - Thurs. (except holidays)
- **Hours of the Day**
  All day . Valid April 1 to June 25 and after Labor Day. 24 hr. Advance tee times and power cart required.

Coupon expires 12/04. Can not be combined with any other offer.

Olde Scotland Links
Bridgewater, MA (508) 279-3344

- **Type of Discount**
  1 riding cart with purchase of 2 green fees.
- **Days of the Week**
  M-Th (Except holidays)
- **Hours of the Day**
  All day Not to be used during league, group or tournament play

Coupon expires 12/04. Can not be combined with any other offer.

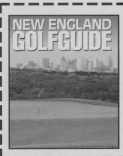

Pine Grove Golf Club
Northampton, MA (413) 584-4570

- **Type of Discount**
  2 players with cart/ $20 each player
- **Days of the Week**
  Weekdays only (except holidays)
- **Hours of the Day**
  Before 1:00pm. Starts on May 1st, 2004.

Coupon expires 12/04. Can not be combined with any other offer.

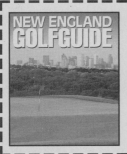

Pine Ridge Country Club
Pleasant St., N. Oxford, MA (508) 892-9188

- **Type of Discount**
  $5.00 off 18 holes greens fee for up to 2 players
- **Days of the Week**
  7 days a week
- **Hours of the Day**
  All day

Coupon expires 12/04. Can not be combined with any other offer.

Golf Course Coupons

NEW ENGLAND
GOLFGUIDE

2 0 0 4

NEW ENGLAND
GOLFGUIDE

2 0 0 4

NEW ENGLAND
GOLFGUIDE

2 0 0 4

NEW ENGLAND
GOLFGUIDE

2 0 0 4

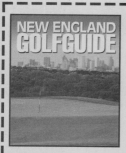

Pontoosuc Lake CC
Pittsfield, MA (413) 445-4217

- **Type of Discount**
  Buy 1 greens fee. Get second greens fee at one-half off.
- **Days of the Week**
  Weekdays only (except holidays) all day.
  Weekends and holidays after 2pm.

Coupon expires 12/04. Can not be combined with any other offer.

✂

Poquoy Brook GC
Lakeville, MA (508) 947-5261

- **Type of Discount**
  20% off non sale golf apparel
- **Days of the Week**
  7 days a week
- **Hours of the Day**
  All day

Coupon expires 12/04. Can not be combined with any other offer.

✂

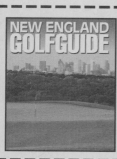

Quaboag Country Club
Monson, MA (413) 267-5294

- **Type of Discount**
  Free Golf Cart with 2 paid Greens Fees
- **Days of the Week**
  7 days a week
- **Hours of the Day**
  All day

Coupon expires 12/04. Can not be combined with any other offer.

✂

Quail Hollow Golf & CC
Old Turnpike Rd., Oakham, MA (508) 882-5516

- **Type of Discount**
  One greens fee free with one paid
- **Days of the Week**
  Weekdays only (except holidays)
- **Hours of the Day**
  All day

Coupon expires 12/04. Can not be combined with any other offer.

Golf Course Coupons

NEW ENGLAND
GOLFGUIDE
2 0 0 4

NEW ENGLAND
GOLFGUIDE
2 0 0 4

NEW ENGLAND
GOLFGUIDE
2 0 0 4

NEW ENGLAND
GOLFGUIDE
2 0 0 4

Quashnet Valley CC
Mashpee, MA (508) 477-4412

- **Type of Discount**
  $4.00 off Greens Fee
- **Days of the Week**
  M - Th (except holidays)
- **Hours of the Day**
  All day

Coupon expires 12/04. Can not be combined with any other offer.

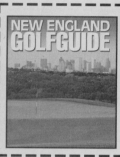

Rowley Country Club
Rowley, MA (978) 948-2731

- **Type of Discount**
  Earlybird & Twilight rates $12 before 8 and after 5pm. Lunch specials 2 players w/carts $37.99.
- **Days of the Week**
  Weekdays only (except holidays)
- **Hours of the Day**
  5:30 am till dusk.

Coupon expires 12/04. Can not be combined with any other offer.

Sagamore Spring GC
Lynnfield, MA (781) 334-3151

- **Type of Discount**
  Free bucket range balls after you buy one bucket
- **Days of the Week**
  7 days a week
- **Hours of the Day**
  All Day. With coupon only

Coupon expires 12/04. Can not be combined with any other offer.

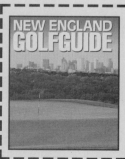

Sassamon Trace Golf Course
Natick, MA (508) 655-1330

- **Type of Discount**
  $5.00 off greens fee for up to 2 players
- **Days of the Week**
  Weekdays only (except holidays)
- **Hours of the Day**
  All day

Coupon expires 12/04. Can not be combined with any other offer.

Golf Course Coupons

NEW ENGLAND GOLFGUIDE

2 0 0 4

NEW ENGLAND GOLFGUIDE

2 0 0 4

NEW ENGLAND GOLFGUIDE

2 0 0 4

NEW ENGLAND GOLFGUIDE

2 0 0 4

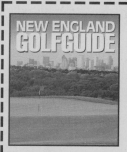

Scottish Meadow Golf Club
Warren, MA (413) 436-5108,

- **Type of Discount**
  Two players for the price of one
- **Days of the Week**
  Monday thru Thursday only
- **Hours of the Day**
  8 am to 12 pm. Must take a cart

Coupon expires 12/04. Can not be combined with any other offer.

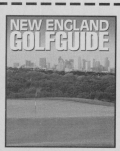

Shadow Brook Golf Course
So. Attleboro, MA (508) 399-8400

- **Type of Discount**
  Buy 3 rounds, get one free.
- **Days of the Week**
  7 days a week
- **Hours of the Day**
  All day

Coupon expires 12/04. Can not be combined with any other offer.

Sheraton Hotel & Colonial Golf Club
Lynnfield, MA   (781) 876-6031

- **Type of Discount**
  25% discount for 2-4 players
- **Days of the Week**
  Weekdays only (except holidays)
- **Hours of the Day**

Coupon expires 12/04. Can not be combined with any other offer.

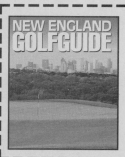

Skyline Country Club
Rt. 7, Lanesborough, MA (413) 445-5584

- **Type of Discount**
  One player at 1/2 price
- **Days of the Week**
  Weekdays only (except holidays)
- **Hours of the Day**
  All day

Coupon expires 12/04. Can not be combined with any other offer.

NEW ENGLAND GOLFGUIDE

2 0 0 4

- - -

NEW ENGLAND GOLFGUIDE

2 0 0 4

- - -

NEW ENGLAND GOLFGUIDE

2 0 0 4

- - -

NEW ENGLAND GOLFGUIDE

2 0 0 4

Southers Marsh Golf Club
Plymouth, MA (508) 830-3535

- **Type of Discount**
  Free Golf Cart with 2 paid greens fees
- **Days of the Week**
  7 days a week
- **Hours of the Day**
  All day

Coupon expires 12/04. Can not be combined with any other offer.

Southwick CC
Southwick, MA (413) 569-0136

- **Type of Discount**
  18 Holes: 2 players with cart $48.00. 2 Seniors with cart $40.00
- **Days of the Week**
  Weekdays only (except holidays)
- **Hours of the Day**
  Before 1:00pm

Coupon expires 12/04. Can not be combined with any other offer.

Squirrel Run CC
Plymouth, MA (508) 746-5001

- **Type of Discount**
  Senior Golf w/ Lunch $23.00
- **Days of the Week**
  Weekdays only (except holidays)
- **Hours of the Day**
  Monday - Friday

Coupon expires 12/04. Can not be combined with any other offer.

Sun Valley CC
Rehoboth, MA (508) 336-8686

- **Type of Discount**
  $2 off 1 round of golf ($1 seniors)
- **Days of the Week**
  Weekdays only (except holidays)
- **Hours of the Day**
  7 AM to 1 PM

Coupon expires 12/04. Can not be combined with any other offer.

Golf Course Coupons

NEW ENGLAND GOLFGUIDE

2 0 0 4

NEW ENGLAND GOLFGUIDE

2 0 0 4

NEW ENGLAND GOLFGUIDE

2 0 0 4

NEW ENGLAND GOLFGUIDE

2 0 0 4

Swansea Country Club
Swansea, MA (508) 379-9886

- **Type of Discount**
  Lunch Special - 18 holes with cart and lunch.
  $37.50.
- **Days of the Week**
  Weekdays only (except holidays)
- **Hours of the Day**
  11:00 am-1:00 pm.

Coupon expires 12/04. Can not be combined with any other offer.

Swanson Meadows
Billerica, MA, (978) 670-7777

- **Type of Discount**
  Free Golf Cart with 2 paid Greens Fees
- **Days of the Week**
  7 days a week
- **Hours of the Day**
  All day

Coupon expires 12/04. Can not be combined with any other offer.

Tekoa Country Club
Westfield, MA (413) 568-1064

- **Type of Discount**
  Buy 1 greens fee. Get 1 free with the purchase
  of a 2 rider cart.
- **Days of the Week**
  Weekdays only before 1 pm
- **Hours of the Day**

Coupon expires 12/04. Can not be combined with any other offer.

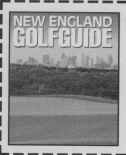

Templewood Golf Course
Templeton, MA (978) 939-5031

- **Type of Discount**
  $5.00 off greens fee for up to 2 players
- **Days of the Week**
  Monday through Friday only, except holidays.
- **Hours of the Day**
  All day

Coupon expires 12/04. Can not be combined with any other offer.

Golf Course Coupons

NEW ENGLAND GOLFGUIDE

2 0 0 4

NEW ENGLAND GOLFGUIDE

2 0 0 4

NEW ENGLAND GOLFGUIDE

2 0 0 4

NEW ENGLAND GOLFGUIDE

2 0 0 4

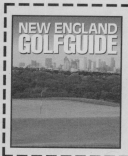

Twin Brooks GC At Sheraton
Hyannis, MA (508) 775-7775

- **Type of Discount**
  4 players for the price of 3
- **Days of the Week**
  7 days a week
- **Hours of the Day**
  Does not apply during twilight

Coupon expires 12/04. Can not be combined with any other offer.

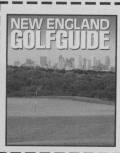

Twin Springs Golf Club
Bolton, MA (978) 779-5020

- **Type of Discount**
  Two players for the price of one
- **Days of the Week**
  Monday - Thursday (except holidays)
- **Hours of the Day**
  6:30am to 3pm

Coupon expires 12/04. Can not be combined with any other offer.

Village Links
Plymouth,MA (508) 830-4653

- **Type of Discount**
  Senior: Golf + Cart for $23.00
  Regular: Golf + Cart for $30.00
- **Days of the Week**
  Monday through Friday (except Holidays)
- **Hours of the Day**

Coupon expires 12/04. Can not be combined with any other offer.

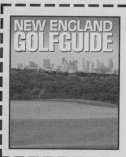

Waubeeka Golf Links
So. Williamstown, MA (413) 458-8355

- **Type of Discount**
  $5.00 off each greens fee for up to 2 players
- **Days of the Week**
  Weekdays only (except holidays)
- **Hours of the Day**
  After 1pm

Coupon expires 12/04. Can not be combined with any other offer.

NEW ENGLAND
GOLFGUIDE

2 0 0 4

NEW ENGLAND
GOLFGUIDE

2 0 0 4

NEW ENGLAND
GOLFGUIDE

2 0 0 4

NEW ENGLAND
GOLFGUIDE

2 0 0 4

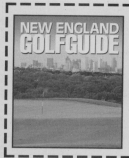

Wentworth Hills Golf & Country Club
Plainville, MA (508) 699-9406

- **Type of Discount**
  $5.00 off greens fee for up to 2 players
- **Days of the Week**
  Weekdays only (except holidays)
- **Hours of the Day**
  All day. Must present coupon to qualify.

Coupon expires 12/04. Can not be combined with any other offer.

Winchendon School CC
Winchendon, MA   (978) 297-9897

- **Type of Discount**
  $5.00 off greens fee
- **Days of the Week**
  Weekdays only (except holidays)
- **Hours of the Day**
  Call for tee times.

Coupon expires 12/04. Can not be combined with any other offer.

Woodbriar CC
Falmouth, MA (508) 495-5500

- **Type of Discount**
  Only pay $15.00
- **Days of the Week**
  7 days a week
- **Hours of the Day**
  After 4:00 p.m.

Coupon expires 12/04. Can not be combined with any other offer.

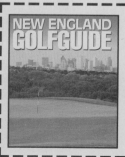

Woods of Westminster CC
Westminster, MA (978) 874-0500

- **Type of Discount**
  $31.00 18 Holes, Cart, and Lunch
- **Days of the Week**
  Weekdays only (except holidays)
- **Hours of the Day**
  Before 1 pm

Coupon expires 12/04. Can not be combined with any other offer.

NEW ENGLAND GOLFGUIDE

2 0 0 4

NEW ENGLAND GOLFGUIDE

2 0 0 4

NEW ENGLAND GOLFGUIDE

2 0 0 4

NEW ENGLAND GOLFGUIDE

2 0 0 4

Worthington GC
Worthington, MA (413) 238-4464

- **Type of Discount**
  Buy one greens fee, get one free.
- **Days of the Week**
  Weekdays only (except holidays)
- **Hours of the Day**
  Before 12 pm. Power cart required.

Coupon expires 12/04. Can not be combined with any other offer.

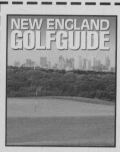

Bar Harbor Golf Course
Rt. 204, Trenton, ME (207) 667-7505

- **Type of Discount**
  Free Golf Cart with 2 paid Greens Fees
- **Days of the Week**
  7 days a week
- **Hours of the Day**
  All day.

Coupon expires 12/04. Can not be combined with any other offer.

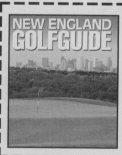

Barren View
Rt. 1, Jonesboro, ME (207) 734-6531

- **Type of Discount**
  25% discount for 2-4 players
- **Days of the Week**
  7 days a week
- **Hours of the Day**
  All day

Coupon expires 12/04. Can not be combined with any other offer.

Bath Country Club
Bath, ME (207) 442-8411

- **Type of Discount**
  Free Golf Cart with 2 paid Greens Fees
- **Days of the Week**
  Weekdays only (except holidays)
- **Hours of the Day**
  After 12:00 pm

Coupon expires 12/04. Can not be combined with any other offer.

Golf Course Coupons

NEW ENGLAND GOLFGUIDE

2 0 0 4

NEW ENGLAND GOLFGUIDE

2 0 0 4

NEW ENGLAND GOLFGUIDE

2 0 0 4

NEW ENGLAND GOLFGUIDE

2 0 0 4

Bethel Inn & Country Club
Bethel, ME (207) 824-6276

- **Type of Discount**
  2nd greens fee at 50% off
- **Days of the Week**
  Weekdays only (except holidays)
- **Hours of the Day**
  All day. Must make tee time no more than 48 hrs. in adv.

Coupon expires 12/04. Can not be combined with any other offer.

Birch Point Golf Club
Madawaska, ME (207) 895-6957

- **Type of Discount**
  Power cart 1/2 price with 2 paid greens fees
- **Days of the Week**
  7 days a week
- **Hours of the Day**
  All day

Coupon expires 12/04. Can not be combined with any other offer.

Boothbay Region CC
Boothbay, ME (207) 633-6085

- **Type of Discount**
  18 holes with cart after 1:00 pm: $50.00 pp. Min. of 2 players.
- **Days of the Week**
  7 days a week
- **Hours of the Day**
  After 1:00 pm. No exceptions.

Coupon expires 12/04. Can not be combined with any other offer.

Bridgton Highlands CC
Bridgton, ME (207) 647-3491

- **Type of Discount**
  2 for $50.00 after 1 pm - includes greens fees
- **Days of the Week**
  7 days a week
- **Hours of the Day**
  After 1:00 pm

Coupon expires 12/04. Can not be combined with any other offer.

NEW ENGLAND
GOLFGUIDE

2 0 0 4

NEW ENGLAND
GOLFGUIDE

2 0 0 4

NEW ENGLAND
GOLFGUIDE

2 0 0 4

NEW ENGLAND
GOLFGUIDE

2 0 0 4

Cape Neddick Country Club
Ogunquit, ME (207) 361-2011

- **Type of Discount**
  Bring a foursome for $50.00 per person.
  Includes: 18 holes, cart, range balls.
- **Days of the Week**
  Weekdays only (except holidays)
- **Hours of the Day**
  All day Valid April. May, June, Sept. Oct., Nov.
  Not for July and August

Coupon expires 12/04. Can not be combined with any other offer.

✂

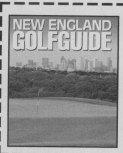

Caribou Country Club
Caribou, ME (207) 493-3933

- **Type of Discount**
  Free Golf Cart with 2 paid Greens Fees
- **Days of the Week**
  7 days a week
- **Hours of the Day**
  All day

Coupon expires 12/04. Can not be combined with any other offer.

✂

Country View GC
Rt. 7, Brooks, ME (207) 722-3161

- **Type of Discount**
  1/2 price Golf Cart with 2 paid Greens Fees
- **Days of the Week**
  7 days a week
- **Hours of the Day**
  All day

Coupon expires 12/04. Can not be combined with any other offer.

✂

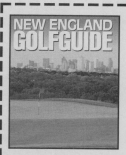

Deep Brook Golf Course
Saco, ME (207) 283-3500

- **Type of Discount**
  4 players for the price of 3
- **Days of the Week**
  Weekdays only (except holidays)
- **Hours of the Day**
  All day

Coupon expires 12/04. Can not be combined with any other offer.

Golf Course Coupons

NEW ENGLAND GOLFGUIDE

2 0 0 4

NEW ENGLAND GOLFGUIDE

2 0 0 4

NEW ENGLAND GOLFGUIDE

2 0 0 4

NEW ENGLAND GOLFGUIDE

2 0 0 4

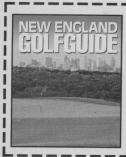

Dexter Municipal GC
Sunrise Ave., Dexter, ME (207) 924-6477

- **Type of Discount**
  Two players for the price of one
- **Days of the Week**
  Weekdays only (except holidays)
- **Hours of the Day**
  Best before 4:00

Coupon expires 12/04. Can not be combined with any other offer.

Dunegrass Golf Club
Old Orchard Beach, ME (207) 934-4513

- **Type of Discount**
  25% discount for 2-4 players
- **Days of the Week**
  Weekdays only (except holidays)
- **Hours of the Day**
  After 1 pm

Coupon expires 12/04. Can not be combined with any other offer.

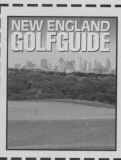

Dutch Elm Golf Course
Arundel, ME (207) 282-9850

- **Type of Discount**
  $5.00 off greens fee
- **Days of the Week**
  Weekdays only (except holidays)
- **Hours of the Day**
  PM only. Coupon to be used before Memorial Day or after Labor Day

Coupon expires 12/04. Can not be combined with any other offer.

Fox Ridge Golf Club
Auburn, ME (207) 777-GOLF(4653)

- **Type of Discount**
  $5.00 off greens fee for up to 2 players
- **Days of the Week**
  Monday - Thursday
- **Hours of the Day**
  All day

Coupon expires 12/04. Can not be combined with any other offer.

Golf Course Coupons

NEW ENGLAND GOLFGUIDE

2 0 0 4

NEW ENGLAND GOLFGUIDE

2 0 0 4

NEW ENGLAND GOLFGUIDE

2 0 0 4

NEW ENGLAND GOLFGUIDE

2 0 0 4

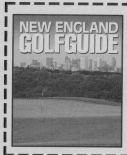

Frye Island Golf Course
Raymond, ME (207) 655-3551

- **Type of Discount**
  $5.00 off greens fee for up to 2 players
- **Days of the Week**
  Weekdays only (except holidays)
- **Hours of the Day**
  All day

Coupon expires 12/04. Can not be combined with any other offer.

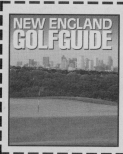

Hermon Meadow GC
Bangor, ME (207) 848-3741

- **Type of Discount**
  Free Golf Cart with 2 regular 18 hole greens fee.
- **Days of the Week**
  Weekdays only (except holidays)
- **Hours of the Day**
  All day

Coupon expires 12/04. Can not be combined with any other offer.

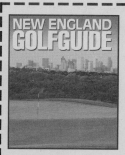

Hidden Meadows Golf Course
Old Town, ME (207) 827-4779

- **Type of Discount**
  Two players for the price of one
- **Days of the Week**
  7 days a week
- **Hours of the Day**
  All day

Coupon expires 12/04. Can not be combined with any other offer.

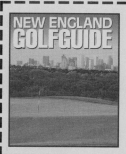

Highland Green Golf Club
Topsham, ME (207) 725-6318, Winter

- **Type of Discount**
  $5.00 off greens fee for up to 2 players
- **Days of the Week**
  Weekdays only (except holidays)
- **Hours of the Day**
  All day

Coupon expires 12/04. Can not be combined with any other offer.

Golf Course Coupons

NEW ENGLAND GOLFGUIDE

2 0 0 4

NEW ENGLAND GOLFGUIDE

2 0 0 4

NEW ENGLAND GOLFGUIDE

2 0 0 4

NEW ENGLAND GOLFGUIDE

2 0 0 4

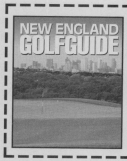

Hillcrest Golf Club
Millinocket, ME (207) 723-8410

- **Type of Discount**
  Two players for the price of one
- **Days of the Week**
  7 days a week
- **Hours of the Day**
  All day

Coupon expires 12/04. Can not be combined with any other offer.

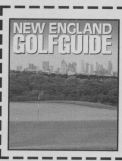

Houlton Community GC
Houlton, ME (207) 532-2662

- **Type of Discount**
  4 players for the price of 3.
- **Days of the Week**
  7 days a week
- **Hours of the Day**
  All day Call for tee times.

Coupon expires 12/04. Can not be combined with any other offer.

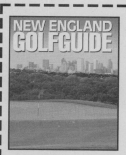

Island Green Golf Course
Holden, ME 207-989-9909

- **Type of Discount**
  Two players for the price of one
- **Days of the Week**
  7 days a week
- **Hours of the Day**
  All day

Coupon expires 12/04. Can not be combined with any other offer.

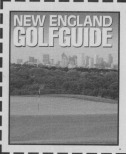

Johnson W. Parks GC
Pittsfield, ME (207) 487-5545

- **Type of Discount**
  Two players for the price of one with cart
- **Days of the Week**
  7 days a week
- **Hours of the Day**
  All weekdays, weekends and holidays after 1pm

Coupon expires 12/04. Can not be combined with any other offer.

Golf Course Coupons

NEW ENGLAND GOLFGUIDE

2 0 0 4

NEW ENGLAND GOLFGUIDE

2 0 0 4

NEW ENGLAND GOLFGUIDE

2 0 0 4

NEW ENGLAND GOLFGUIDE

2 0 0 4

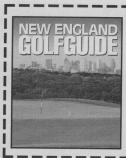

Kenduskeag Valley GC
Kenduskeag, ME (207) 884-7330

- **Type of Discount**
  Free Golf Cart with 2 paid Greens Fees
- **Days of the Week**
  Weekdays only (except holidays)
- **Hours of the Day**
  All day

Coupon expires 12/04. Can not be combined with any other offer.

Limestone CC
Limestone, ME (207) 328-7277

- **Type of Discount**
  $5.00 off greens fee. Cart rental required.
- **Days of the Week**
  Weekdays only (except holidays)
- **Hours of the Day**
  All day

Coupon expires 12/04. Can not be combined with any other offer.

Lucerne-in-Maine Golf Course
Dedham, ME (207) 843-6282

- **Type of Discount**
  Free Golf Cart with 2 paid Greens Fees
- **Days of the Week**
  7 days a week
- **Hours of the Day**
  All day, valid through September 7, 2004.

Coupon expires 12/04. Can not be combined with any other offer.

Maple Lane Inn and Golf Club
Livermore, ME (207) 897-6666

- **Type of Discount**
  18 holes of golf, golf cart & lunch for $20. Stay and Play includes golf & breakfast $70 per couple.
- **Days of the Week**
  Weekdays only (except holidays)
- **Hours of the Day**
  All day

Coupon expires 12/04. Can not be combined with any other offer.

Golf Course Coupons

NEW ENGLAND GOLFGUIDE

2 0 0 4

NEW ENGLAND GOLFGUIDE

2 0 0 4

NEW ENGLAND GOLFGUIDE

2 0 0 4

NEW ENGLAND GOLFGUIDE

2 0 0 4

Mars Hill Country Club
Mars Hill, ME (207) 425-4802

- **Type of Discount**
  20% off greens fee
- **Days of the Week**
  Weekdays only (except holidays)
- **Hours of the Day**
  All day

Coupon expires 12/04. Can not be combined with any other offer.

Merriland Farm Par 3 Golf
Wells, ME (207) 646-0508

- **Type of Discount**
  Two players for the price of one
- **Days of the Week**
  Weekdays only (except holidays)
- **Hours of the Day**
  All day

Coupon expires 12/04. Can not be combined with any other offer.

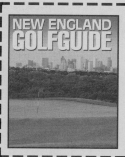

Naples Golf and Country Club
Route 114, Naples, ME. 207-693-6424

- **Type of Discount**
  25% discount for 2-4 players
- **Days of the Week**
  Weekdays only (except holidays)
- **Hours of the Day**
  After 1 PM

Coupon expires 12/04. Can not be combined with any other offer.

Nonesuch River Golf Club
Scarborough, ME (207) 883-0007

- **Type of Discount**
  Free small bucket of range balls with every 18
  holes of golf and power cart paid for.
- **Days of the Week**
  7 days a week
- **Hours of the Day**
  All day.

Coupon expires 12/04. Can not be combined with any other offer.

Golf Course Coupons

NEW ENGLAND GOLFGUIDE

2 0 0 4

NEW ENGLAND GOLFGUIDE

2 0 0 4

NEW ENGLAND GOLFGUIDE

2 0 0 4

NEW ENGLAND GOLFGUIDE

2 0 0 4

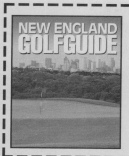

Northeast Harbor GC
N.E. Harbor, ME (207) 276-5335

- **Type of Discount**
  Golf and cart for two, for $40.00
- **Days of the Week**
  7 days a week
- **Hours of the Day**
  All day. Not valid Memorial Day to Labor Day.

Coupon expires 12/04. Can not be combined with any other offer.

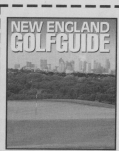

Palmyra Golf Course
Palmyra, ME (207)938-4947

- **Type of Discount**
  Free Golf Cart with 2 paid Greens Fees
- **Days of the Week**
  Weekdays only (except holidays)
- **Hours of the Day**
  All day

Coupon expires 12/04. Can not be combined with any other offer.

Paris Hill Country Club
Paris Hill Rd., Paris, ME (207) 743-2371

- **Type of Discount**
  $5.00 off greens fee for up to 2 players.
  10 % Discount in Pro Shop.
- **Days of the Week**
  7 days a week
- **Hours of the Day**
  All day.

Coupon expires 12/04. Can not be combined with any other offer.

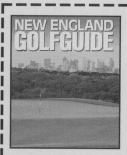

Pine Hill Golf Club
Outer Mill St., Brewer, ME (207) 989-3824

- **Type of Discount**
  $5.00 off greens fee for up to 2 players
- **Days of the Week**
  7 days a week
- **Hours of the Day**
  All day

Coupon expires 12/04. Can not be combined with any other offer.

Golf Course Coupons

NEW ENGLAND GOLFGUIDE

2 0 0 4

NEW ENGLAND GOLFGUIDE

2 0 0 4

NEW ENGLAND GOLFGUIDE

2 0 0 4

NEW ENGLAND GOLFGUIDE

2 0 0 4

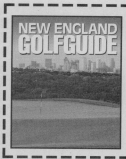

Piscataquis CC
Dover Rd., Guilford, ME (207) 876-3203

- **Type of Discount**
  $39 for 2 people and a cart.
- **Days of the Week**
  Weekdays only (except holidays)
- **Hours of the Day**
  All day Call 24 hours in advance

Coupon expires 12/04. Can not be combined with any other offer.

Point Sebago Golf Club
Route 302, Casco, ME (207) 655-2747

- **Type of Discount**
  $5.00 off greens fee for up to 2 players
- **Days of the Week**
  Weekdays only (except holidays)
- **Hours of the Day**
  After 1 pm

Coupon expires 12/04. Can not be combined with any other offer.

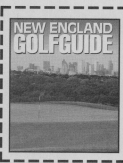

Presque Isle CC
Presque Isle, ME (207) 764-0430

- **Type of Discount**
  Two players, 18 holes for the price of 9 holes each.
- **Days of the Week**
  M,W,Th,&F only (except holidays)
- **Hours of the Day**
  Anytime Power cart required at regular rate.

Coupon expires 12/04. Can not be combined with any other offer.

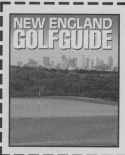

Prospect Hill GC
So. Main St., Auburn, ME (207) 782-9220

- **Type of Discount**
  $5.00 off greens fee for up to 2 players
- **Days of the Week**
  Weekdays only
- **Hours of the Day**
  Before Noon. Proper dress required. Spikeless course.

Coupon expires 12/04. Can not be combined with any other offer.

Golf Course Coupons

NEW ENGLAND GOLFGUIDE

2 0 0 4

NEW ENGLAND GOLFGUIDE

2 0 0 4

NEW ENGLAND GOLFGUIDE

2 0 0 4

NEW ENGLAND GOLFGUIDE

2 0 0 4

Province Lake Golf Club
Parsonfield, ME Route 153 (800) 325-4434

- **Type of Discount**
  $5.00 off greens fee for up to 2 players
- **Days of the Week**
  7 days a week
- **Hours of the Day**
  After 1 pm

Coupon expires 12/04. Can not be combined with any other offer.

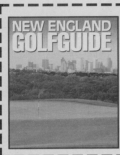

River Meadow GC
Lincoln St., Westbrook, ME (207) 854-1625

- **Type of Discount**
  Free Golf Cart with 2 paid Greens Fees
- **Days of the Week**
  Weekdays only (except holidays)
- **Hours of the Day**
  All day

Coupon expires 12/04. Can not be combined with any other offer.

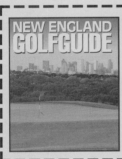

Rockland Golf Club
Old County Rd, Rockland, ME (207) 594-9322

- **Type of Discount**
  $10.00 off per player up to 4 players
- **Days of the Week**
  7 days a week
- **Hours of the Day**
  All day

Coupon expires 12/04. Can not be combined with any other offer.

Rocky Knoll Country Club
River Rd., Orrington, ME (207) 989-0109

- **Type of Discount**
  25% discount for 2-4 players
- **Days of the Week**
  Weekdays only (except holidays)
- **Hours of the Day**
  All day

Coupon expires 12/04. Can not be combined with any other offer.

NEW ENGLAND GOLFGUIDE
2 0 0 4

NEW ENGLAND GOLFGUIDE
2 0 0 4

NEW ENGLAND GOLFGUIDE
2 0 0 4

NEW ENGLAND GOLFGUIDE
2 0 0 4

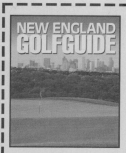

Sable Oaks Golf Club
S. Portland, ME (207) 775-6257

- **Type of Discount**
  $10.00 off 18-hole greens fee
- **Days of the Week**
  Monday-Thursday, except holidays
- **Hours of the Day**
  All day Power cart required

Coupon expires 12/04. Can not be combined with any other offer.

Salmon Falls GC
Hollis, ME (207) 929-5233 or 1-800-734-1616

- **Type of Discount**
  $60.00 for 2 players and golfcart for 18 holes seasonal.
- **Days of the Week**
  7 days a week
- **Hours of the Day**
  All day

Coupon expires 12/04. Can not be combined with any other offer.

Samoset Resort GC
220 Warrenton St., Rockport, ME (207) 594-1431

- **Type of Discount**
  25% discount for 2-4 players (In-house rates)
- **Days of the Week**
  Weekdays only (except holidays)
- **Hours of the Day**
  All day

Coupon expires 12/04. Can not be combined with any other offer.

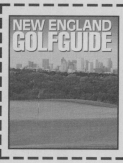

Sanford Country Club
Rt. 4, Sanford, ME (207) 324-5462

- **Type of Discount**
  Free Golf Cart with 2 paid Greens Fees
- **Days of the Week**
  Weekdays only (Except Holidays & Fri)
- **Hours of the Day**
  11:00 am to close

Coupon expires 12/04. Can not be combined with any other offer.

Golf Course Coupons

NEW ENGLAND GOLFGUIDE

2 0 0 4

NEW ENGLAND GOLFGUIDE

2 0 0 4

NEW ENGLAND GOLFGUIDE

2 0 0 4

NEW ENGLAND GOLFGUIDE

2 0 0 4

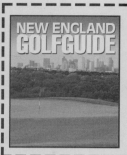

Searsport Pines Golf Course
Searsport, ME (207) 548-2854

- **Type of Discount**
  $5.00 off greens fee for up to 2 players
- **Days of the Week**
  Weekdays only (except holidays)
- **Hours of the Day**
  All day

Coupon expires 12/04. Can not be combined with any other offer.

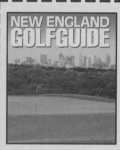

Sebasco Harbor Resort Golf Club
Sebasco Estates, ME 800-225-3819

- **Type of Discount**
  Two players for the price of one
- **Days of the Week**
  Weekdays only (except holidays)
- **Hours of the Day**
  All day

Coupon expires 12/04. Can not be combined with any other offer.

Spring Meadows GC
Gray, ME (207) 657-2586

- **Type of Discount**
  $5.00 off greens fee for up to 2 players
- **Days of the Week**
  7 days a week
- **Hours of the Day**
  All day Not during July and August

Coupon expires 12/04. Can not be combined with any other offer.

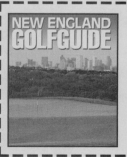

Sugarloaf Golf Club
Carrabassett Valley, ME (207) 237-2000

- **Type of Discount**
  Free Golf Cart with 2 paid Greens Fees
- **Days of the Week**
  Weekdays only (except holidays)
- **Hours of the Day**
  All day

Coupon expires 12/04. Can not be combined with any other offer.

Golf Course Coupons

NEW ENGLAND GOLFGUIDE

2 0 0 4

NEW ENGLAND GOLFGUIDE

2 0 0 4

NEW ENGLAND GOLFGUIDE

2 0 0 4

NEW ENGLAND GOLFGUIDE

2 0 0 4

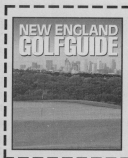

Sunset Ridge
Westbrook, ME (207) 854-9463

- **Type of Discount**
  25% discount for 2-4 golf players.
  2 for 1 unlimited tennis.
- **Days of the Week**
  7 days a week
- **Hours of the Day**
  All day

Coupon expires 12/04. Can not be combined with any other offer.

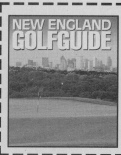

The Links at Outlook
South Berwick, ME (207) 384-4653

- **Type of Discount**
  Free Golf Cart with 2 paid Greens Fees
- **Days of the Week**
  7 days a week (except holidays)
- **Hours of the Day**
  All day (except holidays.)

Coupon expires 12/04. Can not be combined with any other offer.

Toddy Brook Golf Course
North Yarmouth, ME (207) 829-5100

- **Type of Discount**
  Free Golf Cart with 2 paid Greens Fees
- **Days of the Week**
  Weekdays only (except holidays)
- **Hours of the Day**

Coupon expires 12/04. Can not be combined with any other offer.

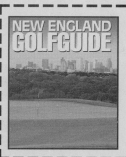

Turner Highland Golf Course
Turner, ME (207) 224-7060

- **Type of Discount**
  Two players for the price of one
- **Days of the Week**
  Weekdays only (except holidays)
- **Hours of the Day**
  After 10 am.

Coupon expires 12/04. Can not be combined with any other offer.

NEW ENGLAND GOLFGUIDE

2 0 0 4

NEW ENGLAND GOLFGUIDE

2 0 0 4

NEW ENGLAND GOLFGUIDE

2 0 0 4

NEW ENGLAND GOLFGUIDE

2 0 0 4

Va-Jo-Wa Golf Club
Walker Settlement Road, Island Falls, ME (207) 463-2128

- **Type of Discount**
  Two players for the price of one
- **Days of the Week**
  7 days a week
- **Hours of the Day**
  All day. Cart rental required

Coupon expires 12/04. Can not be combined with any other offer.

✂

Western View Golf Club
Augusta, ME (207) 622-5309

- **Type of Discount**
  Two players for the price of one, Cart rental required
- **Days of the Week**
  7 days a week
- **Hours of the Day**
  All day.

Coupon expires 12/04. Can not be combined with any other offer.

✂

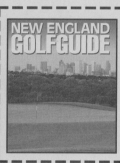

Androscoggin Valley CC
Route. 2, Gorham, NH (603) 466-9468

- **Type of Discount**
  $50.00 for 2 (includes cart)
- **Days of the Week**
  7 days a week
- **Hours of the Day**
  All day with tee times only. Must mention coupon in NEGG

Coupon expires 12/04. Can not be combined with any other offer.

✂

Apple Hill Golf Club
E. Kingston, NH (603) 642-4414

- **Type of Discount**
  $5.00 off greens fee for up to 2 players
- **Days of the Week**
  Weekdays only (except holidays)
- **Hours of the Day**
  All day

Coupon expires 12/04. Can not be combined with any other offer.

NEW ENGLAND GOLFGUIDE

2 0 0 4

NEW ENGLAND GOLFGUIDE

2 0 0 4

NEW ENGLAND GOLFGUIDE

2 0 0 4

NEW ENGLAND GOLFGUIDE

2 0 0 4

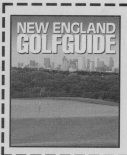

Applewood Golf Links
Range Rd., Windham, NH (603) 898-6793

- **Type of Discount**
  Two players for the price of one
- **Days of the Week**
  Weekdays only (except holidays)
- **Hours of the Day**
  Before 4:00 pm

Coupon expires 12/04. Can not be combined with any other offer.

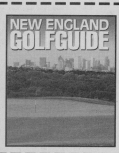

Balsams Panorama GC, The
Dixville Notch, NH (603) 255-4961

- **Type of Discount**
  Two players for the price of one, Power cart rental required.
- **Days of the Week**
  7 days a week
- **Hours of the Day**
  After 11:30am

Coupon expires 12/04. Can not be combined with any other offer.

Balsams-Coashaukee Golf Course
Dixville Notch, NH (603) 255-4961

- **Type of Discount**
  Two players for the price of one, power car rental required.
- **Days of the Week**
  7 days a week
- **Hours of the Day**
  After 11:30 AM.

Coupon expires 12/04. Can not be combined with any other offer.

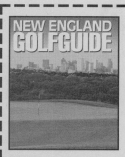

Beaver Meadow GC
Concord, NH (603) 228-8954

- **Type of Discount**
  2 Greens Fees and Cart for $58.00
- **Days of the Week**
  Mon-Wed (Except Holidays)
- **Hours of the Day**
  After 12:00pm

Coupon expires 12/04. Can not be combined with any other offer.

NEW ENGLAND GOLFGUIDE

2 0 0 4

NEW ENGLAND GOLFGUIDE

2 0 0 4

NEW ENGLAND GOLFGUIDE

2 0 0 4

NEW ENGLAND GOLFGUIDE

2 0 0 4

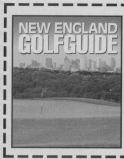

Bethlehem CC
Bethlehem, NH (603) 869-5745

- **Type of Discount**
  Siesta Special: $30 includes cart pp.
- **Days of the Week**
  Weekdays only (except holidays)
- **Hours of the Day**
  12:00 to 4:00pm non-holidays

Coupon expires 12/04. Can not be combined with any other offer.

Blackmount Country Club
N Haverhill, NH (603) 787-6564

- **Type of Discount**
  $3.00 off power cart rental with paid greens fee.
- **Days of the Week**
  Weekdays only (except holidays)
- **Hours of the Day**
  All day

Coupon expires 12/04. Can not be combined with any other offer.

Bramber Valley Golf Course
Greenland, NH 03840 (603) 436-4288

- **Type of Discount**
  $2.00 off 18 holes
- **Days of the Week**
  7 days a week
- **Hours of the Day**
  All day through Nov. 1, 2004

Coupon expires 12/04. Can not be combined with any other offer.

Breakfast Hill Golf Club
Greenland,NH (603) 436-5001

- **Type of Discount**
  $5.00 off greens fee for up to 2 players
- **Days of the Week**
  Weekdays only (except holidays)
- **Hours of the Day**
  Before 4 pm

Coupon expires 12/04. Can not be combined with any other offer.

Golf Course Coupons

NEW ENGLAND GOLFGUIDE

2 0 0 4

NEW ENGLAND GOLFGUIDE

2 0 0 4

NEW ENGLAND GOLFGUIDE

2 0 0 4

NEW ENGLAND GOLFGUIDE

2 0 0 4

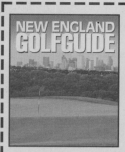

Campbell's Scottish Highlands
Brady Ave., Salem, NH (603) 894-4653

- **Type of Discount**
  18 holes of Golf, Cart, & Bag Lunch for 2 golfers-$80
- **Days of the Week**
  M-Th (Except holidays)
- **Hours of the Day**
  Not valid for group outings. Valid only April 1 - May 27, Oct. 12 - Nov. 24

Coupon expires 12/04. Can not be combined with any other offer.

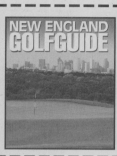

Candia Woods
Candia, NH (603) 483-2307

- **Type of Discount**
  $38.00 Golf fee and Cart for one player. One coupon per player.
- **Days of the Week**
  Monday thru Thursday
- **Hours of the Day**
  All day

Coupon expires 12/04. Can not be combined with any other offer.

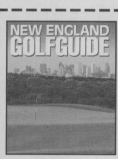

Carter Country Club
Lebanon, NH (603) 448-4483

- **Type of Discount**
  Two players for the price of one
- **Days of the Week**
  Weekdays only (except holidays)
- **Hours of the Day**
  All day

Coupon expires 12/04. Can not be combined with any other offer.

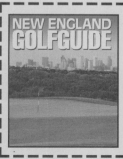

CC of New Hampshire
N. Sutton, NH (603) 927-4246

- **Type of Discount**
  $5.00 off 18 hole greens fee
- **Days of the Week**
  Monday-Thursday (except holidays)
- **Hours of the Day**
  All day. Power cart required.

Coupon expires 12/04. Can not be combined with any other offer.

Golf Course Coupons

NEW ENGLAND GOLFGUIDE

2 0 0 4

NEW ENGLAND GOLFGUIDE

2 0 0 4

NEW ENGLAND GOLFGUIDE

2 0 0 4

NEW ENGLAND GOLFGUIDE

2 0 0 4

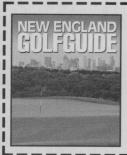

Colebrook CC
Colebrook, NH (603) 237-5566

- **Type of Discount**
  Two players for the price of one
- **Days of the Week**
  Weekdays only (except holidays)
- **Hours of the Day**
  All day Power Cart Required

Coupon expires 12/04. Can not be combined with any other offer.

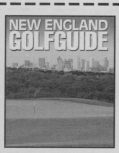

Den Brae Golf Course
Sanbornton, NH (603) 934-9818

- **Type of Discount**
  25% discount for 2-4 players
- **Days of the Week**
  Weekdays only (except holidays)
- **Hours of the Day**
  All day

Coupon expires 12/04. Can not be combined with any other offer.

Eagle Mountain House
Jackson, NH (603) 383-9090

- **Type of Discount**
  Free Golf Cart with 2 paid Greens Fees
- **Days of the Week**
  Weekdays only (except holidays)
- **Hours of the Day**
  All day

Coupon expires 12/04. Can not be combined with any other offer.

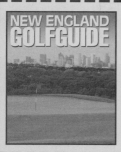

Exeter Country Club
Exeter, NH (603) 772-4752

- **Type of Discount**
  25% discount for 2-4 players
- **Days of the Week**
  Weekdays only (except holidays)
- **Hours of the Day**
  7:00am - 3:00am Valid April thru October. Must make tee time.

Coupon expires 12/04. Can not be combined with any other offer.

Golf Course Coupons

NEW ENGLAND GOLFGUIDE

2 0 0 4

NEW ENGLAND GOLFGUIDE

2 0 0 4

NEW ENGLAND GOLFGUIDE

2 0 0 4

NEW ENGLAND GOLFGUIDE

2 0 0 4

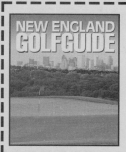

Fore-U-Golf Center
West Lebanon,NH (603) 298-9702

- **Type of Discount**
  Two players for the price of one
- **Days of the Week**
  7 days a week
- **Hours of the Day**
  All day

Coupon expires 12/04. Can not be combined with any other offer.

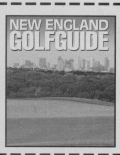

Hales Location Golf Course
North Conway, NH (603) 356-2140

- **Type of Discount**
  $5.00 off with purchase of two 18 hole greens fees and carts.
- **Days of the Week**
  Weekdays only (except holidays)
- **Hours of the Day**
  All day

Coupon expires 12/04. Can not be combined with any other offer.

Hidden Valley R.V. and Golf Park
Derry, NH (603) 887-PUTT

- **Type of Discount**
  Two players for the price of one
- **Days of the Week**
  Weekdays only (except holidays)
- **Hours of the Day**
  All day

Coupon expires 12/04. Can not be combined with any other offer.

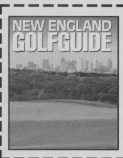

Highlands Links GC
Plymouth, NH (603) 536-3452

- **Type of Discount**
  Two players for the price of one (at regular adult fee)
- **Days of the Week**
  7 days a week
- **Hours of the Day**
  All day

Coupon expires 12/04. Can not be combined with any other offer.

NEW ENGLAND
GOLFGUIDE

2 0 0 4

NEW ENGLAND
GOLFGUIDE

2 0 0 4

NEW ENGLAND
GOLFGUIDE

2 0 0 4

NEW ENGLAND
GOLFGUIDE

2 0 0 4

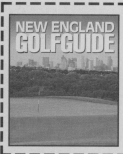

Indian Mound GC
Center Ossipee, NH (603) 539-7733

- **Type of Discount**
  $60.00 for two players and cart for 18 holes
  (Call for tee times)
- **Days of the Week**
  Monday - Thursday, except holidays.
- **Hours of the Day**
  1 pm-3 pm

Coupon expires 12/04. Can not be combined with any other offer.

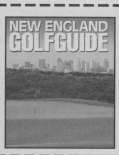

Lakeview Golf Club
Ladd Hill Road, Belmont, NH 03220 (603-524-2220)

- **Type of Discount**
  Free golf cart with 2 paid greens fees
- **Days of the Week**
  Weekdays only (except holidays)
- **Hours of the Day**
  All day

Coupon expires 12/04. Can not be combined with any other offer.

Lisbon Village Country Club
Bishop Road, Lisbon, NH (603) 838-6004

- **Type of Discount**
  Free Golf Cart with 2 paid Greens Fees
- **Days of the Week**
  Weekdays only (except holidays)
- **Hours of the Day**

Coupon expires 12/04. Can not be combined with any other offer.

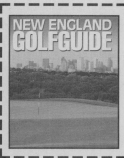

Lochmere Golf & CC
Rt. 3, Tilton, NH (603) 528-4653

- **Type of Discount**
  2 players with power cart/ 18 holes, $38.00 pp
- **Days of the Week**
  Mon-Thurs (Except Holidays)
- **Hours of the Day**

Coupon expires 12/04. Can not be combined with any other offer.

NEW ENGLAND GOLFGUIDE

2 0 0 4

NEW ENGLAND GOLFGUIDE

2 0 0 4

NEW ENGLAND GOLFGUIDE

2 0 0 4

NEW ENGLAND GOLFGUIDE

2 0 0 4

Maplewood Casino & CC
Bethlehem, NH (603) 869-3335

- **Type of Discount**
  $5.00 off greens fee
- **Days of the Week**
  Weekdays only (except holidays)
- **Hours of the Day**
  7:00-6:00. Cart required for 18 holes only

Coupon expires 12/04. Can not be combined with any other offer.

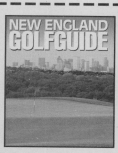

Mojalaki Golf Club
Franklin, NH (603) 934-3033

- **Type of Discount**
  $5.00 off greens fee for up to 2 players
- **Days of the Week**
  Weekdays only (except holidays)
- **Hours of the Day**
  Before 3pm

Coupon expires 12/04. Can not be combined with any other offer.

Mountain View Grand Resort & Spa
Whitefield,NH (800) 438-3017

- **Type of Discount**
  Two players for the price of one based on availablity.
- **Days of the Week**
  Mid-week, except holidays.
- **Hours of the Day**
  Coupon must be presented at time of play. Advance tee times recommended.

Coupon expires 12/04. Can not be combined with any other offer.

Mt. Washington Hotel G.C.
Bretton Woods, NH (603) 278-4653

- **Type of Discount**
  Two players for $99
- **Days of the Week**
  Sunday thru Thursday (Except Holidays)
- **Hours of the Day**
  After 2 pm.

Coupon expires 12/04. Can not be combined with any other offer.

NEW ENGLAND GOLFGUIDE

2 0 0 4

NEW ENGLAND GOLFGUIDE

2 0 0 4

NEW ENGLAND GOLFGUIDE

2 0 0 4

NEW ENGLAND GOLFGUIDE

2 0 0 4

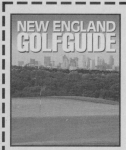

Nippo Lake Golf Club
Barrington, NH (603) 664-7616

- **Type of Discount**
  $5.00 off each greens fee for up to 2 players for 18 holes.
- **Days of the Week**
  7 days a week
- **Hours of the Day**
  After 1 pm

Coupon expires 12/04. Can not be combined with any other offer.

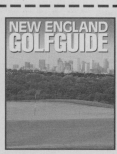

Oak Hill Golf Course
Meredith, NH (603) 279-4438

- **Type of Discount**
  $5.00 off greens fee for up to 2 players over 18 holes
- **Days of the Week**
  7 days a week (except holiday weekends)
- **Hours of the Day**
  All day

Coupon expires 12/04. Can not be combined with any other offer.

Owl's Nest Golf Club
Campton,NH (603) 726-3076

- **Type of Discount**
  $5.00 off each greens fee up to 2 players
- **Days of the Week**
  7 days a week
- **Hours of the Day**
  All Day

Coupon expires 12/04. Can not be combined with any other offer.

Passaconaway CC
Litchfield, NH (603) 424-4653

- **Type of Discount**
  Sr.,Lady, and Jr. discounts weekdays only.
- **Days of the Week**
  Weekdays seniors, ladies juniors.
  Weekends/holidays for inner club.
- **Hours of the Day**
  Weekdays 7am to 6 pm. Weekends, 6am to 6pm.

Coupon expires 12/04. Can not be combined with any other offer.

NEW ENGLAND GOLFGUIDE

2 0 0 4

NEW ENGLAND GOLFGUIDE

2 0 0 4

NEW ENGLAND GOLFGUIDE

2 0 0 4

NEW ENGLAND GOLFGUIDE

2 0 0 4

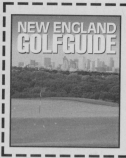

Pheasant Ridge CC
Gilford, NH (603) 524-7808

- **Type of Discount**
  $5.00 off 18-hole greens fee
- **Days of the Week**
  Monday-Thursday (except holidays)
- **Hours of the Day**
  All day Power cart required

Coupon expires 12/04. Can not be combined with any other offer.

Pine Grove Springs CC
Rt. 9A, Spofford, NH (603) 363-4433

- **Type of Discount**
  Free Golf Cart with 2 paid Greens Fees
- **Days of the Week**
  Weekdays only (except holidays)
- **Hours of the Day**
  All day

Coupon expires 12/04. Can not be combined with any other offer.

Pine Valley Golf Links
246 Old Gage Rd., Pelham, NH (603) 635-7979, (603) 635-8305

- **Type of Discount**
  1/2 Price golf cart w/ 2 Paid greens fees
- **Days of the Week**
  Weekdays only (except holidays)
- **Hours of the Day**
  Between 10 am and 2 pm

Coupon expires 12/04. Can not be combined with any other offer.

Ponemah Green
Amherst, NH (603) 672-4732

- **Type of Discount**
  Two players for the price of one
- **Days of the Week**
  Weekdays only (except holidays)
- **Hours of the Day**
  All day. Offer valid Sept. 8, 2004 through end of season

Coupon expires 12/04. Can not be combined with any other offer.

Golf Course Coupons

NEW ENGLAND GOLFGUIDE

2 0 0 4

NEW ENGLAND GOLFGUIDE

2 0 0 4

NEW ENGLAND GOLFGUIDE

2 0 0 4

NEW ENGLAND GOLFGUIDE

2 0 0 4

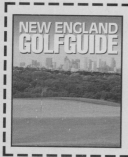

Ragged Mountain Golf Club
Danbury, NH, (603) 768-3600

- **Type of Discount**
  25% discount for 2-4 players
- **Days of the Week**
  7 days a week
- **Hours of the Day**
  Does not include 9-Hole, twlight or any other offer.

Coupon expires 12/04. Can not be combined with any other offer.

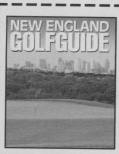

Sagamore-Hampton GC
N. Hampton, NH (603) 964-5341

- **Type of Discount**
  4 players for the price of 3
- **Days of the Week**
  Mon-Thur. Only (except holidays)
- **Hours of the Day**
  All day

Coupon expires 12/04. Can not be combined with any other offer.

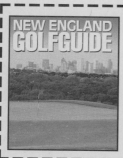

Shattuck GC, The
Jaffrey, NH (603) 532-4300

- **Type of Discount**
  $5.00 off greens fee for up to 4 players
- **Days of the Week**
  7 days a week
- **Hours of the Day**
  All day

Coupon expires 12/04. Can not be combined with any other offer.

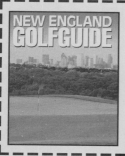

Souhegan Woods GC
Amherst, NH (603) 673-0200

- **Type of Discount**
  $5.00 off 18-hole greens fee
- **Days of the Week**
  Monday-Thursday only (except holidays)
- **Hours of the Day**
  All day Power cart required

Coupon expires 12/04. Can not be combined with any other offer.

NEW ENGLAND GOLFGUIDE

2 0 0 4

NEW ENGLAND GOLFGUIDE

2 0 0 4

NEW ENGLAND GOLFGUIDE

2 0 0 4

NEW ENGLAND GOLFGUIDE

2 0 0 4

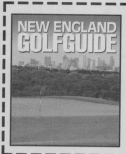

Stonebridge Country Club
Goffstown, NH 603-497-T-OFF (8633)

- **Type of Discount**
  $10.00 off a twosome with a riding cart.
- **Days of the Week**
  Monday thru Thursday
- **Hours of the Day**
  All day

Coupon expires 12/04. Can not be combined with any other offer.

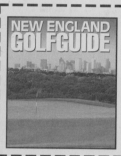

Tory Pines Resort
Rt. 47, Francestown, NH (603) 588-2923

- **Type of Discount**
  Two players for the price of one
- **Days of the Week**
  Mon-Thur
- **Hours of the Day**
  All day Cart not included

Coupon expires 12/04. Can not be combined with any other offer.

Waterville Valley
Waterville, NH (603) 236-4805

- **Type of Discount**
  1 player at half price.
- **Days of the Week**
  Weekdays only (except holidays)
- **Hours of the Day**
  All day. Tee times required.

Coupon expires 12/04. Can not be combined with any other offer.

Waukewan Golf Club
Meredith, NH (603) 279-6661

- **Type of Discount**
  4 players for the price of 3.
- **Days of the Week**
  7 days a week
- **Hours of the Day**
  All day.

Coupon expires 12/04. Can not be combined with any other offer.

NEW ENGLAND GOLFGUIDE

2 0 0 4

NEW ENGLAND GOLFGUIDE

2 0 0 4

NEW ENGLAND GOLFGUIDE

2 0 0 4

NEW ENGLAND GOLFGUIDE

2 0 0 4

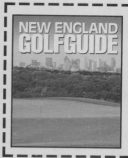

Waumbek CC, The
Jefferson, NH (603) 586-7777

- **Type of Discount**
  $5.00 off greens fee for up to 2 players
- **Days of the Week**
  Monday-Thursday (except holidays)
- **Hours of the Day**
  All day. Power cart rental required.

Coupon expires 12/04. Can not be combined with any other offer.

Wentworth Resort GC
Rt. 16, Jackson, NH (603) 383-9641

- **Type of Discount**
  $25pp for 18 holes including cart
- **Days of the Week**
  Weekdays only (except holidays)
- **Hours of the Day**
  After 1:00 pm. Must call ahead. Must notify of coupon when making tee time

Coupon expires 12/04. Can not be combined with any other offer.

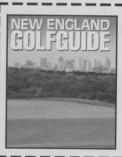

Whip-Poor-Will GC
Hudson, NH (603) 889-9706

- **Type of Discount**
  $5.00 off 18-hole greens fee
- **Days of the Week**
  Monday-Thursday (except holidays)
- **Hours of the Day**
  All day. Power cart required

Coupon expires 12/04. Can not be combined with any other offer.

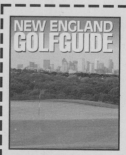

White Mountain CC
N. Ashland Rd., Ashland, NH (603) 536-2227

- **Type of Discount**
  $5.00 off 18-hole greens fee
- **Days of the Week**
  Monday-Thursday (except holidays)
- **Hours of the Day**
  All day. Power cart required

Coupon expires 12/04. Can not be combined with any other offer.

Golf Course Coupons

NEW ENGLAND
GOLFGUIDE

2 0 0 4

NEW ENGLAND
GOLFGUIDE

2 0 0 4

NEW ENGLAND
GOLFGUIDE

2 0 0 4

NEW ENGLAND
GOLFGUIDE

2 0 0 4

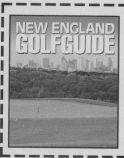

Windham Country Club
1 Country Club Rd., Windham, NH, (603)-434-2093

- **Type of Discount**
  Free Golf Cart with 2 paid Greens Fees.
  Free bucket of balls w/ round.
- **Days of the Week**
  Weekdays only (except holidays)
- **Hours of the Day**
  All day

Coupon expires 12/04. Can not be combined with any other offer.

Woodbound Inn GC
Woodbound Rd., Jaffrey, NH (603) 532-8341

- **Type of Discount**
  Two players for the price of one
- **Days of the Week**
  Weekdays only (except holidays)
- **Hours of the Day**
  All day.

Coupon expires 12/04. Can not be combined with any other offer.

Country View Golf Club
Burrillville, RI (401) 568-7157

- **Type of Discount**
  2 Players for the Price of 1 with the purchase of
  cart fees.
- **Days of the Week**
  Mon-Thurs (except holidays)
- **Hours of the Day**
  AM only

Coupon expires 12/04. Can not be combined with any other offer.

Fairlawn Golf Course
Lincoln, RI (401) 334-3937

- **Type of Discount**
  $2.00 off greens fee
- **Days of the Week**
  Weekdays only (except holidays)
- **Hours of the Day**
  Before noon

Coupon expires 12/04. Can not be combined with any other offer.

Golf Course Coupons

NEW ENGLAND GOLFGUIDE

2 0 0 4

NEW ENGLAND GOLFGUIDE

2 0 0 4

NEW ENGLAND GOLFGUIDE

2 0 0 4

NEW ENGLAND GOLFGUIDE

2 0 0 4

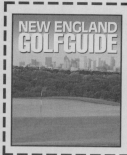

Foxwoods Golf CC
Route 138, Richmond, RI 02898 (401) 539-4653)

- **Type of Discount**
  15% off discount for 2-4 players.
- **Days of the Week**
  Weekdays only (except holidays)
- **Hours of the Day**
  After 12:00 Noon

Coupon expires 12/04. Can not be combined with any other offer.

Midville Country Club
W. Warwick, RI   (401) 828-9215

- **Type of Discount**
  Free Golf Cart with 2 paid Greens Fees
- **Days of the Week**
  Weekdays only (except holidays)
- **Hours of the Day**
  All day. Starts 9/16/04, expires 12/31/04

Coupon expires 12/04. Can not be combined with any other offer.

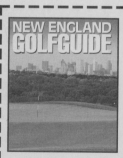

North Kingstown Muni.
N. Kingstown, RI (401) 294-0684

- **Type of Discount**
  4 players with carts for the price of 3
- **Days of the Week**
  M-TH; April, May, Sep, Oct
- **Hours of the Day**
  All day

Coupon expires 12/04. Can not be combined with any other offer.

Rose Hill Golf Course
South Kingston, RI (401) 788-1088

- **Type of Discount**
  $2.00 off greens fee.
- **Days of the Week**
  Monday thru Friday
- **Hours of the Day**
  All day. Not to be combined with any other offers.

Coupon expires 12/04. Can not be combined with any other offer.

NEW ENGLAND GOLFGUIDE

2 0 0 4

NEW ENGLAND GOLFGUIDE

2 0 0 4

NEW ENGLAND GOLFGUIDE

2 0 0 4

NEW ENGLAND GOLFGUIDE

2 0 0 4

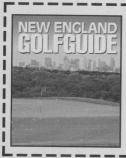

Washington Village Golf Course
Coventry, RI (401) 823-0010

- **Type of Discount**
  2 Golfers with Power Cart: $25.00/9 $44.00/18
- **Days of the Week**
  Mon/Tues: June and September.
- **Hours of the Day**
  10am - 2pm Excludes July-Aug

Coupon expires 12/04. Can not be combined with any other offer.

Windmill Hill Golf Course
Warren, RI (401) 245-1463

- **Type of Discount**
  Free Golf Cart with 2 paid Greens Fees
- **Days of the Week**
  Monday - Wednesday
- **Hours of the Day**
  7:00 am - 10:00 am

Coupon expires 12/04. Can not be combined with any other offer.

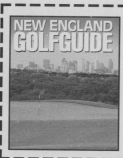

Wood River Golf
Hope Valley, RI (401) 364-0700

- **Type of Discount**
  Free Golf Cart with 2 paid Greens Fees
- **Days of the Week**
  Weekdays only (except holidays)
- **Hours of the Day**
  All day

Coupon expires 12/04. Can not be combined with any other offer.

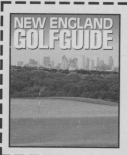

Bakersfield CC
Rt. 108, Bakersfield, VT (802) 933-5100

- **Type of Discount**
  $5.00 off greens fee for up to 2 players
- **Days of the Week**
  7 days a week
- **Hours of the Day**
  All day

Coupon expires 12/04. Can not be combined with any other offer.

NEW ENGLAND GOLFGUIDE

2 0 0 4

NEW ENGLAND GOLFGUIDE

2 0 0 4

NEW ENGLAND GOLFGUIDE

2 0 0 4

NEW ENGLAND GOLFGUIDE

2 0 0 4

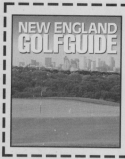

Barton Golf Club
Barton, VT (802) 525-1126

- **Type of Discount**
  Two players for the price of one, cart rental required.
- **Days of the Week**
  7 days a week
- **Hours of the Day**
  All day

Coupon expires 12/04. Can not be combined with any other offer.

Bellows Falls CC
Rt. 103, Rockingham, VT (802) 463-9809

- **Type of Discount**
  Free golf cart with 2 paid greens fee
- **Days of the Week**
  Weekdays only (except holidays)
- **Hours of the Day**
  All day

Coupon expires 12/04. Can not be combined with any other offer.

Blush Hill CC
Waterbury, VT (802) 244-8974

- **Type of Discount**
  Two players for the price of one
- **Days of the Week**
  Weekdays only (except holidays)
- **Hours of the Day**
  Before 2 PM. Cart rental required.

Coupon expires 12/04. Can not be combined with any other offer.

Cedar Knoll CC
Hinesburg, VT (802) 482-3186

- **Type of Discount**
  Mon- Men's day, Wed- Ladies Day, Thur- Senior's Day. $21+tax.
- **Days of the Week**

- **Hours of the Day**
  All Day

Coupon expires 12/04. Can not be combined with any other offer.

NEW ENGLAND GOLFGUIDE

2 0 0 4

NEW ENGLAND GOLFGUIDE

2 0 0 4

NEW ENGLAND GOLFGUIDE

2 0 0 4

NEW ENGLAND GOLFGUIDE

2 0 0 4

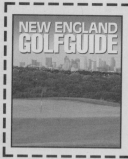

Crown Point CC
Springfield, VT (802) 885-1010

- **Type of Discount**
  Two players for the price of one
- **Days of the Week**
  Weekdays only (except holidays)
- **Hours of the Day**
  All day

Coupon expires 12/04. Can not be combined with any other offer.

Enosburg Falls CC
Enosburg Falls, VT (802) 933-2296

- **Type of Discount**
  $95.00 + tax for 4 players, 2 carts for 18 holes.
- **Days of the Week**
  7 days a week
- **Hours of the Day**
  All day

Coupon expires 12/04. Can not be combined with any other offer.

Farm Resort GC
Rt. 100, Morrisville, VT (802) 888-3525

- **Type of Discount**
  25% discount for 2-4 players
- **Days of the Week**
  7 days a week
- **Hours of the Day**
  After 1 pm, Call for tee times. Cart rental
  required.

Coupon expires 12/04. Can not be combined with any other offer.

Green Mountain National G. C.
Barrows Town Rd., Sherburne, VT (802) 422-GOLF

- **Type of Discount**
  $5.00 off greens fee for up to 2 players
- **Days of the Week**
  Weekdays only (except holidays)
- **Hours of the Day**

Coupon expires 12/04. Can not be combined with any other offer.

NEW ENGLAND
GOLFGUIDE

2 0 0 4

NEW ENGLAND
GOLFGUIDE

2 0 0 4

NEW ENGLAND
GOLFGUIDE

2 0 0 4

NEW ENGLAND
GOLFGUIDE

2 0 0 4

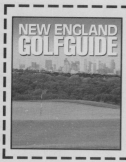

Killington Golf Resort
Killington, VT (802) 422-6700

- **Type of Discount**
  Two greens fees for the price of one.Cart rental rquired.
- **Days of the Week**
  Weekdays except holiday periods.
- **Hours of the Day**
  All day

Coupon expires 12/04. Can not be combined with any other offer.

Lake Morey CC
Fairlee, VT (802) 333-4800

- **Type of Discount**
  $5.00 off greens fee for up to 2 players
- **Days of the Week**
  7 days a week
- **Hours of the Day**
  All day. Valid April 1 to June , Sept 15 to Oct 31

Coupon expires 12/04. Can not be combined with any other offer.

Montague Golf Club
Randolph, VT (802) 728-3806

- **Type of Discount**
  Two players for the price of one
- **Days of the Week**
  Weekdays only (except holidays)
- **Hours of the Day**
  All day

Coupon expires 12/04. Can not be combined with any other offer.

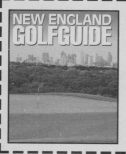

Mount Snow Golf Club
Mount Snow, VT (802) 464-4254

- **Type of Discount**
  $35.00 per person fee includes golf and shared cart
- **Days of the Week**
  Monday - Thursday, any time. No weekend play.
- **Hours of the Day**
  All day. Not valid on Power Lunch or other packages.

Coupon expires 12/04. Can not be combined with any other offer.

NEW ENGLAND GOLFGUIDE

2 0 0 4

NEW ENGLAND GOLFGUIDE

2 0 0 4

NEW ENGLAND GOLFGUIDE

2 0 0 4

NEW ENGLAND GOLFGUIDE

2 0 0 4

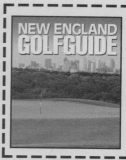

Neshobe Golf Club
Brandon, VT (802) 247-3611

- **Type of Discount**
  $5.00 off greens fee
- **Days of the Week**
  Weekdays only (except holidays)
- **Hours of the Day**
  After 8 AM , Call for tee time. Course may be closed for special events.

Coupon expires 12/04. Can not be combined with any other offer.

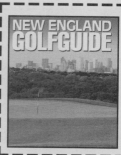

Newport CC
Newport, VT (802) 334-2391

- **Type of Discount**
  Free golf cart with 2 paid greens fees
- **Days of the Week**
  Weekdays only (except holidays)
- **Hours of the Day**
  After Noon. Not Valid, June, July and August

Coupon expires 12/04. Can not be combined with any other offer.

Okemo Valley Golf Club
Ludlow,VT (802) 228-1396

- **Type of Discount**
  Two greens fee for the price of one. Valid May and June, September and October only.
- **Days of the Week**
  Monday through Thursday only
- **Hours of the Day**
  After 1:00 pm

Coupon expires 12/04. Can not be combined with any other offer.

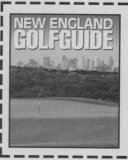

Orleans Country Club
Orleans, VT (802) 754-2333

- **Type of Discount**
  Two players for the price of one
- **Days of the Week**
  Weekdays only (except holidays)
- **Hours of the Day**
  All day. No holidays or Tournament days

Coupon expires 12/04. Can not be combined with any other offer.

Golf Course Coupons

NEW ENGLAND GOLFGUIDE

2 0 0 4

NEW ENGLAND GOLFGUIDE

2 0 0 4

NEW ENGLAND GOLFGUIDE

2 0 0 4

NEW ENGLAND GOLFGUIDE

2 0 0 4

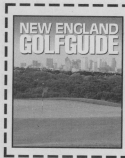

Proctor Pittsford CC
Pittsford, VT (802) 483-9379

- **Type of Discount**
  $5.00 off full price greens fee
- **Days of the Week**
  Weekdays only (except holidays)
- **Hours of the Day**
  All day

Coupon expires 12/04. Can not be combined with any other offer.

Rocky Ridge Golf Club
Rt. 116, St. George, VT (802) 482-2191

- **Type of Discount**
  Free Golf Cart with 2 paid Greens Fees
- **Days of the Week**
  7 days a week
- **Hours of the Day**
  All day

Coupon expires 12/04. Can not be combined with any other offer.

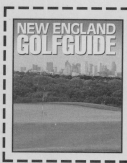

St. Johnsbury CC
St. Johnsbury, VT (802) 748-9894

- **Type of Discount**
  $5.00 off greens fee
- **Days of the Week**
  Weekdays only (except holidays). Must present coupon.
- **Hours of the Day**
  After 12 Noon - call for times

Coupon expires 12/04. Can not be combined with any other offer.

Stratton Mt.
Stratton Mountain, VT (802) 297-4114

- **Type of Discount**
  $5.00 off greens fee for up to 2 players
- **Days of the Week**
  Weekdays only (except holidays)
- **Hours of the Day**
  All day

Coupon expires 12/04. Can not be combined with any other offer.

Golf Course Coupons

NEW ENGLAND GOLFGUIDE

2 0 0 4

NEW ENGLAND GOLFGUIDE

2 0 0 4

NEW ENGLAND GOLFGUIDE

2 0 0 4

NEW ENGLAND GOLFGUIDE

2 0 0 4

Sugarbush Golf Club
Warren, VT (802) 583-6725

- **Type of Discount**
  Free Golf Cart with 2 paid Greens Fees
- **Days of the Week**
  Weekdays only (except holidays)
- **Hours of the Day**
  All day

Coupon expires 12/04. Can not be combined with any other offer.

Vermont National CC
S. Burlington, VT. 802-864-7770

- **Type of Discount**
  25% discount for 2-4 players
- **Days of the Week**
  7 days a week
- **Hours of the Day**

Coupon expires 12/04. Can not be combined with any other offer.

White River Golf Club
Rt. 100, Rochester, VT (802) 767-4653

- **Type of Discount**
  Free Golf Cart with 2 paid Greens Fees
- **Days of the Week**
  7 days a week
- **Hours of the Day**
  All day. Tee time required.

Coupon expires 12/04. Can not be combined with any other offer.

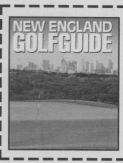

Wilcox Cove GC
Hgwy. 314, Grand Isle, VT (802) 372-8343

- **Type of Discount**
  Two players for the price of one
- **Days of the Week**
  Weekdays only (except holidays)
- **Hours of the Day**
  All day. N/A July 1 thru Labor Day

Coupon expires 12/04. Can not be combined with any other offer.

Golf Course Coupons

NEW ENGLAND GOLFGUIDE

2 0 0 4

NEW ENGLAND GOLFGUIDE

2 0 0 4

NEW ENGLAND GOLFGUIDE

2 0 0 4

NEW ENGLAND GOLFGUIDE

2 0 0 4

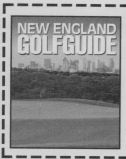

Woodstock Inn & Resort
Woodstock, VT (802) 457-6674

- **Type of Discount**
  Free golf cart with 2 paid greens fees
- **Days of the Week**
  7 days a week
- **Hours of the Day**
  All day

Coupon expires 12/04. Can not be combined with any other offer.

Airways Golf Course
1070 S. Grand, West Suffield, CT (860) 668-4973

- **Type of Discount**
  18 holes of golf, cart, sleeve of golf balls, and $4.00 lunch for $24.00 per person.
- **Days of the Week**
  Weekdays only (except holidays)
- **Hours of the Day**
  All day

Coupon expires 12/04. Can not be combined with any other offer.

Blackledge CC
180 West St., Hebron, CT (860) 228-0250

- **Type of Discount**
  Free Golf Cart with 2 paid Greens Fees
- **Days of the Week**
  Monday thru Thursday (except holidays)
- **Hours of the Day**
  All day Not valid from 5/15/04 to 9/15/04, expires 12/1/04.

Coupon expires 12/04. Can not be combined with any other offer.

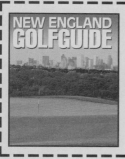

Blue Fox Run
Nod Rd., Avon, CT (860) 678-1679

- **Type of Discount**
  Free golf cart with 2 paid greens fees (Rates may change without notice)
- **Days of the Week**
  M-Th except holidays
- **Hours of the Day**
  7 AM - 10 AM

Coupon expires 12/04. Can not be combined with any other offer.

Golf Course Coupons

NEW ENGLAND GOLFGUIDE

2 0 0 4

NEW ENGLAND GOLFGUIDE

2 0 0 4

NEW ENGLAND GOLFGUIDE

2 0 0 4

NEW ENGLAND GOLFGUIDE

2 0 0 4

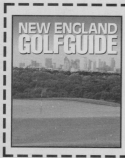

East Hartford GC
Long Hill St., E. Hartford, CT (860) 528-5082

- **Type of Discount**
  Two players for the price of one with rental of power cart
- **Days of the Week**
  Weekdays only (except holidays). From 10/1 to end of season.
- **Hours of the Day**
  All day

Coupon expires 12/04. Can not be combined with any other offer.

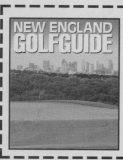

Fairchild Wheeler GC
Fairfield, CT (203) 373-5911

- **Type of Discount**
  Two players for the price of one with one cart.
- **Days of the Week**
  Daily (except holidays)
- **Hours of the Day**
  $50.00 M-Thurs 10:00 - 2:00
  $60.00 Fri/Sat/Sun 11:00-2:00

Coupon expires 12/04. Can not be combined with any other offer.

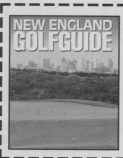

Fox Hopyard Country Club
East Haddam, CT (860) 434-6644

- **Type of Discount**
  $25.00 off green fees prior to May 15th and after October 15th.
- **Days of the Week**

- **Hours of the Day**

Coupon expires 12/04. Can not be combined with any other offer.

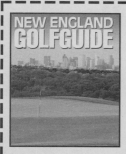

Fox Run at Copper Hill
E. Granby, CT (860) 653-6191

- **Type of Discount**
  18 holes with a cart, sleeve of balls, lunch - $22.50 per person.
- **Days of the Week**
  Monday and Thursday
- **Hours of the Day**
  All day

Coupon expires 12/04. Can not be combined with any other offer.

Golf Course Coupons

NEW ENGLAND GOLFGUIDE

2 0 0 4

NEW ENGLAND GOLFGUIDE

2 0 0 4

NEW ENGLAND GOLFGUIDE

2 0 0 4

NEW ENGLAND GOLFGUIDE

2 0 0 4

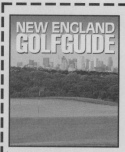

Goodwin Golf Course
Maple Ave., Hartford, CT (860) 956-3601

- **Type of Discount**
  Two players for the price of one (Power cart rental required)
- **Days of the Week**
  Weekdays only (except holidays)
- **Hours of the Day**
  All day

Coupon expires 12/04. Can not be combined with any other offer.

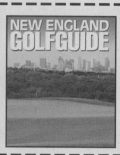

Harrisville GC
Woodstock, CT (860) 928-6098

- **Type of Discount**
  Free Golf Cart with 2 paid Greens Fees
- **Days of the Week**
  Weekdays only (except holidays)
- **Hours of the Day**
  All day

Coupon expires 12/04. Can not be combined with any other offer.

Hawk's Landing CC
Southington, CT (860) 793-6000

- **Type of Discount**
  $2.00 off a round or golf cart.
- **Days of the Week**
  7 days a week
- **Hours of the Day**
  All day

Coupon expires 12/04. Can not be combined with any other offer.

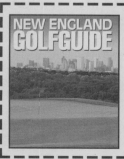

Hillside Links LLC
Deep River, CT (860)526-9986

- **Type of Discount**
  Two players for the price of one
- **Days of the Week**
  Weekdays only (except holidays)
- **Hours of the Day**
  All day

Coupon expires 12/04. Can not be combined with any other offer.

Golf Course Coupons

NEW ENGLAND GOLFGUIDE

2 0 0 4

NEW ENGLAND GOLFGUIDE

2 0 0 4

NEW ENGLAND GOLFGUIDE

2 0 0 4

NEW ENGLAND GOLFGUIDE

2 0 0 4

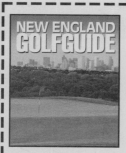

Indian Springs GC
Middlefield, CT (860) 349-8109

- **Type of Discount**
  Free Golf Cart with 2 paid Greens Fees
- **Days of the Week**
  Weekdays before 3:00 pm
- **Hours of the Day**

Coupon expires 12/04. Can not be combined with any other offer.

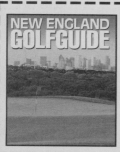

Leisure Resort At Banner Lodge
10 Banner Rd., Moodus, CT (860) 873-9075

- **Type of Discount**
  One player at 1/2 price
- **Days of the Week**
  7 days a week
- **Hours of the Day**
  All day

Coupon expires 12/04. Can not be combined with any other offer.

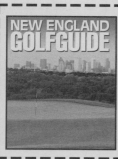

Miner Hills Family Golf, LLC
Middletown, CT (860)635-0051

- **Type of Discount**
  Two with motor cart: $12 each for 9 holes
- **Days of the Week**
  Weekdays only
- **Hours of the Day**
  Before 1 pm

Coupon expires 12/04. Can not be combined with any other offer.

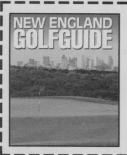

Pequot Golf Club
Wheeler Rd., Stonington, CT (860) 535-1898

- **Type of Discount**
  $5.00 off greens fee for up to 2 players
- **Days of the Week**
  Monday - Thursday
- **Hours of the Day**

Coupon expires 12/04. Can not be combined with any other offer.

NEW ENGLAND GOLFGUIDE

2 0 0 4

NEW ENGLAND GOLFGUIDE

2 0 0 4

NEW ENGLAND GOLFGUIDE

2 0 0 4

NEW ENGLAND GOLFGUIDE

2 0 0 4

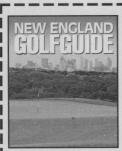

Pomperaug Golf Club
Southbury, CT (203) 264-9484

- **Type of Discount**
  $5.00 off greens fee for up to 2 players
- **Days of the Week**
  Weekdays only (except holidays)
- **Hours of the Day**
  All day

Coupon expires 12/04. Can not be combined with any other offer.

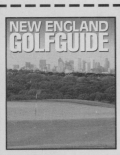

Putnam Country Club
Putnam, CT (860) 928-7748

- **Type of Discount**
  Two players for the price of one
- **Days of the Week**
  M-Th (Except holidays)
- **Hours of the Day**
  7 AM - 2 PM. Cart rental required.

Coupon expires 12/04. Can not be combined with any other offer.

Rolling Greens GC
Rocky Hill, CT (860) 257-9775

- **Type of Discount**
  4 players for the price of 3
- **Days of the Week**
  Weekdays only (except holidays) from 7am to 2pm
- **Hours of the Day**
  Must call the day before.   Power cart required.

Coupon expires 12/04. Can not be combined with any other offer.

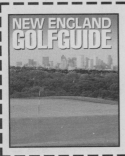

Sunset Hill GC
Brookfield, CT (203) 740-7800

- **Type of Discount**
  Two players for the price of one (cart rental required)
- **Days of the Week**
  Weekdays only (except holidays)
- **Hours of the Day**
  All day

Coupon expires 12/04. Can not be combined with any other offer.

Golf Course Coupons

NEW ENGLAND
GOLFGUIDE

2 0 0 4

NEW ENGLAND
GOLFGUIDE

2 0 0 4

NEW ENGLAND
GOLFGUIDE

2 0 0 4

NEW ENGLAND
GOLFGUIDE

2 0 0 4

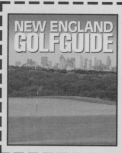

Western Hills GC
Waterbury, CT (203) 756-1211

- **Type of Discount**
  Green Fees, Cart, & Lunch, $27.50 each player
- **Days of the Week**
  Weekdays only (except holidays)
- **Hours of the Day**
  7-10 am Foursomes only, Tee times required 1-3 days adv.

Coupon expires 12/04. Can not be combined with any other offer.

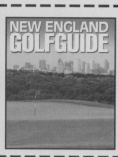

Woodstock Golf Course
S. Woodstock, CT (860) 928-4130

- **Type of Discount**
  25% discount for 4 players
- **Days of the Week**
  Weekdays only (except holidays)
- **Hours of the Day**
  11:00 am- 3:00 pm

Coupon expires 12/04. Can not be combined with any other offer.

Golf Course Coupons

Index to Golf Courses
Alphabetically by State and Course

NEW ENGLAND GOLFGUIDE

NEW ENGLAND GOLFGUIDE® 2004

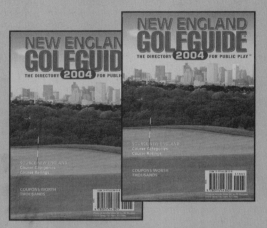

THE PERFECT GIFT!

For your boss, your employees, your husband, your wife, your kids, your best friend, your father, mother, father-in-law, mother-in-law, your brother, brother-in-law, sister, sister-in-law, your significant other, and for **ANY GOLFER ON YOUR GIFT LIST!**